AMERICA'S ANCIENT TREASURES

AMERICA'S ANCIENT TREASURES

A Guide to Archeological Sites and Museums
in the United States and Canada

THIRD REVISED, ENLARGED EDITION

Franklin Folsom
Mary Elting Folsom
Illustrations by Rachel Folsom

University of New Mexico Press : *Albuquerque*

Library of Congress Cataloging in Publication Data

Folsom, Franklin, 1907–
    America's ancient treasures.

    Bibliography: p.
    1. Indians of North America—Museums—Guide-books.
2. Indians of North America—Antiquities—Guide-books.
3. United States—Antiquities—Guide-books. 4. Canada—
Antiquities—Guide-books. 5. Archaeological museums and
collections—United States—Guide-books. 6. Archaeological museumes and collections—Canada—Guide-books.
7. United States—Description and travel—1981–   —
Guide-books. 8. Canada—Description and travel—
1981–   —Guide-books. I. Elting, Mary, 1906–
II. Title.

Library of Congress Cataloging in Publication Data

E56.F64 1982   970.01'074   82–20303
ISBN 0–8263–0650–0
ISBN 0–8263–0651–9 (pbk.)

Designed by Emmy Ezzell

This book about their roots
is dedicated to
Native Americans, past and present

CONTENTS

LIST OF FEATURES

PREFACE
TO THE THIRD EDITION

Prehistoric Americans north of Mexico had not yet developed their own symbols for the sounds of speech at the time when writing arrived from Europe, only a few hundred years ago. The early Indians could not set down in lasting words any account of the richness of their experience. They could not record in unmistakable form the problems they faced or describe the solutions they worked out. This meant that the First Americans could not communicate fully with their present-day descendants—or, for that matter, with those later Americans with whom their descendants were forced to share their land. The ancient ones have scarcely been able to whisper across the centuries. As a result, the million or so Native Americans living north of Mexico today have not been able, as many other peoples have been, to draw a full measure of strength from their forebears. And other Americans have often not known and valued the creativity of those who for thousands of years elaborated life on this continent. Both Immigrant Americans and Native Americans were deprived as long as there was no breach in the wall of silence between the Indian past and the industrial present.

Archeology has assumed the task of doing what can be done to break down this barrier. Here and there, archeologists have given some voice to a few of the millions of people who once were a part of the life on this land. Using a variety of techniques, borrowed from a dozen other sciences, they have recalled fragments out of the past.

They have literally recreated dwellings and places of worship and indeed whole villages, and in the United States they have done so under a variety of auspices. On the federal level the National Park Service, the Bureau of Land Management, the Forest Service, and other agencies have all joined in the work of protecting and presenting what Indians once built and archeologists have now studied and rebuilt. Certain state, county, and city agencies also have joined in the work of preservation, as have some privately financed institutions. All are saving some of the fast-disappearing past for the benefit of present and future generations. Thanks to these efforts we can move toward the world created by our predecessors and enjoy moments of close proximity to the people of yesterday while we listen to what they have to tell us. In archeological parks and monuments we can stand where Indians once built their dwellings or cooked their meals or said their prayers or made love. We can visit their ancient villages, revived for our delight. We can see the implements of their daily life, their works of art, their games, their religious paraphernalia.

Here, in the pages that follow, you can find your way to archeological sites that have been prepared for public view in the area north of Mexico. Here, too, are the museums which tell with some clarity about America's aboriginal yesterdays. However, you will not find any road directions to sites for which adequate protection does not exist.

There are, of course, many more museums than you will find listed here. A considerable number have good Indian exhibits. However, some of these have been omitted because they lack displays which illuminate *prehistoric* Indian life. By prehistoric is meant that period before the art of writing came to North America and made possible the keeping of written records.

There are also many archeological sites which reflect human experience after European and Indian met. These places, often called historic sites, are not included here, nor are museums devoted solely to materials recovered by workers in historic archeology. Another guidebook will have to be prepared to cover them.

This, the third edition of *America's Ancient Treasures,* appears at a time when archeology has been booming, thanks in good part to new federal legislation. A great many sites have recently been excavated, and a number of these new ones, and some older ones, too, have been prepared for visitation by the public. Museum curators have revised many exhibits to reflect the increased knowledge we have about what life was like when Native Americans were the sole human occupants of this continent. At the same time, a few sites once open to the public have been closed for one reason or another. Some museums have ceased operation or transferred their prehistoric holdings to other institutions. At least one has been burglarized and had its collection stolen.

Because museums, parks, and monuments often make minor adjustments in their fees and the hours and even days when they are open, we have tried to give the information on these points in terms that should remain valid for some time. And as we have brought entries about sites and museums up to date, we have also tried to make the text as a whole consistent with the current understanding of prehistory.

Finally we must point out that we have not been able to resolve confusion about the spelling of a word that is central to our endeavor. We have compromised and followed the *United States Government Printing Office Style Manual* in using the spelling *archeology* in our text and wherever it appears in that form in the writings of others. Where *archaeology* is used by others in titles or in quotations that we make use of, we have kept that form of the word.

August 1981   Franklin Folsom
                                                Mary Elting Folsom

Keet Seel Ruin in Navajo National Monument lies under a great, overhanging sandstone cliff at the end of a trail eight miles beyond the end of the road. Tree-ring dates show that trees for ladders were cut between A.D. 1274 and 1284. National Park Service photo by George A. Grant.

INTRODUCTION

Human beings have been trying to manage life on Planet Earth for upwards of two million years. For much of that time their complex and uncertain venture seems to have taken place in Africa. Only recently, on the geological time scale, did they expand their effort at survival onto the Eurasian land mass, and it was only yesterday on that scale that they moved their enterprise into the Americas.

When did the oldest immigrants reach this continent? The experts don't agree on the answer. Some say no solid evidence exists that they arrived more than 13,500 years ago. Others say excavation of stone tools in Peruvian caves indicates that hunters reached the high Andes by 20,000 years before the present. Still other scientists point to tempting hints that people were here 40,000 or 50,000 or more years ago. There are indeed responsible advocates of a still earlier date. Evidence to support such speculation is elusive, to say the least, but evidence does continue to mount that people have made their homes in the Americas for much longer than we usually think.

Support for a date of at least 50,000 years ago comes from several sources. For instance, in 1976 archeologists discovered many crude artifacts buried under a deep, 50,000-year-old deposit in Yuha Pinto Wash in California. Skeletons dated by geochemist Jeffrey L. Bada suggest that human beings were in California at least 48,000 years ago. Some critics, however, feel his dates are much too old.

No matter what date turns out to be right, one thing is clear:

people learned and invented a great deal after they settled in the Americas. Largely without teachers, they became experts at living among the wonderfully varied environments in what Europeans later called the New World.

This learning went on, slowly at first, then often at a quickening pace. It continued until a wave of immigrants from Europe, bringing a different experience in life, overwhelmed the American continents. Then much of what had taken 13,500 or 50,000 or 200,000 years to evolve was destroyed in a short 400 years.

The great collapse came not because the learning accumulated by Native Americans was faulty in relation to their world. The collapse came primarily because the invading people were—by chance—enabled to spurt ahead in control of energy. While two great water barriers separated American Indians from the learning attained by other people, a land bridge linked people around the Mediterranean to energy developments in Mesopotamia, in Africa, in China. People in Mesopotamia and Africa discovered that the energy released by fire could separate certain metals from rock. They also discovered that tools and weapons shaped from those metals could multiply human muscle power many times over.

People around the Mediterranean also learned from China that a certain mixture—a powder—could be made to explode. By combining this powder with tubes made of metal, inventors made guns. Here was a new way of bringing together and concentrating certain new energies. Those who possessed this technology found that they could impose their will on others, who did not happen to be present when someone brought iron and gunpowder together to form weapons. The possessors of guns could force people who had not yet obtained them to do their bidding—and their bidding was to provide land or labor or the products of both.

All this meant that the possessors of the new forms and products of energy could also possess capital, and capital itself became a source of great power on the social scene. Together with material power, this social power made it possible for European culture to displace Native American culture. It was not a question of the greater serviceability in the American environment of European culture, which as a whole in 1492 was very little more advanced than the high Indian cultures of Mexico and Central America and Peru. Energy and power, and the social cohesion they imposed, alone determined the outcome of the struggle which still affects all of us—including the more than one million Indians who survive in the United States and Canada.

The losers in the unequal contest were largely silenced. Their voices have generally not carried to present day ears. This has meant that what people learned in millenia about living where Canadians and Americans now live, has been lost. The heirs of the conquerors have had to learn anew how life can be carried on richly among the great resources of a great part of the surface of the earth. The conquered find it difficult to remember.

Belatedly, a search has started to find the essence of the experience of Native Americans, who managed so well on the terrain that others now occupy. The search is not really to find something more to be borrowed from Indians. It is simply for knowledge. Perhaps by understanding a form of humanity that is different from the one that now prevails, the prevailers will better know themselves. At the very least the gain can be something at which to marvel. For Indians the search can be for their roots—and it is from roots that strength can come.

In one sense, this search for Indian roots is the business of American archeology, and more and more fragments of the pre-European past of America are being rescued and returned to view. For a long time the interpreters of archeological materials did not look for any overall meaning in the history of Native Americans. It seemed enough to classify and try to date the artifacts of each region, and when change or development appeared, it was generally attributed to fresh ideas from somewhere else. Recently, however, the study of cultural change in the Americas has itself been evolving. The New Archeology (capital letters indicate the importance its practitioners attach to their work) is concerned with the dynamics of change and development.

For these scientists really to achieve their purpose it is necessary to bring sympathetic imagination to the potsherds and ruined walls and spent projectile points that have come out of the soil. These products of skill and planning must be extrapolated into the activities of societies that were full of intelligence and striving and love and sorrow.

The search has not been easy or simple. Excavation destroys the very clue the archeologist is looking for, and if he or she makes a mistake, there is no going back to correct the error. Moreover, tomorrow there may be new techniques which will make it possible to squeeze more information out of dry fragments of the past. So, paradoxically, diggers want to dig as little as possible. Although they are all greedy for facts, they feel they must give tomorrow's excavators a chance to use new methods that will gain better results than are possible today.

In an effort to get the maximum of data with a minimum of destruction, the New Archeologists began in the 1960s to use a variety of mathematical devices for learning a lot from a little evidence. These same investigators were bent on discovering as much as they could about the processes of social change that went on yesterday. They tried to find action in the inactive artifacts that came from the earth, and they sought all they could learn about the relationships of human beings to the plants and animals and soils and climates among which they lived. "Cultural ecology," they called it, because they paid much attention to the interrelationships of people with all the rest of nature—and with each other.

The reports that some of the New Archeologists issued often seemed very remote from the humanity they sought. Mathematical formulas, computer printouts, statistical tables and charts, abstractions, and a bewildering variety of jaw-breaking terms littered their pages, tripping up unwary professionals and stopping amateurs dead in their tracks. But this always contentious, sometimes uncommunicative, new group had moved a long way from the early days of archeology, when the main goal of excavators was to recover handsome objects to put on display in museums. With the aid of an ever-growing battery of devices from other sciences, the New Archeologists were discovering something about people, not just accumulating things or tabulating types or traits. And in an age which offers fewer and fewer sites to dig, they were producing more and more ideas.

Even the most refined search for past ways of living and changing will never bring searchers as close as they would like to be to those who have gone before us, but thanks to the abstractions—and to the insistence of the New Archeology on democratic study of the ancient lowly as well as the ancient rich—we do know much more each year about past groups of people. One device of the New Archeology has given notable help. The practitioners of this form of science have put great store on forming hypotheses, then checking the facts to see if their trial theories make sense. The New Archeologists have also learned a great deal from the Old Archeologists. Thanks to both, the search for understanding of human beings has gathered momentum, and it certainly has become more exciting to watch.

Of course, researchers today cannot fully know life as Native Americans once lived it, but archeologists are trying to give Indians—and non-Indians also—a better chance at such knowledge than we have hitherto had.

Probably the ancestors of the first human beings to make the western hemisphere their home had already learned to deal with Ice-Age climate, when glaciers covered much of the northern hemisphere. Bordering the ice sheets was a treeless zone of tundra, and in this zone lived enormous herds of mammals. Caribou grazed there. So did the huge elephants called mammoths. A male mammoth could achieve a weight of six or seven tons, living on a diet of arctic herbs and grasses. Far to the south, extensive prairies also furnished nourishment for mammoths, for giant bison, and for bands of horses and camels. Ground sloths and mastodons grew to great size near the edges of forests, where they lived on a diet of leaves and twigs. Smaller game, too, was abundant—deer, elk, antelope, rabbit, and most of the other animals we know today. Apparently men hunted all these creatures but found it most efficient to kill the largest ones whenever they could. One spear thrust into the heart or lungs of a mammoth produced thousands of times as much meat as one spear that brought down a bounding rabbit.

To reap the harvest of Ice-Age meat, men needed good spears, tipped with ivory or bone or stone, that could pierce the thick skins of large mammals and reach the vital organs. For butchering, hunters found various ways to put sharp edges on certain kinds of stone, thus shaping knives. These stone knives would cut

What Was It Used For?

How can archeologists be sure what stone tools were used for, thousands of years ago? They started with educated guesses based on the shapes of tools and the contexts in which many of them were found. A sharp flint object between the ribs of a bison certainly indicated it was a projectile point. Then in 1962 the Russian scientist S. A. Semenov reported that, under a microscope, even the hardest stone revealed traces of the use to which it had been put. Americans doubted his results until they realized they did not have good enough microscopes to duplicate Semenov's findings. Later experiments with modern replicas of tools convinced them that each kind of work produces its own kind of polish on the stone—and the polish is permanent. A knife used to cut wood takes on a bright polish; bone gives a bright, but less smooth polish than wood, and different from that made by cutting into antler. Sawing shows up in polish, striations, and wear on the edges of a tool. The effect of cutting hide is bright polish with characteristic wear on the edge.

Examination of projectile points found at a buffalo kill site in Colorado indicated that, in addition to bringing down the animals, some of the points had then served as knives for butchering.

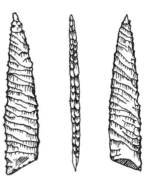

The three views above show a flint blade that has been turned into a point only 1⅜ inches long. This delicate workmanship was done by pre-Eskimo craftsmen at Cape Denbigh, in Alaska. After Giddings.

---

easily through hides that were far too tough for fingers to tear or for teeth to pierce.

Besides food, families needed fire and shelter against the cold, as well as clothing which would produce a miniature warm climate close to their bodies. To make animal-skin clothing, they needed special tools: scrapers of stone or bone to remove from the inside of a skin the tissue that would make it unmanageable when it dried and hardened, awls for punching holes, and needles for sewing.

By burning animal fat and the long bones of mammals, which were rich storehouses of marrow, people could keep warm, even when there was no wood for fires. They could make shelters from the skins of most of the large animals they hunted, although mammoth skins, as thick as automobile tires, were quite unusable. However, in treeless country, mammoth ribs and the leg bones as big around as tree trunks could take the place of wooden frameworks, over which skins could be spread to make houses. With these inventions and a few others, human beings learned the trick of living under arctic conditions. And having learned it, they wandered far, following the herds of big game that were a good source of food.

This wandering, according to the prevailing theory, took some of them from Siberia into Alaska at a time when a vast stretch of prairie joined Asia to North America. In those days the ocean was lower than it is today because there was actually less water in it. Billions of tons of water had evaporated from the earth's seas, had then fallen in the form of snow, and remained unmelted. Each year more snow piled up on the land. There it was compressed into ice, which formed enormous ice sheets. Deprived of water, the oceans shrank, and land which had been close to the surface was now exposed.

One such area, known as the Bering Land Bridge, or Beringia, between Siberia and Alaska, was sometimes more than 1,000 miles wide, covered with arctic vegetation which fed game animals. Getting to Alaska was no special problem for hunters, and it was possible to live there because much of the land was never covered by ice, although most of Canada was.

No one knows how many people moved into Alaska during the Ice Age, or how long they remained there. Possibly some of these people went south along the edge of the ocean, where seafood was plentiful. Sea level was lower than it is today, and the coastline was different. During the times when glaciers did not reach the water, migration along the edge of the land might have been easier than it would be today. More likely, at least once, perhaps more than once, the ice sheet which covered Canada melted, until a long strip of land, just east of the Rocky Mountains, became ice-free all the way from Alaska and northern Canada to the Great Plains. Vegetation invaded the strip. Then animals followed the plants, and at least once, perhaps many times, a band of hunters passed through this corridor, following game southward. After reaching the Great Plains they remained. The hunting was good, and it didn't matter that the glaciers grew again and met, closing the corridor behind them.

Because the food supply was ample, each band grew in size until it had to subdivide. On the Plains the number of bands steadily increased, and from this central starting point people spread out over all of North and South America.

In the heartland of North America the Big-Game Hunters, who are called Paleo-Indians, continued to use tools of the kind they had brought with them. But in time they made innovations and improvements. One very distinctive tool became popular—a type of spearpoint which the hunters fashioned from certain kinds of stone, such as flint, chalcedony, jasper, and chert. With great skill a point-maker thinned a fragment of hard rock and chipped its edges precisely. Then, striking two perfectly aimed blows, he knocked off flakes to form a groove, or channel, down its front and back. The groove, called a flute, set the point apart from others, and for this archeologists are grateful. Such an easily identifiable tool is almost a fingerprint of Early Man. Early Woman's creations, including Early Children, were less able to survive the ravages of time than were the stone tools that males made. Furthermore, the introduction by men of the term Early Man has proved exceedingly durable and pervasive. We all have to use it as if we were ignoring woman's role in human prehistory.

One kind of fluted point has been named the Clovis point because archeologists first excavated it near Clovis, New Mexico. The exca-

In 1927, when excavators near Folsom, New Mexico, found this projectile point between two bones of an extinct bison, they left it in position and summoned experts to observe it. Here was proof that people had lived in America at the same time as animals that had been extinct for about 10,000 years. This Folsom point opened new vistas to archeologists. Denver Museum Natural History photo by Robert R. Wright.

vation offered clear proof that hunters had used points of this kind to kill mammoths about 9220 B.C. In excavations elsewhere evidence has appeared that people worked in groups when they hunted the huge elephants.

Wherever mammoth hunters went, they left points of the Clovis type. Literally thousands have been found in Kentucky, Tennessee, and Alabama, an area in which Paleo-Indians were relatively numerous. Between the years 11,500 B.P. (meaning Before Present) and 11,000 B.P., a thin film of humanity spread over most of the United States and part of Canada. In the next thousand years (11,000–10,000 B.P.) a different kind of fluted point, called the Folsom point, replaced the Clovis point in popularity. Then fluting went out of fashion, and for 2,500 or 3,000 years Big-Game Hunters brought down their quarry with points that were not fluted. All these hunters were Paleo-Indians, and all seem to have lived in much the same way. Their activities did not vary a great deal whether they lived in southern Arizona or the southeastern states or Massachusetts or Alberta or Nova Scotia.

Perhaps the most famous Paleo site is one near Folsom, New Mexico. Here a spearpoint was found between the ribs of a bison of a type that has long been extinct. It was this find, made in 1927, which established beyond a doubt the great antiquity of human beings in America. Up to that time most scientists did not dare to think that people had arrived here more than 3,000 years ago. The Folsom spearpoints pushed the date back to 10,000 years ago, and subsequently the Clovis point discoveries pushed it back even further. The state of New Mexico made the Folsom Site into a State Monument, but the monument has now been closed to the public. Too many visitors dug there in the portion of the site that had not been scientifically excavated. Pending further professional work, it has been placed off limits to the public.

From time to time a Paleo dig is open to the public while excavation is going on, but the chances are that you will have to visit museums if you want to see what archeologists encounter when they excavate Paleo sites. Fortunately the museum exhibits are numerous and illuminating—perhaps more rewarding even than a visit to a site itself would be. Paleo-Indians left few tools or weapons in any one place, and really fine examples of such artifacts (archeologists call them "goodies") don't turn up every day in a dig.

On the archeologist's calendar, the Paleo-Indian Period came to an end about 6,000 B.C. By that time the great glaciers of the Ice Age had disappeared. So had most of the great animals. The mammoths of North America were all gone. A little later the mastodons disappeared. Then ground sloth and the giant bison that roamed the prairies vanished, as did the horses and camels.

Scientists disagree among themselves about the causes of this extinction. Some believe that the animals could not adjust to the changes in vegetation that came when the ice melted and the land grew warmer. Other investigators think that the reproductive cycle of larger animals was geared to Ice-Age seasons, and when the length of the seasons changed with warmer weather, offspring may have been born at times of the year when they could not survive. Still others believe that the Paleo-Indians developed hunting techniques that were so efficient that they killed off the largest of their quarry.

At any rate people could no longer make use of food that came in the biggest units. They had to depend on smaller game. Men and women both began a more intensive search for things to eat. They developed new lifeways and fashioned new tools to provide a livelihood. To supplement their meat diet more than in the past, they gathered berries and plant food of various kinds, particularly seeds. By now the population had increased from a few bands to many thousands of individuals. All over America it had become necessary to exploit even the smallest kinds of food resource. This new stage, with its new developments, has become known as the Archaic. It began in some places before the last vestiges of Paleo culture had disappeared, and in parts of the continent it continued right up to historic times.

In the beginning, as now, the East differed greatly from the West. In the East heavy rains flowed off in numerous streams filled with fish and shellfish. Forests grew thick, and they sheltered smaller animals which were relatively fewer in number than the grazing herds on the grass-rich prairies. Nevertheless, ingenious

About A.D. 850 Indians at Mesa Verde lived on the mesa top in dwellings built in a row. From a diorama in the museum at Mesa Verde National Park, Colorado.

fish weirs, extensive use of shellfish, or one-man hunting methods geared to the tree-congested forest all produced an ample food supply in certain places. There the people of the Archaic could live in larger groups than had been possible in Paleo times.

One Eastern Archaic site open to the public is Russell Cave National Monument in Alabama, where people first began to live 8,5000 or 9,000 years ago. Another Eastern Archaic site is Graham Cave State Park in Missouri. But most Archaic artifacts, like those of Paleo times, are best displayed in museums.

The Archaic lifeway in the West has been called Western Archaic by some archeologists. Others prefer the name Desert culture, and well they might. The West had grown more arid as the Ice Age ended. Large areas had very little rainfall in the course of a year, and this lack of water shaped the kinds of plant that grew there. The plants determined the kinds of animal that lived on them, and these creatures differed markedly from those which lived on and amid lusher vegetation to the east. In turn, the people who lived on both animals and plants in the West worked out patterns of behavior which differed from those in the East. Men whose predecessors had hunted mammoths came more and more to depend on small animals, even the smallest, such as crickets and grasshoppers. But meat of any kind was scarce, and plant food became very important, particularly small seeds. People invented baskets for holding seeds and tools for grinding them. In the whole world no basketry has been dated as early as that found in the Great Basin of the West.

Out of the Western Archaic, or Desert Culture, developed a number of different and highly specialized ways of living. None of them, of course, followed the modern political state lines, and some in northern Mexico extended into the United States. As time went on, many ideas and institutions flowed from Mexico into the southern parts of the present states of Arizona and New Mexico. Some experts believe it was primarily the ways in which people lived which shifted northward. Others believe that immigrants from the south filtered in, bringing ideas and inventions which affected patterns of local life.

A variety of Western Archaic culture which has been named the Cochise (ko-CHEES) developed in that area before 5000 B.C. Most important of the ideas the Cochise received from Mexico was the concept that by planting seeds in garden patches people could create food, not just find it. The result was that several hundred years before the Christian era there began a series of changes toward settled village life.

In what is now northern Arizona, northern New Mexico, and southern Colorado and Utah, there seems to have been an independent and different sort of development. Excavation and research by archeologist Cynthia Irwin-Williams in one part of this area have yielded a continuous picture of evolution from a hunting-and-gathering culture to a sedentary, town-dwelling way of life. In this area, too, the origins of settled communities go back at least 7000 years, and it has been possible for the archeologist to trace through stage after stage an almost unbroken record of human occupation up to Pueblo Indian times. This cultural development has been given the name Oshara Tradition, to distinguish it from the cultures which arose father south.

Many prehistoric sites throughout the Southwest are open to the public, and finds from these sites may also be enjoyed in museums all over the country.

VISITABLE ARCHEOLOGICAL SITES
IN THE UNITED STATES AND CANADA

Many of the sites listed below are included in the National Register of Historic Places, which means that they are protected by the federal government. These are indicated by the initials NRHP. The initials NHL indicate that a site is also a National Historic Landmark and is automatically included in the National Register.

Southwest

Arizona

Canyon de Chelly National Monument NRHP
Casa Grande Ruins National Monument NRHP
Glen Canyon National Recreation Area
Grand Canyon National Park (Tusayan Ruins)
Grasshopper Ruin
Hardy Site
Kinishba Pueblo NHL
Kinlichee Tribal Park
Montezuma Castle National Monument
Navajo National Monument NRHP (Betatakin, Keet Seel)
Newspaper Rock Petroglyphs NRHP
Old Oraibi NHL
Painted Rocks State Park
Petrified Forest National Park NRHP
Picture Rocks Retreat
Pueblo Grande Museum NHL

Three Turkey Ruin
Tonto National Monument NRHP
Tuzigoot National Monument NRHP
Walnut Canyon National Monument NRHP
Walpi
Wupatki National Monument NRHP

Colorado (southwestern)

Chimney Rock
Curecanti National Recreation Area
Dominguez and Escalante Ruins NRHP
Lowry Pueblo Ruins NHL
Mesa Verde National Park NRHP
Ute Mountain Tribal Park NRHP
Yucca House National Monument NRHP

New Mexico

Abo NHL
Acoma Pueblo NHL
Aztec Ruins National Monument NRHP
Bandelier National Monument NRHP

Carlsbad Caverns National Park
Casamero Ruins
Chaco Culture National
    Historical Park NRHP
Coronado State Monument
El Morro National Monument NRHP
Gila Cliff Dwellings National
    Monument NRHP
Gran Quivira NRHP
Hawikuh
Indian Petroglyphs State Park
Jemez State Monument NRHP
Palace of the Governors NHL
Pecos National Monument NRHP
Picuris Pueblo NRHP
Puyé Cliff Ruins NHL
Quarai NHL
Salmon Ruin NRHP
Sandia Man Cave NHL
San Juan Pueblo NRHP
Santa Clara Pueblo NRHP
Taos Pueblo NHL
Three Rivers Petroglyphs
Village of the Great Kivas
Zia Pueblo NRHP
Zuni Pueblo

Utah

Alkali Ridge NHL
Anasazi Indian Village State
    Historical Monument
Arch Canyon Indian Ruin
Arches National Park (Courthouse
    Wash Pictographs) NRHP
Big Westwater Ruin
Buckhorn Wash Pictographs and
    Petroglyphs
Calf Creek Recreation Site
Canyonlands National Park NRHP
    (Salt Creek in E. Section of Park)
Capitol Reef National Park
Clear Creek Canyon Rock Art
Danger Cave Historical Site NHL
Dinosaur National Monument
Edge of the Cedars State Historical
    Monument NRHP
Grand Gulch Archeological
    Primitive Area
Hog Springs Picnic Site
Horseshoe Canyon Pictograph Panels
    NRHP
Horse Canyon
Hovenweep National Monument
    NRHP
Mule Canyon Indian Ruins
Natural Bridges National Monument
Newspaper Rock, Indian Creek State
    Park NRHP
Nine Mile Canyon Rock Art
Parowan Gap Indian Drawings NRHP

Sand Island Petroglyphs
Thompson Wash Petroglyphs/
    Pictographs
Three Kiva Pueblo
Westwater Ruin

Great Basin and California

California

Anza Borrego State Park
Big and Little Petroglyph Canyons
    NHL
Blythe Intaglios NRHP
Calico Mountains Archaeological
    Project NRHP
Channel Islands National Park
Chumash Painted Cave NRHP
Clear Lake State Park
Coyote Hills Regional Park
Death Valley National Monument
Hospital Rock Pictographs NRHP
Indian Grinding Rock State Historic
    Park NRHP
Inscription Canyon
Joshua Tree National Monument
Kule Loklo
Lava Beds National Monument
    Petroglyph Section
Miwok Park
Potwisha Camp Pictographs
Sierra Miwok Village
Topoc Maze

Nevada

Grimes Point Archaeological Area
    NRHP
Hickison Summit Petroglyphs
Lake Mead National Recreation Area
Petroglyph Trail
Rocky Gap Site
Valley of Fire State Park
Willow Springs

Northwest Coast

Alaska

Katmai National Monument
Sitka National Historical Park NRHP

Idaho

Alpha Rockshelter
Lenore Site NRHP
Lolo Trail NHL
McCammon Petroglyphs
Midvale Quarry
Nez Perce National Historical Park
    NRHP
Weis Rockshelter
Wilson Butte Cave NRHP

Oregon

Fort Rock Cave Historical Marker
    NHL

Washington

Ginkgo Petrified Forest State Park
Hoko River Site
Indian Painted Rocks (near Yakima)
Indian Painted Rocks (near Spokane)
Kettle Falls NRHP
Lake Lenore Caves
Manis Mastodon Site
Neah Bay Shell Mound Site
Old Man House
Ozette Site
Roosevelt Petroglyphs
Wakemap Mound

Great Plains

Alberta

Early Man Site
The Ribstones
Writing-on-Stone

Colorado (eastern)

Ute Trail

Kansas

El Cuartelejo Site NHL
Indian Burial Pit
Lake Scott State Park
Pawnee Indian Village NRHP

Manitoba

Bannock Point Petroform Site

Montana

Madison Buffalo Jump NRHP
Pictograph Cave State Monument
    NHL

Nebraska

Ash Hollow State Park

North Dakota

Double Ditch Indian Village State
    Historic Site NRHP
Fort Clark State Historic Site NRHP
Huff Indian Village State Historic
    Site NHL
Knife River Indian Villages National
    Historic Site
Medicine Rock State Historic Site
Menoken Indian Village State
    Historic Site NHL
Molander Indian Village State
    Historic Site
Slant Indian Village

Standing Rock State Historic Site
Writing Rock State Historic Site

Oklahoma

Indian City, U.S.A.
Spiro Mounds State Archeological
Park

South Dakota

Crow Creek Village Site NRHP
Mitchell Prehistoric Indian Village
NHL
Sherman Park Indian Burial Mounds

Texas

Alibates Flint Quarries and Texas
Panhandle Pueblo Culture
National Monument NRHP
Big Bend National Park
Caddoan Mounds State Historical
Site
Hueco Tanks State Historical Park
NRHP
Lubbock Lake Site NRHP
Panther Cave
Seminole Canyon State Historical
Park NRHP
Washington Square Mound Site

Wyoming

Bighorn Medicine Wheel NRHP
Medicine Lodge State Archeological
Site NRHP
Obsidian Cliff

Southeast

Alabama

Fort Toulouse NHL
Indian Mound Park
Mound State Monument NHL
Russell Cave National Monument
NRHP

Arkansas

Toltec Mounds State Park (Knapp
Mounds) NHL

Florida

Crystal River State Archaeological
Site NRHP
Fort Matanzas National Monument
NRHP
Lake Jackson Mounds State
Archaeological Site NRHP
Madira Bickel Mound State
Archaeological Site NRHP
Safety Harbor Site NHL
Temple Mound Museum NHL
Turtle Mound NRHP

Georgia

Etowah Mounds Archeological Area
NHL
Kolomoki Mounds State Park NHL
Ocmulgee National Monument
NRHP
Rock Eagle Effigy Mound
Track Rock Archaeological Area,
Chattahoochee National Forest

Louisiana

Marksville State Commemorative
Area NHL
Poverty Point State Commemorative
Area NHL

Mississippi

Bear Creek Mound
Boyd Mounds
Bynum Mounds
Chickasaw Village Site
Emerald Mound
Grand Village of the Natchez
Indians (Fatherland Plantation
Site) NRHP
Mangum Mound
Nanih Waiya Historic Site
Owl Creek Indian Mounds NRHP
Pharr Mounds
Winterville Mounds State Park
NRHP

North Carolina

Oconaluftee Indian Village
Town Creek Indian Mound State
Historic Site NHL

South Carolina

Charles Towne Landing Site
Santee Indian Mounds (Scott's Lake
Site)
Sewee Mound Archaeological Area
NRHP

Tennessee

Chucalissa Indian Town and
Museum NRHP
Old Stone Fort State Park NRHP
Pinson Mounds State Archaeological
Area NHL
Shiloh Mounds NRHP

North Central

Illinois

Cahokia Mounds State Historic Site
NHL
Dickson Mounds Museum NRHP
Mississippi Palisades State Park

Pere Marquette State Park
Starved Rock State Park NHL

Indiana

Angel Mounds State Memorial NHL
Mounds State Park NRHP
Wyandotte Cave

Iowa

Effigy Mounds National Monument
NRHP
Fish Farm Mounds
Pikes Peak State Park
Toolesboro Mounds National
Historic Landmark Site NHL

Kentucky

Adena Park
Ancient Buried City
Ashland Central Park
Mammoth Cave National Park

Michigan

Great Lakes Indian Museum
Isle Royale National Park
Norton Mounds NHL
Sanilac Petroglyphs State Park

Minnesota

Grand Mound Center
Itaska State Park NRHP
Jeffers Petroglyphs NRHP
Kathio State Park NHL
Minnesota Man Site
Mounds Park
Pipestone National Monument
NRHP

Missouri

Graham Cave State Park NHL
Line Creek Site
Mastodon State Park
Thousand Hills State Park NRHP
Towosahgy NRHP
Van Meter State Park
Washington State Park NRHP

Ohio

Campbell Mound NRHP
Flint Ridge Memorial NRHP
Fort Ancient State Memorial NHL
Fort Hill State Memorial NRHP
Inscription Rock NRHP
Knob Prairie Mound (Enon Mound)
Leo Petroglyph
Marietta Mound
Miamisburg Mound State Memorial
NRHP
Mound City Group National
Monument

Newark Earthworks NHL
Piketon Mounds NRHP
Seip Mound
Serpent Mound State Memorial NHL
Story Mound NRHP

West Virginia

Blennerhassett Island NRHP
Cemetery Mound
Grave Creek Mound State Park NHL
    (Mammoth Mound)
South Charleston Mound NRHP
    (Criel Mound)

Wisconsin

Aztalan State Park NHL
Copper Culture State Park
Devils Lake State Park
Gullickson's Glen
High Cliff State Park
Ice Age National Scientific Reserve
Lizard Mound State Park NRHP
Man Mound
Menasha Mounds
Mendota State Hospital Mound
    NRHP
Muscoda Mounds
Nelson Dewey State Park

Panther Intaglio
Perrot State Park
Roche-a-Cri State Park
Sheboygan Mound Park
University of Wisconsin Arboretum
University of Wisconsin Campus,
    Madison
Wyalusing State Park

Northeast

Delaware

Island Field Site NRHP

Maine

Colonial Pemaquid Restoration
    NRHP
Damariscotta River Shell Mounds
    (Oyster Shell Banks) NRHP
Old Fort Site

Massachusetts

Cape Cod National Seashore
Dighton Rock State Park NRHP

Newfoundland

L'Anse aux Meadows
Port au Choix Cemetery

New Jersey

Watson House (Abbott Farm Site)

New York

Nichols Pond
Owasco Stockaded Indian Village

Ontario

Serpent Mound
Sheguiandah Site

Pennsylvania

Sommerheim Site

Prince Edward Island

Micmac Indian Village

Rhode Island

Fort Ninigret NRHP

Virginia

Flowerdew Hundred NRHP

Thunderbird Museum and Park NHL

AMERICA'S
ANCIENT
TREASURES

More than 600 years ago 12 or 15 families lived in this 19-room, five-story apartment house at Montezuma Castle National Monument.

SOUTHWEST

North of Mexico no places offer more abundant archeological remains than do Arizona, New Mexico, southwestern Colorado, and southern Utah. Millions, possibly billions, of pottery fragments lie in and on the soil. Surveys have revealed thousands of habitation sites. All these are reminders that creative people have long lived here, and all have a common history. The once-lived-in villages, of which the potsherds are evidence, came into existence largely as a result of one special development that took place six or seven thousand years ago. At that time people in the Tehuacan Valley of present-day Mexico, and possibly elsewhere, began to domesticate a certain wild grass. The discovery that they could plant its seeds in garden plots changed their lives and the whole of Indian life in large sections of the American continents.

As this wild grass was cultivated, it changed greatly and evolved into the grain we call corn, or maize. It developed husks that wrapped more and more tightly around the seed-bearing cob, until at last maize could no longer sow its own seeds. It could not live from year to year unless humans removed the husks and planted the corn kernels. At the same time, people became so accustomed to eating corn, prepared in many ways, that their lives revolved around planting, cultivating, and harvesting the helpless but nourishing cereal. Corn and humankind became mutually dependent.

The idea of gardening spread northward. So did a knowledge of how to make long-lasting pots for cooking and storing the new food. With the ability to keep food in reserve, diet changed. Dwellings, too, changed under influences which swept into northern Mexico, then into New Mexico and Arizona. Along with corn there came a whole constellation of customs and ceremonies, such as corn dances and other planting and harvest-time rituals. Some of these are still observed today.

Perhaps as early as 1000 B.C. the Western Archaic people known as the Cochise had begun to add corn to their diet. They also added squash and beans. The beans were most important because they furnished protein which would have been lacking if farmers had tried to depend entirely on corn. People could not live by maize alone. Although life changed greatly with the arrival of this extraordinary plant, the changes were not identical throughout the Southwest. They varied from place to place, as communities learned the new ways of creating food while continuing to be a part of the special kind of ecological system in which they had already found a place for themselves. In one sense, of course, all farmers were alike. They could give up the wandering existence of the hunter or gatherer and build more or less permanent dwellings. The differences in the details of how they built and created and elaborated on life are among the things that make Southwestern archeology fascinating to both the scientist and the layperson.

Broadly speaking, four different lifeways developed under the stimulating influences that came with agriculture from Mexico: The Mogollon (MOH-goh-YOHN), the Hohokam (ho-ho-KAHM), the Patayan (PAH-tah-YAHN), and the Anasazi (AHN-ah-SAH-zee). Eventually there developed several variations or combinations of these four basic cultures.

The Mogollon Culture
By about 100 B.C. the new agricultural way of life had taken on a distinct identity in the highlands of the Mogollon Mountains, which lie across the present border between Arizona and New Mexico. In certain places the slopes of these mountains were ideal for raising corn. They duplicated to a considerable extent the conditions in the part of Mexico where corn was domesticated. Here in the mountains the Cochise had long based their pattern of existence on plant food. They were accustomed to grinding wild seeds in order to make them easy to chew and digest, and it was no problem for women to begin grinding corn as well. We know that the Cochise began to raise corn at a very early date; archeologists have excavated the tiny cobs and husks and even a few seeds of extremely ancient corn in Bat Cave and Tularosa Cave in New Mexico. (Neither of these sites is visitable, but some of the material from Bat Cave is on exhibit at the Peabody Museum, Harvard University, in Cambridge, Massachusetts).

After the Cochise settled down and developed the characteristics now called Mogollon, they began to live in dwellings known as pithouses. To make such a house, they dug a circular pit two or three feet deep and set a strong, upright post in the center. Then over the pit they made a cone-shaped roof of saplings which leaned against the center pole from around the upper edge of the pit. Over the saplings they laid or wove small branches, and on top of the branches they spread a thick layer of mud. On one side of the pithouse a ramp led from ground level down to the floor inside.

A pithouse, part below ground and part above, and covered with a thick, insulating layer of earth, was relatively cool in summer and warm in winter. As time went on, its shape changed from circular to oval to rectangular, and it came to be roofed in various ways, but it remained the standard home until very late in Mogollon history.

The pottery that Mogollon people made was at first red or brown without decoration. Later they invented or borrowed many different designs, and those who lived along the Mimbres River developed a unique style. They painted sophisticated, often humorous representations of animals, insects, fish, birds, and human beings on the white surfaces of their dishes. Examples of Mimbres pottery may be seen in the Millicent Rogers Museum in Taos, New Mexico, in the Colorado University Museum in Boulder, Colorado, and in the Southwest Museum in Los Angeles.

The Hohokam Culture
People who lived along the Salt, the Gila, and the San Pedro rivers in southern Arizona also felt the influence of Mexican ideas and inventions. There is no doubt that a great deal of trade went on between Mesoamericans and these Cochise desert dwellers, and much of it passed through a large community in northern Mexico now known as Casas Grandes.

Excavation at Casas Grandes revealed that by the eleventh century A.D. there were enormous warehouses for goods that people to the north wanted in exchange for turquoise and other gemstones. Copper bells made by a process that had not reached the Southwest, millions of small shells for beads, and large ones for trumpets were stored in the mud-brick rooms of the trading center. Parrots and scarlet and green macaws, much in demand farther north, were actually raised in breeding pens at Casas Grandes.

Before the days of intensive trade, probably as early as 300 B.C., people in the area near present-day Phoenix were developing a special way of life. Known now as the Hohokam (a Pima word for "ancient ones"), they grew corn and other plants from seeds that had come from Mexico, and they brought water to their crops through irrigation canals—a Mexican invention. Later they and neighbors along the rivers diverted water to fields far out on the semiarid land. Rich harvests resulted from irrigation, and the River Hohokam not only had enough to eat, they also had time to spare. Some of them became adept at crafts, making lovely jewelry and

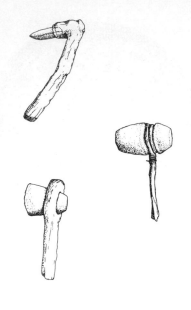

Top to bottom: An adze. A grooved ax. An ungrooved ax, or celt. After Linda Murphy in *Indians of Arkansas,* by Charles R. McGimsey, III.

Ax, Adze, and Celt

Prehistoric Indians cut and shaped wood with all three of these tools, which they fashioned from stone. Each was attached to a handle in its own special way. The ax was shaped by chipping, or by chipping and grinding and polishing. It was sometimes sharpened on one end, sometimes on both ends, and it had a groove which made it easier to attach a handle. (This is called hafting.) The groove might go all the way around the ax or only partway.

A celt was usually polished, had no groove, and was hafted as the illustration shows.

Although neither an ax nor a celt looks very efficient to anyone who is used to steel tools, both work surprisingly well. Archeologists who have tried stone axes found they could chop down a six-inch tree in less than twenty minutes.

The cutting edge of an ax or a celt is parallel to the handle; the cutting edge of an adze is at right angles to its handle. An adze is not designed for chopping down trees, but it is effective, for example, in hollowing out logs to make dugout canoes.

---

figurines. The early Hohokam pottery was buff colored, with red geometric decorations. Later potters made designs in the forms of birds or animals or people.

Early Hohokam houses were somewhat like Mogollon pithouses, except that the builders did less excavation. Later they made large structures several stories high, possibly for storage or defense. They also built ball courts, where they played a kind of ceremonial game with a solid rubber ball, apparently derived from a similar Mexican game.

Did descendants of the ancient Cochise simply adapt ideas and technology that came with traders from the south? Many—perhaps most—archeologists think so. Others, who have done a great deal of work in the Hohokam areas, believe that the Hohokam culture resulted from the actual immigration of people from Mesoamerica. At any rate traces of Mexican interaction with Southwesterners can be clearly seen in such things as food crops, irrigation, building styles, and evidence of religious beliefs.

In the days of the Hohokam there was apparently somewhat more rainfall than there is today in southern Arizona. With more moisture people had more to eat with less work. So life was a little easier than it is for the present-day Pima and Papago Indians, who may be the descendants of the ancient Hohokam.

Left to right: Basketry pad, found at Echo House, Mesa Verde, made for use in carrying heavy water jars on the head. Broken arrowhead, found with its hafting intact, showing how a point was attached to a shaft. Original in Colorado Heritage Center, Denver. Mesa Verde bowl, with a design made in black on a white background.

The Patayan Culture

In the valley of the Colorado River, which includes the western part of Arizona, lived a people to whom agriculture came later than it did to the Mogollon and the Hohokam. Here farming began only about A.D. 600. In the lowlands on the banks of the great river, and in the high plateau country through which the Colorado had cut its deep channel, distinct lifeways developed.

Not a great deal is known about these prehistoric people, who are called Patayan by some archeologists and Hakataya by others. The reason is simple: much evidence of life along the riverbanks has been buried under layers of silt brought down by the Colorado River. Other sites have been washed away and now lie, lost forever, in the Gulf of California.

At the time when corn reached them from Mexico, the Patayan lived in flimsy shelters made of poles covered with brush. Later they began to make more permanent structures covered with mud. Finally some of them borrowed an architectural idea from neighbors to the north and began to build stone dwellings.

People who live along the Colorado River today—the Havasupai, the Maricopa, and the Yuma, among others—are probably descendants of the ancient Patayan people.

These pinnacles, known to Navajos as Spider Rock, are near White House ruins in Canyon de Chelly National Monument. National Park Service photo by Fred Mang, Jr.

The Anasazi Culture

Still farther north of Mexico lies rugged country where high plateaus are cut by deep canyons and rimmed with steep cliffs. Here, through the southern part of Colorado and Utah and the northern part of New Mexico and Arizona, still other groups of Western Archaic people made their homes, beginning about 7000 years ago. In one region of northwestern New Mexico, Cynthia Irwin-Williams and her colleagues have studied a group whose lifeways belonged to what is now called the Oshara Tradition. Like other prefarming, preceramic peoples, they hunted and harvested wild crops, moving about in roughly this one area in an annual round. Sometime after 2800 B.C. these people learned about the maize plant and began to grow it in small patches on the floors of canyons. A more settled way of life was now possible, and with it more structured social and ceremonial customs, which finally evolved into the fully sedentary lifeways now called Anasazi. (This is a word from the Navajo language, meaning "ancient ones.")

As the Anasazi culture developed, changes were so very marked that archeologists have given special names to each of the stages. The first stage is usually called Basketmaker II. There is no Basketmaker I; the archeologists who named it have been disappointed. They expected some day to find evidence of a stage they could call Basketmaker I. They never did. At any rate these first Anasazi corn farmers tended to live in caves or recesses in the cliff walls,

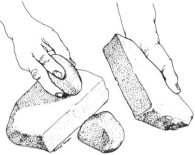

Ancient masonry methods: First, with a sharp-edged blade of chert, a deep groove was scratched on the surface of a slab of sandstone. Next the slab was placed over a pebble. Then, the groove was tapped with a hammerstone, directly above the pebble, to break the slab cleanly in two. *Photo:* Section of a wall built of stone shaped by this method, in Aztec Ruins National Monument. National Park Service photo by George A. Grant.

where their nomadic ancestors had often camped. Sometimes they may have put up brush shelters in the caves, and they certainly stored food in slab-lined pits in cave floors. Later they learned to build pithouses for their own use. These resembled in many ways the pithouses of the Mogollon, but in Anasazi country the half-subterranean dwellings had an interesting later history, which is best told at the museum in Mesa Verde National Park.

The Basketmakers did indeed make marvelous baskets. Thanks to the dry climate and their taste for living in caves, a great deal of their fine handiwork was protected from the weather and has survived for nearly 2000 years. For the same reason we also know what these people looked like. They buried their dead in empty storage pits, and in the dry air bodies became desiccated. Men wore their hair long, sometimes in braids; women cut theirs from time to time and used the hair to make bags or rope.

By A.D. 700 the Anasazi had learned more about farming and had drawn together in larger groups than before. They were building houses of stone, one against another in communal dwellings. The Spanish word for these apartment-house villages was pueblo, and so archeologists have given the name Pueblo to the next stages in Anasazi culture.

In the next 600 years the Anasazi grew more and more skilled at building and pottery making and other crafts, such as the creation of jewelry and fine cloth. Even at this distance, trade brought

An Anasazi jar lid. Museum of Anthropology, University of Missouri, photo.

influences from Mesoamerica. Dams and ditches conserved water for crops. Shell beads and ornaments, macaw and parrot skeletons have turned up in excavations at Anasazi sites.

Within the large, general region where they lived, there began to appear three major centers of development. Each had a style of pottery and masonry and architecture that distinguished it from the others.

One center was near present-day Kayenta, in Arizona. There the finest achievement of the Kayenta Anasazi are preserved in the Navajo National Monument. A second center was at Mesa Verde, in Colorado. The third was in Chaco Canyon, in New Mexico. From all these developments among the Anasazi one important fact emerges. Using corn, beans, and squash as sources of energy in an area which was far from ideal for agriculture, people managed to shape lifeways which became more and more sophisticated with the passage of time. They gathered together in villages and seemed to be approaching urban life, just as the agriculturists did in the Tigris-Euphrates Valley at the beginning of the era of Middle Eastern civilization. Then a great convulsion affected the Anasazi world. In one village after another, men put aside their tools and women abandoned their cooking pots. With only what they could carry on a long journey, they set out to make new homes elsewhere.

A Park Ranger shows how an Indian woman pushed a mano back and forth on a metate to crush hard kernels of corn, making corn meal. National Park Service photo by Robert W. Gage.

Archeologists do not agree on what caused the change which left most Anasazi pueblos deserted forever and turned an expansive people to looking inward. Certainly there was such a change, and it must have been brought on by great stress of some kind. The Anasazi withdrew from the wide area they occupied and went to live in a narrower one. From that time on they seemed to live with less energy. They grew protective of what they had and knew. Surviving, and surviving very skillfully, they became the ancestors of the Pueblo Indians of today.

Perpendicular sandstone walls tower above small clusters of masonry buildings in niches or on the canyon floor in Canyon de Chelly. National Park Service photo.

Many artifacts, such as these effigy vessels recovered from Snaketown, a large Hohokam village site in southern Arizona, can be seen in the Arizona State Museum. National Park Service photo.

Arizona

AMERIND FOUNDATION, INC.

From Tucson (TOO-sahn) drive 64 miles east on Interstate 10, then 1¼ miles on local road toward Dragoon. Open free, by appointment only, Saturday, Sunday all year. Mail address: Dragoon, AZ 85609.

This private museum contains a superb collection of prehistoric material from the area once called Pimeria Alta, which included southern Arizona and the northern part of the Mexican state of Sonora.

ARIZONA STATE MUSEUM
(See University of Arizona)

ARIZONA STATE UNIVERSITY MUSEUM OF ANTHROPOLOGY

In the Anthropology Building, on the campus, Tempe. Open free, Monday through Friday.

Exhibits, which are designed and installed by university students, contain a wide variety of material from the collection of the anthropology department and borrowed from other institutions. A number of displays emphasize archeological techniques for studying artifacts and the material culture of prehistoric people.

Of special interest are exhibits on dental anthropology, showing how the teeth of ancient Americans reveal the areas in Asia where various groups probably originated. Dr. Christy G. Turner II of the anthropology department has examined the special characteristics of thousands of teeth, both in the New World and in the Old, and has concluded that there were three migrations of people from Asia, beginning at least 14,000 years ago and perhaps earlier. First the ancestors of all Paleo-Indians crossed into North America from the area of the Lena River in Siberia; then came the ancestors of the Aleuts and Eskimos from the Amur River area; and third, the ancestors of some Northwest Coast people and of the Navajos and the Apaches moved from a forested area of Siberia across the Bering Landbridge before it was covered by the sea.

Squash seeds were found in Canyon de Chelly, wrapped tightly in corn husk. Drawn from a National Park Service photo.

BESH-BA-GOWAH
(See Gila County Historical Society)

BETATAKIN
(See Navajo National Monument)

CANYON DE CHELLY NATIONAL MONUMENT
(CAN-yuhn duh SHAY)

From Gallup, New Mexico, drive north 8 miles on US 666, then 52 miles west on New Mexico–Arizona 264 through Ganado, then 33 miles north on Navajo 63 to monument headquarters and the Visitor Center at Chinle (chin-LEE). Open free daily, all year. Camping.

Protected by spectacular red sandstone walls, prehistoric Indians built hundreds of small villages and cliff dwellings in this canyon over a period of nearly a thousand years. Visitors can walk to a cliff dwelling called White House Ruin, following a trail that winds down from the canyon rim for about a mile. Other ruins can be seen only when visitors are accompanied by a park ranger or other official guide.

The Story. Beginning about A.D. 350, the canyon was occupied by people now known as the Anasazi, ancestors of the present-day Pueblo Indians. Then about A.D. 1300 the Anasazi moved out, leaving the canyon to occasional visits from their descendants or from the Navajo Indians, who began to take possession of the area. During their thousand-year stay, the Anasazi gardened in small plots on the canyon bottom, where there was flowing water at certain times each year. At other seasons the stream bed must have seemed completely dry, although there was usually enough moisture beneath the surface for crops of corn and squash.

The Anasazi also hunted—at first with spears, then with bows and arrows. Over the years house structures changed as much as hunting methods. Early inhabitants of the canyon lived in houses built partially underground. Their later dwellings, made of stone and entirely above ground, were joined one to another, so that the whole village was one big apartment house. Still later they build some of their apartment houses in large, dry caves in the cliffs.

Rings, bracelets, bone whistle, pottery sculpture, and carved stone found at Casa Grande. National Park Service photo by George A. Grant.

Opposite:
A Park Ranger examines the demolished walls of an ancient pueblo in Canyon de Chelly. This ruin had stood for perhaps a thousand years before it was destroyed in a rock slide caused by a sonic boom. National Park Service photo.

About A.D. 1300 the Anasazi abandoned Canyon de Chelly, just as they moved out of other villages in the Four Corners area—the area where Arizona, Utah, Colorado, and New Mexico meet. Why they left is still something of a mystery. Archeologists have discovered that there was a severe drought at about this time, and for many years before they moved away the Anasazi had great difficulty raising crops. Quite possibly this was not their only reason for deserting the canyon. Internal dissension may have caused villages to break up. Or pressure from outsiders may have induced people to migrate elsewhere.

Little groups of Navajos settled in the canyon nearly 300 years ago, and some of the paintings they made on its rock walls can still be seen.

The Museum. Contains exhibits of Southwestern archeological finds in the Four Corners area and also artifacts from later Navajo culture.

The Name. De Chelly (duh SHAY) is a mispronunciation in English of a mispronunciation in Spanish of the Navajo word *tsegi,* which means "a rocky canyon."

Special Interest. Here, in January of 1864, Colonel Christopher "Kit" Carson directed a military expedition that destroyed all food supplies and forced large numbers of Navajos to choose between death by starvation and surrender. The United States Army then drove the Navajos to Fort Sumner, New Mexico, over 300 miles away. There, for four years, about 8000 Navajos were confined in what amounted to a prisoner-of-war camp. In the end, their insistence on returning to their homeland prevailed, and they came back to Canyon de Chelly and the surrounding area. This traumatic episode in their history is known to the Navajos as the Long Walk.

Fort Sumner, also known as Bosque Redondo, is one of the New Mexico State Monuments, located 2 miles east of the town of Fort Sumner on US 60.

CASA GRANDE RUINS
NATIONAL MONUMENT
(KAH-suh GRAHN-day)

Halfway between Phoenix and Tucson, 1 mile north of Coolidge on Arizona 87. (Note: the National Monument is

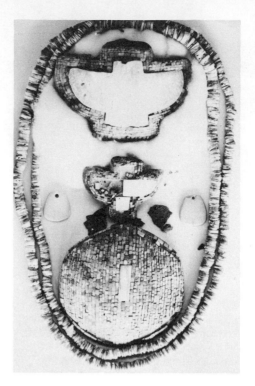

Hohokam craftsmen at Casa Grande glued tiny bits of shaped turquoise onto seashells with mesquite gum. These are in the museum at the site. National Park Service photo by George A. Grant.

not in the town of Casa Grande.) Open daily, all year. Admission charged. Camping nearby.

This site offers an excellent introduction to the lifeway of the ancient irrigation farmers now known as the Hohokam. There are guided tours through one part of the ruins, 9:15 a.m. to 4:15 p.m., and a self-guided tour through another part.

The Story. The impressive, four-story structure which gives the site its name (*Casa Grande* means big house) was probably built about A.D. 1350 and was used until 1450. It may have been a ceremonial center or fortress or both. Its massive walls, made from a special kind of clay, are not typical of the Hohokam. The building is much more like those seen farther south, in Mexico. The usual Hohokam dwellings were separate, single-room houses, made of brush and mud.

Throughout the semiarid Gila River Valley, the Hohokam managed to raise crops by irrigation. They built more than 250 miles of canals, which were between two and four feet wide and about two feet deep. Some can still be seen today.

The Museum. Here may be seen artifacts of the Hohokam people and panels which explain their life.

The Name. The ruins were visited in 1694 by Father Kino, a Spanish explorer-priest, who named the place Casa Grande. The great size of the main building made it a landmark for later visitors, and the name has remained in use.

CLARA T. WOODY MUSEUM
(See Gila County Historical Society)

EASTERN ARIZONA MUSEUM AND HISTORICAL SOCIETY

Main and Center streets, Pima. Open free, Monday through Friday.

Salado and Hohokam artifacts from the vicinity of Pima are on display here, together with some material from northern Arizona, which is not identified.

FORT LOWELL MUSEUM

2900 North Craycroft Rd., near intersection with Fort Lowell Rd., in Old Fort Lowell County Park, Tuc-

This massive structure at Casa Grande Ruins National Monument is made from a kind of clay that contains a cement-like material called caliche. The builders shaped the mud by hand in a layer about two feet thick, let it dry, then added another layer. A protective roof now covers the building to prevent erosion. National Park Service photo by George A. Grant.

son. Open free, daily. Closed certain holidays.

Twelve outdoor panel exhibits tell the story of the Hardy Site, a prehistoric Hohokam village that now lies beneath the park and the surrounding neighborhood. Partial excavation of the site revealed the remains of pithouses, outdoor roasting pits, work areas where stone tools were made, and pits where calcium carbonate was mined for mixing with mud and water, to form plaster for house floors and walls. For other Hohokam sites, see Index.

GILA COUNTY HISTORICAL SOCIETY, CLARA T. WOODY MUSEUM

From the center of Globe take US 60 west to Mine Rescue Building at north end of city. Open free, Monday through Friday; afternoon, Saturday. Closed certain holidays.

Here may be seen artifacts from the ruins of a large village at a site called Besh-Ba-Gowah, which was inhabited from about A.D. 1225 to 1400 by the Salado people. Urban development has now swallowed most of the site. Before its partial destruction, the city of Globe had excavated and done restoration work on some of its hundred rooms. Another Salado village has been preserved in Tonto National Monument, about 40 miles northwest of Globe.

The Name. Besh-Ba-Gowah is the Apache Indian name for Globe, meaning "place of metal."

GLEN CANYON NATIONAL RECREATION AREA

Headquarters and Visitor Center in Page, 134 miles north of Flagstaff on US 89. Visitor Center open daily, all year. Closed certain holidays.

After construction of the Glen Canyon dam across the Colorado River, the waters of Lake Powell destroyed hundreds of archeological sites dating from A.D. 500 or earlier to the late 13th century. Extensive surveys, conducted before flooding, led to the discovery of many Anasazi ruins and also of many petroglyph and pictograph sites.

The rock art turned out to be particularly interesting to archeologists.

Some of their studies made use of the help of modern Hopi Indians whose ancestors probably drew or pecked or scratched many of the pictures on boulders and on the walls of canyons in the Recreation Area. The meaning of these petrographs (a term that includes both petroglyphs and pictographs) is obscure. The numerous representations of sheep very likely had to do with hunting. Some abstract designs probably represent patterns in woven cloth, since it is generally supposed that men were the rock artists and it was men who did Hopi weaving. In some places, where rather crude work appears low down on rock surfaces, children were possibly copying older people's designs.

Fortunately some of the archeological sites in the region lie above the present water line and are still accessible by boat on Lake Powell. Commercial boat trips do not regularly include visits to the sites, but private craft are available for renting. Maps showing the locations of sites can be bought at the Visitor Center, and rangers there will give further information.

In Grand Canyon National Park, Tusayan Ruin, built about A.D. 1185, was occupied for less than 50 years. Then, for some unknown reason, it was abandoned. National Park Service photo by J. M. Eden.

GRAND CANYON NATIONAL PARK

The park is divided by the canyon into two parts, reached by very different routes. For the South Rim drive 59 miles north from Williams on Arizona 64 to park headquarters. For the North Rim drive 30 miles south from Jacob Lake on Arizona 67 to the park entrance, then 12 miles farther to the rim. Open (South Rim) all year; (North Rim) mid-May to mid-Oct. Admission charged. Camping.

Prehistoric people lived in and around this incredible canyon for a very long time. Some climbed into caves in the cliffs and left artifacts there. In recent years Dr. Robert Euler has explored the canyon walls and bottom lands by helicopter and has found a great many archeological sites which no one knew about before. (About half a million acres in the Grand Canyon have still not had an archeological survey.)

A ruined village called Tusayan (too-say-YAHN) on the South Rim may be visited all year. There are guided tours in summer.

On the North Rim a site called Cape Royal Ruin (G.C. 212) has been excavated and is open to the public.

A third site, Bright Angel Pueblo (G.C. 624) on the canyon bottom near the Colorado River, may be visited all year. The eight-mile Bright Angel Trail leads to the site from the South Rim. Hikers are advised to make the trip in two days. Camping reservations required. Mule trips are also available.

The Story. People of the Western Archaic, or Desert culture moved into the Grand Canyon area three or four thousand years ago. They lived by gathering wild plant food and by hunting, and they did what other hunters have sometimes done—they made figurines of deer or mountain sheep and left them in caves, apparently in the hope that this practice would bring them luck. A figurine was fashioned of a single long willow twig, split down the middle and bent in an ingenious way into the form of the animal. Sometimes the figurines were pierced by a twig spear, for good measure. Archeologists have found a number of these split-twig animals in caches in now almost inaccessible caves in the limestone

cliffs. Radiocarbon dates indicate that they were left there between 3100 and 4100 years ago. Almost no other artifacts were found with the figurines, so the culture of their makers has remained something of a puzzle.

More than 370 specimens have now been found, not only in the Grand Canyon, but also in Nevada, Utah and California, and at some of these latter sites they were associated with artifacts of various kinds, such as projectile points, sandals, and skin bags. These sites appear to have been used at a later date than were the Grand Canyon caves. The differences in time and the associated material have led to speculation that the non-cave figurines may have served a different purpose. Perhaps they may even have been playthings rather than ritual objects.

Certainly people of the Grand Canyon area changed their patterns of living and, in time, became more like the Anasazi farmers who lived to the east and north. Some found their way down the canyon's high walls, built small villages, and raised their crops close to the thundering Colorado River. Others made their

The Southwest

Only from the point of view of *norteamericanos* (Spanish for people north of Mexico) is the southwestern part of the United States "the Southwest." From the point of view of Mexicans the area lies to the north. Moreover, in prehistoric times the area received great attention from people in Mexico and was widely influenced by Mexican culture.

To prehistoric Mexicans, and also to the later Spanish *conquistadores,* the region was part of a large area that was known as the Gran Chichimeca, which extended northward from the Tropic of Cancer to the vicinity of present-day San Francisco, California, on the northwest, and to Wichita, Kansas, in the northeast. The word *chichimeca* was descriptive. It meant, among other things, "nomad." It also meant "son of the dog," or "outlander." Gran Chichimeca was the Great Land of Nomads—people who were barbarians from the point of view of the more sophisticated inhabitants of the Valley of Mexico. Some United States archeologists want to revive the name Gran Chichimeca and apply it to both northern Mexico and the southwestern United States. Other archeologists, having no less respect for ancient Mexican culture and for present-day Mexican sensibilities, believe that the term "Southwest" is so deeply imbedded in usage that it is practically impossible to substitute the older name. So, bowing to current custom in the United States, this book calls the Gran Chichimeca the Southwest.

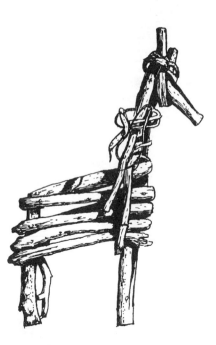

Figurine of a deer, made from split twigs about 3000 years ago in the Grand Canyon area. Original in the Arizona State Museum, Tucson.

homes along the canyon rim. Tusayan, built between A.D. 1185 and 1200, housed about 30 people, but they did not stay long. By 1250 they had moved away, probably to the Kayenta region. One by one the other villages down near the river were also abandoned, and by the time the first Spanish explorers arrived the only Indians living in the canyon were the Havasupai, who have remained there to this day.

There is some evidence that conflict may have accounted for abandonment on the South Rim, and curious settlements on so-called islands in the canyon indicate pressure of some sort. The islands are large areas on top of sections of rock that have been isolated by erosion all around them. These almost inaccessible spots may have been chosen as habitation sites when it became necessary to defend hoards of food at times when bad weather restricted crops. Study of the islands is being continued.

Helicopter rides take visitors close up to canyon walls. At one point below Point Sublime on the North Rim, it is possible to see a former settlement, so protected from weathering that the original roofing on the dwellings appears to be intact.

Visitors to the Tusayan Ruin can take a self-guided tour, aided by a pamphlet that tells about the life and culture of those who built this small village.

The Museums. At Tusayan Ruin the museum has exhibits with special emphasis on the culture of the people who lived there. Displays show how artifacts and pottery vessels were made. There are also exhibits of artifacts made and used by Patayan people called the Cohonina, who lived on the South Rim about A.D. 750 to 1100. The museum is open 8 a.m. to 5 p.m. in summer.

At the Visitor Center the museum is open all year, 8 a.m. to sunset. Displays here show artifacts of most people and periods in the area. Of special interest are the split-twig figurines.

GRASSHOPPER RUIN

From Showlow drive south 29 miles on US 60, then west 14 miles to Cibicue. The site and field school are 11 miles farther west on local roads 21 then 25. For exact directions to the

site, inquire at the cafe in Cibicue. Open free, in summer.

This large village, occupied from about A.D. 1275 to 1400, is being excavated by the University of Arizona. Visitors are welcome to watch ongoing work.

HARDY SITE
(See Fort Lowell County Park page 000)

HEARD MUSEUM OF ANTHROPOLOGY AND PRIMITIVE ART

22 E. Monte Vista Red., Phoenix. Open Tuesday through Saturday; afternoon, Sunday. Closed certain holidays. Admission charged.

Collections in this museum are built around artifacts of Indians of the Americas, including the Hohokam of southern Arizona.

HOHOKAM-PIMA NATIONAL MONUMENT

This unit of the National Park System, which preserves remains of the Hohokam culture, is not open to the public. For information apply at Casa Grande Ruins National Monument, PO Box 518, Coolidge, AZ 85228.

KEET SEEL
(See Navajo National Monument)

KINISHBA PUEBLO

Drive 15 miles west of Whiteriver on Arizona 73. Open free, all year.

This partly restored Mogollon-Anasazi pueblo housed a thousand or more people between A.D. 1100 and 1350. It is one of the largest ruins in the Southwest. Despite its importance, the pueblo can only be viewed through a barbed-wire fence, which the White Mountain Apache Tribe has put up for the safety of visitors and for the protection of the site. When funds become available the tribe hopes to stabilize and restore the entire town, which includes two enclosed courtyards, and to reestablish the museum it once operated here.

Special Interest. An early excavator at Kinishba found the skeleton of a child,

Montezuma Castle. National Park Service photo by Dave Roberts.

Opposite:
This excavated mound at Snaketown was probably a dance platform. A model of Snaketown is in the Heard Museum in Phoenix. National Park Service photo.

around which was wrapped a necklace almost six feet long, made of 2,534 carefully polished turquoise beads. This astonishing piece of work is now in the Arizona State Museum at Tucson. Also in the necklace were 11 larger beads made of catlinite (pipestone), which may have been brought by traders from far-away Minnesota. Many other necklaces at Knishba included coral, which came from either the Gulf of Mexico or Baja California, and shells from the Pacific Coast. Trade was obviously extensive in prehistoric America.

KINLICHEE TRIBAL PARK

On the Navajo Indian Reservation, drive west from Window Rock 22 miles on Navajo 3 (Arizona 264) to Cross Canyon Trading Post, then 2½ miles north on gravel road to Kinlichee and Cross Canyon Ruins. Open free, at all times. Camping nearby.

Anasazi people lived in this area for more than 500 years. Today, in a Tribal Park, the Navajo Indians are preserving the ruins of Anasazi dwellings, the oldest of which is a pithouse dated

at about A.D. 800. Other ruins belong to the various Pueblo periods up to about 1300, when the large, apartment-house villages were abandoned. Wayside exhibits and a trail take the visitor on a self-guided tour, which gives an opportunity to see how Anasazi architecture evolved. To help visitors visualize the life of the past one of the ruins has been completely reconstructed.

MONTEZUMA CASTLE
NATIONAL MONUMENT

From Flagstaff drive 50 miles south on Interstate 17, then 2½ miles east to the Visitor Center. Open daily, all year. Admission charged.

The monument is in two sections —Montezuma Castle and Montezuma Well, 9.5 miles apart. Footpaths from headquarters building lead toward the beautifully preserved "castle," a cliff dwelling built a hundred feet above the valley floor. Along the walk is a diorama with audio tape that explains what life was like in the dwelling more than 600 years ago. The ledge that supports the buildings has wea-

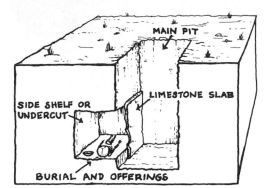

Diagram of an undercut grave at Montezuma Castle National Monument. After Schroeder and Hastings.

Montezuma Castle ruin was given its name by early white settlers, who guessed that Aztec Indians had built the cliff dwellings here. Santa Fe Railway photo.

thered so greatly that visits to the castle itself are no longer permitted. Ruins of other dwellings at the foot of the cliff, farther along the trail, may be visited.

At Montezuma Well two ruins overlook a sunken lake, about 400 feet across and 55 feet deep. The well is fed by a huge spring, from which flow 1½ million gallons of water every day.

The Story. Several groups of farmers with different customs contributed to the development of a distinct way of life in the valley of the Verde River. About A.D. 600 a group of Hohokam people moved into the valley from the desert country near modern Phoenix, where they lived in one-family, one-room houses made of poles covered with brush and mud. The Hohokam were farmers who dug irrigation canals to water their crops of corn, squash, beans, and cotton.

A second group of farmers lived north of the Verde Valley. These people, who raised crops without irrigation, have been named the Sinagua (sin-AH-wah), Spanish for "without water."

In A.D. 1065 both these groups apparently heard news that at a place now called Sunset Crater a volcano had erupted and covered a large area with a layer of cinders. These cinders helped the dry soil to retain moisture and made it good for farming. The result was a land rush, which brought in from the east a third group of people, called the Anasazi. Unlike the other farmers, these people built multiple dwellings of stone, often several stories high.

Some of the Hohokam from Verde Valley joined in the land rush, and they mingled with the Anasazi and the Sinagua. But before long the cinder-covered land became crowded. There may also have been a drought. At any rate, the area no longer seemed attractive to some of its inhabitants, and about A.D. 1100 a group of Sinagua moved south into the Verde Valley. There they began to build the Anasazi type of stone house they had learned about during the land rush. Because they found water in the valley, they irrigated their fields, Hohokam-fashion, grew cotton along with food crops, and became excellent

Anasazi Religion

Archeologists can't dig up a religious belief. All that comes out of the earth is an object. If the object resembles a prayer stick used by Pueblo Indians today, it seems reasonable to suppose that the object may have been a prayer stick in prehistoric times.

There are many similarities between present-day Pueblo religious objects and prehistoric objects which excavators have found.

The basic beliefs of modern Pueblo Indians have been studied. All things considered, it seems likely that the ancestors of the Pueblos had very similar views on life. If this was the case, the Anasazi religion said: "People must live in harmony with nature."

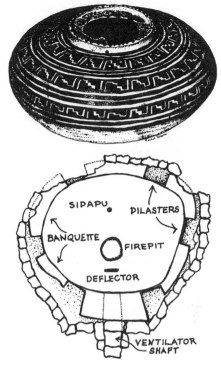

Above: A jar used in kiva ceremonies. The design was painted with a brush of yucca fiber and paint made of boiled plant juices. Original is in the museum at Mesa Verde. *Below:* The ground plan of a kiva. After a drawing in the trail guide to Spruce Tree House, Mesa Verde.

---

weavers. They also mined salt, which is always in demand wherever people's diet consists mainly of grain and other plant foods.

As a result of trade in salt and cotton and other products, new ideas came into the valley. So did many settlers, who were attracted by the wealth there. One new idea served as a protection against rivals—the notion of building dwellings in cavities in cliffs. About 1250 the Sinagua began construction of a stone apartment house, with one room above another, in a cave overlooking Beaver Creek, which flows into the Verde River. This is the five-story habitation called Montezuma Castle.

For 200 years descendants of the original builders lived here in the valley. Then competition for the farmland along the creek and nearby river became too rough for the farmers, who seem to have been peaceful folk.

As aggressive newcomers—possibly the ancestors of the present-day Yavapai—moved into the valley, the Sinagua moved out. Very likely they went north and joined the ancestors of the present-day Hopi.

The Name. Early white settlers in the Verde Valley mistakenly thought that Aztec Indians had built the dwellings at this site. So the five-story apartment house and the well, several miles away, were both named in honor of Montezuma, last Aztec emperor. The name, although misleading, has stuck.

Special Feature. The prehistoric farmers here built irrigation canals from Montezuma Well to their garden plots. Because the water contained lime, the ditches became lined with a hard cement-like crust, which has survived to this day.

MONUMENT VALLEY TRIBAL PARK

From Kayenta drive 24 miles north on US 163 to directional sign, then 5 miles east on local road to Visitor Center. Open free, daily, June to September.

At the Visitor Center in this Navajo Tribal Park arrangements can be made for guided four-wheel-drive trips to prehistoric ruins in the Monument Valley area.

Reproduction of a painting of the Squash Blossom Girl from the Awatovi kiva. Museum of Northern Arizona photo.

MUSEUM OF NORTHERN ARIZONA

Fort Valley Rd. (US 180), Flagstaff. Open free, Monday through Saturday; afternoons, Sunday. Closed certain holidays.

Excellent displays on prehistoric and contemporary native cultures of the Colorado Plateau. Exhibits cover all periods from the Paleo-Indian, Anasazi, and Pueblo, through present-day Hopi and Navajo cultures.

NAVAJO COMMUNITY COLLEGE NED HATATHLI CENTER

On the college campus. From Arizona 63 at Round Rock drive south 16 miles to Lukachukai Trading Post, then 10 miles farther south to Tsaile. Open free, Sunday through Friday; mornings Saturday, during the college year.

Displays contain Navajo sand paintings and other materials, together with artifacts from other Indian cultures.

This college is the first to be located on a reservation and controlled by Native American people.

NAVAJO NATIONAL MONUMENT

From Tuba City drive 56 miles northeast on US 160, then 9 miles northwest on a paved road to Visitor Center. Open free, daily, all year. Camping.

Here several superb cliff dwellings may be visited. Tours are conducted in spring, summer, and fall to the most accessible ruin, Betatakin (be-TAH-tah-kin), which means "ledge house" in the language of the Navajos, who inhabit the region today. This is a village of 135 rooms, built in an immense cave, which reaches 500 feet in height.

Another ruin, one of the largest in Arizona, is Keet Seel, which means "broken pottery" in the Navajo language. An eight-mile trail leads down into a canyon and along a stream to this splendid cliff village, which has a

Betatakin is one of three well-preserved Anasazi cliff dwellings in Navajo National Monument. National Park Service photo by Natt N. Dodge.

remarkably new appearance, although its 160 rooms have not been lived in for more than 600 years. A visit to Keet Seel takes a full day on horses, which can be rented from Navajos or two days on foot, with an overnight stay in the campground near the ruin. Only 1500 visitors a year are allowed at Keet Seel. Tours of the ruin are conducted by a park ranger. Make advance arrangement for horses and/or a tour by writing to Monument Headquarters, Tonalea, AZ 86044.

The Story. About 1500 years ago a special way of life began to develop in northern Arizona and New Mexico and in southern Colorado. People there had learned to farm, and so they could settle in small, permanent villages, which were scattered over a very large area. Little by little these communities joined to form bigger ones, and finally the population became oriented around three distinct cultural regions. One centered at Mesa Verde, in Colorado, another at Chaco Canyon, in New Mexico, and the third near Kayenta, in Arizona. All of these

people shared certain characteristics, and they have been given the general name Anasazi.

The Kayenta branch of the Anasazi built Betatakin, Keet Seel, and a dwelling called Inscription House (not open to visitors). Like many Anasazi villages these were abandoned in the late 1200s for reasons that are little understood.

Modern Navajo Indians, for whom the monument is named, avoided the ruins because they feared all things dead. Then in the nineteenth century John Wetherill, a trader with the Indians, and Byron Cummings, an archeologist, visited Betatakin and Inscription House, John Wetherill's brother Richard later discovered Keet Seel.

Special Feature. In the museum at the Visitor Center a slide program shows how the Anasazi lived and what they made. In summer there are campfire programs, which introduce visitors to the history and archeology of the monument.

A view in the Keet Seel ruin, Navajo
National Monument. National Park
Service photo by Fred E. Mang, Jr.

Inscription House ruin, in Navajo
National Monument, is not open to
the public. National Park Service
photo by Fred E. Mang, Jr.

Betatakin Ruin, in Navajo National Monument. National Park Service
photo by Fred E. Mang, Jr.

Nokachok kachina doll from the Keams Canyon area. These dolls are made by Hopi and Zuni Indians. Field Museum of Natural History photo.

Kachinas

When the Spanish invaders arrived in the Southwest in 1540, every Indian pueblo except one had what the Hopis called kachinas. These were men, costumed, masked, and painted with elaborate symbolism, who participated in ceremonies in the village plazas or in the kivas. They represented supernatural spirits that were themselves called kachinas, and the dancers were believed to have supernatural powers. Some of the dancers were very earthy clowns. Others were impersonators of spirits both good and evil. Occasionally paintings of kachinas were made on the walls of prehistoric kivas.

To teach children all the symbolism of the costumes, and to help them learn the stories about supernatural beings, men often carved and painted wooden dolls in the form of kachinas. Today the Pueblo Indians still have kachina dancers, and they make kachina dolls for children—and for anyone interested in buying them. Archeologists sometimes find kachina dolls in excavations.

NAVAJO TRIBAL MUSEUM

Navajo Arts and Crafts Enterprise Bldg., on Arizona 264, Window Rock. Open free, Monday through Friday, October through April; Monday through Saturday, afternoons, Sunday, May through September. Closed national and tribal holidays.

Exhibits in the museum include both Navajo artifacts and prehistoric Anasazi artifacts. Group tours can be arranged by appointment.

NEWSPAPER ROCK PETROGLYPHS
(See Petrified Forest National Park)

ORAIBI
(oh-RYE-bee)

From Tuba City at junction of US 164 and Arizona 264, drive southeast 50 miles on Arizona 264. Open only to visitors who obtain permission from village officials. Camping nearby.

Oraibi—or as it is sometimes called, Old Oraibi—has been inhabited continuously since about A.D. 1100. When

scientists were working out a way to date ruins by studying tree rings, some of the most important information came from the wooden beams in ancient buildings in Oraibi. Visitors should respect the desire of the Hopi people for privacy in their homes and should honor their request that no photographs be taken or paintings or drawings made in the village.

PAINTED ROCKS STATE PARK

Drive 9 miles west of Gila Bend on Interstate 10, then 9 miles north on marked access road. Open, daily, all year. Admission charged.

Within the park is a group of Indian rock-art drawings of snakes, lizards, men, and geometric figures. The meaning of the drawings is uncertain, but they may represent a system of record keeping.

PETRIFIED FOREST NATIONAL PARK

From Gallup drive 69 miles southwest on Interstate 40 to northern park en-

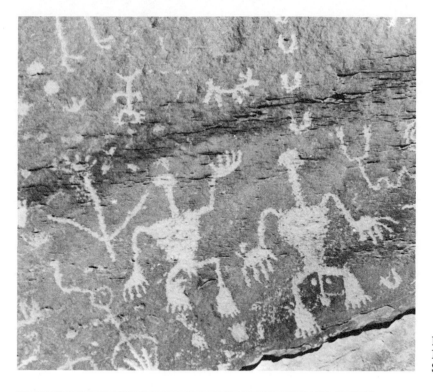

Petroglyphs in Petrified Forest National Park. National Park Service photo by George A. Grant.

trance and Visitor Center. Or from Holbrook drive 19 miles southeast on US 180 to Rainbow Forest entrance and museum. Park open daily. Visitor Centers closed some holidays. Admission charged.

This area, notable for its petrified wood, was farmed by the Anasazi, ancestors of the modern Pueblo Indians. Three of the more than 300 archeological sites are easily reached by the 28-mile park road. The Puerco Indian Ruins, 11 miles south of the Painted Desert Visitor Center, had about 150 rooms when it was occupied, up to 600 years ago. One mile south of the ruins, Newspaper Rock is covered with petroglyphs—pictures and symbols which people at various times pecked with a hard rock into the dark patina called desert varnish that covers the sandstone.

A ruin called Agate House, near the Rainbow Forest entrance, has been partially restored. Here the ancient builders used chunks of petrified wood in their construction. A spur off the Long Logs trail leads to the site.

PICTURE ROCKS RETREAT

From Interstate 10 at north edge of Tucson turn west on Ina Rd. At intersection with Wade Ave., turn left and drive about a mile to entrance. Open free, daily, during daylight hours. Inquire at office for directions to site.

A short, well maintained path leads to a tall exposed rock area on which a variety of petroglyphs can be seen. The Redemptorist Fathers maintain the site and welcome visitors.

PUEBLO GRANDE MUSEUM

4619 E. Washington St., Phoenix. Open free, Monday through Saturday; afternoons, Sunday. Closed certain holidays.

Here, inside the city of Phoenix, are a large archeological site and a museum, which illuminate the life of the Hohokam from about 300 B.C. to A.D. 1400. Trails with explanatory signs lead to a large platform structure—a mound built of earth—upon which small buildings once rested. They may have served for defense or

Petroglyphs made by Indians long ago on a sandstone cliff in Petrified Forest National Park. National Park Service Photograph by George A. Grant.

for ceremonial functions or for storage of food. Around this structure a village spread over an 80-acre area.

From the mound it is possible to see remnants of irrigation canals. A whole system of canals, totaling possibly 250 miles in length, once made the Phoenix area a very productive farming region. Corn, jackbeans, lima beans, kidney beans, tepary beans, amaranth, two kinds of squash, cotton, and possibly tobacco grew well here. Besides raising crops, the Hohokam people of Pueblo Grande gathered wild plant food and hunted desert animals of many kinds. They produced beautiful pottery and other artifacts, and made ornaments of shell, imported from the Gulf of California.

Irrigation farming began about 300 B.C. in and around Phoenix. No one knows whether the Hohokam invented this practice themselves or borrowed the idea, but as soon as water flowed onto the dry land, food increased greatly and so did population. This abundance, however, brought problems. The irrigation necessary for dependable crops caused the ground to

become waterlogged and salt saturated.

In addition to waterlogging, other problems beset the Hohokam around Phoenix. Salt in the water damaged the walls of their buildings. Life became increasingly difficult, and by A.D. 1400 the residents of Pueblo Grande and the surrounding area had all migrated from the Salt River Valley to the valley of the Gila River. Probably the Pima and the Papago Indians of today are descendants of the ancient Hohokam.

The Museum. Exhibits consist of materials recovered from this large site. Much of the excavation was done with the help of crews who were on work relief during the Depression. The museum building was designed after the truncated pyramids of Mexico, reflecting the influence of Mexico on the ancient Southwest. The structure incorporates sophisticated equipment and research laboratories, which will contribute to continuing investigation of the Hohokam. The museum and the archeological site are maintained by the city of Phoenix.

Special Feature. Visible here is a court in which the inhabitants may

Ball Courts

The Spanish who came to Mexico and Central America in the sixteenth century saw Indians playing a game with a solid rubber ball that weighed about five pounds. The players, divided into teams, tried to keep the ball in the air and scored points by bouncing it off the sloping side walls of a specially built court. The biggest score in the game seems to have been made when a player bounced the ball through the hole in one of the doughnut-shaped stone rings which were fixed high in the wall on either side of the court. Players were forbidden to hit the ball with their hands or feet. They could direct it only with blows from their hips or knees or elbows. Apparently the game had ceremonial significance, although it is not known exactly what this was.

In Arizona archeologists have found in Hohokam settlements a number of large areas of hard-packed earth with sloping side walls which somewhat resemble the ball courts of Mexico and Central America. Excavation near one of the Arizona courts turned up a large ball similar to those used in Mexico.

---

have played a ball game that was popular in prehistoric times in much of Mexico and Central America.

SHARLOT HALL
(SHAR-lot)

415 West Gurley, Prescott. Open free, Tuesday through Saturday; afternoons, Sunday. Closed holidays except Memorial Day, July 4, and Labor Day.

One room in this museum is devoted to prehistoric cultural material from Arizona, particularly from the area around Prescott.

SMOKI MUSEUM
(smoke-eye)

100 North Arizona, Prescott. Open free, Tuesday through Saturday; afternoons, Sunday, June 1 to Sept. 1.

A group of non-Indians, calling themselves the Smoki, have devoted a great deal of energy to the study and preservation of Native American cultures in the Southwest. They have gathered in this small museum some prehistoric Arizona artifacts, together with ethnological material.

SUNSET CRATER
NATIONAL MONUMENT

From Flagstaff drive 15 miles northeast on US 89, then follow directional signs on the paved loop road. Visitor Center open free, daily. Closed certain holidays. Camping.

Although archeological sites which have been excavated here are not visitable, Sunset Crater is of archeological interest because of the volcanic eruptions that took place between the growing seasons of A.D. 1064 and 1065. Indians who followed the Sinagua way of life, living in pithouses in the vicinity of the volcano, moved to the southern margin of the cinder fall, where they resumed farming. A little later a group of the Sinagua people moved to the cinder-covered Wupatki area and began farming there. The stone pueblos they built can be seen in Wupatki National Monument.

THREE TURKEY RUIN
TRIBAL PARK

From Chinle, at the edge of Canyon de Chelly National Monument, drive south 5 miles on Arizona 7 to directional sign, then 5 miles west on a primitive road to the Three Turkey Overlook. Open free, daily, except in bad weather.

This Anasazi site was occupied for only a little more than 50 years, apparently by people who came from Mesa Verde at about the time that area was being abandoned. The ruin can be viewed from the overlook and is accessible by a hiking trail into the canyon.

Artifacts made by the Salado people at Tonto National Monument. National Park Service photo.

TONTO NATIONAL MONUMENT

From Globe drive 4 miles west on US 60, then 28 miles northwest on Arizona 88 to the monument entrance, then 1 mile to the Visitor Center. Open daily. Admission charged.

Visits to the Upper Ruin can be made only by guided tours, which must be arranged four days in advance.

On a self-guided tour to the Lower Ruin, which closes at 5:20 p.m. in summer and at 4:20 p.m. in winter, visitors follow a trail to cliff dwellings in which people lived 600 years ago. These ruins are particularly interesting for the richness of the details they have revealed about the lives of those who inhabited them.

The Story. At about A.D. 1100, farming people from the north and east moved into Tonto Basin—the area around Tonto Creek, which flows into the Salt River. Here they lived peacefully with the Hohokam, who already farmed on irrigated land along the stream. The newcomers and the old-timers quickly learned from each other, and the result was vigorous

development. Pottery-making flourished. Expert weavers made cloth in intricate patterns, with fancy designs or colored stripes, and they used some dyes not found anywhere else.

For some reason, perhaps for defense, some of the people moved from the lower land about the year 1300. They built dwellings in several caves in the cliff, using chunks of very hard rock, which they embedded in mortar of adobe clay. The outside was then plastered with clay to give a smooth finish. The cliff villages were lived in for only about 50 years, and then inhabitants moved away—no one knows where or why.

The unique lifeway of these people, and especially their pottery style, extended over much of the valley of the Salt River, and so archeologists have called them the Salado (sah-LAH-doh), the Spanish word for salty.

The Museum. At the Visitor Center can be seen many of the things that the Salado people made and used—pottery, beautiful cloth, tools, and weapons.

Special Feature. Those who lived here apparently remodeled their houses dur-

On a self-guided tour at Tonto National Monument visitors can enter this ruin, built in the middle of the fourteenth century by the Salado people. National Park Service photo.

Salado people built this and other dwellings in rockshelters in what is now Tonto National Monument. National Park Service photo by Jack Tourney.

At Tuzigoot National Monument the ancient town covered a ridge which rose 120 feet above the floor of the Verde Valley. In places the building was two stories high. National Park Service photo by Paul V. Long, Jr.

ing cold weather, when farming was over. In several places the wet clay they used to plaster the walls shows clear imprints, at shoulder height, of the fabrics in clothes worn for warmth.

TUSAYAN RUIN
(See Grand Canyon National Park)

TUZIGOOT NATIONAL MONUMENT
(TOO-zee-goot)

From Flagstaff drive 49 miles southwest on US 89A to Cottonwood, then 3 miles northwest to Monument entrance. Open daily. Admission charged.

Visitors follow a trail on a self-guided tour of this prehistoric hilltop town, which once consisted of nearly a hundred rooms.

The Story. The earliest settlers of Tuzigoot were related to the Hohokam farmers, who lived more than a thousand years ago near Phoenix. Later, about A.D. 1125, they were joined by people called Sinagua, who also settled at Montezuma Castle. The

newcomers, and others who arrived later, built a village of stone houses along a ridge, with a square, two-story structure on the hilltop. The village flourished and grew until the 1400s, when for some unknown reason it was abandoned. Perhaps there was an epidemic. Or the land may have ceased to be productive. Archeologists think that some of the people migrated northward, because modern Hopi and Zuni legends say that some of their families came from the neighborhood of Tuzigoot.

The Museum. Here are displays of artifacts recovered during the excavation of the site. One exhibit shows burial practices. Adults were placed, along with pottery and jewelry, in holes scooped from the village trash heaps. Children were buried beneath the floors of rooms.

The Name. Tuzigoot comes from a modern Apache word meaning "crooked water," referring to Pack's Lake, an oxbow lake caused by a meander in the nearby Verde River, which winds back and forth through the valley.

UNIVERSITY OF ARIZONA, ARIZONA STATE MUSEUM

N. Park Ave. at University Blvd., Tucson. Open free, Monday through Saturday; afternoon, Sunday. Closed certain holidays.

This remarkable museum has illuminating exhibits of all major cultures in Southwest prehistory. Displays include artifacts from Ventana Cave, which was occupied for almost 10,000 years; Snaketown, occupied for a long time by the Hohokam people; and from the Naco and Lehner sites.

The latter site was discovered when a rancher in the San Pedro Valley saw some large bones exposed in an arroyo. He reported the find to Emil Haury, of the Arizona State Museum. Haury excavated and found evidence that hunters, more than 11,000 years ago, killed nine mammoths and roasted some of the meat nearby.

An exhibit in the museum shows mammoth bones and the tools of mammoth hunters exactly as archeologists found them in the earth. Another display explains how prehistoric people

On the ridge in the distance stand the ruins of a village in what is now Tuzigoot National Monument. National Park Service photo by Parker Hamilton.

made their stone tools. Dioramas show a mammoth kill, life around Ventana Cave 10,000 years ago, people of the Desert Culture engaged in food collecting and later people at work farming.

The museum also has rich collections of materials from all the Indian tribes that have lived in Arizona in historic times. A major exhibit on the Tarahumara Indians of Chihuahua, Mexico, recreates a full-scale environmental setting of scenes and activities from Tarahumara daily life, using objects and clothed-manikins to show their lifestyle.

WALNUT CANYON NATIONAL MONUMENT

From Flagstaff drive 7½ miles east on Interstate 40 to directional sign, then 3 miles southeast to Visitor Center. Open daily. Admission charged.

Visitors can take a self-guided tour along the rim of Walnut Canyon, then down to 25 cliff-dwelling rooms. From the trail about 100 other dwellings can be seen.

The Story. Very few people seem to have lived in this beautiful spot before the eruption in A.D. 1065 of Sunset Crater, a volcano about 15 miles to the north, near present-day Wuptaki National Monument. Fifty or sixty years later groups of farmers called Sinagua moved into Walnut Canyon and built their stone houses in recesses in the cliffs. Here they lived for almost 200 years. Then, like their neighbors in this part of Arizona, they abandoned their homes and moved elsewhere. Possibly some of their descendants are now members of Pueblo Indian groups.

Special Feature. In addition to the cliff house, visitors can see a pithouse, which shows a way of life that was common before people began to build multiple dwellings of stone in the canyon.

Mimbres women painted these fish on pottery, although their desert home was far from any fish-producing body of water. Redrawn from Gladwin.

A "mobile" painted on a pot by a Mimbres woman in southern Arizona. Redrawn from Gladwin.

WALPI
(WAHL-pee)

From Tuba City at junction of US 164 and Arizona 264, drive southeast 68 miles on Arizona 264, then north at directional sign. Camping nearby.

Walpi is a Hopi Indian village, built on top of a high mesa. Some of the dwellings go back at least to 1680, and remains of prehistoric houses lie on the slopes below the present village. They are not open to exploration by visitors. No photographing is allowed in Walpi, and visitors are requested not to enter private homes.

Special Feature. Visitors may see at Walpi the Snake Dance ceremony, in the late summer of odd-numbered years. This ceremony had its origin in prehistoric times. Information about the exact date and the place where the dance is held in even-numbered years may be obtained at the Hopi Indian Agency, Keams Canyon, or at Tribal Headquarters, New Oraibi.

WUPATKI NATIONAL MONUMENT
(woo-POT-key)

From Flagstaff drive 32 miles north on US 89 to the Wupatki-Sunset Crater Loop Rd. entrance, then 14 miles east to the Visitor Center. Open free daily, all year. Camping in a nearby Forest Service campground, May to Sept.

There are about 800 ruins in the monument, nearly 100 of them within an area of one square mile. Visitors can take self-guided tours to the largest site, Wupatki, which has been partially excavated, and to one called the Citadel, which has not been excavated. At Wupatki archeologists have uncovered an ancient ball court, one of several in northern Arizona.

The Story. In A.D. 1065 a great volcano exploded and formed what is now called Sunset Crater. Volcanic cinders spread over 800 square miles. Instead of devastating the land, the cinders formed a kind of mulch, which conserved moisture and so promoted the growth of plants. This encouraged Indian farmers to move into the area.

Dogs and Prehistoric Americans

No one knows when dogs first appeared in North America. They had already been domesticated by people who camped at the Koster Site in Illinois, about 5000 B.C. They may have been used by hunters to help in pursuing game, but there is no doubt that they were companions for adults and playmates for children. Among some tribes they had an important place in religious ceremonies. Occasionally they were sacrificed, in somewhat the same way that animals were sacrificed in biblical times, and were ritually buried. Sometimes they were eaten ceremonially—or simply as food in some areas, particularly in the Southwest. On the Northwest Coast people raised a special, long-haired breed and used the hair in weaving blankets and belts.

Dogs were known throughout much of America, especially where men were hunters. In some farming areas archeologists have found no skeletons at all to indicate their presence, but wherever they existed they were the most important domesticated animal—often the only domesticated one. In the Plains area they carried loads on special pole frames called travois (truh-VOY).

One curious fact: In many places the very earliest dogs were very small. Later, dogs in the warmer parts of the continent were small, but farther north they were large, and the largest of all lived farthest north.

Pottery in the form of a dog made by an artist of the Mississippian culture in Tennessee. Original in the Peabody Museum, Harvard University.

From the east and north came the Anasazi. Hohokam people who had farmed by irrigating crops came from the south. From the southeast came the Mogollon. And from the west came others, who belonged to a group we call the Patayan.

All of these groups moved in upon farmers now called the Sinagua, who had been living in the neighborhood before the eruption. Archeologists can be sure of this, because they have excavated Sinagua dwellings, which had been buried under a layer of cinders. And they have been able to calculate the year of the eruption by the tree-ring dating of the wood used in Sinagua houses.

The area around the volcano became a melting pot of Indian peoples. Several very different groups lived together and learned from each other for about 150 years. Perhaps by then the land was exhausted. For whatever reason, the last inhabitants left about A.D. 1225.

The Museum. Exhibits here show methods that prehistoric Indians used in making artifacts.

The Name. Wupatki, a Hopi Indian word, means "tall house." It refers to a multistory dwelling which, during the 1100s, had more than 100 rooms, housing perhaps 150 people.

Special Feature. Eighteen miles from Wupatki National Monument Headquarters, by the Loop Road, is Sunset Crater National Monument. Here may be seen the dead mouth of the volcano which spewed out cinders to cover the surrounding area.

Pot Hound and Grave Robber

A rock hound is a collector of rocks and minerals and harms no one. A pot hound is a collector of pots and other prehistoric Indian artifacts and harms everyone. Usually a pot hound is a grave robber, because Native Americans often buried their honored dead with beautiful vessels as well as ornaments and tools. Whether or not graves are desecrated, the pot hunter is always a vandal, and a collector who buys artifacts from a pot hunter encourages vandalism which destroys forever information that may help us understand other human beings.

Amateur archeologists rightly object to pot hunters, but amateurs and professionals are no better than vandals if they dig without keeping careful, complete records of everything they do and find. Each object, no matter how seemingly insignificant, that is encountered in the ground should be recorded fully, so that all relevant detail will be available when needed.

Collecting artifacts from the surface of privately owned land is not illegal if the landowner gives permission, but such collecting can be harmful from a scientific point of view. Clues on the surface may lead to important evidence beneath the surface. The best thing an amateur can do when he or she finds any ancient object anywhere is to notify a museum or the state archeologist, giving as much exact information as possible about what was found and where. Artifacts left in place can be useful. The same objects moved can be useless. And people who collect artifacts but do not keep them in some kind of order—or simply order them into outlines of hearts or wheels—show a good deal about their own personalities but reveal nothing about those who made the artifacts.

For storage purposes the great virtue is orderliness, but artifacts can also be arranged to show stages in their manufacture, to show how they lay in relation to each other in the ground, how they related historically to other artifacts, or how they related to the environment in which they were made and used. In other words, artifacts can be arranged so that they reveal something about people, and this after all is what archeology is all about.

Pot hunting—grave robbing—on public land has been forbidden since 1906 by the federal Antiquities Act. In addition many states have had their own laws to protect cultural resources. In 1979 a new federal law with more teeth was passed. It is the Archeological Resources Protection Act, which provides that pot hunters can be imprisoned for up to ten years and fined up to $10,000. Some violators have been convicted, and more convictions can be expected. Government agencies responsible for protecting our national heritage are acutely aware that the damage done to ancient sites in 1979 alone was greater than the damage done to such sites in the preceding 600 years.

A. Some of the pots which came out of excavations on Wetherill Mesa in Mesa Verde National Park. National Park Service photo by Fred Mang. B. Mogollon people who lived in the Mimbres Valley, in southwestern New Mexico, decorated their pottery imaginatively with figures of animals and human beings. C. An Anasazi woman made this bowl about 700 years ago. Original in the museum at Mesa Verde National Park. D. An unusual black and white jar found at Mesa Verde. Original in the Colorado Heritage Center in Denver. E. A Mogollon pottery canteen made in the Tularosa style in Arizona about A.D. 1200. Original in the Southwest Museum, Los Angeles.

B

C

D

E

A

Classifying the Anasazi Cultures

The culture of the Anasazi people in the Southwest developed in rather clearly defined stages. You will find these stages referred to under two different sets of names, depending on which archeologist you are reading at the moment.

One set of names was agreed on at Pecos, New Mexico, in 1927, when a group of archeologists met there to exchange information and to work out terms they could all use. The arrangement of terms they adopted for the various stages in Anasazi culture is known as the Pecos Classification.

Later another archeologist, Frank H. H. Roberts, proposed a somewhat different classification, and his terminology is used by some writers.

Basketmaker mothers carried babies in cradles made of fiber. The child's head rested on the round pillow, and a pad of soft, shredded cedar bark served as a diaper. After a Mesa Verde photo by Faha.

Colorado
(southwestern)

For additional Colorado listings see Great Plains.

ANASAZI HERITAGE CENTER

Planned for construction near Dominguez and Escalante Ruins 3 miles west of Dolores, adjacent to Colorado 147. For information write to Dolores Project, PO Box 758, Dolores, CO 81323.

Here, at a date not yet known as this book went to press, the Bureau of Land Management will operate a center devoted to interpreting the Anasazi culture. The center will display materials recovered by the Dolores Project, a massive archeological investigation of the once heavily populated area which will be flooded at the completion of McPhee Reservoir dam being built by the Water and Power Resources Service, formerly called the Bureau of Reclamation.

CHIMNEY ROCK

Reached by an access road off Colorado 151 west of Pagosa Springs. Open free, one conducted tour per week in June, two per week in July, and in August as many as the Forest Service wishes to arrange. The number of visitors allowed on each tour is limited, and appointments should be made in advance. Apply to San Juan National Forest, Pagosa Ranger District, Pagosa Springs, CO 81147. Phone: (303) 259-2727. The site, which is sometimes closed to protect rare peregrine falcons nesting there, is reached by a short uphill walk on a prepared trail.

Here, a thousand feet above the valley floor, on a ridge with a magnificent view in all directions, perhaps as many as 500 Anasazi people lived between A.D. 925 and 1125. The population of neighboring, related villages may have been 1500. Archeologists believe that a colony of male priests from Chaco Canyon, 90 miles away, joined this community about A.D. 1076 and found wives among the resident villagers. After the colonists arrived, in the spring or fall of the

Here are the two systems of classification, put down side by side for convenient reference (adapted from Jennings):

	Pecos	Roberts
A.D. 1700 to the present	Pueblo V	Historic
A.D. 1300 to 1700	Pueblo IV	Regressive (and Renaissance)
A.D. 1100 to 1300	Pueblo III	Great (Classic)
A.D. 800/850 to 1100	Pueblo II	Developmental
A.D. 750 to 900	Pueblo I	Developmental
A.D. 450 to 750	Basketmaker III	Modified Basketmaker
A.D. 1 to 500	Basketmaker II	Basketmaker
pre-A.D. 1	Basketmaker I	Basketmaker

One of the authors of this book standing by Chacoan masonry at Chimney Rock.

year, construction was begun on new rooms and a large kiva. The building was laid out carefully in an L shape, with the kiva to one side of a block of rooms. Tons of rock were then brought in to be chipped and fitted together in fine, even courses.

A great deal of archeological detective work recently done in the Southwest makes this Chimney Rock scenario likely. It is clear that the colonists came from Chaco Canyon, because the construction of new buildings at the site is typical of Chaco towns. The place was laid out according to a predetermined plan characteristic of Chaco, and the beautiful masonry was Chacoan, much finer than that of local buildings near by. The details of the kiva could only have been engineered by people—most likely priests—who were familiar with religious architecture. The pottery that was found at the site gives evidence of intermarriage with local women. None of it was made in the Chacoan style. Since women in Pueblo societies were traditionally the potters, it is safe to assume that women did not accompany the colonists from Chaco.

The unusual, even improbable, location for the town, high above the valley and, during the summer months, a mile or more from the nearest drinking water, may have been chosen for religious reasons. Ample snow decreased the water problem in late fall and winter, and this leads to the idea that building must have been done in fall or spring, when water for making mud mortar and plaster did not have to be carried in jars uphill from valley streams. Additional evidence for the religious aspect of the prehistoric Chimney Rock settlement is a historic Taos Indian legend. The two spectacular pinnacles, or chimneys, which rise beside the site were supposedly dedicated to deities known as the Twin War Gods.

The Chimney Rock community was one of a number of outliers or colonies related to the large center in Chaco Canyon (see New Mexico listing). Among other outliers were the Salmon Ruin, in New Mexico, and the Dominguez and Escalante Ruins, in Colorado. The motivation for the colonies is still not fully understood.

Some archeologists believe they were established to encourage production of resources for the center. Others think they may have served to relieve over-population at the center.

Colonists from Chaco Canyon, in New Mexico, built rooms and circular kivas a thousand feet above the surrounding valley here at Chimney Rock, in Colorado. Photo by Frank W. Eddy.

COLORADO NATIONAL MONUMENT

From Grand Junction drive 4 miles southwest on Colorado 340. Visitor Center open daily, all year. Admission charged in summer.

A panel in the Visitor Center gives information about the Fremont culture and displays some artifacts.

CURECANTI NATIONAL RECREATION AREA

From Gunnison drive 16 miles west on US 50 to entrance and Visitor Center. Open free, daily, early June to end of September. Camping.

Surveys and excavation here have led to some unusual finds. Sites in the area show continued re-occupation for an enormously long period—the earliest with a Carbon-14 date of 10,100 before the present, the most recent about A.D. 1500. Obviously the resources along the nearby banks of the Gunnison River (now partially flooded by a dam) brought people back time after time. But what were the special attractions of the place? Archeologists are not quite sure.

Another intriguing puzzle has been the discovery of several kinds of structure made of poles and mud—a method known as wattle and daub. These have been dated at the Archaic period (between 6000 and 4000 years ago), but exactly what kind of structure they were has not been determined.

At a site more than 200 miles north and east of Curecanti similar structures were unearthed in 1981 by salvage archeologists and dated at about 8000 years ago, amazingly early for wattle and daub.

Testing, excavation, and study of Curecanti will be ongoing, and visitors are welcome to watch the work. Interpretive displays in the Visitor Center give an idea of discoveries at the site, and some days of the week a guide will lead interpretive walks. For information about dates and hours of walks, phone the Visitor Center: 303-641-0403.

DOLORES PROJECT
(See Anasazi Heritage Center)

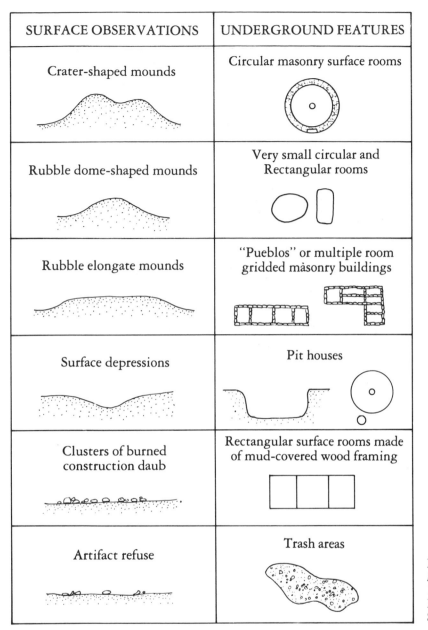

SURFACE OBSERVATIONS	UNDERGROUND FEATURES
Crater-shaped mounds	Circular masonry surface rooms
Rubble dome-shaped mounds	Very small circular and Rectangular rooms
Rubble elongate mounds	"Pueblos" or multiple room gridded masonry buildings
Surface depressions	Pit houses
Clusters of burned construction daub	Rectangular surface rooms made of mud-covered wood framing
Artifact refuse	Trash areas

Redrawn from *Archaeological Investigations at Chimney Rock Mesa: 1970–1972,* by Frank W. Eddy. Boulder, Colorado Archeological Society, 1977.

Surface Surveys

When archeologists walk over an area, they can often find evidence that tells them what lies below the surface. This diagram shows (left) features of the kind found on the surface near Chimney Rock and (right) what lay hidden in the ground below.

Right, and opposite: Excavation and stabilization of the Great Kiva in the Escalante portion of Dominguez and Escalante Ruins.

DOMINGUEZ AND ESCALANTE RUINS

From Dolores drive 3 miles west on Colorado 147 to site entrance marker. Open free, daily, all year.

This Anasazi site intrigues archeologists because it seems to have been occupied simultaneously by people from two different cultural backgrounds. On top of a hill are the ruins, called Escalante, of a large, preplanned village, built in the style of Chaco Canyon, in New Mexico. Dominguez, downhill from Escalante, is one of half a dozen small, rather simple sites in the neighborhood, built in the tradition of Mesa Verde, which is much closer by.

Some archeologists believe that colonists from Chaco came here as traders in the late eleventh century and built their four-sided village of large masonry rooms surrounding a ceremonial kiva, with another kiva just outside the walls. Since few articles of trade were discovered in the excavation, another theory is that the Chacoans may have moved here because the population had increased too much at home.

Dominguez Ruin consists of a kiva and four rooms, one of which was small and not very well constructed. These dwellings seem to have been occupied by no more than two or three families. Yet excavation of one room in the modest site revealed the burial of a woman, together with grave goods of extraordinary quality and quantity. Among other things were three elaborate pendants, turquoise and shell mosaics, ceramic vessels, and thousands of beads made from turquoise, jet, and shell. Burials of this sort were not characteristic of Mesa Verde people. Is it possible that a woman of wealth and high rank from Escalante was buried at more humble Dominguez? If so, what were the other relationships between the two different peoples? Perhaps the Chacoans brought to the area more elaborate religious and social patterns than the indigenous people were used to, and they in turn provided the Chacoans with sur-

plus food or other things which could have been taken back to Chaco Canyon to supply the people there.

The large-scale interaction—here and elsewhere in the region—between Mesa Verde people and those of Chaco Canyon is still not entirely clear, and archeologists hope that the study of Dominguez and Escalante Ruins will lead to solving some of the puzzles.

The Name. In 1776 two Franciscan explorers, Father Dominguez and Father Escalante, set up camp near the present town of Dolores. Dominguez was ill, and while he rested Escalante climbed a hill and came upon the ruin which, he said, "was . . . of the same form as those of the Indians of New Mexico." The site was later named for him, and in 1976 the neighboring site was named for his partner, Dominguez.

FORT LEWIS COLLEGE LIBRARY

On the campus, Library Bldg., third floor, Durango. Open free, afternoons, Monday through Friday. Closed certain holidays.

In a limited display area here are exhibits of Anasazi pottery and other artifacts, together with modern Indian rugs and baskets.

Shifting sands at Great Sand Dunes National Monument sometimes reveal artifacts and campsites buried as long as 10,000 years ago. National Park Service photo by Robert Haugen.

GREAT SAND DUNES NATIONAL MONUMENT

From Alamosa drive 14 miles north on Colorado 17, then 18 miles east on Colorado 150 to Visitor Center. Open at all times. Admission charged to the park. Camping.

People have been leaving tools and weapons around the Sand Dunes for 10,000 years. Two archeological sites in the area have revealed the campgrounds of people who hunted giant bison, which are now extinct. Bones of the animals have been excavated, together with fluted Folsom points.

Later, hunters belonging to various groups, including some Pueblo Indians, once followed great herds of bison, antelope, deer, and elk which roamed the San Luis Valley near the Sand Dunes. Archeologists have discovered indications that whole families traveled along definite routes on these hunting expeditions from the south into the valley. Exhibits in the Visitor Center show artifacts of several prehistoric cultures.

Special Feature. Winds blowing across the San Luis Valley for thousands of years deposited sand at the foot of the mountains along the valley's eastern side, forming some of the world's highest dunes. Hiking is allowed on the dunes, which shift constantly and from time to time uncover a spot where Indians once lived and left artifacts. Visitors may look at but not loot such sites.

LOWRY PUEBLO RUINS

From Cortez drive north 18 miles on US 666 to Pleasant View, then 9 miles west on gravel road. Open free, at all times.

About A.D. 850, possibly earlier, people began to garden at this site. Then for some reason the village was abandoned. Around 1090 it was reoccupied, and eventually it grew to be a community of 40 rooms, in part three stories high, with eight small kivas in addition to a great kiva. In the next 30 years villagers repeatedly altered, rebuilt and added to their dwell-

The painted kiva, Lowry Pueblo
Ruins.

ings. They filled old rooms with trash and constructed new ones adjoining. The last remodeling was done by masons whose stonework was different from that of earlier builders. Possibly they were newcomers from Chaco Canyon. Soon they, too, deserted the pueblo for what reason archeologists have not determined. People may have left because the land was not able to support the increased population. They seem to have moved without pressure from hostile invaders or from any catastrophe such as fire or drought.

Special feature. During their first 20 years at the site, villagers built a kiva with a plastered wall on which they painted designs. At least four subsequent coats of plaster were added and decorated. Later this ceremonial room was filled in and a new one built on top of it. Archeologists discovered the painted kiva in the course of excavating the ruins, and the Bureau of Land Management, which administers the site, has built a shelter over it which protects the paintings but allows visitors to observe them.

MANCOS CANYON
INDIAN PARK
(See Ute Mountain Tribal Park)

MESA VERDE NATIONAL PARK
(MAY-suh VER-day)

Midway between Cortez and Mancos on US 160 turn south to park entrance, then drive 21 miles on the park road to Headquarters and museum. Open all year. Admission charged at park entrance. Museum open free, daily. Camping, May 1 through Oct. 14, within the park, 5 miles from entrance. *Note:* The hours for tours, museum, and other visitor services are subject to change. For the latest information consult Park Headquarters.

Mesa Verde is really a huge outdoor archeological museum, which contains many different sites. The park occupies a stretch of high tableland, or mesa, which is cut by deep canyons with steep cliff walls. In many of the canyons prehistoric people found caves and rockshelters, and there they built some of the most beautiful and interesting villages to be found in the

Southwest. On the mesa top other ruins can be visited. Because there is such a large number of visitable sites, each with its own special interest, each will be discussed separately in the following pages. All, however, share the same general history.

The Story. At about the beginning of the fifth century A.D., people started to cultivate small gardens in the semiarid Mesa Verde area. For 800 years they lived here, improving their farming techniques, eventually building dams and storage ponds and irrigation systems. Through one stage after another they developed a special style of architecture, and their pottery took on a beauty and quality that distinguished it from other pottery made in the Southwest in prehistoric times. Now and then the women, who did the work of shaping and decorating pots, adopted new ideas or fads, and these changes in fashion were often very marked. As a result archeologists have been able to use pottery types as an aid in determining the dates of certain events in the region.

Cliff Palace, in Mesa Verde National Park, seen from about the place where two cowboys first saw it in 1888. National Park Service photo by Leland J. Abel.

Richard Wetherill (third from right in background), discoverer of Cliff Palace in Mesa Verde, sometimes conducted tourists into the area. Here he rests with some of them in Spruce Tree House. National Park Service photo.

Before: When archeologists began excavation in Long House, on Wetherill Mesa, this is what it looked like. *After:* As Long House appears now, cleared of debris, walls stabilized. National Park Service photo.

Mesa Verde was one of the three regions where Anasazi culture reached a very high point before A.D. 1276. (The others were Chaco Canyon and Kayenta.) The year 1276 was important. At about that date people began to abandon the mesa top and the canyons where they had been living. Experts disagree on the reasons for the wholesale migration away from this ancient homeland. Some say that a 23-year-long drought set in; others believe raiders began to attack the villagers, seeking the food stored there. Possibly the Mesa Verde people began to have quarrels among themselves and to develop rival factions. They may have moved to other regions because of a breakdown in the general social structure on the mesa.

For whatever reason, everyone did move away over 600 years ago, and what you see now is the evidence of achievement in a far from lush environment, over a period of eight centuries. For glimpses of the life led by descendants of the Mesa Verde people, visitors can go to present-day pueblos along the Rio Grande River and to the Hopi villages on the Hopi

mesas. It was in these areas that the emigrants made their homes after they left Mesa Verde.

For a clear and detailed picture of Mesa Verde life at each of its stages, visitors should start at the museum in Park Headquarters.

The Museum. Here well-arranged displays give an orderly and illuminating introduction to prehistoric life in the Mesa Verde area. Exhibits lead the visitor on a journey through time, beginning with the days when Basketmaker women ground corn kernels into usable cornmeal by rubbing them between a small stone called a mano and a large stone called a metate. For cooking, these women used baskets in special ways. Corn or other dry food might be placed in a broad, flat basket along with heated rocks and stirred till it was parched. Some baskets were so finely woven that they could hold water. To cook food in such a vessel, a woman dropped hot rocks into the water to make it boil.

Later at Mesa Verde women continued to weave baskets, but they also learned to make pottery. Men hunted with bows and arrows instead of de-

One of the striking architectural features of Cliff Palace, in Mesa Verde National Park, is the square tower with its t-shaped doorway in the fourth story. National Park Service photo by Fred Mang.

pending on spears and spear-throwers as their ancestors had done. They were adept at manipulating fibers—yucca fibers, dog hair, human hair—all of which they made into cord. Using the cord they wove sandals, bags, belts, and nets for catching game. Combining cord and strips of rabbit fur they wove blankets. (The magnificent dog-hair sashes in the museum were not found at Mesa Verde but in Obelisk Cave, in nearby northeast Arizona.)

By A.D. 600 people had begun to live in the kind of dwelling called a pithouse. This was a pit two or three feet deep, roofed over with branches and mud and entered by a ladder through a hole in the roof.

From this half-underground house, Anasazi architecture evolved in two different and fascinating ways, as an exhibit in the museum shows. Step by step, people learned to build homes of stone entirely above ground, but still with entrances through the roof. At the same time they dug deeper rooms entirely underground, and these they used as ceremonial chambers, now called kivas.

For a long time the stone houses clustered together in villages on the mesa top. Then people began to build in caves in the cliffs. For 75 or 100 years they lived in the cliff dwellings and tossed their trash down over the side. Refuse piled up, and very often it was entirely sheltered by the overhanging rock. In the dry Southwestern air the refuse did not decay, and the result was that archeologists found the trash heaps a mine of relics from the past. Many of their finds can be seen in the museum.

Very often the heaps were used as burial places, for it was much easier to dig a grave in trash than in hard clay. Bodies soon dried and became mummylike. Most of the mummies were carried away by collectors in the late nineteenth century, along with quantities of other material, before Mesa Verde became a National Park. Exhibitions of their loot were often sensationalized by the inclusion of one of the desiccated bodies.

Some of the best Mesa Verde exhibits must now be seen far from the Park. A large new one is scheduled to open in autumn, 1982, in the Colo-

Spruce Tree House is usually the first ruin seen by visitors to Mesa Verde National Park. National Park Service photo.

rado Heritage Center in Denver. A beautiful woven blanket can be seen in the University Museum in Philadelphia, and most remote of all is an important collection in Helsinki, Finland.

Spruce Tree House

Open daily, summer, self-guided trip; two guided tours per day, winter.

From the museum a good trail (walking time 45 minutes to one hour) leads to the Spruce Tree House ruin in the canyon nearby.

This is an unusually good place to examine a kiva, a type of ceremonial room which was hollowed out of the rock or dug into the earth. Such underground chambers were common at Anasazi sites in the Southwest.

Entrance to a kiva was by ladder through a hole in the courtyard floor. This entrance hole also allowed smoke to escape from the fire, which furnished heat and some light. Fresh air came down into the chamber through a ventilator shaft, built at one side. In front of the opening to the shaft

inside the kiva, an upright slab of rock deflected the incoming air and kept it from scattering ashes and smoke across the room. At intervals around the wall of the kiva stood masonry columns called pilasters.

The roof of a kiva rested on these pilasters, and it was ingeniously built. First, a row of logs, with their ends supported by the pilasters, was laid around the room. Then another row of logs was laid on top of this. In this second row the ends of each log were placed in the middle of the logs below them. On top of this second row another was similarly placed. The result of this cribbing was a dome-shaped structure. After the logs were all in place, they were covered with earth which was leveled off to serve as part of the courtyard floor.

In the kiva male members of a clan or a society held their ceremonies. Here also they lounged and sometimes worked at their looms. Apparently it was the men and not the women who did the fine Mesa Verde weaving. For special ceremonies women and children were sometimes admitted to these small male sanctuaries. In many places

The archeologist at the left is using surveying instruments as he maps a site on Wetherill Mesa, in Mesa Verde National Park. Atop the tripod the photographer is recording with care every stage of the excavation of the site. National Park Service photo by Al Hayes.

in the Anasazi Southwest there were also great kivas, each large enough to serve a whole community.

The history of the kiva seems to be something like the following. Early Mogollon people lived in semi-subterranean pithouses. They may have conducted certain clan or society ceremonies in these dwellings. Or they may have had special large pithouses for community-wide ceremonies.

Then among the Anasazi the type of house changed. People began to build their dwellings entirely above ground. At the same time, following a conservative impulse, they continued to hold their ceremonies in the old-fashioned type of pithouse. Later apparently, they got the notion that if holding ceremonies partly underground was a good idea, it would be an even better idea to hold them in rooms that were all the way underground. So, fully subterranean kivas were built.

Ruins Road

(Two loops totaling 12 miles in length). Open 8 a.m. to 8 p.m. in summer; closed in winter. If you follow this road, which runs along the mesa top, you will see ruins in the order in which development took place during the course of Mesa Verde history.

1. A Modified Basketmaker pithouse built in the A.D. 500s.

2. Modified Basketmaker pithouses built in the A.D. 600s and 700s.

3. Pueblos of the Developmental Period, A.D. 850, 900, 950, 1000, and 1075.

4. Sun Point Pueblo, built in the early part of the Classic Period (A.D. 1100 to 1300). People then moved down into the canyon, taking with them material from the roofs and walls of their old homes to use in building new ones.

5. Sun Temple, a large ceremonial center, from the late Classic Period.

6. Cliff Palace (Classic Period). Open 9 a.m. to 5 p.m. summer; self-guided tours. Ranger-guided tours in spring and fall start at the Viewpoint on the road. (Inquire about hours at

Two kivas in the south courtyard in Mesa Verde's Balcony House. National Park Service photo by Jack E. Boucher.

Park Headquarters.) Total walking distance, one-quarter mile; time required, 45 minutes to one hour.

Mesa Verde people built their homes in this cave in the cliff, apparently seeking protection from enemies. Here, and at other cliff dwellings during the 1200s, the arts of weaving and pottery making reached their peak. When Mesa Verde was abandoned, people left most of their possessions behind, and no invaders seem to have disturbed the vacant dwellings. Then one snowy winter day in 1888 two cowboys, Richard Wetherill and Charles Mason, discovered the pueblo and named it Cliff Palace. Although many walls had tumbled and dust had filled some rooms, Wetherill and Mason found treasures of pottery and other artifacts in the ruins.

7. Viewpoints. Along Ruins Road are a number of turnouts from which it is possible to see structures of several kinds in the canyon walls. Some are small granaries, or storerooms. Others are pueblos of various sizes. One is a ceremonial site. These sites are not now accessible. To enter and leave many of them, the Mesa Verde

people had to use small handholds and footholds they had chopped in the rock with hammerstones, or axes, made of harder rock.

8. Balcony House (Classic Period). Ranger-guided trips start at the Viewpoint sign in the Balcony House parking area on the hour and half-hour from 9 a.m. to 5 p.m. in summer. The total walking distance is one-half mile. The trip takes one hour.

In this village there is a second-story walkway or balcony, left intact from prehistoric times, which suggested the name for the ruin. Visitors may walk today through the courtyards, high above the canyon floor, protected by the original wall, which has been reinforced for safety. However, archeologists have found evidence in the ruins that cliff dwellings were not always safe for those who lived in them. Skeletons of people whose bones had been broken have turned up in burials, as have crutches and splints.

9. Cedar Tree Tower (Classic Period). After completing the trip to Balcony House, visitors should stop at Cedar Tree Tower on the drive back toward the park entrance. A road one-

Before: This photograph, taken by one of the Wetherill brothers, probably in the early 1890s, shows Cliff Palace as it looked when Richard Wetherill and Charles Mason discovered it in 1888. Courtesy of Library, State Historical Society of Colorado.

After: Cliff Palace, in Mesa Verde National Park, as it looks today, after archeologists excavated and stabilized the structures. National Park Service photo by Jack E. Boucher.

half mile long on the mesa top leads to this curious structure, which was used for ceremonial purposes. From the round tower an underground passage led to a circular kiva, which is also connected to a small niche under an overhanging rounded rock.

No one knows exactly what ceremonies went on here—or elsewhere in Mesa Verde. Archeologists do know that among the Anasazi there were people who practiced healing and magical arts. A kit used by one of them has been excavated and is on display in the museum. Archeologists also know how such kits are used in modern times, for they have studied the ceremonies of present-day Pueblo Indians, some of whom are descended from Mesa Verde people. It seems likely that ancient ceremonies resembled in some ways the modern Pueblo ceremonies. If so, they expressed the desire to have all the elements of the world working together in harmony.

10. Far View Ruins (Developmental Pueblo). Off the road between the park entrance and the museum, a short side road leads to this group of ruins on the mesa top. The pueblos here were inhabited before people moved down into cliff dwellings.

Near the ruins is Mummy Lake, which can be reached by a short trail leading past the ruins of another small pueblo. The dry basin called Mummy Lake was once an artificial reservoir. In ancient times a series of barriers or dams higher up on the mesa collected rainwater and channeled it into ditches which ultimately led into the reservoir. The water in the ditches was muddy, and to keep some of the silt out of the reservoir, the stone-age engineers who designed this facility worked out an ingenious device. They made a sharp curve near the end of the last ditch. The curve slowed the flow of water, and some of the silt settled out before the water entered the reservoir. From Mummy Lake a bypass ditch ran along the sloping mesa, carrying water several miles to the area where Park Headquarters is now located.

Close to Far View Ruins another Developmental Pueblo group of dwellings, with a round tower next to a kiva, has been excavated.

Mug House, one of the ruins on Wetherill Mesa, Mesa Verde National Park. National Park Service photo by Fred E. Mang, Jr.

Wetherill Mesa

This area of the park, first opened to the public in 1973, is reached by a free bus from the Far View Visitor Center, then by minitrain to the top of the cliff. No private cars are permitted. Guided tours are offered daily, June 9 through Labor Day. Inquire about hours at Park Headquarters.

Several Classic Period ruins in the Wetherill Mesa area have been excavated. One of them, which has been prepared for visitors, is Long House. Built in an enormous rockshelter, it has 150 rooms and 21 kivas. Only Cliff Palace is larger.

Pictograph Point

Hikers who register with the ranger on duty in the park office near the Visitor Center may follow a trail to a place where Mesa Verde people made paintings on rock surfaces.

Campfire Programs. The last stop on any day in Mesa Verde should be at one of the campfire programs, either in the Morfield Campground or in the amphitheater near Headquarters.

Nightly at 8:30, from early June through Labor Day, a ranger talks on some aspect of Mesa Verde life. After Labor Day and until the campground closes talks begin at 8 p.m.

The Future. The Park Service has a large site at Goodman's Point, about 10 miles northwest of Cortez, in Montezuma Valley below Mesa Verde. When funds become available this site will be developed and open to the public.

Top to bottom: Anasazi double mug. The original is in the Mesa Verde National Park museum. Mesa Verde women used the beveled edges of bone tools to scrape flesh from hides. Originals of these fleshers are in the Colorado Heritage Center, Denver. A black-on-white pottery ladle. A pot made in the shape of a duck by a woman at Mesa Verde, between A.D. 750 and A.D. 1100. The ladle and the pot are in the Mesa Verde National Park museum.

Left:
Archeologists photograph artifacts in situ, meaning in exactly the situation in which they are found. Here is a bowl, broken by a fallen rock, in a cave on Wetherill Mesa, Mesa Verde National Park. National Park Service photo.

Right:
The routes used by ancient Anasazi people at Mesa Verde as they entered and left caves have often weathered so much they are not usable today. Here an archeologist descends into a cave on Wetherill Mesa by rope ladder. National Park Service photo by Al Hayes.

To aid in the study of prehistory, archeologists often put back together things that have been broken. On the left, a laboratory technician reconstructs a large, corrugated cooking pot found on Wetherill Mesa, in Mesa Verde National Park. On the right, the pot restored, with its yucca-fiber harness and sitting on its original doughnut-shaped rest. National Park Service photos by Fred Mang.

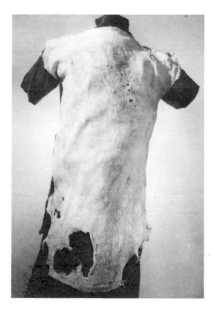

Left:
This finely woven cotton shirt was found on a mummy in Mesa Verde National Park. National Park Service photo by Fred E. Mang, Jr.

Right:
A crew of University of Colorado students digging a test trench in the trash heap beside a Pueblo II ruin on the mesa top in Mesa Verde National Park in 1968.

SOUTHWEST: Colorado *(southwestern)*   57

These ruins at Yucca House National Monument have been surveyed but not excavated. National Park Service photo.

UTE INDIAN MUSEUM

From Montrose drive 4 miles south on US 550. Open daily, approximately May 1 through Labor Day. Admission charged.

The collection here consists mainly of ethnographic material, but includes stone tools and baskets made by the prehistoric inhabitants of Colorado and Utah. Some of the material has been dated as early as 2000 B.C.

UTE MOUNTAIN TRIBAL PARK

Near Towaoc (TOY-akh). Tours guided by members of the Ute Mountain Ute Tribe leave at 9 a.m., Monday through Friday, May 15 to Oct. 1, from the Ute Mountain Tribal Pottery Building, 15 miles south of Cortez on US 160 and 666. On weekends, tours are by appointment only. Phone Mr. Arthur Cuthair, (303) 565–3751, Ext. 282. The tours are free, but a donation to the park development fund is requested. Primitive camping on the Mancos River is available to groups only, and only by advance reservation. Tours end about 4:30 p.m.

and are subject to cancellation if it rains. Those taking the tour must bring lunch and drinking water and drive their own cars. Some roads in the park are dirt, others gravel surfaced.

A back country trip in this colorful, 125,000-acre park includes visits to many surface sites, cliff dwellings, and sites of rock art. Ancient settlements here were Anasazi, similar to those in Mesa Verde National Park, which is adjacent.

At the tribally owned Ute Mountain Pottery it is possible to see not only finished pottery for sale, but to watch the entire process of manufacture.

YUCCA HOUSE NATIONAL MONUMENT

From the intersection of Colorado 160 and US 666 in Cortez, follow US 666 South 8.5 miles. Turn west on Road B, which is a good dirt road identified only by a small green street sign with white lettering. Follow Road B across its intersection with Road 21 to the junction of Road 20.5. Turn north on Road 20.5 and follow it to a small group of buildings, including a

white house with a red roof. Across the road from this house is a parking lot. Enter the small corral through the gate; use the stile over the far corral fence to enter the monument proper. Open free, daily, all year.

This unexcavated Anasazi pueblo ruin, within sight of Mesa Verde National Park, is open to the public, but the National Park Service does not encourage visitations because for the casual visitor there is little to see, and the approach road is often almost impassable in wet weather. Anyone who does make the trip is urged, in the words of the Park Service, to "leave only footprints and take only photographs."

A ranger at Yucca House
National Monument.
National Park Service photo.

New Mexico

ABO
(unit of Salinas National Monument)
(ah-BOH)

Drive 9 miles west of Mountainair on US 60 to a directional sign, then 1 mile north on a local road.

Here, in addition to a seventeenth-century Spanish mission, is a prehistoric archeological area, largely unexcavated, which appears to include two adjacent pueblos of different ages. The people who lived here spoke the now extinct Piro language and were related to the Tompiros, who lived at Gran Quivira (see entry, below) and in pueblos along the middle Rio Grande. The Piros here made an architectural innovation that has intrigued archeologists. Within the Roman Catholic Church complex the Native Americans built a kiva suitable for use in continuing their traditional religion. Also here, unique in the region, were the buttressed curtain walls of the church.

Formerly a New Mexico state monument, Abo has become part of the Salinas National Monument (see entry, below). The church area, enclosed in a fence as this book went to press, will be opened to the public after the National Park Service has completed stabilization work. In the meantime a series of interpretive panels in both English and Spanish explain the site.

ACOMA PUEBLO
(AH-koh-mah)

Between Albuquerque and Gallup leave Interstate 40 at Casa Blanca and drive south 14 miles on New Mexico 23. Open daily, all year. Closed for certain religious activities. Admission charged.

Acoma, often called Sky City, is on top of a high sandstone rock. About A.D. 900, people began to live on or near the site of the present village. Even since A.D. 1075, the pueblo has been continuously occupied. This means that visitors at Acoma are seeing a lived-in prehistoric site, although most of the structures which are visible are obviously of recent origin.

Visitors should respect the privacy of the people of Acoma and should obtain permits from the governor of the pueblo if they wish to take photographs or do painting or drawing. The graveyards, the kivas, and the waterholes are out of bounds to tourists.

AZTEC RUINS NATIONAL MONUMENT

From Farmington drive 14 miles east on US 550 to directional marker in the town of Aztec, then one-half mile north on Ruins Road to monument entrance. Open daily, all year. Closed certain holidays. Admission charged. Camping nearby.

This huge ruin was once a town built in the form of an apartment house around an open plaza. The beautiful masonry walls of its 500 rooms rose two and three stories high in places. A number of kivas—small round ceremonial rooms—were constructed within the building itself, and in the plaza was a very large kiva surrounded by a number of small rooms. This great kiva has been completely restored to show what the im-

This screen made of reeds slid up
and down over a doorway at Aztec
Ruins National Monument.
National Park Service photo by
George A. Grant.

Right:
Archeologists found this old ladder
when they were excavating Aztec
Ruins. National Park Service photo.

Inside the Great Kiva at Aztec Ruins
National Monument, after restoration.
The t-shaped doorway in the center
was popular in many Anasazi
pueblos. The pits to the left and
right may have been covered with
boards and used as dance platforms
or foot drums. National Park Service
photo by George A. Grant.

In Bandelier National Monument, three-story dwellings once stood at the base of this cliff, which is a soft rock called tufa. Builders could easily hollow it out to make storage rooms at the rear of their masonry houses. The small holes held the ends of beams. National Park Service photo by A. H. White.

pressive ceremonial room must have been like 800 years ago.

The Story. Aztec lies between two major areas of the Anasazi culture— Mesa Verde and Chaco Canyon. By A.D. 600 people at Aztec had begun to farm, and by A.D. 1000 they were being strongly influenced by their neighbors.

The design of the town, its fine masonry work, and the great kiva were of the kind that originated in Chaco Canyon. Apparently a group from Chaco had come as colonists to Aztec. (Aerial photography has revealed the existence of an ancient road between the two settlements.) Whether the immigrants moved to Aztec because the population at home was growing too large for the available resources, or whether they intended only to implement trade between home and outlying areas, is still an unsettled question. Whatever their motivation, the Chacoans left not long after their building at Aztec was completed, in the middle 1100s. By A.D. 1225 new people had moved in, bringing with them pottery designs and customs that were similar to those at Mesa Verde.

Fifty years later the Aztec pueblo was again abandoned. This time the inhabitants left, never to return.

The Museum. Here are exhibits of pottery, baskets, various utensils, and tools made and used in the pueblo. Displays explain architectural features and show how the people once lived.

The Name. Early pioneers, who were much impressed by what they had heard about the Aztec Indians in Mexico, called this ruin Aztec. There is, however, no known connection between the inhabitants of this pueblo and the Aztecs, who lived in the Valley of Mexico.

Special Feature. One of the great archeologists of the Southwest, Earl Morris, who was born near Aztec, excavated this site and reconstructed the great kiva. When he began his careful work, he found evidence that the once-important ceremonial chamber had been used as a garbage dump before the pueblo was abandoned. Finally the roof caught fire and collapsed. Nevertheless, Morris was able to figure out details of construction and rebuild the chamber.

BANDELIER NATIONAL MONUMENT
(ban-duh-LEER)

From Santa Fe drive 18 miles north on US 285 to Pojoaque (po-WAH-kay) then 28 miles west on New Mexico 4 to the monument entrance. It is 3 miles farther to the Visitor Center. Open daily, all year. Admission charged. Camping.

This beautiful and unusual site at the bottom of a deep gorge stretches out along a little stream called Rito de los Frijoles (REE-toh day lohs free-HO-lays), Spanish for "bean creek." Along a two-mile trail visitors can see ruins of dwellings built near the cliff walls, and behind them man-made caves. In a separate section of the monument, 11 miles north of Frijoles Canyon, is an unexcavated ruin called Tsankawi (zahn-KAH-wee). Here visitors may take a self-guided tour on a two-mile trail.

The Story. At the end of the thirteenth century there was a great drought in much of the Southwest. Many Anasazi people moved from their homes, seeking water. Some of them found it here in the deep can-

Prehistoric people, walking from place to place in Bandelier National Monument, wore down trails in the soft rock. National Park Service photo by Natt Dodge.

Some of the dwellings in Frijoles Canyon had subterranean rooms. National Park Service photo by George A. Grant.

Artist Paul Coze's conception of life in one of the human-made caves in Frijoles Canyon. Photo by Glen Haynes, used by permission of Paul Coze.

Prehistoric homes in Bandelier
National Monument, part masonry
and part artificial caves hollowed out
of the soft rock. National Park
Service photo by Fred E. Mang, Jr.

Ruins of a large village with three
kivas, in Bandelier National
Monument.

Left:
Pictograph in a cave, Bandelier National Monument. National Park Service photo by K. Chapman.

Right:
A pictograph at the base of a cliff in Frijoles Canyon, Bandelier National Monument. The Park Service has installed a glass cover to protect it. National Park Service photo by George A. Grant.

yons that cut into the Pajarito (PAH-hah-REE-toh) Plateau. (Pajarito is Spanish for "little bird.") In the bottom of Frijoles Canyon farmers planted fields of corn, beans, and squash and built a large pueblo called Tyuonyi (chew-OHN-yee), which means "a meeting place." At the same time, some inhabitants dug storage rooms and also living quarters in the walls of the canyon. This was not too difficult because the rock is very soft—actually compressed volcanic ash.

People continued to live in the canyon until the late 1500s. Then for some reason they left, as did others from various parts of the Pajarito Plateau. Today people who are probably their descendants live at the Cochiti and San Ildefonso pueblos along the Rio Grande.

The Museum. A slide program at the museum in the Visitor Center interprets life in the canyon in ancient times. Exhibits show the arts and crafts of the people who lived there.

The Name. The first archeologist who came west to make a study of sites in New Mexico was Adolph Bandelier. In the late nineteenth century he walked thousands of miles over roadless areas of the state, learning Indian languages, often sleeping on the ground without a blanket, sometimes eating only the parched corn that was a food of the Indians among whom he lived. One of Bandelier's discoveries was the prehistoric settlement in Frijoles Canyon. To explain what he thought life must have been like in this spot he wrote a novel, *The Delight Makers,* which is still very readable and informative. Because of his important services to archeology and his particular connection with Frijoles Canyon, the national monument was named in his honor.

Special Feature: Ninety percent of Bandelier National Monument is a wilderness in which roads will never be built. There are trails, however, and some of them lead to fascinating archeological sites. At one place, 12 miles from Monument Headquarters, there are carved stone mountain lions unlike anything found elsewhere in the Southwest. At another site, 19 miles from Headquarters, is a very large cave, where prehistoric people made paintings in color on the rock.

This enormous cave lies at the end of an arduous trail in Bandelier National Monument. Across the back of the cave are colored paintings, left there in prehistoric times. National Park Service photo.

Indians used cooking pits like this in both prehistoric and historic times. Hundreds of these pits are scattered throughout Carlsbad Caverns National Park. National Park Service photo.

BLACKWATER DRAW MUSEUM

Midway between Clovis and Portales on US 70. Open free, afternoons, Tuesday through Sunday.

This museum is devoted exclusively to the story of humans, from their entry into America until the end of the Archaic period, 2000 years ago. Dioramas show the life of the Paleo-Indians and the mammoths and other animals they hunted. Other displays show how artifacts were made and used. The museum contains many originals and replicas of material recovered from the very important Blackwater Draw Site nearby.

This site was discovered by C. W. Anderson and George Roberts, amateur archeologists, at the time when professional archeologists were just realizing that people had been in America for many thousands of years. On the surface, amid old sand dunes, Anderson and Roberts found some distinctive projectile points, together with mammoth bones. Then in August of 1932, Anderson met a professional archeologist, Edgar B. Howard, in

Carlsbad, New Mexico. He showed him the points, and told him about the bones. Howard immediately went to the site. He was much interested in what he saw, and scientific excavation soon began at Blackwater Draw. It has continued to the present time. The distinctive points found there have been called Clovis points after the nearby town.

Hunters who used spear points of the Clovis type roamed widely about 11,000 years ago. Traces of their camps have been found in other parts of the United States as well as at the dig in Blackwater Draw.

It is not yet possible to visit the excavation, but a trip to the museum gives an excellent idea of what has been going on there for many years.

CAPULIN MOUNTAIN NATIONAL MONUMENT

From Capulin drive 3 miles north on New Mexico 325 to Visitor Center which is open free, daily, all year. Closed certain holidays. Admission charged to the monument.

The archeological display in the

Visitor Center relates to the Folsom culture. On exhibit are two Folsom points and two reproductions.

At Post 22 on the road up Capulin Mountain in the monument, there is a view of the country around the Folsom site, where artifacts of prehistoric people were first found associated with fossil bones of extinct animals. This site, preserved as Folsom Man State Monument, is unmarked and not accessible to the public.

CARLSBAD CAVERNS NATIONAL PARK

From Carlsbad drive 18 miles south on US 62, then 7 miles west on park road to Visitor Center. Open daily, all year. Admission to the park is free; fees are charged for tours of the caverns. Camping outside park.

Prehistoric Indians apparently never ventured far into Carlsbad Caverns, although they did camp near the cave entrance. They made black and red paintings on the rock wall of the entrance, and they prepared some of their foods in rock-lined cooking pits. Many such pits have been found in

Archeologists carefully record pictographs in Painted Grotto, in Carlsbad Caverns National Park. National Park Service photo.

the area, some constructed later by Apache Indians.

Along the park road in Walnut Canyon visitors may take a self-guided tour, which follows an ethnobotanical trail that identifies plants and the uses to which they were put by Indians of the area. There is also a self-guided trail to Goat Cave.

In the Slaughter Canyon area of the park is Painted Grotto, a pictograph site. Permission to visit this site must be obtained from the superintendent, at Park Headquarters.

CASAMERO RUINS

From Grants drive 20 miles west on Interstate 40 to Prewitt exit, then 1 mile east on US 66, then north on unpaved county road for about 4½ miles toward a large electric generating plant. Open free, at all times.

This site was excavated in the course of salvage archeology conducted at the time the generating plant was being planned. The beautifully made masonry walls and the remains of a great kiva identify it as one of the outlying townships where colonists from Chaco Canyon settled in the mid-eleventh century (see Chaco Canyon entry). The kiva—about 70 feet in diameter—is one of the largest known. A number of interpretive signs have been put up by the Bureau of Land Management, which administers the ruins.

Three examples of the beautiful and distinctive pottery made by the Anasazi people who once inhabited Chaco Canyon. National Park Service photo.

CHACO CULTURE NATIONAL HISTORICAL PARK
(CHAH-koh)

From US 64 at Bloomfield drive south 28 miles on New Mexico 44, then at Blanco Trading Post take unpaved New Mexico 57, 30 miles to the Visitor Center. Or from Interstate 40 at Thoreau drive north 44 miles on paved New Mexico 57, past Crownpoint, then 20 miles on unpaved New Mexico 57 to the Historical Park. Before leaving Blanco Trading Post or Crownpoint check the condition of the unpaved road ahead. It is sometimes impassable after a rain. Open free, daily, all year. Camping; water is available but no other supplies.

Here, far from any present-day town, are a dozen large pueblos and about 2,500 smaller sites, the spectacular ruins of one of the three Anasazi culture centers. Easy trails from the main road lead to a number of the most important sites, and there are self-guided tours at those which have been named Pueblo Bonito, Chetro Ketl, Casa Rinconada, and Pueblo Del Arroyo. In summer park rangers conduct guided tours through a number of sites, and there are campfire programs from about Memorial Day to about Labor Day.

Any visit to Chaco Canyon should begin at the Visitor Center, where exhibits in the museum tell the story of human life here. Dioramas and displays help to make clear how people could have prospered in a land which now seems dry and desolate.

The Story. The 800 rooms of Pueblo Bonito, a planned, multistory village built in the form of a huge D around a courtyard, could house about a thousand people. In this pueblo, and in others in the canyon, the art of stone-masonry reached its highest development in the Southwest. Great stretches of wall made from precisely cut and shaped stone remain standing today.

In Chaco Canyon, as elsewhere in the Southwest, a long history of development lay behind great achievements. It began in the canyon with the Basketmaker people, who by A.D. 400 were building dwellings of the kind called pithouses. They were farmers and craftsmen, quick to adopt new ideas from neighbors or strangers.

Left:
In the Southwest archeologists find countless potsherds. These broken bits of pottery usually tell who lived at a certain place and even when they lived there. These sherds are all from Chaco Culture National Historical Parks. National Park Service photo.

Right:
Stone tools left these marks at the base of a cliff in Chaco Canyon when they were sharpened on a slab of softer sandstone. National Park Service photo by George Grant.

The dotted lines mark the edges of a 25-foot-wide road, part of the Chacoan communication system. In the background hand-hewn steps carry the road up a slope behind Dr. Robert H. Lister, former director of the Chaco Center. National Park Service photo by Thomas H. Wilson.

Different masons worked to build this high building. The walls show four types of stonework, ending with the most painstaking and beautiful in the top story. National Park Service photo by George A. Grant.

After building these walls, masons in Chaco Canyon covered their elegant stonework with a coat of plaster. National Park Service photo.

A wall and door with the ends of three original beams still in place, Chaco Canyon. National Park Service photo by Fred E. Mang, Jr.

Apparently the villages in the canyon were hospitable to outsiders. Immigrants from other parts of the Southwest may have come in steadily. By the eleventh century A.D. as many as 5000 people were making their homes in and around the canyon. Craftsmen worked in turquoise and shell, fashioning mosaics, beads, and ornaments of various sorts. Chaco became a sort of trading center, exporting handcrafted goods and redistributing food and raw materials. Traffic to and from the large settlements in the canyon flowed along 300 miles of roads, that linked outlying villages with each other and with the center. Some led to distant sources of supply, even toward Mexico, where traders got copper bells and macaws and other exotic things valued by Chacoans. Although they had no burden-carrying animals or wheeled vehicles, travelers found that wide, straight roads were practical, energy-saving communication routes.

It was not only trade goods that Chaco exported. Colonists from the canyon migrated to other places in the region, taking with them social customs and ceremonial practices and the idea of building preplanned pueblos. About 70 of these outlying townships have been located and studied. Some archeologists believe that the outliers were settled in order to produce food, which was then transported along the roads to the Chaco center. The settlements consisted of one or more groups of small dwellings and one great kiva, plus a large structure, built in the classic Chaco masonry style, which may have served as a public storehouse for food.

Other archeologists think that the main purpose of the migration to outlying villages was to relieve population pressure at the center. It is generally agreed that at some point the number of people in the canyon grew too large for the agricultural resources of the area. As R. Gwinn Vivian reported to the Society for American Archeology, "Redistribution of population was economically more feasible with primitive transport systems than large-scale redistribution of foodstuffs."

One of these Chacoan outliers may be visited at Salmon Ruins (see entry, below), another at Dominguez and Escalante Ruin (see entry, above), a

Two of the many examples of rock art which appear on cliff faces in Chaco Canyon and many other places in the Southwest. National Park Service photo.

The Great Kiva, Chetro Ketl, Chaco Canyon, after excavation and stabilization. This large ceremonial chamber, once roofed, served a whole community; small kivas were used by local groups. National Park Service photo by George A. Grant.

A group of kivas at Pueblo Bonito seen from the cliff which towers above the site. National Park Service photo by George A. Grant.

This is how Pueblo Bonito (in Chaco Canyon) looks when viewed from the top of the cliff which towers above it. National Park Service photo by George A. Grant.

Prehistoric Astronomers

Because it was important for prehistoric people to know when migrations of game would take place or when the time was at hand for planting crops, early hunters and farmers took a keen interest in the sun and moon and stars. Their recurring movements could be correlated with recurring events on earth, and people in widely separated parts of the world developed ways of noting major astronomical events.

In North America modern astronomers and archeologists working together have discovered ancient devices by which it was possible for prehistoric people to know exactly the days of the solstices and equinoxes and other regular occurrences. Sometimes these devices were alignments of stones, as at Bighorn Medicine Wheel in Wyoming. At Cahokia in Illinois circles of posts forming woodhenges were used. In the Southwest some astronomical observations were made by watching where beams of light fell through specially designed windows.

In the Chaco Canyon area of New Mexico ingenious ancient astronomers constructed a sophisticated calendrical device on top of a high butte. In this observatory large slabs of rock were arranged so that shafts of sunlight fell between them onto a group of spiral markings carved into a cliff wall. As the position of the sun changed with the seasons, the shafts of light traversed the face of the markings, indicating important dates to those who knew how to read them.

---

third at Chimney Rock (see entry, above), and still another at Aztec (see entry, above).

Besides their architectural and road-building skills, the Chacoans had a talent for constructing irrigation systems and a technical knowledge which enabled them to establish a remarkable astronomical observatory (see above, this page).

In the late part of the twelfth century the greatness of Chaco Canyon came to an end. Archeologists are still debating exactly what pressures led to the abandonment of the canyon. It may well have been that the needs of the people exceeded the resources available, and what Vivian calls "redistribution of population" went on slowly over a number of years. Perhaps the Chacoan phenomenon did not just suddenly and mysteriously collapse. Instead it may have trickled away.

At any rate, the inhabitants of the canyon did eventually depart. After they left, their great buildings filled up gradually with windblown sand and dust, and many of them were only mounds when the first United States soldiers passed through the canyon on an exploring expedition in 1849.

Pueblo Bonito (Spanish for "beautiful town") is by no means all there is to wonder at in Chaco Canyon, but it was the first to be thoroughly excavated and stabilized. Several other ruins have been explored and studied. Across the arroyo from Pueblo Bonito is Casa Rinconada, where a great kiva has been excavated and sufficiently restored to give an idea of the beauty and majesty of this ceremonial room. Behind the ruin called Kin Kletso an ancient trail leads up through a cleft in the cliff wall to a ruin called Pueblo Alto, on the mesa top.

Many sites in the canyon remain for future archeologists to study, including parts of a possible long-distance, line-of-site signaling network, and there are many aspects of the Chacoan phenomenon still to be understood, even after the recent completion of an ambitious, ten-year program, in which a number of "space-age" techniques were used.

Skeptical archeologists at first found it hard to believe that accurate observations could be made using three rough-looking stone slabs and some seeming squiggles cut into a cliff. But after careful study they could find no reason to doubt that this was a true astronomical device invented by some Chacoan genius—or geniuses—700 or more years ago.

One geologist made a study of the slabs and concluded that there was no way in which they could have moved accidentally from their original position in the rock of the butte to their present location. In his opinion the slabs must have been moved and positioned by people. Other geologists disagree. They say the ancient Chacoans utilized rocks that had fallen naturally and created from them a marker for the seasons.

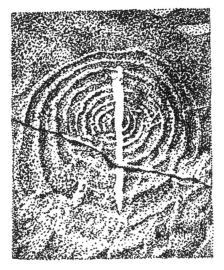

The existence and nature of this device, called the Sun Dagger Calendar, was made known to the world by Anna Sofaer, an artist and photographer, who found it while recording the rock art of Chaco Canyon. Whether the slabs were positioned by Chacoans or by nature, Sofaer says, their use indicates remarkable sophistication. To protect the calendar, the Park Service limits visitation at the site to supervised groups.

Archeoastronomy is the name used for the growing new field of study concerned with the astronomical knowledge of prehistoric peoples. This study is making an important contribution to understanding the intellectual achievements of Native Americans.

At the right is a drawing of the shaft of light which has been called the Sun Dagger.

The treasures of pottery and jewelry that archeologists found here have been removed to museums elsewhere. The National Geographic Society in Washington, D.C., has a large and very beautiful turquoise necklace. Some of the pottery is in the American Museum of Natural History, in New York.

CORONADO STATE MONUMENT

From Albuquerque drive north 20 miles on Interstate 25 to Cuba-Farmington Exit, then 3 miles west on New Mexico 44 to monument entrance. Open free, Thursday through Monday. Closed certain holidays. Camping.

Here, on the west bank of the Rio Grande River a group of Anasazi people began to make their home about A.D. 1300. By the time the Spanish invaders arrived, in 1540, the pueblo, known as Kuaua (KWAH-wah) had grown tremendously. There were about 1200 ground-level rooms, and above them many other rooms, in places several stories high. The walls of the houses were made of adobe clay, which was moistened and built up in layers, each layer being allowed to dry before the next was added.

In the courtyards of the pueblo were a number of underground ceremonial chambers, or kivas. When archeologists excavated one of them they found murals painted on its plastered walls. Further investigation revealed 17 other layers of plaster underneath, and on each layer were more mural paintings of ceremonial activities. The archeologists worked out an ingenious method of removing the murals a layer at a time. An exhibit in the Visitor Center at the Monument tells how they did it. Accurate reproductions of some of the paintings have been put on the wall of a reconstructed kiva at the site.

The people of Kuaua, which means "evergreen" in the Tiwa language, were farmers who grew corn, squash, tobacco, and cotton. They were good weavers and good potters, and they also made fine baskets. Many of their artifacts and religious objects can be seen in the museum at the Visitor Center.

The Name. The monument is named for the leader of the Spanish *conquistadores* who stayed somewhere in the vicinity of Kuaua for a while in the winter of 1540–41.

EASTERN NEW MEXICO UNIVERSITY, ANTHROPOLOGY MUSEUM

On the campus of the university, Portales. Open free, Monday through Friday. Closed certain holidays.

One large room in this museum emphasizes Early Man on the High Plains, with explanations of the Paleo way of life. The director of the museum, Dr. George A. Agogino, who is also director of the Miles Museum and the Blackwater Draw Museum, has arranged an unusual exhibit of photographs of Paleo-Indian sites throughout the western hemisphere, together with material about the archeologists who discovered and excavated the sites.

Atop the mesa in El Morro National Monument are these ruins of a pueblo built by ancient Zuni Indians. National Park Service photo.

EL MORRO NATIONAL MONUMENT

From Grants drive 43 miles west on New Mexico 53; or from Gallup drive south 30 miles on New Mexico 32, then 24 miles east on New Mexico 53. Open free, daily, all year. User fee charged for hiking trails. Camping.

Although devoted primarily to preserving inscriptions made in historic times on a 200-foot-high sandstone promontory, this monument includes hundreds of petroglyphs—symbols and designs which Zuni Indians pecked in the rock long before the first Spaniards arrived. On the mesa behind the cliff stand the ruins of two Pueblo villages, one of which has been partially excavated and stabilized. Visitors may take a self-guided tour of the site, which includes a huge pool that is fed by rains and melted snow, where inhabitants of the pueblos came for water. Handholds and footholds pecked in the rock show the route they followed up and down the cliff.

Exhibits in the Visitor Center interpret the history of the monument, both ancient and modern.

ERNEST THOMPSON SETON MUSEUM
(See Seton Museum)

FLORENCE HAWLEY ELLIS MUSEUM OF ANTHROPOLOGY

At Espanola leave US 285 and follow US 84 northwest for 33 miles. At a sign marking "Ghost Ranch Road" (on which is a design of a cow's skull) drive right on a gravel road for 2 miles. *Note:* the museum is *not* at the Ghost Ranch Visitors' Center on US 84. Open free, April 1–Sept. 30, daily except Monday; Oct. 1–March 30, afternoon Saturday, Sunday. Other days by appointment. For information about holiday closings phone (505) 685–4333. Camping.

Exhibits here show the various local peoples and different types of land use from 14,000 B.P. to the end of the nineteenth century. Included are Paleo and Archaic materials, and materials from a nearby site of the Gallina culture (eleventh to thirteenth centuries) where Ghost Ranch sponsors excavation for two weeks in August every summer.

One exhibit is devoted to Sapawe Pueblo (A.D. 1350–1550), the largest clay-walled pueblo known in New Mexico. According to tradition the people abandoned Sapawe because of drought and moved to the part of the still-existing San Juan Pueblo that lies on the west bank of the Rio Grande.

This museum is named in honor of one of the most active Southwestern archeologists.

FOLSOM MUSEUM

In the town of Folsom. Open free, daily, June 1 to Oct. 1; Saturday, Sunday, Oct. through May.

This small, local history museum includes exhibits related to George McJunkin, the Black cowboy who discovered the nearby Folsom Site, which is of great importance to archeology but is not open to the public.

Fluted Points

When a projectile point has a channel, or depression, running lengthwise on one or both of its faces, it is said to be fluted. Clovis points, used by mammoth hunters about 11,000 years ago, and Folsom points, used by hunters of very large bison about 10,000 years ago, were fluted.

If fluting had any practical value, it was apparently that the thinned base could easily be inserted into the split end of a spear shaft. However, the labor involved in preparing these points was greater than the labor required to shape an unfluted point. In addition there was a great deal of breakage during manufacture. On the other hand, unfluted points seem to have been equally effective weapons, and they were more durable. This has led some archeologists to suggest that fluting may have had a ceremonial purpose.

How or when or where the practice of fluting began is not known. H. Müller-Beck, a Swiss archeologist, believes it may have started in Europe, possibly in southern Russia, at least 26,000 years ago. Other students of Early Man in America think fluting may have developed on the Bering Land Bridge, where men once hunted mammoths. The Land Bridge is now submerged, so all evidence of what went on there is lost. Still other archeologists believe that fluted points were first made in Alaska or on the southern Great Plains in the United States.

No matter where the custom began, it did not last long, as archeologists measure time. By about 9000 years ago point-makers had shifted from the fragile Folsom points to sturdier points, which were easier to manufacture and less likely to break.

Paleo and Archaic

Paleo-Indian is the term used for the first First Americans. They got their subsistence from various sources, but their special achievement seems to have been as hunters of herding animals, which were often very large. The Paleo way of life ended as the herds of big game disappeared. By 6000 B.C. it was necessary to exploit every available food resource to the maximum.

Smaller animals, edible plants, fish, and shellfish now became the fare of people who followed what is called the Archaic lifeway. They hunted and foraged characteristically in forested areas in the East and in semiarid regions in the West, but their lifeways spread over the entire continent.

Out of the Archaic, beginning about 1000 B.C., or perhaps a little earlier, there developed cultures that practiced gardening. People in many places began to create at least part of their food supply, and this meant that they became more and more settled village dwellers. The older lifeways persisted in areas not suited to food growing, but Indian farms and towns were widespread by the time Europeans mistakenly labeled them Indian.

Above: A Folsom point. *Below:* Two Clovis points. Clovis points vary in measurement. These (which are pictured here about half actual length) were found along with mammoth bones at the Lehner Site in Arizona. After Haury et al.

Some of the houses built in caves at Gila Cliff Dwellings National Monument. National Park Service photo by Parker Hamilton.

FORT BURGWIN RESEARCH CENTER

From Taos (TOWSS) drive south 10 miles on New Mexico 3. The Research Center is east of Ranchos de Taos, on New Mexico 3. Open free Monday through Friday; afternoons, Saturday, Sunday, June, July, Aug.

On display here are materials obtained from Pot Creek Pueblo, a 700-room site which was occupied between A.D. 1000 and 1350. Archeologists believe that the ancestors of both the Taos and Picuris (pee-koo-REES) Indians probably came from this Pot Creek Pueblo. Of special interest are the black-and-white pottery, corrugated utility ware, and manos and metates used in prehistoric times, together with tools and projectile points that were popular.

Several unusual exhibits are designed to show the techniques and methods that archeologists use for getting information about prehistoric cultures. Many of the materials which illustrate these archeological techniques come from local sites.

Other displays show cultural sequences and changes that developed in the pottery and stone tools and buildings from the Pueblo II period onward.

GALLUP MUSEUM OF INDIAN ARTS

From Gallup drive 3 miles east on US 66 to New Mexico 566, then north to Red Rock State Park. Open free, Monday through Friday. Closed certain holidays. Camping in the park.

The archeology of the park is shown in exhibits from 13 sites ranging from Paleo-Indian through Basketmaker and Anasazi to nineteenth-century Navajo Indian hogans.

Special Feature. The second weekend of August every year the public may observe Native American dances at the Inter-Tribal Indian Ceremonial held here in the outdoor arena. On occasion dances may also be held in the indoor auditorium.

GHOST RANCH
(See Florence Hawley Ellis Museum)

GILA CLIFF DWELLINGS NATIONAL MONUMENT
(HEE-lah)

From Silver City drive 44 miles north on New Mexico 15. Open free, daily, all year. Closed certain holidays. Camping.

From the Visitor Center, a half-mile trail leads along a tree-shaded stream to ruins built in large caves, high above the canyon floor. In summer on Saturday nights, there are evening campfire talks explaining the archeology of the region. Visitors take self-guided tours. Displays in the Visitor Center interpret prehistoric life in the area.

The Story. Perhaps as early as A.D. 100 Mogollon people began to live within the borders of the present monument. They grew corn and beans, and for about 900 years they built dwellings that archeologists call pithouses because the floor was below ground level. About A.D. 1000, new ideas began to filter in from the Pueblo Indians to the north. Square stone houses above ground took the place of pithouses. New kinds of white pottery, decorated with black designs, were also borrowed from the north, replacing the older red-on-brown ware.

The Mogollon built some of the new, square-roomed dwellings in caves in the cliffs, and some of these are the structures that have been stabilized and prepared for visitors to the monument.

About A.D. 1400 the houses were all abandoned. No one knows why the inhabitants left or where they went. After they moved away, Apache Indians settled in the area, but they did not become cliff dwellers.

Some of the houses built in caves at Gila Cliff Dwellings National Monument. National Park Service photo by Parker Hamilton.

One of the well-protected buildings in Gila Cliff Dwellings National Monument. National Park Service photo by W. H. Shaffer.

Excavators at work at Gran Quivira, a unit of Salinas National Monument, where ruins of both Spanish and prehistoric Indian structures have been preserved. National Park Service photo by Fred E. Mang, Jr.

GRAN QUIVIRA
(unit of Salinas National Monument)
(grahn kee-VEE-rah)

From Mountainair on US 60 drive south 26 miles on New Mexico 14. Open free, daily, all year.

The Story. People built pithouses of the Mogollon type in the Gran Quivira area about A.D. 800. About A.D. 1100 they began to get many ideas from the Anasazi, and soon black-on-white pottery became popular at Gran Quivira. So did underground ceremonial rooms called kivas, and much the same lifeways were observed here as in the pueblos in the Rio Grande Valley.

There was also some interaction with Plains Indians, who lived to the east. Perhaps as many as 10,000 people inhabited the area at the time of Spanish occupation.

One mound at the site contains dwellings built between A.D. 1300 and A.D. 1400, which consist of six concentric circles of rooms. Above these are rectangular room blocks of later periods.

The Museum. In the Visitor Center are display cases, with explanations in both Spanish and English, showing artifacts in their relation to the development of the culture of the people who lived here. An award-winning, forty-minute film of the excavation of one of the 21 house mounds at the site will be shown on request.

HAWIKUH
(hah-wee-KOO)

About 12 miles south of Zuni Pueblo, Zuni Indian Reservation. For permission to visit the site, for the services of a guide, and information about fee, apply to Zuni Tribal Office, Zuni, NM 87327, or phone (505) 782–4686.

Archeologists investigated this site in the early twentieth century, but did not do anything to stabilize the ruins they found here. As a result there remain for the most part only mounds of rubble, covered with potsherds and debris. However, a visit may be worthwhile in view of the history of the place.

Ranger Virginia Pecos at the home of her ancestors in Pecos National Monument. National Park Service photo by Fred E. Mang, Jr.

The Story: Hawikuh was a town of perhaps 1500 people when Spanish explorers entered the Southwest in 1539, led by a Franciscan monk, Friar Marcos. With him came the famous Black slave, Estevan, who had accompanied Cabeza de Vaca on a seemingly impossible journey from the Gulf coast north through Texas, then south to Mexico City.

While Marcos and Estevan were still in Mexico, they heard from Indians that there were seven fabulously rich cities of Cibola to the north. Marcos sent Estevan on ahead of his expedition, and at Hawikuh the Black explorer met his death.

Estevan had traveled far, had visited many people who lived as hunters and gatherers, and was skilled at getting along with them. A persuasive explanation of his death at Hawikuh seems to be that he arrived there in the company of wandering Indians who had joined Marcos and who belonged to groups that had given the sedentary Zunis a great deal of trouble. More important, Estevan looked different from any people the Zunis had ever seen—black skin, curly hair and beard—and he was dressed as if he might be a shaman or medicine man. The priests at Hawikuh, who were not shamans, were taking no chances with potential rivals in the field of religion, and Estevan's large following gave the impression that he might be regarded as having special powers. So the first Black explorer in North America, who happened also to be the first explorer from the Old World to enter New Mexico from Old Mexico, was killed by Zuni arrows.

Meanwhile Friar Marcos returned to Mexico City with tales of the Seven Cities of Cibola, one of which—Hawikuh—he claimed he had seen, although he had not been near the place. It was this hoax that sparked Coronado's expedition through the Southwest and changed the history of the people who lived there.

INDIAN PETROGLYPHS STATE PARK

In Albuquerque, on Atrisco Drive NW, about one-half mile north of Volcano Cliffs. Open free, Thursday through Monday, all year. Open certain holidays. Camping nearby.

At some time, perhaps 900 years ago, hunters camped in this area and carved a variety of realistic and symbolic drawings in the face the basalt escarpment created by a lava flow from a nearby volcano. Several concentrated groups of the petroglyphs are protected and interpreted within the park.

One of the Jemez Indian rangers who interpret Giusewa, which was built by their ancestors.

Ruins at Jemez State Monument. Museum of New Mexico photo.

JEMEZ STATE MONUMENT
(HEM-ess)

From Bernalillo drive 23 miles northwest on New Mexico 44, then northeast on New Mexico 4 to monument entrance on the northern edge of the town of Jemez Springs. Or from Los Alamos drive 38 miles west and south on New Mexico 4. Open free, Thursday through Monday. Closed certain holidays.

Here are the ruins of the pueblo of Giusewa (jee-SAY-wah), which dates from about A.D. 1300. It is known to have been very large, but how large is uncertain, because only part of it has been excavated. In places the buildings are three stories high. The prehistoric inhabitants used the nearby hot springs as baths. Today their descendants live several miles down the canyon, in Jemez Pueblo. They are the only people who now speak the Towa language.

Rangers at the monument are members of Jemez Pueblo, and they have participated in preparing the museum exhibits at the Visitor Center. Displays interpret the life and history of Giusewa from the Indian point of view, with an audio accompaniment of traditional Jemez music. There are additional interpretive panels along the trail through the ruins.

The monument, a unit of the Museum of New Mexico, also preserves the seventeenth-century Franciscan mission of San José de los Jemez.

KIT CARSON HOME AND MUSEUM

On Old Kit Carson Rd., one-half block east of the plaza, Taos (TOWSS). Open daily, all year. Closed certain holidays. Admission charged.

One room in this museum is devoted to Indian culture and includes exhibits of prehistoric material from the Taos area dating back as far as 3000 B.C. Most of the archeological material is Anasazi from after the year A.D. 1.

LABORATORY OF ANTHROPOLOGY

Just outside Santa Fe. From center city drive south on Old Santa Fe Trail to Camino Lejo, then right to laboratory entrance. Open free, Monday through Friday. Closed certain holidays.

This research center houses rich collections of prehistoric Southwestern material, from which exhibits are drawn.

MAXWELL MUSEUM OF ANTHROPOLOGY
(See University of New Mexico)

MILES MUSEUM

On the campus of Eastern New Mexico University, Portales. Open free, afternoons, Monday through Friday. Closed certain holidays.

Exhibits include general Southwestern archeological materials, and a large collection of prehistoric pottery.

The Palace of the Governors, Santa Fe, containing archeological exhibits, is the oldest governmental building on the soil of the United States. Spanish colonial authorities established it about A.D. 1609. In the arcade along the front of the building Indians from various pueblos sell their craftwork. Photo by Russell D. Butcher.

MILLICENT ROGERS MUSEUM

From Taos drive 4 miles north to directional sign near the junction of US 64 and New Mexico 3. Open daily, May 1 to October 31; Tuesday through Sunday, November through April. Admission charged.

In addition to modern Native American material, this museum exhibits some fine Mimbres and Anasazi pottery.

NEW MEXICO STATE UNIVERSITY MUSEUM

On the campus of New Mexico State University, on University Ave., off US 80, Interstate 25, and Interstate 10, Las Cruces. Open free, afternoons, daily, or by appointment.

This general museum contains Mogollon pottery and stone tools from the period A.D. 800 to 1350, together with a considerable quantity of Casas Grandes pottery from northern Mexico. Exhibits also include local archeological finds and much ethnological material.

PALACE OF THE GOVERNORS

Palace Ave., on the plaza, Santa Fe. Open free, daily, mid-March to mid-Oct.; Tuesday through Sunday, mid-Oct. to mid-March. Closed certain holidays. Administered by the Museum of New Mexico.

This handsome building, which now houses one of the best museums in the Southwest, was formerly the governor's residence under Spanish colonial, territorial, and present-day rule. Erected in 1610, it has been in use continuously since then.

Many of the objects in the archeological exhibit are drawn from the museum's exceptionally rich collections. A series of interpretive displays entitled "The Rio Grande World," in the Hall of the Southwestern Indian, emphasizes the prehistory of Indians in the Rio Grande region from the vicinity of Albuquerque to the vicinity of Taos. The exhibit spans the time from the days of Paleo-Indians through Oshara (Archaic) hunters and gatherers and continues with the Anasazi up to A.D. 1600, when the Native Am-

erican culture was changed by the Spanish conquest and the people became known as Pueblo Indians.

PECOS NATIONAL MONUMENT (PAY-kohs)

From Santa Fe drive southeast 25 miles on Interstate 25 to Glorieta-Pecos interchange, then 8 miles on US 84A to the monument. Or from Las Vegas drive west on Interstate 25 to Rowe interchange, then 3 miles on US 84A to the monument. Open free, daily. Camping nearby.

Here, near the Pecos River, are the ruins of a pueblo that housed one of the largest town populations north of Mexico, when Coronado entered the area in 1541. Visitors may follow a trail on a self-guided tour of the ruins.

The Story. In the ninth century people began to settle in small groups along the upper reaches of the river. In time these small settlements grew together into larger settlements, and by 1540 Pecos was a huge, multi-storied pueblo, constructed around

Pecos Indians built this wall not for defense but to outline the area of the town which was closed to visitors at night. National Park Service photo.

Pecos ruins, which were first investigated by Adolph Bandelier, who drove out in a buggy from Santa Fe, 25 miles away. National Park Service photo.

an open plaza. At least 660 rooms provided living quarters for about 2000 people.

The Pecos people were farmers, like all the Anasazi, but their geographic location led them into special activities. Their pueblo stood at a crossroads, where Plains Indians met Pueblo Indians from the Rio Grande Valley, and where Indians from north and south along the Pecos River met. The pueblo was a great center for trade. Many strangers came there. Possibly to define an area within which Pecos residents wanted privacy at night, they built a wall around the town. The wall appears not to have been for defense.

Sometime in the 1620s the Franciscans built a huge church near Pecos and set about Christianizing the inhabitants. Apparently their success was incomplete. The pueblo continued to use ceremonial kivas. Some, at least, of the converts seem to have lived in a separate pueblo near the mission church. Possibly unconverted Pecos people also lived here, but this dwelling area, called the South Pueblo, had no kivas.

In 1680 the Pecos people joined most of the other Pueblo Indians in a general revolt against the Spanish. They burned the church and drove the friars out. The church building which stands at Pecos today is much smaller than the original mission, signs of which were discovered only in 1967, during archeological excavations.

By 1838 the population of Pecos had dwindled from 2000 to 17. Disease had killed many. Warfare killed others. The survivors moved to Jemez Pueblo, where their descendants live today.

Between 1915 and 1929 Dr. A.V. Kidder made very important excavations at the Pecos site. A vast number of interesting artifacts came from the dig. Some of them can be seen in the Phillips Academy, Peabody Foundation, in Andover, Mass. Dr. Kidder's discoveries made it possible to bring order into the chronology of a large area in the Southwest. In 1927 all archeologists who had been working in the area came to Pecos to exchange information and to adopt a terminology that all of them could use and understand. Honoring that first Southwestern conference, archeologists still meet every year for a Pecos Conference at some place in the Southwest.

PICURIS PUEBLO
(pee-koo-REES)

From Taos drive southwest on New Mexico 68 to Embudo, then east about 16 miles on New Mexico 75. Open daily, all year. Admission charged.

Archeological excavations at Picuris have established that the pueblo was founded between A.D. 1250 and 1300. Those who built their homes at the present site moved from another pueblo that once stood near Talpa (on New Mexico 3). The excavated features at Picuris are open to the public and may be photographed.

PUYÉ CLIFF RUINS, SANTA CLARA INDIAN RESERVATION
(poo-YAY)

From Espanola on US 84 drive southwest on New Mexico 30 to directional sign, then 9 miles west on New Mexico 5 to entrance gate. Open all year. Admission: a fee is collected by a rep-

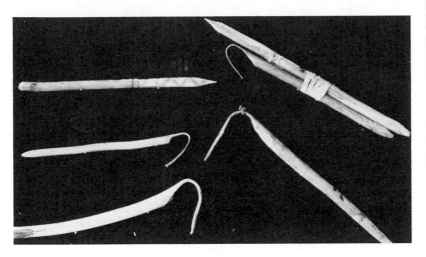

Ancestors of the present-day inhabitants of Santa Clara Pueblo once lived in these rooms at Puyé Ruins. Photo by Ellen Conreid Balch.

A general view of Puyé Cliff, showing some of the masonry structures at the base together with holes leading into artificial caves in the cliff itself. Photo by Ellen Conreid Balch.

Ruins of the old Quarai mission stand amid remains of a prehistoric pueblo in Salinas National Monument. Museum of New Mexico photo.

resentative of the Santa Clara Pueblo, which supervises the ruin. Camping nearby.

Ancestors of the present-day Santa Clara Indians lived at Puyé Cliff. Some of their masonry dwellings were built along the base of the rock wall; other rooms were dug into the soft stone of the cliff itself, and on top of the cliff were several hundred additional rooms. Apparently the inhabitants moved away from Puyé Cliff seeking more fertile and better-watered lands, which they found near the site of the present Santa Clara Pueblo.

Parts of this very large ruin have been excavated and prepared for view by the public. The site is one of the few large prehistoric ruins administered by the descendants of the people who once lived there. Every year, in midsummer, the Santa Clara Indians hold an elaborate ceremonial at Puyé Cliff. The public is admitted.

QUARAI
(unit of Salinas National Monument)
(car-EYE)

From Mountainair on US 60 drive north on New Mexico 14, 8 miles to Punta de Agua, then 1 mile west from directional sign. Open free, Thursday through Monday. Closed certain holidays. Camping nearby.

In addition to walls of a seventeenth-century Spanish mission that can be seen here, there is a rubble heap—the remains of a largely unexcavated but partly stabilized pueblo ruin. Archeological tests show that part of the site was inhabited in the fourteenth century. Other parts were used at least as far back as the thirteenth century. People here spoke the Tiwa language.

Before Indians and Spaniards abandoned Quarai in 1675, it served as the center in New Mexico for the Inquisition. Although Indians, considered inferiors, were not subject to the Inquisition, they did not escape punishment if they failed to pay tithes to the state or if they continued to practice their ancient religion.

In the Visitor Center at the site, which was formerly a state monument and is now part of the Salinas National Monument, are displays explained in both Spanish and English, of prehistoric artifacts and of materials that interpret life at Quarai in the historic period.

RED ROCK STATE PARK
(See Gallup Museum of Indian Arts)

SALINAS NATIONAL
MONUMENT
(sah-LEE-nus)

This monument consists of three separate units, located in three places: Abo (see entry, above) and Quarai (see entry, above), which were formerly New Mexico state monuments, and Gran Quivira (see entry, above), which was formerly a National Monument by itself. As this book went to press, the National Park Service, which administers Salinas, was in the process of setting up monument headquarters in Mountainair, where there will eventually be an interpretive center. For

Part of the museum at Salmon Ruin, which was financed by a bond issue approved by citizens of San Juan County.

Archeologists excavating Salmon Ruin. Photo by Peter B. George.

information write to Superintendent, Salinas National Monument, PO Box 496, Mountainair, NM 87036.

SALMON RUIN
(SOL-mun)

From Bloomfield drive 2.5 miles west on US 64 to entrance and museum. Open daily, all year. Closed certain holidays. Admission charged. Camping nearby.

The Salmon pueblo was one of several built by people who went out as colonists from the Chaco Canyon area, about 50 miles to the south. Tree-ring dates taken from roof beams show that the massive masonry structures were put up between A.D. 1088 and 1095. Built in the form of a squared C, the pueblo measured 430 feet along the back wall, 150 feet along the arms and was two stories high. In this pre-planned, multiple dwelling were about 250 large, high-ceilinged rooms, arranged in groups for family units. Underground in the plaza was a ceremonial great kiva and, at the highest point in the structure, an unusual tower kiva.

After about 60 years of occupation, most of the Chacoan people left the pueblo. Only a few of the original inhabitants remained, until in the thirteenth century new people moved in, probably from the San Juan River valley. They made pottery in the style of Mesa Verde, and their culture seems to have been simpler than that of the Chacoans. They divided the large, original rooms into smaller units, by constructing poorly made masonry walls. By the beginning of the fourteenth century, these people, too, had abandoned the pueblo.

The ruin has been partially excavated and is undergoing stabilization. It can be visited on a self-guided tour. The San Juan County Archaeological Research Center and Museum at the site has exhibits of materials found there, and regular, daily slide-tape programs give details of the archeological exploration. The museum is the result of a cooperative endeavor by the citizens of San Juan County, who voted a $275,000 bond issue to finance construction of the Research Center and Library.

Excavation and interpretation of this important site were directed by Dr. Cynthia Irwin-Williams.

The Name. Salmon Ruin was named for George Salmon, who homesteaded in the area in the late 1800s and protected the site from vandals and pot-hunters.

Fanciful Archeology

The Swiss writer Erich von Daniken has started a fad that attracts people who are more interested in believing than in knowing. Without any evidence, often citing data inaccurately, and with disrespect for the abilities of Native Americans, he claims that many archeological features in the Americas were created by visitors from outer space. Although a carefully researched television program demonstrated to millions of viewers that there is no basis in fact for von Daniken's theories, believers persist.

Other theories, too, have been based on the racist notion that Indians had to get their ideas from somewhere else. At one time or another the Celts, the Welsh, the Irish, Phoenicians, Egyptians, the Africans were all put forward as originators of great achievements in the New World. The American Indians themselves were supposed by some to have been descended from the Ten Lost Tribes of Israel. For none of these theories is there any evidence that withstands scientific scrutiny.

That fancies flourish where facts are few
Is true of Atlantis and also of Mu.

A tourist rests at the entrance to Sandia Man Cave, after climbing the spiral stairway from the path, far below.

SANDIA MAN CAVE
(san-DEE-ah)

From Albuquerque drive north 16 miles on Interstate 25, then east 12½ miles on New Mexico 44 to the parking area for the cave. Or from Tijeras on US 66 drive north 6 miles on New Mexico 14, then northwest on New Mexico 44 about 12½ miles to the parking area. From the parking area a trail leads one-half mile to the cave itself. Camping nearby.

This cave is of interest because for many years archeologists believed that it had contained the oldest artifacts found in America. The remains of human occupation were originally dated at about 20,000 years B.P. (before present). Recent re-study of the material has cast doubt on this early date, but the cave does remain of interest as one of the two places in which Sandia points have been found. These points seem to be at least as old as the Clovis points that have been associated with the hunting of mammoths.

Material from the excavation may be seen at the Museum of Anthropology, University of New Mexico, Albuquerque.

Sandia Man Cave is administered by the Forest Service of the U.S. Department of Agriculture.

SAN JUAN PUEBLO
(san HWAN)

About 5 miles north of Espanola on New Mexico 68 and US 285. Open free, daylight hours. A visitor's permit must be obtained from the governor of the pueblo. Camping nearby.

This pueblo was in existence when the first Spaniards arrived. The name San Juan is a shortened form of San Juan de los Caballeros, the name given the pueblo by the Spanish conquerors.

SANTA CLARA PUEBLO

From Santa Fe drive north 24 miles on US 84-285 to Espanola; cross the Rio Grande and turn south on New Mexico 5, 1 mile to pueblo. Open free, daily, all year. Camping nearby.

This pueblo has apparently been on its present site since about 1500. Before the coming of the Spanish it was called Kapo. In earlier prehistoric times the Santa Clara people lived on the Pajarito Plateau, in the region of Puyé.

SETON MUSEUM

From Cimarron drive 5 miles south on New Mexico 21 to Philmont Camping Headquarters. Open free, June 1 through Aug. 31 and Monday through Friday, Sept. 1 through May 31.

From its large collections of archeological and ethnological artifacts the museum offers exhibits that depict the life and culture of the Southwest.

TAOS PUEBLO
(TOWSS)

From Taos drive north 3 miles on New Mexico 3. Open daily, all year. Parking fee required. Visitors may take photographs on payment of a fee. Camping nearby.

This pueblo has existed on its present site since prehistoric times, and the architecture of the buildings resembles the architecture of the pre-Spanish pueblo.

Prehistoric Firepower

Stone weapons changed a great deal in the millenia of their use. Very early in the Old World people learned to extend their grasp by jabbing a pointed stick into small creatures they could not easily reach with their bare hands. They also learned how to break certain kinds of stone to get sharp edges that were good for cutting or gouging. Then came a big innovation. Someone fastened a stick and a sharpened rock together—and made a spear.

At first this new tool was probably used only for poking, but it was effective. In America humans could apparently kill even mammoths with thrusting spears. They increased the range of their weapons when they found they could hurl a spear as well as thrust it. The spear had become a javelin—a projectile. Next its range was extended with the aid of a spear-thrower, also called a throwing stick or atlatl (AT-ul-AT-ul). People who used atlatls often made the shafts of their spears lighter than the shafts of thrusting spears, and these small spears, or javelins, are often called darts. Dart points, too, were likely to be smaller than the points on heavy thrusting spears.

For thousands of years American Indians got much of their protein food with the aid of darts and atlatls. Then came a device with which a person could put still more power behind projectiles—the bow. The bow acted as a spring: it stored up muscle power and then released a lot of it all at once.

As people increased the power behind the projectile, they were often able to decrease the size of the projectile shaft. For the sake of balance, the lighter shaft was equipped with a light point. Even reeds were used as the forepart of dart shafts and also for arrows, and some arrow points were very small.

Since arrows were easily transported in quantity, they made possible a great increase in firepower, and human destructiveness multiplied. Not only could they kill more animals and thus obtain more food; they could also kill more people. So, paradoxically, as soon as human beings were better able to provide for themselves, they also became less sure of surviving.

Archeologists may never know how it happened that some genius in the Old World invented the bow. They do know that it spread from the Old World to the New. Exactly how it got here is not clear, but it had appeared in the New World by 5500 years ago.

The wood that went into making bows varied from place to place, depending on what was available. Some were made of several small pieces of wood ingeniously fitted together. Some were reinforced with sinews. Bows were long. Bows were short. Bows curved in different ways.

Some arrows may have been only sharpened wooden sticks. Some shafts were made of sturdy reeds. Very often a man identified his own arrows by painting some special mark or symbol on them.

Arrow points are abundant in areas where people depended heavily on hunting for food. In other areas, where most of the food came from agriculture, arrow points may be much less frequently found. In the largest ruins of the Southwest, for example, they are often far from numerous.

The spear thrower, also called a throwing stick or atlatl, extended the distance a spear could be hurled. Men who used atlatls often made the shafts of their spears lighter than the shafts of javelins or thrusting spears. The projectile launched by an atlatl is often called a dart. A dart point was smaller than the point of a thrusting spear but was larger than the point of an arrow used with a bow. After Indians discovered the greater accuracy and efficiency of the bow and arrow, they stopped using the atlatl and dart.

Taos Pueblo as it appears today.

THREE RIVERS PETROGLYPHS

Drive 28 miles south from Carrizozo (care-ee-ZO-zo) on US 54, then 5 miles east at Three Rivers, following signs on a gravel road. Open free, all year. Camping nearby.

A 1400-yard surfaced trail, with shaded rests along the way, leads through an area where people of the Jornada branch of the Mogollon culture made more than 500 rock carvings between the years A.D. 900 and 1400. Pictured on the jumbled boulders here are ceremonial figures, geometric figures, and animals—birds, frogs, lizards, mountain sheep, insects, and even an inchworm. Especially interesting are large, decorative pictures of fish in this very arid part of the country. Found here and almost nowhere else is a recurring design, made of a circle surrounded by dots.

UNIVERSITY OF NEW MEXICO, MAXWELL MUSEUM OF ANTHROPOLOGY

On the campus, at University and Ash, N.E., Albuquerque. Open free, Monday through Saturday; afternoon, Sunday.

This excellent museum emphasizes archeology of the Southwest and has in addition exhibits of archeological and ethnological material from other parts of the world. Permanent exhibits include *Man in the Southwest, Bands,* and *Human Evolution.* A special display contains material from the Gilbert and Dorothy Maxwell Collection of kachina dolls. Rotating exhibits feature various subjects, including archeology.

VILLAGE OF THE GREAT KIVAS

On the Zuni Indian Reservation. For road directions and permission to visit the site, write Zuni Tribal Office, Zuni, NM 87327, or phone (505) 782–4686.

This small, ruined settlement is notable for the two great kivas which identify it as one of the outliers, or colonies, established by people from Chaco Canyon (see entry, above) in the eleventh century.

Prehistoric Indian rock art in Horse Canyon, Canyonlands National Park.
National Park Service photo by N. Woodbridge Williams.

ZIA PUEBLO
(TSEE-ah)

From Bernalillo drive northwest 18 miles on New Mexico 44. Open free, during daylight hours. Visitors are not allowed to photograph, draw, or paint in the pueblo. Camping nearby.

This pueblo has been on its present site since about A.D. 1300. Recent excavations by Dr. Cynthia Irwin-Williams suggest that the ancestors of the Zia people, like the ancestors of some other Pueblo people, have lived in the same general area for nearly 8000 years.

The symbol for the sun that the ancient Zia used has been adopted as the design at the center of the New Mexico state flag. These are the words of the official salute to the flag: "I salute the flag of the State of New Mexico, the Zia symbol of perfect friendship among united cultures."

ZUNI PUEBLO
(ZOON-yee or ZOON-ee)

From Gallup drive south 30 miles on New Mexico 32, then 11 miles west on New Mexico 53. Open free at any time. Arrangements must be made for photographing. Camping nearby.

Zuni Indians have lived on or near the site of the present town since prehistoric times. About 50 miles south of the pueblo is the sacred Zuni Salt Lake, in the crater of an extinct volcano. Since ancient times the Zuni and other Indians have gathered salt there.

Utah

ALKALI RIDGE

From Monticello drive 13 miles south on US 163 to directional marker, then 8 miles to site. Or from Blanding drive 5 miles north on US 163 to directional marker, then 2 miles to site. Open free, at all times. Camping nearby.

Although no exhibits have been prepared for the public here, the site has long been of interest to archeologists. More than a thousand years ago a band of people settled in this land of cliffs and canyons. They hunted bighorn sheep, planted small fields of corn, and found it a good place in which to live. Their descendants continued to make their homes there for 500 years.

The firstcomers belonged to an early group of Anasazi people, called Basketmakers because they were very skilled at weaving baskets of many kinds. As time passed they developed new skills, following the general pattern of all the Anasazi in the region. Students of archeology are especially interested in this settlement at Alkali Ridge, because they can trace Anasazi life there, stage by stage, and also because the ceremonial kivas, which mark Anasazi culture in the Southwest, may have evolved in this particular area.

Alkali Ridge was excavated between 1931 and 1933 by J.O. Brew, of the Peabody Museum, at Harvard. Afterward, the site itself was covered over, and there is little for the casual visitor to see.

Fremont Culture

In Utah about A.D. 900, many people began to live in somewhat the same way as the Anasazi farther south. Some archeologists call this Utah lifeway the Fremont culture and regard it as a subdivision of the Anasazi. Fremont people lived on the northern periphery of the Anasazi area and gathered wild foods, as their ancestors apparently had done for thousands of years, but they also raised corn. Unlike the Anasazi they wore moccasins rather than sandals. Much of their pottery was rather plain, and experts can easily distinguish it from Anasazi pottery, which was often more decorated. Like the Anasazi the Fremont people built dwellings of stone and adobe masonry.

In the eastern part of Utah the lifeway of the Fremont people differed somewhat from that of their neighbors in the western part, who are called Sevier (suh-VEER)-Fremont. Both the Fremont and the Sevier-Fremont left rock art on cliff walls throughout the area.

At the beginning of Classic Pueblo times (about A.D. 1100), the Fremont culture began to disappear. A recent theory suggests that Fremont people moved out of Utah, some to the south, where they merged with the ancestors of the present-day Pueblos, some to the east, onto the Plains, probably through South Pass. According to this theory, which is based on cultural, skeletal, and linguistic evidence, the Shoshoni Indians, whom the first white settlers found in Utah, were not descendants of the Fremont people but were fairly recent immigrants to the area.

ANASAZI STATE HISTORICAL MONUMENT

In Boulder on Utah 12. Open free, daily, all year.

The Utah Division of Parks and Recreation maintains a Visitor Center at the site of an Anasazi village (A.D. 1050 to 1200) excavated by University of Utah archeologists. Some of the buildings have been reconstructed, and artifacts are on display in the Visitor Center.

ARCH CANYON RUIN

From Blanding drive south on US 163 to intersection with Utah 95, then about 20 miles west to the bottom of Comb Wash marked by a small sign, then north 3 miles on a graded road which ends at the head of a trail leading ¼ mile to the site. Open free, at all times. Camping nearby.

This small interesting Anasazi ruin has been partially stabilized and fenced to keep out cattle, but can be entered through a gate. For more information inquire at the Monticello office of the Bureau of Land Management, which administers the area.

ARCHES NATIONAL PARK

From Moab drive 5 miles north on US 163 to Park Headquarters. Open daily, all year. Admission charged. Camping.

There are a number of pictograph and petroglyph sites in the park, the most accessible of which is the Courthouse Wash Panel. For directions to the site inquire at the Visitor Center. Some of the unusual paintings here are five feet or more tall, and are similar to paintings in Horseshoe Canyon (see entry, below). On a portion of the same cliff are petroglyphs which have been carved in the sandstone. Unfortunately, because of its accessibility the site has been badly vandalized.

BARRIER CANYON
(See Horseshoe Canyon)

BIG WESTWATER RUIN

From Blanding drive 6½ miles south on US 163, then west for about 1 mile on a secondary road, then north for about ¾ mile. Open free, daily, all year.

At this Anasazi site there are several masonry rooms in a large rockshelter. Tree-ring dates indicate that the dwellings were built between A.D. 1150 and 1250.

A few miles north of this site is Westwater Ruin, a large rockshelter occupied from as early as A.D. 800 to A.D. 1250.

BRIGHAM YOUNG UNIVERSITY, MUSEUM OF ARCHEOLOGY AND ANTHROPOLOGY

On the campus, Provo. Open free, daily, all year.

This museum contains archeological materials of the Fremont culture in Utah, as well as ethnographic materials from the Southwest.

Cliff dweller ruins on Westwater Creek near Blanding. Bureau of Land
Management photo.

Handprints in Canyonlands National Park. National Park Service photo.

BUCKHORN WASH PICTOGRAPHS AND PETROGLYPHS

From Castle Dale drive east 13 miles on a local road to Buckhorn Flat, then follow signs 8 miles to Buckhorn Wash. Open free, daily, all year.

Here are paintings and carvings on stone left by people of the Fremont culture between A.D. 900 and 1300.

CALF CREEK RECREATION SITE

On Utah 12 midway between Boulder and Escalante. Open free, at all times. Camping.

Anyone who plans to visit both Capitol Reef National Park and Bryce Canyon National Park may wish to make the trip via Utah 12 (partly unpaved), which passes the ruins of two Anasazi villages. For information inquire at Kanab office, Bureau of Land Management, which administers the site.

CANYONLANDS NATIONAL PARK

To reach Island in the Sky district of the park, turn west from US 163, 11 miles north of Moab. To reach Needles district, drive west on Utah 211. Other districts require a four-wheel drive vehicle. Open free, at all times. Primitive camping.

Throughout the park there are numerous small ruins of dwellings, granaries, and kivas built by the Anasazi people between A.D. 900 and 1250. Visitors are invited to look at the ruins, but are forbidden to enter them. The rock walls of the canyons offered innumerable flat surfaces for prehistoric artists, and a great deal of their work has been preserved. Visitors may see both pictographs, which are paintings on rock, and petroglyphs, which are pictures pecked or scraped on rock. Some of these, archeologists think, may have been made to mark game trails.

Anasazi people made their homes in areas such as this in Canyonlands National Park. National Park Service photo by George A. Grant.

Many small structures like this can be seen in protected areas in what is now Canyonlands National Park. National Park Service photo.

Prehistoric shields made of buffalo hide, which were found packed in juniper bark in a burial in the Capitol Reef National Park area. National Park Service photo by George A. Grant.

Petroglyphs in Capitol Reef National Park. National Park Service photo by Parker Hamilton.

CAPITOL REEF NATIONAL PARK

On Utah 24, 75 miles southeast of the junction of Utah 24 with US 89. The museum at the Visitor Center is open free, daily. Closed certain holidays. Camping.

The Fremont people once lived in this area, and a portion of the Visitor Center is devoted to them. Petroglyphs, probably made by Fremont people, may be seen near the highway.

CLEAR CREEK CANYON ROCK ART

Between Sevier and Cove Fort on Utah 44. Open free, at all times.

Many panels of petroglyphs may be seen along the walls of Clear Creek Canyon. The main concentration is between the mouths of Mill Creek and Dry Creek.

COLLEGE OF EASTERN UTAH, PREHISTORIC MUSEUM

City Hall, Price. Open free, Monday through Saturday. Closed certain holidays.

The museum contains artifacts of the Fremont culture.

COURTHOUSE WASH PANEL
(See Arches National Park)

DANGER CAVE STATE HISTORICAL SITE

One mile north of Wendover off US 40. Open free, at all times.

This famous site, although so far undeveloped, has been opened to the public by the Utah Park system. For its significance see introduction to Great Basin section.

DINOSAUR NATIONAL MONUMENT

From Jensen on US 40, drive north 7 miles on Utah 149 to Visitor Center. Open free, daily, all year. Camping.

Prehistoric people may have been in this area as early as 11,000 years ago, although archeological excavation has revealed few details about them. Fremont people made their homes from A.D. 900 to 1200 along rivers and creeks, hunting, gathering, and farming. Their petroglyphs (rock carvings) and pictographs (rock paintings) may be seen in several areas in the monument. The best and most accessible are east of the dinosaur quarry on a park road. For information about their location, inquire at Dinosaur Quarry Visitor Center.

More recently, Ute Indians lived in one part of the area, Snake and Shoshone Indians in another, known as Browns Park. Descendants of the Utes now occupy a reservation nearby.

DINOSAUR NATURAL HISTORY MUSEUM
(Formerly Utah Field House of Natural History)

235 East Main St., Vernal. Open free, daily, all year. Closed certain holidays.

Within this natural history museum are archeological displays of prehistoric

Edge of the Cedars Ruin, Blanding. Edge of the Cedars State Historical
Monument photo.

artifacts. The cultures represented are primarily the Fremont, Basketmaker, and Ute Indian.

EDGE OF THE CEDARS MUSEUM

660 West 400 North, Blanding. Open free, daily. Closed certain holidays.

Here are dioramas and materials from Anasazi as well as from historic Ute and Navajo cultures. Demonstrations of pottery making are given from time to time. An Anasazi ruin may be visited in adjacent Edge of the Cedars Historical Monument.

GOULDING'S TRADING POST

At just about the point where US 163 crosses the border between Arizona and Utah, 24 miles north of Kayenta, drive west 3 miles on a local road.

Although its post office address is in Utah, this trading post and motel has long been associated with Navajoland in Arizona. Visitors who want to see prehistoric sites in Monument Valley can arrange for guided, four-

wheel-drive day or half-day trips. For information, from April to November, write to Box 1, Monument Valley, Utah 84536

GRAND GULCH ARCHEOLOGICAL PRIMITIVE AREA

From Blanding drive south on US 163, then 35 miles southwest on Utah 95 to intersection with Utah 261, then 4 miles south on Utah 261 to Kane Gulch. A hiking trail leads down Kane Gulch to Grand Gulch, about a five hour trip. Open free, at all times, but visitors must register at the Kane Gulch Ranger Station and must carry drinking water.

This is a deep canyon, rich in archeological remains, with many large, well-preserved Anasazi dwellings. There are three entrances, fenced for protection, and the area can only be traversed on foot or horseback. Guide service is available in Monticello. Inquire there at the Bureau of Land Management, which administers the site.

Pottery from Grand Gulch is now

Detail showing masonry of round towers at Hovenweep National Monument.

in the Museum of the American Indian, New York City. It was collected by Richard Wetherill, a member of a Quaker family who settled near Mancos, Colorado, in the 1880s. From the home ranch he and his brothers, John and Clayton, went out on many exploring expeditions and made many archeological discoveries. In a cave in Grand Gulch Richard found, underneath layers of dust and debris containing things left by Pueblo people, artifacts made by Basketmaker people. This surely meant, said Wetherill, that the Basketmakers lived in the Southwest earlier than the Pueblos. Today the idea seems obvious, but at that time American archeologists had not made use of the principle of stratigraphy (the study of strata or layers in the earth), which had long been used in European archeology.

HOG SPRINGS PICNIC SITE

From Hanksville drive 37 miles south on Utah 95. Open at all times. Admission charged.

Near the picnic site is a rockshelter containing Indian pictographs, one of which is called the Moki Queen by local residents. Administered by the Bureau of Land Management.

HORSESHOE CANYON
(Barrier Canyon)

Accessible only by four-wheel drive vehicle and foot trail. From Green River drive 9 miles west on Interstate 70 to Utah 24, then south to sign for Goblin Valley State Park; continue to unimproved dirt road (next left), and follow Maze District signs to Hans Flat Ranger Station, where further directions to the canyon can be obtained.

Throughout Horseshoe Canyon and Barrier Canyon, which is part of the area, are large paintings of human figures on sandstone cliff walls. Archeologists believe they may have been done by shamans and that they had religious significance to those who at some prehistoric time lived in the small villages in what is now Canyonlands National Park.

HOVENWEEP NATIONAL MONUMENT

From Cortez, Colorado, drive north 18 miles on US 666 to Pleasant View; turn west at the Hovenweep directional sign and follow the graded road 27.2 miles to Square Tower Group, which is in Utah. Open free, all year. Camping.

In this extremely isolated spot are imposing and well-preserved towers and other structures built by people who followed about the same lifeway as the ancient farmers of Mesa Verde. Exact dates and many details about the Hovenweep people are not yet known, because there has been no excavation at this site. Visitors take self-guided tours on a number of trails leading to the most interesting of the ruins. A ranger on duty at the Visitor Center will answer questions.

The Name. On September 13, 1874, a party exploring for the United States Government camped at this place. Ernest Ingersoll, a zoologist, and W. H. Jackson, a photographer, were members of the expedition. Ingersoll noted in his journal that the place was named

Above and opposite: Many towers at Hovenweep National Monument are
square. Others are circular or oval or d-shaped. Until scientific excavation is
done, there can only be speculation about the meaning and use of the towers.
National Park Service photos by Fred E. Mang, Jr.

The symbols on this stone slab, called Newspaper Rock, may have had real meaning to the people who put them there, but experts agree that they do not constitute true writing. The symbols cover an area 25 feet long and 25 feet high in Indian Creek State Park. Photo by Norman Van Pelt.

by the explorers from two Indian words meaning "deserted canyon."

Special Feature. Hovenweep is a kind of bank in which archeological riches are being kept for future generations of scientists to excavate and study. Archeologists approve this policy, because new techniques are constantly being developed, which make it possible to learn more and more from the materials recovered at a site. When Hovenweep is excavated in the future, it will yield information that might be lost if digging went on today. Once a site is excavated it is destroyed as a source of scientific information.

MULE CANYON INDIAN RUINS

From Blanding drive south on US 163, then west 20 miles on Utah 95 to site entrance. Open free, all year.

This site was discovered and excavated during a survey prior to the construction of the new Utah 95. After the ruins were stabilized, the Bureau of Land Management built trails, rest rooms, and a protective shelter over one structure.

Anasazi people lived here shortly before A.D. 1300. The small complex consists of rooms for dwelling and storage, a kiva for religious ceremonies, and a tower which might have been used for defense or as a platform for sending signals with fire or smoke. A crawlway led from the kiva to one of the house rooms. The site was probably the home of an extended family of about eight adults and their children.

On the canyon rim nearby are the ruins of several round stone towers, probably associated with the settlement in the canyon below. The site, marked on some maps as Cave Towers Ruins, has not been prepared for visitation.

NATURAL BRIDGES NATIONAL MONUMENT

From Blanding drive 40 miles west on Utah 95. Or from Mexican Hat drive north on Utah 261, then west on Utah 95. Open all year except when closed by rain or snow. Admission charged in summer. Camping.

Within the monument are 200 sites once occupied by Anasazi people.

Hikers who follow the trails will pass a cliff dwelling with several rooms, granaries, and kivas, which may be viewed but not entered. Federal laws protecting antiquities are enforced.

NEWSPAPER ROCK, INDIAN CREEK STATE PARK

Drive 12 miles north of Monticello on US 163, then 12 miles west on Utah 211. Open free, all year. Camping.

Here a large cliff wall is covered with Indian rock art that may have accumulated over a period of 1500 years. It seems likely that most of the petroglyphs were made by the Fremont people between A.D. 900 and 1200. Drawings depicting horses were clearly done in the historic period.

Tree-Ring Dating

Trees grow by adding layers of wood outside the layers that are already there. Some trees add a layer each year, and in years that are wet during the growing season, the layers are thick. In dry years they are thin. In an area where weather conditions are uniform, all trees that are weather-sensitive in this way tend to have the same pattern of thick and thin rings. By matching the ring pattern in a living tree with the ring pattern in a tree that was felled some time ago, it is often possible to tell the exact year in which the dead tree was cut.

Working backward from living trees, scientists have found a pattern of tree-ring growth in much of the Southwest that prevailed for more than 2000 years. They have made a master chart showing patterns of clusters of thick rings and thin rings. These patterns are called signatures, and each tree-ring signature differs from every other just as each handwritten signature differs from every other. By comparing the pattern of growth rings in a tree with the master chart it is possible to determine the exact years during which the tree was alive. In this way you can find out the exact year when the tree died or was cut down.

If the tree was used as a beam in a room, you can be sure it was not used before it was cut down. You have the beginning of a date for the room. If you find other beams in the same room all with the same date, you can be fairly sure when the roof was put on the building. If you find charcoal in the fireplace of the building that gives the same date as the roof beams, you can be reasonably sure that the building was finished and used in about the year given by the tree rings in the beams. This also means that you have some idea about the date of artifacts found in the room. The entire contents of the room were not likely to have been placed there before the room was built.

Tree-ring dating is also called dendrochronology.

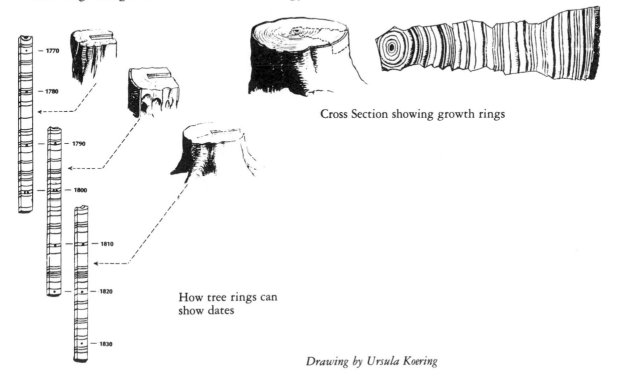

Cross Section showing growth rings

How tree rings can show dates

Drawing by Ursula Koering

Weather Prediction

Archeologists have developed many strategies for determining what the weather was like at various periods in the past—and how it affected the lives of Native Americans. Growth rings in trees, for example, reflect periods of drought and heavy rainfall which brought bad or good crops. The remains of various types of vegetation in layers of earth, which geologists can date, indicate whether plants that were tolerant of cool and dry or warm and wet weather were flourishing at one period or another.

Certain snails proliferate in wet climates, others in dry. By determining which type is found in a particular layer of earth associated with human remains, an archeologist can tell whether much or little rain fell on the people who lived there.

Most archeologists have theorized that from about 8000 B.C. to 4000 B.C. the weather in the Southwest was cool and dry. This notion has been challenged recently by an ingenious method of linking climate to the remains of the meat that people ate. Analysis of the faunal bones found in caves used by hunters in the Southwest indicate that many of these same animals now exist only in warmer, wetter environments to the north and east of the caves. Therefore, it is assumed, the Southwest in ancient times must have been a warmer and wetter than it is now, and so was more attractive to hunters than archeologists previously thought.

NINE MILE CANYON ROCK ART

Between Price and Myton on Utah 53. Open free, at all times.

Many rock-art panels are visible along the walls of this canyon. Occasional granaries and other structures, attributed to the Fremont culture, may also be seen.

PAROWAN GAP INDIAN DRAWINGS
(pair-oh-WAN)

From Cedar City drive north 18 miles on Interstate 15 to Parowan turnoff, then west on county road toward Utah 130. The site is next to the road. Open free, at all times. Camping nearby.

Drawings and designs seem to have been placed on the rock here by the Fremont people sometime between A.D. 900 and 1150. Administered by the Bureau of Land Management.

SAND ISLAND PETROGLYPHS

From Bluff drive 2 miles southwest on US 163 to directional marker. Open free, at all times. Camping.

A large panel of petroglyphs, protected by a wire fence, overlooks the San Juan River. The carvings of animals, human beings, and abstract designs probably date back to Anasazi times. One of the figures is that of Kokopelli, the humpbacked flute player, who appeared frequently in Southwestern rock art. His exact significance is not known. Some interpret him as a trader, possibly with a pack on his back. Others believe he was a fertility figure.

SEGO CANYON PETROGLYPHS
(See Thompson Wash Petroglyphs)

THOMPSON WASH PETROGLYPHS

From Thompson drive 3.4 miles north on a local road. The site is marked on Utah highway maps as "Sego Canyon Petroglyphs."

There are extensive panels of both carving and painting on the rocks in this area.

THREE KIVA PUEBLO

From Monticello drive south on US 163 about 4 miles to Montezuma Canyon Rd., then 3 miles into canyon to an interpretive sign. Four-wheel-drive vehicle recommended because of deep sand in places. For information inquire at Monticello office of the Bureau of Land Management.

This village, the ruins of which have been stabilized by the Bureau of Land Management, was occupied at least three different times from A.D. 900 to 1300. Close to the dwellings is an area which archeologists believe was a turkey pen.

Diorama showing what a prehistoric village, now in ruins, may have looked like when people lived in Zion National Park. National Park Service photo.

UNIVERSITY OF UTAH, UTAH MUSEUM OF NATURAL HISTORY

On the campus, Salt Lake City. Open daily. Admission charged.

Archeological exhibits in this museum include dioramas and materials from the important excavations at Hogup Cave and Danger Cave. For the story of Danger Cave, see introduction to Great Basin section.

UTAH MUSEUM OF NATURAL HISTORY
(See University of Utah)

WESTWATER RUIN
(Five Kiva House)

From Blanding drive 2 miles south on Utah 163. Follow directional signs on a paved road leading to a dead end immediately opposite the ruin which is on land owned by the Navajo Development Council.

This Anasazi ruin, the largest excavated rockshelter site in the area, consists of many masonry structures. The site was occupied in the Basketmaker III period and in later Pueblo II and Pueblo III periods. Tree-ring dates indicate that many of the masonry structures were built between A.D. 1243 and 1250. The people were farmers who relied heavily on corn, beans, and squash.

Although the site has been excavated and prepared for visitation, access to it crosses private land which is not always open. For information inquire at the Blanding office of the Bureau of Land Management.

ZION NATIONAL PARK

From Kanab (kah-NAB) drive 17 miles north on US 89, then 24 miles west on Utah 9 to Park Headquarters.

The deep canyons and towering cliffs of this area were known to ancient Basketmaker and Pueblo people. A number of sites have been excavated, but none have been prepared for the public. An archeological diorama in the Visitor Center museum depicts prehistoric settlements in the park.

The holes in this slab of rock were used by prehistoric California women as mortars for grinding seeds, particularly acorns, to prepare them for eating.

THE GREAT BASIN AND CALIFORNIA

The peaks of the Rocky Mountains were a familiar sight to many a band of Big-Game Hunters 11,000 years ago. As they tracked mammoth and bison along the western edges of the Great Plains, they may have felt that the mountain range set a definite limit to their world. And indeed it usually did. At a few places, however, the Rockies presented no barrier to the hunters who wandered on foot. South Pass in Wyoming, for example, offered a route that rose like a broad gentle ramp, up and over the Continental Divide. Hunters could follow game across it without any sense that they were leaving the meat-rich Plains far behind, heading toward places where life would have to be lived in new ways.

Slowly little groups of people filtered across the Divide and down into a land which scientists call the Great Basin, an enormous stretch of country lying between the Rockies and the Sierra Nevada. Today this is a desert region, broken by short chains of rugged mountains. From much of the desert land there is no outlet to the ocean. Any water that flows down from the mountains must remain landlocked in swamps or in lakes, only one of which—the Great Salt Lake in Utah—is now very large.

In the days of the Big-Game Hunters the landscape looked quite different. Each of several basins within the Great Basin was filled with a huge body of water. But even in those days much less rain fell there than on the Great Plains, and people found desert shrubs growing instead of prairie grass. The reason for this seeming contradiction of little rain and vast expanses of water is simple: the basin lakes had been formed by the meltwater from Ice-Age glaciers and mountain snowfall. Following the Ice Age there was a rainy period for a while, at least in the mountains, and the runoff fed the lakes: One of them, called by geologists Lake Bonneville, which once reached a depth of about 900 feet, was still 90 feet deep by the time a small band of people began to visit its shore, more than 10,000 years ago.

In this land of sparse vegetation, game was less abundant than on the Plains. Mammoth hunting did not offer a way of life. Nor did bison roam in large herds. As a result human invaders had to look for other sources of food, and they had to try out new materials for some of their equipment.

Only two kinds of material existed in relative abundance— stone and fibrous plants—and people made the most of them. To the hunter's kit of stone tools, such as knives, scrapers, and projectile points, they added, in the course of time, flat stone implements for grinding small seeds. From plant fiber they fashioned a variety of things that Big-Game Hunters had never found necessary. To hold the seeds that had become essential foods in the new environment they made deep carrying baskets. Other baskets served for parching the seeds. Thin fibers could also be twisted into cord for nets, with which they caught small animals or birds. Other plant material went into sandals and aprons. Some who lived near the lakes clearly fashioned reeds into the shapes of ducks, which they floated on the water as decoys.

Those who came to the shores of Lake Bonneville sometimes took shelter in a cave now known as Danger Cave (so called because one of the archeologists who excavated it was almost buried beneath rock falling from its roof). There and in nearby caves people left signs of the extraordinary ways in which they managed to use whatever their harsh world offered. From layer after layer of debris archeologists reconstructed a picture of people constantly on the move, but not aimless wanderers. They had learned to take advantage of every edible thing in its own season, and they traveled from place to place according to a well-worked-out plan. Danger Cave, apparently, was a late-summer stopping place, where they harvested the tiny pickleweed seeds. Tons of dried stems from the plants accumulated over the years, after the seeds had been beaten out on the cave floor.

A Desert Culture
In other areas in the Great Basin groups of people adapted to the desert world in generally similar ways, although they may have come originally from different backgrounds. Some may have entered the far northern end of the Basin, then migrated southward, bringing with them a set of tools and a lifeway that has been called Old Cordilleran. Others, possibly descendants of the mammoth hunters, drifted across low passes in the Southwest. Wherever they came from, they developed a Western Archaic lifeway, known as the Desert culture, throughout the very large area that includes

southwestern Wyoming, Utah, Nevada, and parts of California, Oregon, and Idaho.

After this desert way of life had taken shape, precarious though it was, it continued. The vast lakes, however, did not persist. As they dwindled, many groups of people moved on. Some of them migrated westward through passes into California, and in this new kind of country they found themselves forced to make adjustments in many different ways.

At this point there is disagreement among specialists on one important question. Did the migrants from the Great Basin find people already resident in California?

Did some of these earlier people have a way of life so simple that it revolved around the use of large, clumsy tools made by chipping flakes from big pebbles or cobbles? The evidence is not all in and not all clear. Readers who wish to examine some of it firsthand may visit the Calico Mountains Project, near Barstow, California.

When Europeans first reached California, they found many distinct groups of people, speaking a great number of different languages or dialects. This probably meant that time after time a band of Indians, each with its own language, moved into the area, found a niche for itself between the territories of other groups, and gradually took on some of the traits of its neighbors. (Some archeologists call this the "fish-trap" pattern of settlement, because the various bands seeking food entered California but never made their way out again.)

Prehistoric Indians shaped this gigantic figure, which is 105 feet long, and outlined it in gravel on the desert near Blythe, California. Photo by Michael J. Harner.

Migration for Food

All up and down the coast, and inland, too, people found life attractive, and many of them continued an ancient pattern of local, seasonal migration in search of food. Wherever they stayed they left evidence of their habits. At various places on the coast they gathered oysters and clams, and great heaps of discarded shells remained for the archeologist to use in reconstructing the past. Some groups came to depend almost entirely on the sea for their living. They fished with spears and hooks, and hunted sea lions and dolphins.

Elsewhere the early Californians gouged out pits in the rock to use as mortars for grinding seeds and nuts, and hundreds of these food-processing places are still visible. Like many other prehistoric Americans, these early Californians decorated rock surfaces and cave walls with paintings and peckings which are intriguing but not very well understood.

For all the variety in their languages and in the details of their lives, the California people remained gatherers of seeds and sea foods and hunters of small animals. In other words, their lifeway up until historic times remained at the stage we have called Western Archaic. Unlike the people of the Southwestern pueblos, they never became farmers with solid, permanent dwellings and all the habits that go with the raising of crops. Some Californians did live in good-sized villages, where they had a year-round supply of food from the sea, but many continued their seasonal migrations, moving from one harvest to another. So, too, did the people who remained in the Great Basin. Like their ancestors thousands of years before, they journeyed from place to place, harvesting first one kind of food and then another, as it ripened.

For a brief time some groups in one part of Utah and at the southernmost edge of Nevada did try farming. But by A.D. 1200 they had given up. Apparently subsistence agriculture was not worth the struggle in this land of little rain. Those who had tried it seem to have departed, leaving the inhospitable region to newcomers who found it easier to forage for food than to grow it.

Baskets and Steatite Vessels

Because most of the Indians of California and the Great Basin were not farmers, the evidences of their lives are not easily seen today. They made lightweight, perishable baskets for gathering and storing their food, instead of manufacturing pottery, which was both cumbersome and fragile. And so the landscape is not littered with potsherds as it is in the Southwest. In a few places people did carve bowls and vessels from a soft rock called steatite, and a California people who lived near Santa Barbara, called Canaliño by the Spaniards, made elegant, large steatite jars for storing water and for cooking. The latter were not placed over the fire. Instead they were filled with water, which women kept at the boiling point by dropping in hot stones. It is interesting to note that on the East Coast of the United States some people also used steatite vessels before they made pottery.

Dwellings, like basketry, were made for the most part from perishable material, and people who stopped in caves did not build stone houses there as they did in the Southwest. The result has been that many archeological sites have not tempted park officials to restore them for visitors. Fortunately there are excellent museums to supplement the growing number of reconstructions.

The Great Basin and California are particularly rich in a special kind of artifact that intrigues and puzzles archeologists. In many places prehistoric artists used rock surfaces as backgrounds for paintings, called pictographs, and/or carvings in the stone, called petroglyphs.

For the most part this rock art cannot be accurately dated by the usual methods. It is almost always exposed, not buried together with other material that can be dated. Specialists who study it can sometimes associate it with datable habitation sites or with symbols that appear in connection with certain cultures. Occasionally ingenious techniques can be used. For example, dates have been found for petroglyphs which were pecked in rock around the Salton Sea in California.

The level of water in the sea has risen and fallen at various times in the past, and each time that a rock surface has been under water it has received a deposit of calcium carbonate. Because of the carbon content of these deposits, they can be dated by the C-14 method. During one dry period, some petroglyphs were scratched in a layer of deposit on a Salton Sea rock. Then the sea rose, and the petroglyphs were covered by a new deposit. Now, by dating the layer just above and the layer just below these petroglyphs, scientists estimate that they were made about 9000 years ago.

Many petroglyphs and pictographs are more recent. Some of those in the West show horses and men with rifles. Obviously these could not have been made before people from Europe introduced horses and guns. One recent example of rock art even shows a truck.

There has been much speculation about the meaning of petroglyphs and pictographs. One theory is that a great deal of rock art may reflect the visions of shamans. The elaborate, multicolored Chumash Indian paintings near Santa Barbara, California, may have been done by shamans under the influence of datura, which causes colorful hallucinations. Possibly the Blythe, California, intaglios also had their origin in the mystical beliefs and visions of shamans.

Although many rock-art sites have been opened to the public, archeologists and park officials have ambivalent feelings about encouraging visits to them. Since most are unguarded and unprotected, they are vulnerable to the peculiar kind of vandal who delights in defacing them. Wherever possible barriers of some kind have been put up to discourage too close an approach, and visitors are urged to honor whatever means of protection has been installed.

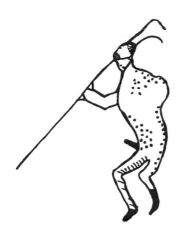

Kokopeli, also known as the Humpbacked Flute Player, frequently appears in rock art in the Southwest. The figure is sometimes regarded as a fertility symbol and sometimes is interpreted as a wandering trader carrying on his back a pack containing his goods. Redrawn from Renaud.

At the Calico Mountains Site, excavators dig in squares 5 feet on a side. As they proceed, they leave exposed what they call a witness column which shows the kind of material through which they have dug. Photo by Fred Budinger.

California

ANZA BORREGO STATE PARK PICTOGRAPH SITE

At State Park Headquarters, 2 miles northwest of Borrego Springs inquire for exact directions to site. Open free, at all times.

At the end of a well maintained mile-long trail a small group of symbols, painted in red, cover the vertical face of a large boulder. Although Indian remains are abundant in the park, only this site has been prepared for the public.

BIG AND LITTLE PETROGLYPH CANYONS

At the Naval Weapons Center, Main Gate, in China Lake, obtain road directions. The access road is 45 miles long, about half of it hard surfaced. Some parts of the area can be reached only by four-wheel-drive vehicles. Open free, 9 a.m. to nightfall, Saturday and Sunday, when range firing is not going on and when two vehicles, both sponsored by the Naval Weapons

Center, make the trip together.

Possibly the largest concentration of petroglyphs in the world may be seen here. More than 20,000 have been counted. Apparently the carving was done over a long period of time and by people from at least two different cultures.

Visitors must leave everything in the area undisturbed.

BLYTHE INTAGLIOS

From Blythe drive 17 miles north on US 95 to a roadside marker, "Giant Desert Figures," then west ½ mile on a dirt road to one fenced area; for a second area continue to the top of a rise and follow on foot a trail for ¼ mile south.

An intaglio is a figure or design carved below the surface of the surrounding material. At this site Native Americans created gigantic intaglios on the desert floor by scraping the gravel away to reveal the lighter soil beneath and piling the gravel so that it formed the outline for the figure or design. Some in the shape of a man measure as much as 175 feet

from head to toe. Others represent animals with long tails.

The age and significance of the intaglios are not known. Possibly they represent visions of shamans. Or they may illustrate a religious story similar to that of Yuman people, who believed that if they dreamed of a certain god which had two forms—one of a man, the other of a panther—they would be lucky in hunting. In the intaglios these two forms often appear together.

These rare forms of Native American art here and elsewhere in the desert have been vandalized by drivers of off-road vehicles, who have almost obliterated some of them with wheel cuts. To protect those remaining, members of the Sierra Club and other organizations have put up fences. More fencing is needed, and anyone interested in helping with the work should write to Desert Watch, Sierra Club, 2410 Beverly Blvd., Los Angeles, CA 90057.

Although it is possible to see the intaglios from the ground, a much better view can be had from the air. Addresses and phone numbers of char-

Archeologists call the objects at the left, hand axes; those in the center, cutting and scraping tools; those at the right, blades and blade cores. All come from deep in the Calico Mountains dig. Photo by Dan Griffin.

tered plane services can be found in the yellow pages of phone books in Lake Havasu City and Yuma, Arizona, and other nearby communities.

BOWERS MUSEUM

2002 N. Main St., Santa Ana. Open free, Tuesday through Saturday, afternoons Sunday; evenings Wednesday, Thursday. Closed certain holidays.

As this book went to press, the Indian Gallery of the Charles E. Bowers Memorial Museum was scheduled to reopen in 1982 with exhibits of Southern California Indian material (Chumash, Gabrielino, and Luiseño), along with Alaskan Eskimo artifacts. The two culture areas will be compared.

CALICO MOUNTAINS ARCHAEOLOGICAL PROJECT

From Barstow on Interstate 15 drive east to Mineola Overpass, then past a cafe and north on a local road to the Visitor Center near the excavation. Open free, Wednesday through Sunday with hourly guided tours.

Beginning in 1964 excavation here was under the supervision for several years of the late L. S. B. Leaky of Nairobi, Kenya, widely known for his discoveries of very early hominids in Africa. In immediate charge of the project are Ruth Dee Simpson, San Bernardino County Archaeologist, and Fred Budinger, Site Curator.

The site was discovered during an archeological survey of Manix Basin in which there had been a lake in the Ice Age. What appeared to be very old artifacts lay on the surface of the site above the basin. Were these objects made by human beings or by natural forces?

Some scientists have said they were made by nature and called them "geofacts." Other experts disagreed.

Excavation in a deposit at the site that is undisturbed has yielded large numbers of what Dr. Leaky and others insist are products of human craftsmanship. Dr. Clay R. Singer of California State College at Northridge has conducted intensive micro-analyses of these objects and reports the presence on them of use wear patterns. Uranium-thorium tests made in the facilities of the United States Geological Survey and the University of Southern California have indicated the astonishing age of 200,000 ± 20,000 years. The material tested was calcium carbonate which, it is claimed, had formed on the specimens *after* they were covered by a developing alluvial fan.

On the basis of these tests, archeologists connected with the site believe it is the oldest site in the Americas. Obviously the date of 200,000 years, which many archeologists regard with great skepticism, would have enormous implications for prehistory.

Dwarf Mammoths

On Santa Rosa Island off the California coast near Santa Barbara, excavators have found the remains of mammoths that apparently never attained a height of more than six feet. Elsewhere the crown of a mammoth's head was as much as 12 feet above the ground.

Some archeologists believe that men hunted the dwarf mammoths on Santa Rosa as far back as 29,000 years ago. Others think that the evidence for this is shaky and that fires attributed to men were really brush fires. Perhaps more excavation on the island will remove all doubt.

Santa Rosa is one of eight Channel Islands that lie between San Diego and Santa Barbara. It is privately owned and can be visited only by obtaining permission in advance from Vail & Vickers, 123 West Padre St., Santa Barbara, CA 93105; by phone (805) 682–7645. No archeological site has been prepared for visitation either on Santa Rosa or on any of the islands that make up Channel Islands National Park (see entry), but walking trails do pass some sites in the park.

CALIFORNIA STATE INDIAN MUSEUM

2618 K St., Sacramento. Open free, daily. Closed certain holidays.

This museum is devoted to the life of California Indians, past and recent, and includes many archeological exhibits. It has an excellent basket collection.

Special Feature. Indian legend puppet shows are presented every weekend.

CATALINA ISLAND MUSEUM

In the Casino Building at Avalon, on Santa Catalina Island. Can be reached by boat from Los Angeles harbor or by plane from Long Beach airport. Open free, afternoons and evenings, Easter through October; Saturday, Sunday, and holidays, November to Easter. For detailed information about transportation, phone (213)-510-2414.

In prehistoric times people who had mastered the use of boats lived on Santa Catalina and others of the eight Channel Islands, which lie off the coast of southern California. When Spaniards first arrived, those who occupied the northern islands were Chumash Indians, and groups who spoke a Shoshonean language lived on the southern islands. However, archeologists often refer to the culture of all the islands at that time as Canaliño.

Included in the Catalina Island Museum are materials covering a period of about 4000 years. Artifacts in the displays were excavated by archeologists from California universities and from the Museum of the American Indian, in New York. The exhibits have been arranged to answer these questions: What did people use for dress and decoration? What did they use to make a living? What did they use in religious ceremonies?

CHANNEL ISLANDS NATIONAL PARK

Park Headquarters, 1699 Anchors Way Dr., Ventura, can give up-to-date information about transportation to the islands. Commercial boat service is available from many southern California ports. Or visitors may use personally owned boats. Open free, daily, all year. No permit is needed for Anacapa and Santa Barbara islands, but a permit to land on San Miguel must be obtained from park headquarters in advance of any trip. Primitive camping on East Anacapa and Santa Barbara islands. Campers must register in advance at Park Headquarters.

Included in this National Park are Santa Barbara Island, San Miguel Island, and three small islands that make up Anacapa. Archeologists believe that at least 5000 years ago, prehistoric hunters lived here and on three privately owned islands outside the park. Remains of their habitation, and of Chumash Indian occupation

Painted Cave, San Marcos Pass, near Santa Barbara. A well-preserved example of prehistoric Indian rock art, probably painted by Chumash Indians. Santa Barbara Museum of Natural History photo.

before and after the Spanish conquest, have been found at about 600 sites throughout the park. Self-guided and ranger-led walks take visitors past some of the sites. The Visitor Center, at Park Headquarters, in Ventura, has a variety of artifacts on display.

CHAW'SE INDIAN GRINDING ROCK
(See Indian Grinding Rock State Historic Park)

CHUMASH PAINTED CAVE

From Santa Barbara, drive on San Marcos Pass Road (California 154) to junction with Painted Cave Rd., then 4 miles to marker. Open free, at all times.

In a rock outcropping 20 feet above the road is a grotto about 15 feet deep. Here prehistoric artists painted on the stone many brilliant, colorful figures and designs that have given the cave its name. The cave itself is not open to the public but may be viewed from outside the grilled gate.

CLEAR LAKE STATE PARK

From Lakeport on California 29 drive south on local road to Kelseyville, then northeast 4 miles on Soda Bay Rd. to park entrance. Open at all times. Admission charged. Camping.

A group of prehistoric Indians, who lived in much the same way as the Pomo Indians, once had a settlement on this lake. From the few traces they left, archeologists can reconstruct something of their customs and daily activities.

Here, as in much of North America, a sweathouse was important in prehistoric Indian life. In California it was usually a substantial, earth-covered structure, a little smaller than the dwellings people lived in. Men came to the sweat house, often at night, much as men of other cultures go to clubs. They took the baths together and often slept all night in the house. Apparently sweat baths were as much for pleasure as for reasons of health or because they had ceremonial significance. And men really sweated. They built a very hot fire, inside the house, and if the smoke got too thick

they lay down on the floor, where they could breathe fresh air. Often the houses were near streams or lakes or the ocean. After getting up a good sweat, the bathers plunged into the water. Then to dry themselves, some of them, in historic times at least, rolled in the sand.

Another structure that once existed at Clear Lake was a ceremonial house. It, like the sweathouse, was earth-covered, but it was a great deal larger. People met here for dances and religious activities. California Indians never developed a priesthood. They had shamans, or medicine men, and they had at least two religious cults that survived into historic times. One, in north central California, is called the Kuksu. Men who belonged to the cult impersonated mythological characters, and initiations were very important. Another cult, in southern California, called the Toloache, also placed great emphasis on initiation rites and on the use of jimsonweed, which has hallucinogenic properties.

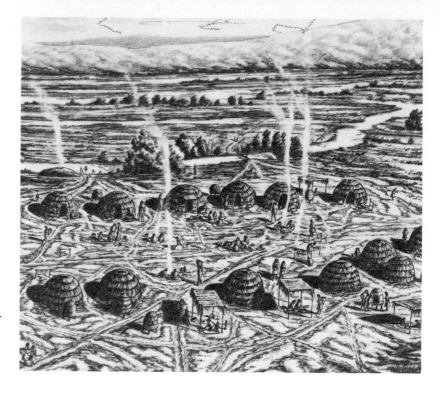

This is an artist's reconstruction of an Ohlone village, which once stood at the place now called Coyote Hills. Illustration by Michael Harney from *The Ohlone Way: Indian Life in the San Francisco–Monterey Bay Area,* by Malcolm Margolin. 1978.

No one knows what cult was connected with the ceremonial house at Clear Lake, but we can be sure that the religious beliefs and practices here did not differ greatly from those in neighboring areas. Although California Indians spoke many different languages, their ceremonial lives were patterned in similar ways.

A nature trail in the park, for which a folder has been prepared, identifies many plants in the area and tells how they were used by the Indians who lived here. Along the trail is the site of an Indian village. It is marked by a mortar hole and a grinding slab. When a woman wanted to grind acorns, she took a special basket that had a hole in the bottom and placed it in the mortar hole. Then she filled this receptacle with acorns, and used a stone pestle to crush them.

One of the plants identified along the nature trail is the California buckeye. This plant produces a fruit which is poisonous when eaten raw, but the Indians learned how to bake it and then soak it in a way that removed

the poison. Roasted buckeyes were mashed or whipped, much as we mash or whip potatoes.

COYOTE HILLS REGIONAL PARK

From Newark, near Fremont in Alameda County, drive north on Newark Blvd. Turn left onto Patterson Ranch Rd. into the park. Open daily. Parking fee charged on weekends. Tours are conducted on weekends except in the rainy season. Program hours are posted in the park.

Four shell mounds in this park indicate that Ohlone (Costanoan) Indians lived here from about 400 B.C. to perhaps A.D. 1800. Visitors may enter the site when accompanied by interpretive personnel of the East Bay Regional Park District.

One of the mounds has been made into an outdoor museum with an ongoing village reconstruction project and a display which makes clear the time periods of occupation. Here visitors have the experience of listening, in a small outdoor amphitheater, to a

program on the life of hunting-and-gathering people who once inhabited the spot.

At times volunteers take part in projects in the park. As this book went to press, volunteers had been asked to make a reconstruction of a two-person reed Ohlone boat.

CUYAMACA RANCHO STATE PARK
(KOO-yah-MAH-ka)

From San Diego drive east on US 80, then north on California 79 to museum. Open free, daily. Camping.

An Indian exhibit in the former Dyar residence in the park deals with the story of the Diegueño Indians of the area.

DEATH VALLEY NATIONAL MONUMENT

From Las Vegas, Nev., drive northwest 85 miles on US 95 to Lathrop Wells, then south 23 miles on Nevada 29 to Death Valley Junction, then west 30 miles on California 190 to

Examples of Indian rock art can be seen in many canyon areas in California. These drawings were cut into a soft tufa cliff at Emigrant Wash, in Death Valley National Monument. National Park Service photo.

DESERT PEOPLE

For the last 2,000 years the people of have been people of the desert.

An exhibit in the museum at the headquarters of Death Valley National Monument sketches the life of Indians who lived in this desert area for 2000 years. National Park Service photo.

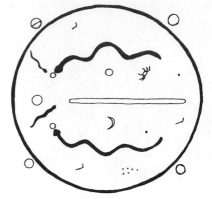

This design represents the world, the sun and moon, and snakes and animals with special powers. The Diegueño Indians used it in the puberty ceremony held for boys. After Waterman and Underhill.

Whale effigy carved from stone, California.

Visitor Center and museum at Furnace Creek. The museum is open free, daily. Camping.

Exhibits in the museum tell briefly the story of human habitation of Death Valley from 6000 or 7000 B.C. to the present.

Petroglyphs may be seen at many places in the monument, notably at Klare Spring, in Titus Canyon, and along the ridges of Greenwater Canyon, near the Mesquite Springs Campground, and in Emigrant Canyon.

HOSPITAL ROCK PICTOGRAPHS
(See Sequoia and Kings Canyon National Parks)

INDIAN GRINDING ROCK STATE HISTORIC PARK

From Jackson drive northeast 10 miles on California 88 to Pine Grove, then 1.3 miles northwest on Pine Grove–Volcano Rd. Open at all times except when closed by snow. Admission charged. Camping.

The Story. Miwok Indians once lived at this site, which they called Chaw-se (sha-tze). Here, on an outcrop of limestone 173 feet long and 82 feet wide, are 1,185 circular pits which have been worn in the rock. These pits are chaw-se—that is, stationary basins in which women used pestles to grind up seeds, particularly acorns, as one step in preparing them to be eaten.

On the same outcrop are 363 petroglyphs which have been pecked in the limestone.

The Indians who lived at Chaw-se no doubt had many of the customs of other Miwoks. They probably used money made of shell or of small polished and baked cylinders of a rock called magnesite. They built cone-shaped dwellings, some wholly above ground, others partly below ground. Often they dug large pits and then erected structures over them to serve as assembly places or dance houses. Men had special houses in which they took sweat baths.

Certainly the grinding of acorns was not all that went on at Chaw-se. For such large facilities there must also have been large storage arrangements. Wherever they lived the Miwoks seem to have erected granaries, which they built on posts, using a kind of basketry technique. Like other Indians of California, they had developed the art of basketmaking to a very high degree.

The baskets and other artifacts made by prehistoric Miwoks can be seen in various California museums. But nowhere is there a better example of the way these people turned bedrock into a tool essential to their livelihood.

There are several developed trails in the park, one leading to an exhibit that consists of reconstructions of eight bark dwelling houses, a ceremonial roundhouse, an acorn granary, a large shelter, and a hand-game house. Two display cases show where Miwok Indians lived in California and how they processed food.

Special Interest. On the Saturday and Sunday following the fourth Friday in September, Miwok people hold an Acorn Festival here, with traditional dancing and games.

INSCRIPTION CANYON

Northwest of Barstow, mostly on graded dirt roads. For detailed road directions consult Ms. Simpson or Mr.

Students from the University of Southern California excavating a site at Squaw Tank, in Joshua Tree National Monument. National Park Service photo.

Reynolds at San Bernardino County Museum in Redlands, California.

Beautiful and unusual petroglyphs carved on basalt cliffs may be seen in the canyon, also called Black Canyon, and at other spots along the road.

JOSHUA TREE NATIONAL MONUMENT

74485 National Monument Drive, Twentynine Palms. The monument is open free, at all times. The Visitor Center is open free, daily except Dec. 25. Camping.

The Story. The Visitor Center has cases of archeological material devoted to the Pinto Basin culture, which once dominated the region and which takes its name from Pinto Basin, in southeastern California. According to some specialists this culture may have begun as early as 6000 or even 7000 B.C. One archeologist, however, does not believe it began until about 3000 B.C. All agree that it lasted until at least 1000 B.C., and it is important because it marked for this region the beginning of the intensive use of crushed, hard-shelled seeds for food. Evidence of this new adjustment to the arid environ-

ment—or evidence of adjustment to a newly arid environment, whichever the case may be—is that milling stones and manos appeared here for the first time, just when the distinctive Pinto Basin projectile points first appeared. Earlier people in the region, who belonged to the Lake Mohave culture, seem not to have made use of tools for pulverizing seeds.

The Pinto Basin people shared the tendency to engage in intensive exploitation of resources which marked the Archaic lifeway in every part of the continent. How, within this widespread Archaic pattern, they made their special adjustment can be seen here at the Joshua Tree National Monument. Exhibits at the Visitor Center also include one devoted to more recent Indians, who lived in the area from approximately A.D. 1000 to historic times: the Serrano, the Chemèhuevi, and the Cahuilla people.

Within the monument visitors can see numerous examples of rock art in addition to archeological sites of other kinds. Rangers can give directions to some of the petroglyphs as well as other areas of archeological interest.

KERN COUNTY MUSEUM

3801 Chester Ave., Bakersfield. Open free, daily. Closed certain holidays. Admission charged.

Random local archeological finds are included here with more recent artifacts, which are representative of Yokuts and other cultures in southern San Joaquin Valley. A diorama shows Yokuts basketweaving techniques.

Children's class at the Marin Miwok Museum, which features hands-on exhibits. Photo by Joan Fray.

Prehistoric Indians pecked a great many animal figures and designs on the rocks in Little Petroglyph Canyon near China Lake, California. Maturango Museum photo.

KULE LOKLO

In Bear Valley, Point Reyes National Seashore, off California 1 at Olema. Open free, daily, all year. Hike-in camping nearby.

Kule Loklo is an authentic replica of a Coast Miwok Indian village. Such buildings as a ceremonial dance house, dwellings, and a sweathouse are based on archeological evidence and on the accounts of early European visitors to the area. The village is being constructed by volunteers, young and old, and visitors are invited to participate in activities. Guided tours are available for school groups. Students are encouraged to learn how to do such things as weave mats, construct bird traps, and make shell beads or ceremonial rattles.

For centuries before Europeans reached California, the peaceful Coast Miwok people lived along the shore, fishing, hunting, and gathering acorns and wild plants. In 1579 the English pirate Francis Drake landed somewhere near Point Reyes, but it was almost 200 years before Spanish colonists and missionaries arrived. They made the Miwok people leave their homes to work at the missions, and the coastal Indian villages were abandoned. Archeologists have studied some of these village sites, but none are open to the public. Instead, Kule Koklo has been built to give a more vivid picture of Miwok life than would be offered by an actual site.

LAVA BEDS NATIONAL MONUMENT, PETROGLYPH SECTION

The petroglyphs are nine miles south of Tule Lake, off California 139. Open free, daily. Camping in the main part of the monument.

The petroglyphs are carvings of abstract, animal and human figures, made at some unknown time in the past on boulders in a volcanic cone.

LOMPOC MUSEUM

200 S. H St., Lompoc. Open free, afternoons, Tuesday through Sunday. Closed certain holidays.

Exhibited here is material from 50 Chumash sites in northern Santa Bar- bara County. Among the displays are fine stone tools, sculptured steatite effigies, and Indian basketry collections. Material from southwestern, western and midwestern states, Alaska and Canada is also represented in the prehistoric artifact collections. Special exhibits change throughout the year. One gallery is devoted to the history of the Lompoc Valley.

LOWIE MUSEUM OF ANTHROPOLOGY
(See University of California)

MALKI MUSEUM

On the Morongo Indian Reservation, 11–795 Fields Rd., Banning.

The collections here include artifacts of the Cahuilla and other Southern California people.

MARIN MIWOK MUSEUM

2200 Novato Blvd., Novato. Open Tuesday through Saturday; afternoons, Sunday. Closed certain holidays. Admission by donation.

Rock art in Little Petroglyph Canyon. Maturango Mueum photo by R. T. Sandberg.

Rotating exhibits on the prehistory, culture, and art of Indians of the San Francisco Bay Area include stone, bone, and shell materials, basketry, textiles, and a native plant garden. The museum features hands-on exhibits involving visitor participation and a classroom program, "The Indian as Environmentalist," which may be booked in advance. Eighty-one Edward S. Curtis photogravures of Indians are also on display.

In Miwok Park, where the museum is located, is the site of a Coast Miwok village.

MATURANGO MUSEUM

For road directions inquire at the Naval Weapons Center, Main Gate, in China Lake, north of Ridgecrest. Open free, afternoons, daily. At other times by appointment.

In the Maturango Museum of Indian Wells Valley are exhibits of materials which span the period from Pinto Basin culture to recent Shoshonean culture in the Upper Mojave Desert. Displays include examples of Indian rock art from nearby Big and Little Petroglyph canyons.

MIWOK PARK
(See Marin Miwok Museum)

NATURAL HISTORY MUSEUM OF LOS ANGELES COUNTY

900 W. Exposition Blvd., Exposition Park, Los Angeles. Open free, Tuesday through Sunday. Closed certain holidays. Admission charged.

A large collection illustrates American Indian cultures of the West and Alaska. Archeological materials from 8000 B.C. to historic times can be seen. There is special emphasis on ancient California, its offshore Channel Islands, and the prehistoric Southwest. Dioramas depict Indian life of the Pueblo, Southwest California, the Northwest Coast, and Alaska. Some artifacts have been arranged to demonstrate the making of baskets, stone tools, and pottery.

OAKLAND MUSEUM, HISTORY DIVISION

On Oak St., between 10th and 12th streets, Oakland. Open free, Tuesday through Sunday. Closed certain holidays.

Archeological materials from several Bay area sites are part of a large exhibit devoted to the ethnography and cultural ecology of California Indians. One exhibit is a reconstruction of an Alameda County shell midden.

PALM SPRINGS DESERT MUSEUM

101 Museum Dr., Palm Springs. Open Tuesday through Saturday; afternoons, Sunday, Sept. 1 through May 31. Admission charged.

This museum displays some local archeological material.

POINT REYES NATIONAL SEASHORE
(See Kule Loklo)

POTWISHA CAMP PICTOGRAPHS
(See Sequoia and Kings Canyon National Parks)

Acorns

The prehistoric population was more dense in California than in many other parts of America north of Mexico. Some specialists believe that about 300,000 people were living in the present area of California when the Spanish began to settle there. Obviously these Indians had a food supply ample for maintaining such a population, and the most important single element in their diet was acorns.

Most varieties of oak tree produce acorns that contain tannic acid and are bitter tasting in their natural state. However, if acorns are soaked in water long enough, the tannic acid disappears, and the nut that is left is sweet and nourishing. Archeologists don't know when Indians discovered this source of food; they do know that the technique of preparing it spread along the West Coast wherever oak trees grew.

The process of leaching whole acorns was slow. It took months to get out all the tannic acid. Finally someone made an invention to speed up the work. Using mortar and pestle of the kind that crushed hard-shelled

---

RANDALL MUSEUM

199 Museum Way, San Francisco. Open free, Tuesday through Saturday; afternoons, Sunday.

The Josephine D. Randall Junior Museum is designed primarily as a teaching aid for school groups and includes a variety of specially selected material on loan from the Robert H. Lowie Museum of Anthropology, University of California, Berkeley.

One exhibit identifies prehistoric artifacts found in an Ohlone (Costanoan) shell mound and demonstrates the techniques used in excavating it. This model suggests how it is possible for archeologists to trace the development of Costanoan culture from the time when people began to live around San Francisco Bay in small, scattered clusters of dwellings made of poles covered with brush or mats. By studying the contents of the mounds, scientists have found that the Costanoans lived on or near these big heaps of oyster and clam shells only at certain seasons. This meant that people were elsewhere part of the time, gathering

food that was different from the kind they could get along the shore.

Many aspects of Costanoan culture could not be preserved in the mounds. Baskets, for example, rotted and left little or no trace. So did canoes or rafts made of reeds. We know, however, from accounts written by early Spanish missionaries, that the Costanoans made beautiful baskets and were clever at constructing watercraft from plants that grew in marshy places.

Beliefs, stories, myths, patterns of social organization are only dimly reflected in the artifacts that people discarded, but here again we can reconstruct some details from the accounts of Europeans. So the mounds, together with direct observation of historic people, give some depth to our picture of a lifeway that has vanished.

Special Interest. In cooperation with the San Francisco State College Department of Anthropology, the museum offers school children the experience of excavating an archeological site, finding artifacts, and recording data.

SAN BERNARDINO COUNTY MUSEUM

2024 Orange Tree Lane, Redlands. Open free, Tuesday through Saturday; afternoons, Sunday. Closed certain holidays.

Although this museum has displays covering the Northwest Coast and Southwest, its main concern is with the prehistoric and historic Indians of San Bernardino County. The Serrano, Cahuilla, Chemehuevi, Panamint, and Mohave Indians are represented, as are ancient prehistoric cultures including Basketmakers, Amargosa, Paleo-Indian, and Calico. The Calico Horizon, represented by materials from an excavation in the Calico Mountains near Yermo, Calif., is creating widespread discussion in archeological circles. If the age of Calico material proves to be as great as some archeologists think it may be—200,000 years—then this museum will contain the oldest dated artifacts in the Americas.

seeds to make them edible, a woman ground the soft acorns into a flour. When this acorn flour was soaked in hot water, the tannic acid disappeared very quickly.

To do the leaching, a woman often made a small hollow in the sand beside a stream. In the hollow she placed a lining of leaves and poured in acorn flour. Then she filled a water-tight basket with water and dropped hot stones in it. When the water was hot, she poured it over the acorn flour. Several dousings completely carried the acid away. What remained was a moist cake that could be eaten without delay or dried and saved for future use. Dried acorn flour, mixed with water, was served as a kind of thick soup, or mush.

Acorn flour was not only tasty but nourishing. It contained about 21 percent fat, 5 percent protein, and 62 percent carbohydrate. Its fat content was much greater than that of either maize or wheat; its protein and carbohydrate content somewhat less.

The holes in this slab of rock were used by prehistoric California women as mortars for grinding seeds, particularly acorns, to prepare them for eating.

SAN DIEGO MUSEUM OF MAN

Balboa Park, San Diego. Open daily. Admission charged, except on Wednesday.

This museum has rich resources of southern California and Southwestern material. The exhibits change frequently.

As you go through California museums or read about Indians, you may be puzzled by two names which look somewhat alike—San Dieguito and Diegueño. San Dieguito refers to a very early culture. Diegueño refers to a late culture, which extended into historic times.

The San Dieguito culture began perhaps 11,000 years ago in the southern part of the Great Basin. At that time the people apparently did not specialize in any one method of getting food. They hunted, did some fishing, and dug up edible roots. As the centuries passed, they became gatherers and grinders of small seeds. Later, about 7000 or 8000 years ago, when some of them moved to the coastal regions in southern California, they became adjusted to a diet of food

from the sea, which supplemented their vegetable foods. Apparently because our first knowledge of this culture comes from sites close to San Diego, archeologists gave it the name San Dieguito. However, some important San Dieguito sites are a great distance from San Diego. One, for example, is at the lowest level of Ventana Cave, in southern Arizona.

The Diegueño Indians, who have lived in the San Diego area for the last 1000 years, introduced pottery making and practiced cremation of their dead. During their ceremonials they made paintings on the ground, using fine powders for pigments. They used ground soapstone for white, iron oxide for red, charcoal for black, and dried seeds for other colors.

The museum displays a large collection of bows and arrows, including examples from North, Central, and South America.

SAN FRANCISCO STATE UNIVERSITY, TREGANZA ANTHROPOLOGY MUSEUM

1600 Holloway Ave., San Francisco. Open free, Monday through Friday.

American archeological materials in the Adán E. Treganza Anthropology Museum represent most of the cultural areas of the state, beginning with Early Horizon times and coming up to the historic period.

A diorama in the Santa Barbara Museum of Natural History shows prehistoric cave dwellers in Southern California. Santa Barbara Museum of Natural History photo.

SANTA BARBARA MUSEUM OF NATURAL HISTORY

2559 Puesta del Sol Rd., Santa Barbara. Open free, Monday through Saturday; afternoons, Sunday. Closed certain holidays.

Archeological exhibits here are devoted largely to the Chumash Indians of southern California. Displays include culture history, tracing the ancestors of these people back to the Canaliño (A.D. 1000–1769), Hunting People (2000 B.C.–A.D. 1000), Oak Grove people (5000–2000 B.C.), and even to the more distant Mammoth Hunters, reported to have lived on the Channel Islands (30,000–10,000 B.C.). Several displays show life on the eve of historic contact, focusing upon economy, food preparation, technology, arts in shell, stone, and wood, as well as basketry, music, games, rituals, social organization. Dioramas show scenes of Canaliño, Oak Grove, and Chumash life. A full-size Chumash plank canoe is on exhibit.

SEQUOIA AND KINGS CANYON NATIONAL PARKS

Good roads lead to these two contiguous National Parks from either Fresno or Visalia. Open daily, all year. Admission charged. Camping.

In Sequoia interesting pictographs can be seen at Hospital Rock and at Potwisha Camp. As with most rock art, the meaning and date of these paintings are not known.

At Hospital Rock, in addition to pictographs, there are curious small pits carved in the rock, which may have been made by shamans or medicine men. Prehistoric people also camped here and probably built small, thatched houses. Archeologists have excavated their refuse heap, which was about six feet deep, and have found artifacts suggesting that the site may have been occupied as early as A.D. 1000. One of the tools recovered was a grooved, stone arrow straightener, an invention of people who used cane for arrow shafts. The crooked joints in the cane had to be straightened so that arrows would fly true. To accomplish this the stone was heated and

the joint was placed in the groove. The heat made the joint relax, and it could then be pressed out straight.

SHERMAN MUSEUM

9010 Magnolia Ave., Riverside. From the Van Buren offramp of the Riverside Freeway, turn onto Magnolia Ave. Open weekday afternoons. Closed certain holidays. Voluntary contribution.

In this museum in the Sherman Indian High School, along with Indian material from the historic period, are prehistoric stone implements, potsherds from Arizona and southern California, and Hohokam, Salado, Mimbres, and Four Mile Polychrome bowls.

SIERRA MIWOK VILLAGE

In Yosemite National Park, near the Visitor Center, Yosemite Valley District. Open free, daily, all year. Admission to park charged. Camping.

This replica of a village interprets Sierra Miwok Indian culture. There is a Native American museum nearby.

Petroglyphs at Hospital Rock in Sequoia National Park. From *Indians of Sequoia and King's Canyon.* Courtesy National Park Service.

SOUTHWEST MUSEUM

234 Museum Dr., Highland Park, Los Angeles. Open free, afternoon, Tuesday through Sunday. Closed certain holidays and from mid-August to mid-September.

Extensive exhibits are devoted to the Indians of all the Americas, with rich archeological materials from all areas of the New World.

There are particularly good exhibits of artifacts from California and the Southwest. Dioramas show prehistoric Indian life and structures. Artifacts on display include Sandia, Clovis, and Folsom projectile points. Fine exhibits included Anasazi material and Hohokam and Mimbres pottery.

TOPOC MAZE

From Needles drive south on Interstate 40 to Park Moabi exit, then west ½ mile on a gravel road to its end. There turn left on a second gravel road; at a Y keep left, then left again 200 yards to a parking lot.

This curious huge artifact consists of parallel rows of gravel, which pre-

historic people scraped into heaps a few inches high, forming paths three to four feet apart. Some of the paths cross each other, although they do not form a real maze, and they originally covered about 18 acres, almost half of which has been vandalized.

The meaning of the lines can only be guessed. Some archeologists think they may have been made by people who shared the later Mojave Indian belief in the need for running along certain paths as part of a purification rite.

TREGANZA ANTHROPOLOGY MUSEUM
(See San Francisco State University)

TULARE COUNTY MUSEUM
(too-LAIR-ee)

27000 Mooney Blvd., Visalia. Open daily, June 1 through Labor Day; Thursday through Monday, Labor Day through May 31. Closed certain holidays. Admission charged.

Exhibits illuminate the life of the Yokuts Indians, particularly as it was about 1800, before it was much influ-

enced by European culture. A leaflet available at the museum gives a great deal of information about the activities, crafts, and skills of these inhabitants of the San Joaquin Valley.

UNIVERSITY OF CALIFORNIA, LOWIE MUSEUM OF ANTHROPOLOGY

College Ave. and Bancroft Way, Berkeley. Open Tuesday through Friday; afternoons, Saturday, Sunday. Closed certain holidays. Admission charged.

The Robert H. Lowie Museum has a vast collection of California and other American archeological material, parts of which are on display from time to time. There is no permanent display on North American prehistory.

YOSEMITE NATIONAL PARK
(See Sierra Miwok Village)

Baskets, Bags, and Pots

Two examples of basketry from the Mesa Verde area. *Above:* An intricately woven pillow. *Below:* A basket that contained charms used by a religious leader in performing healing ceremonies.

Almost everywhere Indians sooner or later found that they could take grasses or shredded bark or other plant fibers and fashion them into implements that enriched life or—in very poor areas—made survival possible. Weaving and plaiting, they made baby carriers, nets to catch game or fowl or fish, containers for food, and baskets so fine they could be used as canteens or as pots for cooking.

The art of basketmaking seems to be older than the art of shaping and baking clay to form durable pots. Baskets were light and easily carried from place to place. On the other hand, pottery was heavy, and it broke easily. So people tended to cling to basketmaking as long as they were on the move, looking for sustenance. When they had a food supply from farming, they could settle down—indeed, they had to settle down—and then they could economically use heavy pots.

The art of pottery making had reached the Southwest by A.D. 300. Curiously, in Florida, it appeared much earlier—about 2500 B.C.

In California and along the Northwest Coast, where food was relatively abundant without agriculture and where people lived together in large groups, they clung to basketry up to historic times. Apparently they felt satisfied with their old way of life and saw no great need for change. Pottery making did come into southern California in relatively recent times, when knowledge of the art spread from the Southwest and Mexico.

In the Great Basin basketry was the skill people used above all others. Strips of rabbit skin, woven basket fashion, formed their robes. Even their simple shelters were rather like big, crude baskets.

Baskets and baked clay pots were by no means the only kinds of container. In areas where steatite (soapstone) was available, some people carved vessels from this soft material. In other places they carved bowls of wood or shaped wood into boxes or used tough-skinned gourds as canteens for holding water. In the northern woodlands they often shaped tree bark into containers. Hunters on the Plains made pouches and bags and boxes from the stomachs and intestines and hides of buffalo. They even used hollow buffalo horns as containers for the live coals they carried from one campground to another.

Prehistoric Indians mined steatite for cooking vessels. Smithsonian Institution photo.

Vast numbers of petroglyphs (drawings pecked in rock) show the elusive bighorn sheep, greatly prized by ancient hunters but hard to get. The petroglyphs may have been connected with the belief that a hunter could win magical power over an animal by drawing its likeness. Those shown here were found in the Lake Mead National Recreation Area. National Park Service photo.

Nevada

GRIMES POINT ARCHAEOLOGICAL AREA

From Fallon drive 10 miles east on US 50 to roadside marker. Open free, daily, all year.

Grimes Point was first visited by Native Americans about 8000 years ago, when much of the now arid region was covered by ancient Lake Lahontan. Some of these early hunters and others who followed them left traces of camps—stone scrapers, bits of matting, scraps of bone. Many of them also spent time making petroglyphs in the boulders of the area. At one spot, which archeologists think may have been used 7000 years ago, numerous small pits have been carved in the rock, along with long grooves. At other places the rock engravings are abstract designs, or possibly markers for ancient game trails. No one is sure of their meaning or their exact age.

The boulders at Grimes Point are a deep, dark brown, but under the surface the color of the rock is much lighter. The dark color, called patina, or desert varnish, was caused by long-term chemical changes in the rock. Any scratch reveals the lighter surface beneath. In time scratches themselves acquire patina—the older they are, the darker. Thus students of rock art believe they can tell at least the relative ages of the engravings.

Visitors may see a good deal of rock art along the Grimes Point Petroglyph Trail, which was built by the Youth Conservation Corps and is administered by the Bureau of Land Management. An illustrated booklet is available, free, at the entrance to the site, and trail markers explain points of special interest.

HICKISON SUMMIT PETROGLYPHS

In Hickison Petroglyph Recreation Site. From Austin drive 24 miles east on US 50 to site entrance. Open free, daily, all year. Camping.

Here, at some time between 1000 B.C. and A.D. 1500, five different groups of Native Americans pecked designs and pictures of animals on the cliff at the south edge of the present picnic ground. Archeologists believe that hunters may have made the carvings to indicate that this was a migration route for deer and antelope. A game trap for ambushing the animals seems to have been located nearby.

LAKE MEAD NATIONAL RECREATION AREA

Good highways lead into the area from Kingman, Arizona; Needles, California; Las Vegas and Glendale, Nevada. Open free, all year, Camping.

People have lived in Nevada for at least 11,000 years, and the tools and weapons that indicate their presence at an early date have been found in many places in the Lake Mead National Recreation Area. The waters of Lake Mohave and Lake Mead have now covered nearly all the campsites or petroglyphs left by humans before the dawn of history.

Left and opposite:
Some of the petroglyphs in
Grapevine Wash, Lake Mead
National Recreation Area. National
Park Service photo.

The easiest place to see petroglyphs is in Grapevine Wash, on the Christmas Tree Pass Road, near Davis Dam, on Lake Mohave. Christmas Tree Pass can be reached from either Nevada 77, west of Bullhead City, Arizona, or from US 95 south of Searchlight, Nevada. It is not known when or by whom the petroglyphs in this area were made, but they may be very ancient.

Not far from the recreation area, near Las Vegas, archeologists have excavated Gypsum Cave. In it they found a fairly complete collection of the implements that Western Archaic people had developed in the desert area for use in gleaning an existence from so unpromising a terrain. Some of this material is in the Southwest Museum in Los Angeles.

The cave also yielded two quite unusual discoveries. One was a type of diamond-shaped projectile point that had not been seen before. The point seemed to be associated with the other novel feature—an unfamiliar kind of animal dung, apparently of great antiquity. Some very large

animal had inhabited the cave and had left droppings on the floor; this happened after one group of men had been there and before another group took up residence. But what animal?

M. R. Harrington, who was excavating the cave, suspected the animal was a giant ground sloth, a creature that lived in the Americas at about the same time as mammoths. To make sure, he sent off samples of the dried dung to experts in natural history museums, and they agreed: a sloth had lived in the cave.

Since there were dates for sloths from other places, and since human use of the cave seemed to be contemporaneous with the existence of the sloth, the time for human use of Gypsum Cave appeared to have been more than 10,500 years ago. Long after the dung was discovered in Gypsum Cave, a radiocarbon date was obtained for it, and the date suggests that it may have been at least 10,500 years old.

Not all specialists are now convinced that the Gypsum Cave discovery proves that people hunted—or even lived—at the same time as sloths. But the discovery of sloth dung there does call

attention to the importance of fossil fecal matter. Scientists are able to discover an amazing amount about the lifeways of prehistoric people by studying their droppings, which are called coprolites.

LEHMAN CAVES NATIONAL MONUMENT

From US 6–50 follow signs through Baker and on to the monument. Open free, daily, all year.

The entrance tunnel to one cave passes through a room in which prehistoric Indians once lived, but there is no exhibit of material at the monument.

LOST CITY MUSEUM OF ARCHEOLOGY

On Nevada 169 in Overton, near Lake Mead. Open free, daily, all year. Closed certain holidays.

This museum, operated by the Nevada State Museum, has extensive exhibits of materials, which begin with the artifacts made by Gypsum Cave people. There are also materials here

from ancient Basketmaker and Pueblo cultures. Of special interest are materials excavated in the Lost City area, along the nearby Muddy River. Several hundred sites, which have been dated between A.D. 500 and 1000, were once inhabited by people who built pueblo-like dwellings. Many of these sites were covered by water after the building of Boulder Dam (now named Hoover Dam).

The museum also contains materials from the culture of the Paiute people, who apparently entered the area about A.D. 1100 and who still live in southern Nevada.

NEVADA STATE HISTORICAL SOCIETY

1650 N. Virginia St., Reno, on the campus of the University of Nevada. Open free, daily, all year. Closed certain holidays.

In this museum are exhibits of artifacts from three important Nevada archeological sites.

Material from Lovelock Cave includes artifacts left there over a long period of time, beginning about 2500

Plants for the World

Indians in the Americas domesticated more than a hundred kinds of plant. Some of these have become major sources of nourishment throughout much of the world. They include corn (maize), potatoes, peanuts, beans in many varieties, squash, pumpkins, manioc (cassava), chili peppers, sunflowers, sweet potatoes, avocados, pineapples, tomatoes, and cacao. Coca has given the world cocaine, for better or for worse, and tobacco has spread from the tropics to the arctic to the benefit of no one. Much commercially grown cotton is derived from cotton domesticated by Native Americans.

All of these plants originated south of what is now the United States, but Indians north of Mexico adapted at least 58 imports to suit their needs. Another two dozen plants were independently cultivated either in the Southwest or in the East, among them pigweed, goosefoot, and marsh elder. Altogether, counting wild plants as well as cultivated plants, people north of Mexico used an astounding total of 1,112 different species. Many of these served as medicines, some for fiber or for smoking, and others as dyes, beverages, or seasonings.

Today, according to geographer William Denevan, three-fifths of the world's agricultural wealth comes from plants that Native Americans domesticated. They exceed in commercial value the cultigens of any of the other three places where agriculture was developed—Mesopotamia, Southeast Asia, and sub-Saharan Africa.

B.C. Archeologists who have studied baskets, clothing, and weapons from the cave believe that its early visitors were probably ancestors of the Paiute Indians who were living in Nevada when Europeans first arrived.

The oldest artifacts from Fishbone Cave, also called Winnemucca Lake Cave, seem to have been used by hunters and gatherers who entered this desert area about 11,000 years ago. Later people who used the cave as a storage place left fishing and hunting gear similar to that used near Lovelock Cave.

Pottery from Lost City, also called Pueblo Grande de Nevada, was made by farming people who built stone dwellings along the Muddy River, in southern Nevada, about A.D. 500. Their experiments with corn raising were apparently not successful on a long-term basis, and they abandoned the villages. Archeologists located several hundred sites in the area, many of which are now covered by water impounded by Hoover Dam. (The Lost City Museum, near the dam, also has on exhibit a good deal of material

left by these people when they moved away about a thousand years ago.)

Since neither Fishbone Cave, nor Lovelock Cave, nor the actual Lost City sites can be visited, the displays in both museums are of special importance.

NEVADA STATE MUSEUM

N. Carson St., Carson City. Open free, daily. Closed certain holidays.

This museum has exhibits of archeological materials from Nevada, California, the Southwest, and the Great Plains. In addition to a life-size display of a Paiute camp scene, there are dioramas of a Paiute fishing camp, of salt mining, of pine-nut harvesting, of a mud hen drive, and of an antelope hunt.

PETROGLYPH TRAIL

In Humboldt National Forest. From Baker drive west on Nevada 488 toward Lehman Caves National Monument. Just before crossing into the monument, turn south on Baker Creek road (graded dirt) and continue for

about 3 miles to a small parking lot on the left side of the road.

Interpretive signs take the visitor on a self-guided tour of rock carvings along the trail. The site has been developed and is supervised by the Forest Service.

RED ROCK CANYON RECREATION LANDS
(See Willow Springs)

ROCKY GAP SITE
(See Willow Springs)

UNIVERSITY OF NEVADA, LAS VEGAS, MUSEUM OF NATURAL HISTORY

4505 S. Maryland Parkway, Las Vegas, on the university campus. Open free, weekdays. Closed certain holidays.

Archeology exhibits here focus on the southern Nevada region. There are special exhibits of pre-Columbian pottery.

Lovelock Cave

In northwestern Nevada, Lovelock Cave once opened out on Lake Lahonton, an immense body of water that existed during and after the rainy period at the end of the Ice Age. About 4500 years ago, people began to visit this cave, and for a long time they used it as a place in which to store equipment. The implements they left there show how they exploited plant and animal life along the lakeshores. To attract ducks, for example, they used decoys fashioned from reeds that grew around the lake and sometimes made realistic with duck feathers woven along the sides. From reeds and a dozen other fibers, the cave's visitors made sandals, fishnets, mats, and baskets of various kinds. They used shredded fiber in clothing and wove blankets from animal fur and bird skins.

The concern these people felt for weaving and basketry appeared in another way. In the cave they left sickles made of bone and mountainsheep horn that helped them harvest the grasses they used as fibers.

Few sites in the Great Basin area have yielded more information about the early people who lived there. Lovelock Cave itself has not been prepared for visitation by the public. Fortunately, however, some of the materials excavated there are on exhibit in the Nevada State Historical Society Museum.

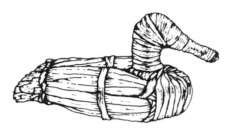

This duck decoy, made of reeds, was found in Lovelock Cave, Nevada. Some duck decoys were decorated with feathers. After Loud and Harrington.

VALLEY OF FIRE STATE PARK

From Las Vegas drive northeast on Interstate 15 to Valley of Fire exit, then on Nevada 40–169 to the park; total distance 55 miles. Or from Overton drive south on Nevada 12–169 to Nevada 40–169; total distance 15 miles. Visitor Center open, free, daily. Closed certain holidays. Camping.

The Story. Because of the very limited water supply, there was apparently never a large or continuous occupation of the Valley of Fire. However, archeologists have found evidence that Anasazi people visited the area occasionally from about 300 B.C. to A.D. 1150. At various times, which cannot be exactly determined, the Indians left a large number of petroglyphs in the valley. Some of the designs are geometric. Others portray hands, feet, mountain sheep, birds, snakes, lizards, and atlatls—the throwing devices used by hunters before the introduction of bows and arrows.

Petroglyph Canyon may be visited on a half-mile, self-guided trail, which has markers to explain the examples of prehistoric rock art.

In the Visitor Center is a small display of material of archeological interest. A much larger archeological exhibit representing the area is in the Lost City Museum at Overton.

WILLOW SPRINGS
(Rocky Gap Site)

From Interstate 15 in Las Vegas, turn west on Charleston Blvd. and drive 15 miles to Red Rock Canyon Recreation Lands directional markers. Open free, daily, all year. Camping.

As this book goes to press, a Visitor Center with interpretive exhibits is scheduled to open. Meantime an interpretive trail takes visitors to agave-roasting pits used by prehistoric people and to the pictographs and petroglyphs they left on rocks in the area. The site is jointly administered by the Nevada Division of Parks and the Bureau of Land Management.

Animal symbols of ancient origin
were often the figures which
Northwest Coast Indians carved on
totem poles.

NORTHWEST COAST

At 4 o'clock in the afternoon, on March 28, 1778, the first white American to visit the Northwest Coast had his first glimpse of the Indian Americans who lived there. He was John Ledyard, aboard the *Resolution,* one of two ships with which Captain Cook was exploring the Pacific.

Ledyard had a special interest in Indians. He had lived for several months among the Iroquois in the Northeast, after dropping out of Dartmouth College, which was primarily a college for Indians. Now he was keen to observe the Nootkas whose village he had reached at the end of a sea voyage more than halfway around the world from New England. In the journal which he kept with his own unique spelling, he had this to say:

"It was a matter of doubt with many of us whether we should find any inhabitants here, but we had scarcely entered the inlet before we saw that hardy, that Intriped, that glorious creature man approaching us from the shore. . . . In the evening we were visited by several canoes full of the natives. . . . The country around this sound is generally high and mountainous . . . intirely covered with woods. . . . We saw no plantations or any appearance that exhibited any knowledge of the cultivation of the earth, all seemed to remain in a state of nature. . . . We purchased while here about 1500 beaver, besides other skins, but took none but the best . . . Neither did we purchas a quarter part of the beaver and other furr skins we might have done. . . ."

Of the Nootka canoes he saw, Ledyard wrote: "They are about 20 feet in length, contracted at each end, and about 3 feet broad in the middle . . . made from large . . . trees. . . . I had no sooner beheld these Americans than I set them down for the same kind of people that inhabited the opposite side of the continent. They are rather above the middle stature, copper-coloured, and of an athletic make. They have long black hair, which they generally wear in a club on the top of the head, they fill it when dressed with oil, paint and the downe of birds. They also paint their faces with red, blue and white colours . . . Their clothing generally consists of skins, but they have two other sorts of garments, the one is made of the inner rind of some sort of bark twisted and united together like the woof of our coarse cloaths, the other . . . is . . . principally made with the hair of their dogs, which are mostly white, and of the domestic kind: Upon this garment is displayed very naturally the manner of their catching the whale—we saw nothing so well done by a savage in our travels. . . . We saw them make use of no coverings to their feet or legs, and it was seldom they covered their heads: When they did it was with a kind of basket covering made after the manner of the Chinese . . . hats."

Top left: A stone club from British Columbia, that may have been used in battle or ceremonies. *Top right:* Ancient Northwest Coast Indians were expert carvers in bone, wood, and stone. This figure, made of steatite (soapstone) represents a guardian spirit. *Below:* British Columbian Indians used this ceremonial mask, which represents a bear. Originals are in the Museum of the American Indian.

Cannibalism

Ledyard then went on to describe an event for which Europeans, for all their experience with killing in warfare, were not prepared: "[the Nootkas] are hospitable and the first boat that visited us . . . brought us what no doubt they thought the greatest possible regalia, and offered it to us to eat: This was a human arm roasted."

It is not clear what dark notion prompted the Nootkas to make this cannibalistic offering to strangers whose civilization would soon devour theirs. There is no doubt, however, that a form—or forms—of religious cannibalism existed on the Northwest Coast. Another coastal tribe, the Kwakiutl, had established a Cannibal Society. Members of this group in moments of religious frenzy took bites out of the arms of living people. They also ate the flesh of the dead, often of slaves killed for the purpose.

This cannibalism had nothing in common with the cannibalism practiced by some farming people who sacrificed things of great value—such as human life—in an effort to obtain good crops. Nor was the Kwakiutl custom like that of people who ate brave enemies, hoping thus to gain courage. Something different was involved. The Kwakiutls loathed the flesh they ate. Very often they spat it out, and the practice was regarded with revulsion by the community which also regarded it with awe. After eating flesh a man was isolated for a long time and then had to go through elaborate rituals before he could resume normal life.

It is difficult today to imagine what religious frenzy accompanied the Kwakiutl cannibal rite, or what prized result it was supposed to bring. But one thing is clear:. The Kwakiutls, and probably the Nootkas, did not consider human flesh a delicacy.

And they certainly did not consume it because they were hungry. No people in America ate so well as the Indians who lived on the Pacific coast from northern California to southern Alaska. These people had rich resources in shellfish and fish—salmon, halibut, cod, herring, candlefish. They could get quantities of meat from seals, sea otters, porpoises, and whales. They also had a wide choice of land animals and birds, and they could vary their diet with berries of several different kinds.

The Northwest Coast Indians were indeed wealthy by prehistoric standards. Besides ample food they had the beautiful skins of a number of animals to make into clothing. They could weave garments from the shredded bark of certain plentiful trees, and they fashioned rainproof hats of fibers from cedar tree roots.

As Ledyard noted, they wove garments from the long hair of dogs, which they kept especially to be shorn. Women in certain coastal areas made expeditions inland to collect the mountain-goat wool that clung to bushes when it was shed. This they combined with dog hair to make fine blankets. Alone among North American Indians they wove with wool, and alone on the Northwest Coast the women around Puget Sound and in adjacent British Columbia used true looms. Where they got the idea no one knows. The nearest looms in America were in the distant Southwest, and there cloth was made from cotton, not wool, until the Spanish brought sheep to this continent.

Boards for Building

Another resource, one as important as food and just as available on the Northwest Coast, was a special kind of wood of exactly the right kind for making boats and houses. In the forests that grew down almost to the water's edge stood tall cedar trees with unique properties: the grain of the wood was straight, and men using wedges could split it into flat, even planks. These thick cedar boards made possible the huge buildings that impressed the artist who accompanied Captain Cook and Ledyard. Each dwelling—it might be 40 by 30 feet with a high, gabled roof—was large enough to house several families, and in some villages the massive structures stood row on row along the beach. Those who lived farther north than the Nootka—the Haida and Tlingit people—built the grandest houses of all. A dozen families could live in one of them.

The social relations between these villagers were unlike those in most parts of prehistoric North America. The differences were largely due to the fact that their easy food supply allowed them time to accumulate a wealth of possessions. One custom based on their economy of abundance was known as the potlatch, or gift-giving ceremony. This is how it went. Suppose a chief's son was growing up and approaching the time when he was to be given a new name. Far in advance the chief would make preparations to celebrate the occasion by giving away property. When he had accumulated piles of blankets, furs, boxes of whale oil, containers

Indians made innumerable pictures and designs on rock surfaces, particularly in western North America. Archeologists differ about the meaning of this rock art, but agree that it is not a form of writing. These designs were pecked into a rock in southeastern Oregon. Photo by Donald Martin, courtesy of Campbell Grant.

filled with berries, and vast quantities of food, he sent out messengers in canoes to deliver invitations to people in other villages up and down the coast. At the appointed time the guests assembled, and the big plank house was taxed to capacity. Between great meals the chief ceremoniously gave away everything he had—and much that he had borrowed from relatives. The biggest gifts went to the most important guests, and everyone present remembered who got what.

Anthropologist Wayne Suttles says the potlatch was a way of "coping with abundance." If people in one village were short of supplies—because of bad luck in fishing or hunting, for example, or because too much rain spoiled salmon smoking—the giveaways evened things out.

"Gifts," Ruth Kirk and Richard Daugherty say in *Exploring Washington Archaeology,* "dealt with surplus in a way that brought honor far beyond that of selling or trading, yet in economic terms they amounted to a redistribution of food and goods. . . . Prestige lent momentum to the whole system." A man could assert his importance by gift giving. The more lavish his gifts the higher his status, and nothing in Northwest Coast life was more essential than status. Those who had received the gifts, of course, had to proclaim their own importance by holding potlatches to which the giver was invited. And so in the end a man was likely to get back what his potlatch had cost him. Among the Kwakiutl this way of asserting superiority had a special quirk. The potlatch was often used to embarrass and humiliate a rival by giving him more costly gifts than he could possibly give in return. A man could not refuse a gift, even though he might have to sell himself into slavery to make a reciprocal gift.

Totem Poles

In historic times the rich men among the Haida often held potlatches to commemorate the raising of totem poles. A totem was an animal which was associated in some way with a man's family. Or it might be a monster or a supernatural being. Figures of these creatures were carved on masks or worn as crests on helmets. An important family might be entitled to a number of different crests. In prehistoric times people may have made small carvings to represent their totems, and later—in the eighteenth century—when they got steel tools, they began to carve the figures, one above the other, on huge wooden poles.

A totem pole could be rather like a coat of arms—advertising the ancestry of the man who raised it beside his house. Other totem poles were memorials to people who had died. Still another type, the ridicule or shame pole, might be set up to shame an important person who had failed to carry out some obligation, with a portrait of him carved upside down.

The property-conscious Northwest Coast Indians were aggressive and competitive in many ways. They were also creative. They had many ingenious implements for fishing, for hunting, for storing food, for killing whales, for keeping off rain, and their art was highly developed and unique in style.

Establishing the date at which their elaborate culture began is a problem which archeologists are not sure they have solved. Certainly it took time to develop, and certainly it was based on earlier lifeways. Much of American prehistory apparently began in Alaska during the latter part of the Ice Age, when Siberia was joined to North America by the Bering Land Bridge, a thousand miles wide. Some of those who wandered across the bridge continued eastward, following game.

It is possible that one or more of these small groups may have moved southward following the food-rich coast of the Pacific Ocean. This could have happened if some of the wanderers were skilled at using seaworthy canoes or if there were times when the great continental glacier met two seemingly contradictory conditions. The glacier had to be big enough, withholding enough water from the sea, to lower the ocean level and make the shoreline very different from the cliff-walled coast we know today. The coastline had to be one along which it was possible to walk. This required a second condition. The behavior of the glacier had to be such that extensions of it did not at all times block foot travel by flowing right down into the ocean, as happens in places today. Understandably no evidence has been found that people used this Pacific Coast route. If such evidence exists it lies covered by so much water that it is not likely to be retrieved until another great ice age again lowers the sea level.

However, people were not trapped in Alaska. Along the shore of the Arctic Ocean some groups found an easy travel route, and when they reached the mouth of the Mackenzie River, good hunting led them south. After traveling the whole length of the river valley, they crossed where there was no natural barrier, from the headwaters of the Mackenzie into Alberta. There the open Plains spread out endlessly to the south.

Archeologists have found sites where these hunters camped and dropped their tools. One, known as Kogruk, is on the slope of the Brooks Mountains near the Arctic coast, in Alaska. Another, called Engigsciak, is at the mouth of the Firth River, in the Yukon. At the latter site, excavation indicates that hunters who followed the British Mountain lifeway perhaps 18,000 years ago, when the local climate was warmer, killed bison of a kind that has long been extinct. Neither of these sites is open to the public. Indeed, visitors to Alaska and northwest Canada will find little evidence of prehistory on display. For one thing, travel is difficult in much of the area. For another, archeologists have only begun to examine this vast but little-inhabited portion of the continent.

Other southward-moving groups sifted into the high plateau region between the Continental Divide on the east and the coastal ranges on the west. In this Interior Plateau region those who began to live along rivers found an abundance of fish. As early as 11,000 years ago fishermen left tools at Five Mile Rapids on the Columbia River. Not far away, at a place called The Dalles, people also camped and caught salmon that ran in the river for nine months of the year. Farther up one of the river's tributaries, at the Marmes Site, archeologists have found the bones of people who arrived between 10,000 and 13,000 years ago. In Idaho radiocarbon dates show that stone and bone tools were left at Wilson Butte Cave at least 14,500 years ago.

Very early, in other words, human beings found a way of living in the Interior Plateau by exploiting the food resources of the rivers that cut through it. They also gathered camas bulbs in spring and summer and ate them raw or cooked. Roots and tubers of other plants were another source of nourishment. Women ground some of them into a kind of flour, which they made into cakes and stored. They also harvested berries, sunflower seeds, and wild carrots.

As far as archeologists can now tell, these Riverine Plateau people eventually moved down the rivers to the coast. There they met other people who came more directly from the north. These two groups stimulated each other and became the ancestors of the Northwest Coast Indians. Once they reached the food-rich ocean they developed new tools, new food-gathering techniques, and social customs that were unique in all America. Their unusual lifeway spread throughout the long, narrow coastal region between northern California and southern Alaska.

Because steep mountains and thick woods came down to the edge of the water in the fjords which cut deeply into the land, travel had to be almost entirely by water. People paddled great distances in canoes, and in time they met others to the north who had their own ways of managing life along the shore. From these northern people, who were Aleuts and Eskimos, the Northwest Coast tribes learned many things. The Aleuts and Eskimos, for their part, had ideas which had probably come from people who lived in the Amur River region of Siberia. Thus some of the ideas borrowed by the Northwest Coast Indians came indirectly from Asia. In addition, it is possible that some Asian traits reached them directly. Fishermen, possibly from Japan, may have been blown off course and drifted to America on the Japan current, which also brought the warmth and rain that distinguish the climate of the Northwest Coast from the cold and snowy inland climate in the same latitudes.

By combining the ways of living that they had developed along the rivers on the Interior Plateau with ideas that came from Asia, the Northwest Coast people produced a unique culture. Ideas even came from coastal dwellers in California, but there is no hint of Mexican influence. This absence of Mexican traits is one thing that sets the Northwestern lifeway apart from much of the rest of prehistoric Indian life in North America.

The stimuli coming from Alaska reflected an adjustment to coastal living that may have begun when the Bering Land Bridge still joined Siberia and Alaska. The coast of the Land Bridge curved around the North Pacific, with one end at a mountain which now appears on the map as Umnak Island, in the Aleutians. At the other end lay the Japanese island of Hokkaido. Along the intervening shore people spread out, exploiting bird and fish and sea-mammal resources. Before the end of the Ice Age, some of these wanderers from Asia had reached the vicinity of the Umnak Island mountain. Then the ocean rose, swollen by water from melting glaciers, and forced people onto higher ground. Some of them took refuge on the mountain, which the sea eventually surrounded and cut off from adjacent land.

Among the descendants of these settlers on Umnak Island two separate traditions developed, beginning perhaps 4,500 years ago. Some of them, seeking new places to live, spread out along the other Aleutian islands, where the ocean remained open all year. There they developed a dialect, then a distinct language, Aleut. Other groups moved north from Umnak. Their language, too, changed, becoming Inuit, or Eskimo.

Most of the Eskimo people lived on the edge of water which was covered over with ice for much of each year. Intense cold required them to make adjustments quite unlike those of their relatives on the Aleutian Islands.

This drift of Umnak people in two different directions, and along two different types of shore, resulted in two separate cultures—the Aleut and the Eskimo. Both of them were distinct from any Indian cultures, and both the Aleuts and Eskimos were physically different from Indians. They were more Mongoloid in appearance

This mask, carved of wood, with abalone-shell eyes, was worn by a shaman on the Northwest Coast.

than any Indians, and they differed in blood type. No Indian has blood type B, but this type is not uncommon among Eskimo-Aleuts, and it is present in modern Mongoloid people in Asia. Differences in their teeth also distinguished the Aleut-Eskimos from neighboring Indians.

Physical anthropologists believe that the Mongoloid race appeared relatively recently and was still evolving when the earliest ancestors of the Indians entered North America. Mongoloids then continued to evolve in Asia and reached their characteristic present-day form less than 15,000 years ago. It was apparently from this modern Asian base that the ancestors of the Eskimos and Aleuts split off when they migrated to North America.

New Skills and Inventions

Later, when the Umnak people split and some of them took up residence on the Aleutians, they developed certain special skills. They made elegant baskets from the fine grasses that grew on the windswept islands. Since sea mammals were less abundant than they had been on Umnak Island, the Aleuts made increased use of fish and birds. Although Aleuts were largely dependent on driftwood for any wood they had, they developed a unique custom of carving wooden hats, and they were skilled carvers of masks for their ceremonies, some of which were very much like those of the Northwest Coast Indians farther south. Apparently the Aleuts borrowed ideas from their southern neighbors, who in turn borrowed from them.

The Umnak people who moved to the mainland—the Eskimos' ancestors—learned to protect themselves from the cold in a variety of ingenious ways. They invented clothes capable of retaining body heat, thus creating a microclimate in which they could survive. They developed sleds, and some Eskimos trained dogs to pull them. They learned how to harpoon seals in every season—in spring as the animals basked on shore, in summer on the open ocean, where hunters pursued them in light skin boats called kayaks. In winter they searched out the holes in the ice where seals came to breathe and drove their harpoons down from above. Many Eskimos also hunted caribou.

Wherever they were, at any time of year, Eskimos were able to build dwellings. In summer they used tents made of poles, possibly collected as driftwood, over which they stretched a cover made of skin. Some developed the dome-shaped winter igloos made of snow. Others made semisubterranean winter houses roofed with driftwood covered with earth or sod. For light and heat they had lamps—shallow stone dishes filled with seal oil, in which a burning wick floated.

To judge from the discoveries archeologists have already made, a surprising amount of material left by Aleuts and Eskimos and their ancestors still lies in the earth waiting to be excavated. But there are great areas of Alaska and Canada that have not yet been studied, and for the most part visitors to this area of few roads

A prehistoric Eskimo woman's knife,
called an ulu, from Cape
Krusenstern in Alaska. National
Park Service photo by Robert
Belous.

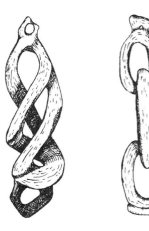

Left to right: An unusual stone bowl
with a human effigy carved into the
bottom, in which Eskimos burned
oil for heat and light. For protection
against the glare of sun on snow,
prehistoric Eskimos carved these
goggles from antler horn. Redrawn
from Giddings. Two carvings of
ivory from a burial at Ipiutak Site,
Point Hope, Alaska. Redrawn from
Larsen and Rainey.

will not be able to see archeological sites. There are, however, some excellent museum exhibits. The University of Alaska Museum displays artifacts from three particularly important sites—St. Lawrence Island, Ipiutak, and Cape Denbigh. At the Haffenreffer Museum in Rhode Island, there are fine displays of material which gives insight into Arctic prehistory.

Included in this prehistory are Indians as well as Aleuts and Eskimos and their predecessors. In southwest Yukon, people who hunted in the subarctic forest made distinctive tools from tiny blades of flint, which they struck from larger chunks. No one knows with certainty who they were, but some archeologists suspect they may have been the ancestors of the Athapascan Indians who still live in the area. The Athapascans seem to have arrived long after the ancestors of the Paleo-Indians.

One other type of culture existed in part of the area included here with the Northwest Coast and Interior Plateau—that is, in southeastern Oregon and southern Idaho. This region is geologically part of the Great Basin, and the prehistoric Indians who lived there developed lifeways similar to those of Desert culture people to the south. Indians who lived along the rivers of the Interior Plateau seem to have borrowed some traits from their Great Basin neighbors, but since they are described elsewhere in this book, there is no need to dwell on them here.

Native people who live in the Far North today call themselves Inuit, a name they prefer to Eskimo, which is a word from an American Indian language meaning "those who eat raw flesh." As long ago as 2500 B.C. Inuit hunters began making their camps close to the edge of the permanent ice cap in northern Canada. Because of the distinctive, tiny, sharp stone blades they used, their culture has become known as the Arctic Small Tool Tradition. Within the tradition, which lasted for nearly 3500 years, some archeologists like to distinguish two stages. The later one, which began about 600 B.C. is called the Dorset; the other, simply pre-Dorset.

Around A.D. 1000 this ancient culture suddenly disappeared, and another, known as the Thule, took its place. Whether new bands of people from the region around the Bering Sea conquered the earlier hunters, or whether the two cultures simply merged is still to be puzzled out.

Dorset sites on a Canadian island north of Greenland have yielded evidence that in summer the hunters lived in great long-houses (about 16 by 148 feet) roofed with skins anchored to stone foundations. Outside the communal dwelling, which may have housed 100 people, stood a row of cooking hearths.

Food was apparently abundant and the people "had eaten well, judging by our excavations," says Dr. Peter Schledermann of the University of Calgary, who has located more than 150 Inuit sites. "We unearthed an assortment of bones of birds and animals, geese, ducks, foxes, arctic hares, seals, walruses, belugas, and even nar-whales." It was the bones, in fact, that led archeologists to the campsites. Even after several thousand years, the bones still nourished patches of lichens and mosses, marking the spots where leftovers from Dorset Inuit meals lay buried.

Archeologists believe the Dorset people may have spent the winters in snow houses out on the ice, where they hunted seals. Their successors, the Thule Inuit, had year-round settlements. Living in tents in summer, they built winter huts partially underground and dome-roofed with whale ribs covered with sod.

Excavation of Thule houses has yielded well-preserved bone, wood, and ivory tools—needle cases, ornaments, harpoon points. And surprisingly some Norse artifacts have also turned up. Iron boat rivets, some links from chain mail, pieces of an oak box (oak does not grow anywhere near the area), and a piece of woollen cloth all indicate that the Inuit had contact with Vikings, perhaps as early as the eleventh century. Did Norse artifacts reach the islands north of Greenland by gradual trade? Or did Viking sailors actually land there? Archeologists think either one or both may have happened.

Still to be fully understood also are small, sharp, iron knife blades discovered at ancient sites in north-central Canada. Fashioned from meteoritic iron and hafted to bone handles, the blades seem to have been used for carving and engraving bone. Some iron meteorites are found in Canada, but whether the Inuit who used the small tools got their material on the spot or by trade is a question.

Alaska

ALASKA STATE MUSEUM

Juneau. Open free, Monday through Friday; afternoons, Saturday, Sunday. Closed certain holidays.

Grouped exhibits of major Alaska Native cultures—Eskimo, Aleut, Athapaskan, and Northwest Coast (Tlingit, Haida, and Tshimsian) display a fine collection of native artifacts.

ANCHORAGE HISTORICAL AND FINE ARTS MUSEUM

121 W. 7th Ave., Anchorage. Open free, Monday through Saturday, Memorial Day to Labor Day; Tuesday through Saturday, Labor Day to Memorial Day; Sunday all year.

In addition to historical and contemporary materials, archeological exhibits feature the art and culture of Eskimo, Aleut, and Indian peoples.

DINJII ZHUU ENJIT MUSEUM

In Fort Yukon. Open afternoons, Monday through Friday, in summer; by appointment in winter. Admission charged.

This museum has exhibits of the artifacts of prehistoric Athapascan Indians, who are related to the Navajo and Apache people of the Southwest.

KATMAI NATIONAL MONUMENT (KAT-my)

From the King Salmon Airport on Bristol Bay, scheduled commercial flights go to Brooks River Lodge in the monument. Open free, from about June to Sept. 15. Camping.

National Park Service rangers conduct trips from Brooks River along a nature trail to a reconstructed Eskimo dwelling. This large house was in use about 1,000 years ago. The site has been excavated and roofed over. Some artifacts found in the excavation have been left in place and are open to view.

PRATT MUSEUM

In Homer. Open Monday through Saturday; afternoons, Sunday, in summer; Tuesday through Saturday, in winter. Closed December and January. Admission charged.

In addition to a few archeological exhibits, this museum has some totem poles.

SITKA NATIONAL HISTORICAL PARK

Visitor Center, Metlakahtla and Lincoln streets, Sitka. Open free, Wednesday through Monday.

Though not strictly devoted to a prehistoric site, this park preserves 14 Alaskan totem poles which were part of the Alaska exhibit at the St. Louis Exposition in 1904.

Tlingit Indians occupied the area around Sitka when whites—Russian fur traders—first arrived. Like other coastal people the Tlingits were great craftsmen. Woodcarvers even made into works of art the clubs that they used for killing the seals they harpooned. After they got steel tools from

Left and opposite:
Archeologists digging in Katmai National Monument, Alaska, look up from their work to watch an arctic fox, which has come to see what is going on. National Park Service photo.

Alaskans built this pithouse in Katmai National Monument about A.D. 120. A shelter now protects it, and visitors can see artifacts in the excavation just where they were found. National Park Service photo.

A hat shaped like an eagle's head, used by Tlingit Indians in ceremonies.

An Eskimo hunting through the ice.

traders, they turned their skills to carving the huge totem poles. Artifacts on display in the museum were chosen to illustrate major aspects of Tlingit culture—migration, settlement, subsistence, art, ceremony, and societal relationships.

UNIVERSITY OF ALASKA, UNIVERSITY MUSEUM

On the campus, four miles from Fairbanks. Open free, daily, mid-May to mid-Sept.; afternoons, mid-Sept. to mid-May.

With materials gathered in the course of an active archeological research program, this museum interprets pre-Eskimo and Eskimo lifeways. Artifacts and environmental exhibits show the adjustment people have made to life on the tundra.

The artifacts on display come from many of the most important digs in Alaska, including St. Lawrence Island, a large, treeless island in the Bering Sea southwest of Nome, only 40 miles from Siberia. Eskimos who live there are much like the Siberian Eskimos, and, until recently at least, intermarried with them.

In 1878 Russian traders obtained furs from the 1500 people on St. Lawrence, giving alcohol in exchange. Three years later the naturalist John Muir and an ethnographer visited the island and found the Eskimo dwellings filled with skeletons. Most of the people on St. Lawrence had died in the winter of 1878–79, either of starvation or of an epidemic which accompanied it. Alcohol, brought by the traders, had caused the disaster. The Eskimo men had been drunk during the hunting season when they normally obtained their winter food supply.

None of the traders who visited the island, nor Muir himself, realized that St. Lawrence harbored a rich record of human life, stretching back for at least 2000 years. More recently archeologists have excavated mounds on the island and studied a series of beaches that have been exposed on the Northeast Cape. People have lived on each of these beaches in turn and left the remains of their dwellings, the oldest being farthest from the present seashore. Driftwood used for beams in the dwellings apparently had floated

down the Yukon River, and the wood made it possible to date some of the houses by the tree-ring method. Thus a picture of cultural change could be constructed in a spot which is remote from present-day life but close to the route from Asia followed by some of those who peopled America many thousands of years ago. The archeological sites at Gambell, on the Northwest Cape of St. Lawrence have been made a National Historic Landmark.

Excavated sites on the tiny Punuk Islands near St. Lawrence have yielded artifacts, many carved from ivory, which are on exhibit at the University Museum.

Artifacts from Point Hope Peninsula may also be seen. They come from the Ipiutak Site where the earliest Eskimos lived, and many objects are similar to those found in Siberia. The site itself is large, covering 200 acres and including a cemetery and more than 600 houses, not all of which were lived in at the same time.

Another important area represented in the museum is Cape Denbigh, on Norton Sound. Here archeologists found evidence of a lifeway that flour-

In Sitka National Historical Park, Alaska, are preserved several large totem poles, of which these are two. Totem poles of this size were not made until Indians obtained steel tools. In other words, they are not actually prehistoric. However, the carving tradition and the great interest in the animal symbols are of ancient origin. National Park Service photo by Harry G. Schmidt, Supt.

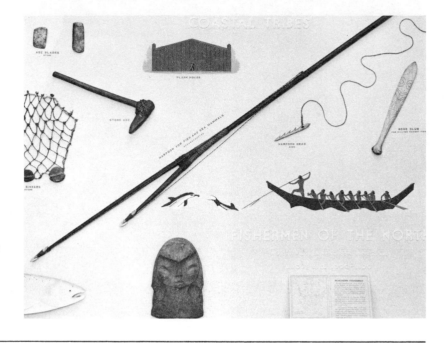

Prehistoric fishers of the Northwest Coast made tools and weapons like those shown in this exhibit in the Field Museum of Natural History, Chicago. Field Museum of Natural History photo.

ished about 2000 B.C. and included the use of very small, very delicate flint blades. The makers of these tools lived in the same area where the Eskimos appeared much later. The Iyatayet Site, where Denbigh artifacts were first found, is a National Historic Landmark.

British Columbia

BRITISH COLUMBIA PROVINCIAL MUSEUM

601 Belleville St., Victoria. Open free, daily. Closed certain holidays.

Displays in the Native Peoples Gallery show both the archeological story of the native peoples and the artifacts of their daily life. There is a completely reconstructed Indian house within this large exhibit.

Special Interest. The museum supervises Thunderbird Park in Victoria, where there are reproductions of totem poles from various parts of British Columbia and a full-scale Kwakiutl Indian house that is sometimes used for Indian ceremonies. Visitors to the park

may watch several Kwakiutl woodcarvers at work on totem poles, masks, and other objects, some of which are for sale in the museum gift shop.

CAMPBELL RIVER MUSEUM

Centennial Bldg., Tyee Plaza, Campbell River. The town of Campbell River is 100 miles north of Nanaimo on British Columbia 19, on the east coast of Vancouver Island. Open, Tuesday through Saturday, May 15 to Sept. 15; afternoons, Tuesday through Saturday, Sept. 16 through May 14. Closed certain holidays. Admission by donation.

Exhibits feature Kwakiutl, Coast Salish, and Westcoast (Nootkan) ethnographic materials, including basketry, masks, totem poles, tools, and trade goods.

CENTENNIAL MUSEUM OF VANCOUVER

1100 Chestnut St., Vancouver. Open daily, all year. Admission charged.

In the archeology section of this museum are random local finds and

excavated materials representative of the lifeways in Fraser Canyon from 11,000 B.C. to 400 B.C. and of lifeways in the Fraser Delta from 1000 B.C. to A.D. 1808. One display shows how adze blades were manufactured from nephrite, sometimes called jade. Many artifacts are grouped by their function—for example, woodworking tools in one display, bone-shaping tools in another. Some exhibits show how artifacts were made.

KAMLOOPS MUSEUM ASSOCIATION

207 Seymour St., Kamloops. Open free, Monday through Saturday, summer; afternoons, Monday through Saturday, winter.

Here are displayed Interior Salish baskets, of both birch bark and the intricately patterned style made from cedar and other roots. Other exhibits include a dugout canoe of cottonwood, a wide range of tools and weapons of stone and bone, and a few items from burials in banks, exposed during roadway or building construction.

Petroglyphs depicting marine creatures, Sproat Lake, Vancouver Island, British Columbia. National Museum of Canada photo. Courtesy of Campbell Grant.

This 64-foot, ocean-going canoe, carved by Haida Indians from a single log, is now at the American Museum of Natural History, in New York.

This engraving from the report of Captain Cook's third voyage, in 1778, shows a communal dwelling of the kind that Indians had long used on Nootka Sound in British Columbia.

KELOWNA MUSEUM AND NATIONAL EXHIBIT CENTRE

470 Queensway Ave., Kelowna. Open free, Monday through Saturday; afternoons, Sunday, July 1 through Aug. 31; Tuesday through Saturday, Sept. 1 through June 30.

Archeological exhibits here emphasize people who were ancestral to the Interior Salish people of historic times.

'KSAN INDIAN VILLAGE AND MUSEUM

Hazelton. Open free, daily, May through Oct. Admission charged for guided tours. Camping.

This is a reconstruction of a Gitksan Indian village staffed by Indians, some of whom can be seen engaged in the practice of ancient crafts, including woodcarving. One of the buildings, called "Stone Age House," is a replica of a large, prehistoric communal dwelling. In it visitors may see how Gitksans used feathers, bone, skins, and especially cedar bark in making clothes, tools, and utensils.

Special Interest. During July, Gitksan Performing Dancers are featured.

MUSEUM OF NORTHERN BRITISH COLUMBIA

First Ave. and McBride St., Prince Rupert. Open free, daily, all year. Closed certain holidays.

This museum preserves and exhibits artifacts used by Northwest Coast Indian groups. Displays include Tsimshian masks, Nootka baskets, fishing implements, ceremonial blankets, woodworking tools, bentwood boxes, and artifacts used in a ceremony called the potlatch. Also on exhibit are Haida totem poles carved from argillite, a soft, black slate. Although large, wooden totem poles everywhere in the Northwest date from the historic period, when steel woodworking tools became available, the traditions and beliefs which inspired the poles had their origins in prehistory.

OKANAGAN MUSEUM AND ARCHIVES ASSOCIATION
(oh-kah-NAG-ahn)
(See Kelowna Museum and National Exhibit Centre)

PENTICTON MUSEUM AND ARCHIVES
(pen-TICK-ton)

785 Main St., Penticton, which is 265 miles east of Vancouver on the southern Trans-Canada Highway. Open free, afternoons, daily, summer; afternoons, Tuesday through Saturday, fall and winter. Closed certain holidays.

In addition to random local finds, some materials from organized excavations are on display here. Most of the artifacts were made by Salish Indians or their predecessors. Some materials were excavated by Washington State University archeologists.

SIMON FRASER UNIVERSITY MUSEUM OF ARCHAEOLOGY

On the campus, Burnaby. Open free, daily.

Displays here are devoted to the archeology and ethnology of the Pacific Northwest.

An archeologist digs through 8000 years of debris accumulated in the Alpha Rock Shelter, near the Salmon River, in Idaho. Idaho State University photo.

UNIVERSITY OF BRITISH COLUMBIA, MUSEUM OF ANTHROPOLOGY

On the campus, Vancouver. Open free, afternoons, Tuesday through Sunday, all year. Closed certain holidays.

On exhibit here are Northwest Coast Indian artifacts from extensive archeological holdings.

Idaho

ALPHA ROCKSHELTER

From Salmon drive 20 miles north on US 93 to North Fork, then follow the Forest Service Road down the north side of Salmon River past Shoup, then cross the Salmon on the Pine Creek Bridge and continue along the south side of the river about 4 miles to a marker which indicates the site. Open free, at all times.

From a platform erected for the convenience of visitors it is possible to look into this rockshelter, which has been excavated. Paintings are visible on the roof of the overhang.

Occupation began here about 6000 B.C. and continued until 1000 B.C. After that it was visited intermittently until about A.D. 1300. Broken animal bones and freshwater mussel shells show that the site was used by hunters and fishermen. Milling stones found among the debris indicate that women collected seeds and ground them to make them edible.

The people who lived in this and other rockshelters followed what is called the Bitterroot way of life. They may have been ancestors of the Northern Shoshone who inhabited the valley when Lewis and Clark visited it in 1805.

IDAHO MUSEUM OF NATURAL HISTORY
(See Idaho State University)

IDAHO STATE UNIVERSITY, IDAHO MUSEUM OF NATURAL HISTORY

On the campus in Pocatello. Open free, Monday through Friday. Closed certain holidays.

Exhibits here are taken from the museum's large collection of prehistoric artifacts from the northern Great Basin and northern mountain regions.

In September 1805 prehistory and history met on this meadow, now Nez Perce National Historical Park, in Idaho, when three Nez Perce boys and six men of the Lewis and Clark expedition came face to face. People in the village from which the boys came fed the strangers and gave them a horse-load of roots and salmon to take back to the main body of the expedition. National Park Service photo by William S. Keller.

LENORE SITE

From Orofino drive 16 miles west on US 12. Open free, at all times.

Native Americans have lived in this area for 10,000 years. A sign interprets the results of archeological excavations at the site.

LOLO TRAIL

From the Idaho-Montana line, this old trail parallels US 12 for 4 miles. Open free, at all times.

This ancient Indian trail generally follows the ridge of the mountains north of the Lochsa River and extends for 150 miles through wilderness. It is not passable for ordinary tourist vehicles. In prehistoric and early historic times, Nez Perce Indians traveled along it to reach buffalo country in Montana. Lewis and Clark followed it in 1805 on their expedition to the West Coast.

McCAMMON PETROGLYPHS

From Pocatello drive about 18 miles southeast on Interstate 15 to a roadside rest between Inkom and McCammon. Open free, at all times. Camping nearby.

Here, protected by a fence, are several large boulders on which prehistoric Indians pecked designs and pictures. A state historical sign reads: "Over much of western North America, Indians made rough drawings like these, mainly in areas where they hunted and gathered food. Often called rock writing, these drawings are really not writing at all: their meaning—if any—could be interpreted only by the people who made them. Some probably are forms of magic, and some may have been made simply for fun. Many of them, including these, range in age from a few centuries to much older, but dating them precisely is difficult at best."

Other examples of rock art in Idaho have been found along the Snake River and in the south-central part of the state.

MIDVALE QUARRY

On US 95 near Midvale.

Here a historical sign labeled "An Early Industry" indicates a nearby quarry that is of archeological interest but is not open to the public. The sign reads: "At the top of this hill 3 to 5000 years ago, prehistoric men had a rock quarry where they made a variety of stone tools. Projectiles, knives, and scrapers were among the tools made by these early people who camped at the foot of the hill. These nomads hunted deer and other game, collected plant foods, and fished in the river here. They had spears and spearthrowers for hunting and fishing, and mortars and pestles for grinding roots and berries. Archaeologists have not yet determined when this industry shut down."

Weis Rockshelter, in Idaho, was excavated between 1961 and 1964 by archeologists from Idaho State University, who discovered evidence of occupation going back 8000 years. Idaho State University photo.

NEZ PERCE NATIONAL HISTORICAL PARK (NEZ-PURS)

Park Headquarters is in Spalding, on US 95, 12 miles east of Lewiston.

The park itself consists of 24 separate areas, two of which—the Weis Rockshelter and the Lenore Site—are archeological sites open to the public. Weippe Prairie, though not strictly an archeological site, has interest because it was here that Lewis and Clark first met Nez Perce Indians, who had never before seen White people.

WEIS ROCKSHELTER

At Cottonwood, on US 95, a Nez Perce National Historical Park interpretive marker calls attention to the site. From this marker drive south 8 miles on the graveled Grave Creek Canyon Road. Camping nearby.

Weis Rockshelter is one of a series of niches in cliffs along the western slope of the Rocky Mountains in Idaho. People lived here for about 8,000 years, but their culture was somewhat different from that of the occupants of Alpha Rockshelter, near Shoup.

During excavation archeologists found many tools, including bone awls and needles for piercing and sewing skins, chipped stone projectile points for hunting, and antler wedges for splitting wood. The hunters who made these tools may have been ancestors of the Nez Perce Indians of historic times.

The Weis Rockshelter is one of many separate areas which make up the Nez Perce National Historical Park.

WILSON BUTTE CAVE

On Idaho 25 near Wilson Lake reservoir.

Here a historical sign labeled "Prehistoric Man" indicates a nearby cave which is of archeological interest, but which is not open to the public. The sign reads: "Archeological excavations show human occupation of the Snake River Plains for more than 10,000 years. Early men left weapons and other gear in a cave in a nearby butte. Bones show that they hunted game which is now extinct—camels, ancient horses, and ground sloths. In succeeding thousands of years, the climate grew extremely dry, much drier than it is today. Still later, it became less arid again. Through all these changes, man succeeded in adapting and remained here."

A radiocarbon date indicates that the earliest visitors left their crude stone tools in the cave between 14,500 and 15,000 years ago.

"Some of the earliest known inhabitants of this continent made their home in a cave in one of the low knolls dominated by Fort Rock, visible across this basin. Radio-carbon dating indicates that sandals found in the cave may be 9,000 years old. Fort Rock is the remnant of an ancient volcano rising 325 feet above the plain. A great lake covered this entire basin, spreading as far south as Picture Rock. It was in a cave facing that lake that the Fort Rock People lived." This sign on Oregon 31, near the town of Fort Rock, calls attention to Fort Rock, near which archeologists found basketry older than any other that had been found anywhere in the world. Oregon State Highway photo.

Northwest Territories

Archeologists have excavated sites in the upper Arctic, and recently they have done some investigation farther south. Most of the sites in both areas are inaccessible by road, and none are yet open to the public. Some material from the region is in the collections of the National Museum of Man in Ottawa.

Oregon

FORT ROCK CAVE HISTORICAL MARKER

On the east side of Oregon 31, about 18 miles north of Silver Lake.

This roadside marker indicates Fort Rock Cave at the foot of a butte, which can be seen about four miles away, although it is not open to the public. (The cave is named for a nearby volcanic formation called Fort Rock.)

No one knows exactly when Indians first took shelter at this spot. By 9,000 years ago they had already left in the cave some of the baskets and sandals which they wove with great skill from sagebrush fibers. Apparently they did not have a permanent camp there. At least they were all away from home one day when volcanic eruptions at Newberry Craters, north of Fort Rock, filled the air with glowing cinders and ash. The hot layer of ash that settled in the cave charred, but did not destroy, some of the 75 sandals scattered about on the floor. Later, people returned to the cave, and their household debris accumulated on top of the older layers.

When archeologists excavated the cave they could establish a radiocarbon date not only for the charred sandals—and for the people who had made them—but also for the volcanic eruption. The sandals turned out to be the oldest woven artifacts so far discovered in North or South America— or anywhere in the world. Moreover the sandals and basketry found here and at other Oregon caves were not the work of people who had recently taken up the art of weaving. A long period of experimentation, innovation, and practice obviously lay behind the fashioning of any artifact so intricate.

In other Oregon caves, and at open campsites, there is evidence of even earlier visitors to the area. At one place archeologists found very primitive chopping tools. The signs of weathering on these tools indicated that they had been manufactured originally at some unknown date in the distant past. Then about 9,000 years ago they were picked up, sharpened, and reused.

The remains of daily life in caves known as Roaring Springs, Paisley, and Catlow indicate a scene quite unlike the present, semidesert landscape. These caves, like Fort Rock, were all formed by the action of waves at the edges of lakes which filled the valleys at the end of the Ice Age. Eventually the lakes dried up. Until then the people who lived on their shores had food resources different from those available today—and much richer.

In Catlow Cave archeologists found several objects which helped them to remember with a certain poignance that real people lived here. First they came upon two small sandals, about

From the summit of Fort Rock, 300 feet above the prairie, visitors can see the butte in the distance where archeologists, digging in a cave, found sandals and basketry. Oregon State Highway photo.

right for a child of five or six. Nearby were two tiny baskets and a small dart of the kind used in a well-known Indian game. For some reason a little girl one day left her sandals and her toys on the cave floor and never returned. Nor did anyone else disturb them for thousands of years.

HORNER MUSEUM
(See Oregon State University)

McIVER PARK PROJECT

In Milo McIver State Park, 15 miles southeast of Portland, near Estacada on the Clackamas River. Open free, every weekend during summer. Camping.

A group of local citizens devoted to the preservation and enhancement of archeological resources developed this project as a long-range, experimental program. Beginning from scratch in 1978, its first object was construction of a full-size replica of a Chinook plank house. Participants used only Indian tools and techniques, such as woodworking, fiber processing, and flint tool making. The finished house will serve as an interpretive center to en-

courage interest in experimental archeology. Anyone wishing to participate in the project should write to Oregon Archaeological Preservation Committee, 19790 S. Old River Drive, West Linn, OR 97068.

OREGON HIGH DESERT MUSEUM

In Bend, 59000 S. High St. Scheduled to be open daily. Admission will be charged.

This museum devoted primarily to science and natural history emphasizes contemporary management of resources, with both indoor and outdoor habitat exhibits. Part of its indoor interpretive displays will depict the lifeway of Native Americans in the northern Great Basin and high desert areas during the 3000 years before contact with Europeans. How they adjusted to the environment will be a large part of the story. Original artifacts from Oregon sites will be supplemented by replicas of material from such sites as Fort Rock. There will be educational and participatory programs for both adults and children.

OREGON STATE UNIVERSITY, HORNER MUSEUM

Gill Coliseum, on the campus, Corvallis. Open Tuesday through Friday; mornings, Saturday; afternoons, Sunday, Sept. through May; Monday through Friday; afternoons, Sunday, June through Aug. Closed certain holidays. Donation requested.

Exhibits here include basketry, pottery, stone pipes, and other artifacts, together with a map of Native American prehistoric culture areas and languages of Oregon.

PORTLAND ART MUSEUM

Southwest Park and Madison, Portland. Open afternoons, Tuesday through Sunday; evenings, Friday. Admission free except for major exhibitions.

Materials chosen primarily for esthetic value make up the collections devoted to Northwest Indian art and prehistoric art from elsewhere in America.

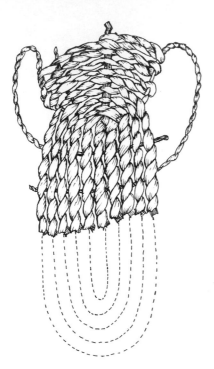

This remnant of a sandal from Roaring Springs Cave, in Oregon, shows a type of weaving mastered by early people in the Great Basin. After Cressman.

When water rises behind a new dam it often covers evidences of prehistoric life. People salvage what they can before the waters rise. Here, for instance, is a fragment of a larger stone that is now covered by the water behind the Dalles Dam in Washington. On this fragment is a pecked representation of a supernatural being. The fragment can be seen in the Winquatt Museum. Photo, courtesy of Campbell Grant.

SCHMINCK MUSEUM

129 S.E. St., Lakeview. Open afternoons, Monday through Saturday. Closed certain holidays. Admission charged.

On display are artifacts from random local finds.

TILLAMOOK COUNTY PIONEER MUSEUM
(TILL-ah-mook)

2106 2nd St., Tillamook. Open free, Monday through Saturday; afternoons, Sunday. Closed Monday, Oct. 1 to May 1 and certain holidays. Donations accepted.

On display here are materials from Umnak Island in the Aleutian Islands, together with surface finds and material excavated from Oregon sites.

UNIVERSITY OF OREGON, MUSEUM OF NATURAL HISTORY

On the campus, Eugene. Open free, Monday through Friday, during the academic year.

The museum staff has conducted significant excavations, and archeological material from the Northwest Coast, Columbia Plateau, and Great Basin is on display, along with material from other regions of North America. One exhibit contains material from Fort Rock Cave. Another deals with a large site now flooded by the dam pool at The Dalles.

WALLOWA COUNTY MUSEUM

In Joseph. Open free, daily, mid-May to Sept. 30. Donations accepted.

In the Nez Perce room here are Nez Perce artifacts which are not dated.

WINQUATT MUSEUM

In Seufert Park 3 miles east of The Dalles. Open, free, Tuesday through Sunday, May through Sept.; afternoons, Wednesday through Friday; all day, Saturday, Sunday, Oct. through April.

Archeological material from numerous prehistoric Indian campsites along the Columbia River are displayed here. Many different cultures are represented because many different peoples came from great distances to fish and to trade in this area. Among the exhibits are bowls, pestles, projectile points, and other artifacts.

A group of petroglyphs, which prehistoric Indians carved on basalt rock, are preserved in the museum. Sections of rock bearing the petroglyphs were removed from their original site near the Columbia River, before rising water behind The Dalles Dam flooded them.

The Name. Winquatt is a word used by local Indians meaning "high hills."

Washington

CHENEY COWLES MEMORIAL MUSEUM
(*See Eastern Washington State Historical Society*)

DRY FALLS INTERPRETIVE CENTER

From Coulee City on US 2 drive 2 miles west to junction with Washington 17, then follow directional markers. Open free, at all times.

The lifeway of prehistoric people in a cave in the Grand Coulee area is recreated in a diorama at the Interpretive Center in Dry Falls, Washington. Washington State Parks photo.

This building with a spectacular view of the Grand Coulee area contains exhibits intended chiefly to explain geological phenomena. However, one display is devoted to the nearby Lake Lenore Caves, which were inhabited in prehistoric times.

EASTERN WASHINGTON STATE HISTORICAL SOCIETY, CHEYNEY COWLES MEMORIAL MUSEUM

West 2316 First Ave., Spokane. Open free, Tuesday through Saturday; mornings, Sunday. Closed certain holidays.

This museum draws on its large collection of archeological as well as modern Indian material for exhibits that interpret regional history from prehistoric times to the present.

EAST MUSEUM

Civic Center, 5th and Balsam, Moses Lake. Open free, Tuesday through Friday; afternoons, Saturday, Sunday, May through Aug.; afternoons, Tuesday through Friday, Sept., Oct., March, April. Closed certain holidays.

This museum houses a large number of artifacts collected by Adam East along the Middle Columbia River. Detailed information about these finds is often lacking, but many of the objects were made by Salish Indians and their prehistoric predecessors.

Some very crude scrapers on exhibit are said to have come from *under* a moraine. Since a moraine is a mass of rock and gravel deposited by a glacier, these tools would be evidence of man's presence in the area before the last glacier of the Ice Age. Scientists are not sure with what care the scrapers were excavated and are cautious about accepting them as proof that people were present in America in preglacial times.

FORT SIMCOE MUSEUM

Fort Simcoe (SIM-kwee) State Park. From Toppenish drive 28 miles west on Washington 220. Open mornings, April 15 through Sept. 30; mornings, Saturday, Sunday, Oct. 1 through April 14.

Some prehistoric but undated artifacts appear here among local ethnological materials.

GINKGO PETRIFIED FOREST STATE PARK INTERPRETIVE CENTER

From Ellensburg drive 27 miles east on Interstate 90 or US 10 to Vantage, then follow signs to park. Open free, daily, all year.

At an unknown date early inhabitants of the Columbia Plateau region pecked many designs and pictures into basalt cliffs along the Columbia River. The rising water of Lake Wanapum, behind Wanapum Dam, would have covered all of these had not some been removed and placed where they are now, south of the balcony in the Interpretive Center. An exhibit in the center shows how the petroglyphs were made.

HOKO RIVER SITE

North of US 112, west of Sekiu. For information and directions to the site inquire at Makah Cultural Research Center, Neah Bay.

Here at the mouth of the Hoko River, 15 miles east of Neah Bay, mud has preserved from decay many

Prehistoric Indians on the Interior Plateau and the Northwest Coast often gave artificial shapes to the heads of their babies. This Chinook woman had her head flattened when she was very young, and now she is giving her own baby a fashionable head shape. Apparently this practice had no ill effects on the brain. Redrawn from Catlin.

artifacts of wood and fiber made by people who lived in the area at least 2500 years ago. For the first time archeologists have found at this site a set of tiny, sharp, stone blades, called microliths, imbedded in a wooden handle for use probably in cutting up fish. Microliths are known from other sites, but never before hafted. Many of the artifacts at Hoko River are so fragile that ordinary excavating tools would destroy them, so they are freed from the mud with gentle streams of water from hoses. Visitors are welcome to watch excavation during summer.

INDIAN PAINTED ROCKS

From Yakima city limits drive 3 miles northwest on US 12. Open free, at all times. Camping nearby.

Present-day Indians in the area have no idea who may have made paintings on the cliffs at this spot. They resemble many others found in western North America and are sometimes interpreted as depicting religious experiences. They may also have been records of hunts or of meetings between people of different tribes. This particular display of rock art stands beside a modern highway that follows an old Indian trail leading to the Wemas Mountains.

INDIAN PAINTED ROCKS

Northwest of Spokane near the Rutter Parkway Bridge over Little Spokane River. Open free, at all times.

Pictographs on the rocks here are similar to those found at Indian Painted Rocks near Yakima.

KETTLE FALLS

In Coulee Dam National Recreation Area, near junction of US 395 and Washington 25. Open free, May through Oct. Camping.

The present town of Kettle Falls was built some distance from the falls themselves, which are now submerged beneath Lake Roosevelt. Before the lake was formed by a dam across the Columbia River, the area was one of the largest Indian salmon fishing grounds, and had been since prehistoric times. Recent archeological work has revealed that people lived here for at least 9000 years, making this one of the oldest continuously occupied sites in the Northwest. In addition to permanent inhabitants, as many as a thousand others from many different tribes visited the falls in summer, when the salmon were migrating upstream to spawn. Using willow baskets, men caught the fish as they leaped up the falls. Women then smoked them or preserved the meat with fat and berries in a food called pemmican.

A hiking trail around the St. Paul's Mission site in the recreation area offers a view of the former fishing grounds.

The Name. The word "kettle" probably refers to the basins formed by the force of falling water in the rocky bed of the river.

LAKE LENORE CAVES

From Coulee City on US 2 drive 2 miles west, then 10 miles south on Washington 17 to directional sign, then ½ mile east to parking area. Open free, at all times. Camping nearby.

"Cave shelters such as found here were used by prehistoric man for temporary housing during hunting and gathering trips. The caves were formed by the plucking of basalt from the coulees by the rush of melt water during the Ice Age." An interpretive sign with this message has been placed near the Lake Lenore Cave Shelters, in Washington. Washington State Parks photo.

A trail leads to seven caves in Lower Grand Coulee that were inhabited by prehistoric Indians who apparently used them as temporary shelters while on hunting expeditions. Many small stone scrapers have been found in the caves and these are taken as evidence that people who lived here prepared skins.

At Dry Falls Interpretive Center, an exhibit is devoted to Lake Lenore Caves.

MAKAH CULTURAL RESEARCH CENTER
(mah-KAH)

Neah Bay, at the western end of Washington 112, the northwestern-most settlement in the contiguous 48 states. Open daily, June 1 to Sept. 15; Wednesday through Sunday, Sept. 16 to May 31. Closed certain holidays. Admission charged. In Neah Bay, which is in the Makah Indian Reservation, visitors should be careful not to invade the privacy of the residents.

The Makah Cultural Research Center, built at a cost of $2 million,

houses 55,000 artifacts recovered from the 2500-year-old Ozette archeological site.

Ozette was a village on the far tip of what is now called the Olympic Peninsula. Migrating whales passed by it every year, not far out at sea, and the men of Ozette became great whale hunters. In large canoes that held eight men each, they were able to kill and bring in whales that weighed as much as 30 tons.

At other times of the year Ozette people exploited the area's other rich resources, such as fish and plant roots and berries for food, and various kinds of wood for dishes, tools, and the large planks they used in house building. Each dwelling was big enough for several families, and it was constructed in such a way that it could be dismantled and moved to a new location for a seasonal harvest.

Much is known about these houses because the village stood at the foot of a bluff, and it was partially covered more than once by mud flows. The heavy, wet earth preserved entire dwellings, together with their contents.

Excavation of the site was done by a team of scientists led by Richard Daugherty, of Washington State University, working with a group from the Makah Indian Nation. Because perishable materials were found intact, much unusual information could be gathered about everyday life here. For example, a fragment of textile showed that a woman had woven it from threads made of cedarbark, plus dog wool mixed with cattail fluff. Other artifacts included harpoon blades of mussel shell, adzes and chisels for wood carving, beautifully carved clubs, combs, boxes, weaving equipment, spindle whorls, baskets, nets, and much more.

In addition to displays of objects from Ozette, the Makah Cultural Research Center offers dioramas, a full-size longhouse, some hands-on exhibits, and an audio program. The Ozette excavations have stimulated a renaissance of traditional Makah craftsmanship, examples of which are on sale at the center. On certain days the Ozette site, which is 15 miles away, is open to visitors. For information inquire at the Center, phone: (202) 645-2711.

On Visiting Excavations

Archeologists usually like to encourage people who want to learn about the science which they find so fascinating. But at an excavation everyone is usually too busy to explain what goes on. So, although they don't like to be rude, archeologists very often have to make an absolute rule that visitors may not come to their digs.

There are exceptions. If you want to watch the slow and painstaking work that goes into an excavation, you should ask the proper authorities if visitors are allowed. In national parks, ask park rangers. It may be possible for you to see a dig from a good vantage point. There may even be a ranger assigned to explain what is happening.

If you want to take part in an organized dig, the American Anthropological Association publishes in February every year a list of archeological field schools—about ninety of them in the 1982 issue. There is

---

MANIS MASTODON SITE

In Sequim (SQUIM), on US 101, turn south on 3rd Ave., then west on Happy Valley Rd., then left at directional sign. Open Tuesday through Sunday, early May through Labor Day; other times by appointment. Admission charged.

This site, on the property of Clare and Emanuel Manis, is one of the few places where archeologists have discovered proof that prehistoric Americans hunted mastodons. In 1977 the Manises decided to build a duck pond in a low-lying spot in a field, and quite by chance chose the exact place where a partly butchered mastodon skeleton had been lying under layers of peat and earth for about 12,000 years. Digging with a backhoe, Manis turned up bones and tusks, realized they were something special, and immediately began searching for experts to take a look. Richard Daugherty, of Washington State University, and other scientists responded.

Examination of a rib brought up by the hoe showed something very special indeed—a bone spear tip im-

bedded in the rib. Apparently a hunter, long ago, had thrust the spear through the mastodon's thick skin and muscle, and it had broken off in the rib without killing the animal. The wound had partly healed when hunters either drove the mastodon into a mud hole or found it mired there. Then, the scientists believe, the hunters dispatched it, possibly by breaking its skull with rocks. At any rate excavation turned up the cracked head bones nearby, along with other bits of bone that had obviously been shaped into tools of some sort.

The kill may have been possible in part because the mastodon was old and feeble. Its bones showed signs of arthritis, and its teeth were worn down to the gumline—the result of much chewing on the woody plants on which mastodons browsed. (Unlike their cousins the mammoths, they were not grasseaters.) The body had lain on its side, and the uppermost bones showed butchering marks where the flesh had been stripped away. A stone chopping tool lay close by.

Excavation at the Manis Site has continued. Recently, at a 10,000-year

level, archeologists discovered a harpoon point and other evidence of human occupation. Visitors are offered a guided tour and a slide show of the entire dig.

MUSEUM OF NATIVE AMERICAN CULTURE
(Formerly Pacific Northwest Indian Center)

E. 200 Cataldo (reached by way of Boone St.), Spokane. Open Monday through Saturday; afternoons, Sunday. Admission charged.

This museum houses a collection of prehistoric artifacts from many Western areas. The building is located on the site of an early camping area of the Spokane Indians.

NEAH BAY SHELL MOUND SITE
(See Makah Cultural Research Center)

OLD MAN HOUSE

East of Poulsbo, north of Agate Pass bridge. Open free, at all times.

This is the site of a very large communal dwelling, built of hand-adzed cedar slabs, which existed at the time a charge for the list. For information about it write to the American Anthropological Association, 1703 New Hampshire Ave., N.W., Washington, DC 20009, and include a stamped, self-addressed, business-size envelope.

The Archaeological Institute of America, 260 W. Broadway, New York, NY 10013, publishes *Fieldwork Opportunities Bulletin,* giving information about organizations that offer archeological programs. There is a charge for the bulletin.

Earthwatch, Field Research Corps, 10 Juniper Rd., Belmont, MA 02178, conducts summer volunteer expeditions to help at various sites in the United States and elsewhere around the world. Team members pay a share of the cost.

---

the first settlers arrived in the area. Chief Sealth, for whom the city of Seattle was named, once lived here. The house survived until 1870, when it was destroyed by order of the U.S. Army.

OLYMPIC NATIONAL PARK, PIONEER MEMORIAL VISITOR CENTER

2800 Hurricane Ridge Rd., Port Angeles. Open free, daily, except Dec. 25. Camping in the park.

A large amount of ethnological and archeological material from Northwest Coast tribes is stored here and is available for scientific study. A small selection of this material is exhibited in the museum.

OZETTE SITE

This site, on the Makah Indian Reservation, was backfilled after excavation by Washington State University, and much of the extensive material recovered is now on exhibit at the Makah Cultural and Research Center (see entry, above). The site can be

reached by a 4½-mile foot trail from the Olympic National Park Ranger Station on Hoko River Rd., which intersects US 112 just beyond Sekiu. In summer there are sometimes Indian guides at the site, and the Makah are planning to open an interpretive center there. For information, phone: (202) 645–2711.

PACIFIC NORTHWEST INDIAN CENTER
(See Museum of Native American Culture)

ROCKY REACH DAM VISITOR CENTER

Seven miles north of Wenatchee on US 97. Open free, daily, all year.

Some exhibits here give information about prehistoric people in the now flooded river valley.

ROOSEVELT PETROGLYPHS

On Washington 14 about a mile east of Roosevelt. Open free, at all times.

Here, in a special park, the citizens of Roosevelt have installed and

A projectile point from the Marmes Early Man Site. Marmes Rockshelter Project photo, Laboratory of Anthropology, Washington State University.

One of the most important Early Man sites was the Marmes Rockshelter, dated at more than 10,000 years ago, which was covered by water before excavation could be completed. This view shows the shelter after excavation had begun. Marmes Rockshelter Project photo, Laboratory of Anthropology, Washington State University.

protected a group of petroglyphs collected from nearby sites along the Columbia River. These sites have been flooded by the reservoir behind John Day Dam.

SAKAJAWEA STATE PARK MUSEUM
(SOCK-ah-jah-WEE-ah)

From Pasco drive 6 miles southeast on US 395 to directional sign. Open free, daily.

One wing of this museum features stone artifacts; the other interprets the Lewis and Clark expedition, emphasizing the Indian woman, Sakajawea, who accompanied the expedition.

SEATTLE ART MUSEUM

14th Ave. E. and E. Prospect St., Volunteer Park, Seattle. Open Tuesday through Sunday. Closed certain holidays. Admission charged.

In a large general collection are some archeological objects from the Northwest Coast and the Upper Mississippi Valley.

SNOQUALMIE VALLEY HISTORICAL MUSEUM
(sno-KWAL-mee)

222 North Bend Blvd., North Bend. Open free, afternoons, Saturday and Sunday, March through Oct. Tours by appointment.

Included here with historical exhibits are a display of undated Snoqualmie Indian artifacts.

STATE CAPITOL MUSEUM

211 W. 21st Ave., Olympia. Open free, Tuesday through Sunday. Closed certain holidays.

Here are examples of Northwest Indian art and material culture.

THOMAS BURKE MEMORIAL STATE MUSEUM
(See University of Washington)

Large trenches were dug at right angles by bulldozer to remove sterile soil above the evidence of human occupation. Marmes Rockshelter Project photo, Laboratory of Anthropology, Washington State University.

UNIVERSITY OF WASHINGTON, THOMAS BURKE MEMORIAL STATE MUSEUM

On the campus, Seattle. Open free, Tuesday through Saturday; afternoons, Sunday. Closed certain holidays.

In addition to large displays on historic Indian cultures, this museum has some exhibits of prehistoric materials.

WAKEMAP MOUND
(WAH-kem-up)

In Horsethief Lake State Park, east of Wishram, off Washington 14. Drive through the park to the river, then from the end of the road walk west on the path from which petroglyphs and pictographs are visible. Open free, at all times.

The mound here is actually an ancient village site, occupied at various times from the tenth century to the period of contact with Lewis and Clark. Each succeeding group of people built houses on top of former house sites, producing a mound of rubble. More interesting to the casual visitor

now are examples of rock art, which may be seen on boulders along the river.

WANAPUM TOUR CENTER
(WAHNA-pum)

From Ellensburg drive 27 miles east on US 10 to Vantage, then 5 miles south on Washington 243 to the Wanapum Dam. Open free, daily, April 15 through Oct. 31.

Displayed here are projectile points, net sinkers, knives, scrapers, pipes, drills, needles, and other prehistoric artifacts found in the vicinity of the Wanapum and Priest Rapids reservoirs.

WASHINGTON STATE HISTORICAL SOCIETY

315 North Stadium Way, Tacoma. Open free, Tuesday through Saturday; afternoons, Sunday. Closed certain holidays.

This museum, which emphasizes Northwestern history, displays some prehistoric artifacts.

WASHINGTON STATE UNIVERSITY, ANTHROPOLOGY MUSEUM

In Johnson Tower, on the campus, Pullman. Open free, Monday through Friday, during the academic year.

In this general teaching museum archeological materials are used in an exhibit of artifacts from Ozette (see entry, above), a site on the Washington coast, from St. Lawrence Island in Alaska, and from the Snake River area. The latter includes material from the Marmes (MAR-muss) Site, one of the most important early human sites in the United States, which cannot be visited because it now lies under water in a reservoir in the southeastern corner of Washington.

The Story. For several years Washington State University conducted excavations in the Marmes Rockshelter, named for the owner of the property. Here, in the Palouse River Valley, near its junction with the valley of the Snake River, archeologists found layer after layer of debris which indicated people had first used the shelter 10,000 years ago, possibly even earli-

Strata in the walls of the excavation.
Marmes Rockshelter Project photo,
Laboratory of Anthropology,
Washington State University.

er. Digging revealed food-storage pits lined with matting, shell beads, grinding implements, projectile points, tools of various kinds, and more than a dozen burials.

One skeleton lay beneath a thick layer of volcanic ash, which geologists identified as having resulted from the eruption of Mount Mazama, at Crater Lake, in Oregon, about 6700 years ago. This was especially interesting in view of an Indian legend about Crater Lake. It was formed, according to the Indians, when a battle took place between the underworld chief who lived inside Mount Mazama and the chief of the world above. The underworld chief hurled out fiery rocks and great clouds of ash, and the earth shook, but in the end his rival succeeded in pushing him down into the mountain, forming the great hole which then filled up with water, to create the lake. The discovery that a human being had lived in the rockshelter before the eruption suggested that Indian storytellers based their tale not on fantasy but on the 6700-year-old fact that an eruption really had happened.

One day a member of the Marmes expedition—a geologist—decided to have a trench dug in the terrace below the shelter. He called in a bulldozer to clear away the soil quickly, and as he walked behind the machine, he saw a fragment of bone. It turned out to be human bone. The bulldozer was replaced by trowels, and careful digging revealed portions of three skulls. Since they lay underneath material which was dated at 10,000 years B.P., the bones had to be older than that. Since they lay on top of soil known to have been deposited no more than 13,000 years ago, the bones were somewhere between 10,000 and 13,000 years old.

Near the skulls were found a spearpoint made of animal bone and a tiny, delicately made bone needle with an eye in it. This was taken to mean that the people who lived here a hundred centuries ago sewed animal-skin clothing. Indeed the needle was so small that experts think it may have been used to sew watertight seams, as Eskimos are known to have done in much later times.

A bone tool, called a flesher, for scraping hides of freshly killed animals, found at the Old Crow Site in Yukon, Canada. The left half of the artifact was cut off to be used in carbon-14 dating, which indicated that the bone was 28,000 years old; present-day carbon-14 methods would have left more of the bone intact. Whether the scraper was actually made 28,000 years ago or by a later craftsworker who used ancient bone is a disputed question. National Museum of Man, Ontario. Photo by Richard Garner.

The Marmes discovery was very important, but those who made it were able to excavate only part of the site. A dam was under construction downriver, and when it was completed water rose rapidly behind it and approached the level of the rockshelter. People who were interested in the scientific importance of the site persuaded President Johnson to instruct the Army Corps of Engineers to protect it. A coffer dam was built around the site, but someone had overlooked the nature of the soil under this barrier. It was gravel, through which the water from the reservoir seeped very readily. Nevertheless, optimistically, the archeologists lined the sides of their excavation with plastic and then had the hole filled with gravel, to prevent slumping. Someday, they hope, if several million dollars are forthcoming to pump out water and retrieve the site—or if the reservoir silts in so much that it has to be drained—scientists may return to finish their work.

WILLIS CAREY MUSEUM

Off US 2, in Cashmere. Open free, Monday through Friday; afternoons, Saturday, Sunday.

Both prehistoric and historic Native American artifacts are on exhibit here.

YAKIMA VALLEY MUSEUM (YAK-i-maw)

2105 Tieton Dr., Yakima. Open Wednesday through Friday; afternoons, Saturday, Sunday. Admission charged. Closed certain holidays.

The principal Indian exhibits here are Yakima, Klickitat, and Sioux (Dakota). A small amount of undated prehistoric material is included.

Yukon Territory

MacBRIDE CENTENNIAL MUSEUM

First Ave. and Steele St., Whitehorse. Open, daily, late May to early Sept. Admission charged.

Although no archeological sites in Yukon Territory are open to the public, some finds of prehistoric materials are exhibited in this museum, which also displays more recent Indian materials, along with relics of pioneer and Gold Rush times.

An aerial view of part of the Bannock Point Petroform Site, in Whiteshell Provincial Park, Manitoba, where prehistoric people used rocks to create designs on the ground.

GREAT PLAINS

"I observed the remains of an old village which had been fortified," Captain William Clark wrote in his journal on Oct. 19, 1804. He and other members of the Lewis and Clark Expedition noted several of these abandoned sites along the Missouri River before they stopped at a vigorous and hospitable settlement of Mandan Indians near present-day Bismarck, North Dakota. There for the next five months the exploring party camped on the very edge of prehistory.

The daily lives of the Mandans, their ceremonies and rituals, may well have resembled those of Indians whose villages and garden plots had been sprinkled along rivers in the flat heart of America for the preceding thousand years. Even before that, transient hunters left evidence of their wanderings over the Great Plains, just as they had in other parts of the country. The Plains environment, however, was unique. Accordingly human adjustments to it had special qualities.

This huge region extends from central Texas northward to southern Alberta, Saskatchewan, and Manitoba. On the west it begins at the foothills of the Rocky Mountains, and its stretches eastward through much of Oklahoma, all of Kansas and Nebraska, part of Iowa, and all of South and North Dakota. A feature common to most of the Plains is grass. In the east it grows tall, and the tall-grass country is often called prairie. The west, where the land is higher and rainfall less, is short-grass country.

A diorama showing how hunters drove buffalo over a cliff to make possible a large kill. Many such buffalo jumps have been studied on the Plains. Smithsonian Institution photo.

When Europeans began to explore here they assumed, as have most people since then, that the prairies were very ancient. However, this may not have been the case. In the not too distant past, trees grew in some places where whites found only grass. Forests covered large sections of the Plains at certain periods. Just when or why they disappeared is not altogether clear. Possibly a slight decrease in rainfall, together with forest fires, destroyed much of the tree cover. The grasses could survive, but perhaps the slower-growing trees then succumbed to the Indians' habit of setting grass fires to make hunting easy.

This change in vegetation had its effect on animal life. It gave bison a virtually limitless supply of food. Herds multiplied and roamed freely. Perhaps 30 million of the big animals were grazing on Plains grasses by the time Europeans first saw them. With such a resource people, too, could make the grasslands their home. Bison fed the Plains dwellers. Their hides gave them robes for warmth and material for shelter and for containers. Sinews were useful for sewing. Horns could be made into spoons, certain bones into scrapers. Dried bison dung (buffalo chips) made excellent fuel.

Even before the buffalo hunters, there were small groups on the Plains who followed the giant bison. These huge creatures— they were probably four times as heavy as modern buffalo— furnished an abundance of meat, as did mammoths, camels, and other game that is now extinct. Mammoth kill sites have been found in Oklahoma, Colorado, and Wyoming, and associated with the bones were projectile points of the kind first discovered at Clovis, New Mexico. A whole series of other points were also used to kill large game animals on the Plains. These too are identified in museums by the names of the sites where they were first found— Scottsbluff, Eden, Milnesand, Hell Gap, and others. Although they vary in shape, all are of beautifully worked stone. Perhaps it was the efficient use of these points that helped to bring extinction to several species of animal. At any rate the big game of Paleo-Indian times disappeared, and by about 6000 B.C. the lifeway of hunters on the Great Plains began to undergo change.

Archaic Period

Hunting continued in the next period, the Archaic, but in the absence of the large meat animals people ate more of the smaller ones, even squirrels, rats, and mice, which already had a place in their diet. They also accepted plants as food. Grinding stones to make seeds edible now appear in places where Archaic campsites come to light. Not many of these sites have been found. Perhaps no one has looked hard enough for them; or the climate may have been to blame. According to some weather experts a hot, dry period began about 5000 B.C., and vegetation declined in the western sections of the Plains. This could have meant that animal life was scarce, and people who depended on both plants and animals would have had little reason to stay in the area. Some dispute this idea, but archeologists have found only limited traces of human presence during the next 2500 years.   Eastern sections of the Plains were not arid, and there the lifestyle resembled that of Archaic people who inhabited the heavily wooded areas from the Mississippi to the Atlantic coast. (Although archeological material from eastern Oklahoma is listed in this section of the book, it is culturally related to the Southeast.)

No mountain barrier separated the Plains from the woodlands. On the contrary, waterways linked the entire region from the Rocky Mountains to the Appalachians, and Woodland people could and did move freely along them. Ideas traveled too, but not always very fast. Pottery making, for example, had appeared as early as about 2400 B.C. in Florida, and in the Northeast by about 1000 B.C. It then took about a thousand years for the useful art of ceramics to reach the eastern Plains and even longer for it to spread into short-grass country.

Partly because pieces of broken pottery are numerous and easy to see, the human record on the Great Plains becomes clearer. The advent of gardening and corn raising makes the record clearer still, because farmers stay longer in one place and hence leave more debris in one place than hunters do.

How agriculture entered the Plains is a matter of discussion among the experts. Some believe it came from the south and west. Others think it may have been brought by people who moved westward out of the valleys of the Ohio and Illinois and Mississippi rivers. Apparently a migration did begin about A.D. 1, when a group settled on the Missouri River where Kansas City

Strange stone heads from the southern Plains may be among the earliest works of art in the New World. *Left to right:* The Frederick Head was carved from sandstone. Original now in the Museum of the Great Plains, Lawton, Oklahoma. The Malakoff Heads (only the faces are shown here in reproduction). Originals in Texas Memorial Museum, Austin.

now stands. With them came customs typical of a lifeway known as Hopewellian, that centered in Ohio and Illinois. After that, settlements appeared farther and farther up the Missouri.

As the people moved northward the women, who did the planting, had a basic problem—the farther they went, the shorter was the dependable weather for crop growing. This meant that not all of their corn seeds would produce mature plants before frost. Nevertheless, along the Missouri River and elsewhere, they managed to save some hardy, early-ripened seeds each year, and gradually, by a process of selection, they developed strains suited to the climate of each area they settled.

Wherever corn became a successful crop, village life was possible for at least part of the year. Although these Plains settlements had much in common, they varied in many ways that intrigue the archeologist. Life in regions where farming developed early differed from life where it came late or not at all. And so, for convenience in reporting, archeologists who have been most concerned with the Great Plains area divide it into five subareas: Southern Plains, Central Plains, Middle Missouri, Northeastern Periphery, and Northwestern Plains.

There are several reasons why the Middle Missouri has yielded the most archeological "goodies." Along this stretch of the river, as it crosses South Dakota and North Dakota to its junction with the Yellowstone, the land was suited to the needs of village dwellers. It offered good soil for gardens. There was access to hunting grounds and plenty of timber for building the distinctive Plains Village houses. These are known as earth lodges because their framework of poles and upright logs was banked with earth or sod. A frequent house shape was a half dome, like those which Lewis and Clark saw among the Mandans, with roofs which sometimes covered a surprisingly big area. A hole in the center provided an escape for smoke and a source of light. In bad weather the smoke hole could be covered with an inverted bull boat—a circular craft made of bison skin stretched around a wooden frame.

In varying sizes and shapes—sometimes round, sometimes rectangular or square—the earth lodges housed Plains Village Indians along the Missouri from about A.D. 1000 to historic times. After they were abandoned the earth lodges attracted little attention until, at the end of World War II, dam building for flood control began along the Missouri. A program of salvage archeology in this rich area yielded much fascinating material that may be seen in the National Museum of Natural History in Washington, D.C., and also in western museums and at a few sites noted in this section.

Archeologists have done less excavating in the eastern Dakotas and southern Manitoba (the Northeastern Periphery subarea). As a result they are not altogether sure what happened there during the Plains Village period. They do know that at some time people built a good many burial mounds. Just when they began is not certain, but they may have continued into historic times. Perhaps the first mounds were the work of people who shared in the widespread Woodland lifeway. Almost certainly they were not farmers but hunters.

Woodland people did inhabit the long-grass part of the Central Plains subarea, which includes the westernmost part of Iowa, all of Kansas and Nebraska, eastern Colorado, and a little of southeastern Wyoming. Here were resources for men who hunted and for women who may have done a little gardening but who certainly had the knack of gathering seeds and roots. What happened to these groups after about A.D. 500 remains a mystery. All we know is that people with an entirely different life style moved in and stayed.

Changing Lifeways
These newcomers were village dwellers. Like their predecessors they hunted bison, but they were also gardeners, and they made new use of one particular part of the bison—they turned the shoulder blades into hoes for their cornfields. Along one river valley after another the Plains Village communities spread westward through the Central Plains. Proof that they were not transients appeared when archeologists dug into a site inhabited by people of the Mill Creek culture in Iowa. During the years they spent here— from perhaps A.D. 800 to 1400—they piled up a rich collection of trash 12 feet deep over a two-acre area.

Somewhat less wealthy were the earth-lodge builders who settled in the upper valley of the Republican River in Nebraska. However, they must have had large surpluses of corn, beans, squash, and sunflower, for they dug innumerable food storage pits both inside and outside their dwellings. The Upper Republican women were good potters; the men efficient hunters of deer, antelope, and bison. Why they disappeared shortly before the arrival of Europeans, archeologists cannot say. Possibly nomadic raiders from the west stole their surplus food and forced them to move toward safer places in the east. Or perhaps it was drought that robbed them of food.

A little farther to the west, where the prairie gives way to the short-grass country of the High Plains, lived the Dismal River people, who did little gardening but lived primarily by hunting. Instead of building earth lodges they made shelters of poles with roofs of skin or bundled grass. Probably they were the ancestors of the Plains Apaches who followed the buffalo herds on horseback in historic times.

Farther south in the Oklahoma and Texas panhandles, which are part of the Southern Plains subarea, people of the Antelope Creek culture had an interesting mixture of traits. Some of their patterns of living seem to have come from Upper Republican contacts; another custom—their way of building square houses of masonry and adobe mud—certainly reached them from the Pueblo people, across the mountains in New Mexico.

Close by these settlements lay the Llano Estacado—the Staked Plains—where, long before, Paleo-Indians hunted mammoths. Because the hard sod and the uncertain climate made farming almost impossible, this remained hunting country. Countless bison roamed there, and in late prehistoric times Comanche Indians made it their home.

Elsewhere in northern Texas and Oklahoma, village Indians resembled in many ways those of the Central Plains. The Washita River people, for example, built rectangular houses but daubed the outside with clay instead of banking the walls with earth. They gardened and hunted and also did some fishing. Similar villages dotted parts of north-central Texas.

Although south Texas is not strictly a part of the Great Plains, it is included here for convenience. This was not a hospitable or comfortable land. Along the coast plenty of rain fell in the course of a year, but it often did not fall at the right time for corn growing. Inland the climate was very dry. As a result, people who lived either on the coast or inland never took up agriculture, and so they did not gather in permanent farming villages. They simply subsisted on what was at hand—roots, nuts, seeds, and the fruit and stems of cactus. Along the coast they found fish and mollusks, and shell heaps accumulated as they did along the Pacific and Atlantic coasts. Their way of life, in short, was a continuation of the Desert culture from which the farming cultures of the Southwest developed. Possibly these South Texans were immigrants who came to North America very early and were pushed into so harsh a land by later people. One basis for this theory is their language. It resembles the Hokan tongue which survived into historic times in California and which scholars believe is the oldest of all California languages.

Almost as difficult as south Texas are some parts of the Northwest Plains, which include Wyoming, Montana, the western Dakotas, and the southern end of Alberta and Saskatchewan. Corn did not prosper here, and people could not base their lives on farming. Instead they continued to live century after century much as their ancestors had in Archaic times. Some pottery did appear about A.D. 500, but it was never very useful to nomadic hunters because it was fragile and awkward to transport. More suitable containers could be made from hide and from the stomachs and intestines of bison.

Ways of hunting bison varied. The most spectacular was also the most productive—and wasteful. To secure a large quantity of meat with least trouble, men would drive a whole herd over a cliff. Indians used this technique, called the buffalo jump, both before and after they obtained horses.

Some of the buffalo hunters of historic times—the Blackfeet, Arapaho, and Assiniboine—were probably descendants of the prehistoric Northern Plains people. Others who hunted here after the arrival of horses had different origins. The Cheyenne and the Sioux were latecomers. Their ancestors had been Plains Village dwellers farther east—farmers who gave up farming and moved about living entirely by the chase, once horses were available.

From the colorful riders of historic times to the early makers of simple stone tools, the range of Plains life was wide and, like the Plains themselves, surprisingly varied. Our knowledge of it is far from complete but has accumulated very rapidly in recent years. As a result of decisions to build huge flood-control dams in the Missouri River Basin, the Smithsonian River Basin Survey and the National Park Service undertook a large and intensive salvage archeology program, especially in the Dakotas. The work done by the survey—and work done everywhere else on the Plains—has been well summarized and interpreted by Waldo R. Wedel in a very illuminating book, *Prehistoric Man on the Great Plains.*

Very Old Sites in Alberta

In 1961, about three miles north of Taber, Alberta, a geological field party found fragments of the bones of a young child buried under 70 feet of earth and gravel. Unfortunately the fragments were too small to permit dating by the radiocarbon method, but scientists have ways of estimating how long ago the gravel was deposited at the site. A geologist, A. MacS. Stalker, who studied the deposits, came to the conclusion that the bones were at least 37,000 years old, and perhaps as much as 60,000 years old. If Stalker is correct, these human remains may be the oldest so far found in the Americas.

At another site, near Medicine Hat, in Alberta, Stalker's attention was called to a gravel bed in which chipped stones appeared. Some of these showed that they had been additionally flaked as if to sharpen a knife edge. The sharpening, Stalker believes, must have been done by people, because he knows of no natural process that could have accomplished the flaking. In this same bed appeared wood and mollusk shells. Radiocarbon dates for this material indicate an age of between 30,000 and 36,000 years. Stalker also found the bones of mammoth and other extinct animals in this bed, but there was no proof that they were associated with the tools of humans who might have hunted them.

Alberta

EARLY MAN SITE

From Fort MacLeod drive 12 miles northwest on Alberta 2. Open free, at all times.

A cairn erected by the provincial government marks the site where Indian hunters built an enclosure, or pound, into which they drove bison. In this trap they could conveniently slaughter the animals, which were difficult to kill when on the run.

LUXTON MUSEUM

Birch Ave., Banff. Open daily, last week in June to Sept. 7; Tuesday through Sunday in other seasons. Closed certain holidays. Admission charged.

Included with western Canadian ethnographic material in the museum are archeological specimens from the area. A diorama shows a buffalo jump.

THE RIBSTONES

From Viking drive 6 miles east on Alberta 14. Open free, at all times.

Here on a farm is a provincial cairn which points out the ribstones—a kind of artifact found more in Alberta than in any other Plains province or state. A ribstone is a boulder on which prehistoric hunters pecked grooves which often resemble animal ribs. The Cree Indians in historic times thought that these petroglyphs represented buffalo ribs and that the boulders were dwelling places of the animals' guardian spirits. Sometimes a buffalo head was pecked near the grooves in a ribstone, along with circular depressions. These holes, according to the Crees, allowed arrows (and bullets in historic times) to pass through without harming the guardian spirit within the stone.

Excavation at the Olsen-Chubbuck site in Colorado revealed this "river of bones," which remained after prehistoric bison were driven into an arroyo and butchered. Photo by Joe Ben Wheat, University of Colorado, Boulder.

UNIVERSITY OF ALBERTA, ANTHROPOLOGY EXHIBITS

Henry Marshall Tory Bldg., on the campus, Edmonton. Open free, Monday through Saturday, when the university is in session.

In the hallway on the main floor of the building are display cases of archeological material representing all stages of Alberta's prehistory, from Paleo times up to the period of contact with Europeans. There are also recent Eskimo artifacts. Displays are changed once or twice a year.

WRITING-ON-STONE

Off Alberta 4, on the Milk River 75 miles southeast of Lethbridge. Open free, at all times.

Here in the valley of the Milk River, near sandstone cliffs, the provincial government has erected a cairn to indicate where Indians pecked various designs in the rock.

Some of the petroglyphs show men on horseback. Although horses roamed the Plains in Paleo-Indian times, they disappeared and were reintroduced by the Spanish in the sixteenth century. The pictures showing men on horseback must have been made sometime after A.D. 1730, which is thought to be the date when horses reached Alberta. Representations of men with bows and shields may have been made earlier.

Archeologists who have examined the site believe that much of this rock art is prehistoric. Possibly the figures of animals were made by young men as part of a religious rite called the guardian spirit quest. A youth in search of a guardian spirit went off alone to some remote spot, where he fasted and tried to dream of an animal which would become his protector and helper in later life.

Colorado
(eastern)

COLORADO HERITAGE CENTER

1300 Broadway, Denver. Open free, daily. Closed Dec. 25.

The Heritage Center museum, run by the Colorado Historical Society, has a great deal of prehistoric Native American material, including a superb collection of pottery, textiles, sandals, basketry and other objects from Mesa Verde cliff dwellings in southwestern Colorado. As this book went to press, a new exhibit on Mesa Verde was scheduled to open in the near future. It will include dioramas and displays of much of the material from the center's collection.

DENVER ART MUSEUM

100 West 14th Ave. Parkway, Denver. Open free (except for some traveling exhibitions), Tuesday through Sunday. Closed certain holidays.

On exhibit in the Native Arts Department are examples of North American material, mostly ceramic, from both the Southwest and the Southeast. The collection includes a few examples of prehistoric basketry, stone sculpture, textiles, and engraved shell.

Ginsburg and Margie and Paleo-Indians

One day in March 1978, archeologists learned a good deal about how stone and bone tools helped Paleo-Indians obtain food. They used replicas of such tools to butcher an elephant, named Ginsburg, that had died in the Boston Zoo. Ginsburg, except for her smaller size, closely resembled a mammoth, and all of her, except for certain parts kept for study in Boston, was trucked to Front Royal, Virginia. There Dr. Dennis Stanford of the Smithsonian Institution directed very precise studies of how projectile points penetrated the thick skin of the elephant and how stone and bone knives cut the hide and flesh. One finding made on the spot was that tools fashioned from elephant bone were very effective. "It might have been possible to kill and butcher a mammoth without using stone tools," Stanford said.

A similar opportunity to try out replicas of prehistoric tools on an elephant came in Denver in June 1979. Dr. Bruce Rippeteau, then Colorado State Archeologist, got a dead circus elephant named Margie on loan from a rendering plant, and with the aid of a hastily gathered group of experts proceeded to experiment with spears and other tools made of wood, stone and bone. They proved that thin, fluted Clovis points could penetrate the animal's underbelly, provided their hafting was carefully tapered. Thin, slightly serrated blades were best for slicing meat, and a stone hand axe effectively peeled off the thick hide. The angles at which tools were held also affected their efficiency.

DENVER MUSEUM OF NATURAL HISTORY

City Park, Denver. Open Monday through Saturday; afternoons, Sunday and most holidays. Admission charged.

This museum first gained fame in the world of archeology for its excavation of the Folsom Site in New Mexico (see above), and it displays the original Folsom point, as it was found, between the ribs of an extinct bison.

A number of exhibits in the newly arranged North American archeology section emphasize sites in Colorado and the Southwest. Much of the material here resulted from H.M. Wormington's field work on Early Man which was sponsored by the museum.

One display contains material from a site with an interesting history: A summer cloudburst in 1932 exposed some large bones along the South Platte River near the Dent railroad station 39 miles from Denver. Railroad workers reported the bones to Reverend Conrad Bilgery, S.J., a teacher at Regis College near Denver. Father Bilgery excavated and found under the pelvis of a mammoth a large spear point that had short flutes on each face near the base. This was identified as a Clovis point—a type of projectile discovered that same year at Blackwater Draw Site near Clovis, New Mexico. Dating of the Clovis point finds revealed that hunters had been in the Plains areas at least 11,000 years ago—earlier than archeologists had previously thought. The Dent Site is not open to the public, but the Clovis point found there is on exhibit in the Denver Museum. The mammoth from the site is in the Cleveland Museum of Natural History.

FORT COLLINS MUSEUM

200 Mathews St., two blocks north of Mulberry St. (Colorado 14), Fort Collins. Open free, Tuesday through Saturday; afternoons, Sunday.

On display is an extensive collection of Folsom artifacts collected in the 1920s and 1930s at the Lindenmeier Site, in northern Colorado. This Paleo-Indian culture existed about 10,000 years ago.

KOSHARE INDIAN MUSEUM, INC. (ko-SHAH-ray)

From US 50 in La Junta drive south 18 blocks on Colorado Ave., then west 1 block. Open free, daily, summer; afternoons, winter.

This museum on the campus of Otero Junior College contains archeological materials and dioramas showing prehistoric Indian life. The collections have been assembled partly through the activities of an extraordinary troop of Boy Scouts who call themselves Koshares. The Koshares also perform Indian dances in authentic costumes on Saturday nights and at varying other dates in July and August and at the end of December. Inquire at the museum for a schedule of appearances.

ROCKY MOUNTAIN NATIONAL PARK, MORAINE PARK VISITOR CENTER

From Estes Park drive 2 miles west on Colorado 36 to park entrance, then follow directional signs within the

Margie's big leg bones provided a chance to see just how a twenty or thirty pound hammerstone, with or without a stone anvil, splintered the bone so that fragments could be shaped into tools. Dennis Stanford was on hand to join in experiments with bone. The archeologists also peered through microscopes at their tools after they had used them, to find out how wear had affected the implements.

Here scientists in Denver engage in experimental archeology as they butcher a 9,480 pound dead elephant using replicas of the prehistoric tools that Paleo hunters of mammoths used 13,000 years ago. This study became known as the Denver Elephant Project. Photo courtesy of Dr. Bruce Rippeteau.

park 4 miles to Moraine Park Visitor Center, which is open free, daily, June to Sept. Admission charged to the park. Camping.

The main exhibit theme of the museum is change brought about by glaciers, beavers, and people. On display are some artifacts made by prehistoric people in the area, who may have been ancestral to the Utes and Arapahoes of historic times.

TRINIDAD STATE JUNIOR COLLEGE MUSEUM

Library Bldg., on the campus, Trinidad. Open free, Monday through Saturday when the college is in session.

Here on display along with ethnological materials are archeological exhibits from the Trinidad area and also from the Southern Plains and the Texas Panhandle. The early history, geology, paleontology, and anthropology of the local region are shown in detail. A diorama shows the Trinchera Rock Shelter with artifacts which date from the Archaic period.

UNIVERSITY OF COLORADO MUSEUM

On the campus, Henderson Bldg., Boulder. Open free, Monday through Friday. Closed certain holidays.

The Hall of Man in this museum includes numerous displays that illuminate North American prehistory, particularly in the Plains area and the Southwest.

One exhibit dramatizes a mass bison kill at the Olsen-Chubbuck Site in Colorado, which was excavated under the direction of Joe Ben Wheat, the museum's curator of anthropology. In this dig archeologists exposed about 200 bison skeletons and recovered 27 projectile points and a few stone tools. That, plus a study of the terrain, was all Dr. Wheat and his colleagues needed for putting together a complete scientific detective story.

The Story. In May or June about 6500 B.C. a band of perhaps 150 hunting people sighted a herd of buffalo. Because the wind was blowing toward the hunters, the animals were not alarmed. This gave time for men, women, and children to station them-

selves in two long lines leading up to a steep-banked arroyo. With the trap arranged, a few men stampeded the buffalo across the prairie, between the lines, straight into the gulch, where they were killed either by the fall or by hunters' spears.

Butchering and feasting started immediately. Tongues and tender favorite cuts were eaten first, while the tough parts were dried for future use. Probably the fresh meat lasted for three weeks before it spoiled. After that the band moved on, carrying loads of preserved meat and fat to eat until the next big kill.

A few of the clues to the story are these. Buffalo calves are born in May or June, and the calf skeletons at the site were those of animals only a few days old. Projectile points told the approximate century of the kill; they were similar to points found at other sites which had been dated by the radiocarbon method. The positions of skeletons in the arroyo led to reconstruction of the stampede procedure. All of the big bones were laid in more or less orderly piles after the meat was cut off, but tongue bones were scat-

Paleo-Indian Big-Game Hunters of the Plains used these projectile points: Midland (left); Hell Gap (center); and Scottsbluff (right). Redrawn from Irwin and Wormington.

Outlines of Kokopelli, the humpbacked flute player, appear in many places throughout the Southwest, but never before 1981 had anyone discovered the mythological figure on the floor of a kiva. Here is what Joe Ben Wheat found in a dig at Yellow Jacket, Colorado. University of Colorado Museum photo by Joe Ben Wheat.

tered about, suggesting that people ate the fresh tongues as they worked. The size of the band was estimated by calculating the amount of meat cut from the carcasses, taking into account how much of it could be eaten fresh and how much was tough and had to be dried for future use.

The Olsen-Chubbuck display is one of many in the museum. Others are devoted to the Fremont and Anasazi cultures. One exhibit shows how archeologists have been able to determine the age of material found at Southwestern sites by the use of tree-ring dating. Another display presents various types of Hopi kachina dolls.

Special Interest. The Anasazi material on exhibit was collected by Earl Morris, famous for his archeological work in the Southwest and Yucatan. His papers are in the custody of the museum, and his biography has been written by Robert Lister, formerly a member of the Anthropology Department of the University of Colorado, in collaboration with Mrs. Lister.

UTE TRAIL

Rocky Mountain National Park. From Estes Park drive 2 miles west on Colorado 36 to park entrance, then follow directional signs to Trail Ridge Road. Open free, daily, in summer when Trail Ridge Road is open. Admission charged to the park. Camping nearby.

This ancient Indian trail crosses Trail Ridge Road above timberline. It is possible to explore the trail for some distance on foot, following cairns which mark a portion of the route which prehistoric Utes took when they crossed the continental divide in this area.

Visitors should stop at Park Headquarters for a map and directions to the trailhead.

Kansas

BARTON COUNTY HISTORICAL SOCIETY

Main St. across River Bridge, Great Bend. Museum open free, afternoons, Tuesday through Sunday, May through Dec. Closed certain holidays.

On display here are dioramas and archeological material from Barton County, covering the period from Folsom times until contact with Europeans.

BENEDICTINE COLLEGE MUSEUM

Science Hall, on the north campus, Atchison. Open only by appointment.

Here are Hopewellian artifacts from Easton, Kan., from Weston, Mo., and from the important Renner Site in Kansas City, Mo. Other materials come from a village site in Doniphan, Kan., and from a Mimbres site in the Southwest.

This diorama in the Pawnee Indian Village Museum in Kansas depicts a moment of contact between White traders and a Pawnee village group. Kansas State Historical Society photo.

CLINTON LAKE VISITOR CENTER

As this book went to press the Army Corps of Engineers was planning a Visitor Center at the dam that forms the lake, just outside Lawrence, with exhibits explaining the archeology of the area which will be covered by the lake water.

EL CUARTELEJO RUINS
(See Lake Scott State Park)

ELLSWORTH COUNTY MUSEUM (HODGDEN HOUSE)

Main St., Ellsworth. Open free, Tuesday through Saturday; afternoons, Sunday.

One room here is devoted to about 20 replicas of petroglyphs which prehistoric Indians pecked in sandstone outcroppings in central Kansas. Some prehistoric artifacts are also on display.

A number of the figures in the petroglyphs represent animals. Although their exact meaning is not known, archeologists have speculated that they may be of religious significance. Quite possibly the petroglyphs were symbols of the visions young men had or sought during their guardian spirit quests.

HILLSDALE LAKE PROJECT

From Paola drive north on US 169 to Hillsdale exit. Information Center open free, daily, all year.

Excavation at this site, now covered by water, revealed occupation at different periods: between 5000 and 4000 B.C. (Nebo Hill Culture); through the Late Archaic and Plains Woodland to about A.D. 1300. Exhibits in the Visitor Center, maintained by the Army Corps of Engineers which constructed the Hillsdale dam, include graphic displays of the history of the various peoples who inhabited the site.

INDIAN BURIAL PIT

From either Niles exit or Camp Webster Corner exit on Interstate 70, near Salina, follow directional signs to the site. Or from Salina follow directional signs on old US 40, now Kansas 140, about 4 miles to the site. Open daily, all year. Admission charged. Camping nearby.

El Cuartelejo, the only known
Indian pueblo in Kansas, as it may
have looked when it was occupied at
the time of contact with a Spanish
expedition. Drawing courtesy Scott
State Park.

More than a thousand years ago,
farming people built a little village
here near the Smoky Hill River. They
were not especially wealthy, but they
did make a practice of burying gifts
with the dead—shell ornaments, stone
tools, and sometimes a piece of pottery. Graves in their cemetery came
to light after modern farmers began
to cultivate the land. More than 140
of these have been meticulously excavated and protected inside a building,
so that visitors may now see the burials just as they were found.

Excavation at the village site has
only begun. However, enough is
known about it and similar ham-
lets along the river to give a general
picture of the Smoky Hill lifeway.
Houses were sturdy structures of poles
against which earth or sod was banked.
The men did some hunting of deer
and antelope and bison to supplement
the crops that were raised in garden
plots. For winter use, corn, beans,
and sunflower seeds were stored in
grass-lined, underground caches.

Indian Burial Pit, which is operated
as a private commercial enterprise, is
known in archeological literature as

the Whiteford Site, or the Price Site,
named for successive owners. No place
in Kansas has been more carefully preserved to give a glimpse into the past.

KANSAS HISTORICAL SOCIETY

Memorial Bldg., 120 W. 10th St.,
Topeka. Open free, Monday through
Saturday; afternoons, Sunday. Closed
certain holidays.

In a gallery devoted to Kansas Indians are dioramas of Indian life and
displays of archeological specimens
from Paleo, Archaic, Middle Woodland, and Central Plains cultures.

LAKE SCOTT STATE PARK

From Scott City drive north 12 miles
on US 83, then 3 miles west on Kansas 95. Open daily, all year. Admission charged to the park. Camping.

Here may be seen the ruins of a
small pueblo, known as El Cuartelejo,
built by Taos Indian refugees who in
1664 escaped from Spanish rule in
New Mexico and joined a band of
Plains Apache. There are interpretive
markers at the site.

The Pawnee Indian Village Museum in Republic County, Kansas, is constructed over and around the remains of a large Indian dwelling. The village of which it was a part was in use during historic times, but it closely resembled those of prehistoric times. The museum building is designed to resemble a Pawnee earth lodge, and it houses artifacts recovered in the course of excavating the site. Kansas State Historical Society photo.

McPHERSON COUNTY OLD MILL MUSEUM

120 Mill St., Lindsborg. Open Tuesday through Saturday; afternoons, Sunday. Closed certain holidays. Admission charged.

On display here are prehistoric artifacts, some from the period when Coronado was exploring nearby, in search of Quivira.

PAWNEE INDIAN VILLAGE MUSEUM

From Belleville drive 15 miles west on US 36, then 7 miles north on Kansas 266. Open free, Tuesday through Saturday; afternoons, Sunday. Closed certain holidays.

Here on the carefully excavated site of a Pawnee village, is a museum which the Kansas Historical Society has constructed over and around the remains of a large dwelling. Although the village was inhabited after the arrival of Europeans, it closely resembled those of prehistoric times.

Like many other people of the Central Plains, the Pawnees and their pre-decessors lived a divided life. Twice a year the entire community picked up and left for buffalo country, to the west. During the buffalo hunts they camped in tipis. Afterward they returned to their home base, a settlement of perhaps 20 huge, circular houses built near the fields where they raised corn, beans, and squash. Each of these dwellings, called earth lodges because the framework of logs was covered with blocks of sod, sheltered as many as 40 people.

In the museum building, which somewhat resembles an earth lodge, display cases contain artifacts recovered in the course of excavating the site. Outside the museum a walk takes the visitor past underground storage pits and lodge floors.

RICE COUNTY HISTORICAL MUSEUM

221 East Ave. South, Lyons. Open free, Tuesday through Saturday; afternoons, Sunday. Closed certain holidays.

Here is material from the Quivira Indians who lived in the area when Coronado entered it in 1541.

RONIGER MEMORIAL MUSEUM

In Cottonwood Falls, on Courthouse Square, Union and Oak streets. Open free, Tuesday, Wednesday, Friday through Sunday. Closed certain holidays.

Displayed here is a large number of artifacts from the surrounding area, some collected by two brothers excavating on their farm near Cottonwood Falls.

STERNBERG MEMORIAL MUSEUM

On the campus, Fort Hays State University, Hays. Open free, Monday through Friday; afternoons, during vacations. Closed certain holidays.

Some exhibits here include prehistoric Indian materials.

UNIVERSITY OF KANSAS, MUSEUM OF ANTHROPOLOGY

Dyche Hall, on the campus, Lawrence. Open free, Monday through Saturday; afternoons, Sunday.

Official university expeditions on the Great Plains produced most of the archeological material on display here. Dioramas show reconstructions of activities of prehistoric people.

Manitoba

BANNOCK POINT PETROFORM SITE
(Formerly Ojibway Boulder Mosaics)

In Whiteshell Provincial Park. From Trans-Canada Highway 7 at the Manitoba-Ontario border, which is also the border of the park, drive about 20 miles west on Manitoba 44, then follow Manitoba 307 about 20 miles north to the site. Open from about the third weekend in May to about the last weekend in Sept. Admission charged to the park. Camping.

Exposed here are granite expanses which are interesting because the rock is perhaps the oldest in the world. It was scoured clear of soil by glaciers of the Ice Age. This bare granite serves as a background for large designs, called petroforms, which prehistoric people laid out, using both small rocks and huge boulders which had been pushed along by glaciers and left when the ice melted. Some of the designs are geometric; others are effigies, which include turtles and snakes. The snakes vary in length from a few feet to about 300 feet. One human figure is 90 feet long.

Who built the effigies and when is not known. Estimates, based on slight evidence, date them variously at a few hundred years ago or at as much as 3000 years ago.

Recent studies have shown that some of the stones are aligned to the summer solstice and to a point one lunar month past the summer solstice.

In addition to these visitable effigies, there are many others in Whiteshell Provincial Park which are not accessible to the public.

Above and opposite:
Figures and designs, outlined on the ground with rocks, were made by
prehistoric people in Manitoba. Called petroforms, they are of unknown age
and meaning. Manitoba government photo.

A close-up view of one of the petroforms in Whiteshell Provincial Park, Manitoba. Manitoba government photo.

The Museum. Near the petroforms a log building houses exhibits of tools, weapons, and ornaments made by prehistoric inhabitants of the area.

MANITOBA MUSEUM OF MAN AND NATURE

190 Rupert Ave., Winnipeg. Open Monday through Saturday; afternoons, Sunday and holidays. Admission charged.

Displays here center around the relation of people to their environment—in the arctic, subarctic, boreal forest, parkland, and grassland areas. Used in the exhibits are materials from a far-northern culture known as pre-Dorset, from burial mounds, and from Eskimo sites. Paleo-Indian and Copper culture artifacts are also featured, along with rock paintings and boulder effigies.

OJIBWAY BOULDER MOSAICS
(See Bannock Point Petroform Site)

UNIVERSITY OF WINNIPEG, ANTHROPOLOGY MUSEUM

515 Portage Ave., Winnipeg. Open free, daily.

Archeological exhibits in this museum concentrate on prehistory in the Boreal Forest and Northern Plains areas.

WHITESHELL PARK
(See Bannock Point Petroform Site)

Montana

GALLATIN COUNTY COURT HOUSE
(GAL-ah-tun)

Bozeman. Open free, Monday through Friday.

In the second floor lobby is a collection of artifacts from the Madison Buffalo Jump, together with a display of projectile points from other sources.

The hunting technique of driving buffalo herds over a cliff and then harvesting the meat began among the Indians about 4000 years ago. At Madison Buffalo Jump, a Montana State Archeological Site, there is much information about this ancient practice. Montana Fish and Game Department photo.

MAC'S MUSEUM OF NATURAL HISTORY

At Powder River County High School, Broadus. Open free, on request at any hour, any day.

This private collection includes more than 4000 Indian items, some of which are prehistoric. A few are like artifacts which have been radio-carbon dated at about 2500 B.C. Others are more recent. Most of the Montana material has come from bison traps in Powder River country.

MADISON BUFFALO JUMP

From Interstate 90 at Logan drive 7 miles south on a local road to Visitor Center. Open free, at all times.

On the eastern approaches to the Rocky Mountains, between central Wyoming and southern Alberta, several hundred places have been found where Indians killed bison by driving them over cliffs or bluffs. More than half of these sites are in Montana. The Madison Buffalo Jump is one of the first to be preserved and prepared for the public.

Whenever possible, Indians chose for the drive a gently rising stretch of prairie ending in a steep dropoff, which the bison could not see until it was too late to turn back. To guide the animals' approach, the hunters set up piles of rocks in two lines—far apart on the open prairie and funneling in toward the cliff. At some jumps the lines stretched out for as much as two miles. The rock piles were often large enough to conceal and protect the men who would spring up suddenly, wave blankets, and frighten the bison on toward the jump. Smaller rock piles would support a pole with something attached to flutter in the wind. Once started into the funnel, a herd ran faster and faster, then plunged over the brink. Any animals that were not killed by the fall could be dispatched with weapons.

In some places, where the jump was not very high, hunters might build a sort of corral, or pound, at the foot of the embankment. This would contain the bison until they could be killed with spears or shot with arrows.

At Madison Buffalo Jump, archeologists found evidence that Indians made

Figures and designs outlined on the ground with rocks, were made by prehistoric people in Manitoba. Called petroforms, they are of unknown age.

A Plains Indian Garden

A living garden can scarcely be prehistoric, but it can be a reasonable facsimile of an ancient Indian's vegetable patch—provided the modern gardener can find authentic seeds. Most varieties of vegetables grown today are very different from the ancestral plants which Indians cultivated. The new, improved types of corn, beans, and squash have become so widely used that the older types have almost disappeared. To save them from extinction became the hobby of Charles E. Hanson, Jr., an engineer in the U.S. Department of Agriculture. With the help of his wife and children, he collected and planted seeds of the old-time varieties, some of them rare or even the last in existence. Now a flourishing garden which resembles those of the Plains Indians is sponsored by the Nebraska Historical Society. It can be seen at the Museum of the Fur Trade, three miles east of Chadron, Nebraska, on US 20.

---

their last drive about 200 years ago. They may have used it at intervals for about 2000 years before that.

Nearby stand dozens of tipi rings—stones arranged in circles, supposedly to hold down the edges of skin tipis. Here the hunters camped while they butchered and dried the buffalo meat, cured the skins, and made implements of bone and horn. As they worked they feasted. Some of the meat they roasted over fires, and some they stewed in skin containers. To make a stew a woman filled a skin pouch with water, then heated it and kept it boiling by dropping hot rocks into it. Many of these rocks have been found at the site.

At the top of the cliff are other tipi rings. Perhaps these mark shelters for lookouts who watched for bison or for enemies. Other small stone enclosures are something of a mystery here, as they are elsewhere on the Plains. Some archeologists think they may have been eagle traps. Covered with brush they could conceal a man who waited for an eagle to dive for bait—perhaps a rabbit—fastened outside. When the bird struck, the man could seize its legs.

The stone enclosures may equally well have been shelters for young men who were fasting and seeking religious visions. Indians in historic times said they were fireplaces used in smoke signaling.

MONTANA STATE UNIVERSITY, MUSEUM OF THE ROCKIES

On the campus, South Seventh and Kagy Blvd., Bozeman. Open free, Monday through Friday; afternoons, Saturday, Sunday. Closed certain holidays.

The museum interprets the natural, social, and technological heritage of Montana, Idaho, Utah, and parts of adjacent states and Canadian provinces. Among the exhibits are materials excavated by Montana State University archeologists. Of special importance is the skeleton of an imperial mammoth, discovered by a farmer who noticed fragments of tusk eroding from a borrow pit along a county road and called the site to the attention of archeologists. Marks on the bones, and the fact that the skull had been bashed in and the thigh bones piled

on top of one another, indicate that hunters came upon an animal that was dead or dying and butchered it, about 11,700 years ago.

MUSEUM OF THE ROCKIES
(See Montana State University)

PICTOGRAPH CAVE STATE MONUMENT

From Billings drive southwest toward Hardin across an overpass, then turn right and follow directional signs about 7 miles to monument entrance. Open free, at all times. Camping nearby.

When this large cave was discovered in 1937 its most obvious features were the pictographs on its walls—designs and figures of men and animals painted in red, white, and black. Interesting though these were, material that was even more valuable to archeologists lay in the cave floor. When they dug down through 23 feet of earth and debris that had accumulated there, they uncovered evidence of at least three different periods of occupation.

An exhibit in the Museum of the Rockies: bones of a mammoth from a kill site in Central Montana. Cut marks on the bones and the way some bones were broken indicate that the animal was butchered by people.

The first visitors were hunters who took shelter in the cave perhaps 5000 years ago. Next came hunters who made baskets, ornaments, and later the paintings on the cave walls. The upper layers of trash indicated the presence of still other hunters in late prehistoric times.

After Pictograph Cave had been excavated, a museum and trail for visitors were prepared. Unfortunately the museum was vandalized, but the paintings, still in fair shape, are worth a visit.

Nebraska

ASH HOLLOW STATE PARK

From Ogalalla drive 22 miles northwest on US 26 to directional sign for park entrance. Open free, in daylight hours, all year. Visitor Center open daily, May 24 through Labor Day. Camping.

Exhibits in the Visitor Center explain the use during Paleo times and by later prehistoric hunters of rockshelters in what is now the park.

FORT ROBINSON MUSEUM

Fort Robinson, 4 miles west of Crawford on US 20. Open free, Monday through Saturday; afternoons, Sunday; April 1 through Nov. 15. By appointment, winter.

Exhibits include the story of prehistoric peoples' occupation of the Great Plains. A free, guided tour includes the Red Cloud Indian Agency Site. A Trailside Museum of Natural History exhibits the skeleton of a mammoth and other features of the environment in which prehistoric Indians lived.

HASTINGS MUSEUM

1330 N. Burlington Ave., Hastings. Open Monday through Saturday; afternoons, Sunday and holidays. Admission charged.

Some prehistoric artifacts are exhibited here along with historic Indian material.

An exhibit in the Museum of the Nebraska State Historical Society, Lincoln, shows the interior of a reconstructed Pawnee earth lodge. At the right are a paddle and a round bullboat made from a framework covered with buffalo hide. The kettle is from contact times. Nebraska State Historical Society photo.

NEBRASKA STATE HISTORICAL SOCIETY

1500 R St., Lincoln. The museum is open free, Monday through Saturday; afternoons, Sunday.

Various prehistoric periods in Nebraska are represented here in exhibits and dioramas.

PLATTE RIVER MUSEUM

203 East 6 St., Cozad. Open free, Sunday through Friday, May through Oct.; afternoons, Sunday through Friday, Nov. through April. Closed all of Jan. and certain holidays.

Exhibits include material from the Platte River area and various Wyoming sites.

UNIVERSITY OF NEBRASKA STATE MUSEUM

Morrill Hall, 14th St., on the city campus, Lincoln. Open free, Monday through Saturday; afternoons, Sunday and holidays.

A systematic collection of Nebraska artifacts, including stone tools, bone tools, and pottery, is available for study in the newly developed Encounter Room. These artifacts may be compared with specimens brought by the visitor or with materials in a "Discovery" box available from a staff member in the room.

An excavated block from the Lipscomb site, a Folsom-period bison kill in the Texas Panhandle, is on exhibit on the main floor. The cast of a Folsom point among the bones marks the spot where the real point was found.

The Lipscomb Site seemed puzzling at first. There the skeletons of a dozen bison lay in a very small area, most of them facing in the same direction and actually overlapping each other. In among the bones were projectile points, scrapers, stone knives, and charcoal from fires. Had hunters managed to lay out their game so neatly? If so, why—and why the charcoal?

Probably, the archeologists decided, the Indians had simply been lucky enough to find the animals caught in a deep snowdrift, huddled together and headed away from the wind. After the kill, the hunters apparently built fires, made camp on the spot, took some of the meat, but left most of the carcasses as they had fallen.

North Dakota

DOUBLE DITCH INDIAN VILLAGE STATE HISTORIC SITE

From Bismarck drive north on US 83 to marker. Open free, at all times.

One of the largest Mandan villages in North Dakota once stood here, on the east bank of the Missouri River. Apparently the site had been abandoned by 1804, when Lewis and Clark visited the area. The outlines of earth lodges, refuse heaps, and two dry fortification ditches are clearly visible. A shelter has been constructed by the State Historical Society to protect maps, drawings, and a description of the site.

FORT CLARK STATE HISTORIC SITE

From the intersection of North Dakota 48 and US 200A, drive 1 mile east,

Like their prehistoric ancestors, Mandan Indians lived in round earth lodges along the Missouri River in North Dakota. A. When the artist George Catlin visited them in 1832 they allowed him to watch and sketch their ceremonies. From Catlin's *Eight Years,* Vol. 1.

then 1 mile north to Fort Clark. The site is just north of the post office. Open free, at all times.

A Mandan village was standing here when Fort Clark was built, in 1829. The location of the village is clearly visible, and a small shelter constructed by the State Historical Society contains maps and a description of the area. The Mandans here all died in a smallpox epidemic in 1837. Arikara Indians occupied the site after that date.

HUFF INDIAN VILLAGE STATE HISTORIC SITE

From Interstate 94 at Mandan drive south on North Dakota 1806 to Huff, on the west bank of the Missouri River. The site is one mile south of Huff. Open free, at all times.

A marker describes the large Mandan village which once stood here. The rectangular outlines of individual house sites are clearly visible, as is a dry moat. At one time, in addition to the moat, there was a protective palisade, along which ten bastions were built.

KNIFE RIVER INDIAN VILLAGES NATIONAL HISTORIC SITE

From Stanton follow directional signs north on local road to visitor contact station. Open free, all year. Camping nearby.

At three major sites in the area—Big Hidatsa, Lower Hidatsa, and Sakakawea—earth lodge rings of prehistoric villages are still visible, and one travois trail is well defined. The National Park Service, which is developing an interpretive program for visitors, offers guided tours.

By using a remote sensing device called a magnetometer, archeologists have been able to locate at one site a number of earth lodges that were buried, completely out of sight, underneath later earth lodges. The early villages were made up of small rectangular lodges, occupied by Hidatsa and Mandan people. These were later replaced by circular lodges, of which there were more than 100 in the largest villages. Archeologists estimate that at the time Europeans arrived, there were probably more people living along the Missouri River in North

Tipi Rings

This circle, the significance of which is unknown, is outlined in boulders in Stutsman County, North Dakota. Redrawn from *American Anthropologist*.

One form of evidence of human presence on the Northern Plains is a large number of sites where Indians collected stones and laid them in circles. There are perhaps half a million of these circles in the Canadian province of Alberta alone. What were they for? Many archeologists think that the stones held down the edges of tents or tipis. Hence the name "tipi rings." Some rings, however, seem too small for tipis. Were they made to hold down children's play tents? Or were they small tipis in which medicine men held ceremonies? Other rings seem too big and elaborate for tipis. Did they have ritual significance? That was certainly true of other outlines made of rocks in the shape of animals, men, and women.

Aerial photography in the Central Plains has disclosed another type of ring made by digging a circular trench and heaping the earth into a mound inside the ring. Each such circle seems to have had a central position at a village site, and each one has signs of breaks in the circle at just the spots where the sun's rays would fall at sunrise at the time of the equinoxes. Were they calendar rings? Some archeologists think so.

Dakota than live there today. These villagers were successful farmers, with cultivated fields along terraces above streams. They also fished and hunted small and large game and engaged in a great deal of trade with Indians to the west.

With Europeans came diseases which killed as many as two-thirds of the population, and by 1862 the villages along the Knife River had been abandoned.

There seems to be no evidence for any major epidemics in the Americas before Europeans brought in measles, smallpox, and other diseases. One reason, archeologists think, may have been that New World villages had better sanitation that those in the Old World, because they lacked large numbers of penned-up, disease-carrying, domesticated animals.

MEDICINE ROCK STATE HISTORIC SITE

From Elgin on North Dakota 21, drive 8 miles south on local road. Open free, at all times.

At this site, preserved by the North Dakota Historical Society, are petroglyphs carved on a large rock and what is called a "dance ring," 200 feet in diameter.

MENOKEN INDIAN VILLAGE STATE HISTORIC SITE

From Menoken on Interstate 94 drive 1¼ miles north on county road. Open free, at all times.

A marker describes this former Mandan village which occupied 14 acres. House sites and a dry moat are clearly visible.

MOLANDER INDIAN VILLAGE STATE HISTORIC SITE

From Interstate 94 at Mandan drive north on North Dakota 1806 on the west bank of the Missouri River to Price. The site is 3 miles north of Price. Open free, at all times.

Here, clearly visible, are the remains of an earth-lodge village, which was once surrounded by a dry moat.

NORTH DAKOTA HERITAGE CENTER
(See State Historical Society Museum)

SLANT INDIAN VILLAGE

Fort Lincoln State Park. From Mandan drive 4 miles south on North Dakota 1806. Open free, daily, all year. Camping nearby.

Mandan Indians, who were living at this site about A.D. 1750, chose an unusual location for their houses. Instead of building on level ground, they placed their dwellings on a slope. Hence the name Slant Village. Five of the dwellings have been restored and are much like the circular earth lodges of late prehistoric times.

The Indian collection in the museum interprets the history of North Dakota tribes, with special attention to Mandan agriculture, hunting, home activities, and social life.

The Story. At some unknown date, perhaps a thousand years ago, people began to cultivate gardens around little communities along the Missouri River in central North Dakota. They grew sunflowers, beans, squash, and

A Plains Indian tipi of this kind was easily put up and taken down. After Spanish horses became common on the Plains it was possible to have large tipis carried from place to place. Before that dogs were trained to carry smaller burdens. Photo National Museum of Man, Ottawa.

a remarkable variety of corn. Ordinary corn is a plant that needs warm temperatures and a long growing season. Certainly this was the kind the Indians first tried to raise in this cool, northern climate. They must have been disappointed and hungry very often before they managed to develop a new variety, which ripened in only a little more than two months.

Perhaps it was the ancestors of the Mandans who became corn experts. At any rate, they were prosperous farmers when white traders first met them here and at other large, neighboring villages. By 1837, as the result of a devastating epidemic of smallpox that spread to the villages from a passenger on a river boat, only a few Mandans remained.

Special Interest. Fort Lincoln was the headquarters of Lt. Col. George Custer, whose campaign against the Plains Indians ended in his defeat at the battle of the Little Bighorn in Montana.

STANDING ROCK STATE HISTORIC SITE

From the town of Ft. Ransom drive one mile west on local road to the site. Open free, at all times.

At this site is a complex of burial mounds dating from Woodland times. The rock, which in historic times has been considered sacred by Sioux (Dakota) Indians, is shaped like an inverted cone and stands in the midst of the mounds.

STATE HISTORICAL SOCIETY MUSEUM

In North Dakota Heritage Center, off Court Rd., State Capitol grounds, Bismarck. Open free, Monday through Saturday, all year; afternoons. Sunday, June through Aug. Closed certain holidays.

This museum has conducted excavations for many years, and its exhibits reflect its work. Among its activities has been salvage archeology, aimed at saving valuable information before it was lost under rising water behind dams on the Missouri. Now in a new location in the Heritage Center, its developing exhibits include one on the exploitations of the bison by Native Americans and, in the historic period, by Europeans.

WRITING ROCK STATE HISTORIC SITE

From the junction of US 85 and North Dakota 5, drive west to Fortuna, then southwest on county road to the site. Or from Grenora on North Dakota 50 drive north on county road. Open free, at all times.

Here the State Historical Society preserves two large glacial boulders, on which are carved Indian petroglyphs probably representing the mythical thunderbird.

A mammoth kill site was excavated at Domebo, in Oklahoma, by the Museum of the Great Plains. This is an artist's conception of how the kill took place, displayed in a diorama at the museum. Museum of the Great Plains photo.

Oklahoma

A. D. BUCK MUSEUM OF SCIENCE AND HISTORY
(See Northern Oklahoma College)

ARROWHEAD MUSEUM

On West 24 St., ¼ mile west of Murray State College, Tishomingo. Open free, daily.

Collections of prehistoric Native American stone artifacts are on exhibit.

CHISHOLM TRAIL MUSEUM AND GOVERNOR SEAY MANSION

605 Zellers Ave., Kingfisher. Open free, Monday through Saturday; afternoons, Sunday. Closed certain holidays.

In this primarily historical museum are exhibits of prehistoric Indian material.

CHOCTAW TRAIL OF TEARS MUSEUM

In Eagletown 6 miles east of Broken Bow, off Interstate 70. Open April 30 to Labor Day, Monday through Saturday; afternoons, Sunday. Admission charged.

The museum is in the former home of Choctaw Chief Jefferson Gardner. Prehistoric Native American artifacts are included in the exhibits.

CREEK INDIAN MUSEUM

On the Town Square, Okmulgee. Open free, Tuesday through Saturday. Closed certain holidays.

In the archeology room are displays of prehistoric artifacts of the Caddoan culture and material which was excavated from the Eufaula and Spiro Mounds.

CULTURAL CENTER MUSEUM

1000 East Grand Ave., Ponca City. Open free, Monday and Wednesday through Saturday; afternoons, Sunday. Closed certain holidays.

Housed in the municipally owned former mansion of an oil millionaire, the museum features an archeological laboratory and collections of historic and prehistoric Native American artifacts.

EAST CENTRAL COLLEGE MUSEUM

East Central College Library, Ada. Open free, Monday through Friday; by appointment, Saturday, Sunday. Closed certain holidays.

Exhibits in this museum are devoted to the Anasazi culture of the Southwest, the archeology of Texas and Arkansas, and six sites in Oklahoma, all dated at about 1000 years ago. One display presents prehistoric carvings and a reproduction of a painted wall in a cave about 6 miles from Ada. Another identifies different types of projectile point from various parts of the United States, and gives the time periods during which they were used. There is also an exhibit showing how prehistoric Indians made artifacts of stone.

RISE AND DECLINE OF THE
WICHITA INDIANS

From contact with Coronado in 1541, the Wichita slowly drifted south across Oklahoma to Spanish Fort on the Red River by 1750. In 1834, a small group lived at Devil's Canyon.

An exhibit in Museum of the Great Plains, Lawton, Oklahoma. Museum of the Great Plains photo.

INDIAN CITY, U.S.A.

From Anadarko drive 2 miles south on Oklahoma 8. Open daily, all year. Admission charged. Camping.

Here visitors may see reconstructions of various house types which were common in early historic and late prehistoric times. In a kind of large outdoor museum the living arrangements of the Navajo, Chiricahua Apache, Wichita, Kiowa, Caddo, Pawnee, and Pueblo Indians are brought to life. Many of the houses are furnished with typical tools, household equipment, toys, weapons, and musical instruments. A herd of buffalo grazes in a pasture adjoining the Indian City grounds.

An indoor museum contains material, some of it prehistoric, which supplements the outdoor exhibits.

All buildings here were constructed under the supervision of the Department of Anthropology, University of Oklahoma. Indians serve as guides through the outdoor area.

KERR MUSEUM

From Poteau drive 7 miles southwest on US 271. Open Monday through Friday; afternoons, Saturday and Sunday, April to Dec. Admission charged.

Exhibits of prehistoric Native American artifacts include a collection of materials from the Spiro Mounds, located about 20 miles northeast of Poteau.

MEMORIAL INDIAN MUSEUM

Allen and Second streets, Broken Bow. Open free, daily.

Exhibits include Native American artifacts from prehistoric times to the present. Especially interesting is the large collection of Caddoan pottery.

MUSEUM OF THE GREAT PLAINS

In Elmer Thomas Park, off US 62 West, in Lawton. Open free, Monday through Saturday; afternoons, Sunday. Closed certain holidays.

This museum offers exhibits of Paleo-Indian, Plains Archaic, and prehistoric Plains farmer materials. Some displays interpret the relationship between prehistoric peoples and the Plains environment. One diorama shows how women in a Wichita Indian village constructed a typical grass house. Another shows hunters who have trapped a mammoth. This is based on the museum's excavation of the Domebo (DUM-bo) Site, in Oklahoma, where a mammoth skeleton was recovered in association with artifacts. Dating of the bones indicated that hunters had killed the animal about 11,000 years ago. It was a female about 14 feet tall at the shoulder, and archeologists quipped that she may have had "a quarrelsome disposition," for the right shoulder had been previously broken, possibly in a fight with another mammoth.

A unique artifact on display is a naturally rounded ball of sandstone, in which human features have been pecked. This crudely sculptured head was found near Frederick, Oklahoma; it may be very old. It was discovered more than 15 feet below the surface

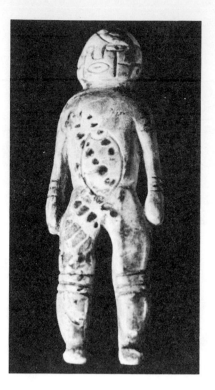

A shell figurine from Spiro Mounds. Department of Anthropology, University of Oklahoma, photo.

in a gravel bed, but unfortunately no datable material accompanied it, so archeologists can only speculate about its origin and age. Somewhat similar carvings, called the Malakoff Heads, are now in the Texas Memorial Museum, Austin, Texas.

MUSEUM OF THE RED RIVER

In Idabel (on US 70 bypass), 812 Southeast Lincoln. Open free, Tuesday through Saturday; afternoons, Sunday. Closed certain holidays.

Special exhibits from the museum's collection of archeological and anthropological materials are on display from time to time.

NO MAN'S LAND MUSEUM
(See Panhandle State University)

NORTHERN OKLAHOMA COLLEGE, A. D. BUCK MUSEUM OF SCIENCE AND HISTORY

1220 East Grand, on the campus, Tonkawa. Open free, Sunday through Friday. Closed during winter.

In this general museum are exhibits of prehistoric artifacts.

NORTHERN OKLAHOMA STATE UNIVERSITY MUSEUM

In Jesse Dunn Hall on the campus, Alfa. Open free, on request, Monday through Friday. Closed certain holidays. For appointment call (405) 327-1700.

The museum maintains research facilities in anthropology, archeology, natural history, and other disciplines. Activities include guided tours, films, and educational programs. Exhibits include Native American artifacts.

OKLAHOMA HISTORICAL SOCIETY

Lincoln Blvd., Capitol Complex, Oklahoma City. Open free, Monday through Saturday.

In this historical museum are several archeological exhibits. One is devoted to materials excavated at the Spiro Mounds, in eastern Oklahoma.

PANHANDLE STATE UNIVERSITY, NO MAN'S LAND MUSEUM

On the campus, Goodwell. Open free, Tuesday through Friday; afternoons, Saturday and Sunday. Closed certain holidays.

Archeological exhibits include Oklahoma Basketmaker material and artifacts of the Plains area, from Folsom times up to the contact period.

PHILBROOK ART CENTER

2727 S. Rockford Rd., Tulsa. Open Tuesday through Saturday; afternoons, Sunday. Closed certain holidays. Admission charged.

In this museum devoted to art there is Anasazi, Hohokam, Salado, and some Mimbres pottery.

SPIRO MOUNDS STATE ARCHAEOLOGICAL SITE
(SPY-roh)

11 miles east and north of Spiro on the Lock and Dam Rd. Open free, daily, all year. Closed certain holidays. Camping.

Above, left: Front and side views of a tobacco pipe made of clay, found at Spiro Mounds, in Oklahoma. The pipe represents a human sacrifice. After Hamilton. *Above, right:* Three of the many pots from Spiro Mound. Originals in the Stovall Museum, Norman, Oklahoma. *Below, left:* Prehistoric people often used masks in ceremonies. In the Southeast many were carved from wood. This one from Spiro Mounds is of red cedar, with shell inlays for eyes and mouth. Original in the Museum of the American Indian. *Below, center:* Mississippian people made intricate carvings on pieces of conch shell. Found at Spiro Mounds, this is in the Stovall Museum at the University of Oklahoma. *Below, right:* A gorget, a neck ornament, has the weeping-eye symbol which often appears in art of the Southeast. It was carved from conch shell and found at Spiro Mounds. Original in the Museum of the American Indian.

Lucifer Pipe from Spiro Mound,
University of Oklahoma Collection.
University of Oklahoma photo.

The Story. On the bank of the Arkansas River near what is now the town of Spiro, a remarkable village stood in late prehistoric times. Unlike the farming villages in the neighborhood, this one seems to have been inhabited by an elite group of priests and/or political leaders who somehow won the allegiance—and the labor—of large numbers of the farming people. Men and probably women from surrounding communities carried basketload after basketload of earth to build nine large mounds for their leaders. Some were topped with buildings—possibly temples or dwellings for priests. Others were burial mounds. At the same time a group of excellent craftsworkers developed and became particularly adept at carving intricate designs on conch shells, which came all the way from the Gulf of Mexico. Women fashioned beautiful pottery in a great variety of styles, and much of it was buried with the dead, together with other grave goods. The elaborately furnished Spiro burials were a rich storehouse of information about one way of living on this earth—

until the day when a modern farmer's plough exposed the handiwork of an earlier farming people.

Soon a business operation began. The Pocola Mining Company was formed to extract artifacts from the mounds for commercial sale. Using dynamite and road scoops the miners dug out great quantities of pottery, pearls, and other material which they transported by the wheelbarrow load to the roadside and sold. Before long the mounds had been gutted, to the modest enrichment of the diggers and to the enormous impoverishment of science.

Later, two amateur archeologists, Mr. and Mrs. Henry W. Hamilton, set about undoing what little of the damage could be undone. For 16 years they traced artifacts to their buyers and recovered them whenever possible. The result of this patient endeavor was a surprisingly large amount of material, which revealed a culture akin to, but also distinct from, the cultures at Etowah in Georgia and Moundville in Alabama.

Thanks to the Hamiltons and to various scientific excavations that

managed to glean data from part of the site not totally destroyed, it is now possible to get glimpses of Spiro culture. Here at the site are a reconstructed house, two reconstructed mounds, and a walking trail with interpretive plaques. In the Interpretive Center are exhibits of artifacts, some formerly in the Stovall Museum, and some replicas of material in other museums. Slide shows at the center are a good introduction to the site. Excavation goes on here from May through July, and visitors are invited to watch archeologists at work.

Collections of Spiro artifacts may be seen also in the Stovall Museum, the Oklahoma Historical Society Museum, the University of Arkansas Museum, and the National Museum of Natural History of the Smithsonian Institution.

STOVALL MUSEUM
(See University of Oklahoma)

The Pocola Mining Company made a business of vandalism at the Spiro Mounds Site. Here miners are destroying evidence of a fascinating culture as they dig in Craig Mound looking for goodies to sell. Photo courtesy Dr. William E. Bell and the University of Oklahoma Stovall Museum.

THOMAS GILCREASE INSTITUTE

2500 West Newton, Tulsa. Open free, Monday through Saturday; afternoons, Sunday and holidays. Closed Dec. 25.

The Thomas Gilcrease Institute of American History and Art has in three galleries extensive displays of American Indian artifacts from 12,000 years ago to the arrival of Europeans. The exhibits are arranged in chronological sequence, with one gallery containing Meso-American materials. One section illustrates techniques of manufacture; another, which is changed periodically, contains special exhibits of projectile points, pottery, and engraved shell. Displays may also compare artifacts in time or in geographic relationships. Material from specific sites includes Spiro Mounds in Oklahoma and the Snyders Site in Illinois.

UNIVERSITY OF OKLAHOMA, STOVALL MUSEUM

On the campus, 1335 Asp Ave., Norman. Open free, Monday through Fri-

day; afternoons, Saturday, Sunday. Closed certain holidays.

Permanent and changing exhibits drawn from the museum's extensive archeological collections focus on Oklahoma's Indian past. Materials are included from the first mammoth hunters to early contact sites of the historic Caddo and Wichita. Of particular interest are artifacts from the Spiro Mounds Site, including engraved shell, carved stone effigy pipes, and copper ornaments. Also displayed are artifacts from more recent American Indian people.

Among the museum's publications are pamphlets on the Domebo Site, the Packard Site, the Roy Smith Site, and the Spiro Mounds Site in the *Prehistoric People of Oklahoma* series.

WASHITA VALLEY MUSEUM

1100 North Ash St., Pauls Valley. Open free, Tuesday through Sunday afternoons.

Prehistoric and historic Native American artifacts are on display here.

WESTERN TRAILS MUSEUM

Just southwest of Clinton on US 66 and Interstate 40. Open free, daily, Monday through Saturday; afternoons, Sunday.

Although the museum is devoted primarily to pioneer White exhibits, it displays some prehistoric archeological material.

WOOLAROC MUSEUM
(WOOL-ah-rock)

From Bartlesville drive 14 miles southwest on Oklahoma 123 to entrance to the Frank Phillips Ranch, then 2 miles on ranch road to the museum. Open free, daily.

In addition to historic displays this museum tells the story of prehistoric people in America, particularly in Oklahoma. Included in the archeological exhibits are materials 3000 years old representing the Oklahoma Basketmaker culture in the neighborhood of Kenton. Several cases contain artifacts from the Spiro Mounds, from Washita culture sites in western Oklahoma, and from Hopewell culture sites

The Tales That Old Bones Tell

How old was this person when he died—and how do we know he was *he*? Specialists in the study of human bones can tell approximate age by the sawtooth-shaped edges of the various parts of the skull. At birth there are spaces between the skull bones. These spaces decrease at a known rate until, at about age 55, the parts are fused. A male skull usually has prominent eyebrow ridges and jaws; a female skull is usually more delicate. A female pelvic bone has a bigger opening (which facilitates childbirth) and a different shape. Children's arm and leg bones grow from the middle part outward toward the ends, and not until about age 15 in girls and later in boys are the center parts and the knobby ends completely fused. A child at birth has 270 bones, some of which fuse at a fairly regular rate until by adulthood the skeleton is made up of only 206 bones.

---

in northeastern Oklahoma. Other exhibits contain materials from Alaska and from the vicinity of Phoenix, Arizona.

The Name. Woolaroc comes from the first letters of *woods*, *lakes*, and *rocks*—all common in the surrounding landscape.

Special Interest. In rugged woodland adjoining the museum, herds of bison, elk, and deer graze just as they did in prehistoric times.

Saskatchewan

BATTLEFORD NATIONAL HISTORIC PARK

E. 13th St., Battleford. Open free, daily, May 1 through Thanksgiving weekend.

In addition to Cree and Sioux (Dakota) ethnological material, this museum displays some random local finds of prehistoric artifacts.

SASKATCHEWAN MUSEUM OF NATURAL HISTORY

Wascana Park, College Ave. and Albert St., Regina. Open free, daily, May through Sept.; Monday through Friday and afternoons, Saturday, Sunday, Oct. through April.

Here in the Hall of Man are ten cases devoted to prehistory in Saskatchewan. In addition to random local finds, there is considerable material from excavations conducted by the museum staff. Exhibits include artifacts from various periods and cultures from Paleo-Indian to historic times. Special displays pertain to hunting, religion, ceremonies, and customs.

South Dakota

BADLANDS NATIONAL MONUMENT

From Rapid City drive 75 miles east on Interstate 90, then 9 miles south on US 16A to Visitor Center. Or from Kadoka drive 18 miles west on Interstate 90 to US 16A, then 9 miles south to Visitor Center. Visitor Center is open free, daily, all year. Camping.

In the course of trying to stamp out a religious movement known as the Ghost Dance, which was spreading among Plains Indians, a unit of the U.S. Army arrested more than 250 Sioux three days after Christmas in 1890. All night these people, two-thirds of whom were women and children, camped at Wounded Knee Creek in South Dakota, surrounded by 500 soldiers. In the morning the soldiers disarmed the Sioux men and then proceeded to shoot indiscriminately, using rapid-fire guns. Almost all the unarmed captives were killed on the spot, but a few women escaped and ran for several miles before soldiers overtook and shot them. This was the massacre of Wounded Knee, and one of the two Indian exhibits in the Visitor Center here is devoted to it. The other exhibit traces Indian life in the Badlands from 10,000 years ago through the Woodland culture of about A.D. 500, the Village Indians of about A.D. 1500, and the Sioux of A.D. 1800.

Was a man a hunter or a farmer? Teeth can often give the clue. Eaters of tough meat wear down their teeth by middle adulthood. The teeth of those whose diets are chiefly bread or mush made from corn ground into meal on sandstone show different deterioration. They, too, are worn away, but before that happens they are likely to have many more cavities than do meat eaters' teeth.

Was this man a member of an upper or a lower class? The bone specialist at the Koster Site, Jane Buikstra, has studied the skeletons of men whose graves in nearby burial mounds contained artifacts of many kinds. She discovered that those whose elaborate grave goods indicated high status often had signs of arthritis in the elbow bones. Those in lower-class burials were likely to have arthritis in the hands. This means to her that upper-class men were hunters, whose elbows suffered from the use of spears or bows. Lower-class men were probably artisans, who used their hands for tool and weapon making.

CROW CREEK VILLAGE SITE

On the Crow Creek Indian Reservation, east of Ft. Thompson, off South Dakota 34. Open free, at all times.

This is one of the few large, prehistoric sites in the region that have not been covered by water impounded behind dams on the Missouri River. Excavation in the 1950s revealed that some of the large, earth-lodge dwellings that once stood here had been burned. Probably they were destroyed at the time of abandonment of the village, which was surrounded by two ditches, presumably for defense. Later, erosion at one side of the site exposed human bones, and archeologists returned in 1978 for further investigation. What they discovered was a mass burial of 500 or more men, women, and children. From detailed examination of many bones they were able to piece together the following story.

The dry summer of the year 1325 followed a long period of droughts. Indian farmers along Crow Creek and other tributaries of the Missouri River began to suffer from malnutrition as crops failed year after year. Here, as elsewhere, bones show dietary deficiency in several ways. In adults they may become pitted with small holes. A well-nourished child's arm and leg bones grow at a regular rate from the center portion outward toward the ends, but in times of famine, growth stops, and this interruption results in a detectable line. Alternating periods of adequate and inadequate diet show up in alternating areas of growth and tell-tale lines. At Crow Creek one youth's bones showed 14 such periods of malnutrition, and those of almost all the other children indicated four or five hungry years.

It was not hunger, however, that killed about a third of the village's inhabitants. Probably they were raided by starving neighbors, who found that the Crow Creek people had not yet finished the new moat and fortification around their homes. Desperate to get at stored food, the raiders massacred all who could not or did not flee. Later the survivors must have returned and buried their dead in one huge grave, then left forever.

A regular pattern of feuds or warfare among these farming people seems not to have developed. Rather the Crow Creek raid was probably an act of extreme desperation. Among themselves, scientists think, these Indians were cooperative and compassionate. Evidence for this is the number of skeletons of handicapped and crippled people who survived in the community until the raid.

Excavation by the University of South Dakota Archeology Laboratory has been completed, though study of the site goes on. The Army Corps of Engineers, which administers the Missouri River dams, will stabilize the eroded bluff, and may install an interpretive sign. Both the archeologists and the Crow Creek Indians have been pressing to have the site made a National Monument, and would welcome the support of the public to this end. Meantime the site is open to visitors. Souvenir hunting, however, is forbidden, and a guard is on hand for protection against looters.

This diorama shows Archaic people in a rockshelter in Texas. Texas Memorial Museum photo.

MITCHELL PREHISTORIC INDIAN VILLAGE

From South Dakota 37 at north edge of Mitchell, turn west on Cemetery Road. Proceed ¼ mile and turn north on Indian Village Rd., 0.7 mile to site. Open daily, June through Aug. Admission charged.

At this site of a mid-eleventh-century fortified farming community archeological research is going on. The project is funded jointly by the city and the federal government. Visitors may watch an archeological crew excavating. There are exhibits and video tapes, and guides will explain the site and the research.

OVER DAKOTA MUSEUM
(See University of South Dakota)

SHERMAN PARK INDIAN BURIAL MOUNDS

Sherman Park, West 22nd St. and Kiwanis Ave., Sioux Falls. Open free, at all times. Camping nearby.

In this municipal park are several mounds built by people who followed the Plains Woodland lifeway, 1600 years ago. One mound has been excavated by the W.H. Over Dakota Museum of the University of South Dakota. Material recovered by the dig, including artifacts and the skulls and large bones of four people, is at the museum at Vermillion.

SHRINE TO MUSIC MUSEUM
(See University of South Dakota)

SOUTH DAKOTA STATE HISTORICAL MUSEUM

Soldiers Memorial Bldg., Pierre. Open free, Monday through Saturday; afternoons, Sunday.

A fairly extensive exhibit of Indian artifacts, some of them prehistoric, can be seen in this essentially pioneer-history museum.

UNIVERSITY OF SOUTH DAKOTA, OVER DAKOTA MUSEUM

Clark and Yale streets, Vermillion. Open free, Monday through Saturday; afternoons, Sunday.

The W.H. Over Dakota Museum, in its Hall of Man, emphasizes the development of implements and their uses from Paleo times to the historic period. People who followed the Big-Game Hunters and the Archaic Foragers in this part of South Dakota began to build conical burial mounds. Later they built large rectangular houses in groups of 25 or more along terraces above major streams. These people certainly did some hunting, for they left implements made of buffalo bone. And they must have done some gardening, because one of their implements was the hoe made from the shoulder blade of the buffalo.

In many respects their lifeway, called the Middle Missouri, resembled that of the historic Plains Indians. But their pottery and their tobacco pipes were more characteristics of groups who lived to the east, in Wisconsin. Some archeologists think they may have been ancestors of the Mandans, who stopped here on their way westward.

Other exhibits are devoted to a much later people, who also combined elements of two cultures. Their life-

Henry Hertner (at left), an amateur archeologist, led the campaign to have the Alibates Flint Quarry made into a National Monument. In this area prehistoric Indians made projectile points, knives, and scrapers from multicolored flint that they found there in large deposits. Texas Highway Department photo.

way, called Coalescent, was studied at the Scalp Creek Site. A diorama of the Scalp Creek village shows round earth lodges surrounded by a stockade and a ditch.

UNIVERSITY OF SOUTH DAKOTA, SHRINE TO MUSIC MUSEUM

Clark and Yale streets, Vermillion. Open free, Monday through Saturday; afternoons, Sunday. Closed certain holidays.

In this museum's collection of North American musical instruments are some that are prehistoric.

WIND CAVE NATIONAL PARK

From Hot Springs drive 11 miles north on US 385. Or from Custer drive 19 miles south on US 385. Visitor Center open free, daily. Closed certain holidays. Camping May 15 through Oct. 1.

One exhibit case here includes Arikara and Mandan pottery and projectile points. There are also a few random finds of points and other artifacts from earlier periods.

Texas

ALABAMA-COUSHATTA INDIAN MUSEUM

From Livingston, drive 17 miles east on US 190 to the Alabama-Coushatta Reservation. Open free, Monday through Saturday; afternoons, Sunday.

This museum, on the only Indian reservation in Texas, has exhibits relating to the history of the Alabama and Coushatta tribes and of other Texas tribes as well. There is a continuous slide show.

ALIBATES FLINT QUARRIES AND TEXAS PANHANDLE PUEBLO CULTURE NATIONAL MONUMENT
(AL-ah-bates)

From Amarillo drive 35 miles northeast on US 136 to Alibates Rd., then 6 miles on Alibates Rd. to contact station. Open free, daily. Memorial Day through Labor Day. Visits to the prehistoric flint quarries are by guided tour only, and guides are available

daily, in season. During the off-season tours are by reservation only. Requests for reservations should be received at least 5 days before the tour date. Write to Superintendent, Lake Meredith Recreation Area, Box 1438, Fritch, TX 79036, giving date and number of persons in party. The tour is 1.3 miles round-trip, over rough terrain and loose stones.

The Story. Here above the Canadian River, Paleo-Indians found a large outcrop of excellent stone—a varicolored flint which has an easily recognized marbled appearance. About 12,000 years ago people began to quarry it for use in making projectile points, knives, and the scrapers with which they removed hair and tissue from hides. Many Clovis points used for hunting mammoths in New Mexico were made of Alibates flint. It remained popular with the Paleo-Indians who lived in the Texas Panhandle up to 7000 years ago. It was also sought by people who followed the Archaic lifeway at a later time. Hunters of the Woodland Period obtained flint at the quarries, and they left evidence of their presence nearby.

Natural hollows in the rock in these semiarid hills formed reservoirs or tanks that provided a water supply for prehistoric hunters in Texas. Photo Hueco Tanks State Park, Texas Parks and Wildlife Department.

About A.D. 1300, Plains Village Indians settled near the flint outcrop. Their dwellings, made of mud and stone, resembled somewhat those of the Pueblo Indians of New Mexico. Like the Pueblos, these people were farmers who raised corn, beans, and squash. They also hunted buffalo, antelope, and other game, and they combined those two activities with exploiting the quarries. The flint they dug out was exchanged, sometimes over great distances, for such things as pottery, obsidian, catlinite, sea shells, and turquoise.

Evidence of the extent of mining of Alibates flint is impressive. Over the centuries, prehistoric Indians dug out hundreds of tons of the hard, beautiful stone. Several hundred quarry pits are still visible on the mile-long ridge in the national monument.

Alibates flint continued to be sought by Indians of the Plains. Even in historic times they made it into weapons whenever they could not get metal.

The Name. The word "Alibates" is derived from the name of Allie Bates, a cowboy who worked in this area in the early ranching days.

BAYLOR UNIVERSITY, STRECKER MUSEUM

West Basement, Sid Richardson Science Building, on the campus, Waco. Open free, daily. Closed certain holidays.

Exhibits emphasize the cultural heritage of central Texas from 12,500 B.C. to the arrival of the Spanish. There is an extensive research collection of prehistoric central Texas Indian artifacts.

BIG BEND NATIONAL PARK

From Marathon on US 90 drive south on Texas 385, 69 miles to Park Headquarters. Open free, daily, all year. Camping.

Along the Hot Springs Nature Trail in the park pictographs may be seen. On this trail and on two others are mortar holes in the rock, used by prehistoric people for grinding seeds.

CADDOAN MOUNDS STATE HISTORICAL SITE

On Texas 21, 6 miles southwest of Alto. As this book went to press, the site was not yet ready for the public. For information about the schedule for opening, inquire of Texas Parks and Wildlife Dept., 4200 Smith School Dr., Austin, TX 78744.

At this site are two mounds and a village area inhabited from about A.D. 780 to 1250 by Caddo Indians, perhaps the most prominent of the prehistoric inhabitants of Texas.

A confederation of Caddo groups occupied a large area between the Trinity River and the Red River and spread into what is now Arkansas and Louisiana. These groups referred to each other as Taychas, which meant "allies," or "friends." At first they mistakenly included Spaniards among their friends, and ironically the Spanish name for the whole of what is now the state of Texas was based on the Caddoan word.

The Caddo were farmers who hunted in winter, had a rich ceremonial life, and were famous for their pottery. At one stage they build large, earthen temple mounds, but by historic times had given up this practice. In many ways their culture resembled the Mississippian tradition, which flourished

Artifacts characteristic of the prehistoric Caddo Indians, and stages through which their culture passed, are shown in this exhibit in the Texas Memorial Museum, Austin. Texas Memorial Museum photo.

farther to the east. But whether Caddoan culture simply influenced—or was also influenced by—the Mississippian is still a matter of dispute.

CADDO INDIAN MUSEUM

In Longview, between Texas 80 and Harrison Rd. Open daily. Admission charged.

Exhibits include both prehistoric and historic Caddo Indian material. The influence of ancient Caddoan culture extended far to the east, and to the north as far as Spiro, in Oklahoma. (See Spiro Mounds entry, above).

EL PASO CENTENNIAL MUSEUM
(See University of Texas)

FORT WORTH MUSEUM OF SCIENCE AND HISTORY

1501 Montgomery St., Fort Worth. Open free, Monday through Saturday; afternoons, Sunday. Closed certain holidays.

Both the Hall of Medicine and the Hall of Man in this museum contain archeological material, including a collection of pre-Columbian ceramics and stone implements.

HUECO TANKS STATE HISTORICAL PARK

From El Paso drive 32 miles northeast on US 62 to intersection with Ranch Road 2775, then to Park Headquarters. Open daily, all year. Admission charged. Camping.

The word *hueco* in Spanish means hollow. Throughout the park many huecos—natural hollows in hard rock— form reservoirs, or tanks, which provided a water supply for people as long ago as 8000 B.C. At that time Big-Game Hunters, using projectile points of the type called Folsom, camped near the tanks and left the bones of now extinct giant bison. Later, when there were no more big-game animals, people of the Desert Archaic culture hunted small animals and gathered seeds and plants around the tanks. Still later, Mogollon people lived in villages and did farming in the area. Except at times when rains have filled the tanks, this semi-arid

land seems too inhospitable for permanent settlement. However, in rats' nests dated at 13,000 years ago, scientists have found piñon nuts, which prove that there were once trees around the tanks, and until recent times there may have been enough moisture to support crops.

Many of the people who frequented the tanks painted pictures and designs on the walls of caves and shelters. Some of the paintings are lively and graphic, others are mainly designs. Archeologists who specialize in rock art believe that the various styles are characteristic of the different cultural groups that came to the area. A number of these pictograph sites are accessible to visitors.

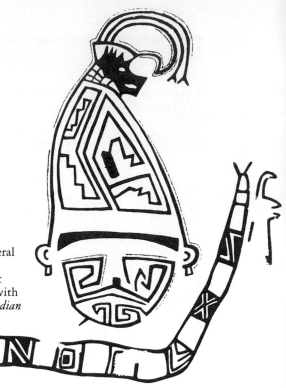

Hueco Tanks, a complex of three massive granite outcrops rising several hundred feet above the desert floor, has numerous rock paintings. Above: A figure 23 inches tall that is an elaborate mask with abstract decoration and conical cap. Below: A horned serpent painted in red with decorated body. Illustrations by Wes Jernigan in Polly Schaafsma, *Indian Rock Art of the Southwest.*

INSTITUTE OF TEXAN CULTURES

Southeast corner of HemisFair Plaza, San Antonio. Open free, daily.

The Institute uses some prehistoric Indian material in exhibits of Texas ⋅life, past and present. Through a plan of borrowing artifacts or copying art from other museums or private collections, exhibits are changed frequently, and it is possible to present new material that might not be easily seen otherwise.

JOHN E. CONNER MUSEUM
(See Texas A&I University)

LAKE MEREDITH RECREATION AREA
(See Alibates Flint Quarries)

LUBBOCK LAKE SITE

North of Clovis Rd. (US 84) off Loop 289, in Yellow House Canyon and Comanche Park, which is being developed near Lubbock. As this book went to press, an on-site museum was being planned. For information about visiting excavations at the site, inquire at Texas Tech University Museum, in Lubbock.

The university museum reports that it has found evidence at this site of very early human activity. Buried under deep layers of earth were spearpoints and the fossil bones of extinct animals, indicating visits by Paleo hunters, 12,000 years ago. Visits by later people continued at intervals.

MONAHANS SANDHILLS

On US 80, 5 miles east of Monahans. Open daily, all year. Admission charged.

At the Interpretive Center here is a small exhibit of local finds relating to prehistoric Indian shelters, projectile points, and foodstuffs.

MUSEUM OF THE BIG BEND
(See Sul Ross University)

PANHANDLE-PLAINS HISTORICAL MUSEUM

2401 Fourth Ave., Canyon. Open free, Monday through Saturday; afternoons, Sunday. Closed Dec. 25.

In addition to a large collection of Comanche and Kiowa ethnological material, this museum displays random local finds and artifacts excavated by the Works Progress Administration in the 1930s. In the archeological exhibits are Clovis, Folsom, and Plainview projectile points, used by hunters in Paleo times; also Archaic materials, artifacts from the Adobe Walls site, and artifacts of the Panhandle culture from the South Canadian River, dated about A.D. 1300 to A.D. 1540.

PANTHER CAVE

In Amistad Recreation Area. From Comstock drive northwest on US 90 to Pecos River boat-ramp exit. Open free, daily, all year. Camping nearby.

The Amistad Recreation Area was created after the construction of Amistad Dam on the Rio Grande River. Within the area Panther Cave is the only visitable prehistoric pictograph site. It is accessible only by private boat. Visitors must bring their own boats or make arrangements for use of private boats. From the Pecos River boat ramp the cave is approximately

Near Lubbock, Texas, the Texas Tech University Museum has excavated and opened for the public a stratified site at Lubbock Reservoir. Here Dr. W. C. Holden, former director of the museum, points to a layer deep in the canyon wall, indicating the great age of the site. Texas Tech University Museum photo.

a 25-minute ride downstream, at the junction of the Rio Grande and Seminole Canyon. The National Park Service provides a courtesy dock at Panther Cave. The site is protected by a cyclone fence.

Remarkably rich and detailed pictures cover the whole wall and part of the ceiling of the cave. Archeologists believe the people who made the paintings relied on hunting for much of their food, because herds of deer appear frequently in the paintings here and in other, neighboring caves. The panthers, which give the cave its name, are large and realistically drawn—one is so big that it can be seen clearly from the top of the cliff on the opposite side of Seminole Canyon.

SEMINOLE CANYON STATE HISTORICAL PARK

From Del Rio drive 40 miles northwest on US 90 to directional sign, between Comstock and Lantry. Open daily, all year. Admission charged.

Very large rockshelters in the park contain unusual painted murals. The Visitor Center has interpretive exhibits.

STRECKER MUSEUM
(See Baylor University)

SUL ROSS UNIVERSITY, MUSEUM OF THE BIG BEND

On the campus, Alpine, entrance from US 90. Open free, afternoons, Tuesday through Sunday.

The archeological collections here relate to prehistoric Big Bend Basketmaker culture. There is also some Plains Indian material.

TEXAS A&I UNIVERSITY, JOHN E. CONNER MUSEUM

On the campus, Texas A&I University, on Santa Gertrudis, between Armstrong and University, Kingsville. Open free, Monday through Friday; afternoons, Sunday. Closed certain holidays.

Although this museum is not primarily concerned with archeology, it does display material from the La Paloma Mammoth Site, and the exhibits here include prehistoric artifacts.

TEXAS MEMORIAL MUSEUM
(See University of Texas)

TEXAS TECH UNIVERSITY MUSEUM

Indiana Ave. and 4th St., Lubbock. Open free, Monday through Friday; afternoons, Saturday and Sunday. Closed certain holidays.

Some exhibits and dioramas here deal with Early Man, dating back to Clovis times, principally in Texas.

TEXAS WILDERNESS MUSEUM

In El Paso, 2000 Transmountain Rd. Open free, Tuesday through Saturday; afternoons, Sunday.

In this museum, administered by the city, are dioramas showing a Folsom hunt, a pithouse scene, and a scene from the Hueco Tanks area (see entry, above). Other displays feature pottery, tool making, food plants, and basketry. As this book went to press, reconstructions of a pithouse, a kiva, and a three-room pueblo were scheduled to open along a nature trail in the area adjoining the museum.

Everyday prehistoric Caddoan life appears in this diorama in the Texas Memorial Museum. Texas Memorial Museum photo.

UNIVERSITY OF TEXAS, EL PASO CENTENNIAL MUSEUM

2400 Trinity St., Austin. Open free, Monday through Friday; afternoons, Saturday and Sunday. Closed certain holidays.

Exhibits emphasize prehistoric cultures of the El Paso area, including material from caves in the nearby Hueco Mountains. Other displays are devoted to the Mogollon culture and to pottery and ornaments from the Casas Grandes area of northwestern Mexico. A diorama shows prehistoric Pueblo life near El Paso.

UNIVERSITY OF TEXAS, TEXAS MEMORIAL MUSEUM

2400 Trinity St., Austin. Open Monday through Friday; afternoons, Saturday and Sunday. Closed certain holidays. Admission charged.

This large museum has many archeological exhibits of several different kinds. Dioramas show a central Texas flint quarry. Archaic life, and Bonfire Shelter, which was the site of a bison jump. Technological exhibits demonstrate flint chipping and the manufacture of pottery and baskets. Other exhibits introduce North American archeology as a whole or concentrate on specific subjects, such as the Paleo, Archaic, and later periods. A cross section of an Archaic midden appears in one exhibit; in another, Archaic points are identified. A display is devoted to influences that came into Texas from the Southwest. Another shows Caddoan cultural stages.

The museum as a whole is undergoing extensive renovation. One new area will be devoted to exhibits of sites, some well known, some being excavated. These will be changed often.

Of particular interest is material from the Plainview Site in Texas. Here archeologists found the skeletons of about a hundred giant bison—a type now extinct. With them were 18 points, which resembled Clovis points except that they did not have a flute or groove down the center. Apparently the bison had become mired at a waterhole or stream crossing, where hunters found and dispatched a good many of them with their stone-tipped weapons. Later this same type of pro-

Bighorn Medicine Wheel, which prehistoric people made by laying out rocks in a pattern on the ground, is thought to be an astronomical device. Parts of the wheel are aligned with the rising sun at the summer solstice. USDA Forest Service photo.

jectile point—called the Plainview point, after the site where it was first identified—was found elsewhere on the Great Plains, as far away as the Dakotas.

WASHINGTON SQUARE MOUND SITE

In Washington Square, Nacogdoches, near the old high school. Open free, daily, all year.

In this well-preserved Caddoan ceremonial complex there may be on-going excavation. For information write to James E. Corbin, Box 13047 SFA Station, Nacogdoches, TX 75962.

WITTE MEMORIAL MUSEUM

3801 Broadway, Brackenridge Park, San Antonio. Open daily. Closed certain holidays. Admission by donation.

This museum, which has an active archeological program, grew up around materials from the Pecos River area and now displays material from many parts of Texas and the Southwest.

Wyoming

BIGHORN CANYON NATIONAL RECREATION AREA, VISITOR CENTER

Off US Alternate 14, near Lovell, on Wyoming 37. Open free, daily, all year. Closed certain holidays.

In the Bighorn Visitor Center is an archeological display.

BIGHORN MEDICINE WHEEL

On Interstate 90 drive northwest from Sheridan to Ranchester exit, then west on Wyoming 14 to Burgess Junction, then west on Alternate 14 toward Lovell. About 30 miles west of Burgess Junction, turn north on Medicine Wheel access road. Open free, July 1 to Sept. 15. The access road is not maintained during inclement weather.

The Medicine Wheel is a large, circular arrangement of stones, with a central hub and radiating spokes. There are rock cairns at intervals around the circumference of the wheel.

The U.P. Site

In 1960 Ivan Hayes was operating a dragline on the Union Pacific Railroad's right-of-way near Rawlins, Wyoming. In the muck, around the spring he was clearing, the dragline caught on some huge bones. Hayes reported this to Dr. George A. Agogino, at that time professor of anthropology at the University of Wyoming. Agogino quickly got money from the National Geographic Society. Then he persuaded Henry and Cynthia Irwin, a brother-sister team of archeologists, to bring their student crew from a dig elsewhere in Wyoming. Battling against mud and water, the excavators unearthed proof that hunters had butchered a mammoth at this spot. Its crushed skull indicated that they had probably killed it by hurling down rocks from the top of a bank above the stream where it had come to drink. Materials from the U.P. Mammoth Kill Site are in the Peabody Museum at Harvard University.

Astronomer John Eddy has discovered that the wheel is aligned to the position of the rising sun at the time of the summer solstice. Eddy and archeologists Tim and Alice Kehoe have found that other medicine wheels in the West also mark the summer solstice.

Bighorn Medicine Wheel, in the Bighorn National Forest, is administered by the U.S. Forest Service, which has provided parking space and interpretive signs.

BUFFALO BILL HISTORICAL CENTER

720 Sheridan Ave., Cody. Open daily, May through Sept.; afternoons, Tuesday through Sunday, March, April, Oct., Nov. Closed Dec., Jan., Feb. Admission charged.

This is a four-part complex, of which the Plains Indian Museum is one part. One wing contains prehistoric artifacts found in the Cody area.

GATCHELL MEMORIAL MUSEUM

10 Fort St., Buffalo. Open free, daily, June 1 to Labor Day. Closed July 4.

In addition to random local finds the Jim Gatchell Museum displays prehistoric artifacts recovered in a dig conducted by the University of Wyoming at a buffalo jump in the area.

MAMMOTH VISITOR CENTER, YELLOWSTONE NATIONAL PARK

From the north entrance to the park on US 89, drive south to Mammoth Hot Springs. Open free, daily. Camping.

Five exhibits in the Visitor Center contain material about Indians in the park. One exhibit concentrates on prehistoric artwork and artifacts collected in the park.

MEDICINE LODGE STATE ARCHEOLOGICAL SITE

From Hyattville follow signs on gravel county road 4 miles north to site. Open free, at all times.

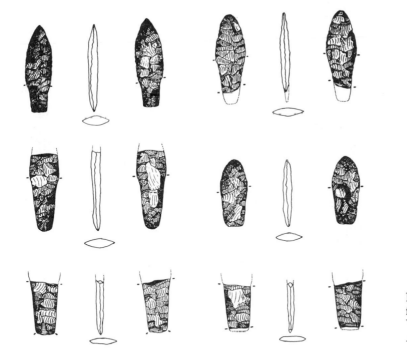

Drawings of various projectile points found at the Hell Gap Site, in Wyoming. Photo courtesy of George Agogino.

Excavation was done here by the University of Wyoming. The site has been filled, to be reopened at a future time.

OBSIDIAN CLIFF

In Yellowstone National Park. From Mammoth Hot Springs drive about 12 miles south toward Norris. Park gates are always open. Most roads are open May through Oct. Over-the-snow vehicles, Oct. to May. Admission charged to the park. Camping nearby.

East of the road may be seen a dark mass of stone known to pioneer explorers as Glass Mountain. It is quite literally that—a mountain of volcanic glass, or obsidian.

Prehistoric hunters made projectile points and knives of obsidian, which are sharper than steel. However, sources of the material are rather rare, and early archeologists were puzzled when many obsidian artifacts turned up in the burial mounds of Ohio and Illinois. Was it possible that people had brought the volcanic glass all the way from Yellowstone? It was. One of the trails

they followed to the quarry at Obsidian Cliff was worn so deep into the earth that it could still be seen in historic times.

Few present-day archeologists have doubted that Indians carried on trade and traveled great distances for things they wanted. Nevertheless, James B. Griffin, of the University of Michigan, decided to test various obsidian samples by a process called neutron activation. Working with members of the university's chemistry department, he has proved that Obsidian Cliff and two other places in Yellowstone are the sources of obsidian used in many artifacts found at midwestern sites.

PLAINS INDIAN MUSEUM
(See Buffalo Bill Historical Center)

UNIVERSITY OF WYOMING MUSEUM

On the campus, Old Law Building, 14th and Ivinson, Laramie. Open free, Monday through Friday. Closed certain holidays.

Exhibits in the museum's recently opened new quarters contain material

from the university's extensive collection of Paleo-Indian artifacts and of material from late prehistoric sites.

WYOMING STATE MUSEUM

Barrett Bldg., 23rd and Central avenues, Cheyenne. Open free, daily, summer; closed Sunday, winter.

Interpretive displays in this primarily historical museum include archeological material dating from early prehistoric times.

The debris in Russell Cave, Alabama, contained so many nutshells that archeologists think the cave was not a year-round shelter but was visited mainly in fall, when nuts would be ripe.

THE SOUTHEAST

At the end of the Ice Age people wandered eastward as well as westward from the Plains, following the trails of big game. By 10,000 B.C. (possibly earlier) these Paleo hunters had appeared east of the Mississippi River and south of the Ohio. Perhaps they crossed the great water barriers on the ice in winter, or perhaps they had watercraft made of logs or of skins stretched around a framework of branches. No one knows how they reached the Southeast, but there is evidence that early Americans were not limited to land in their travels. Paleo-Indian artifacts 7000 years old have been found on islands in the Caribbean Sea, obviously left there by people who had watercraft, although no vestiges of their boats or rafts have been found.

Paleo-Indian Period
No glaciers ever reached into the Southeast, but there was heavy rainfall, which nourished a dense forest cover. In the shady woods mastodons could find enough to eat, for they were browsers, living on twigs and leaves. In open, unshaded areas there was grass for mammoths. Both animals must have been game for Paleo-Indians in the Southeast, and collectors have picked up innumerable projectile points of the kind that the Big-Game Hunters alone used. Indeed, the concentration of fluted points of the Clovis type is greater at certain places in the Southeast than it is anywhere in the Southwest.

Prehistoric people in the Macon, Georgia, area modeled this head as part of a pottery vessel. Original in the museum, Ocmulgee National Monument, Macon.

Archaic Period

After the big game disappeared, descendants of Paleo-Indians gradually had to make adjustments to a changing climate and to many new environments. At first hunters of the next—the Archaic —period faced their changing world with no better equipment than that of their ancestors. In time, however, they elaborated new tools and new ways of getting nourishment in a land no longer rich in the huge animals that had brought such great rewards for a single kill. Sometime between 6000 B.C. and 4000 B.C. knowledge became widespread that mollusks could be harvested. People who camped often or long on the same site near rivers began to eat freshwater clams and mussels, and here the change in climate played a special role. Rainfall was decreasing. As a result, rivers dwindled and grew sluggish, and in the shallow, slow-moving waters shellfish were easy to gather. Since it took a great many mollusks to feed a family, the piles of discarded shells grew higher and higher as long as the weather remained warm and dry. But when rainfall increased again, streams grew deeper and their currents sped up. It was more difficult now to pick shellfish off the bottom. People turned to other food sources, and the inland shell mounds ceased to grow.

Along the coasts of the Atlantic Ocean and the Gulf of Mexico the harvest of saltwater mollusks continued uninterrupted. There the shell mounds kept increasing in size right into historic times. Their extent in some places is monumental. Even though centuries of habitation contributed to their growth, it is hard to believe that so many oysters and clams could have been consumed.

This is not to say that all Archaic people concentrated on shellfish. They didn't. Many were meateaters, hunters of deer and smaller game, who supplemented their diet with nuts, roots, and seeds. They, too, left debris where they camped, and many a hummock in a modern farmer's field has turned out to be a mound of Archaic garbage, partially converted into soil.

The Eastern Archaic hunters differed from Paleo-Indians in their social relationships. Big-Game Hunters probably worked together in groups as they pursued large animals. But people who lived in wooded areas found it more efficient to search as individuals for their smaller quarry. For them hunting was a solitary, not a collective, enterprise. So, too, was a good deal of the foraging that went on. Large-scale cooperation was not required for harvesting nuts, seeds, and roots. Moreover, these were usually not abundant enough to support a large band that remained long in one place.

An exception was the shellfish eaters. During at least part of each year, they could live in larger groups than had ever been possible in the past. But at certain seasons many of them seem to have dispersed, as they turned away from mollusks and sought other foods.

Life changed in many ways in the Archaic period. There was a general, very intensive search for new things to eat. At the same time there was an increase in the number and variety of implements used to gather and process the new foods. For example, Archaic people harvested hard-shelled seeds, for which they needed crushing tools. To make nutcrackers they first pecked several small depressions in a stone. Nuts fixed in these depressions could then be easily cracked by a blow from a hammerstone. Grinding stones and mortars and pestles came into use for pulverizing small seeds. In pots carved from steatite (soapstone) tough seeds could be cooked to a soft mush.

Still further specialization marked the end of this stage. The old, simple and rather fluid ways of the hunter began to disappear. Instead of depending entirely on what grew naturally, people created a new source of food by planting gardens. Larger groups could now live together, for part of the year at least, in semi-permanent villages. In some places women began to make a crude sort of pottery from clay that was mixed with grass or moss and then baked in a fire. (This is called fiber-tempered pottery.)

With the arrival of squash, beans, and corn from Mexico, there was a large jump in available calories. Population increased. So did the activities and responsibilities that men and women invented for themselves. As settled communities developed, some individuals could now spend a good deal of time in pursuits other than foodgetting, and many of the activities they chose centered around burials and burial ceremonies.

At the same time, women had more leisure for making pottery in better and more beautiful forms than before. Good pottery vessels, in turn, increased the available food by providing better means of storing it. They also made cooking easier and so brought a more varied diet. The quality of life changed.

The winged serpent appears in a variety of forms in many prehistoric Indian cultures. A follower of the Mississippian lifeway made this design. After Clarence B. Moore.

Woodland Period

With the appearance of agriculture, there began what is known as the Woodland period. Within this widespread general cultural pattern, some interesting developments came to many parts of the Southeast. One was the custom of building earthen mounds over the bodies, the bones, or the remains from cremations of the dead.

At first, during Early Woodland times, burial mounds in the Southeast were small and conical in shape. They were heaped up by the thousand, often a little way outside villages, wherever people dwelt along rivers, large streams, or the ridges of hills. As time passed, mound construction grew more complex. First a low platform was built, in preparation for a mass funeral. After bodies were placed on it, they were covered with earth. Later burials might be made in the mound and more layers added, until the structure rose as much as 20 feet.

The burial-mound idea seems to have spread to the Southeast from Illinois and Ohio, where it had already become very important in the lives of people who followed a lifeway called Hopewellian. For mortuary offerings, which they placed in graves, these people required a great deal of material obtainable only in distant

These figurines, each two feet high and carved from marble, were found at Etowah Mounds Archeological Area, Cartersville, Georgia, and are on display there. They may be portraits of the man and woman with whom they were buried.

places—shells from the seacoast, for example. Perhaps the Hopewellians made long journeys for the shells, or they may have got them by trade. In either event, information about their religious customs traveled along the routes that led to the source of the shells. And where the burial-mound idea spread, so, too, did its trappings—elaborate ornaments, tobacco pipes, tools and weapons of polished stone, ornaments of mica, and specially made mortuary vessels.

The intense activity of burial-mound rituals finally began to wear out in one place, then in another. But as this stage was ending another had already begun.

The Mississippian Period
Religious and ceremonial practices in much of the Southeast now centered around a new kind of mound. Possibly inspired by ideas from Mexico, people constructed large, flat-topped, earthen pyramids which served as platforms for temples—buildings with thatched roofs, on which effigies of birds were sometimes perched. Since the temple-mound idea took form and then spread out vigorously from places along the Mississippi River, the cultural developments that went with it have been called Mississippian.

Those who followed the Mississippian lifeway became expert farmers and organizers. Population grew tremendously around ceremonial centers, and huge pyramids were built by people who moved vast quantities of earth in baskets. Sometimes 20 or more large mounds marked a great ceremonial site. Arts and crafts flourished as the Mississippian cultures reached a climax.

In some areas temple-mound building became associated with a complex of human activities called the Southern Cult. This final development in ceremonial and religious practices was possibly stimulated by the arrival of new notions from Mexico. It has also been called the Southern Death Cult, or the Buzzard Cult, and with good reason. Those who practiced it were preoccupied with death.

A great proliferation of grave goods accompanied the spread of the cult, and many of the new artifacts were both elaborate and most skillfully made. Native copper was hammered into ornate headdresses, plaques, ear spools, and celts (a kind of ax). Craftsmen engraved intricate symbolic designs on shell, which was imported from the Gulf Coast. Sculptors shaped stone into excellent likenesses of people and animals. They also carved and polished stone axes, complete with stone handles. Such monolithic axes were useless for real work, but were obviously important for some ceremonial purpose. Symbols abounded—among them skulls, bones, an eye in the palm of a hand. An eye that wept appeared everywhere in engravings and on pottery. So, too, did spiders and warriors with wings. Workers in flint created graceful fantasies in this intractable material—ceremonial knives adorned with crescents and curlicues.

Human sacrifice was illustrated in various ways on artifacts, and it obviously was practiced in this death-centered culture. Pottery appeared in a great variety of nonutilitarian forms, made only for burial with the dead. Exuberant life was expressed in many ways—all celebrating the negation of life. The Death Cult seemed to be imaginative about preparing for its own death, and die it did.

With a dramatic suddenness that still baffles investigators, the building of earthen pyramids ceased, and the lifeway associated with them vanished. Various theories have been put forward to explain what happened. Perhaps some great prehistoric epidemic sapped the vitality of the people. (This disease theory still lacks supporting evidence.) Perhaps the shock of the European invasion spread panic and sealed the fate of the culture, which was already in decline. Certainly the presence of Spanish troops under De Soto was disastrous to large numbers of Indian people in the Southeast. When De Soto arrived in 1539, some moundbuilding was still going on, but little if any was done after his men withdrew at the end of their vain search for loot—a search which led them from Florida to Georgia, then all the way west into Arkansas. Not only did the Europeans disrupt Indian life by killing and enslaving great numbers of people, they were also an enormous drain on food resources. Wherever the Spanish army went, the Indian economy had to provide food for 700 soldiers, for a large number of slaves, for 200 horses, and for hogs that ate corn and multiplied much faster than the Spanish butchered them.

The invaders also brought with them diseases to which the Indians had not developed any immunity, and as a result the population suddenly began to dwindle. If there was still vitality in the customs and beliefs that encouraged people to build temple mounds and to pursue the ecstasies of the Death Cult, that vitality soon disappeared.

Historic Indian tribes lived on in the vicinity of the mounds, which soon became as ancient and mysterious to them as to the Europeans who were overwhelming the land. It is these huge, earthen structures that make up most of the archeological sites now open to the public in the Southeast.

Some of the historic Indian tribes in the Southeast were surely descendants of the people who once engaged in the prodigious labor of piling up mounds. However, proof is usually lacking that a particular tribe is related to the builders of mounds near which it lived. On the other hand, scientific excavation has been able to disprove one myth: There was no mysterious vanished race of Mound Builders.

Indians who followed the Mississippian lifeway pecked these designs on a rock in Alabama. Frank Jones and Spencer Waters photo, courtesy Campbell Grant.

This pottery bottle is from Mound State Monument, Alabama. Original in the Museum of the American Indian.

Alabama

ALABAMA DEPARTMENT OF ARCHIVES AND HISTORY

624 Washington Street, Montgomery. Open free, Monday through Friday; afternoons, Saturday, Sunday. Closed certain holidays.

In the State of Alabama Department of Archives and History are random local archeological finds, reflecting the culture of one or another of the tribes in the Creek Indian Confederacy. Displays are not primarily interpretive, and are exhibited with Choctaw, Chickasaw, and Seminole ethnological materials.

Special Interest. Some artifacts on exhibit were collected by a man who accompanied John James Audubon on a trip through the West.

ALABAMA MUSEUM OF NATURAL HISTORY
(See University of Alabama)

BIRMINGHAM MUSEUM OF ART

2000 Eighth Ave. N., Birmingham. Open free, Monday through Saturday; afternoons, Sunday; evenings, Thursday. Closed Dec. 25.

Permanent exhibits here include North American Indian art, along with pre-Columbian art from Central and South America. There are changing exhibitions each year.

FORT TOULOUSE PARK

Off US 231, 12 miles northeast of Montgomery. Open daily, all year. Admission charged. Camping.

On the grounds near the site of an eighteenth-century French fort, early hunting people once camped. Later inhabitants built several large temple mounds here, one of which remains today. Some prehistoric artifacts are exhibited in the Visitor Center.

HORSESHOE BEND NATIONAL MILITARY PARK

From Danville drive 12 miles north on Alabama 49. Open free, at all times. Camping nearby.

Although not concerned with prehistoric archeology, this park is of interest because here, in March 1814, a thousand Red Stick Creek warriors faced a two-thousand-man army, led by Andrew Jackson. Jackson's superior forces won and decisively broke the power of the Creeks, which extended far back into prehistoric times.

INDIAN MOUND

South end of Court St., Florence. Open Tuesday through Sunday. Closed certain holidays. Admission charged.

This is one of the largest Mississippian mounds in the Tennessee Valley, built about A.D. 1200. It is 43 feet high and originally had steps on one side. A museum near the base contains artifacts collected in the area.

This black pottery vessel from Mound State Monument has incised designs, shown here in white to make them more visible.

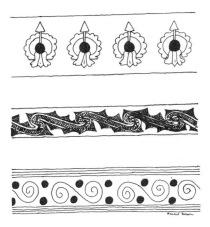

Three designs used on pottery made by Mississippian Indians. Pots are on display in the museum at Mound State Monument.

MOUND STATE MONUMENT

From Tuscaloosa drive 13 miles south on Alabama 69 to the monument at Moundville. Open daily, except Dec. 25. Admission charged. Camping.

This combination archeological site and museum is a division of the University of Alabama Museums. The museum building is constructed over two actual excavations. Artifacts from these and other digs in the area illustrate the cultural traits and physical characteristics of the prehistoric people who lived here. On top of the principal mound in the monument is a restoration of a temple, which includes a life-size exhibit of a ceremony of the kind that once went on there. A reconstructed village of five huts shows people performing the everyday tasks of Moundville Indians in prehistoric times.

The Story. Between the years A.D. 1200 and A.D. 1400 a large settlement prospered in peace at this site. People in the village were, by present-day, non-Indian standards, good-looking, muscular, and of medium height. Though naturally handsome, they often followed a custom which they probably thought improved their appearance: they altered the shapes of babies' heads by strapping them to wooden cradleboards. The soft baby bones were readily and permanently flattened.

Men and women wore clothing made of woven fabrics and cured animal skins. For warmth in cold weather they had robes made of feathers. They adorned themselves with delicate shell necklaces and pendants, copper bracelets and armbands, and ear decorations called earplugs. Hairdos received a good deal of attention, and women used long bone hairpins.

The houses in this community consisted of frames made of logs, over which there was a covering of reeds and canes woven into mats and then plastered with mixed clay and sand.

Food was plentiful. Men hunted in the nearby forest and fished in Black Warrior River, on the banks of which their village stood. They shaped barbless fishhooks of bone, wove fishnets, and made traps, snares, bows, and arrows. Corn, beans, and pumpkins grew readily in soil that was exceed-

A Park Ranger at Russell Cave National Monument, Alabama, indicates the layers of debris accumulated in more than 8000 years of human occupation of the cave. National Park Service photo.

This diorama in the museum at Mound State Monument shows how archeologists think the village may have looked 500 years ago. The structure on top of the mound at right was a religious and political center of the community. University of Alabama, Museum of Natural History photo.

ingly fertile. To harvest their various crops they made tools much like those used by Indians elsewhere in eastern America. They also had woodworking tools and grinding implements for making cornmeal. Eating utensils were cut from shell.

Women apparently had time and energy for making pots, that were often very lovely. Everyone seems to have had the time necessary for ceremonies and rituals and for the labor of building the 40 mounds on which they placed temples and other important structures. Although they did not build burial mounds, these people were followers of the Southern Cult and devoted a great deal of effort to mortuary customs. As in many other Indian societies, precious belongings were buried with the dead. These grave goods give us much of our information about the lifeway of the people who made and used them.

Examples of the material culture and technology of these people are on display in the museum. Still other artifacts recovered at Moundville are on exhibit in the Museum of the American Indian, in New York.

RUSSELL CAVE NATIONAL MONUMENT

From Bridgeport on US 72 drive west on County Road 91 to Mt. Carmel, then turn north onto County Road 75, which leads to the monument entrance. Total distance from Bridgeport about 8 miles. Open free, daily. Closed Dec. 25.

A record of more than 8000 years of human life is preserved in this monument. In Russell Cave itself an exhibit shows how archeologists did the excavation. There is also an audiovisual presentation, and, nearby, a self-guided ethnobotanical trail. The museum near the cave contains interpretive exhibits.

The Story. Long ago hunters found that the gaping hole now called Russell Cave provided shelter, and they camped on its rock-strewn floor. Bits of charcoal, dated by the carbon-14 method, show that men, women, and children warmed themselves at fires here sometime between 8000 and 9000 years ago. Usually their visits were in fall and winter, when quantities of nuts could be harvested in the neighboring forest. Hunting at that

Busk

For many eastern Indians in historic times the most important ceremony of the year was the summer corn festival. Among the Creeks, who may be directly descended from one group of temple-mound builders, the ceremony was called the "pushkita." English-speaking people shortened this word to "busk."

Apparently some of the ideas for the busk came from Mexico, where there were temple mounds. The ceremony, a kind of New Year celebration, took place when corn first ripened. People put out all fires and engaged in various rites which were supposed to purify. They drank the Black Drink, took ceremonial baths, and then, as a sign that they had rid themselves of evil, they started new fires. Boys who had reached puberty took new names during the busk and were thenceforth regarded as men. The ceremonies lasted for eight days and ended with dancing.

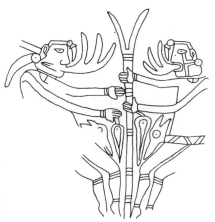

One element of the busk ceremony is shown in this design, which was engraved on a conch shell found at Spiro Mounds, Oklahoma. The symbols coming from the men's mouths may represent speech. Original in the Museum of the American Indian in New York City.

---

time of year was good, too, and fish and shellfish were easy to harvest in the nearby Tennessee River.

Year after year families kept visiting the cave, cooking over fires, dropping trash, losing tools. After a while the floor on which they camped was so littered that tidying-up seemed necessary. Loads of dirt were brought in to cover the debris, and the cave floor slowly rose high above its original level.

At last, about 500 B.C., the lifeway of the cave's visitors changed a great deal. They began to make pottery, and many sherds littered the floor. The favorite weapon was now the bow and arrow instead of the spear and spear-thrower, which had been used until then. Tools became more varied as people learned to garden as well as hunt.

Farming increased in importance, and beginning about A.D. 1000, people stopped at Russell Cave less and less often. This was a time when many communities in the Southeast were building temple mounds. Some evidence of the temple-mound lifeway was left in the cave, but not a great

deal. The final occupants, Cherokee Indians, took shelter there even in historic times.

During all these centuries of occupation, debris piled up on the floor until it reached a depth of 14 feet. In 1953 four members of the Tennessee Archaeological Society began to dig into the litter. A little excavating was enough to tell them that the job was too big for such a small crew and too important to be left undone. The amateurs called in the Smithsonian Institution, which, together with the National Geographic Society, excavated the cave and by so doing added greatly to our knowledge of the early inhabitants of the Southeast. In all of North America no excavation before this had provided such a detailed record of human life over such a long period. No excavation in the Southeast had provided an earlier date. The National Geographic Society later bought the cave property and donated it to the public. In 1961 it was made a national monument.

UNIVERSITY OF ALABAMA, ALABAMA MUSEUM OF NATURAL HISTORY

University of Alabama, on the campus, Tuscaloosa. Open free, daily, when the university is in session.

Exhibits here emphasize worldwide ethnology and geology.

Special Interest. A traveling exhibit traces Indian life in Alabama from Paleo times, before 8000 B.C., through all the major cultural developments, including the historic period. Information about the schedule of the exhibit may be obtained from the museum.

The museum also conducts a field school in archeology at Mound State Monument, in Moundville, and an expedition and other scientific endeavors for high school and younger students. Enquiries should be directed to John Hall, PO Box 5897, University, AL 35486.

Left to right: An effigy vessel in the shape of a frog, found in a burial mound in Arkansas. Original in the Museum of the American Indian. This unusual-shaped water jar was found in Arkansas. Original in the Museum of the American Indian. The winged-serpent design was engraved on a conch shell found at Spiro Mounds. Original in the University of Arkansas Museum, Fayetteville.

Arkansas

ARKANSAS STATE UNIVERSITY MUSEUM

On the campus, Jonesboro. Open free, Monday through Friday. Closed certain holidays.

The archeological exhibits in this general museum serve as an excellent introduction to prehistory in northeastern Arkansas, from the Paleo through the Archaic, Woodland, and Mississippian mound-building stages. Maps indicate the various culture areas and tell which artifacts are related to which time period.

A large display is devoted to the Ballard Site, an early burial mound dating from A.D. 700 to 800. A cutaway in this display shows various strata, the artifacts associated with each one, and tools used by archeologists in excavating a burial and grave goods. Another exhibit explains the five steps in making pottery.

Cooking pots were not decorated, but they often had a corrugated finish. A note in the museum offers this explanation: The rough surface kept the pot from slipping out of a woman's hands when it was slick with grease.

HAMPSON MUSEUM

From West Memphis drive 34 miles north on Interstate 55, then 7 miles east on local road to Wilson, and follow directional signs to museum. Open free, Tuesday through Saturday; afternoons, Sunday. Closed certain holidays.

Material from Nodena Mound, which has been declared a National Historic Landmark, is on display here in the Henry Clay Hampson II Memorial Museum of Archaeology. The museum, 7 miles from the mound, is owned by the state of Arkansas and operated by the Department of State Parks.

Dr. J. K. Hampson, who excavated the material, began collecting artifacts when he was 9 years old and continued in this avocation for 70 years. His greatest activity centered at the Nodena site, which covers more than two acres of the Hampson family plantation. In the course of his excavation he uncovered many burials, and because he was a physician he was par-

ticularly interested in what the study of bones could tell him about prehistoric people and their customs and diseases. He found, for one thing, that they were apparently peaceful. In all the burials he discovered only two evidences of death by violence.

Numerous pots, including many effigy jars, are on display in the museum, along with other artifacts that represent the Mississippian lifeway at Nodena Mound and elsewhere.

HENDERSON STATE COLLEGE MUSEUM

On the campus, Arkadelphia. Open free, during college semesters and by appointment.

This museum has over 600 pieces of Caddoan pottery. About 100 are on display, along with Caddoan stone, bone, and shell tools and ornaments.

The Caddoan archeological area is named after the Indians of historic times who spoke a Caddoan language and who apparently were descendants of prehistoric groups in Texas, Arkansas, Louisiana, and Oklahoma. The Caddoans shared religious and politi-

Model Archeology Program

Anyone who wants to watch a dig—or to do volunteer work in one—may be able to do so in Arkansas.

Arkansas has what is perhaps the best archeology program in any state or province north of Mexico. The Arkansas Archeological Survey employs a staff of full-time archeologists, with one of them attached to each state-supported college and university. This network is salvaging a great deal of valuable information that would otherwise be lost, as grading machines turn scores of thousands of acres of land into absolutely level fields. Any farmer or amateur archeologist who finds material that may be of scientific interest can phone the nearest college, and an expert will normally be out to investigate within two hours. In addition, of course, the Archeological Survey team gathers information from places where roads are being made or foundations dug or artifacts discovered by amateurs.

If a dig is visitable, Dr. Charles R. McGimsey III, director of the Arkansas Archeological Survey, can send you to it. Write to Arkansas Archeological Survey, P.O. Box 1249, Fayetteville, AR 72601, or phone 505–575–3556.

---

cal ideas with their neighbors to the east, built mounds, and buried their honored dead with a wealth of grave goods. Caddoan pottery vessels are elaborately made, engraved with intricate designs, and are among the most beautiful in the prehistoric southeastern tradition.

HOT SPRINGS NATIONAL PARK MUSEUM

In the Visitor Center, Central and Reserve avenues, Hot Springs National Park. Open free, daily. Closed Dec. 25.

In the Visitor Center a few Caddoan artifacts are on display, together with explanations of the prehistoric human use of the water from the hot springs. Drawings show how Indians made implements from a very hard stone called novaculite.

MUSEUM OF SCIENCE AND NATURAL HISTORY

MacArthur Park, 500 E. 9th St., Little Rock. Open free, Tuesday through Saturday; afternoons, Sunday.

One hall in this museum is devoted to material found in prehistoric sites in Arkansas.

TOLTEC MOUNDS STATE PARK
(Knapp Mounds)

From North Little Rock drive 15 miles southeast on Arkansas 130, then ½ mile west on Arkansas 386. Open free, daily.

Various groups of people occupied this site for over 1000 years, beginning about A.D. 400. Some of them built large, earthen mounds, probably for ceremonial purposes—18 altogether, of which 9 are still visible. An earthen embankment 6 feet high and a mile long once surrounded the site.

In the Visitor Center are archeological exhibits, audiovisual programs, and an archeological laboratory. Full-time research goes on here, and when excavation is in progress, visitors may watch. Guided tours are available.

The Name. Former owners of the site thought the mounds had been built by Toltec Indians from Mexico. Although this was discovered not to be so, the name persisted.

UNIVERSITY OF ARKANSAS MUSEUM

338 Hotz Hall, on the campus, Fayetteville. Open free, Monday through Saturday; afternoons, Sunday. Closed Dec. 25.

Unusual material in this museum comes from what are called bluff shelters in the Arkansas Ozark Mountains. These shelters are areas at the bases of overhanging rock ledges under bluffs or cliffs. Many are quite dry—completely protected from rain and snow —and for that reason they attracted prehistoric people. The absence of moisture also meant that baskets, sandals, clothing, garbage—any organic material left there—did not decay. Things which ordinarily would have been lost to the archeologist have survived, and they tell a story of the life of nonfarming people who inhabited the shelters from about 8000 B.C. to about 1000 B.C.

Ozark Bluff hunters used spears and darts tipped with large stone points.

Florida Key Dwellers

Visitors to the keys and glades of southern Florida in the late nineteenth century were often amazed at the vast deposits of shells which had been left there by prehistoric people. In some places these refuse heaps had been turned into built-up living and ceremonial areas. On one key, for example, early inhabitants had constructed a monumental sea wall more than ten feet high, mostly of conch shells. It was "as level and broad on top as a turnpike," said the archeologist Frank Cushing, who explored it. Beyond the wall were terraces, with a graded way leading to five large mounds and an especially big pyramidal mound, which probably supported a temple.

Cushing speculated that at first people built up the keys with shells, then extended the sea walls to make enclosures that served as fish traps, into which they paddled their canoes, driving the fish ahead of them. As mud and debris accumulated in canals between shell heaps, they dug it out and formed little garden patches. They also built platforms for dwellings and cisterns to catch rain for drinking water. As time passed the settlements grew more and more elaborate, and so did the lives of the people who occupied them. At Key Marco, where Cushing did a famous job of excavating, he uncovered a wealth of beautiful and fascinating material. Much of it looked as if it had just been finished. Even perishable things such as cordage, mats, and objects made of wood had been preserved in the salty bogs.

Women gathered nuts and wild plants, made excellent baskets and mats, and wove blankets of feather and hemp. Some of their textiles, cordage, and baskets are on display in the museum. Unfortunately the Ozark Bluff people did not bury grave goods with the dead. A blanket, a mat, and a basketry pillow are about the only offerings found in the graves, and so less is known about this culture than about some others. Perhaps a little more could have been found out if collectors had not looted the shelters before archeologists got there.

Several displays in the museum contain material from the famous Spiro Mounds Site in Oklahoma, which yielded much fascinating material even after extensive vandalizing. Featured are pearl and shell beads, engraved shell cups and gorgets, a stone earspool and monolithic axe, and the famous "Big Boy" pipe, which is often considered the best prehistoric Native American stone sculpture.

Other exhibits include Paleo-Indian stone points, an interpretation of the Burial Mound period in Arkansas, material from the three major cultures

of the Temple Mound period, and illustrations of the wide trade networks developed by Native Americans.

Florida

CASTILLO DE SAN MARCOS NATIONAL MONUMENT

1 Castillo Dr., St. Augustine. Open daily, all year. Closed Dec. 25. Admission charged. Camping nearby.

The castillo, a seventeenth-century Spanish fort, was built on a very large prehistoric midden.

CRYSTAL RIVER STATE ARCHAEOLOGICAL SITE

From the town of Crystal River drive northwest a short distance on US 19 to directional sign, then turn west on a paved road which leads directly to the museum. Open daily, all year. Admission charged.

In addition to housing interpretive exhibits and artifacts excavated in the vicinity, the museum in this Florida

state park offers a view through its windows of three different types of mound—refuse mounds, burial mounds, and a temple mound. Trails lead from the museum to the mounds.

The Story. Beginning about 2100 years ago, Indians developed a settlement here on the bank of the Crystal River. In time this became a very important ceremonial center, and activities continued here for about 1600 years.

In the course of excavations, which began in 1903, more than 450 burials have been found. Some of the grave goods have proved that there was trade between Crystal River Indians and Indians who lived in distant places—as far north as Ohio. Two stone slabs may indicate that these people were also affected by ideas from Mexico. Carvings on one of the slabs resemble those on stones called steles, which were erected in ancient Mexico to commemorate special events.

FLORIDA STATE MUSEUM
(See University of Florida)

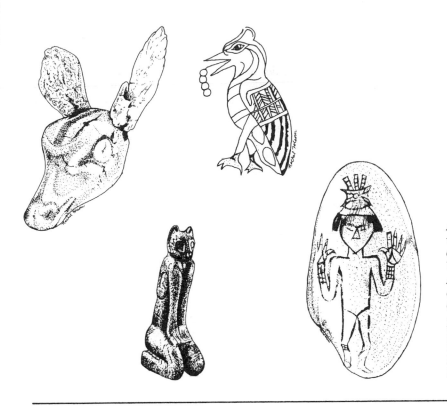

Above, left: The Key Marco artist who carved this deer's head made the ears movable. Original in the University Museum, Philadelphia. *Above, right:* A woodpecker painted on wood, from Key Marco. After Cushing. *Below, left:* This panther-like figure was carved by a Key dweller. *Below, right:* A humorous shell painting from Key Marco. Original in the University Museum, Philadelphia.

FORT CAROLINE NATIONAL MEMORIAL

12713 Fort Caroline Rd., Jacksonville. Open free, daily, all year. Closed certain holidays.

In the museum at the Visitor Center are exhibits of Timucuan Indian artifacts from excavations at the fort and elsewhere in Florida.

FORT MATANZAS NATIONAL MONUMENT

From St. Augustine drive 14 miles south on Florida A1A. Open free, daily, all year. Closed Dec. 25. Camping nearby.

Within the park are several large prehistoric middens.

GULF ISLANDS NATIONAL SEASHORE

Planned for some time before 1985 are a museum exhibit and a wayside display about the Santa Rosa—Swift Creek Indian Culture. For information write to PO Box 100, Gulf Breeze, FL 32561.

HISTORICAL MUSEUM OF SOUTHERN FLORIDA

3280 S. Miami Ave., Bldg. B., Miami. Open free, Monday through Saturday; afternoons, Sunday. Closed Dec. 25.

Random local finds and materials professionally excavated throw light on the lifeways of the Calusa and Tesquesta Indians from about 600 B.C. to the historic period. The Calusas lived on the west coast of Florida, south of Tampa Bay; the Tequestas on the east coast, from the upper Florida keys to what is now Martin County. The exhibits show how people adjusted to an environment that lacked metal and hard stone by substituting seashells and wood for materials that would have been used in other areas.

INDIAN TEMPLE MOUND MUSEUM
(See Temple Mound Museum)

JACKSONVILLE MUSEUM OF ARTS AND SCIENCES

In Jacksonville, 1025 Gulf Life Drive. Open free, Tuesday through Friday; afternoons, Saturday, Sunday. Closed September and certain holidays.

Some exhibits here are devoted to the prehistoric Indians who lived in the Everglades.

LAKE JACKSON MOUNDS STATE ARCHAEOLOGICAL SITE

Four and one-half miles north of Tallahassee off US 27. Open free, daily.

Excavations at this ceremonial mound site have revealed that people lived in the area from about A.D. 1300 to historic times. A nature trail leads to one visitable mound.

MADIRA BICKEL MOUND STATE ARCHAEOLOGICAL SITE

From Bradenton drive 5 miles north on US 41 and US 19, following US 19 to left and state park directional signs to the mound site, which is on Terra Ceia Island. Open free, daily, all year.

Some Indians occupied this site, which is near present-day St. Petersburg, apparently from about A.D. 1 to about 1600. The earliest inhabit-

People who lived on Weeden Island, Florida, about 1000 years ago, modeled this clay bottle in the shape of a dove. Original in the Museum of the American Indian.

A clay figure on display in Temple Mound Museum, Fort Walton Beach. Florida News Bureau, Dept. of Commerce photo by Eric Tournay.

ants lived as shellfish harvesters. Abundant food from the sea nourished them, and they left only a few tools behind in their piles of discarded shells. Slowly their lifeway changed, and they began to adopt customs that made existence a good deal more complicated. Like many others in the Southeast, they became greatly occupied with burying the dead.

After about A.D. 700 their rituals and their pottery closely resembled those of the Weeden Island people, who also lived close to St. Petersburg. Sometimes single bodies of the dead were placed within low mounds of sand. Often the bones from a number of skeletons would be bundled together for burial in a mound. Artifacts associated with these burials included specially made pottery, polished stone celts, shell beads, and shell cups. Pottery of the Weeden Island type is unusually attractive, and it was found here in abundance.

Sometime after A.D. 1400 this area came under the influence of dynamic new ideas associated with the building of temple mounds. The people became much more proficient farm-

ers, adopted a new style of pottery making, and spent a great deal of time and energy heaping up an earthen pyramid on which they placed a ceremonial structure. At the time the Spaniards first visited Florida, temple-mound builders still lived here.

SAFETY HARBOR SITE

In Philippe Park, 1 mile northeast of Safety Harbor on County Road 30. Open free, daily.

Here, on a point of land which extends into Tampa Bay, Timucua Indians built a temple mound in late prehistoric times. The mound, which is 150 feet in diameter and 25 feet high, is protected by the Pinellas County Park Department.

Part of the area has been excavated and a large amount of material recovered. Some of it is on display in the County Courthouse in Clearwater.

SAINT PETERSBURG
HISTORICAL SOCIETY

335 Second Ave., N.E., St. Petersburg. Open Monday through Satur-

day; afternoons, Sunday. Admission charged.

Included in this historical museum are some prehistoric skulls, artifacts, and potsherds, collected in Pinellas County. Some materials reflect the important Weeden Island and Safety Harbor cultures, which developed nearby. Most are from the early 1500s.

SOUTH FLORIDA MUSEUM
AND PLANETARIUM

201 Tenth St. W., Bradenton. Open Tuesday through Friday; afternoons, Saturday, Sunday. Closed certain holidays. Admission charged.

Prehistoric artifacts are on display here, together with information about the different types of mounds built in Florida before the arrival of Europeans. Dioramas give an artist's interpretation of a Calusa village scene and of a wedding among the Timucua people in Florida in prehistoric times.

TEMPLE MOUND MUSEUM

At intersection of US 98 and Florida 85, in Fort Walton Beach. Open Tuesday through Saturday; afternoons, Sunday. Admission charged.

This museum, which is operated by the city of Fort Walton Beach, introduces the visitor to 10,000 years of Indian life on the Gulf Coast. Beginning with artifacts from Paleo-Indian times, the exhibits carry prehistory forward chronologically to historic time. Of particular interest are the Weeden Island culture ceramic artifacts. There is also a large exhibit of Fort Walton pottery.

The mound, on top of which a temple once stood, has been restored. Archeologists have estimated that Indians constructed the mound by moving 500,000 basketloads of earth.

TURTLE MOUND

From New Smyrna Beach drive 9 miles south on Florida A1A. Open free, all year. Camping nearby.

A very large mound grew up here as Indians harvested oysters and dis-carded the shells over a period of several thousand years.

The site is largely unexcavated, and doubtless contains much material that can throw light on prehistoric Florida. It would now be lost to science had it not been for a campaign by local citizens when an attempt was made to quarry its shells for road construction. Their efforts brought state protection to the site, but other mounds have disappeared as road builders hauled their contents away. Acquired by the federal government, Turtle Mound in 1975 became a part of Canaveral National Seashore and is now administered by the National Park Service.

Special Feature. A self-guided nature trail, complete with a booklet and a boardwalk, leads to the top of Turtle Mound, providing a good view of the Atlantic Ocean and the lagoon behind. Yaupon plants, which belong to the holly family, grow near the trail. It was from the leaves of this plant, or its close relative the cassina holly, that Indians in the Southeast made the Black Drink, which played an important part in certain ceremonies. First the leaves were parched, then steeped

Left: This clay vessel was created in the form of a kneeling figure. Original in the Museum of the American Indian. *Right:* Turtle Mound, south of New Smyrna Beach, Florida, grew to its present height of 50 feet as prehistoric Indians of the area harvested oysters and discarded the shells. Several years ago it was threatened with destruction, but a campaign on the part of local citizens led to state protection of the site. Turtle Mound Historic Site photo.

Indians pecked these circular designs on a granite boulder near Etowah Mounds, in Georgia. The boulder is now on the campus of Reinhardt College, Waleska, Georgia. Margaret Perryman Smith, photo, courtesy Campbell Grant.

in a large jar of water. The result was a liquid containing a great deal of caffein.

Before performing certain ceremonies, Indians drank some of this Black Drink from conch shell cups. Sometimes other herbs were added to make it an emetic. The vomiting it induced was supposed to have a purifying effect. Without the emetic herbs, people often used the Black Drink just as we use coffee or tea today.

UNIVERSITY OF FLORIDA, FLORIDA STATE MUSEUM

On the campus, Gainesville. Open free, Monday through Saturday; afternoons, Sunday and certain holidays.

In this museum, which emphasizes hands-on exhibits and calls attention to concepts spanning different cultures, visitors can walk through life-size reconstructions—for example, a Florida cave or a Mayan palace. Of particular interest to those concerned with prehistory north of Mexico is a reconstruction of a 500-year-old Timucuan village.

Georgia

ALBANY AREA JUNIOR MUSEUM, INC.

516 Flint Ave., Albany. Open free, Monday through Friday. Closed in August and on certain holidays.

This museum, in which ethnographic exhibits emphasize Creek and Cherokee material, also displays artifacts of Paleo, Archaic, Woodland, and Mississippian cultures.

COLUMBUS MUSEUM OF ARTS AND SCIENCES

1251 Wynnton Rd., Columbus. Open free, Tuesday through Saturday; afternoons, Sunday. Closed certain holidays.

Here are displays of artifacts from Paleo through Mississippian cultures. Dioramas show how a site is excavated and how Archaic and Mississippian people lived.

ETOWAH MOUNDS ARCHEOLOGICAL AREA (ET-oh-wah)

From US 41 at Cartersville, drive 1 mile west on Georgia 61 Spur, then continue 2 miles following directional signs to museum and headquarters. Open free, Tuesday through Saturday; afternoons, Sunday. Closed certain holidays. Camping nearby.

The museum at this site gives an excellent general view of prehistoric life in the area, beginning about 5000 B.C., and at the same time it provides real insight into what archeologists do as they search for information about the past. Of special interest is the period beginning about A.D. 1000, when Etowah was occupied by people who built temple mounds and practiced the rituals associated with the Southern Cult.

During excavation archeologists were astonished at the richness of the grave goods they found buried in tombs, particularly those discovered at the foot of one of the mounds. Exhibits in the museum show something of the society that produced this wealth

Present-day visitors at Etowah Mounds Archaeological Area, in Georgia, can climb steps on the same ramp used by prehistoric Indians when they went to the building which stood on the flat top of the large mound, at right in this aerial photograph. Georgia Historical Commission photo.

As archeologists dug at Etowah Mounds Archaeological Area, they came across evidence of an ancient structure. The rows of holes show where upright wall posts once stood. Georgia Historical Commission photo.

and the gorgeous costumes worn by some of the inhabitants of Etowah. This relatively small group must have had high status in the community, though exactly what it was is not entirely clear. Members of the group certainly had special privileges, including the right to be buried with ritual objects.

Ornaments and ceremonial paraphernalia found in the graves were often made of materials from distant places, and one exhibit in the museum traces the amazing extent of trade—obsidian and grizzly bear teeth from the Rocky Mountains, for example, and turtle shell and shark's teeth from the seacoast. Very similar grave goods have been found in burials at other Southeastern sites, indicating that finished objects may have been traded among various communities. Beautifully worked stone axes, engraved copper headdresses, and large stone knives unsuited for work of any kind indicate that skilled craftsworkers created the objects for ceremonial purposes, and perhaps they themselves were among the elite group. The fact that objects of this kind were found

at other sites suggests that perhaps the spread of the Southern Cult was really the spread of specially made objects, rather than a spread of an actual religious ritual.

Exhibits in the museum include explanations of the ceremonial paraphernalia. The grounds outside are worth a walk, and a superb view of the entire area rewards the visitor who makes the steep climb to the top of the largest mound in the Etowah complex.

KOLOMOKI MOUNDS STATE PARK
(koh-loh-MOH-kee)

From Blakely drive 2 miles north on US 27, then follow directional signs 4 miles to the Visitor Center Museum and mounds. Open free, Tuesday through Saturday; afternoons, Sunday. Closed certain holidays. Camping.

This site includes the largest mound group in the Gulf Coast area and is also noteworthy because of the very careful detective work done by the archeologists who have excavated and interpreted it.

The Story. Hunters probably camped here several thousand years ago, beside

an artesian spring near Little Kolomoki Creek, but the earliest visitors left only the scantiest of traces. Then a succession of peoples visited the area, at least briefly, during a period of several thousand years. By about A.D. 700 a small village had been established, and women were making pottery that resembled the kind made at Weeden Island, farther south. From then on the population grew, and a distinct Kolomoki lifeway developed.

The daily existence of the ordinary people must have differed greatly from that of the leaders. Commoners did the work of farming, doubtless following patterns of behavior that were widespread throughout the Southeast. The leaders, on the other hand, probably did no farm work. Rather they acted as executives who directed public projects and supervised and organized ceremonies and rituals in the temple on top of the platform mound or in the plaza at the foot of the mound.

One of the complex operations connected with ritual activity was the manufacture of grave goods. First the raw material had to be obtained—

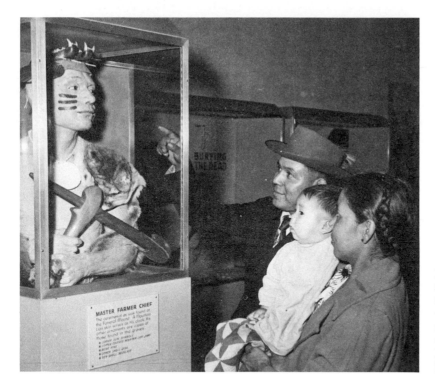

Modern Creek Indians, who came from Okmulgee, Oklahoma, to visit Ocmulgee National Monument, where their ancestors once lived, inspect the likeness of a chief from whom they may be descended. National Park Service photo by Drinnin, Inc.

shell from the Gulf of Mexico, copper, galena, and mica from much more distant places. These materials were transformed by craftsworkers into ornaments and other artifacts buried with the bodies of important people.

All of this activity was coordinated by members of the ruling group. They supervised at least a thousand men, women, and children, who must have been involved in the final construction of the pyramid. At that time the work force dug, carried, and dumped the heavy clay necessary to create a cap six feet thick, covering the top of the pyramid, which measured 325 feet by 200 feet at its base.

An almost equally large crew of workers had to be directed when it came time to raise a mound for the burial of an important personage at Kolomoki. For such a burial laborers first dug a large pit, about seven feet deep. Then the cremated bones were laid in the bottom, together with ornaments, beads, and precious possessions. Next, large rocks were brought in (one measured 6 × 3 × 2 feet) to fill the hole about halfway. When this had been covered with a large,

rounded heap of clay and more stones, graves at the side were made for wives and other members of the household, who were sacrificed. Quantities of specially made mortuary pottery accompanied these burials. Continuous processions of workers added layers of earth and clay, some of which they had to bring from a spot half a mile away, in the side of a steep bluff.

The finished burial mounds were as much as 50 feet in diameter and from 6 to 20 feet high. To complete the mortuary ceremonies more people were sacrificed. Why do archeologists suspect there were sacrifices? Excavation shows that numerous heads with no bodies attached had been buried in the mounds. Many of the heads bore decorations in just the positions they would have had if held there by skin and hair. Where copper ornaments were present, there were even bits of skin and hair left on the bone as a result of the preservative action of the copper. In other words, recently severed heads had been buried, not fleshless skulls. A likely explanation was that the heads were cut off in the course of human sacrifice.

The Museum. To show how archeologists work and what they find, one of the burial mounds, with skeletons and grave goods in place, has been roofed over and made part of the museum. Exhibits here and elsewhere in the building illustrate many aspects of Kolomoki life—hunting, cooking, fishing, planting, house building, pottery making, working with copper, and making decorations of shell. Dioramas and paintings show construction of mounds, and there are fine displays of pottery, especially the kind used only as mortuary ware. Exhibits also give an idea of life in several earlier periods, when people with quite different cultural patterns lived here.

OCMULGEE NATIONAL MONUMENT
(ohk-MULL-ghee)

At the southeast edge of Macon on US 80. Open free, daily. Closed certain holidays. Camping nearby.

Ocmulgee was the first large site in the Southeast to be scientifically investigated. Temple mounds, a reconstructed ceremonial building, and

This ceremonial earth lodge at Ocmulgee National Monument has been reconstructed over the original clay floor. National Park Service photo.

exhibits in the museum at the Visitor Center recreate the whole history of Indian life in central Georgia.

The Story. The first people to enter Georgia seem to have arrived about 8000 B.C. They were Paleo-Indians, hunters of mammoths and other Ice-Age game. A very small, wandering population remained in the area for about 3000 years. Some who camped near Ocmulgee left behind a projectile point, many scrapers, and a few other tools.

When the big game disappeared, hunters turned to new ways of getting food. In some parts of the Southeast they discovered they could lead an easier life by harvesting freshwater clams and mussels. However, those who camped at Ocmulgee did not become shellfish eaters. The equipment they left behind shows that they continued hunting, although the game now consisted of smaller animals. When game was scarce in one place the hunters moved on to another, following a route that brought them back repeatedly to their old campsite at Ocmulgee.

Not long after 1000 B.C. a whole new way of life began in this part of Georgia. People had learned to grow food in gardens. They cultivated pumpkins, beans, and sunflowers, and this food supply made it possible to live in villages. Settlement allowed women to adopt an invention that had been in use much earlier in other parts of the Southeast—crude pottery. These Early Farmers, as they are called in the Ocmulgee Museum (or Swift Creek people, as they are also called), gradually expanded their gardens, and now they had more free time. Arts and crafts developed. Their pottery improved.

About A.D. 900 some aggressive people (called by the museum Master Farmers and also referred to as Macon Plateau people) invaded the area. Just where they came from no one knows for sure, possibly from the Mississippi Valley near the mouth of the Missouri River, possibly from Tennessee. Whatever their origin, they drove out the earlier inhabitants and began intensive and very successful corn farming.

The newcomers also brought along elaborate political and religious cus-

Interior view of the earth lodge at the Ocmulgee National Monument. The raised platform, shaped like an eagle or a buzzard, has three places where dignitaries sat during ceremonies or councils. The floor is of a special type of clay. National Park Service photo.

toms and the habit of building very large ceremonial lodges entirely covered with earth. Here at Ocmulgee one of these earth lodges, constructed rather like a huge Eskimo igloo, has been restored. The roof is new, but it was possible to keep the original floor intact. This was made of a special clay called kaolin, which packs down very hard when walked on—or danced on—-as this floor no doubt was.

Meticulous work in excavating the earth lodge revealed that it was used for about 30 years and then burned—perhaps accidentally, but more probably as part of a ritual or as a safety measure. The earthen roof was heavy and often damp, and the supporting beams must have rotted quickly. Fortunately for archeologists, the burned wood collapsed and preserved the circular floor with its molded seats for 47 people around the edge. At one end is a platform in the shape of an eagle, designed in a way that was popular all over the Southeast in late prehistoric times. Apparently important people sat on the platform, where there are seats for three.

The lodge was a place for religious ceremonies and civic gatherings, particularly those held in winter. Because of its thousand-year-old floor, it has been called the oldest public building site in the United States.

Across an open space opposite the earth lodge stands a large, flat-topped mound nearly 50 feet tall. Like many other great mounds in the Southeast, this one served as the foundation for a temple. The original temple stood on a low platform. After a time this building was burned, perhaps when a leader died, and the site was entirely covered with earth, which served as the foundation for a new temple. This pattern of destruction and rebuilding went on, again and again, as long as the village was occupied by the Master Farmers.

Over a period of 200 years other, smaller mounds supported additional temples, and at one end of the village is a mound which apparently served as a cemetery. All of this building took a vast amount of time. More work, too, went into digging moats or ditches, which may have served for protection. Warfare certainly occupied these people, perhaps because the de-

Diorama of an Indian ceremony at Ocmulgee National Monument. National Park Service photo by Jack E. Boucher.

Women who once lived at Swift Creek, Georgia, used implements like these to press designs into their pottery while the clay was still moist. Archeologists reconstructed these stamps, now on display in Ocmulgee National Monument.

scendants of the earlier inhabitants were trying to return. What happened in the end at Ocmulgee is something of a mystery. For some unexplained reason everyone left, and the site was never occupied again except for one brief period much later.

Possibly descendants of the Early Farmers mingled with the Master Farmers and settled nearby. Certainly people who shared traits with both the Early Farmers and the Master Farmers developed what is known as the Lamar lifeway and built mounds nearby. Some of their descendants became Creek Indians of historic times.

The Museum. All of this story—and much more—is told in the museum. Models and dioramas illuminate various aspects of the lives of those who inhabited the area for 10,000 years. Exhibits display many artifacts, including a large collection of pipes.

Among the special exhibits of pottery of many kinds is one showing how women at Ocmulgee made and decorated their vessels. Visitors who

are familiar with pottery making in other parts of the country will find interesting differences here.

The Name. Ocmulgee comes from a Creek Indian word, the meaning of which is now unknown.

After the Creeks were forced to leave the Southeast in the 1800s, they made new homes for themselves in Oklahoma, where they called one of their towns Okmulgee—the old name, spelled differently.

ROCK EAGLE EFFIGY MOUND

From Eatonton drive 5 miles north on US 441 to the Rock Eagle 4-H Center. Open free, at all times. Camping.

Prehistoric Indians carried great numbers of white, quartz rocks a considerable distance to use in building this effigy. It is in the shape of a huge bird, called an eagle by some archeologists, a buzzard by others. The wings stretch out across a flat hilltop for 120 feet, tip to tip, and the depth of the original rockpile is thought to have been about 10 feet. At the foot of the bird a modern tower has been con-

Mound building took many forms in the Southeast. Rock Eagle Effigy Mound near Eatonton, Georgia, can be seen in its entirety from the top of a tower which has been built for the convenience of visitors. The effigy is made up of thousands of white quartz rocks.

structed so that visitors can see the whole of it, looking down from above. Another bird effigy of this sort is in the vicinity, but it cannot be visited by the public.

The date when the effigy was built and its purpose are not known, but archeologists believe it must have marked a ceremonial gathering place. Excavation revealed some charred bone, but no artifacts.

THRONATEESKA HERITAGE FOUNDATION

In Albany, 100 Roosevelt Ave. Open free, Monday through Friday; afternoons, Saturday. Closed certain holidays.

In this primarily historical museum are some exhibits of prehistoric Creek artifacts.

TRACK ROCK ARCHAEOLOGICAL AREA, CHATTAHOOCHEE NATIONAL FOREST

From Blairsville drive 8 miles south on US 19, then east 5 miles on Forest Service Road 95 to marker. Open free, at all times. Camping nearby.

Here, in a 52-acre area are preserved petroglyphs—rock carvings—of ancient Indian origin; they resemble animal and bird tracks, crosses, circles, and human footprints.

Louisiana

LOUISIANA STATE EXHIBIT MUSEUM

3015 Greenwood Rd., Shreveport. Open free, Monday through Saturday; afternoons, Sunday. Closed Dec. 25 and Jan. 1.

Displays of Paleo-Indian and other projectile points can be seen in the Capitol Historical Gallery of this museum, which is operated by the Louisiana Department of Culture, Recreation, and Tourism, Office of State Parks. Exhibits from mounds, including the Gahagan Mound in Red River Parish, show examples of ornaments, pottery, and other artifacts.

Special Feature. A large diorama, built under the guidance of an archeologist, shows the Poverty Point Site in northern Louisiana when it was a flourishing village. (See entry below.)

Although no one can be sure exactly what the Poverty Point dwellings looked like, those in the diorama show the probable shape of huts thatched with grass, palmetto leaves, or bark. The appearance of the women is based on figurines made of baked clay found at the site. (No male figures seem to have been made.) The women wore short, belted skirts in summer and probably heavier deerskin clothing in cold weather. One of the figurines shows a woman carrying a baby on a cradleboard.

LOUISIANA STATE UNIVERSITY, MUSEUM OF GEOSCIENCE

On the campus, Baton Rouge. Open free, Monday through Friday. Closed certain holidays.

Although this museum is devoted chiefly to earth sciences, it has a section, including some dioramas, on the prehistoric and historic Indians of Louisiana.

Pebble Tools

Knowing the trick, a person can pick up a certain kind of water-worn pebble or cobble, strike it a few times with a hammerstone, and make it into a useful tool for chopping. Pebble tools of this kind were among the earliest created by humans, and they have been found by the ton on the surface of the ground in certain parts of Alabama.

Did recent Indian hunters knock out these artifacts for one-time or emergency use? Or were the choppers made a very long time ago by people whose tool kit was very, very simple? These questions occurred to archeologists, both amateur and professional, as they encountered thousands of rounded stones that had distinct chopping or cutting edges. Often the stones looked very old because they had weathered deeply. Always they resembled tools found in the Old World, which were known to be very ancient. However, there seemed to be no way to discover the exact age of the Alabama artifacts. Even when the tools were found buried in the earth, luck has not been with the diggers. So far dating has been uncertain or impossible.

As a result, a fascinating mystery remains unsolved. Some archeologists suspect that the pebble tools are evidence that people who did not know how to make stone projectile points lived in America before the days of the big-game-hunting Paleo-Indians. Other archeologists think the pebble tools may have been made in a hurry by much later people, who regarded them as expendable. Whatever the true explanation turns

---

MARKSVILLE STATE COMMEMORATIVE AREA

Adjacent to Marksville on Louisiana 5. Open daily.

Prehistoric earthen walls enclose a 40-acre tract in which there are a number of burial and temple mounds and a museum.

The Story. As early as 1500 B.C. people seem to have used this site, which was then close to the Mississippi River. Eventually the river shifted course, and its banks are now 30 miles away. Today Old River Lake is all that remains of the ancient channel. About A.D. 300 a permanent village began to grow here along the riverbank, and in unbroken sequence, until about the time Europeans arrived, the Marksville people increased their food supply and the range and variety of their implements, art forms, and religious customs.

Quite early an ambitious earthen barricade was placed around the village, apparently for defensive purposes. Within this protected area three types of mound were built at different times over a period of two millenia. Some

mounds are refuse heaps or middens, some conical burial mounds, some temple mounds. One, no longer in its original shape, was a conical mound atop a truncated pyramid.

Archeologists have found this site of great interest. Excavation was done by the Smithsonian Institution, and Louisiana State University, in cooperation with the Works Progress Administration.

Exhibits in the museum installed under the supervision of Dr. James A. Ford, of the American Museum of Natural History, and Robert S. Neitzel of the Louisiana State Parks and Recreation Commission, display material recovered in the course of the excavations and illustrate the many changes in the lives of those who lived here for such a long time.

During the period of occupation when people were building burial mounds, they were greatly influenced by the Hopewell lifeway, which centered far to the north. A special variant of Hopewell has been called Marksville, after this site, where it was first identified.

Aerial photographs in the museum show the large number of mounds in and near the area and the relation of these mounds to the former bed of the Mississippi River.

NORTHWESTERN STATE UNIVERSITY, WILLIAMSON MUSEUM

On the campus, Northwestern State University, Natchitoches. Open free, Monday through Friday. Closed certain holidays.

Some exhibits here show artifacts from sites excavated by the university.

POVERTY POINT STATE COMMEMORATIVE AREA

From Interstate 10 drive north on Louisiana 17 to Epps, then northeast on Louisiana 577. Open free, daily.

This site went almost unnoticed until 1953, when an alert archeologist examined an aerial photograph taken by an Army mapmaker. The photograph revealed a mound and long, low hummocks of earth, which had

out to be, interest in the tools is considerable in Alabama and elsewhere, and the Alabama Archeological Society, University of Alabama, Box 5897, University, AL 35486, can tell interested persons where examples of the artifacts may be seen.

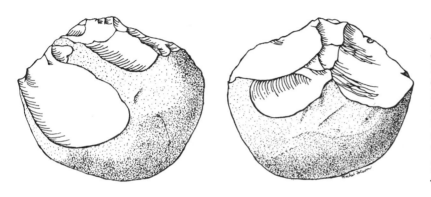

The pebble tool was one of the earliest implements developed by humans. Archeologists have not yet determined who made them in the New World or when, but thousands have been found in various parts of the United States. These two views are of a pebble tool from Alabama, where many such artifacts have been discovered. After Lively and Josselyn.

been laid out in a very definite, geometric pattern. They were a series of artificial terraces, built in the form of six concentric octagons. The whole configuration measured more than half a mile across, and its very size concealed its real nature.

Archeological work at the site soon told an amazing story. Apparently several thousand people at a time lived in this settlement for more than a thousand years, beginning perhaps about 1500 B.C., and the construction they did was remarkable.

To form the terraces, on which they placed their dwellings, people carried earth and heaped it to a height of 6 feet or more. Each terrace was about 80 feet wide at the base, and there were six of them, one inside the other. The total linear measurement of these concentric ridges added up to more than 11 miles.

On the west side of the village these same people built a ceremonial mound, 700 feet by 800 feet at the base and 60 feet high. About a mile away they put up another large mound, also used for ceremonies. Still others, which were smaller and cone-shaped, covered places

where the dead were cremated. Archeologists have estimated that workers transported 20 million basketloads of earth, 50 pounds at a time.

The bow and arrow were not known at Poverty Point. Like other Archaic people, the men used spears, darts, and spear-throwers. Hunters may also have captured large birds with bolas. These were weights, either oval or pear-shaped, tied at the ends of strings in groups of three or more. The hunter whirled the weighted strings around and released them at just the right moment to make them wrap themselves around the birds.

The special heavy stone used for the bola weights had to be imported from northern Arkansas or southern Missouri, some distance away. Other material that Poverty Point people wanted came from even more remote places. They got flint from Ohio, slate from the vicinity of Lake Michigan, and copper from Lake Superior. Soapstone for making pots may have come by dugout canoe or raft as much as 500 miles, from a quarry in North Carolina.

The soil close to the Mississippi River had almost no stone—a fact which led to a curious invention called the Poverty Point object. Each of these objects was molded from a small handful of clay, then baked as hard as rock. Some were roughly spherical. Others were carefully made in other geometric shapes. When hot, the baked clay balls were used in the way stones were used elsewhere: possibly they were dropped into a vessel containing stew or mush to make it boil. Lacking pottery vessels, women cooked in watertight baskets or carved stone bowls.

There is also evidence that cooking was done in another way. First the women dug a pit in the ground. Next they fashioned some of the balls from clay, laid them in the pit, and built a fire over them. Presently they raked out the coals and the hard-baked balls, lined the hot pit with grass, laid food on the grass, covered it with the heated balls and left it to cook, clam-bake style. Whichever way the objects were used, women made, according to estimates, 24 million of them during the period the village was occupied.

Right: Pottery bowl made in the Mississippian Period. Original at Mississippi State University.

Left: The Museum of the American Indian has this water jar from Louisiana in its collection. The prehistoric potter incised the intricate design on the moist clay before firing the vessel.

Another unusual trait of Poverty Point people was their use of very small, sharp stone tools called microflints.

Some archeologists have speculated that the Poverty Point mounds were inspired by pyramid building in Mexico. Recent research, however, seems to indicate that the mounds do not really resemble Mexican structures and that they were a local phenomenon.

No direct evidence of agriculture has been found at Poverty Point, but its inhabitants no doubt raised crops. They lived on fertile land and had many customs characteristic of farmers elsewhere. For example, they made female figurines, probably thinking thus to encourage fertility. They had grinding implements as did people who raised corn in Mexico. The very fact that they built geometric mounds suggests agriculture. Their mounds were so constructed that the equinox could be recognized when the sun rose directly in line with certain features of the earthworks. Such information about the seasons was always of importance to farmers.

Details of the Poverty Point lifestyle may be seen in exhibits at the museum in the Visitor Center. There are also sight-seeing trails and an observation tower where visitors may view the overall design of the site.

WILLIAMSON MUSEUM
(See Northwestern State University)

Mississippi

BEAR CREEK MOUND

At milepost 308.8 on the Natchez (NATCH-ez) Trace Parkway. Open free, daily, all year.

At this site is a ceremonial mound and an adjacent village occupied as early as 8000 B.C. by hunters who stayed only a short while.

BOYD MOUNDS

At milepost 106.9 on Natchez Trace Parkway. Open free, at all times.

This village site with several burial mounds is marked with an interpretive sign.

BYNUM MOUNDS

From Tupelo drive 34 miles southwest on Natchez Trace Parkway to directional marker. Open free, during daylight hours. Camping nearby.

Here is a group of burial mounds, two of which can easily be seen from a hard-surfaced path. An interpretive panel gives information about the far-flung trading activities of the Indians who once lived at the site.

The Story. About A.D. 700, people who followed the Middle Woodland way of life settled here and built circular houses thatched with grass. They hunted, fished, and gathered wild fruits and nuts, and they may also have maintained small gardens. After a time they adopted the custom, popular elsewhere at this period, of building earthen mounds over the remains of the dead. Altogether six of these burial mounds were constructed in the neighborhood of their village.

Gradually life became richer and more complex for the Bynum people. They obtained materials for weapons, ornaments, and tools by trading with other Indians who lived in distant plac-

Emerald Mound, a ceremonial site near Natchez Trace Parkway. National Park Service photo by Don Black.

es. Flint came from Ohio; marine shells, from the Gulf Coast; greenstone for their grooved and polished axes, from Alabama. Like the people at Emerald Mound, which is also on the Natchez Trace Parkway, they imported copper from Lake Superior. Why and exactly when they abandoned this site no one yet knows.

CHICKASAW VILLAGE SITE

On the Natchez Trace Parkway, 7 miles south of the Tupelo entrance (from US 78). Open free, daily, all year.

In exhibits at the site of an ancient village, the daily life of Chickasaw Indians is described. A quarter-mile nature trail with interpretive signs describes Indian uses of plants.

COBB INSTITUTE OF ARCHAEOLOGY
(See Mississippi State University)

EMERALD MOUND

From Natchez drive 12 miles northeast on the Natchez Trace Parkway. Open free, during daylight hours, daily, all year.

Emerald Mound is the third largest temple mound in the United States. Its base measures 730 × 435 feet and covers nearly eight acres. Only Monks Mound, in Cahokia Mounds State Park in Illinois, and Poverty Point Mound, in Louisiana, are larger. Two interpretive panels at the site tell how Indians constructed this immense earthwork.

The Story. People who followed the Mississippian lifeway began to build Emerald Mound about A.D. 1300, and they continued to live here until about A.D. 1600. After finishing the huge, flat-topped platform, they went on to add at one end of it a second mound, itself as large as many of those in the Southeast which rest directly on the ground. On the principal mound there may once have been many ceremonial structures, and on top of the second one there was certainly a temple.

The whole Emerald Mound complex served as a ceremonial center for farmers who lived nearby in thatch-covered houses, which had walls plastered with clay. These people made fine pottery and were skilled at fabricating a variety of tools and ornaments. As did the earlier farmers at Bynum Mounds, they obtained some of their materials from the Gulf Coast, and their copper came from far away to the north, near Lake Superior. What happened to them in the end is something of a mystery, but Emerald Mound, like many others, was still in use when De Soto's marauding expedition passed through the Southeast in A.D. 1540–1541. Many other mounds, including the important Anna Mound group, dot this vicinity, but since none of them have been prepared for the public they cannot be visited.

GRAND VILLAGE OF THE NATCHEZ INDIANS
(Fatherland Plantation Site)

In Natchez, 400 Jefferson Davis Blvd. Open free, daily, all year.

At this site, which was inhabited

Underwater Sites in Florida

Near Charlotte Harbor in southwest Florida are two small bodies of water, one called Little Salt Spring, the other called Warm Mineral Springs. Though they are rather shallow at the edges, they fall away toward the center, where a kind of chimney in the limestone, called a sinkhole, leads down to a water-filled cavern far below (Little Salt Spring is about 200 feet deep). These were ideal spots for scuba divers, who some years ago began bringing up stone projectile points and the bones of animals and human beings. By the time scientists were called on to identify and date the finds, Warm Mineral Springs had been greatly disturbed, and the material from it was not as useful to archeologists as it might have been. However, human bones and the bones of a saber-toothed tiger from the site proved to be about 10,000 years old. Whether one killed the other could not be determined. A small exhibit of material from the site can be seen in the entrance to Warm Mineral Springs Spa, 12 miles south of Venice on Florida 41.

Fortunately a foundation grant and cooperation from the University of Miami have given archeologists a chance to work at the much less disturbed Little Salt Spring site, which has turned out to be very rich and exciting. There are actually two phases to the work, one under water and one on land. Deep in the spring itself divers found a ledge which was dry land 12,000 years ago, when sea level and the water-table level in Florida were much lower than today. On the ledge lay the shell of a

---

about A.D. 1200, are plaza areas and platform mounds, three of which have been restored. An audiovisual program in the museum and Visitor Center interprets the life of the people who built the mounds.

MANGUM MOUND

From Natchez drive 46 miles northeast on the Natchez Trace Parkway. Open free, daily, all year.

Copper ornaments and other artifacts found in burials here have revealed much to archeologists about the people who built the mound. Interpretive signs, a map, four exhibits, and an audio station provide explanations of the site.

MISSISSIPPI STATE UNIVERSITY, COBB INSTITUTE OF ARCHAEOLOGY

On the campus, Mississippi State. Open free, Monday through Friday. Closed certain holidays.

Some exhibits contain material of the Mississippian culture.

NANIH WAIYA HISTORIC SITE

From Louisville drive 12 miles south on Mississippi 397, then right on Mississippi 490 to sign for Nanih Waiyah State Park. Open free, at all times. Camping.

There is a mound at this site where Native Americans lived for about 1500 years before contact with Europeans.

OWL CREEK INDIAN MOUNDS, TOMBIGBEE NATIONAL FOREST

From Houston on Mississippi 8 drive 10 miles north on Mississippi 15 to Old Houlka, then east on Forest Service Rd. 903 for 4½ miles to the parking area near the mounds. Open free, at all times. Camping at Davis Lake, 1½ miles from the mounds.

Here, near the place where De Soto made his winter camp, are two reconstructed ceremonial mounds. These, together with three other mounds, once surrounded a village plaza.

PHARR MOUNDS

At milepost 286.7 on the Natchez Trace Parkway, a section that was under construction as this book went to press. For information about date of opening, inquire at Tupelo Visitor Center, 3 miles north of Tupelo entrance to the parkway from US 78.

This is the largest and most important archeological site in northern Mississippi. It consists of eight large, dome-shaped burial mounds, scattered over an area of 90 acres, built and used from about A.D. 1 to 200 by nomadic hunters and gatherers, who returned to the site at times to bury the dead with their possessions. Recent archeological investigations revealed on the same site a Woodland-period palisaded village that was occupied about A.D. 1000 to 1200.

When preparation for the public is completed, there will be interpretive signs and explanations of the archeology of the site.

giant extinct tortoise, obviously killed by a sharp wooden spear that was still stuck in its body. The wood, by C-14 dating, is 12,030 years old.

Nearby on the ledge lay a wooden weapon, shaped much like a boomerang. This killing stick is unique because it is the oldest one ever found anywhere in the world, and the only one so far discovered in the Americas. When archeologists tested a model of the boomerang, it proved capable of bringing down game at a hundred yards.

Divers also found Paleo campgrounds from about the same period, now under water but on dry land before the water level rose, about 8000 years ago, and covered all the remains of human occupancy. Water in the spring is both high in mineral content and low in oxygen, and that accounts for the excellent preservation of wood and of the bones of both people and extinct animals—mammoth, mastodon, and ground sloth.

Excavation in now boggy earth around the sinkhole reveals that people camped there about 6000 years ago and buried their dead nearby. The burials so far excavated lead archeologists to think there may be as many as a thousand graves at the site. From one of them came the remarkably well preserved body of a woman wrapped in a shroud made of a kind of bark cloth and covered with a net woven from grapevines.

As this book went to press, Little Salt Spring was not open to the public, although plans for a visitor center are awaiting the necessary funds.

STATE HISTORICAL MUSEUM

Capitol and N. State streets, Jackson. Open free, Monday through Saturday; afternoons, Sunday. Closed certain holidays.

Within the room devoted to Mississippi Indians are dioramas and random archeological finds from various parts of the state.

TUPELO VISITOR CENTER NATCHEZ TRACE PARKWAY

On Natchez Trace Parkway, 3 miles north of the Tupelo entrance (from US 78). Open free, daily, all year. Closed Dec. 25.

On display here are some of the artifacts and other objects found in the excavation of prehistoric Indian mounds and villages along the Natchez Trace Parkway. A free film program introduces both the prehistory and the history of the trace. A library contains all the research reports on the excavations along the parkway.

The parkway itself follows old Indian trails. It also passes five groups of prehistoric mounds, which have been prepared for visitation. When completed, the parkway will run for about 450 miles between Nashville, Tenn., and Natchez, Miss. As this book goes to press, 380 miles of roadway have been finished. For up-to-date information about the progress of road construction and about any new sites that may have been prepared for the public, write to Natchez Trace Parkway, RR1, NT-143, Tupelo, MS 38801. The completed portions of the parkway are open free, at all times.

WINTERVILLE MOUNDS STATE PARK

From Greenville drive north 10 miles on Mississippi 1. Open Tuesday through Saturday; afternoons, Sunday. Closed Dec. 24 and 25. Admission charged.

A large, Mississippian-period ceremonial center was built here about A.D. 1000. The great main mound is about 55 feet high. A museum in the Visitor Center contains an outstanding collection of artifacts, some of which were excavated from the site by Jeffrey Brain of the Peabody Museum.

At Oconaluftee Indian Village a Cherokee Indian demonstrates how his ancestors made a dugout canoe by hollowing out a log with the help of fire and a stone axe.

North Carolina

CATAWBA COLLEGE, MUSEUM OF ANTHROPOLOGY

At the north edge of Salisbury, off US 601 on Brenner Ave., Heath Hill Forest, South Campus of Catawba College. Open free, most afternoons. For confirmation write, or phone (704) 637–4447.

Archeological exhibits in this museum emphasize the South Atlantic Piedmont. They include lithic technology.

Visitors who have special interests are given free guided tours that include the Research Laboratory of Archaeology.

CHARLOTTE NATURE MUSEUM, INC.

1658 Sterling Rd., Charlotte. Open free, Monday through Saturday; afternoons, Sunday. Closed certain holidays.

Exhibits of projectile points and tools collected in the Carolina Piedmont area are representative of the major culture periods from Paleo-Indian to historic times. There are also artifacts of the Basketmaker people of the Southwest and projectile points from Pennsylvania and Virginia.

GREENSBORO HISTORICAL MUSEUM

130 Summit Ave., Greensboro. Open free, Tuesday through Saturday; afternoons, Sunday. Closed certain holidays.

Exhibits of artifacts collected in the Piedmont area represent 16 culture groups from Paleo-Indian times to about A.D. 1700.

MORROW MOUNTAIN STATE PARK NATURAL HISTORY MUSEUM

From Albemarle on US 52 drive to junction with North Carolina 740, follow directional signs to park entrance. Open free, daily, all year.

In this small natural history museum an archeological display contains artifacts from each of the local cultures, along with explanations of their use.

In the reconstructed Council House, Oconaluftee Indian Village, a Cherokee woman describes the social and cultural life of the Cherokees, 250 years ago.

MUSEUM OF MAN
(See Wake Forest University)

MUSEUM OF THE CHEROKEE INDIAN

In Cherokee, Open daily, all year. Admission charged.

Exhibits and audiovisual programs tell the story of Cherokee life from prehistoric times to the present.

OCONALUFTEE INDIAN VILLAGE

From Cherokee drive north on US 441 to intersection with North Carolina 19; turn at directional sign and drive ½ mile to village entrance. Open daily, mid-May through Oct. Admission charged. Camping nearby.

In this reconstructed Cherokee Indian village an ancient way of life is recreated in authentic detail. Well-informed Cherokee guides escort the visitor through the village, where live demonstrations of Cherokee skills, crafts, and arts as practiced over 200 years ago are demonstrated. In the council house and on the squareground, lecturers explain important points of Cherokee culture. Plants used by the Indians are identified in an herb garden and along a nature trail.

ROANOKE INDIAN VILLAGE

On Roanoke Island, 5 miles from Manteo on North Carolina 54. Open Monday through Saturday, Memorial Day through Labor Day. Admission charged.

This is a reconstruction of the Native American village that was nearby at the time the unsuccessful attempt was made by English colonists to settle here. Exhibits show various crafts.

SCHIELE MUSEUM OF NATURAL HISTORY

1500 E. Garrison Blvd., Gastonia. Open free, Tuesday through Friday; afternoons, Saturday, Sunday.

Materials from sites in North Carolina illustrate Paleo, Archaic, and Woodland cultures. Dioramas show the domestic activities of Mesa Verde, pre-Columbian Cherokee, and other peoples.

At Town Creek Indian Mound is a reconstructed palisade, surrounding a temple that looks the same as it did 400 years ago. North Carolina Department of Agriculture photo.

TOWN CREEK INDIAN MOUND STATE HISTORIC SITE

From Mount Gilead drive east on North Carolina 73, then north on State Rd. 1160 toward North Carolina 731 to directional sign; total distance, about 5½ miles from Mount Gilead. Open free, Tuesday through Saturday; afternoons, Sunday. Closed certain holidays. Guided tours on weekdays by reservation. Camping nearby.

The Story. Midway in the fifteenth century a group of energetic, aggressive people entered this area, driving out the earlier inhabitants. These newcomers, like the invaders who took over Ocmulgee in Georgia, had been influenced by the Mississippian culture. They were farmers who had extraordinary ability to make the land productive. They also had some very distinctive customs. Along with their practical skill they brought a whole constellation of religious ideas, building habits, ceremonial practices, and even a game called chunkey.

On a high bluff, near the place where a stream now called Town Creek joins the Little River, the newcomers made a clearing and surrounded it with a high palisade of logs interwoven with cane. Two openings in the palisade served as entrances, but there was also a third, half underground, along the bluff. Inside the palisade they leveled off a plaza and around it, as time passed, they built ceremonial structures. The main one was a mound, constructed in one layer after another, starting with a low platform on which a religious building or temple stood. Later the mound was enlarged and made higher, as a base for another temple. At the center of the plaza stood a group of ceremonial buildings arranged in a square. Across the plaza from the major temple is a reconstruction of a minor temple which probably served as the home of the high priest.

The newcomers occupied their village at Town Creek for only about 200 years. During that time they seem to have been at war often with their neighbors. But whether they gave up in defeat or left for some other reason no one knows. After their departure in the early seventeenth century, bands of people who had very different customs moved in. They spoke a language related to the language of the Sioux Indians of the West, and they were living there when Europeans first came.

The Museum. In the museum in the Visitor Center are an audiovisual program and displays of material discovered during excavation of the site. Archeologists have investigated most of the ceremonial area, and based on their data and on historical records, reconstructions have been built of the major temple, the earthen mound, a minor temple, a mortuary, a game pole, and a palisade surrounding the ceremonial area.

UNIVERSITY OF NORTH CAROLINA, RESEARCH LABORATORIES OF ANTHROPOLOGY

Person Hall, on the campus, Chapel Hill. Open free, Monday through Friday; mornings, Saturday.

Displays here include bones, pottery, and artifacts found in North Carolina.

A restored painting in the temple, also restored, at Town Creek Indian Mound. North Carolina Department of Agriculture photo.

WAKE FOREST UNIVERSITY, MUSEUM OF MAN

114 Reynolda Village, Winston Salem. From Interstate 40 take Silas Creek Parkway north to Reynolda Rd., then east to Reynolda Village. The Museum of Man is located in Barn 2. Open free, Tuesday through Friday; afternoons, Saturday, Sunday. Closed certain holidays.

In an exhibit entitled "The History of Human Experience" is a display explaining life in North Carolina 600 years ago in the Yadkin River Basin.

South Carolina

CHARLES TOWNE LANDING SITE

From Interstate 26 in Charleston, drive south on South Carolina 7 to South Carolina 171, then southeast on 171 to the Charles Towne Landing sign. Open daily, all year. Admission charged.

In addition to a reconstruction of an English colonial settlement and for-

tification, there are exhibits and pictorial displays here, together with artifacts, of a sixteenth-century Indian settlement that once occupied the area. The site was excavated and interpreted by the Institute of Archeology and Anthropology of the University of South Carolina.

SANTEE INDIAN MOUND
(Scott's Lake Site)

From the town of Santee take Interstate 95 north to turnoff just beyond the Lake Marion Bridge; turn left on dirt road at the sign to Fort Watson and Santee Indian Mound; continue through the U.S. Fish and Wildlife Refuge, about 1 mile, to the site. Open free, at all times.

A large temple mound was built here in prehistoric times by people who followed the Mississippian lifeway. Long after the site was abandoned it was reoccupied by the British, during the American Revolution. The British camped near the foot of the mound and fortified its top. An interpretive sign tells something of the history of the site.

SEWEE MOUND ARCHAEOLOGICAL AREA, FRANCIS MARION NATIONAL FOREST

From Charleston drive 21 miles north on US 17, then turn right and drive southeast 4 miles on South Carolina 432. Open free, at all times. Camping.

The U.S. Forest Service has opened this well-preserved shell mound to the public. Visitors are reminded that the Antiquities Act provides severe penalties for collecting any artifacts from the area.

Part of the reconstructed village area at Chucalissa Indian Town and Museum, Memphis, Tennessee. Memphis State University photo.

Tennessee

C.H. NASH MUSEUM
(See Chucalissa Indian Town and Museum)

CHUCALISSA INDIAN TOWN AND MUSEUM
(CHOO-kah-LEE-sah)

From US 61 at the southern edge of Memphis, drive 4½ miles west on Mitchell Rd. and follow directional signs to museum entrance. Open Tuesday through Saturday; afternoons, Sunday,. Admission charged. Camping at T.O. Fuller State Park, which adjoins the site.

The Story. People settled here about A.D. 900 and occupied the site repeatedly for more than 700 years. Their village developed in two parts—one for ordinary folk, the other for religious and political leaders. The houses of the leaders bordered a large plaza in front of a huge platform mound and were made of poles or posts, finished outside with mud-and-straw plaster, and roofed with overlapping bundles of long, heavy grass.

The principal chief's house and another structure, possibly a temple, stood on the large platform mound made of earth, which at first was low. As years went by, one set of buildings after another was purposely burned, perhaps when a leader died, and the whole platform was then covered with a mantle of new earth. Each mantle added height and breadth to the foundation for the next buildings that were constructed, until at last a sizable mound dominated the village.

The women of Chucalissa cooked and wove baskets, mats, and textiles. They also made quantities of pottery, some of it very lovely, some very plain, for use as kitchenware.

The men did some hunting, made tools of bone and stone and wood, and cared for crops in their fields. Like other people who built temple mounds at this time, they must have been expert farmers. They may even have raised a variety of corn that was unusually productive. At any rate, they had adequate food to support a community of about a thousand common people, as well as a large number of religious and political leaders, who spent much time and energy on ceremonies.

Probably a fire was kept burning in the temple day and night, and people in relays had to tend it carefully. For rituals and festivals crowds gathered in the plaza and shared in such events as the busk, or ripe corn ceremony.

For some reason not known, these people left their homes and temples before the arrival of the first French explorers in 1673, and so we cannot be certain which, if any, modern Indians are their descendants. Today Choctaw Indians, originally from central Mississippi, act as guides and conduct tours around the site.

The Name. Chucalissa is a word from modern Choctaw which means "house abandoned."

The Museum. A large part of the Chucalissa site has been made into an outdoor museum. Eight of the prehistoric houses and a corncrib have been reconstructed. Three of these have life-size exhibits showing a variety of daily activities of the prehistoric vil-

Excavation at Chucalissa, Tennessee, revealed this pattern of post holes, showing where a building once stood. Memphis State University photo.

lagers. A long archeological trench, showing a cross section of the village deposits, has been roofed over and serves as an entryway to the village reconstruction area.

An indoor museum displays material recovered from the site and also from other sites in the Southeast. Some of the most informative exhibits to be found anywhere show the "how's" of archeology: how a scientist-sculptor can reconstruct the face of a prehistoric man after examining a skull carefully; how potsherds tell a story of the people who made the pots; how cane was split and woven into baskets; how blowguns were made. In one room of the museum visitors may hear a lecture, illustrated with slides, about the archeology of the site and the life of its former inhabitants.

Special Feature. The site is being continuously excavated by Memphis State University, and during the summer months visitors may see archeologists and students at work. The first excavation here began with the support of the Tennessee Division of State Parks and with the help of prisoners from the Penal Farm. According to

an article in the *Tennessee Historical Quarterly,* "Undoubtedly it was, for many, the most creative work they had ever undertaken, and they dug carefully, painstakingly, taking enormous and justifiable pride in their digs. . . . One particular prisoner—Driver by name—found the archeologist's conventional tools totally unacceptable and so devised and made his own, instruments which now form the backbone of our tool kit!"

CUMBERLAND GAP NATIONAL HISTORICAL PARK

From the west take the Corbin exit from Interstate 75 and travel about 45 miles on US 25E. From the south take Tennessee 33 from Knoxville, through Tazewell and Harrogate, Tennessee. From the north take the 11 west exit from Interstate 81, connecting with Virginia 58 at Kingsport. Virginia 58 intersects US 25E about 3 miles from the park Visitor Center. Open free, daily, all year. Closed Dec. 25. Camping.

From Cumberland Gap a prehistoric trail ran to the Ohio River. This trail

Above: Small objects of this sort are often called plummets. They may have been used as sinkers on fishlines or fishnets. *Right:* A tobacco pipe, carved in stone, from about A.D. 1600. Found in a mound at Shiloh National Military Park.

Stratigraphy

If a river floods every year and deposits silt on the land, the top layer of silt is the most recent. The bottom layer is the oldest. This fact has been important to geologists in determining the age of rocks and soil.

When people live in the same place a long time and keep throwing rubbish in the same garbage pile, the newest rubbish will be on top. The oldest will be on the bottom. To archeologists this can be very important in determining dates.

When people change their fashions, or adopt new foods, or take up the use of new implements, there is a change in what they throw away. Layers may form in a trash pile, easily distinguished from each other by the differences in objects they contain. Layers may form, too, when some material such as dust or silt or volcanic ash covers a trash heap and clearly separates an old deposit of rubbish from a new deposit later added above it.

By comparing what lies in the layers, which are called strata, it is possible to say that one type of artifact is older or younger in relation to another. You have a relative date. Relative dates are not perfect, by any means, but they do help to arrange events in some kind of order.

---

and others in Kentucky are the subject of an exhibit in the Visitor Center. Other exhibits relate to the entry of Whites into what had hitherto been Indian land.

CUMBERLAND MUSEUM AND SCIENCE CENTER

In Nashville, 800 Ridley Ave. Open Tuesday through Saturday; afternoons, Sunday. Admission charged. Closed certain holidays.

Displays devoted to Native American life from prehistoric times include an exhibit on mound builders.

LOOKOUT MOUNTAIN MUSEUM

From Chattanooga drive south on Tennessee 58 to the top of Lookout Mountain, then follow directional signs to Point Park. The museum is opposite the park entrance. Open daily, all year. Closed Dec. 25. Admission charged.

Some archeological materials in this museum are Paleo-Indian from the LeCroy Site, near Chattanooga. Most of the other prehistoric materials also come from the Chattanooga area. They

include Archaic and Mississippian artifacts collected over a period of 50 years by an amateur archeologist, J. P. Brown. One diorama shows how Indians shaped stone artifacts by flaking, pressure, grinding, and drilling. Another, with life-size models, shows an Archaic family engaged in various domestic activities.

McCLUNG MUSEUM
(See University of Tennessee)

OLD STONE FORT STATE PARK

Just west of the city limits of Manchester, on US 41. Open free, during daylight hours.

The Story. On a high bluff that rises where the Little Duck River flows into the Duck River, early pioneers found sections of a wall that had obviously been built by humans. Legends grew up about the site. Some said it was built by Vikings to protect themselves from Indians. Others said it was constructed by a Welshman named Madoc who they believed discovered America about A.D. 1170.

In 1966 archeologists from the University of Tennessee settled the question. They excavated the site, which includes more than 2000 feet of wall on just one of its sides, and found that the wall had been built over a long period of time, beginning about A.D. 1 and ending sometime before A.D. 400. The people who did all this vast labor were Indians, not Vikings or Welshmen, and they seem to have been influenced by the Hopewell lifeway, centered in the Ohio River valley.

Apparently the builders of the Old Stone Fort did not live at the site, but archeologists have not discovered exactly what they did there. Although it could have served for defense, it also resembled Hopewell ceremonial sites. But what kind of ceremony took place inside the walls? Only further excavation can provide an answer.

PINSON MOUNDS STATE ARCHAEOLOGICAL AREA

From Jackson drive 8 miles south on Tennessee 45 to Pinson, then left on Ozier Rd., 2½ miles to the park. Open

In certain places the layers in archeological sites are very clear and offer excellent clues. In many dry caves, for example, the strata are very helpful, unless pack rats have done a lot of burrowing in the debris. Pack rats and other rodents can dig holes into which material from top layers in the deposit can fall. When this happens recent things can end up under things that are much older. Also, burrowers often bring old things to the surface, where they are found above objects which are much more recent. It is because animals and worms and people keep stirring things up that archeologists have to be very careful as they dig and as they draw conclusions from what they find.

Although it is not always true that new things lie above old things in digs, it is true often enough to be a real help. In looking for clues about time, archeologists don't depend solely on stratigraphy—the study of strata. They use many other ways of dating what they find, and when they find that several different dating methods all produce the same result, they feel fairly confident they have a date on which they can depend.

(Continued on page 246)

---

free, Monday through Friday; by appointment Saturday and Sunday.

This, the site of the second largest mound in the United States, was preserved thanks to the concern of local citizens, who convinced the State of Tennessee to buy the land and make it into a park. There are more than twenty mounds in the group, along with village sites and earthworks. Most of the mounds seem to have been used for burial, although those with flat tops may have been for ceremonial purposes. Archeologists are still working at the site to determine more about the people who probably lived here and constructed the mounds between A.D. 1 and 500.

The Museum. Built to resemble a mound, the museum houses interpretive exhibits and a small theater where archeology programs and films are scheduled from time to time. Several miles of nature trails take the visitor past the most interesting spots in the park.

SHILOH MOUNDS, SHILOH NATIONAL MILITARY PARK (SHY-low)

From Savannah drive 4 miles west on US 64, then 6 miles south on Tennessee 22. Open free, daily. Closed Dec. 25.

About three-quarters of a mile from Park Headquarters is a cluster of mounds on a bluff above the Tennessee River. As early as 1899 a fine effigy pipe was found there, but most of the digging was done in 1934 by Works Progress Administration labor under the direction of Dr. Frank H. H. Roberts, of the Smithsonian Institution.

In all, there are more than 30 mounds in the Shiloh group. Six large ones have flat tops, and temples once stood on them. The seventh large mound, in the shape of an oval dome, was used for burial of the dead. Many smaller mounds were dwelling sites.

The Story. The people who began to live here (perhaps 600 to 800 years ago) followed cultural patterns resembling those of many other mound-building Indians in the Southeast. They

(Continued from page 245)

The first stratigraphic excavation in the United States was begun in 1902 by Dr. Max Uhle, a German, who had worked in Peru. At Emeryville, on the shore of San Francisco Bay, Uhle excavated a mound made up of a vast accumulation of oyster and clam shells. Periodically, over a very long time, prehistoric people had visited this spot, collected oysters and clams, and thrown the shells away. The shells eventually piled up into an immense heap, along with other remnants of living. The contents of the mound varied from bottom to top, showing that cultural changes had taken place through time.

After Uhle had completed his work another archeologist, Nels Nelson, a Dane, also studied shell mounds in the San Francisco area. Nelson maintained that he could not see any significance to the admittedly small differences he found from one stratum to another in the mounds. Later, however, when he excavated in the Galisteo region, south of Santa Fe in New Mexico, Nelson remembered what Uhle had said about stratigraphy. For the first time in the Southwest Nelson used the stratigraphic method to study layers in a trash pile and thereby laid the basis for the first relative chronology in the area.

A. V. Kidder, digging at nearby Pecos, seized on the method and worked out in detail a relative dating for pottery in the Rio Grande Valley and for the cultures which had produced the pottery. Kidder's work brought order on a large scale into Southwestern archeology.

---

constructed platforms for temples, then periodically burned the buildings and added a new layer to the whole outside of the mound. They buried important leaders in graves stocked with pottery, ornaments, and ceremonial objects. Like the inhabitants of Etowah in Georgia they seem to have held great feasts in the plaza between the mounds, and afterward they threw the refuse into deep pits. As a result of studying the remains of the feasts archeologists know that these people must have been corn farmers, that they also fished, gathered clams, and hunted for wild game.

The dwellings near the large mounds were made of upright posts, with saplings and split cane woven in between. This latticework was then daubed over with clay. For roofs, the builders made a close wickerwork of canes and branches, which they covered with leaves and grass, and then over this they plastered clay.

People here, as at many other Southeastern towns, played a game called chunkey, using a discoidal (wheel-shaped) stone. According to Europeans who witnessed the game in historic times, contestants holding greased spears gathered at one end of a long, flat field. A signal was given, and a man rolled the chunkey stone down the field. A moment later the players hurled their spears, each one hoping to estimate the distance the stone would roll before it stopped. The winner—the man who landed his spear closest to the spot where the stone came to a halt—then collected the bets he had made with the other contestants. A number of chunkey stones turned up in the excavations at Shiloh, as did evidence of another gambling game played with marked counters which resembled dice.

By the time Europeans arrived in Tennessee the inhabitants of this site had left. Investigators have not yet been able to say for sure which of the historic Indian tribes may have been descendants of the builders of Shiloh Mounds.

The Name. After driving the Indians from Tennessee, Whites settled in the neighborhood of this group of ancient mounds and built Shiloh Church, named for the biblical Shiloh which, perhaps coincidentally, was the site of a temple on a mountain. In 1862 a bloody Civil War battle was fought here at Shiloh, and to commemorate it the site was made a National Military Park. Visitors to the park can get a glimpse of history and of prehistory as well.

TRAVELLERS' REST HISTORIC HOUSE

From Nashville drive 6 miles south on Farrell Parkway to marker. Open Monday through Saturday; afternoons, Sunday. Admission charged.

In the Indian museum, which is part of Travellers' Rest, is a display devoted to the culture of people who built temple mounds from about A.D. 1200 to A.D. 1600. In addition to artifacts which throw light on the Mississippian culture, a large mural shows an artist's interpretation of village life in the vicinity of Nashville in prehistoric times.

The game of chunkey was popular in prehistoric times in Tennessee and at many other places east of the Rocky Mountains. In 1832 George Catlin made this drawing of Mandan Indians enjoying the sport. Participants threw spears, each one hoping to land his just where the rolling, doughnut-shaped chunkey stone stopped. The man who came closest won. From Smithsonian Report, 1885.

Delicately flaked flint artifacts, apparently for ceremonial purposes, were found in Tennessee. Originals in the McClung Museum, Knoxville.

UNIVERSITY OF TENNESSEE, McCLUNG MUSEUM

On campus, 1327 Circle Park Dr., Knoxville. Open free, Monday through Friday; mornings, Saturday; afternoons, Sunday.

Materials in the Frank H. McClung Museum, gathered by careful scientific excavation, throw light on Archaic, Woodland, and Mississippian cultures in the Southeast. Exhibits show how artifacts were made and used and how they related to their environments at different times. Many important finds came to the museum at the time when the Tennessee Valley Authority was building flood-control dams. In a crash program of salvage archeology, thousands of relief workers dug at many sites in the river basins, saving what could be excavated before the water rose.

Special Feature. The museum houses the collections of Thomas M. N. Lewis and Madeline Kneberg Lewis, archeologists who contributed greatly to knowledge of Southeastern cultures. Their work at the famous Eva Site in Benton County disclosed a long period of development of lifeways in that part of Tennessee, beginning about 5200 B.C. Some of the Eva people who settled along riverbanks harvested tremendous quantities of clams and mussels, and their heaps of discarded shells offered a convenient place for burials. In some of those which the Lewises excavated were found an amazing number of skeletons of adults who lived to be 60 or 70 years old. (Usually prehistoric people died at a much earlier age.) Skeletal remains also indicate a rather inbred population. Apparently people lived here almost undisturbed for generations. However, the different levels of occupation do show changes in food habits from time to time. During some periods a great amount of deer and other meat was eaten, but almost no shellfish.

Serpent Mound in Ohio. It is nearly one-quarter of a mile long, 20 feet wide, and 4 to 5 feet high. The date of construction is not known. Ohio Historical Society photo.

NORTH CENTRAL

A young newspaperman named Ephraim George Squier moved from Connecticut to the small Ohio town of Chillicothe in 1845 and began to edit the newspaper there. Near his new home he saw a number of large earthen mounds—artificial, he was told— and he immediately grew curious about them. A physician, Dr. E. H. Davis, also of Chillicothe, shared Squier's interest.

Working as a team, these two amateurs started to investigate. Inside the mounds they discovered human bones and artifacts. Surveys in Ohio and other states revealed more and more sites where vast quantities of earth had been piled up by human hands. Before long Squier and Davis had dug into more than 200 of the mounds, and these were only a sampling of what existed in the Midwest.

Obviously a sizeable and well-organized population had carried out these tremendous projects. Innumerable craftsworkers must have been engaged in making the grave goods lavished on burials. Why did an apparent obsession with funeral ceremonies move these people? And what mysterious fate overtook them in the end? Neither White settlers nor the Indians they encountered in the area had any clues to offer.

Squier and Davis needed financial help for their investigations, and they got it from the young American Ethnological Society. Within a year Squier had a report ready. Soon it had expanded

A Hopewell man wearing copper earspools, necklace of copper and pearls, and headdress of deer antlers. The reconstructed figurine is in the Field Museum of Natural History, Chicago.

into a big book, and in 1848 the newly established Smithsonian Institution brought it out under the title *Ancient Monuments of the Mississippi Valley*.

The Squier and Davis report was the Smithsonian's first publication. It also marked the beginning of widespread interest in the earthworks which were a very prominent feature in America's nineteenth-century landscape. The two men visited, dug into, and surveyed mound after mound in the central part of the United States. Then Squier drafted beautiful maps of the sites and wrote careful descriptions. In addition, a good many theories came from his facile pen, and here he shared the views of those who were at that time busy driving the original Americans off the land. Indians, in Squier's opinion, were such inferior creatures that they could never have built the great earthen structures in the Mississippi and Ohio valleys. Nor could they have made the sculptured pipes, the pottery, and the handsome ornaments he and Davis were finding in ancient graves. Another people—a separate race of Mound Builders—must have been the creators of such works.

More than a hundred years later archeologists were still plagued with the myth of the Mound Builders, which Squier and Davis and the Smithsonian Institution had done much to circulate. So persistent was the notion of a mysterious, extinct race that Robert Silverberg has found ample material for tracing its history in a fascinating book, *The Mound Builders of Ancient America*.

The fact, of course, is that Indians were quite capable of the esthetic and social achievements which Squier and Davis and a host of other investigators observed. It was also true that by the nineteenth century all mound building had ceased. The art forms associated with mounds were no longer remembered in the central United States, and Indians knew as little as Whites about what had happened to earlier dwellers on the land.

Interpretation of the Mounds

There are still a great many unanswered questions. Archeologists do not all agree in their interpretations of material which continuing excavation turns up. However, what has so far emerged as a result of recent scientific study is roughly this:

Toward the end of the Archaic period, about 3000 years ago, groups of people in parts of the northeastern and north-central United States seem to have developed special burial practices. They covered the dead with mounds of earth. Other customs later came to be linked with mound burial. People began to place offerings in graves—such things as food and weapons and ornaments. Ceremonial activities were added to the making and burying of grave goods. Fire took on importance in these rituals. Bodies were sometimes cremated, and mortuary offerings were broken and burned. In many places bodies were first exposed until the flesh had decayed or had been removed by scavengers. Then the bones were covered with a kind of paint made from the mineral known as red ocher, which is an oxide of iron. Sometimes red ocher powder was sprinkled in quantity over both the remains and the grave goods.

No one knows why this mineral was considered important for burials. One suggestion is that red blood is associated with life, and therefore blood-colored ocher in a burial may have been a wordless way of trying to summon continued life for the person who was being buried.

The Red Ocher people in Illinois made pottery, which they often placed in their small, low, burial mounds, along with projectile points and beads of copper and shell. Pottery, of course, is hard to transport. Those who make it do not usually travel much. This means that Red Ocher people must have been able to get all the food they needed within a small area. They were good hunters and skilled in the use of every kind of wild food. Eventually some of their descendants, whose lifeway is known as the Morton culture, learned to grow food in gardens. The cult of the dead persisted. Bigger mounds were built. Grave goods became more elaborate.

Meanwhile, in the Ohio Valley, to the east, groups of hunters had been developing lifeways that were similar to those in Illinois. They started with simple graves in small mounds. Later they placed the dead in log tombs, over which they heaped earth. On top of the first burial they added others, gradually building up a high structure shaped like a cone. Groups of these conical mounds covered whole mortuary areas near villages. Here, too, ceremonies and the creation of grave goods—including pottery—occupied large numbers of people and led to the distinctive culture now called Adena.

The Woodland Lifeway

Adena people began to make pottery about 1000 B.C., as did many other groups in the eastern two-thirds of North America. For archeologists, pottery marks the beginning of a new period. Some call it Woodland; some call it Ceramic. All agree that it is distinguished also by the development of agriculture. Woodland is perhaps an unfortunate term for a lifeway that extended from the eastern forest lands onto the treeless plains, but since the name appears in most books and museums, it is hard to avoid.

About 100 B.C. another lifeway, called Hopewell, appeared in Ohio. Hopewell was named for a farmer, M. C. Hopewell, on whose land near Chillicothe archeologists excavated one of the richest of all burial mounds. Hopewell grave goods were beautiful, lavish, and sophisticated. Experts have found them baffling, as well. At first the evidence seemed to indicate that this new system had developed from the simpler Adena culture in the Ohio Valley. This proved not to be so. On further study Hopewell traits in Ohio seemed to spring from nowhere, then spread outward with great vigor. Suddenly, in many places, large Hopewell burial mounds were being constructed in groups, often surrounded by earthen walls built in the form of immense circles, octagons, and squares.

These astonishing earthworks required millions of cubic feet of soil to be transported in baskets and piled up to form the mounds and miles of embankments, some as much as 20 feet high. An engineer, James A. Marshall, has studied these ancient engineering projects and has come to the conclusion that they are the product of much mathematical knowledge. A standard unit of measurement was used, and separate earthworks were sometimes precisely lined up, although miles apart.

In each Hopewellian center there must have been an elite group with power and status enough to command enormous labor for building the earthworks and mounds. In the upper ranks of this society, in addition to the ruling group, the priests, and the engineers, were professional artisans who created all of the beautiful objects that went into the burial mounds. Funerary offerings included daggers and knives chipped from huge pieces of obsidian, smoking pipes carved from stone in the shapes of animals and birds, and sheets of mica precisely cut in the outlines of birds or serpents or human hands, possibly for use as stencils. In one mound group alone archeologists found 100,000 freshwater pearls.

A great deal of the raw material for grave goods came from distant places. Mica and quartz crystal were brought from the Appalachian Mountains. The obsidian had to be transported all the way from the Southwest or from the Yellowstone area, in Wyoming. Silver for beads came from Ontario, copper for beads and other ornaments from around Lake Superior. Florida provided shells and the teeth of shark and alligator, while sources closer to home furnished bear teeth for necklaces, feathers for gorgeous feather-cloth robes, and pearls by the hundreds of thousands. And all this was then buried in tombs under earth and stone laboriously heaped up to form the large mounds.

Ceremonies and Trade
Funerals of those who belonged to the highest classes were held with pomp and grandeur. At the same time Hopewell ceremonialism stimulated a very intricate economy, as people from one center engaged in trade with others over a wide area. A relentless search for raw material had to go on because the need could never be satisfied while a steady stream of manufactured objects was disappearing underground.

The dynamic Hopewellian ideas eventually dominated areas from Weeden Island, in Florida, all the way to the Canadian border, and from Kansas City to New York State. But wherever the Hopewell influence went, the local people seem to have kept their own basic patterns of existence while they adopted—or perhaps submitted to—the new system. Villages continued much as they had been before Hopewellian times, and powerful central cities did not form around the mounds themselves.

What exactly was the Hopewell phenomenon? It cannot be called a culture, because people in various regions kept their own ways, rather than being united in a homogeneous set of practices. Nor was it a unified political system, although in various areas large numbers of ordinary folk did participate in the special engineer-

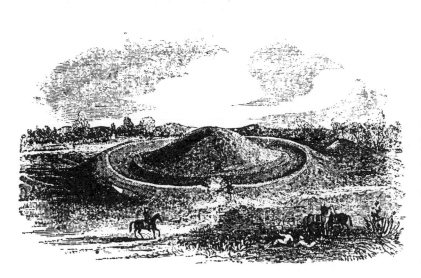

Some conical mounds were surrounded by circular earthworks. This remarkably symmetrical one, in Greenup County Kentucky, had a narrow gateway through the embankment and a causeway across the ditch. From *Ancient Monuments of the Mississippi Valley* by E. G. Squier, A.M., and E. H. Davis, M.D., *Smithsonian Contribution to Knowledge, Volume* I, 1847.

ing projects. Although there were certainly religious elements in Hopewell, it was too complex a mixture to be called simply a cult. The economic, the political and the religious were intertwined, and some sort of socioreligious stimulation seemed to motivate the system.

In the Ohio Valley, Hopewell and Adena existed side by side and probably borrowed notions from each other, although their relationship may not always have been completely friendly. In the end large numbers of Adena seem to have given in to pressure of some sort. Groups of them migrated southward into Kentucky; others went eastward all the way to Chesapeake Bay.

For more than 600 years the Hopewellian elite lived intricate lives that centered around death. Then for reasons no one yet understands, their influence declined and finally disappeared, not only in Ohio but also in all their other centers. What could have happened?

One suggestion is that a slight change of climate may have brought a long period of crop failure. Without a stable food base people could no longer afford to provide the luxuries demanded by the elite. And so the system died, although its practitioners lived on.

Another suggestion is that greatly increased population brought about greatly increased competition for food. This meant raids or warfare. There is evidence of burning and massacre and the building of defenses at several Hopewell centers. Conflict might also have stopped the trading for raw materials that were essential to the manufacture of elaborate grave goods. Without these necessary exotic materials the system itself ground to a halt.

Or it may be simply that everyone got tired of the whole business. Perhaps a kind of disillusionment set in: Why squander life to celebrate death? People may well have found unendurable the contradiction between creating wealth and destroying it for the glory in death of the powerful, who probably weren't very lovable taskmasters when they were alive. Whatever the reason, Hopewell mound building ceased about A.D. 500, and before long the system had vanished, leaving no trace except the great structures that were soon covered with forest or sod.

The period from about A.D. 600 to 800 in Illinois has been called a kind of "Dark Age." People apparently built no mounds, wore no rich ceremonial dress, made no elegant grave goods. Villages housed only small groups, and people who had once been skilled farmers raised only small field crops to supplement their hunting. In other words, they lived much as their ancestors had done 2000 years before.

The Mississippian Culture

Then change began again along the Mississippi River, near the mouth of the Missouri, in the area where several important, age-old travel routes came together. This was also a region where the soil was particularly good for growing corn. Here, about A.D. 800, a new way of life appeared. Before long there was new mound building. Separate social classes developed once more, along with intense ceremonialism, including once again an emphasis on death. However, the new religiosity had many very distinct features. Rituals were aimed at insuring the productivity of crops. The new, flat-topped, pyramidal mounds served chiefly as platforms for religious structures, although priests or leaders were sometimes buried in them. The prosperity of communities often led to a wealth of beautiful artifacts, but they were not all intended primarily to be grave goods.

The origin of this lifeway, which archeologists call Mississippian, has not been established to everyone's satisfaction. It seems to have been based, in part at least, on ideas that came from Mexico, possibly in association with a kind of corn farming that was enormously productive. At any rate, Mississippian habits of farming, of temple-mound building, of pottery making, and of religious ritual spread widely throughout much of the Mississippi drainage system and spilled over into other areas of the Southeast as well.

Between A.D. 1200 and 1500 these people flourished. Then their society, like that of the Hopewell, began to decline. Although temple mounds in some places were still built and used in historic times, by the late seventeenth century all the great centers were abandoned, and Mississippian ceremonialism had withered and died.

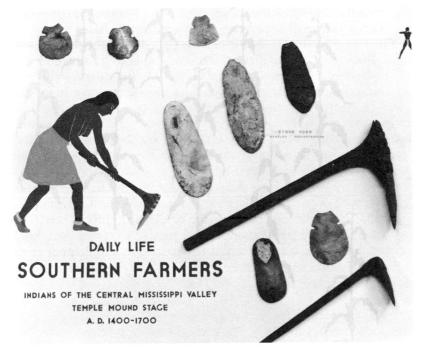

DAILY LIFE

SOUTHERN FARMERS

INDIANS OF THE CENTRAL MISSISSIPPI VALLEY
TEMPLE MOUND STAGE
A. D. 1400-1700

The life of farmers who built temple mounds in the central valley of the Mississippi River is suggested in this exhibit in the Field Museum of Natural History, Chicago. Field Museum of Natural History photo.

In the nineteenth century all these giant earthworks—and the spectacular quantities of loot that came from them—were bound to intrigue both professional and amateur investigators. They also attracted mound-miners, who were animated by the spirit of free enterprise. These men dug up objects not for what they could learn by studying them but for what they could earn by selling them. There was a market for archeological goodies, and much that scientists would like to have in museums has now disappeared. The amazing thing is that unrifled burials do still exist, and very often professional people are called in to excavate them.

Other Lifeways

Mound builders, however, were not the only prehistoric inhabitants of the North Central area. Near the town of Modoc, in southern Illinois, for example, ancient hunters 10,000 years ago discovered a shelter under overhanging rock in the bluffs along the Mississippi River. Off and on, until about 3000 B.C., families slept, ate, and made tools and weapons in this dry, protected spot. Later, small bands of hunters used it in spring and fall. All of them left the trash of daily living, and by the time archeologists discovered the Modoc shelter, 27 feet of refuse had piled up on the floor.

South of Modoc, along the Ohio River, hunters now known as Baumer people settled in semipermanent villages about 3000 years

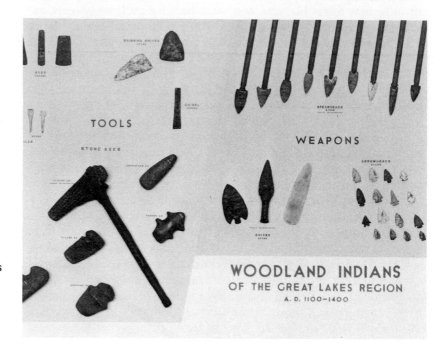

Between A.D. 1100 and A.D. 1400, woodland Indians of the Great Lakes region used tools and weapons like these, which are on display in the Field Museum of Natural History, Chicago. Field Museum of Natural History photo.

ago. Men continued to search for game, but they came home to solid dwellings made of upright logs, where women and children lived the year round. This kind of existence was possible because the Baumer people and some of their neighbors had learned to store large supplies of acorns and hickory nuts in pits underground. In winter, when the earth was frozen, empty pits were sometimes used as graves.

Farther up the Ohio, particularly in Kentucky, hunting-and-gathering people harvested great quantities of freshwater shellfish and established seasonal camps on riverbanks. As the piles of discarded shells grew higher, they were often used as burial places. Very few of these shell mounds can now be seen, but some have been studied by scientists.

More than a thousand burials are known to have been made at Indian Knoll, on the Green River, in Kentucky, and the site has recently been examined with a view to finding out what the mortuary practices could reveal about the social organization of the people who occupied the area between five and six thousand years ago. Artifacts buried with the dead offered clues—shell beads, projectile points, awls, and other implements. The fact that tools customarily used by women were often found in men's and children's graves, and that hunting equipment was buried with women and children, indicated to archeologists that this society was more or less egalitarian. In societies known to have definite classes, mortuary goods are much more likely to be differentiated according to sex and/or status in the community.

Everywhere, as people exploited their environment, they sought not only new foods but also new materials for tools and weapons. Near the Great Lakes, about 3000 B.C., they found one material little known elsewhere—deposits of pure copper, that could be mined with stone tools. By a process of heating and hammering the metal, they fashioned it into knives, projectile points, drills, and adzes. Later they used it—and traded it to others for use—in beads and ornaments and ceremonial objects.

Toward the end of Hopewellian times there appeared in Wisconsin, Iowa, and Illinois mounds of a new kind, less spectacular than the great burial mounds and very different in appearance. Some were simply long, low rod-shaped piles of earth. Others were built in the shapes of lizards, panthers, bears, geese, deer, beaver, birds and other animals, and so they have been called effigy mounds. (In Michigan and Minnesota long, straight plain mounds were also built at this same time.) Burials in effigy mounds were seldom accompanied by elaborate offerings. A little pottery, some shell beads and a tool or two were about all the grave goods usually found in association with an effigy mound. Sometimes the grave was placed at a vital spot of the effigy animal—the heart or head. Often a group of mounds stretched out along a high ridge overlooking a valley. As for the significance of the effigy forms, archeologists can only guess that they may have been connected in some way with clan totems or with some other mythological belief.

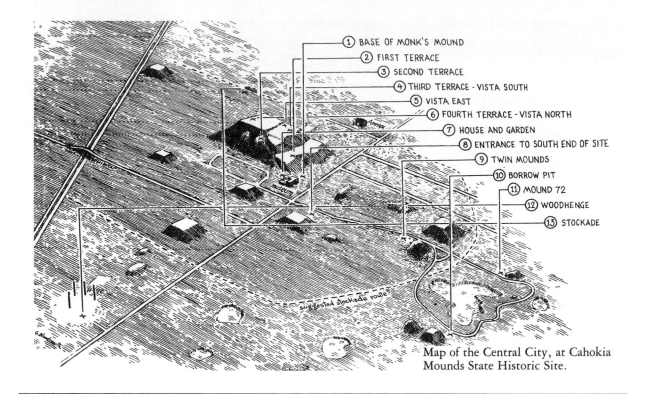

1. BASE OF MONK'S MOUND
2. FIRST TERRACE
3. SECOND TERRACE
4. THIRD TERRACE - VISTA SOUTH
5. VISTA EAST
6. FOURTH TERRACE - VISTA NORTH
7. HOUSE AND GARDEN
8. ENTRANCE TO SOUTH END OF SITE
9. TWIN MOUNDS
10. BORROW PIT
11. MOUND 72
12. WOODHENGE
13. STOCKADE

Map of the Central City, at Cahokia Mounds State Historic Site.

Illinois

BURPEE NATURAL HISTORY MUSEUM

813 N. Main St., Rockford. Open free, Tuesday through Saturday; afternoons, Sunday. Closed certain holidays.

Random finds, identified by county of origin, are on exhibit. These include Paleo, Archaic, and Woodland artifacts from local collections, surface finds, and limited excavations.

CAHOKIA MOUNDS STATE HISTORIC SITE

From St. Louis, Mo., drive 5 miles east on Interstate 55–70 to Illinois 111 exit; then south to US (Business) 40 (Collinsville Rd.); then left 1½ miles to site entrance. Open free, daily, May 1 to Oct. 31; Tuesday through Saturday; afternoons, Sunday, Nov. 1 through April 30. Closed certain holidays. Free guided tours of excavations, mid-June to Sept. 1.

This 1300-acre park contains the central section of the largest archeo-logical site and the first city in North America. It includes the largest mound in the United States (Monks Mound) —an artificial pyramid of earth 100 feet high at its summit—and 40 smaller mounds.

Some archeologists believe that at one time as many as 40,000 people may have lived here—a population more dense than at any other place in America north of the Valley of Mexico. Others believe it is necessary to rethink the population figure. They suggest that Cahokia might have been a great trading and ceremonial center, or a defense fortress, where large numbers of people came and went but did not have permanent homes. The dwelling areas may have been used chiefly by caretakers, civic leaders, and members of the military and the priesthood. At any rate, wealth and vigor made Cahokia a center from which the Mississippian culture spread over a vast area.

The Story. About A.D. 700 Late Woodland people built small villages and planted corn in a fertile area called the American Bottoms along the east side of the Mississippi River, oppo-

Monks Mound, the largest totally earthen mound in the New World, at Cahokia Mounds State Historic Site. It rises in four terraces to a height of 100 feet. A huge temple once crowned its summit. It is named for Trappist monks who farmed its terraces in the early 1800s.

site St. Louis. Later, around A.D. 800–50, another people arrived, bringing with them Mississippian lifeways. Eventually they became dominant. Their corn was an extraordinarily productive variety, and they increased their yields by using an efficient flint hoe to dig deeply and to kill weeds that competed with corn plants.

Raw material for the hoes came from the area near the present town of Mill Creek, in southern Illinois. There, in a deposit of soft clay, people discovered flint nodules which were somewhat flat. This shape easily lent itself to the making of large, oval hoe blades, which could be attached to wooden handles. To get at the nodules, they dug shafts, some almost 30 feet deep, often with side corridors at the bottom.

Convinced that the hoe blade had been an important tool, archeologists did an experiment. They attached blades to long handles and tried to dig up the tough bottomland soil at Cahokia. To their surprise, this turned out to be backbreaking work. The hoes did not seem nearly so efficient as had been expected. Recently this minor mystery may have been solved when excavators near Cahokia discovered a beautifully carved figurine of a woman with a hoe in her hand. The blade was bound to a short stick handle that bent at a right angle, and the woman was kneeling to use it. Perhaps the archeologists would not have found it so hard to dig if they had knelt and used a short-handled hoe.

With good tools to use and good seed to plant, farmers produced large crops on the rich land near Cahokia. There was enough corn, together with abundant resources of fish, game, nuts, and berries, to feed many families. As the population grew, increasing complexities marked the ways in which people related to each other and to their environment. In the larger community certain important structures were used for civic and religious affairs. To emphasize their importance, leaders had these public buildings placed on earthen mounds, which elevated them above the flat landscape. Large open plazas in front of the buildings gave them further distinction. Inspiration for this pattern of construction was once thought to have come from Mexico, where similar towns existed at the time. However, it now seems possible that the mound and plaza idea was a slow, indigenous development rather than a sudden intrusion from Mexico.

From this busy and growing settlement it was possible for traders to take long canoe trips on the Mississippi and its tributaries—the Missouri, Ohio, Illinois, Tennessee, and Arkansas rivers. Raw materials reached Cahokia from the Gulf of Mexico, the Appalachian Mountains, the Great Lakes, and the Rockies. With trade came an exchange of ideas. Cahokians exported art forms, even attitudes toward life, along the routes they used, and they in turn received stimulation from many places, some very distant.

As time passed, the number of mounds at Cahokia increased to about 120 within an area of about 4000 acres. Possibly the region became overpopulated, and resources were depleted. For that reason or some other, groups of Cahokians began to move away. In the new communities they set up they continued to follow the Mississippian way of life.

MOUND OF EARTH BUILT OVER SACRED ENCLOSURE

CREMATION AND BURIAL IN A SACRED ENCLOSURE LATER COVERED BY A MOUND OF EARTH

Two stages in mound building. First, Indians cremated and buried a body within a sacred enclosure. Then they heaped up basketloads of earth over the burial, forming a mound. The lower drawing shows how funerary offerings were placed on the altars, right front and upper right. Part of an exhibit in the Field Museum of Natural History, Chicago. Field Museum of Natural History photo.

Some of these colonies were established in regions where people were still living in Late Woodland ways. One such place was Aztalan, in Wisconsin. Another colony seems to have grown up about A.D. 1200 on the Ohio River, near the place were Brookport, Illinois, is presently located. Here a major temple-mound community developed and apparently served as a trading station on the river. This community, known as the Kincaid Site, is now a National Historic Landmark, but it is *not* open to the public. It in turn seems to have had an important influence on other communities, including Angel Mounds, in Indiana, which is visitable.

Cahokia itself prospered, though not entirely at ease. The center of the city was encircled by a defensive log wall, with bastions at regular intervals, which was reconstructed at least four times between A.D. 1100 and 1300. What enemy was feared is not clear, but the threat of attack apparently existed for 200 years or more. By A.D. 1500 the city was abandoned.

Nineteenth-century settlers found good farmland in the American Bot-

toms, and they leveled some of the mounds with their plows. For a while Trappist monks made gardens on top of the big, main temple mound, now called Monks Mound. At one time there was danger that it might be torn apart to make fill for a railroad bed. Highway builders and industrial developers destroyed many of the other earthworks. Those which remain are now protected by the State Historic Site.

For years both amateur and professional archeologists worked at the site, and since 1960 intensive scientific work has been going on there. Digging will continue in the summer months. Already excavations have established much good information about daily life during the Mississippian occupation. People built their house walls of posts set upright in trenches in the earth, then wove branches in between, basketfashion. Over this they spread a layer of mud plaster. To protect the plaster from rain, they added an outer covering of woven reed mats. Roofs thatched with dried grass were supported by large center poles.

This kind of dwelling didn't last long. The roof caught fire easily, and the whole building might burn. When that happened, or when a house weakened with age or rot, a new one was often put up on the same site. Houses rebuilt on one spot for hundreds of years left a series of understandable hints about household affairs.

Other hints need further study. For example, there seems to be evidence that Cahokians sought good crops by conducting ceremonies that included sacrifice of the most valuable of all things—human life. This practice was known in Mexico, where maize agriculture originated. However, the full extent and meaning of human sacrifice in the Mississippian culture is not yet understood.

Possibly associated with agriculture was another discovery, reported in 1964 by Warren L. Wittry and further studied in 1978–79. Four very large circles, once defined by upright posts, were revealed in the course of excavation. They resemble the Stonehenge circles in England and are called woodhenges. Wittry believes that the circles formed a sort of calendar that indicated the

Featured in the Dickson Mounds Museum exhibits is this reconstructed house of a type built by the native inhabitants of the area a thousand years ago. Illinois State Museum photo by Marlin Rees.

seasons and kept track of important dates—for feast days, ceremonies, and the right times for planting and harvesting. When Wittry checked the alignment of post holes in relation to the rising sun, he found that alignments did mark the solstices and equinoxes. One set of posts lines up with the rise of a very bright star, Capella, during the third week in April, possibly indicating the date on which corn planting was best done.

The Name. When French explorers entered Illinois in 1673 they met several Algonquian-speaking tribes which had formed a confederacy. These Indians called themselves the Illini (ILL-in-ee) or Illiniwek. One tribe, known as the Cahokia, lived in the American Bottoms near the mounds—which by association became known as the Cahokia Mounds. But the Cahokia Indians were latecomers to this area. The true descendants of the people who built the mounds are not known.

The Museum. The Cahokia Mounds Museum in the park gives an introduction to the site and offers an interpretive program, conducted as a service of the Illinois State Museum.

Special Feature. In summer at Cahokia there are showings of archeological films, workshops in Native American crafts, guided tours of ongoing excavation, and an archeological field school. For information write to Ranger, 7850 Collinsville Rd., East St. Louis, IL 62201; or phone (618) 344–5268.

DICKSON MOUNDS MUSEUM

From Lewistown drive 3 miles east on US 24, then 2 miles south on Illinois 78 to directional sign. Or from US 136 just west of Havana drive 5 miles north on Illinois 78 to directional sign. Open free, daily. Closed certain holidays. Camping nearby.

A building, designed to suggest the shape of a prehistoric mound, houses the museum and encloses the burial mound which has made this place famous. Inside the building it is possible to see 234 burials exactly as they were found by archeologists.

Not far from the museum is the Eveland prehistoric village, which can also be visited. Color-slide shows with taped commentaries give a good deal

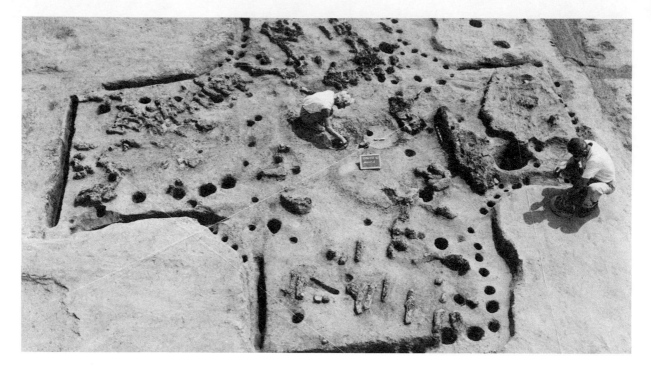

Excavating an unusual, cross-shaped structure in the Eveland Village area, Dickson Mounds. Illinois State Museum photo.

of information about the history of the whole site. The Dickson Mounds Museum is a branch of the Illinois State Museum.

The Story. About 15,000 years ago the front edge of the last major Ice-Age glacier reached into the northern part of Fulton County, in Illinois. On the tundra, which stretched southward from the ice, herds of grass-eating animals grazed, and small bands of Paleo-Indians hunted them. When the ice began to melt and move northward, a forest of fir, spruce, and pine grew up where the tundra had been. Now mastodons, elk, and deer browsed on shrubbery and the lower branches of the trees, and men hunted the browsers.

About 7000 years ago Archaic hunters and gatherers managed existence here, living on smaller game, nuts, seeds, and shellfish. Some of these Archaic people left evidence of their campsites along the Illinois River, near what is now Dickson Mounds Museum.

By 1000 B.C. their successors were following a new pattern of life, which archeologists call Woodland. They made pottery, using designs that were

a little different from Woodland designs elsewhere. They cultivated plants and paid a good deal of attention to the burial of their dead. One such group lived for a while in a village within the museum grounds. Their particular variety of Early Woodland culture has been called Black Sand because some of their burials were found on a sandy black layer of earth.

Between 200 B.C. and A.D. 400, people here followed a new pattern— the Middle Woodland. They buried their important dead in a large mound, and around it they built a pentagonal earthen enclosure or wall 800 feet across. Like others before them, they left tools and weapons and other evidence of their daily lives.

By A.D. 1000 Late Woodland people occupied the nearby hilltop. They constructed a large, permanent village and began burying their dead in mounds along the bluff.

About A.D. 1050 Cahokians, or people like them who followed the Mississippian lifeway, moved in and settled here, merging to some extent with the resident Woodland population. At this point a memorable development

Working from various archeological clues, an artist painted this version of an Oneota harvest ceremony for the Field Museum of Natural History, Chicago. Field Museum of Natural History photo.

began. The Mississippians started a cemetery in the form of a group of mounds, which kept growing as burials were added. Because of the peculiar chemical composition of the wind-blown soil used to cover these burials, large numbers of skeletons were beautifully preserved. More than a thousand have been found.

Farmland was good in this neighborhood. There was also an ample supply of waterfowl and mussels and forest mammals. People lived in relative prosperity until about A.D. 1300, when something upset their relationship with the world around them. Possibly a slight change in climate made farming more difficult. Possibly poor conservation practices, such as the custom of setting fire to forests in order to get farmland, reduced productivity near Dickson Mounds. Whatever the reason, activity at Dickson Mounds ended. Occasional bands of hunters were the only inhabitants until Europeans arrived.

The Name. In 1833 the Dickson family settled on land around the burial mound. In 1927 Dr. Don F. Dickson, a chiropractor, began scientific investigation of the human bones that he found on the place. What started out as medical curiosity about possible evidence of disease in prehistoric skeletons ended in archeological curiosity about all aspects of life here. Dr. Dickson did a great deal of excavating and did it so well that he attracted the interest and admiration of professional archeologists. When it came time to choose an official name for the museum at the site, it was easily agreed that the Dickson name should be used.

Special Interest. Dickson Mounds has proved to be a rich source of information. There is apparently so much more that can be learned here by scientist and layman alike that the Illinois State Museum, with funds provided by the Illinois General Assembly, has established research facilities at the site. Work continues at Dickson Mounds and elsewhere in the vicinity. There are known to be 3000 mounds and village sites in Fulton County alone.

FIELD MUSEUM OF NATURAL HISTORY

Roosevelt Rd. at South Lake Shore Dr., Chicago. Open daily, except Dec. 25 and Jan. 1. Admission charged.

Exhibits and dioramas in Halls 4 through 10 on the main floor are devoted to the Indians of the Americas. Hall 4 tells the story of people in the New World from the time of their arrival from Asia to the time of the arrival of Europeans. In one section are exhibits showing techniques for manufacturing stone tools and the methods used by archeologists in excavating and interpreting prehistoric material.

Other halls also throw some light on prehistory. Hall 5 contains exhibits on Indians of the prairies and woodlands. One feature is a full-size (55'x40'x18') reconstruction of a Pawnee earth lodge. Here from time to time there are programs about Pawnee life.

Separate halls are devoted to the Southwest, the West, and the Northwest. In addition there are halls for Indians of Middle and South America.

Red Paint people of the Archaic Period hunted moose using spears and spear throwers (atlatls). This diorama is in the Field Museum of Natural History, Chicago. Field Museum of Natural History photo.

Visitors may join scheduled guided tours through parts of the Indian exhibits. Those who are seriously interested in archeology may use the museum's excellent library.

Special Interest. Anyone who comes here after visiting sites open to visitors in other parts of the country will find certain things that could not be seen at the sites themselves. For example, the museum has in its collection material from the original Hopewell Site, and its Hopewell exhibit gives a good idea of how these people built their burial mounds, how they dressed, and what their ornaments were like.

ILLINOIS STATE MUSEUM

Spring and Edwards streets, Springfield. Open free, Monday through Saturday; afternoons, Sunday. Closed certain holidays.

Archeological exhibits in this general museum cover the whole range from Paleo-Indian times to the historic period. A series of dioramas shows the major steps in human cultural development.

Archeologists connected with the

museum have excavated many important sites in Illinois and elsewhere, and some of the material they have found is included in exhibits. Of special importance is their work at the Modoc Rock Shelter, where they helped to uncover one of the longest records of human existence in North America.

Modoc Rock Shelter was formed when the Mississippi River, carrying great torrents of water from the melting ice of Pleistocene glaciers, ate into the base of a high sandstone bluff on the Illinois side, south of St. Louis. When the water went down, it left a protected area 25 feet deep and about 300 feet long. Ten thousand years ago Paleo hunters and gatherers began to live under this overhang, which is named for the nearby village of Modoc.

For 5000 years the shelter served groups of people, at first as a permanent base, later as a seasonal campsite. Then for some reason it was not used for a while, until Woodland Indians began to stop there on occasion and to leave broken pottery and other signs of their visits.

Visitors tour the reconstructed Indian village at Kampsville, Illinois. Photo courtesy of Center for American Archeology.

Sheltered from the rain, layer on layer of human history piled up to a depth of 27 feet. Archeologists now read the story with special attention because it reveals that Archaic Indians in the East followed the same general pattern of existence as that of Archaic people in the West. Clear evidence of this had not appeared before the Modoc Rock Shelter was excavated.

Here also was evidence of steadily changing adjustments to an environment that remained essentially unchanged. The people who lived on the bank of the great waterway could pick up ideas from travelers. Theirs was a relatively rich world, and they learned how to get the most out of it. For example, about 5000 years ago they used rough, chipped stone axes to chop down saplings for the frames of the shelters they built even in their sheltered dwelling place. Then they improved the axes and made them more efficient. To reduce the friction of stone against wood, they began to grind and polish the axe to make it smooth. In time they polished other stone artifacts as well.

Modoc Rock Shelter is not open to the public. Nor are other sites such as the Knight burial mounds in Calhoun County, along the Mississippi, where archeologists discovered Hopewell figurines. Reconstructions of these famous figurines can be seen in the museum, along with Hopewell artifacts from other sites.

The Illinois State Museum also directs the Dickson Mounds Museum, near Lewiston.

KAMPSVILLE ARCHEOLOGICAL CENTER

In Kampsville, 60 miles north of St. Louis, Mo., on Illinois 100. The Kampsville Archeological Museum, one of more than 30 buildings in the center complex, is open free, daily in summer.

At the museum, tours can be arranged to an Indian village that has been reconstructed to show what buildings were like in the Mississippian and Woodland period. Special tours of varying lengths, which include much more of the center's varied resources and are tailored to the special interests of any group, can be arranged at any time of year. Information about these tours and fees can be obtained from: Special Tours, 1911 Ridge Ave., Evanston, IL 60201, (312) 492-5300.

At the Kampsville Archeological Center are sophisticated research facilities for professional archeologists, and workshops are conducted here for teachers. Special activities have been developed for junior and senior high school students. There are field schools for young people in these age groups and also for college students. A Native American Studies program approaches prehistoric culture through ethnographic accounts, surviving tradition, and experimental projects in Native American crafts. There is also a program for adult amateur archeologists. A catalog that gives detailed information about these educational programs is available from the Center for American Archeology, PO Box 1499, Evanston, IL 60204.

Material on exhibit at the museum in Kampsville has come from important sites in the area. In all, more than 2500 sites are known within a 60 minute drive of Kampsville. One

of these, the Audrey Site, has been roofed over and heated so that excavation can go on the year round. The entire Kampsville Archeological Center grew up around the Koster Site, now closed.

The Koster Site. This unusual site was named for Theodore Koster, a farmer who for a long time turned up potsherds whenever he plowed his cornfield near the Illinois River. His neighbor, Harlin Helton, thought that archeologists ought to do some serious digging on the Koster farm. Helton persuaded Dr. Stuart Struever, of Northwestern University, to make test excavations in 1969, and that started a most important and rewarding project.

Subsequent digging astonished and delighted both Mr. Koster and Dr. Struever—and crews of helpers. (Workers at the site ranged from junior high-school, college, and graduate-school students to senior citizens in nonacademic work groups.) Excavation revealed that time after time in the last 9,500 years, people lived in this protected spot near the foot of a limestone bluff. Each time its inhabitants

abandoned the site, all the debris they left was gradually covered by earth washed down from the bluff. Thus was formed what Dr. Struever called a "fossilized layer cake"—first a layer of sterile soil untouched by people, then an icing rich in the lost, broken, or buried remains of human activity. Another sterile layer followed, then came another filling of archeological goodies, and so on.

By the time the Koster Site was closed to the public, 13 layers of habitation had been excavated and studied. (The levels are called horizons.) Computer analysis of material recovered at the site later indicated that there were probably more than 20 occupation levels. Digs elsewhere in the United States have also revealed multiple horizons, but this is the first where archeologists have found such extensive Archaic village areas, one above another, so clearly separated and so readily dated.

With the help of men and women skilled in nearly a dozen branches of science, archeologists have been able to elaborate the story of the early inhabitants of Illinois. Geologists studied

the sterile soil, which was fortunately the kind that best preserves bone, seeds, fish scales, shells. An expert on moisture-loving snails used them as clues to the climate at different times. Botanists found that for a long period the staple food was hickory nuts. Later a variety of other nuts and plants was harvested. Bones of deer, small animals, and enormous numbers of fish, analyzed by specialists, helped to reveal the seasons when people lived at the site. Other specialists studied what Koster Site people looked like, what diseases they suffered, and how they related to their environment.

All these and many other scientific findings added up to some surprises. For example, there seems to have been a stable society here as early as 6400 B.C., almost 4000 years earlier than scientists had thought more or less sedentary people could efficiently exploit plant and animal food. Moreover, the early Koster inhabitants apparently chose plants that yielded the most for the least labor and that provided the most nutritious diet.

Horizon 8 at the site disclosed the earliest permanent dwellings in North

Above left:
View of the Koster Site. Center for American Archeology photo by D. R. Baston.

Above right:
Junior high school students enrolled in the field school of the Center for American Archeology excavate a feature at the Answell-Knight Site near Kampsville, Illinois. Photo courtesy of Center for American Archeology.

Students work on trench squares at the Audrey Site dig conducted by the Center for American Archeology. Photo courtesy of Center for American Archeology.

Work at the famous Koster site was begun in 1972. Work at the site was completed and it was backfilled in 1979. Photo courtesy of Center for American Archeology.

Portrait of a Leader

In 1952 archeologists digging at a site on the Illinois River uncovered the skeleton of an Indian who had been buried there at some time between A.D. 900 and A.D. 1200. With only his bones and a few artifacts to study, the scientists have put together an amazingly complete picture of the man.

Evidence that he was a leader is in the articles placed beside him in the grave: two necklaces with a total of 468 beads, each laboriously shaped of shell brought from the Gulf of Mexico; bracelets and anklets of shell beads; four projectile points; a stone for use in grinding red pigment; a pottery jar. Other objects are the sort of thing that might be given to someone who held office—a large stone ceremonial blade, a piece of galena ore imported from the north, a tobacco pipe, an animal rib that had been carved for some purpose, and a long rod made of horn. Negative evidence that the man was important lay in the other burials nearby. They contained much less wealth in the form of grave goods.

After examining the skull, Bartlett Frost, of the Detroit Historical Museum, modeled the bust shown here, basing his work on information that physical anthropologists have put together. Size of facial muscles, for example, is indicated by bony structure where the muscles are attached. Skin thickness and nose shape are determined by other measurements. The result is this portrait of an Indian leader in Illinois a thousand years ago.

Illinois Archeological Survey photo.

America, dated at about 5000 B.C. By 1200 B.C. squash was being cultivated, and there is evidence of some corn by 200 B.C. But it was another thousand years before the villagers began to depend heavily on growing crops for food. Wild food could be obtained much more easily.

Perhaps the change to reliance on corn was not entirely to the farmers' advantage. Their bones often give evidence that they were not so well nourished as their hunting-and-gathering forebears.

Scientists who studied the Koster Site are now inclined to dispute several long-held archeological theories. In the earliest times people there did not always live chiefly by the hunt but depended greatly on plant food. Nor was life so insecure that they had little time for loafing and meditating. They probably had more leisure than we do. But contrary to theory, this leisure did not necessarily breed inventions, art, and ritual.

Why was Koster finally abandoned for good, somewhere between A.D. 1100 and 1200? There are signs of conflict in the region, and Koster, at the foot of a bluff from which attackers could fire projectiles down into the village, was not easily defensible.

Special Interest. An annual contribution to the Center for American Archeology entitles the donor to take part in certain special membership activities, plus a subscription to *Early Man,* a magazine devoted to archeology.

KOSTER SITE
(See Kampsville Archeological Center)

LAKEVIEW CENTER FOR THE ARTS AND SCIENCES

1125 Lake Ave., Peoria. Open free, Tuesday through Saturday; afternoons, Sunday; evenings, Wednesday. Closed certain holidays.

In the gallery of this institution there is a section devoted to Illinois archeology. Exhibits change from time to time.

This drawing of a prehistoric burial mound in Ohio was published in *Ancient Monuments of the Mississippi Valley,* by E. G. Squier and E. H. David. National Park Service photo.

MADISON COUNTY HISTORICAL MUSEUM

715 N. Main St., Edwardsville. Open free, Wednesday and Friday; afternoons, Saturday, Sunday. Closed certain holidays.

Nearly 3000 artifacts in the Indian collection of this museum are grouped by types—axes together, bannerstones together, and so on. Although some of the material seems to be at least 4000 years old, no attempt is made to arrange it chronologically or by cultures. A number of artifacts are from Cahokia Mounds. In addition to Illinois material, mostly from Madison County, there are some artifacts from the prehistoric Southwest.

MISSISSIPPI PALISADES STATE PARK

From Savanna drive 2 miles north on Illinois 84 to directional sign on the right. Open free, all year. Roads may be closed during periods of freezing and thawing. Camping.

Within the park are old Indian trails and numerous mounds in which archeologists have done little excavating.

PERE MARQUETTE STATE PARK
(PEER mar-KET)

From Alton drive 19 miles northwest via Great River Rd. to Grafton, then 5 miles west on Illinois 100 to the park entrance. Open free, all year, except when roads are closed during freezing and thawing. Camping.

Beginning around A.D. 1, Indians left evidence of their presence at 18 different sites in this park, which is named for the seventeenth-century French explorer, Father Jacques Marquette. A folder issued by the Illinois Department of Conservation summarizing the history of Indian occupation of the area is available at park headquarters.

When Marquette traveled the Illinois and Mississippi rivers, two distinct mound-builder cultures had developed, flourished, and died along their banks. A group known as the Jersey Bluff people once made their

The Meaning of a Mound

What does a mound show about the people who built it?

A mound has a definite shape. It is planned. It is not spontaneous or haphazard. This means that there was a social mechanism for planning and for getting plans carried out.

A mound means division of labor. There were planners, or leaders, involved in its construction, and there were those who carried out the plans—who were led. In other words, there were social classes, at least in rudimentary form. There were rulers and ruled.

Rulers had to have time in which to do their ruling. They had to be able to eat without spending all of their days obtaining food. This meant either that leaders were very successful part-time food getters or that they were fed out of the stores grown or collected by others. Moreover the food supply had to be large enough to sustain the common people while they expended an immense amount of energy in piling up huge quantities of earth.

Mounds also meant that their builders had religious beliefs. They had adopted or invented ways to feel comfortable amid the baffling complexities of life and the painfully recurrent fact of death. To judge from what we know has happened among similar groups of people who have been directly observed, the leisure-time activities of some members of the mound-builder community must have gone into developing reassuring myths and shamanistic procedures. As time went by, these may have led to ceremonies and rituals supervised by full-time specialists, whom we would call priests.

The religious beliefs which mound builders held provided motivation for the great trouble they took in burying their dead, often amid riches and almost always under great heaps of earth. By such activity people must have sought either to influence events in some magic way or to do something that seemed to fit the living satisfactorily into the immutable flow of events.

Mound builders also had thoughts for the welfare of loved ones—or feared ones—who had died. They were solicitous for the continuing comfort of those whom they regarded as in some way important. In imagination they created circumstances that lay ahead for those who had ceased to live in the flesh, and then they laid palpable conveniences—garments, meals, weapons, implements, amulets—close to the bodies or bones of the deceased. Here were real objects that could be taken as testimony to the reality of some kind of ongoing existence.

Mounds tell us all this about people who lived within nature and at the same time erected a world outside it—a world of the supernatural. Mounds say that their builders elaborated life in ways that were different from those worked out by earlier people. The simplicity of the shape of the mound belies the intricacy of the society that produced it.

A few of the many artifacts recovered at Angel Mounds State Memorial, Indiana. In twenty years of excavation at this site more than two million pieces of material have been found and examined. Indiana Department of Natural Resources photo.

homes in the rocky palisades near the park, and they may have been the forerunners of the great mound builders at Cahokia, a little way to the south. In adjacent Calhoun County a much earlier people, who followed the Hopewell lifeway, buried their dead in less prominent earthworks. But the gifts they put into the graves were spectacular. At one of the sites—the Knight Mound, which is not visitable —they buried small, baked-clay figurines. These portrait statues were purposely broken at the time of burial, but they have been reconstructed and are one of the chief sources of information about Hopewell appearance and dress. Replicas of the Knight figurines can be seen in the Illinois State Museum.

SOUTHERN ILLINOIS UNIVERISTY, UNIVERSITY MUSEUM AND ART GALLERIES

Faner Hall, on the campus, Carbondale. Open free, Monday through Saturday; afternoons, Sunday. Closed certain holidays.

Here the Center for Archeological Investigations has extensive archeological collections from the Midwest.

STARVED ROCK STATE PARK

From Ottawa drive 6 miles west on Illinois 71 to the east entrance of the park. Or from La Salle drive 6 miles east on Illinois 71, then ¾ of a mile north on Illinois 178 to west entrance. Open free, all year. Camping.

In this beautiful place on the bank of the Illinois River are old Indian trails through the woods, shelter caves and open sites where prehistoric people camped, and the remains of several burial mounds.

The Story. When the first wandering hunters entered Illinois, perhaps 10,000 years ago, a band of them discovered Starved Rock and camped there. The Rock is a section of the Illinois River bluff which rises 125 feet straight up from the water. It can be approached only from one side, and so its flat circular top made it an ideal lookout spot.

During the Archaic Period, people sometimes camped on the Rock. At other times men probably camped below, brought chunks of stone to the top and the bluff, and sat about making projectile points and tools. The remains of their workshops have turned up in archeological excavations. One such group also left behind a copper spearpoint, one of the earliest known. Others, over a period of two or three thousand years, lost or discarded their hammerstones, scrapers, drills, and grinding tools around their campsites on the Rock.

Later, when people began to follow the Woodland way of life, women cooked here and threw away their broken pots. On the flatlands near by, the dead were buried in mounds. Still later, other groups visited the Rock, at least occasionally, up until historic times.

The Name. According to legend, the Illini Indians who lived along the river were attacked by Ottawa and Potawatomi warriors. The Illini fled to the top of the Rock, which they were able to defend until their food gave out. In the end many died of hunger. Hence the name Starved Rock.

This partly reconstructed defensive wall shows how people at Angel Mounds State Memorial, Indiana, built palisades and house walls, using poles, branches, and mud. Indiana Department of Natural Resources photo.

UNIVERSITY OF ILLINOIS, MUSEUM OF NATURAL HISTORY

Natural History Building, on the campus, Urbana. Open free, Monday through Saturday. Closed certain holidays.

In the museum's Hall of the Past several cases display material related to the life of prehistoric Indians in Illinois, beginning with Paleo times, about 8000 B.C. There are exhibits of the tools, clothing, hunting gear, and homes of Archaic people, of Woodland people from 2500 B.C. to A.D. 1300, and of the Mississippian culture, from A.D.. 900 to A.D. 1500. Special displays identify various types of pottery and stone artifacts and tell how certain artifacts were made.

A portion of the hall is devoted to prehistoric people of the Southwest.

Indiana

ANGEL MOUNDS STATE MEMORIAL

From downtown Evansville drive 7 miles east on Indiana 662 to a point 2½ miles west of Newburgh, then south ¾ of a mile on Fuquay Rd. to Pollack Ave., then east ½ mile to entrance. Open Monday through Saturday; afternoons, Sunday. Admission charged. Camping nearby.

People who followed the lifeway which archeologists called Mississippian lived here on the bank of the Ohio River from about A.D. 1300 to 1500. Like others in their day, they were farmers, traders, and builders of temple mounds. What makes this site unusual and important is its fate in modern times. It lies in a spot that industry has not invaded. It escaped extreme depredation by relic hunters, and in 1938 was purchased by the Indiana Historical Society, which deeded it to the State of Indiana. For more than 20 years the site was made available, with adequate financing, to ar-

cheologist Glenn A. Black to excavate. Foot by foot he studied the village, which probably marks the most northeasterly extension of the Mississippian culture.

Black dug into the mounds. He stripped away soil from the living areas, and unearthed more than 2½ million pieces of material. Still there is much to be discovered, and scientists will continue to work at the site for some time to come.

The people who built the mounds were immigrants, probably from Illinois. They may not have been entirely welcome, for they chose to build in a spot that was easy to defend. In front of their village an island in the river shielded them from approach across open water. A stream, now dry, protected the site from the rear. For extra safety the settlers surrounded the village with a palisade. This wall, about a mile in length, was made of stout posts placed upright in the ground. Branches were woven between the posts and then plastered over with mud. At intervals in the palisade were bastions, or lookout towers.

Birdstones have been found throughout the North Central area, and their exact use and function are still disputed. This birdstone may have been used as a weight on an atlatl. Original in the Milwaukee Public Museum.

The bannerstone, also, is an artifact that has thus far defied exact identification. This one was cut from slate and finely polished. It is of the type called "winged"; others were shaped like butterflies. Original in the Museum of the American Indian, New York.

In times of peace the river channel between shore and the island offered an easy place to fish. The surrounding land, which lay above the water level of most spring floods, was good for farming. In the woods not far away there was game.

Inside the palisade these hard-working people built 11 mounds, the largest with three distinct terraces. A religious structure may have stood on the lowest terrace. Possibly the house of the principal chief occupied the terrace above that. Higher still, on the northeast corner, was a conical mound. Perhaps the chief made ceremonial use of this prominence, the top of which was 44 feet above the surrounding land. Some experts think he may have mounted it daily to greet the rising sun.

A second large mound is believed to be the location of the main religious structure in the town. Between this temple mound and the chief's mound was the town square, where important ceremonies took place. On ordinary days people gambled in the square and young men played games. Members of the upper class probably lived close to the square; common people, farther away.

The town as a whole seems to have served as the religious center for an area that extended outward for 50 or 60 miles. What happened to it in the end is not known. Like other Mississippian settlements it was deserted when Europeans reached the Ohio Valley.

The Museum. The Interpretive Center at the entrance offers an orientation program outlining the history and meaning of the site. Exhibits, some permanent and some changing, contain portions of the wealth of archeological material found here.

Reconstructions on the site show different types of thatched dwelling, part of the 20-foot-high defensive stockade, and the temple. A museum in the temple shows and explains how burials were conducted.

The Name. Angel was the family name of people who once owned the mounds. Now the state of Indiana owns the site, and students in archeology at Indiana University dig here.

CHILDREN'S MUSEUM OF INDIANAPOLIS

3010 N. Meridian St., Indianapolis. Open free, Tuesday through Saturday; afternoons, Sunday. Closed certain holidays.

Indian artifacts, both prehistoric and historic, are displayed in this museum. Exhibits and dioramas have been designed to show grade-school children how tools, weapons, and utensils were made and how they were related to the everyday life of the people who used them.

GLENN A. BLACK LABORATORY OF ARCHAEOLOGY

Ninth and Fess streets, Bloomington. Open free, daily, all year.

The museum exhibits here emphasize the archeology of the Great Lakes–Ohio area. Some of the material recovered from Angel Mounds may be seen, as well as other collections from southwest Indiana.

Birdstones, Boatstones, Bannerstones

In 1840 some theological students from Connecticut found in an Indian burial a highly polished stone that somewhat resembled a bird. In 1848 Squier and Davis included illustrations of similar stones in their *Ancient Monuments of the Mississippi Valley*. From that time on farmers and others began to collect these strange objects. Birdstones turned up all over Ohio and Indiana and in western New York, western Pennsylvania, eastern Illinois, southeastern Wisconsin, southern Michigan and lower Canada.

The carefully snaped images sometimes resembled creatures other than birds. Some looked a little like boats (these were called boatstones). Others, less representational in form, got the name bannerstone, possibly because they were thought to resemble the small banners that in some societies were attached to ceremonial staffs. The kind of stone used in these objects was very often attractive. Banded slate was a favorite material. So was porphyry, which has a mottled, varicolored appearance. The range of shades in these artifacts was wide and so was the range of shapes.

But what was their origin, their use, their meaning? Answers to these questions were as numerous as facts about them were scarce. They were called handles for knives, emblems of maternity designed to be worn in women's hair, stone bayonets, totemic emblems, cornhuskers, necklace ornaments, fetishes, decorations for the tops of staffs used by medicine men. One man argued that the birdstones were somehow connected with the widespread thunderbird myth.

Arthur Parker, an archeologist and himself an Indian, speculated that at least one type of bannerstone was attached to the shaft of a spear. Its purpose was to give weight to the spear, and also to keep it on course, as feathers do for an arrow. Parker experimented with this arrangement and discovered that the spear went much straighter, faster, and about 25 percent farther than an unweighted shaft.

Another theory is that a good many bird/bannerstones were used as weights on atlatls (and not on spears themselves), to give added momentum for launching the weapon. Some evidence does suggest that some bannerstones were so used. It also seems possible that some birdstones had no such mechanical value but were for magical or ceremonial purposes.

Archeologist Thorne Deuel believes that bannerstones developed from atlatl weights but were either decorations or ceremonial objects carried by men to show they were good hunters. Later, he thinks, they evolved still further into flat forms that had bannerstone outlines but were worn as gorgets.

Cailup B. Curren, Jr., of the University of Alabama, has speculated that some at least of the "gorgets" may have served as tools which potters used for smoothing and shaping clay vessels. The idea occurred to him when he noticed that a kind of modern ceramic tool called a rib was remarkably like certain of the two-holed, polished stone prehistoric objects. Inquiry revealed that in some places the first appearance of these "gorgets" coincided with the first appearance of ceramics.

Whatever future researchers discover about these problematical objects, one thing is certain: Many forgers have gone into the business of making birdstones and have found it very profitable.

Caveat emptor!

These rounded heaps of earth are part of nine mounds built by Indians nearly 2000 years ago in an area used for ceremonies and funeral rites. The site is now part of Mounds State Park, Indiana. Indiana Natural Resources photo.

Another view of mounds in Mounds State Park, Indiana. Indiana Natural Resources photo by Ken Williams.

INDIANA STATE MUSEUM

202 N. Alabama St., Indianapolis. Open free, daily, all year. Closed certain holidays.

In the prehistoric gallery of this museum, exhibits tell the story of the first inhabitants up to contact with Europeans and before they were influenced by White traders.

INDIANA UNIVERSITY, MATHERS MUSEUM

On the university campus, Bloomington.

A new museum building is scheduled to open in 1983. It will contain some archeological exhibits.

MIAMI COUNTY HISTORICAL MUSEUM

Court House (4th Floor), Peru. Open free, Monday through Saturday. Closed certain holidays.

Prehistoric materials on display here include some artifacts from each of these cultures: Paleo-Indian, Adena, Hopewell, Mississippian, and Fort Ancient.

MOUNDS STATE PARK

From Anderson drive 4 miles east on Indiana 232. Open at all times. Admission charged. Camping.

Of the nine mounds in the park five are circular, two are fiddle-shaped, one is rectangular, and one is somewhat in the shape of a figure eight.

The largest, the Great Mound, seems to have been designed for use as a ceremonial ring. Nearly 16,300 cubic yards of earth were moved to create a circular structure 1200 feet around and almost 15 feet high. This apparently was used for seating around a central platform where ceremonies were held. Excavation of the platform revealed six burials. The best preserved was found in a log tomb, over which an animal skin had been stretched.

Artifacts found at the site include sheets of mica, a smoking pipe, and some rather unusual ornaments, which seem to have been attached to clothing rather than worn around the neck. These and the burials indicate that the people who conducted their ceremonies here probably followed the Hopewell lifeway.

MUSEUM OF INDIAN HERITAGE

6040 DeLong Rd., in Eagle Creek Park, Indianapolis. Open Tuesday through Sunday, June 15 through Labor Day; Saturday, Sunday and afternoons, Tuesday through Friday, fall and spring; Saturday, Sunday, Feb. and March. Closed Jan. Admission charged.

This important museum has archeological material along with material from the historic period.

PUTERBAUGH MUSEUM

11 N. Huntington St., Peru. Open free, Monday through Saturday. Closed certain holidays.

Artifacts on display represent the Paleo-Indian, Woodland, and Mississippian cultures.

At Effigy Mounds National Monument, in Iowa, one young worker digs carefully with trowel and whisk broom. Another shovels loosened earth into a screen which fits over a wheel barrow. The screen catches any small objects missed by the boys in the pit. National Park Service photo.

WYANDOTTE CAVE

From Interstate 64 turn south onto Indiana 66 to intersection with Indiana 62, then east through Leavenworth on Indiana 62 to cave. Open daily, all year. Closed Dec. 25. Admission charged. Camping nearby.

Although people usually visit this state-owned cave to see the cave itself, it is of archeological interest on more than one count. Apparently two different groups of people came here at two different times to do two different types of mining. One group hammered out and carried away large quantities of a soft mineral called calcite. What they used it for is not known, possibly because calcite turns to dust under certain conditions. The other group dug out nodules of flint embedded in the walls in a different section of the cave. The flint was, of course, raw material for projectile points, scrapers, and other tools.

At still another place, in the dried mud on the floor of a corridor that had long been blocked off by a calcite formation, Indian moccasin footprints were found, going farther into the cave

but not returning. One possible explanation is that the footprints led to a cave exit, which was later closed by a rockfall.

Some scientists believe the cave was also used from time to time as a shelter by Indians from 7000 B.C.. to A.D. 1500.

Iowa

DAVENPORT MUSEUM
(See Putnam Museum)

EFFIGY MOUNDS NATIONAL MONUMENT

From Marquette drive 3 miles north on Iowa 76 to monument entrance. Open free, daily, all year. Closed Dec. 25. Camping nearby.

Here on high land, which was bypassed instead of being scoured down by glaciers of the Ice Age., Indians built nearly 200 mounds during a period of at least 1500 years. Some of these mounds are likenesses—effigies—of birds or bears. Others are cone-shaped and were built by people whose

Two students in archeology, working at Effigy Mounds National Monument, in Iowa, prepare to remove a column of earth intact, so that it may be studied in a laboratory. Examining different pollen grains in each layer of the soil discloses what plants grew there at a given time in the past. National Park Service photo.

customs differed from those of the effigy-mound builders. It is possible to see a good sample of both types by walking along a trail that starts at the monument's Visitor Center.

The Story. Twelve thousand years ago in Iowa, Paleo-Indians hunted mammoths and giant bison, which grazed on prairie grasses. But changes in climate brought changes in vegetation, and forest slowly covered much of the land along the banks of the Yellow River, where it flows into the Mississippi. The big game of earlier times disappeared and people turned to hunting smaller animals.

The earliest tools that have been discovered near Effigy Mounds are woodworking impelements—axes, adzes, gouges. Obviously the people who made this kind of tool lived in wooded country. Other evidence shows that they hunted forest mammals, fished, and gathered freshwater mussels. Plants, too, made up part of their diet—wild rice, nuts, fruits, berries. They sewed clothing and wove baskets, using awls that were made of bone or copper. Their religious leaders conducted ceremonies aimed at cur-

ing illness and warding off bad luck, but if they had any special burial customs few signs of them have survived.

Their successors, however, began to take a deep interest in death ceremonials. By 2000 years ago they were following the pattern of many other groups of the North Central area. First they allowed the flesh of their dead to disintegrate. Then they gathered up the bones in bundles, which they buried along with spearpoints and large, knifelike artifacts. Often they covered the bones with red ocher.

Later, knowledge of how to make pottery came into this area, and over the years potters improved their techniques and changed the styles of the vessels they made. Gradually people adopted other new customs and accepted new beliefs. Between 100 B.C. and A.D. 600 they participated in the Hopewell phenomenon.

Hopewell ideas about death and burial included the belief that a wealth of beautiful objects should be placed in graves. To get the material for their grave goods, Hopewellians in Iowa, like those in other places, engaged in trade. Mica for their decorations came

from the distant Appalachian Mountains. They used obsidian from Yellowstone Park, conch shells from the Gulf of Mexico, and copper from the Great Lakes area. As in other Hopewellian settlements, mounds were built over the dead. Three such burial mounds can be seen near the Visitor Center in the monument.

A new fashion in mound building began here about A.D. 500, while the Hopewell ideas were still active. The new style dictated that burial mounds should be in the form of effigies—huge earthen likenesses of birds or bears. Twenty-seven such effigy mounds are in the monument.

The Effigy Mound people apparently lived in ways that resembled those of the Hopewellians, but they differed in some ways too, and not only in the kind of mound they built. They did not bury grave goods with their dead. They put copper to practical use in tools instead of merely shaping it into decorations.

By A.D. 1400, Indians who lived here were following the Oneota lifeway. Now they spent more time farming than earlier people had, and they

Outlined in white in this photo is the Great Bear Group of mounds in Effigy Mound National Monument. National Park Service photo by James E. Mount.

lived in larger communities. Apparently, among the descendants of the Oneota were the Iowa Indians, whom Europeans later encountered in the region and from who the state of Iowa gets its name.

The Museum. Exhibits in the Visitor Center throw light on the prehistory of the monument area, and an audiovisual presentation interprets the archeological findings. Two paintings show what people may have looked like, what they wore, and how they built mounds.

FISH FARM MOUNDS

From New Albin drive 3 miles south on Iowa 26. Open free, daily, all year.

At this site, which overlooks the Mississippi River, are about 30 prehistoric Indian mounds representative of the Woodland culture.

GROUT MUSEUM OF HISTORY AND SCIENCE

Park Ave. at South St., Waterloo. Open free, Tuesday through Friday; afternoons, Saturday, in summer; af-ternoons, Tuesday through Saturday, during the rest of the year. Closed certain holidays.

Four exhibit cases here are devoted to early Big-Game Hunters, bison hunters, Iowa's first farmers, and Indians of Iowa.

IOWA STATE MUSEUM

E. 12th and Grand Ave., Des Moines. Open free, daily, all year.

Early Woodland, Middle Woodland, and Mississippian artifacts are emphasized in the archeological collections here.

PIKES PEAK STATE PARK

From McGregor drive 1½ miles south on Iowa 340. Open free, daily, all year. Camping.

Here, overlooking the Mississippi River, are several mounds, including an impressive effigy mound in the form of a bear.

Figurines like this one, which was found at Knight Mounds in Illinois, have provided archeologists with information about the appearance of Indians who followed the Hopewell lifeway. After a reproduction in the Field Museum of Natural History, Chicago.

PUTNAM MUSEUM
(formerly Davenport Museum)

1717 W. 12th St., Davenport. Open Monday through Saturday; afternoons, Sunday. Admission charged.

Examples of Middle Mississippian pottery of several kinds from Tennessee and Arkansas, together with Hopewell artifacts from Iowa and Illinois, are on display here.

Special Interest. Over a hundred years ago, Jacob Gass, a Lutheran minister and passionate amateur archeologist, managed to get under the skin of some colleagues in the Davenport, Iowa, Academy of Natural Science. To even the score, they concocted an elaborate hoax. On one piece of slate from an old building they drew the signs of the zodiac; on another they scratched letters from various alphabets that they found in a Webster dictionary. Then they buried the slates in a mound and encouraged Gass to excavate there. He did not suspect his find was not genuine, and word spread that he had dug up proof that the mounds were built by people whose written language resembled those of ancient Mediterranean countries. The Davenport tablets became a sensation. Some experts suspected a hoax, but the perpetrators themselves were now ashamed to reveal their plot. Years later some of them confessed, and the records of the affair, together with the tablets, are in the Putnam Museum.

SIOUX CITY PUBLIC MUSEUM

29th and Jackson streets, Sioux City. Open free, Tuesday through Saturday; afternoons, Sunday.

In addition to ethnological exhibits from the Plains and North Central areas, this museum has some archeological material from northwest Iowa.

STATE UNIVERSITY OF IOWA, MUSEUM OF NATURAL HISTORY

Macbride Hall, on the campus, Iowa City. Open free, Monday through Saturday; afternoons, Sunday. Closed certain holidays.

Of the ten cases in this museum which display archeological material, three contain exhibits on cultures north of Mexico. One presents baskets, pottery, and blankets from the Southwest. Another shows clothing, snowshoes, and tools made by Indians of the Far North. The third deals with techniques of pottery decoration. Exhibits in the other cases are changed from time to time.

Archeologists believe that one type of Adena house looked like this. Often mud plaster was added to the walls. No original dwelling now exists, but some were destroyed by fire, which baked the mud and preserved the imprint of posts and interwoven branches. After Webb.

This stone pipe is from the original Adena Mound, in Ohio. Ohio Historical Society photo.

TOOLESBORO MOUNDS NATIONAL HISTORIC LANDMARK SITE

From Wapello drive 6 miles east on Iowa 99. Open free, afternoons, Thursday through Monday. Special appointments any time. Mail address: State Historical Society, 402 Iowa Ave., Iowa City, IA 52240.

A group of Hopewell burial mounds here dates from the Middle Woodland period (200 B.C. to A.D. 400). Near by is the Demonstration Prairie Plot in which grow the plants that flourished in the vicinity when the Hopewell people lived here. The Visitor Center contains displays and photographs which illuminate the Hopewell phenomenon and the vegetation in the prairie plot.

UNIVERSITY OF IOWA, MUSEUM OF NATURAL HISTORY

On the campus, in MacBride Hall, Iowa City. Open Monday through Saturday. Closed certain holidays.

A limited number of archeological exhibits here include Eskimo and Canadian Indian materials.

Kentucky

ADENA PARK

From Lexington drive 8 miles north on US 27, then turn off onto Old Ironworks Rd., and from this turn onto Mount Horeb Pike. The park is on the south side of N. Elkhorn Creek. Open free, by appointment arranged through the Department of Campus Recreation of the University of Kentucky in Lexington.

In the park is a circular earthwork, of the kind known as a "sacred circle," which surrounds a flat area where a structure once stood. A ditch and an embankment crossed by a cause-way form part of the site, which was built and used as a ceremonial center by Adena people. The park is owned by the University of Kentucky.

ANCIENT BURIED CITY
(King Mounds)

From Cairo, Ill., drive across the Ohio River Bridge, then 7 miles southeast on US 51 to directional sign near Wickliffe. Open daily. Admission charged.

Here, close to the place where the Ohio River flows into the Mississippi, was once a large community that followed the Mississippian lifeway. Several of the temple and platform mounds and one burial mound built by these people are protected by buildings, in which they may be viewed in a partially excavated state. The site is administered by a commercial enterprise, profits from which go to the Western Baptist Hospital in Paducah, Kentucky.

Adena

One of the nineteenth-century governors of Ohio lived near Chillicothe on a large estate, which he called Adena. Like other property nearby, his grounds had been occupied in prehistoric times by people who built large, cone-shaped earthen mounds, in which they buried their dead. But unlike most mounds, the one at Adena remained more or less undisturbed until 1901, when an archeologist was allowed to excavate it. The material he uncovered seemed to be the work of a people with very definite and identifiable traits.

When artifacts and burials from other mounds were compared to those at Adena, a general pattern emerged. People with similar traits had lived in prehistoric times throughout most of Ohio, eastern Indiana, northern Kentucky, western Pennsylvania, and parts of West Virginia.

Much of Adena life centered around rituals in honor of the dead. Few people ever had more ways of handling burials. Sometimes they placed an individual in a bark-lined pit on the floor of a house, which was then covered with a mound of earth. They cremated other bodies, then buried the remains. Sometimes part of a body was cremated and part buried. Often bodies were left to decay, perhaps lying on raised platforms, and then the cleaned bones were buried. Ritual bowls were made from some skulls, and bone from the skullcap might be shaped and engraved to make gorgets.

Toward the end of their history, which lasted from about 1000 B.C. to about A.D. 200, the Adena seem to have paid honor mainly to a few important people, who were buried in stout, log tombs, surrounded by their possessions. These grave goods included copper bracelets and rings, beads of shell and copper, smoking pipes, and ornaments of mica, polished stone, and other materials.

Archeologists have found the skeletons in log tombs especially interesting. Many were tall—men and women both over six feet. Almost all the skulls were flattened at the back, as a result of binding to a cradleboard in infancy. Some also had a groove at the sides, which seems, to indicate further binding to give the skull a rounded shape.

Smoking played a part in ceremonies, and the Adena made innumerable pipes, some of clay and some of stone. Often a man's pipe was buried with him, but occasionally archeologists have found large numbers of them associated with a single burial, perhaps because the dead man was a pipe maker.

In some of their ceremonies, possibly designed to bring good hunting, men wore headdresses imitating deer antlers and masks imitating wolf or puma heads. The jaws of bears and other animals were also carefully cut and ground to make ornaments or charms of some sort.

The Adena culture was similar in many ways to the richer, more elaborate Hopewell phenomenon which coexisted with it for centuries and shared some of the same territory. The original Adena mound cannot be visited, but the house on the estate for which it was named is open to the public.

Glacial Kame Culture

When the great ice sheet of the Pleistocene retreated, it left ridges of gravel in many places. Sometimes these ridges are known as glacial kames. *Kame* is a Scottish word for ridge and is pronounced like "came."

Some time after one group of hunting people entered and established themselves in an area which had been glaciated, they began to bury their dead in the gravel ridges. Because they left a distinctive set of grave goods with these burials, archeologists have named them Glacial Kame people. Many of their burials have been found in northern parts of Ohio and Indiana, southern parts of Michigan and Ontario, and also in eastern Illinois and southeastern Wisconsin.

As far as is now known, the people who followed the Glacial Kame lifeway lived at some time between 2000 B.C. and 1000 B.C. Their rather elaborate burials included many ornaments but very few tools, a fact which leads some archeologists to think they may have been forerunners of the Adena and Hopewell people, who placed great emphasis on funerary practices. It is also possible, though not proved, that the whole later tradition of placing burials in artificial mounds derived from the Glacial Kame practice of using natural mounds.

No Glacial Kame sites have been prepared for the public, but Glacial Kame artifacts can be seen in exhibits in the Allen County Museum in Lima, Ohio.

ASHLAND CENTRAL PARK

Two blocks south of US 60 in Ashland. Open free, daily, all year.

In the playground area in this city park, markers indicate five burial mounds. These are a small fraction of the total number that once existed where the city of Ashland now stands, on the bank of the Ohio River. Professional archeologists have not investigated the mounds in Central Park, and it is not known who built them or when.

BEHRINGER MUSEUM OF NATURAL HISTORY

Devou Park, Covington. Open free, Tuesday through Saturday and holidays; afternoons, Sunday. Closed Dec. 1 to April 1.

Included in the archeological displays in this museum is a collection of Adena material.

BLUE LICKS MUSEUM

Blue Licks Battlefield State Park. From Lexington drive 40 miles northeast on US 68 to Blue Licks Spring, then follow directional markers. Open daily, April through Oct. Admission charged. Camping.

Ten thousand years ago a spring of saltwater flowed in the park. Attracted by the salt, mastodons, mammoths, bison, and other animals visited the spring. Big-Game Hunters followed the animals, which sometimes got stuck in the mud and died there.

After the animals of the Ice Age disappeared, hunters continued to camp near the spring from time to time. Finally, about A.D. 1400, people who followed the Fort Ancient lifeway made their homes nearby. Their village, known as the Fox Field Site, has been excavated, and artifacts from it are on exhibit at the museum in the park. Other exhibits contain projectile points used by the early hunters, fishooks, and stone tools made by later people. Bones of some of the extinct animals are also on display.

Gigantic herds of buffalo in ancient times made a regular path, called a trace, to various salt licks in Kentucky. Near the Falls of the Ohio, at Louisville, they had a crossing, as did the mammoths and mastodons. Prehistoric peoples also followed trade routes to the crossing. At least one trading expedition may have made its way to the Falls from the neighborhood of Poverty Point, far down the Mississippi, in Louisiana. Evidence suggesting such a visit was a cache of small, baked clay balls of the kind which Poverty Point people used in cooking. Possibly visitors from Louisiana brought the balls along or they or someone else may have made them on the spot.

On the Indiana side of the river there was once a settlement of shellfish eaters, who left piles of discarded mussel shells ten feet deep for almost a mile along the riverbank. Their tools and those of other groups who lived in the area turn up often near the Falls, but no visitable sites remain.

KING MOUNDS
(See Ancient Buried City)

Two thousand years ago an Indian was mining gypsum 2½ miles from the entrance to Mammoth Cave when a huge rock fell on him. The photo shows archeologists removing the rock. National Park Service photo.

MAMMOTH CAVE NATIONAL PARK

From Bowling Green drive 22 miles north on Interstate 65 to Park City, then north on Kentucky 255 to park entrance; from here it is 5 miles to park headquarters. From points north and east, take US 31W west to Cave City, then Kentucky 70, 10 miles to park headquarters. Open daily, all year. Admission charged. Camping.

Indians knew about and sometimes ventured into Mammoth Cave in Archaic times, 3000 years ago, before they made pottery or did any farming. During one such visit a young girl died. Before moving on, her people buried her in a grass-lined grave at the cave's mouth.

By at least 400 B.C., people had grown bold enough to enter the dark, underground passages. There they found various minerals, such as gypsum and epsomite, which they used in some way. No one knows which minerals they valued or why, but they sought them far underground. Two and a half miles of cave walls show evidence of their mining activity. As tools they used stone hammers and scrapers made of mussel shells. For light they carried torches made from bundles of reeds.

When modern visitors entered, remnants of ancient torches still lay on the cave floor, as did worn-out sandals woven from strips of the inner bark of the pawpaw tree. Here and at nearby Salts Cave, collectors began to find and carry away feather blankets, cloth woven in black and white stripes, dishes made of dried squash rind, string bags, and basket coffins made of cane. Much of this material disappeared into private collections before the caves were put under government protection. A few articles are on exhibit in the museum at Mammoth Cave Park Headquarters.

In 1935 an explorer came upon the body of an ancient miner who had been killed by a falling rock. Instead of decaying, his flesh had simply dried in the cool, pure cave air.

Explorers in nearby Salts Cave in 1875 also came upon the desiccated body of a nine-year-old boy. Recently scientists have determined that the boy lived at least 2000 years ago, during

Prehistoric copper miners at work. Smithsonian Institution photo.

the Woodland period, and was possibly a member of an Adena population. Other signs of human acitivities in Salts Cave have been dated back to about 1500 B.C.

SPEED ART MUSEUM

2035 S. Third St., Louisville. Open free, Tuesday through Saturday; afternoons, Sunday. Closed certain holidays.

Prehistoric material on display in the J.B. Speed Art Museum consists mainly of artifacts made by the Adena people in Kentucky and southern Indiana. There are also some Paleo-Indian artifacts.

UNIVERSITY OF KENTUCKY, MUSEUM OF ANTHROPOLOGY

Lafferty Hall, on the main campus, Lexington. Open free, Monday through Friday. Closed certain holidays.

Exhibits here illustrate the culture history of Kentucky from Paleo-Indian times to the present. Since this was the heartland of the Adena culture, items from Adena tombs are on display.

Michigan

CHIPPEWA NATURE CENTER

400 South Badour Rd., Midland. Open Monday through Saturday; afternoons, Sunday. Closed certain holidays. Admission charged.

Dioramas and exhibits of prehistoric Native American material include artifacts found at nearby sites in an area called the Oxbow Archaeological District, where ongoing excavation is sometimes open to the public.

CRANBROOK INSTITUTE OF SCIENCE

500 Long Pine Rd., Bloomfield Hills. Open Monday through Friday; afternoons, Saturday, Sunday. Admission charged.

This very active, general science museum is interested in archeology and has good exhibits on prehistoric Indian life and culture, including one on Starved Rock (Illinois) stratigraphy and another on the sequence of cultures in Michigan.

FORT MICHILIMACKINAC
(MISH-ill-ee-MACK-in-aw)

On US 75 at the southern end of the Mackinac Bridge, Mackinaw City. Open daily, May 30 through Oct. 12. Admission charged.

Visitors can see archeologists at work in the park from June 1 to Aug. 20, excavating the French (1715–61) and British (1761–81) colonial fur-trading center.

GRAND RAPIDS PUBLIC MUSEUM

54 Jefferson Ave., Grand Rapids. Open free, Monday through Friday; afternoons, Saturday, Sunday, and holidays. Closed Dec. 25.

This museum contains a major exhibit entitled "The People of the Grand," which tells the story of the habitation of the Grand River Valley, in the Grand Rapids vicinity, from Paleo-Indian times through the establishment of the first permanent European settlement. The exhibit includes four life-size, three-dimensional scenes: Paleo-Indians hunting mastodons; a

the haltiner COPPER CACHE

the only known copper cache with finished and unfinished pieces and a large raw copper nugget

the cache was found across the street on the community college site. it was in a mass as if it had been in a container such as a leather pouch when it was dropped or lost. the largest pottery vessel found in northern michigan was discovered on the same site on the same day. it will be on display in the future.

An exhibit in the Jesse Besser Museum, Alpena, Michigan.

Hopewell burial ceremony, at the Norton Indian Mounds; a contact-period scene of an Indian village and fur traders; and a log cabin mission of 1825. Artifacts of the various Indian cultures, with audiovisual accompaniment, provide a picture of what life was like during the past 10,000 years.

GREAT LAKES INDIAN MUSEUM

In Historic Fort Wayne, 6053 West Jefferson Ave., Detroit. Open free, daily in summer.

Interpretive exhibits here trace Native American history from prehistoric times to the present. Of special interest is material from a burial mound on the bank of the Detroit River, which is now on the grounds of the museum. Originally a group of mounds built more than 1200 years ago stood on the site. All had been destroyed except this one, when the fort was constructed. Fortunately the commanding officer forbade unauthorized digging. Then in 1944 the Aboriginal Research Club and the University of Michigan were given permission to excavate.

HISTORIC FORT WAYNE MUSEUM
(See Great Lakes Indian Museum)

ISLE ROYALE NATIONAL PARK

For information on how to reach the park by boat or plane, write to: Superintendent, Isle Royale National Park, Houghton, MI 49931. Camping.

Prehistoric copper mines can be seen on Isle Royale, an island in an archipelago in Lake Superior. Beginning perhaps 4500 years ago, Indians dug pits to expose copper-bearing rock. Then they may have built fires to heat the rock and dashed cold water on it to make it crack into chunks. Finally, using cobbles as hammerstones, they probably broke up the chunks to get at the lumps of pure copper inside.

Some of the lumps were small. Others were very large. In 1874 one solid mass of copper was found on Isle Royale which weighed 5720 pounds. On it were clear marks that showed where prehistoric hammerstones had battered off small chunks of the malleable metal. Obviously it had once been even larger than it was when found by White miners. After this immense nugget was exhibited to the public for a while, it was melted down for commercial use.

There are many of the old mining pits in the park. In or near them has been found evidence that they were worked until historic times. Some of the prehistoric miners may have been ancestors of modern Algonquian and Siouan tribes. There is also evidence of the use of the mines by Iroquois Indians.

JESSE BESSER MUSEUM

491 Johnson St., Alpena. Open free, Monday through Friday; afternoons, Saturday, Sunday. Closed certain holidays.

A collection of 20,000 artifacts traces the story of prehistoric people in the Great Lakes area. The Gallery of Early Man contains many Old Copper Culture artifacts found near the museum, including a cache composed of a large, raw copper nugget, 31 partially worked pieces, and 3 finished artifacts. Loan exhibits from other museums are regularly featured.

The Sanilac petroglyphs. At center, bottom are long-tailed animals which, according to Indians of the Great Lakes area in historic times, represented the water panther. This supernatural creature, by switching its tail, was supposed to create storms and high winds. From *Great Lakes Informant,* Michigan Department of State.

KALAMAZOO PUBLIC MUSEUM

315 S. Rose St., Kalamazoo. Open free, Monday through Saturday; afternoons, Sunday, Sept. through May.

Some prehistoric archeological material from the Southwest and from Eastern Woodland cultures in the United States is exhibited in this museum, which emphasizes history.

MICHIGAN HISTORICAL MUSEUM

In Lansing, 208 North Capitol Ave. Open free, Monday through Friday; afternoons, Saturday and Sunday.

An audiovisual program here, introducing Michigan history, includes prehistoric Indian material. Some exhibits show Native American artifacts from the days of caribou hunters to modern times.

MICHIGAN STATE UNIVERSITY MUSEUM

Circle Dr., East Lansing. Open free, Monday through Friday; afternoons, Saturday, Sunday. Closed certain holidays.

Some of the North American prehistoric exhibits in this museum are devoted to Michigan archeology. Others show the culture areas of the continent and techniques used in archeological excavation.

MUSEUM OF THE GREAT LAKES

1700 Center Ave., Bay City. Open free, Monday through Friday; afternoons, Sunday. Closed certain holidays.

In this general museum, devoted to the history of the Great Lakes area, are small exhibits of projectile points and stone tools used by prehistoric inhabitants of Michigan.

NORTON MOUNDS

From Campau Square in Grand Rapids drive 4 miles south along Grand River on Market St. to the railroad crossing, where Market St. becomes Indian Mound Rd. This is the mound area, and it is undeveloped. Open free, at all times.

Here are 17 mounds, 13 clearly visible, which are all that remain of

about 40 once standing in the vicinity. Although the site lies outside Grand Rapids, it is owned by the city. Local citizens are seeking to have the mounds included in a national monument, which would protect and interpret them. Meantime, to avoid littering, the road through the park is closed, and it is necessary to visit the mounds on foot.

The Story. People who practiced the Hopewell lifeway moved from the Illinois River valley to this place about A.D. 200. Here as elsewhere they began to pile up earth over the bodies of their dead. Around the mounds they built low, earthen enclosures. When a leading member of the community died, lavish funeral ceremonies were held, and gifts were placed in the grave. To get material for their burials, the Hopewell traded with other people in distant places. Copper for beads and tools came from northern Michigan; conch shells for ornaments from the Gulf of Mexico. Decorations and silhouette designs were cut from sheets of mica, which had to be brought from the far-off Appalachian Mountains. Sources close to home provided mate-

Hopewell funeral ceremony is depicted in this diorama in the University of Michigan Exhibit Museum. University of Michigan Museum of Anthropology photo.

rial for polished stone tools, chippped projectile points, headdresses of deer antlers, and beads of beaver teeth.

For 200 years people continued to build their burial mounds here and at a site, now destroyed, in the center of Grand Rapids. Then for some unknown reason mound building stopped.

Archeologists from the University of Michigan have excavated Norton Mounds, and some of the materials they recovered are on exhibit nearby in the Grand Rapids Public Museum. A leaflet about the mounds may be obtained at the museum.

SANILAC PETROGLYPHS STATE PARK

In Greenleaf Township, off Michigan 53, at intersection of Germania Rd. and Bay City–Forestville Rd. Open free, daily. The key to the padlocked gate may be obtained from Len Spencer, on the adjoining farm.

This park, created through the efforts of the Michigan Archaeological Society, protects a very unusual depression in a sandstone outcropping, where at some unknown time in the

past people carved abstract designs and · the figures of animals and human beings. One·curious image seems to link a spiderlike creature to a human umbilical cord. Another depicts a hunter with bow and arrow. Some of the carvings have been almost destroyed by weather and by the shoes of people who walked over them. A shelter now helps to keep them from further damage.

UNIVERSITY OF MICHIGAN EXHIBIT MUSEUM

Geddes St. and N. University Ave., Ann Arbor. Open free, Monday through Saturday; afternoons, Sunday. Closed certain holidays.

In this general natural science museum are exhibits on early Indian sites in Michigan. There are also exhibits of prehistoric Eskimo, Northwest Coast, and Woodland material. Several displays show the manufacture, evolution, and use of Old World tools, some of which were ancestral to prehistoric American tools. Fourteen small dioramas, six of which are devoted to

Michigan, show aspects of various Indian cultures before the arrival of Europeans.

The Museum of Anthropology in this same building conducts archeological research. Its collections are for scientific study and are not open to the public.

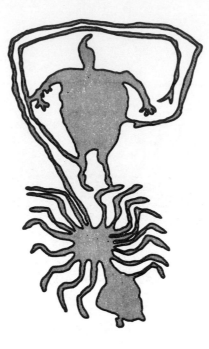

This figure, painted in shades of violet in a Michigan cave, is known as the Spider Man. However, some archeologists believe the lower part of the picture represents not a spider but a campfire. From *Great Lakes Informant,* Michigan Department of State.

Opposite:
The Visitor Center at Jeffers Petroglyph State Park. Photo Minnesota Historical Society.

Minnesota

GRAND MOUND CENTER

From International Falls, drive 17 miles west on Minnesota 11. Open free, daily, May 1 through Oct. 31; Saturday, Sunday, Nov. 1 through April 30.

The Grand Mound is the largest prehistoric burial mound in the northern Midwest, one of the few to survive in Minnesota, where there were once 10,000 or more. Together with three smaller mounds, this immense earthen structure was built by people of the Laurel culture, who occupied the area along the Rainy River from about 200 B.C. to A.D. 800. They were Woodland people, who fished and hunted and made an unusual smoothly finished pottery. Two distinctive types of Laurel tool were a detachable, toggle-head harpoon point and a chisel made from a beaver incisor tooth.

For many years steamboats from Ontario made special trips, bringing people to dig for artifacts in the Grand Mound. The site is now protected by the Minnesota Historical Society and has been investigated by archeologists.

The Interpretive Center at the site offers extensive exhibits, which relate the Rainy River peoples to the larger North American Indian scene. One display, called "How We Know," introduces the visitor to the methods and tools that archeologists use in reconstructing the past. The exhibits surround an indoor forest scene, recreating the environment in which Laurel people lived and adapted to the harsh, northern climate.

An audiovisual program tells the story of fanciful nineteenth-century attempts to explain mound building, which was once supposed to have been done by the Lost Tribes of Israel or other mysterious predecessors of the Indians. Films and lectures are also offered from time to time.

A self-guided nature trail leads from the Interpretive Center to the Grand Mound.

ITASCA STATE PARK

Near intersection of Minnesota 200 and US 71, 21 miles north of Park Rapids. Open daily, May through Oct. Admission charged. Camping.

Here, near the source of the Mississippi River, are numerous ancient burial mounds, a Dakota Indian village site, and a bison kill site. At the latter site aboriginal hunters camped sometime between 8000 and 7000 years ago and waited in ambush to kill bison fording a stream during fall migration. Investigators of the site found many stone tools and animal bones, including the skeleton of a dog—the earliest evidence of that animal to be discovered in Minnesota.

Exhibits at the museum on the north shore of Lake Itasca interpret the archeological finds.

JEFFERS PETROGLYPHS

At junction of US 71 and County Rd. 10, drive 3 miles east on 10, then 1 mile south on County Rd. 2. Open free, daily, May 1 through Labor Day.

This site contains the largest known concentration of aboriginal rock art in Minnesota, consisting of more than 2000 figures, carved on a sloping outcrop of red quartzite about 700 feet long and 150 feet wide at its widest point. Studies indicate that the carvings were made by several groups, over a long period of time. The representations of atlatls—devices used by hunters for throwing darts of spears—indicate that a large number of the carvings may have been made as early as 3000 B.C. Others include characteristic symbols of the Siouan peoples and probably were made between A.D. 900 and 1700.

An interpretive building contains information about the site, which is surrounded by a virgin prairie area, one of the few that remain much as they were before the arrival of Europeans.

KATHIO STATE PARK

On Minnesota 169 near Onamia. Open free, in summer.

The Interpretation Center interprets the archeology of the park, where village sites and mound groups are marked with signs. Archeological excavations are ongoing and are frequently open to the public.

MILLE LACS INDIAN MUSEUM

From Minneapolis drive 29 miles northwest on US 52 to Elk River, then 64 miles north on Minnesota 169 to the museum on the west side of Lake Mille Lacs. Open free, May 1 through Sept. Camping.

This district was the site of an important Sioux (Dakota) village until the 1740s, when the Chippewa, who had obtained guns in the fur trade, drove the Sioux westward onto the plains. The museum, which is operated by the Minnesota Historical Society, has some prehistoric material as part of its displays on the history of the Sioux and Chippewa. Dioramas show Chippewa camps during the four seasons.

Modern Indians in the area still harvest and preserve wild rice as their ancestors did in prehistoric times, and they offer a demonstration of the process on several Sundays during the summer at nearby Mille Lacs Kathio State Park.

A pipe maker at work, using the soft stone called catlinite, quarried in Pipestone National Monument. Only Indians are now allowed to dig the stone. National Park Service photo.

MINNESOTA MAN SITE

Drive 3 miles north from Pelican Rapids on US 59. Camping nearby.

Here, where the highway cuts through an embankment, road workers found a skeleton in a bed of clay that had been laid down during the last part of the Ice Age. If, as some experts believe, this skeleton was covered by clay during the Ice Age, it is very old and very important. Others believe it was buried in recent times and might be a modern Sioux. All agree that Minnesota Man is a young female.

Archeologists agree, too, that it is a pity the excavation of the skeleton was not scientifically done. It is now difficult to tell with certainty whether or not the earth above the burial had been dug or moved. Undisturbed earth would have given clearer evidence of great age.

MOUNDS PARK

Mounds Blvd. and East St., St. Paul. Open free, at all times.

This park preserves 6 burial mounds, all that remain out of 18 or more that once stood in the area.

PIPESTONE NATIONAL MONUMENT

From Pipestone, at the junction of US 76 and Minnesota 23, drive about 1 mile north. Open free, all year. Camping nearby.

Among almost all Indians, pipe smoking had religious meaning. Very often men smoked when an agreement had been made. Thus a pipe was often a symbol for peace. So important was it in ceremonial life that Indians traveled great distances to obtain the material they deemed best for making pipe bowls. Much sought after was a reddish stone that came from a quarry in Minnesota. The quarry was known apparently over a large part of the United States and was considered a sacred spot.

Pipestone is a kind of clay which has been altered by chemical and physical action after having been laid down under water a very long time ago. It is soft and easily carved.

Archeologists do not know exactly when Indians began to visit the Pipestone Quarry, but they feel sure it must have been at least 300 years ago. There was mining at the site when the first Whites appeared in the area. At that time the Dakota Indians, better known as the Sioux, controlled the quarry and had a monopoly of the stone, which they traded to other tribes. Only Indians are now allowed to dig the stone, and they do continue to use it.

Pipes, now almost always associated with tobacco smoking, were long used for smoking other herbs. In the Southeast pipes have been dated at 1590 B.C. But no one knows when tobacco, originally a Mexican plant, reached areas north of the border. The earliest identifiable traces of it have been dated at A.D. 1000, although it probably reached the United States

Pipestone National Monument. Here Indians quarried a soft stone for use in making pipes. National Park Service photo.

Many Indians liked a certain soft, red stone for making the bowls of tobacco pipes. The stone, called catlinite because the artist George Catlin was the first to write about it, occurs in a very large deposit in Pipestone National Monument, Minnesota. This diorama at the monument shows Indians at work quarrying catlinite. National Park Service photo.

area before that. Pipes themselves seem to have been a northern invention that spread south into Mexico.

The long, decorated stem of a smoking pipe played an important symbolic role in the calumet ceremony which Europeans observed in early historic times. This ritual, in which the pipe was passed from one person to another, established strong relationships between different individuals or groups. Some scholars, thinking the practise began after Indians first encountered Europeans, have interpreted it as an assertion of Indian identity. Others, however, point to archeological evidence that the ceremony originated on the Great Plains long before the contact period. The earliest known pipe of the calumet type—a stone bowl set at a right angle to a long stem—has been C-14 dated at 710 years ago. It was associated with a culture called the Nebraska phase which thrived in eastern Nebraska and western Iowa.

Because of its use in forging close bonds, Europeans often called a calumet a "peace pipe." The word *calumet* itself is of French origin and appropri-

ately refers to a reed which was used as the stem of one kind of pipe.

From the Plains the calumet ceremony spread to the Eastern woodlands where it was much elaborated. As it spread, it served to increase bonds between groups of people who traded with each other. It also played a role in the formation of military alliances, and some archeologists have argued that it had an important part in developing the Iroquois Confederacy.

One of the first White people to see Pipestone Quarry was the artist George Catlin, who visited it in 1836. Catlin made a drawing and a painting which show the quarry and Indians at work there, no doubt as they worked in prehistoric times. In his notes, later expanded into a detailed description, he writes that behind the quarry rises a natural wall "two miles in length and thirty feet high, with a beautiful cascade leaping from its top into a basin. On the prairie, at the base of the wall, the pipeclay is dug up at two and three feet depth. There are seen five immense granite boulders, under which there are two squaws,

according to their tradition, who eternally dwell there—the guardian spirits of the place—and must be consulted before the pipestone can be dug up."

Catlin sent a sample of pipestone to a scientist friend, who analyzed it and named it catlinite, in honor of the artist.

Beginning at the Visitor Center, where there is a small museum, a circle trail leads to the quarry pits and other points of interest in the monument.

In 1832 George Catlin saw this very old Minitaree chief smoking a pipe, the bowl of which was carved from the kind of stone geologists now call catlinite. From George Catlin's *Illustrations of the Manners, Customs, and Condition of North American Indians.*

Missouri

ATKINS MUSEUM OF FINE ARTS
(See William Rockhill Nelson Gallery)

CLAY COUNTY HISTORICAL MUSEUM

West side of the square, Liberty. Open free, afternoons, Tuesday through Sunday. Closed certain holidays.

In this museum are some materials representative of the Nebo Hill culture, which the museum dates at 5000 B.C.

GRAHAM CAVE STATE PARK

Take the Danville—Montgomery City exit from Interstate 70, then drive 2 miles west on County TT to park entrance. Open free, daily, Memorial Day to Labor Day. Camping.

Graham Cave is a natural rockshelter 20 fee high and 120 feet wide, in which people camped at intervals for 10,000 years. During that time the cave floor was littered with the waste they left, then with chunks of rock that fell from the ceiling, and quantities of fine dust blown in by wind. All this material piled up to a depth of six or seven feet, forming a series of layers, in which archeologists could read the story of Missouri's early inhabitants.

Hunters first took shelter here at the end of the Ice Age, when prairie vegetation extended from the present Great Plains to the vicinity of the cave. These hunters had weapons like those used father west by Paleo-Indians, who stalked the big-game animals that grazed on prairie grass. Later as forests took the place of grasslands, hunters who followed the Archaic lifeway camped at the cave. Still later, people of Woodland culture stopped here from time to time.

One interesting find in the cave is a large, flat rock around which smaller rocks are arranged. Quite clearly, ancient campers built fires on the big rock, then sat around it on the small ones, perhaps engaging in some kind of ceremony.

Because the cave contains evidence of human life over such a long span of time and because it lies on the western fringe of the Woodland culture area, this site is of great importance to archeologists.

The cave itself may be seen but cannot be entered. Interpretive signs and leaflets give a good idea of what was discovered here and how.

Size of Prehistoric Populations

Estimates of the total Native American population at the time Europeans arrived have varied widely. The documentary data for estimates—such as letters, diaries, official reports of explorers and colonial settlers—are not very reliable and are usually incomplete. We know that after 1492 the decrease in native population in certain areas was rapid and steep, but slower in other places, continuing until recent times. This variation in the amount and rate of depopulation makes it difficult to figure backward to an estimate of original population. However, sophisticated statistical methods have been applied convincingly to archeological, documentary, and ecological evidence. The numbers of villages and of house sites in villages give clues, as do skeletal remains and traces of fields and gardens. After considering all available figures, geographer William M. Denevan has concluded that in 1492 the population of North America was about 4,400,000 and that the total for North, South, and Central America was about 57,300,000.

A bird bowl, found at the Campbell Site, in Missouri.

KIMMSWICK SITE
(See Mastodon State Park)

LINE CREEK MUSEUM

In Line Creek Park, at the intersection of N.W. Waukomis Rd. and N.W. 56 St., Kansas City. Open free, Saturday, Sunday; afternoons, Monday through Friday. Closed certain holidays.

This museum, located near a Hopewell site, features material found at the site, as well as other Hopewell material and artifacts of Archaic, Woodland, and Mississippian cultures. A slide show about the Line Creek Site may be seen at a theater in the building.

LONG BRANCH LAKE VISITOR CENTER

On the east side of the dam, just outside Macon. Open free, daily, all year.

Before construction of the dam by the Army Corps of Engineers, archeologists recovered artifacts indicating that the area had been occupied from Paleo times to the period of contact with Europeans. An audiovisual program and archeological exhibits in the Visitor Center tell the story of the site, which is now covered by water.

MASTODON STATE PARK
(Kimmswick Site)

A museum and interpretive center in the park is planned for sometime in the future. Meantime, a small exhibit of material from the site may be seen in the nearby Kimmswick Museum, about 15 miles south of St. Louis, off US 55 on US 61–69. Tours of the museum are given on weekends, at other times by appointment. For information call Dorothy Heinze in Imperial, (314) 467–5608.

Archeologists have long suspected

Graham Cave in Missouri is formed by an overhanging rock. The cave is 120 feet wide and 20 feet high. It attracted hunters from the time of the Ice Age on, and for more than 10,000 years debris and remains of human life accumulated there. Graham Cave State Park photo.

that early hunters who killed mammoths also found mastodons a source of meat. Proof of mammoth hunting has appeared at many sites, particularly in plains areas, where spearpoints and other stone tools have been found in association with the animals' bones. Although mastodon remains had come to light in several bone beds in formerly forested places, clear proof of a kill eluded searchers until 1977, when the Manis Site was discovered in the state of Washington. Then, in 1979, excavation in Mastodon State Park turned up a Clovis point of the kind used by mammoth hunters 11,000 or more years ago. The point lay on top of some mastodon bones and beneath others—unmistakable evidence that a human being had been involved in the animals' death. Further digging resulted in the discovery of more Clovis spearheads, as well as stone flakes of the kind made by sharpening stone tools, which suggest that this might also have been a hunters' campsite.

The park and the Kimmswick Museum are the work of a group of devoted citizens, who managed to raise enough money to buy the site and save it from commercial development. Excavation of the bone bed in the park continues, but it is not usually open to the public. The area contains much still unstudied material and fragile specimens, preserved from decomposition by minerals in the water.

Eventually the Mastodon Park Committee, which one of its founders proudly says is sparked by housewives, hopes to get together funds for a large interpretive center. What the members call a minimuseum now devotes about half its space to children's programs and half to material that came from the park.

MISSOURI HISTORICAL SOCIETY

Lindell at De Balivere, St. Louis. Open free, Tuesday through Sunday. Closed certain holidays.

Artifacts on display here came primarily from digs in Missouri or the middle Mississippi Valley. Paleo, Archaic, Woodland, and Mississippian periods are represented.

MISSOURI STATE MUSEUM

State Capitol Bldg., Jefferson City. Open free, daily. Closed certain holidays.

The newly renovated History Hall contains exhibits depicting Missouri's Indian cultures. Archeological and historical exhibits are integrated into a chronological sequence illustrating Missouri's development since prehistoric times. The Resources Hall, due to be renovated, will include additional archeological materials relating to Missouri's prehistoric cultures.

MUSEUM OF SCIENCE AND NATURAL HISTORY

Clayton at Big Bend Rd., St. Louis. Open free, daily. Closed certain holidays.

Many midwestern cultures are represented in this museum, which displays prehistoric material dating from 8000 B.C. to A.D. 1500. The greatest concentration of artifacts is Mississippian, and the areas best represented are Missouri and Illinois. Some arti-

Right:
An effigy vase, made by people of the Mississippian culture, found in Mississippi County, Missouri. Southeast Missouri State University Museum photo.

Left:
This pottery vessel, modeled in the shape of a head, was incised before firing. Found at the Campbell Site, in Missouri.

facts are from scientific digs conducted during the Depression, with labor provided by the Works Progress Administration.

RALPH FOSTER MUSEUM
(See School of the Ozarks)

SAINT JOSEPH MUSEUM

Eleventh and Charles streets, St. Joseph. Open Monday through Saturday; afternoons, Sunday, April through mid-Sept.; afternoons, Tuesday through Sunday, mid-Sept. through March. Admission charged except Sunday and holidays.

The American Indian collections in this museum are national in scope and include some archeological material.

SAINT LOUIS ART MUSEUM

Forest Park, St. Louis. Open free, Wednesday through Sunday; afternoons and evenings, Tuesday. Closed certain holidays.

Some prehistoric artifacts are on exhibit here. They include copper plaques from southeast Missouri.

SCHOOL OF THE OZARKS, RALPH FOSTER MUSEUM

From Springfield drive 40 miles south on US 65. The school is 3 miles south of Branson at Point Lookout. Open free, Monday through Saturday; afternoons, Sunday.

This museum has on display 625 pieces of pottery from the Mississippian culture. There are also exhibits of artifacts made by Ozark Bluff Dwellers and materials from other, later cultures.

SOUTHEAST MISSOURI STATE UNIVERSITY MUSEUM

In Memorial Hall, on the campus, Cape Girardeau. Open free, Monday through Friday, all year.

On display here is a collection of Early Middle Mississippian artifacts. Exhibits consist of pottery with small rim effigies, water vessels, ornaments, axes, farming tools, celts, and other implements.

THOUSAND HILLS STATE PARK

From Kirksville drive 3 miles east on Missouri 6, then 2 miles south on Missouri 157 to park. Open free, daily, all year. Camping.

Here a cluster of petroglyphs (rock carvings), protected by a cover, ar interpreted for the public. The carvings depict footprints, crosses, sunbursts, arrows, animals, thunderbirds, and other designs. The people who made them are believed to be associated with the Woodland Tradition in Missouri, which probably dates them earlier than A.D. 900, and earlier than the rock carvings at Washington State Park (see below) associated with the Mississippian Tradition. Interpretations of the petroglyphs vary, but it is generally believed that they served a ceremonial purpose.

TOWOSAHGY STATE PARK
(toe-wah-SOG-ee)

From East Prairie drive 6 miles east on Missouri 80, then 2 miles south on County Rd. AA, then 3 miles south on County Rd. FF; turn east and go 1

Salvaging what they can of the past, archeologists race against rising water in a new reservoir. National Park Service photo.

mile on gravel road, then south 1 mile on gravel. As this book goes to press, the site is not open to the public, but is viewable from the bordering road.

Between A.D. 1000 and 1400 people of the Mississippian culture were living in a 30-acre village and civic-ceremonial center at this site. They built mounds around a large central plaza, and on at least two they placed structures which were probably temples or other important community buildings. A portion of the center was fortified by a system of vertical-log stockade walls and a bastion, or defensive projection, of the wall line. A large borrow pit and several smaller ones furnished the earth from which the mounds were built. The people of the village farmed near by and they made pottery in styles that were popular in other villages in southeastern Missouri.

TRUMAN DAM VISITOR CENTER

In Warsaw. Open free, daily, all year.

Before construction of the dam by the Army Corps of Engineers, excava-tion at the site, which is now covered by water, yielded evidence that mastodons were hunted here in Paleo times. The exhibits in the Visitor Center show replicas of artifacts and bones recovered by archeologists.

UNIVERSITY OF MISSOURI, MUSEUM OF MAN, ART AND ARCHAEOLOGY

100 Swallow Hall, on the campus, Columbia. Open free, Monday through Friday; afternoons, Saturday; tours by appointment for groups during the week, weekends, or evenings.

This museum gives special attention to Indian cultures of Missouri and the Midwest. Its archeological exhibits include artifacts from Paleo-Indian times to A.D. 1800. There is a special wealth of material in the Mississippian period (A.D. 1100 to 1500). Dioramas show a Paleo-Indian hunt, a Woodland mound, and a Mississippian mound. There is also a full-sized reconstruction of a Mississippian house of about A.D. 1200.

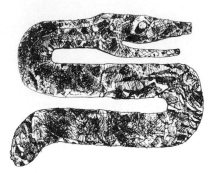

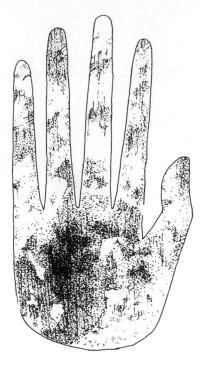

An ornament in the shape of a snake, cut from a sheet of mica. The original, found at Turner Mound, Ohio, is now in the Peabody Museum, Harvard University.

This mica grave offering, in the form of a hand, was made by the Hopewellian people of Ohio. Original in the Field Museum of Natural History, Chicago.

VAN METER STATE PARK

From Marshall drive 8 miles north on Missouri 41 to junction with Missouri 122, then 4 miles west to park. Open free, daily, all year. Camping.

In this park are several visible and interpreted archeological sites. Research indicates that people inhabited the area as early as 10,000 B.C., and the Missouri Indians, for whom the state is named, were the last major tribe to live here. A large earthwork in the park, called the Old Fort, is associated with the Oneota culture and possibly with the Missouri Indians. Just north of the Old Fort site is a cluster of burial mounds.

If ongoing archeological excavation is being done in the park, visitors are invited to watch, though not to participate in the work.

WASHINGTON STATE PARK

From DeSoto drive 15 miles south on Missouri 21. Open daily, all year. Camping fee charged.

In this park are petroglyphs (rock carvings) and a museum which includes archeological exhibits. A folder available at the park gives directions to the petroglyph sites, which are viewable year-round.

At Site 1 several hundred symbols were carved in the rock, presumably between A.D. 1000 and 1600. The designs include birds, arrows, squares, ovals, circles, footprints, claws, and human figures. The birds may represent the eagle, buzzard, or hawk, which were important in many Indian cultures over a wide area. Speech scrolls issue from the mouths of several human figures and one bird. Like the balloons in modern day comic strips, they seem to indicate that talking is going on.

Site 2 has symbols that were connected with the Southern Cult—maces, bilobed arrows, crosses.

Some archeologists believe that ancient trails crossed in this area and that people came together here for spe-

cial rites or ceremonies. Possibly the symbols were associated with such ceremonies. Or they may have been devices to help people memorize certain songs or rituals.

WILLIAM ROCKHILL NELSON GALLERY AND ATKINS MUSEUM OF FINE ARTS

4525 Oak St., Kansas City. Open Tuesday through Saturday; afternoons, Sunday. Closed certain holidays. Admission charged except on Sunday.

Some prehistoric material is included in exhibits devoted to Indian pottery and jewelry.

Ohio

ALLEN COUNTY MUSEUM

620 W. Market St., Lima. Open free, afternoons, Tuesday through Sunday. Closed certain holidays.

A feature of this museum is a diorama showing how Glacial Kame people buried their dead, together with material from a Glacial Kame grave found near Lima. Other displays con-

Top to bottom: The bird of prey often appeared as an element in mound builders' designs. This ornament was cut from a sheet of hammered copper. Original in Ohio Historical Center. The bird motif, sometimes very stylized, was also carved by Adena mound builders on small pieces of stone. These engraved Adena tablets, found in burials, were probably used somehow in funeral ceremonies. After Webb and Baby.

tain materials from Paleo-Indian, Archaic, Adena, Hopewell, Cole Creek, Fort Ancient, and Erie cultures.

CAMPBELL MOUND

On McKinley Ave., ½ mile south of Trabue Rd., Columbus. Open free, at all times.

This example of an Adena mound is administered by the Ohio Historic Preservation Office.

CINCINNATI MUSEUM OF NATURAL HISTORY

1720 Gilbert Ave., Cincinnati. Open Tuesday through Saturday; afternoons, Sunday. Closed certain holidays. Admission charged.

Most of the archeological materials on display here have been collected by the museum's own fieldworkers in the Ohio Valley. The Adena, Hopewell, and Fort Ancient cultures are represented. Leaflets describing the lifeways of these people are available. Some material from the Southwest and the Northwest Coast is also on exhibit.

Special Feature. The museum building stands not far from the site of an ancient Adena burial mound. In the mound was discovered a small, carefully shaped piece of stone, on which a design had been engraved. This tablet, one of 12 found in various mounds, is now in the museum.

Some Adena tablets appear to have been coated with a red pigment. This may indicate that they were used as stamps to print red-colored designs on clothing or on the bodies either of the dead or of those taking part in funeral ceremonies. Some connection with burial practices seems likely because Adena people sprinkled red ocher over the remains of the dead and even over the grave goods placed in tombs.

Careful study of the designs on tablets indicates that many if not all of them represent birds of prey, such as the vulture, duck hawk, and carrion crow. On some tablets the figures are quite realistic. On others, such as the Cincinnati tablet, the design seems to contain very stylized elements of wings, beaks, and eyes. Flesh-eating birds seem to have been important in all the burial mound cults, possibly

Styles in smoking pipes varied from one place to another and changed as time went on. This one, in the form of a fish and a bird, was carved by Hopewellian people in Ohio. Original in the Field Museum of Natural History, Chicago.

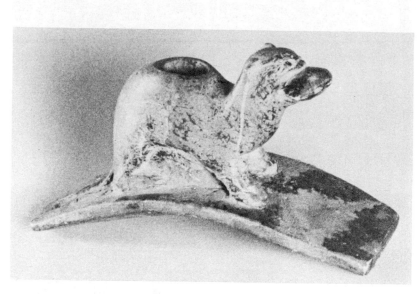

On this platform pipe found in Tremper Mound, Ohio, an artist carved the effigy of an otter. Ohio Historical Society photo.

because they acted as scavengers and helped to clean the bones of bodies which were exposed and allowed to decompose before burial or cremation.

CLEVELAND MUSEUM OF ART

11150 E. Blvd. at University Circle, Cleveland. Open free, Tuesday through Saturday; afternoons, Sunday; evenings, Wednesday. Closed certain holidays.

A number of prehistoric art objects are on display. They include Mimbres and other Southwestern pottery, a Mississippian sandstone pipe, and an Adena sandstone pipe from Ohio.

CLEVELAND MUSEUM OF NATURAL HISTORY

Wade Oval, University Circle, Cleveland. Open Monday through Saturday; afternoons, Sunday. Closed certain holidays. Admission charged.

On display here are materials on prehistoric peoples in Ohio and other North American areas. Dioramas show reconstruction of ancient life. Exhibits of current fieldwork change from time to time.

CLINTON COUNTY HISTORICAL SOCIETY AND MUSEUM

149 East Locust St., Wilmington. Open afternoons, Tuesday through Sunday, March through Dec. Closed certain holidays. Admission charged.

A small collection of archeological material includes an exhibit of projectile points.

DAYTON MUSEUM OF NATURAL HISTORY

2629 Ridge Ave., Dayton. Open Monday through Saturday; afternoons, Sunday and all holidays. Admission charged.

Exhibits include Ohio material from Paleo times (14,000 B.C.) to Fort Ancient (A.D. 1500). There is a large display of material from the museum's ten years of excavation at the Incinerator Site in Montgomery County, Ohio, a twelfth-century Fort Ancient culture village.

FIRELANDS MUSEUM

4 Case Ave. (at the rear of the Public Library), Norwalk. Open every afternoon, May, June, Sept., Oct.—Monday through Saturday; afternoons, Sunday, July and Aug.—afternoons, Saturday, Sunday, April and Nov. Admission charged.

One room here includes archeological materials from the Archaic, Early Woodland, and Hopewell periods.

FLINT RIDGE MEMORIAL

From Brownsville drive 2 miles north on County 668. Open Tuesday through Saturday; afternoons, Sunday, April 1 through Oct. 31. Admission charged.

In hilly country between Newark and Zanesville, Indians once mined the fine translucent, varicolored flint that covered an area of five square miles in deposits from one to ten feet thick. To break off chunks of the flint, they first drove wooden or bone wedges into natural cracks in the rock, using hammerstones, some of which weighed as much as 25 pounds. Then with smaller hammerstones they shaped

A conventionalized bird of prey engraved on a stone tablet. Ohio Historical Society photo.

This imaginary creature, carved in stone, came from Turner Mounds, Madisonville, Ohio. Original in the Peabody Museum, Harvard University.

what are called blanks. Some blanks were chipped to make finished artifacts on the spot. People carried other blanks back to their villages, where they did the painstaking work of chipping them into projectile points or knives or drills or scrapers.

Miners also shaped flint into blocks called cores, which were sometimes carried for considerable distances. When a man wanted a new knife, he struck a flake off one of these cores and had a cutting tool almost as sharp as a steel blade.

In prehistoric times the flint from this huge quarry was so prized that it was traded over great distances—as far east as the Atlantic Coast, as far west as the present site of Kansas City, and as far south as Louisiana.

The Museum. At the quarry the Ohio Historical Society maintains a museum, which tells the geological story of the formation of the flint and the archeological story of the use that people made of it over a very long period of time. Exhibits show how flint was mined and then made into artifacts.

FORT ANCIENT STATE MEMORIAL

From Lebanon drive 7 miles southeast on Ohio 350. The earthworks are open during daylight hours, daily; the museum is open Tuesday through Saturday; afternoons, Sunday, April 1 through Oct. 31. Admission charged.

The Story. Here a bluff rises 275 feet above the Little Miami River. On this natural eminence two different Indian peoples lived at two different times.

The first settlers arrived about 300 B.C. From that time until about A.D. 600 they followed the Hopewell way of life. All around the top of the bluff they built a wall of limestone slabs and earth that varies in height from 4 to 23 feet. Apparently the wall served a defensive purpose, but it was also designed to have some significance in relation to social and religious activities. The Hopewell people here, as elsewhere, enclosed the areas where they performed rituals and conducted elaborate funeral ceremonies.

A model in the museum at Fort Hill State Memorial, in Ohio, shows what a building in a large Hopewell ceremonial area once looked like. Ohio Historical Society photo.

The Hopewell people may have raised some corn, were skilled artisans, and traded widely. The grizzly bear teeth they used in ornaments came from the Rocky Mountains; they got shark teeth from the Atlantic Coast, shells from the Gulf of Mexico, copper from the Lake Superior region. But here, as elsewhere in the Ohio Valley, they came to some sudden and unknown end.

After the Hopewell settlement was abandoned, apparently no one lived on the hilltop for a long time. Then about A.D. 1000 a group of Indians who followed what is called the Fort Ancient lifeway settled on part of the site—the South Fort. They also built homes in the valley below the bluff. These Fort Ancient people grew more corn than had the earlier people, and they hunted and fished and made a variety of artifacts, but none of them were so skillfully fashioned as the earlier Hopewell tools and ornaments.

About A.D. 1600 Fort Ancient people left the site, for what reason no one knows. It was uninhabited when the first Europeans entered the area.

The Museum. Here are exhibits which give a good deal of information about the two distinct cultures connected with the site. Another display deals with the chronology of this area over a 10,000-year span of time.

FORT HILL STATE MEMORIAL

From Hillsboro drive 16 miles southeast on Ohio 124, then 2 miles north on Ohio 41. Or from Chillicothe drive 20 miles southwest on US 50, to Bainbridge, then 12 miles south on Ohio 41. The grounds are open daily during daylight hours—the museum is open Tuesday through Saturday; afternoons, Sunday and holidays. Admission charged. Camping nearby.

At a date not yet known, Fort Hill became an important center for people who practiced Hopewell rituals. Around the flat top of the hill, which stands out from the surrounding land, people built a wall of earth and rock. At its base the wall is about 40 feet thick, and in places it is 15 feet high. Earthworks of this kind were common at Hopewell sites. Many of them seem

to have had only ritual use, but here the embankment may have served also for defense.

On the flat land below the hill two structures were built. One was circular, possibly used as temporary housing for visitors who came for ceremonies. No other such circular building is known in Ohio. The second was exceedingly large—120 feet long and 80 feet wide. It may have been a craft workshop.

The Museum. Archeological exhibits here illuminate the Hopewell lifeway. Models show the site and its structures as they may have looked when it was occupied. One display includes material on older cultures in Ohio.

HANEY ARCHEOLOGICAL MUSEUM

706 Buckhorn St., Ironton. Open free, by appointment.

Artifacts on display include local finds of Paleo, Archaic, Hopewell, and Fort Ancient material.

Rock art attracted the attention of E. G. Squier and E. H. Davis who made the first serious investigation of the prehistory of the Mississippi River drainage. They found petroglyphs, which they called "sculptured rocks," on the banks of the Guyandotte River in West Virginia (left), and they copied one of these (above). From *Ancient Monuments of the Mississippi Valley*.

INDIAN RIDGE MUSEUM

8714 West Ridge Rd., Elyria. Open afternoons, Tuesday through Sunday. Admission charged.

Exhibits include a large private collection of Erie, Hopewell, and Adena artifacts.

INSCRIPTION ROCK

Kelleys Island, in Lake Erie, north of Sandusky. Open free, at all times. Administered by the Ohio Historic Preservation Office. Camping nearby.

Inscription Rock is a large boulder on which prehistoric people carved symbols and figures of animals, birds and humans. No one knows exactly what the inscriptions mean or who made them, but they probably date from A.D. 1000 to 1650. There is an interpretive sign at the site.

KNOB PRAIRIE MOUND
(Enon Mound)

One mile south of Interstate 70 in Enon. Open free, at all times.

This large, remarkably well preserved mound was probably built by Adena people.

LEO PETROGLYPH

From Jackson on US 35 drive 5 miles north on Ohio 93 to Coalton, then northwest on Ohio 337 to Leo. The site is on an unpaved road northwest of Leo. Open free, during daylight hours, all year. Administered by the Ohio Historic Preservation Office.

This site is similar to Inscription Rock. Here prehistoric Indians carved symbols and figures on a stone slab, but their date and meaning are not known.

MARIETTA MOUND

In the cemetery, Marietta.

This large mound, originally part of a complex of mounds and earthworks, was set aside to be the center of the town cemetery when Marietta was first settled, in 1788. Two of the earthwork squares were also fenced. These unusual precautions saved the site from the total destruction that went on when many other Ohio towns were built. Some artifacts from the Marietta complex are in the Peabody Museum, at Harvard.

MIAMI COUNTY ARCHAEOLOGICAL MUSEUM

From Pleasant Hill drive one mile west on Louver Rd. to directional sign just west of the Stillwater River bridge. Open free, the last Sunday of the month, May to Oct.

Some of the materials on display here are random local finds from each of five prehistoric Indian cultures of the area, beginning with Paleo-Indian and ending with Fort Ancient.

MIAMISBURG MOUND STATE MEMORIAL

One mile southeast of Miamisburg on Ohio 725. Open free, during daylight hours, all year. Administered by the

Prehistoric features are clearly visible at Mound City Group National
Monument, in Ohio. Here in the foreground is an enclosure wall. In the
background are mounds. National Park Service photo.

Ohio Historic Preservation Office.
Camping nearby.

This cone-shaped Adena mound, 68
feet high, is the largest of its kind in
Ohio.

MOUND CITY GROUP
NATIONAL MONUMENT

From Chillicothe (chil-ee-KOTH-ee)
drive 4 miles north on Ohio 104. Open
free, daily. Closed certain holidays.
Camping nearby.

The Story. By about 200 B.C. some
Indians here in the Scioto River Valley had begun to follow the Hopewell
way of life. They paid great attention
to personal decoration and became very
skillful at fashioning beautiful ornaments. They also devoted themselves
to performing elaborate ceremonials
and to building earthen mounds over
the remains of the dead. Many burials
were accompanied by fine pottery,
carvings, jewelry, and other objects
made by sophisticated crafts workers
with a variety of materials, some of
which are foreign to the Ohio area.

The location of the Mound City
Group on the bank of the Scioto River
was no accident, for the river provided easy transportation and was a dependable source of food in the form of
fish and clams. But for some reason
the Hopewell lifeway declined, and
by about A.D. 500 it had vanished.

The Mound City site was mapped
and partially excavated by the pioneer
archeologists E.G. Squier and E.H.
Davis. Their work produced spectacular artifacts, which were ultimately
acquired by the British Museum, in
London, where they remain today. In
1920–21 the Ohio Historical Society
did further excavation, and much of
the material discovered at that time is
on exhibit at the Mound City Group
Visitor Center. Recent excavation,
started in 1963 as a National Park
Service program and continuing until
1975, has revealed further information
about the mounds and their ancient
builders. This work has made possible an improved restoration of the site.

A rectangular earthen embankment
encloses the 13-acre mound area.
Within this enclosure visitors may start
a tour. Several of the 23 mounds are

Archeologists excavating at Mound City Group National Monument, in Ohio, found holes in which posts once stood. This was evidence that a structure had occupied the spot where a burial mound was later raised. National Park Service photo.

given specific interpretation. One contained a burial site, in which the cremated remains of four bodies were elaborately buried with sheets of mica. In another, excavators found many beautifully carved pipes, replicas of which are on display in the Visitor Center. Offerings to the dead varied from one mound to another. At one point archeologists, instead of restoring an excavated mound, have created a post pattern outlining the charnel house structure in relation to the mound which later covered it.

Visitor Center. Exhibits here are designed to help visitors understand the Hopewell story. Outdoor audio programs provide explanations of mound construction and a glimpse into the lives of these prehistoric people. An eight-minute videotape program in the museum provides a look at the life and customs of Hopewell times.

MUSEUM OF HEALTH AND NATURAL HISTORY

Toledo Zoological Park, 2700 Broadway, Toledo. Open daily, all year. Admission charged.

Materials here include many random finds in the Toledo area, representing Archaic, Hopewell, and prehistoric Potawatomi, Algonquian, and Iroquoian cultures. Dioramas show prehistoric Wyandot and Algonquian village life on the banks of the Maumee River.

NEWARK EARTHWORKS

Newark Earthworks is the collective name for three separate sections of a huge prehistoric site on which the modern city of Newark has been built. The three areas are now preserved as public parks. Their names, with road directions, are given below. All are open daily.

An amazing group of people settled near Newark about 1800 years ago. They followed the Hopewell lifeway, but apparently with more than usual energy and a taste for grandiose public works. Like other Hopewellians, they buried their dead under mounds of earth in special ceremonial areas. Here they conducted death rituals inside tremendous enclosures made by heaping up earth into walls or embankments 8 to 14 feet high. One of

An aerial view of the Newark Earthworks (right); (opposite) a map of the Earthworks made by E. G. Squier and E. H. Davis before 1847. An engineer, James A. Marshall, has studied various Ohio earthworks and reports that a unit of measurement 187 feet long was commonly used in their construction. The inset at lower left of the map shows how this unit of measurement fits the rectangular area at the center right of the map. Ohio Historical Society photo; map from *Ancient Monuments of the Mississippi Valley;* inset redrawn from *Early Man.*

the enclosures was a square, another an octagon, several were circular. All were linked together by long corridors between high, parallel earthen walls. A separate corridor extended from the site to the bank of the Licking River in an almost straight avenue, two and a half miles long.

For many years, a civil engineer, James A. Marshall, has been studying and surveying Hopewell earthworks, which he believes were the achievement of people with a real knowledge of geometry. Hopewellians, he says, used a consistent unit of measurement, equal to 187 feet. Before starting work, they apparently drew up plans, as engineers do today, and made grids 187 feet on a side that guided them in construction. (This same unit of measurement seems to have been used by builders of the great religious ceremonial center at Teotihuacan, in Mexico.)

A few important individuals seem to have lived at the Newark religious center itself. Possibly they were leaders of the groups that regarded the area as a focal point in their elaborate

ceremonial life. The dwellings of ordinary people were built in outlying areas.

Like Hopewell people in other places, those at Newark were superb craftsworkers. They made personal ornaments of many kinds—earrings, combs, necklaces, headdresses. They were skilled weavers, using thread they made from various plant fibers, including the bark of certain trees. Many if not most of the splendid things they created were made only to be buried with the dead.

When an important personage died, the body was dressed in rich clothing and covered with decorations. It might then be placed in a tomb. More likely it was cremated. At first small mounds of earth were heaped over the remains of the dead. Later, much more earth was added to cover a group of the small heaps, creating one sizeable mound.

Archeologists believe that the ceremonies, which required such great expenditure of effort and great destruction of wealth, were reserved for mem-

bers of an upper class. Funerals for common people were certainly more simple.

Much of the original complex of structures at Newark has been destroyed by the expansion of the city. The three portions that survive are administered by the Ohio Historic Preservation Office. They are:

Mound Builders State Memorial

Enter from the junction of S. 21st St. and Cooper. Museum open Tuesday through Saturday; afternoons, Sunday. Admission charged.

This is the area known as the Great Circle Earthworks. The circular embankment encloses ceremonial grounds 1200 feet in diameter, covering about 26 acres. Within the enclosure are four mounds. High earthen walls once lined a corridor that led from the Great Circle to a smaller, square enclosure now called Wright Earthworks. The museum displays artifacts, chosen for their artistic interest, mainly made by the Adena and Hopewell people.

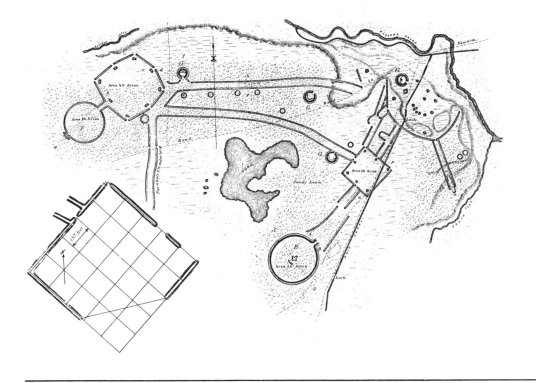

Octagon Mound State Memorial

From Church St. drive south on 30th
St. to Parkview, then west to park
entrance. Open free, daily.

Here an eight-sided enclosure of 50
acres adjoins another which is circular
in form and covers about 20 acres.
Several small mounds stand inside the·
octagon. This well-preserved area is
now the municipal golf course.

Wright Earthworks

From West Main St. drive south on
S. Williams St., then east on Waldo
to park entrance. Open free, all year,
during daylight hours.

Only part of the original, square
enclosure survives here. Before modern settlement began, it was possible
to see that the square was linked by
corridors to another area, of unknown
shape, and by a very long passageway
to still another, built in the shape of
an octagon.

OHIO HISTORICAL CENTER
(Formerly the Ohio State Museum)

Interstate 71 and 17th Ave., Columbus. Open free, Monday through Saturday; afternoons, Sunday and holidays.

This new building opened in August, 1970. Displays of prehistoric
material are arranged in mall areas,
and there is a unique pit system, which
permits visitors to examine objects
without the intrusion of glass separa-
tions.

Excellent exhibits relate to Paleo-
Indian, Archaic, Glacial Kame, Adena,
Hopewell, Cole, Fort Ancient, and
Erie cultures. Materials from many
important sites are on display, including finds from new excavations
which the museum has been conducting in the Mound City Group.

Anyone who has visited Ohio sites
and is eager to know more about them
will find the dioramas of special interest. Some of them interpret prehistoric life at Fort Ancient, Seip Mound,
Hopewell Mound Group, and Harness
Mound. Others show an Adena house,
a rockshelter, a Fort Ancient grave, a

Serpent Mound, Ohio, as it appears today in an aerial photograph (right) and (opposite) as it was mapped in 1846. Ohio Historical Society photo; engraving from *Ancient Monuments of the Mississippi Valley*.

cremation basin. Many cases, each with a distinct theme, introduce the visitor to important archeological ideas and to a great variety of archeological materials.

PIKETON MOUNDS

In the cemetery in Piketon. Open free, daily.

This site was once part of an extensive system of ceremonial and burial mounds, three of which remain.

RAY BEATSON'S INDIAN RIDGE MUSEUM

In Elyria, 8714 West Ridge Road. Open afternoons, Tuesday through Sunday. Admission charged.

Exhibits in this private museum contain artifacts representing Ohio prehistoric Indian periods, including Adena, Hopewell, and Mississippian.

SEIP MOUND (SIPE)

From Bainbridge drive 3 miles east on US 50. Open free, daily, all year. Administered by the Ohio Historic Preservation Office.

This site is part of a Hopewell burial complex that was once extensive. Several mounds are still visible, the largest an oval 150 feet wide, 250 feet long, and 32 feet high. An earthwork in the form of a circle 2000 feet in diameter surrounds the mound. In addition there is a smaller earthen circle and a partly preserved earthen square.

From the Seip mounds came much of the early information about the Hopewell lifeway. One grave yielded a great collection of ornaments made of mica, copper, and silver and so many thousands of pearls that it was called "the great pearl burial."

An exhibit pavilion is located at the site. Material from the mounds can also be seen in the Ohio Historical Center, in Columbus.

SERPENT MOUND STATE MEMORIAL

From Peebles drive northeast about 7 miles to Locust Grove then drive 5 miles northwest on Ohio 73. The mound is open during daylight hours daily, all year. The museum is open free, daily, April 1 through Oct. 31. Closed certain holidays.

At this place long ago (the exact date is not known), Indians used small stones and lumps of clay to trace on the ground an outline of a huge snake. Then they covered these markers with great quantities of yellow clay, which they dug up nearby. The result was a modeled form which resembled a writhing snake with open mouth.

Many Indian groups attached great significance to snakes. Many built snake effigies, but none is larger than this one. It is nearly one-quarter of a mile long, 20 feet wide, and 4 or 5 feet high. The people who labored to pile up so much earth did not leave in the mound itself any clues to their identity or to the time when they did their work. However, archeologists think

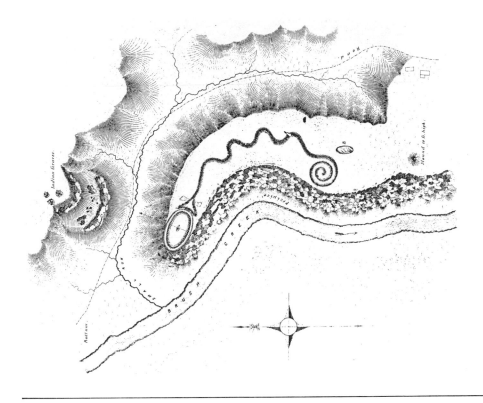

it is likely that whoever shaped the serpent also built the burial mound found nearby, and that mound did offer clues.

Among the things in the mound were some leaf-shaped knife blades, some points that had stems, chunks of sandstone in which there were deep grooves, bone tubes and awls, and a pigment called red ocher. All these were objects that usually are associated with the Adena people, who are known to have lived in this part of Ohio from about 800 B.C. to A.D. 400. The evidence uncovered so far does not prove that people who built the burial mound also constructed Serpent Mound, but archeologists believe they did.

The Museum. Exhibits include an interpretation of the site, models of the steps taken in reconstruction of the effigy and nearby burial mound, some Adena artifacts and their use, and chronology. A diorama shows a conical burial mound with an Adena grave to which another burial was later added by Fort Ancient people.

Special Interest. The preservation of Serpent Mound was one of the first American archeological conservation projects. When White men first learned about the mound, it lay in the midst of a forest and seemed to be in no danger. Then, just before the Civil War, a tornado mowed down the big trees along its whole length. Farmers completed the job and began to cultivate the area. Some years later F.W. Putnam, an archeologist from Harvard University, visited the mound and then went home to talk about the need for protecting it. As he tells it, "Several of Boston's noble and earnest women issued a private circular." They soon collected enough money to buy the mound, which was given in trust to the Peabody Museum, at Harvard. Later the museum turned it over to the Ohio Historic Preservation Office, which now administers it.

A pottery head from Seip Mound, in Ohio, shows how skulls were artificially shaped by binding in infancy. Ohio Historical Society photo.

STORY MOUND

Delano Ave., one block south of Allen Ave., Chillicothe. Administered by the Ohio Historic Preservation Office.

Here, easily visible through a fence, is an Adena burial mound. In size and shape it is similar to the original Adena mound, which has been destroyed by excavation.

WARREN COUNTY HISTORICAL SOCIETY

105 S. Broadway, Lebanon. Open Tuesday through Saturday; afternoons, Sunday. Closed certain holidays. Admission charged.

Prehistoric material exhibited here is from Hopewell and Fort Ancient cultures.

WESTERN RESERVE HISTORICAL SOCIETY

10825 East Blvd., Cleveland. Open free, Tuesday through Friday.

A feature of this historical museum is an introduction to American Indian cultures which has been arranged for children. It includes eight small dioramas, presenting scenes of Indian life from a wide variety of geographic areas. In addition there is special emphasis on Indian life in northern Ohio, both at the time of contact with Europeans and earlier.

WYANDOT COUNTY HISTORICAL SOCIETY

130 S. Seventh St., Upper Sandusky. Open afternoons, Tuesday through Sunday, March 1 to Nov. 1; weekends only in winter. Admission charged.

Here are some random local archeological finds, including some material from mounds.

Delf Norona Museum, Moundsville, West Virginia. Grave Creek Mound in background. Delf Norona Museum photo.

West Virginia

BLENNERHASSETT ISLAND

Excursion boats from the Point, in Parkersburg, take visitors to Blennerhassett Island on Friday, Saturday, and Sunday afternoons. Excavation is usually going on at one of the several archeological sites on the island, where materials being recovered range in age from Paleo-Indian to the contact period. These will be exhibited in a museum scheduled for completion in 1983 in the Visitor Center, Fort Boreman Hill, in Parkersburg. For information write Blennerhassett Historical Park Commission, Parkersburg, WV 26101.

CEMETERY MOUND

City Cemetery, Romney
Here in the municipal cemetery is a prehistoric Indian mound.

DELF NORONA MUSEUM AND CULTURAL CENTRE

801 Jefferson Ave., Moundsville. Open Monday through Saturday; afternoons, Sunday. Closed certain holidays. Admission charged.

The museum is adjacent to Grave Creek Mound State Park and provides access to the grounds on which the mound stands. Grave Creek is the largest of all the mounds known to have been built by Adena people. When first measured in 1838, it stood 69 feet high and had a flat top 60 feet in diameter. Around its summit ran a low wall, or parapet. A circular ditch surrounded the base.

In 1838 some enthusiastic citizens began to excavate the mound, hoping to find archeological treasure that would lure tourists and, as one newspaper story put it, produce admission fees "in copious torrents." Two tunnels and a shaft did reveal graves near the center of the mound. One of these burial vaults was soon turned into a candle-lit museum, with skeletons and artifacts on display.

The prehistoric village of Aztalan in Wisconsin was the most northerly outpost of the Mississippian way of life. This diorama by Arminta Neal, in the Rahr-West Museum in Manitowoc, Wisconsin, shows an everyday scene at Aztalan. Photo by Daryl Cornick.

One object, supposed to have been found in the excavation, was an engraved stone tablet with markings widely believed to be letters in some undeciphered language. The "writing" stirred up a great controversy before scholars came to agree that the tablet was a fake, planted in the mound by some hoaxer.

Neither the tablet nor the exhibit in the tomb brought commercial success to the venture. The original museum was soon abandoned; the tunnels and shaft caved in, and most of the excavated material disappeared. So did the famous tablet.

Fortunately a careful account of the interior of the mound was written by a doctor, in 1839. This and other accounts and records were discovered and collected by Delf Norona, former director of the present museum, who put the story together in an interesting booklet, *Moundsville's Mammoth Mound,* published by the West Virginia Archeological Society.

Grave Creek Mound, also known as Mammoth Mound, is one of about 100 which once stood on the present site of the city of Moundsville. Its builders probably began it in late Archaic times, then in several distinct stages made additions, which they used as burial places for important people. Almost all the other mounds in the area have been destroyed by modern industrial construction. A somewhat similar one, Cresap Mound, ten miles away, was excavated by Don W. Dragoo, of the Carnegie Museum. Material found at Cresap may be seen in that museum in Pittsburgh, although the mound itself is not visible. Another, Natrium Mound, was excavated by Ralph Solecki, of the Smithsonian Institution.

The Museum. A series of exhibits portrays and interprets what is known about the life of the prehistoric Adena people associated with the construction of Grave Creek Mound. The museum's permanent collection includes material from about 1000 B.C. to A.D. 700.

GRAVE CREEK MOUND STATE PARK
(Mammoth Mound)
(See Delf Norona Museum and Cultural Centre)

SOUTH CHARLESTON
(Criel Mound)

In downtown South Charleston, on US 60. Open free, daily, all year.

This prehistoric mound has been greatly altered by modern use. A hundred years ago its top was taken off to make room for a judges' stand at horse races held on the site. Later a bandstand was built into its side.

WEST VIRGINIA DEPARTMENT OF CULTURE AND HISTORY MUSEUM

Capitol Complex, Charleston. From Interstate 77 take State Capitol exit, left at Washington St. to Cultural Center parking lot. Open free, Monday through Friday; afternoons, Saturday, Sunday. Closed Dec. 25.

A major exhibit area here is devoted to prehistoric cultures in West Virginia and to contact period Indians. A large study collection of artifacts is rotated through the displays and is used in educational programs.

Wisconsin

AZTALAN STATE PARK
(AZ-ta-lan)

From Lake Mills drive 3 miles east on County Trunk B to the center of Aztalan, then south to park entrance. Open free, daily. Closed to vehicles Oct. 15 to April 15.

This is one of the most important sites in Wisconsin. Seven hundred years ago a busy town stood here, completely protected by a palisade built of upright poles 12 to 19 feet high, placed close together. Branches were woven between the poles, then the entire structure was covered with a thick plaster of clay. Watchtowers built at frequent intervals reinforced this stockade, which surrounded not only the dwellings but also fields and ceremonial mounds and burial areas as well.

Portions of the stockade have now been restored, as have two large, pyramidal mounds. One of these rises in a series of terraces, the other in an

unbroken slope. Ten conical mounds also remain, although 74 once stood in a double line within the palisade.

An exhibit case in the park interprets Aztalan culture for summer visitors, but is removed in winter. There is no official museum. However, random local finds of material from the Aztalan area are exhibited in the Lake Mills–Aztalan Historical Museum adjoining the park.

The Story. Sometime after A.D. 1100 a group of people, probably from Cahokia in Illinois, started out in search of a new home. Possibly they had been under pressure from newcomers. (Archeologists have evidence that outsiders did invade Cahokia at about this time.) Possibly the emigrants left because there was too large a population at Cahokia to be supported by the surrounding farmlands, rich though they were. Or perhaps some kind of feud had developed in the community.

Nobody is sure why some people moved away, but move they did—up the Mississippi River, then up the Rock River, and finally up a tributary of the Rock, the Crawfish River. Finally,

Working with information supplied by archeologists, an artist painted this view of Aztalan as it may have looked during the period from A.D. 1100 to A.D. 1300. Milwaukee Public Museum photo.

Archeologists at Aztalan State Park uncovered post holes indicating that a square dwelling once stood here.

on the banks of the Crawfish, the wanderers found a site to their liking. It offered good farmland, good fishing, and good hunting in the nearby woods. All around, however, were Indians who followed the Woodland lifeway, which was very different from the Mississippian.

The Woodland people were less advanced than the newcomers. Their arts were less developed. Their ceremonial life was much more simple. The two groups did not get along. This explains the strong outer palisades and watch-towers and the additional inner palisades that divided up the settlement into smaller areas that were easy to defend.

For nearly 200 years the Mississippian farmers, who with their families never numbered more than 500, managed to live on, surrounded by a hostile community. They kept to their own ways and continued to conduct their own kind of ceremonies, including one which may have been religious in nature but was certainly not reassuring to their neighbors. The Mississippians practiced cannibalism, and since the victims in cannibalistic rites were very likely captured Woodland Indians, the latter may have had good reason for taking a dim view of the alien culture in their midst. In the end they seem to have destroyed it completely. The entire town of Aztalan, including the log palisades, was burned to the ground, and no one knows what became of those who once lived there.

The Name. In the early part of the nineteenth century readers of books and magazines in the United States were excited by reports of mysterious pyramids supposedly built by the ancient Aztecs of Mexico. Two men in Wisconsin had these stories in mind when they discovered the flat-topped pyramidal mounds on the banks of the Crawfish. With very little trouble the two enthusiastic pioneers developed the theory that their site was the original homeland of the Aztecs, and they called the place Aztalan.

Special Feature. You may wonder how archeologists can be sure that the log palisade around Aztalan was 12 to 19 feet high and plastered over with clay. After all, the wood should have decayed in 600 years, and clay would long ago have been washed away by rain.

The fact is that the fire which burned Aztalan was so intense that it baked the clay brick-hard. Chunks of this "Aztalan brick" still show the marks of the wooden posts, and when pieced together, they tell exactly how high the palisade was.

BELOIT COLLEGE, LOGAN MUSEUM OF ANTHROPOLOGY

South end of Beloit campus, Beloit. Open free, Monday through Friday; mornings, Saturday; afternoons, Sunday, when college is in session.

Along with extensive archeological displays of materials from many parts of the world, this museum has these Wisconsin exhibits: Paleo-Indian, Effity Mound culture, Archaic Period, Middle Woodland Period, Middle Mississippian, Oneota culture. Dioramas of archeological subjects include one showing an effigy mound on the Beloit campus. On the second floor of the museum are Southwestern exhibits. Among these is a full-scale Pueblo house.

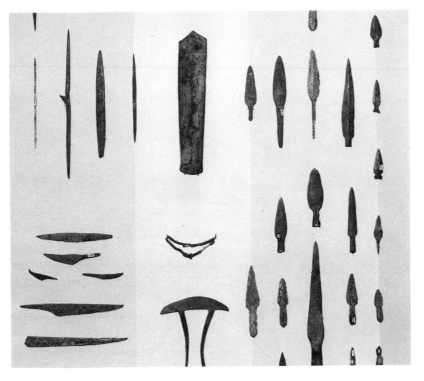

At one time Archaic people in Wisconsin and other northern areas made tools of the pure copper which they found in deposits near Lake Superior. This display of artifacts of the Old Copper culture is in the Rahr-West Museum, Manitowoc, Wisconsin. Photo by Daryl Cornick.

COPPER CULTURE STATE PARK

From junction of US 41 and Wisconsin 22 in Oconto, drive 2/10 mile west on Wisconsin 22 (Main Street), then follow directional signs. Open free, daily, all year. Camping nearby.

This small park contains the undeveloped site of an important archeological discovery.

The Story. For a great many years Midwestern farmers found strange green objects in their fields when they plowed. Nobody was sure what these objects were. Then in 1945 the Mississippi River washed away part of its bank near Potosi, Wisconsin, and exposed what is called the Osceola Site. Excavation revealed chipped stone tools and human burials. With them were some objects which proved to be copper tools turned green by corrosion.

A few years later a boy at Oconto found some bones in a gravel pit. His first thought was that he had stumbled upon evidence of a murder, and he reported his discovery to the sheriff. It was an archeologist, however, who solved the mystery. The bones belonged to an Indian who had been buried for a very long time. In the same gravel pit were other burials, many of them, and made in three different ways. Some of the bodies had been cremated. Some had been buried only after the flesh was removed from the bones. About half had been buried while the flesh was still intact. This was all interesting, but most exciting to archeologists was the discovery of copper tools with many of the burials.

Archeologists now began to talk about an Old Copper culture, because the tools were much more ancient than others made of copper by such people as the Hopewell. Carbon-14 dates show that the Old Copper people lived perhaps 5000 years ago.

This date suggested that Indians in Wisconsin were using metal almost as early as any people in the Old World, but the Indians never learned to smelt it. Nor did they harden it by adding another metal to form an alloy. Perhaps the softness of copper led them to abandon it in favor of stone. Perhaps a hostile group got control of the mines and kept the Old Copper people away from their source of sup-ply until they forgot about the metal. For whatever reason, Indians in Wisconsin had stopped making much use of copper long before the arrival of Europeans in the area.

DEVILS LAKE STATE PARK

From Baraboo drive 3 miles south on Wisconsin 123 to park entrance. Open daily, all year. Admission charged to park. Visitor Center open free, Monday through Saturday, summer. Camping.

Effigy mounds in the park are indicated by explanatory signs. One in the shape of a bear and another which resembles a lynx are at the north end of the lake. A bird-shaped mound is at the south end.

In the Visitor Center a diorama shows Indians building the bear effigy mound.

Reconstructed exterior and cutaway of a house at Aztalan. After R. R. Burke.

GULLICKSON'S GLEN

From Black River Falls drive 2 miles south on Wisconsin 54, then west about 7 miles on C Road. At Disco Store turn south and drive 3 miles to parking lot at the site.

Here in a narrow gorge on high sandstone cliffs a large collection of petroglyphs is preserved in a county park. Among the figures are recognizable bison, elk, cranes, a wild turkey, a human figure with bow and arrow, an eagle dancer, and a thunderbird. Excavation at the site produced numerous artifacts from the late-prehistoric Oneota culture. These included quartzite tools that may have been used in carving the rock. Materials from the dig are in the possession of the Wisconsin Historical Society, at Madison.

HIGH CLIFF STATE PARK

From Menasha (men-ASH-a) drive about ten miles east on Wisconsin 114 to park entrance: or from Stockbridge drive north on Wisconsin 55 to park

entrance. Open daily, all year. Admission charged. Camping April 1 through Nov. 30.

On top of the bluff in the park, 200 feet above Lake Winnebago, prehistoric people built 13 effigy mounds. Some are in the shape of lizards; others represent birds. All are about two feet high, but they vary in length from 25 feet to 285 feet.

HOARD HISTORICAL MUSEUM

407 Merchants Ave., Fort Atkinson. Open free, Tuesday through Saturday; afternoons, first Sunday of each month.

Over 15,000 artifacts found in Jefferson County representing the Old Copper, Woodland, and Mississippian cultures are on display here.

ICE AGE NATIONAL SCIENTIFIC RESERVE

There are visitable archeological sites in some of the nine separate units of the Reserve which is affiliated with the National Park system. For information about road directions, dates, fees, camping write to the Wisconsin

Department of Natural Resources, Bureau of Parks and Recreation, Box 7921, Madison, WI 53707.

LAKE MILLS–AZTALAN HISTORICAL SOCIETY MUSEUM

From Lake Mills drive 3 miles east on County Trunk B to junction with Aztalan Mound Rd. Open Monday through Saturday; afternoons, Sunday and holidays, May 1 to Oct. 1. Admission charged.

Random local finds of Mississippian and Woodland material are displayed in this small historical museum, which adjoins Aztalan State Park. Some of the "brick" from the burned walls of the Aztalan palisade is on exhibit.

LIZARD MOUND STATE PARK

From West Bend drive 4 miles northeast on Wisconsin 144, then 1 mile east on County Trunk A to directional marker. Open free, daily, all year, except when snows are heavy.

In this park there are 31 good examples of effigy mounds, three to four feet high, which represent birds, pan-

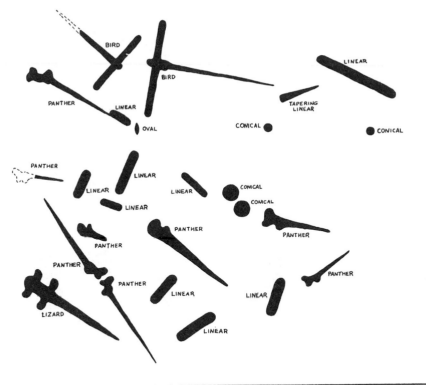

Prehistoric people in Wisconsin built mounds as monuments to the dead. Some were simply linear shapes. The smallest one here is about 100 feet long. Others were effigies in the shapes of animals. This group, in Lizard Mound State Park, takes its name from the unusual lizard effigy, lower left.

thers, and lizards. A number are geometrical—either linear or conical in form.

About 5000 effigy mounds have been found in southern Wisconsin—approximately 98 percent of all that are known in North America. Some of them are so large that is was presumably from the vantage point of treetops that their builders were able to view them as a whole—if they ever did. In any event, they seemed to have had clear patterns in mind as they worked.

The creators of effigy mounds usually buried the dead in them, but often they did not leave offerings in the graves. As a result, archeologists know less about the Effigy Mound people than they do about people who left abundant gifts with burials. One important question is when the building of effigy mounds began. At least one specialist believes the custom may have started in Archaic times. Others say that a more likely date is between A.D. 600 and 1000.

Generally speaking, the people who built effigy mounds were part of the widespread Woodland culture. They had pottery, engaged in hunting and fishing, and also did some farming. In winter and in summer they scattered and lived in small bands. At planting time in the spring, and again at harvest time in the fall, the bands seem to have come together, forming temporary communities. At such times there was a good deal of manpower and womanpower available—enough to do the considerable work involved in building mounds.

No one knows for sure why effigy mounds take the shapes they do. Perhaps they represented creatures sacred to the person buried in them. The burials, incidentally, were often made at spots in the effigies which were possibly considered vital to the creatures whose shapes had been modeled in earth. Skeletons have been found where wings or legs joined effigy bodies, or in the areas of the head, heart, or groin.

LOGAN MUSEM OF
ANTHROPOLOGY
(See Beloit College)

MAN MOUND

From Baraboo drive east on Eighth Ave. (Wisconsin 33), then north on County Trunk T to the first intersection, then east to the mound. Open free, at all times. Camping nearby.

This large effigy mound in a county park is unusual because it resembles a human figure. Most other effigy mounds are likenesses of birds, serpents, or four-legged mammals.

MENASHA MOUNDS

Smith Park, Menasha. Open free, at all times.

In municipally owned Smith Park are three effigy mounds said to resemble panthers. The largest is 180 feet long. A marker in the park indicates that they were built about A.D. 900.

MENDOTA STATE HOSPITAL
MOUND

On the grounds of Mendota State Hospital, Madison. Open free, at all times.

Here, on the hospital grounds, is a

At some time in the distant past this deer head was incised in stone at a rockshelter near Disco, Wisconsin. Photo by Warren Wittry, courtesy Campbell Grant.

A knife and projectile point of copper, typical artifacts of the Old Copper culture. Note sockets for hafting.

6-foot-high effigy mound in the form of a bird which has a wingspread of 624 feet.

MILWAUKEE PUBLIC MUSEUM

800 West Wells St., Milwaukee. Open daily, all year. Closed certain holidays. Admission charged.

In addition to prehistoric material from Mexico and Central and South America, the museum has on exhibit some artifacts from the Southwest and one display of Southeastern material. An exhibit scheduled to open at some future date will focus on the prehistory of the upper Great Lakes region. It will include displays on Paleo-Indian, Red Ocher, Old Copper, Woodland, Hopewell, and Mississippian cultures.

MUSCODA MOUNDS
(MUSS-koh-dah)

From Muscoda drive one mile west on Wisconsin 60 across the Wisconsin River to directional sign. Open free, at all times. Camping nearby.

This group of effigy mounds, on private land, has not been developed, but is open to the public. The mounds can be seen from an unsurfaced road which passes them.

NATURAL BRIDGE STATE PARK

From Devils Lake State Park drive south on US 12 to County Rd. C, then west to Natural Bridge entrance. Open spring to fall. Admission to park charged.

A self-guided trail in the park is devoted to explaining how the Indians used plants.

NELSON DEWEY STATE PARK

From Cassville drive 2 miles northwest on County Trunk VV to the park. Open daily, except when there is snow on the ground. Admission charged. Camping.

In this park overlooking the Mississippi River are a number of prehistoric effigy mounds.

NEVILLE PUBLIC MUSEUM

129 S. Jefferson St., Green Bay. Open free, Monday through Saturday; afternoons, Sunday. Closed certain holidays.

In this general museum is an important display of artifacts from the Old Copper culture. There are also materials from another Archaic culture, the Red Ocher. The North Bay culture of the Middle Woodland Period is represented by material from the Mero Site, and there is Oneota material also.

OCONTO COUNTY HISTORICAL SOCIETY MUSEUM
(oh-KAHN-toh

917 Park Ave., Oconto. Open daily, all year. Admission charged.

In the annex of this museum are examples of Old Copper culture material found at the Oconto Site, on the western edge of the town. This site is now part of Copper Culture State Park.

Prehistoric Indians belonging to a group called Old Copper people hunted deer with spears and spearthrowers, as shown in this diorama by Arminta Neal, in the Rahr-West Museum in Manitowoc, Wisconsin. Photo by Daryl Cornick.

OSHKOSH PUBLIC MUSEUM

1331 Algoma Blvd., Oshkosh. Open free, Monday through Saturday; afternoons, Sunday.

Various members of the staff of this museum have gathered material from several excavations in the area. This material, plus some collected by early Wisconsin archeologists and supplemented by random local finds, illustrates cultures from Paleo-Indian times through Archaic, Woodland, and Mississippian, up to the present.

PANTHER INTAGLIO

From Fort Atkinson drive west on Wisconsin 106 to the site. Open free, at all times. Camping nearby.

Here is a large effigy dug into the earth instead of raised above it. The intaglio effect is created by a depression about a foot deep. No burials have been found at the site. In the vicinity are effigies of the usual kind, modeled in the form of a mound.

PERROT STATE PARK
(pair-OH)

From Trempealeau drive 2 miles west along the Mississippi River. Open daily, all year. Admission charged. Camping.

In this park are a few conical mounds and some Hopewell mounds.

RAHR-WEST MUSEUM

Park St. at N. Eighth, Manitowac (MAN-i-to-WAHK). Open free, Tuesday through Friday; afternoons, Saturday, Sunday. Closed certain holidays.

In the prehistory room of this museum are exhibits based to some extent on random local finds of materials from the Old Copper, Hopewell, Middle and Upper Mississippian cultures. Dioramas show Old Copper and Aztalan life.

Special Interest. At Two Creeks, near Manitowac, a forest grew during a warm period between the last two temporary advances of the last Pleistocene glacier. The final advance covered the trees with rock and clay. This buried forest is of great interest to geologists

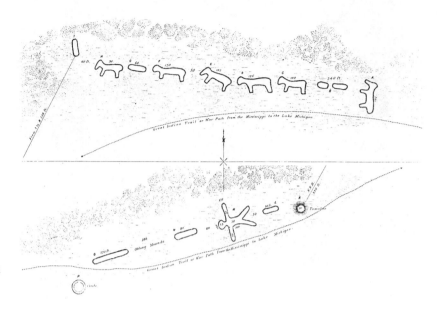

Here, shown in two sections and drawn from an actual survey, is a group of effigy mounds that stretched for nearly half a mile on high prairie ground along a trail in Wisconsin between the Mississippi River and Lake Michigan. Six of the figures may represent bears and vary in length from 90 to 120 feet. The human figure is 125 feet long. From *Ancient Monuments of the Mississippi Valley.*

and archeologists because wood from it has been radiocarbon dated. The trees were living 11,500 years ago. This Two Creeks date establishes the time *after* which the last glacial advance took place. Thus it helps to date events in the lives of Paleo-Indians who once lived in the area but who did not move in until the glacier had moved out.

ROCHE-A-CRI STATE PARK

From Friendship, drive 2 miles north on Wisconsin 13. Open daily, last week of May through Oct. Admission charged. Camping.

In the side of a mound in the park are petroglyphs. There is an interpretive marker at the site.

SHEBOYGAN COUNTY MUSEUM

3110 Erie Ave., Sheboygan. Open Tuesday through Saturday; afternoons, Sunday, April 1 to Sept. 30. Admission charged.

In this museum are random local finds from Old Copper, Hopewellian, and Upper Mississippian cultures.

SHEBOYGAN MOUND PARK

From Sheboygan drive south on US Business 141, then east on County Trunk EE, then south on S. 12th St. to Riverdale Country Club. Here turn east on Panther Ave., then south on S. Ninth St. to the park entrance. Open free, at all times. Camping nearby.

In this city park are 33 effigy mounds, called the Kletzien Group. Some resemble deer and panthers. Others are conical and linear in shape. As with many effigy mound burials elsewhere, there were very few artifacts found in the graves here. Therefore, little is known about the people who built these earthen structures. From carbon-14 dates obtained at other sites, it is supposed that the Sheboygan Mounds were built between A.D. 500 and 1000.

STATE HISTORICAL SOCIETY OF WISCONSIN

816 State St., Madison. Open free, Monday through Saturday. Closed certain holidays.

Turtle Mound as it appeared in 1919 on the University of Wisconsin campus at Madison. State Historical Society of Wisconsin photo by George R. Fox.

This museum has materials from sites that have been excavated by the museum staff. The exhibits represent all periods in Wisconsin prehistory, and separate displays show how pottery, stone, and copper artifacts were made.

Dioramas show the excavation of a rockshelter, prehistoric economic activities in each season, and the life cycle of an Indian man.

STEVENS POINT MUSEUM OF NATURAL HISTORY
(See University of Wisconsin)

UNIVERSITY OF WISCONSIN ARBORETUM

On the shore of Lake Winagra, Madison. Open free, at all times.

There are three groups of mounds in the University Arboretum, all of which can be visited. No effort has been made to interpret them.

UNIVERSITY OF WISCONSIN CAMPUS

Madison. Open free, at all times.

At four places on the campus there are prehistoric mounds, several of them near the Elm Drive dormitories. One is on Observatory Hill, two groups on Picnic Point, and one group near Eagle Heights, the student housing units. Some, but not all, are marked by plaques.

UNIVERSITY OF WISCONSIN, STEVENS POINT, MUSEUM OF NATURAL HISTORY

Learning Resources Bldg., on the campus, Stevens Point. Open free, Monday through Saturday; afternoons, Sunday.

On display in this museum are local Indian artifacts and an exhibit of Eskimo material.

WYALUSING STATE PARK
(WYE-uh-LOOSE-ing)

From Prairie de Chien (duh-SHEEN) drive 6 miles southeast on US 18, then 5 miles west on County Trunk C, then ¾ mile to County Trunk X, then to junction with State Park Road, which leads to park entrance. Open daily, all year. Admission charged. Camping.

Sentinel Ridge, a high divide in the park, was used by prehistoric people as a burial spot. Here they built mounds over the bodies of the dead. One large group, known as "a procession of mounds," stretches out in a line along the ridge and can be reached by auto and an easy trail from the parking lot.

Health was of great interest to prehistoric Indians, who died young as a rule. This diorama in the National Museum of Man, in Ottawa, shows Indians of the Eastern Woodlands culture attempting to drive out disease with a curing ceremony in which some of the participants wear masks called false faces. National Museum of Man photo.

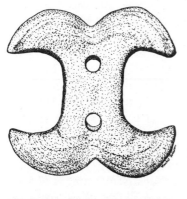

NORTHEAST

After the last Ice-Age glacier disappeared from northern North America, one feature was common to all the land from Labrador south to Virginia. The area became forested. Everyone who lived in the region during the next 10,000 years had to adjust in one way or another to that fact. As a result, there were similarities in the prehistoric cultures of the Northeast, but there were also marked differences in lifeways. These arose in part from necessarily different responses to climate and food resources. They also arose from the influences of diverse cultures in neighboring areas.

People arrived in the northern part of the Northeast even before trees began to grow on land recently laid bare by retreating ice. The first to come were Paleo hunters, who sometimes tracked their quarry very close indeed to the edge of the ice. For example, the Debert (deh-BURT) Site in Nova Scotia yielded evidence that people camped there 11,000 years ago, when snowfields were just five miles away, and it was only 65 miles to the ice itself. Even in such a chilly world tundra vegetation fed herds of grazing animals, which in turn provided food for hunters.

Other groups of Paleo-Indians stayed behind, in the region farther south. After the glaciers contracted, this area was the first to be covered by trees, which eventually spread northward into Canada. What we know about these Big-Game Hunters in the Northeast comes from a small number of sites, including the Williamson Site in Virginia, the Shoop Site in Pennsylvania, Bull Brook and Wapanucket No. 8 in Massachusetts, Reagan in Vermont, and the Vail Site in Maine. The latter is probably unique in the eastern United States because unbroken projectile points were found at a caribou kill very close to the associated campsite. None of these Paleo sites are prepared for the public, but artifacts from some of them can be seen in major northeastern museums.

Archaic Period

As they did elsewhere, Paleo-Indians in all of the Northeast slowly developed new lifeways in the forest environment, and during the next period, known as the Archaic, they learned to exploit new resources. Along some rivers and seashores they harvested quantities of mollusks, and the shells they discarded piled up in heaps. Many of these heaps, all the way from Virginia to the Maritime Provinces of Canada, have now disappeared under water because sea level has risen in relation to the land, but where they survived, archeologists have studied them—along the banks of the Hudson River, for example, and on Cape Cod and the coast of Maine.

At one place, unfortunately not open to the public, the shell middens tell a story of considerable social change. At Ellsworth Falls, Maine, excavation has revealed four distinct stages of social development. In the oldest, known as the Kelley Phase and dated before 3000 B.C., people made heavy, chipped tools. The implements they used for scraping hides or wood were large and crude. Their hammerstones were essentially large pebbles, or cobbles. Flakes struck from the cobbles seem to have served as knives.

By about 2000 B.C. a much more elaborate tool kit had developed at this site. There were adzes and gouges—woodworking tools useful in making dugout canoes, among other things. Six hundred years later they had refined their tools still further—they used plummets, possibly as weights on fishing nets or as bolas. They made weights to improve the balance and efficiency of their atlatls, and in time they began to use pottery. Finally hunters at Ellsworth Falls began to use smaller projectile points. This suggests that they had bows and arrows. They may even have done some gardening. They had entered what is called the Woodland cultural period.

Fish Trapping

In broad outline this one site tells what happened in varying ways at varying times all over the Northeast. Where Boston now stands, Archaic people who depended on the sea for food made an elaborate adjustment to their environment and reached a high level of social organization earlier than did those at Ellsworth Falls. At Boston—and elsewhere—they trapped fish in devices called weirs. These were arrangements of various kinds built so that fish could more easily swim into them than out of them.

The Boston Site, known as the Boylston Street Fish Weir, is now covered by the New England Mutual Life Insurance Company building. When construction workers were digging the foundation for this building they encountered evidence of earlier construction. Archeologists studied the site, dug further, and found that 65,000 wooden stakes had been driven into clay, above which shallow tidal waters once rose and fell. Between the upright stakes branches had been woven basket-fashion, permitting water to pass through but creating an obstacle for fish. Later 12 feet of silt had been deposited above the tops of the stakes. This meant that the water had risen in relation to the land. Then, as Boston expanded in historic times, landfill had been dumped on top of the silt, driving the water away from the area.

Estimates by geologists and dates obtained by the radiocarbon method place the time of construction of the Boylston Street Fish Weir between 4000 B.C. and 2000 B.C. The Archaic people who used the trap had obviously achieved a rather highly organized society; otherwise they could not have built and maintained such a large and complicated device for obtaining food.

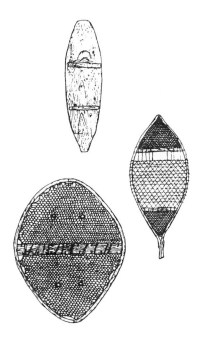

Various types of snowshoe: a bearpaw snowshoe, used by Naskapi Indians, with four eyelets through which lashings were placed to hold it firmly on the foot (bottom); a woven snowshoe made by Onondaga Indians (center); and a wooden snowshoe from Manitoba (top). After Birket-Smith, Turner, Beauchamp.

Snowshoes

A quite different invention—snowshoes—helped those who lived inland to get food in the dead of winter. Some experts think snowshoes may have come into the Northeast from northern Eurasia. Others believe they may have been an independent invention made by northeastern Indians during early Archaic times. Whichever it was, hunters could now walk and even run on top of soft snow. They could actually travel faster than the game they hunted.

At the time when people were harvesting fish in Boston and mollusks at Ellsworth Falls, other groups had begun to develop a lifeway known as Laurentian in northern New York, Ontario, Quebec, and parts of New England and Pennsylvania. Hunters used broad, heavy projectile points, and their meat diet was supplemented with fish, nuts, berries, and seeds. At many Laurentian campsites evidence points to short stays by small groups. Here and there, however, where they found an abundance of fish or waterfowl or acorns, several groups gathered in large settlements for part of the year.

In central New York and northern Pennsylvania a quite distinct lifeway, known as the Lamoka, developed in a few places, paralleling in time and in some of its traits the Laurentian culture. Lamoka people mainly hunted and fished. At one time or another they consumed more than 30 different kinds of animal and left the bones in trash heaps. They were also great eaters of acorns and other nuts and seeds, which they parched and ground into meal. Some of their grinding stones were very large, and they seem to have pounded some of their food with big stone pestles, using hollow stumps for mortars.

Toward the end of the Archaic Period, about 1000 B.C., hunters in some areas began to travel more and more in canoes. In Pennsylvania, New York, and New Jersey, for example, they tended to camp along riverbanks and to make short expeditions into the forests for food.

Three views of a flint point, 1⅝ inches long. This delicate artifact was made by craftsmen at Cape Denbigh, in Alaska, more than 4000 years ago. Similar small tools were made by pre-Dorset people in Canada.

At about this same time women acquired a new kind of cooking vessel. For centuries in the past they had been preparing stews and soups in watertight kettles of skin or wood or bark, into which they dropped hot stones to make the liquid boil. Now they began to use large, heavy vessels carved from a soft stone called steatite or soapstone. The old-fashioned method of stone boiling continued, but it was easier to do in the large steatite pots, which also held heat much better than vessels of wood or skin. Canoes made it possible to take the heavy vessels along when it was necessary to move camp. If a pot broke, it was cut up to make beads, gorgets, ladles, and spoons.

Woodland Period

This time of change, called by some archeologists the Transitional Period, merged into another period known as the Woodland. If any one thing sets off the Early Woodland lifeway it is the acquisition of pottery. Vessels of baked clay replaced the cumbersome steatite pots, and since they could be set directly over the fire they gave new freedom to the women who made and used them.

Another new concern of Early Woodland women was gardening. Just how or when they came by the idea is not known, but between about 1000 B.C. and 500 B.C. they were caring for little patches of sunflowers, Jerusalem artichokes and several other plants which we customarily think of as weeds.

With a more stable food supply came further changes in life. People could settle down near garden patches, although men made constant trips into the forests for game. Before long the gardening areas increased. Trees were cleared along stream banks to make larger fields. Eventually squash, and later, corn and beans began to take the place of older food plants. During these Middle Woodland times, which lasted from about 500 B.C. to about A.D. 700, agriculture became important from Virginia as far north as the St. Lawrence River. Abbott Farm, in New Jersey, which archeologists have been studying for a hundred years, was inhabited during this time. In New York, Ontario, and New England, the lifeway known as Point Peninsula began to develop from a purely hunting culture into one that accepted the idea of farming.

Development of Villages

From now on, with a few exceptions, lifeways all over the Northeast developed slowly but steadily in much the same directions. Villages, some of them quite large, took the place of single farms. Many of these settlements were fortified by log stockades. Corn and beans became more and more important in the diet. In western Pennsylvania one Late Woodland culture is known as the Monongahela. In New York and around the lower Great Lakes the Owasco culture evolved from earlier lifeways.

It was from the Owasco that the prehistoric Iroquois developed. By the time Europeans came to New York and the St. Lawrence

River area, some of their great towns had a thousand inhabitants, with fields covering several hundred acres of cleared and cultivated ground.

From Paleo times until the day when Europeans arrived on the Atlantic coast, the numbers of northeastern Indians increased a great deal. This does not seem to have been the result of large migration from other areas. Rather it was a steady growth of resident populations as they improved their methods of obtaining food.

Although people did not move into the Northeast, ideas and customs and inventions did. From the south in Early Woodland times knowledge of pottery making entered Virginia and moved up the coast. Possibly the pottery idea also entered the northern part of the region from some place far to the west, in Canada. Corn and beans—and some of the notions and social behavior connected with agriculture—came ultimately from Mexico. Cultures, such as the Adena, which were stimulated by agriculture in the Ohio Valley, affected people in part of the Northeast. There were also minor influences from the Hopewell of Ohio. The custom of burying the dead in mounds appeared in a number of places; Virginia was one. There in a burial mound Thomas Jefferson conducted the first scientific excavation in the United States.

Possibly there were influences in pottery styles or implement design that came somehow from northwestern or northeastern Eurasia. Immigration did take place at more than one time across the Bering Strait, and immigrants who followed that route certainly brought their cultures with them. It is not so easy to see how ideas could have crossed westward from northern Europe, but the use of small craft for island-hopping has been suggested as a possibility. Also scholars have suggested that people may have crossed the water barrier in the north when it was covered with ice floes, following the edge of the ice and subsisting, as Eskimos did, on the sea mammals and fish available there.

The Northeast never attained the population density of the Mississippi Valley. Nor did arts and crafts and social organization reach such levels of development as in the major centers of Indian life. But much more happened in 12,000 years in the Northeast than one would guess from the number of visitable archeological sites. These are few indeed, and an important reason is that a humid climate and generally acid soil in the region have conspired to destroy most organic matter left by prehistoric peoples.

But even though site areas are minimal, some of the best museums in America are in the Northeast. They serve as excellent introductions to the area and to Indian life elsewhere as well.

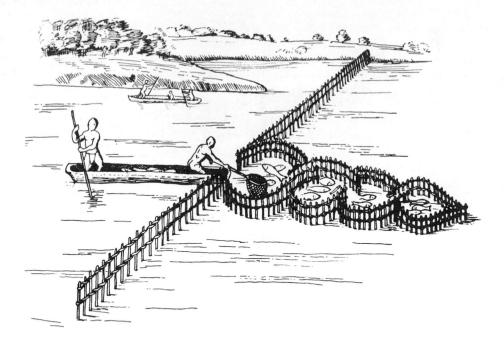

Fish traps of several kinds were used in rivers and estuaries along the Atlantic Coast. This one, built by Indians in Virginia, was sketched by Hariot, one of the first French artists to visit America. Fishermen drove stakes into the river bottom and then wove branches between the stakes, basket-fashion, allowing the water to pass through but creating an obstacle for the fish. After Hariot.

Connecticut

AMERICAN INDIAN ARCHAEOLOGICAL INSTITUTE

From Washington drive south on Connecticut 47 to intersection with Connecticut 199, then 2 miles on Connecticut 199 to Curtis Road. Open daily. Closed certain holidays.

On display here are all of the artifacts from the only known Connecticut Paleo-Indian site, dated at about 10,000 B.C. Other exhibits include material of Archaic through contact periods from Connecticut and adjacent areas. There is also an ethnobotanical herbarium.

Special Feature. By appointment the museum conducts group tours, field trips, and craft demonstrations.

BRUCE MUSEUM

Museum Drive, Greenwich. Open Monday through Friday; afternoons, Saturday, Sunday. Admission by donation.

The museum's Native American displays include such diverse materials as pre-Columbian spindle whorls and Cherokee lacrosse racquets. New archeological materials are frequently added.

CHILDREN'S MUSEUM OF HARTFORD

950 Trout Brook Dr., West Hartford. Open Monday through Saturday; afternoons, Sunday. Closed certain holidays. Admission charged.

Artifacts here interpret the life of Native Americans in Connecticut and elsewhere in the United States. There is also a model display of Indian villages.

CONNECTICUT STATE LIBRARY MUSEUM
(See Museum of Connecticut History)

Dr. Roger Moeller of the American Indian Archaeological Institute directed excavation of this Paleo-Indian site in 1977. From it came evidence that people had been living in Connecticut for 10,190 ±300 years. American Indian Archaeological Institute photo.

MATTATUCK MUSEUM OF THE MATTATUCK HISTORICAL SOCIETY
(MATT-a-tuck)

119 West Main St., Waterbury. Open free, afternoons, Tuesday through Sunday. Closed, Sunday, July and Aug., and certain holidays.

Eight cases contain displays of Indian artifacts, mostly from the Northeast.

MUSEUM OF CONNECTICUT HISTORY

231 Capitol Ave., Hartford. Open free, Monday through Friday; mornings, Saturday. Closed certain holidays.

Some prehistoric artifacts are displayed here.

NEW BRITAIN CHILDREN'S MUSEUM

30 High St., New Britain. Open free, Saturday; afternoons, Monday through Friday. Closed certain holidays and Saturday in summer.

This small but active museum has changing exhibits, which include dioramas and prehistoric Indian material.

Special Interest. The museum prepares display kits on prehistoric Indian life which schools, churches, or other institutions may borrow for educational use. The staff conducts a training program for teen agers in museum work and encourages those interested in archeology.

PEABODY MUSEUM OF NATURAL HISTORY
(See Yale University)

STAMFORD MUSEUM AND NATURE CENTER

High Ridge at Scofieldtown Rd., Stamford. Open Monday through Saturday; afternoons, Sunday and certain holidays. Admission charged.

Several Indian rooms here contain displays of prehistoric artifacts, including local finds. One exhibit demonstrates how stone was chipped to make tools and weapons. Dioramas showing typical village scenes depict the lives

of Woodland people in the Northeast and Southeast, mound builders, and Indians of the Plains, Southwest, California, and the Northwest.

YALE UNIVERSITY, PEABODY MUSEUM OF NATURAL HISTORY

170 Whitney Ave., New Haven. Open Monday through Saturday; afternoons, Sunday. Closed certain holidays. Admission free, Monday, Wednesday, Friday. Admission charged other days.

Money contributed by George Peabody, in the nineteenth century, financed this museum, which bears his name. It houses an extensive archeological collection, from which are taken the material for exhibits both permanent and changing.

A number of displays illuminate prehistoric Indian life in Connecticut, with artifacts, photographs, and drawings of a rockshelter, a soapstone quarry, a shell heap, a burial, and a village site. Other exhibits explain the process of making bone needles, wampum, clay pottery, soapstone vessels, and chipped stone tools. Of particular in-

Detail from a diorama in the Hagley Museum in Wilmington, Delaware, that shows Indian life in a rockshelter. The woman is making cornmeal by breaking up kernels of corn in a hollow tree stump. Hagley Museum photo.

terest is the display of snowshoe making, together with types of snowshoes which were apparently invented in Europe and Asia, as well as in North America.

Some material on exhibit comes from important sites that are not open to the public. There are artifacts from Deer Island, Maine; from Florida shell mounds; and from a Mississippian site in Perry County, Missouri.

Special Interest. The museum has a division which lends material to schools for study and which offers special programs for school children.

Delaware

DELAWARE STATE MUSEUM

316 S. Governors Ave., Dover. Open free, Tuesday through Saturday; afternoons, Sunday.

This museum has a display of prehistoric weapons, implements, and pottery made by Delaware Indians. One exhibit shows a cache of stone blades; another an Indian burial.

HAGLEY MUSEUM

Barley Mill Rd., Greenville, Wilmington. Open free, Tuesday through Saturday and Monday holidays; afternoons, Sunday.

Devoted mainly to industrial history, this museum has some prehistoric material dating back as far as the Archaic Period. A diorama shows an Indian habitation in a rockshelter.

IRON HILL MUSEUM

From Newark drive south on Delaware 896, past the intersection with Interstate 95, then west on the Old Baltimore Pike. The museum is between Cooch's Bridge, Del., and Elkton, Md. Open free, by appointment. Call 737–2363.

In 1964 an all-Black school ceased to operate in this building, and a group of volunteers sponsored by the Delaware Academy of Science turned it into a museum. Since then exhibits designed primarily for school children have been developed, showing the lives of Woodland Indians of the vicinity. One exhibit centers around the Har-

lan Mill Steatite Quarry, where prehistoric Indians obtained soapstone from which they made vessels for cooking. A general exhibit traces the history of Indians from Paleo times to the historic period. Indian foods are displayed, and there are dioramas, on Delaware (Lenni Lenape) village life and trapping methods.

ISLAND FIELD MUSEUM
(Island Field Site)

South Bowers Beach. From U.S. 113 north of Milford, take Delaware 19 to 120 to Delaware 121, thence to South Bowers. Note: There is no bridge from Bowers to South Bowers. Open free, Tuesday through Saturday; afternoons, Sunday, March 1 through Nov. 30.

This museum is at an archeological site which has been occupied by various groups for 3000 years or more, and it is possible to see how archeologists have made a series of discoveries.

First to be excavated were ancient storage pits and trash dumps, where people left artifacts among discarded mollusk shells. During a later dig,

A diorama in the Museum of Natural History of the Smithsonian Institution shows a prehistoric Indian settlement in what is now Washington, D.C. The museum has many dioramas and displays on the major prehistoric cultures of the United States. Smithsonian Institution photo.

rains exposed what turned out to be a large cemetery. Excavation revealed burials made in a number of different ways. Some graves contained skeletons of bodies buried in the flesh. In others were bones that had been bundled together after the flesh was removed. Still others contained the remains of cremations. In several a number of individuals had been buried together.

With many of the burials were grave offerings, including bone awls and needles, harpoons made of deer antler, pipes carved from stone, and a variety of tools, weapons, and ornaments.

The cemetery was apparently used between A.D. 700 and 1000 by people who followed the Woodland lifeway. They were prosperous farmers, hunters and fishers and their grave offerings show that they did widespread trading. Some of their ideas and practices may also have been influenced by trade. Like people in the Ohio Valley and elsewhere in the Midwest, they seem to have valued mica and shark teeth, conch shell, and bits of crystal.

Special Feature. Archeologists are often working at the site during summer months, and visitors are welcome

to watch. Guided tours may be arranged during most of the year by writing in advance to Curator of Archeology, Island Field Museum, R.D. 2, Box 126, Milford, DE 19963.

ISLAND FIELD SITE
(See Island Field Museum)

ZWAANENDAEL MUSEUM
(ZWAN-en-dale)

Savannah Rd. and Kings Hwy., Lewes. Open free, Tuesday through Saturday; afternoons, Sunday. Closed certain holidays.

This museum contains artifacts from the Townsend Site, which dates from A.D. 1550 to 1600.

District of Columbia

NATIONAL GEOGRAPHIC SOCIETY, EXPLORERS HALL

17th and M St. N.W. Open free, Monday through Saturday; afternoons, Sunday.

Permanent and changing exhibits in Explorers Hall depict major exploration and research projects, past and present, sponsored by the society, including Cliff Dwellers in the Southwest. Exhibits of other North American archeological material may appear from time to time.

NATIONAL MUSEUM OF NATURAL HISTORY, NATIONAL MUSEUM OF MAN, SMITHSONIAN INSTITUTION

Constitution Ave. at Tenth St., N.W. on the Mall. Open free, daily. Closed Dec. 25.

In this great museum, at the entrance to the hall devoted to Eskimo and Indian cultures on the second floor, is a mural that shows how individuals from various tribes looked at the time they were first seen by Europeans. The hall is arranged by cultural areas, and precontact material is included in the exhibits. In dioramas the facial features of individuals are based on molds made from living Indians.

On the third floor a large hall holds exhibits of prehistoric North Ameri-

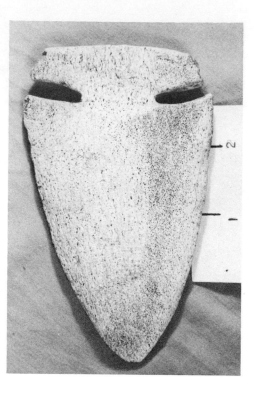

Left: In the eastern woodlands, as well as on the Plains, Indians worked porcupine quills, often dyed, into intricate designs. Here Micmac Indians in Maine have pressed quills into a birch bark box. Robert Abbe Museum of Stone Age Antiquities photo. *Right:* This projectile point from Maine was made of whale bone. Robert Abbe Museum of Stone Age Antiquities photo.

can Indian cultures. Included are dioramas of Mummy Cave in Arizona, a soapstone quarry, flint knapping, Indians of the Potomac area, and a model of Pueblo Bonito in Chaco Canyon.

Wall displays show how archeologists work and date the past. Other exhibits are devoted to the Archaic cultures of the Eastern Woodlands, early horticulture on the Great Plains, cultures on the Pacific Coast and in the Arctic. Also on display are beautiful artifacts of copper, ceramic, stone and shell from the Hopewell and Mississippian cultures.

A separate hall that deals with the biology of human populations explains the distinctive blood types and teeth of the American Indian. An exhibit on population indicates how rapidly the Indians increased in number once they entered the Americas, but also how sparse the population was compared to the total population of the area today.

A large map shows the predominant foods available in prehistoric times: fish, sea and land mammals, wild seeds and nuts, maize and other cultivated plants.

One exhibit is devoted to the ceremonial shell art of eastern Oklahoma, with numerous examples and labels that explain the relationship of this art form to similar work done in copper, stone, and pottery. Exhibits also make clear how shells were used in the Black Drink Ceremony.

SMITHSONIAN INSTITUTION
(See National Museum of Natural History)

Maine

ABBE MUSEUM

Acadia National Park. From Bar Harbor drive south on Maine 3 to Sieur de Monts Spring. Open free, daily, Memorial Day to Labor Day. Camping in Acadia National Park.

The Robert Abbe Museum of Stone Age Antiquities contains materials from Woodland sites, both coastal and interior. One diorama shows summer activity in prehistoric times; another shows an autumn camp and chores associated with salmon fishing.

ANCIENT PEMAQUID RESTORATION
(See Colonial Pemaquid Restoration)

AROOSTOOK HISTORICAL AND ART MUSEUM OF HOULTON

109 Main St., Houlton. Open afternoons, Tuesday through Saturday. Admission charged.

Stone tools on exhibit here were made by people of the Red Paint culture.

COLONIAL PEMAQUID RESTORATION

Pemaquid Beach, next to New Harbor, on the same site as Fort William Henry. Open daily, Memorial Day through Labor Day. Admission charged. Camping nearby.

The Wawenocks, a subtribe of the Abnakis, once lived at this site and left refuse heaped up in a midden. A few artifacts recovered from the midden and an Indian burial are on display in the museum, which is devoted

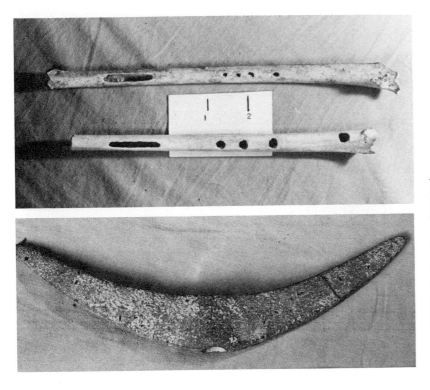

Above: Flutes were popular musical instruments among prehistoric Indians in many places. These, made of bone, come from Maine. Robert Abbe Museum of Stone Age Antiquities photo. *Below:* Weights which Archaic Indians used to increase the efficiency of atlatls were made in different shapes in different places. In Maine, where many people were familiar with whales, some craftsperson made this weight to resemble the tail of one kind of whale. Robert Abbe Museum of Stone Age Antiquities photo.

primarily to the English occupation of the area in the seventeenth and eighteenth centuries.

DAMARISCOTTA RIVER SHELL MOUNDS
(Oyster Shell Banks)
(dam-uh-riss-COTT-uh)

For road directions inquire at Information Booth, US Business 1, Damariscotta. Open free.

Mounds, which consist mostly of oyster shells, were left here by prehistoric people, probably some time after 2000 B.C. The mounds can be seen from across the Damariscotta River. Artifacts from the site are in the Peabody Museum, Harvard University.

MAINE STATE MUSEUM

LMA Bldg., Station 83, Augusta. Open free, Monday through Friday; afternoons, Saturday, Sunday.

One exhibit here presents in chronological order, groups of artifacts from Indian cultures dating from 10,000 B.C. to A.D. 1800. A major new exhibit dealing with prehistoric and historic archeology of northern New England is in the planning stage.

UNIVERSITY OF MAINE, ANTHROPOLOGY MUSEUM

On the campus, Orono. Open free, Monday through Friday. Closed certain holidays.

Exhibits here reflect the archeological work done by the university and include material from sites in the Northeast.

WILSON MUSEUM

Perkins St., Castine (kas-TEEN). Open free, afternoons, Tuesday through Sunday, May 27 to Oct. 1.

Exhibits of prehistoric artifacts represent some of the major Indian cultures in North America. They include material from the Northeast, from Ohio mounds, Southwestern pueblos, the Great Plains, and Eskimo areas in Canada.

Special Feature. One display of material found in a Red Paint grave contains fire lighters. These were pieces of iron pyrite, which were struck with flint to make sparks.

Maryland

CITY HALL MUSEUM AND CULTURAL CENTER

In downtown Salisbury, on West Church St., just off US 50. Open Monday through Friday; mornings, Saturday. Admission by donation. Closed certain holidays.

Interpretive displays here include local artifacts of the major cultural periods of the lower Eastern Shore. An inscribed bone awl is of special interest.

Ross McCurdy (left) and Dr. Maurice Robbins (right) of the Massachusetts Archaeological Society find a cremation burial at the Wapanucket Site. Massachusetts Archaeological Society photo.

DORCHESTER HERITAGE MUSEUM

From Cambridge, drive 3 miles east on Maryland 343 to Horn Point Rd., ½ mile west of entrance to Maryland Center for Environmental and Estuarine Studies. Open afternoons, Saturday and Sunday. Admission by donation.

Interpretive exhibits here feature prehistoric Indian artifacts.

PISCATAWAY PARK
(pis-CAT-ah-way)

From Alexandria, Va., drive east on Interstate 495 to Exit 37, then 12 miles south on Maryland 210 to park entrance. Open free, daily.

About 5000 years ago hunters camped here on the bank of the Potomac River. Later, people buried their dead in a cemetery not far from what is now the site of old Fort Washington. Still later, when George Washington built his home at Mount Vernon just across the river, there were Indians living in the park area, and they continued to do so until almost 1800. Although archeologists have done excavation here, there is no special site prepared for view.

ST. CLEMENT'S ISLAND– POTOMAC MUSEUM

From Maryland 5 east of Leonardtown, take Maryland 244 south, turn right onto Breton Beach Rd., then right onto Abell's Wharf Rd. Open daily, June through August. Admission charged.

Exhibits here emphasize the archeology of southern Maryland and explain the various culture periods and the methods archeologists use to recover information. Many of the artifacts displayed came from excavations in the nearby Potomac Archaeological Park, which was not open to the public as this book went to press.

Tools made of flint were used by Paleo-Indians for preparing animal hides. These scrapers, 9,000 years old, came from the Wapanucket Site at Assawompsett Lake in Massachusetts. Massachusetts Archaeological Society photo.

Massachusetts

BRONSON MUSEUM

8. N. Main Street Building, Attleboro. Open free, Monday, Tuesday, Thursday; other days by appointment.

This unusual museum is operated by the Massachusetts Archaeological Society, and a great deal of its material comes from sites which the society has excavated. For comparative purposes some displays contain artifacts from areas outside New England, but the main concentration is on prehistoric cultures in Massachusetts from Paleo times through the Woodland Period. A large diorama shows a village as it may have looked about 2300 B.C. at Assowampsett Lake, where the society has been excavating for 19 years.

Other dioramas show a quarry where people dug steatite (soapstone), from which they made large cooking vessels; a Woodland burial; a Titicut Site village scene; and a scene based on information gained by the society in excavating a site in Massachusetts known as Wapanucket #6. Exhibits include a number of restored soapstone bowls found with cremations, tools and weapons which are explained, and a group of implements for which hafting has been reconstructed.

Special Interest. The Massachusetts Archaeological Society offers lectures at the museum from time to time and sponsors conducted group visits.

CAPE COD NATIONAL SEASHORE

Follow US 6 on Cape Cod to Eastham, where the Salt Pond Visitor Center is located. Visitor Center open free, daily. Closed Dec. 25, Jan. 1.

The Indians first encountered by the Pilgrims were Wampanoags. These people may have lived on Cape Cod for 8000 years or more before a boatload of the *Mayflower's* passengers disembarked and helped themselves to corn which the Indians had stored underground in a large basket. The Wampanoags hunted and fished as well as farmed. Their arrowheads, fishline sinkers, and other implements are still to be found at sites on Cape Cod, even after more than 300 years of European occupation. A large display in the museum shows how some of the implements were used.

From the Visitor Center it is a short drive to Indian Rock, at Skiff Hill. The rock, a 20-ton glacial granite boulder, has deep grooves where Indians sharpened bone harpoon heads, fishhooks, and stone axes. Originally the giant whetstone stood a hundred feet down the hill at the edge of Nauset Marsh. It was moved when it seemed in danger of being lost in the marsh. Indian Rock is only one of several such sharpening stones in the neighborhood.

Along the beaches and ponds of the National Seashore there are heaps of discarded shells, where prehistoric people camped and ate seafood. These have not been excavated. Visitors are earnestly requested not to disturb them.

CHILDREN'S MUSEUM, INC.

Russells Mills Rd., Dartmouth. Open free, Tuesday through Friday; afternoons, Saturday, Sunday. Closed certain holidays and from late Dec. to early Feb.

Mimbres women often decorated their pottery with pictures of animals. *Top to bottom:* Duck; Turkey; Deer. Redrawn from Gladwin.

Animals for Food

As they explored their different environments on this continent, Indians seem to have tried just about every likely source of nourishment. The food resources in a desert area were of course quite different from those near a large river in the Southeast. Plains dwellers had foods quite unlike those available to inhabitants of the Northwest Coast.

Archeologists study all the animal bones they find in an excavation in an effort to discover the diet of the people who lived there, and also to find out about prehistoric ecology.

Here is a list of animal remains found at one site in Massachusetts, which was inhabited between A.D. 900 and 1500: beaver, dog, red fox, grey fox, black bear, mink, harbor seal, white-tailed deer, red-throated loon, great blue heron, mallard, black duck, red-tailed hawk, bald eagle, great auk, snapping turtle, Plymouth turtle, roughtail sting ray, Atlantic sturgeon, black sea bass, sculpin, sea robin, scup, wolffish, bay scallop, blue mussel, quahog, surf clam, long clam, lobed moon shell, moon shell, boat shell, thick-lipped drill, conch, and channeled conch.

In addition to historic Indian materials from the Plains and the Southwest, this museum has a few prehistoric Wampanoag Indian artifacts from the immediate vicinity.

COHASSET HISTORICAL SOCIETY, MARITIME MUSEUM

Elm St., Cohasset. Open afternoons, Tuesday, Wednesday, Thursday, from the last week in June through the first week in Sept. Admission charged.

This museum devoted to local history includes a case of Indian artifacts found in the area. These are primarily Algonquian and seem to date from about A.D. 1500 to 1700.

DIGHTON ROCK STATE PARK (DIE-ton)

Go north from Fall River on Massachusetts 24, take Main St. exit at Assonet and follow directional signs to the park. Open free, daily during daylight hours.

Dighton Rock is a 40-ton boulder on which inscriptions have been carved. Ever since the seventeenth century,

the rock has inspired study and controversy. Among the theories advanced to explain the inscriptions is the assumption made by Cotton Mather and others that the carvings were made by Native Americans. Another theory, suggested in the book *Dighton Rock* by E.B. Delabarre, of Brown University, is that a Portuguese explorer, Miguel Corereal, visited the spot in A.D. 1511.

These, along with two other theories, are presented on panels in the Dighton Rock Museum, at the site. In 1963 the rock was raised out of the Taunton River and is now housed within the same museum.

Special Interest. At one time certain markings on the rock were supposed to have been made by Vikings. This prompted the nineteenth-century violinist Ole Bull to buy it for the Royal Society of Copenhagen. When scholars disproved the idea of Norse origin, the society gave the rock to the Old Colony Historical Society, of Taunton, which then presented it to the Commonwealth of Massachusetts.

FRUITLANDS MUSEUMS

Prospect Hill, Harvard. Open, afternoons, Tuesday through Sunday, May 30 through Sept. 30, and holiday Mondays. Admission charged.

The American Indian Museum in this complex contains dioramas and a selection of prehistoric implements, arts, and industries.

HARVARD UNIVERSITY, PEABODY MUSEUM OF ARCHAEOLOGY AND ETHNOLOGY

11 Divinity St., Cambridge. Open Monday through Saturday; afternoon, Sunday. Closed certain holidays. Admission charged, except on Monday.

This very important museum exhibits archeological materials from all over the world, but as this book went to press the North American section was undergoing extensive reconstruction which was not scheduled to be completed before 1984. Until then it would be advisable to write or to phone 617-495-2248 to find out what exhibits have been finished and opened to the public.

In addition to the study of plant and animal remains found at sites, analysis of ancient dessicated human feces, called coprolites, can tell archeologists not only what people ate but also something about their environment. The presence of corn indicates farming. Predominance of wild plants may mean that gardening was secondary to gathering.

Researchers at Chaco Canyon were somewhat surprised by what coprolites revealed there. As had been expected, Chacoans ate deer meat, but they also consumed an enormous number of smaller animals— chipmunks, voles and prairie dogs: The chunks of bone that people chewed, apparently not very well, were quite large enough for identification by specialists in animal anatomy.

The corn in the Chacoan diet seems mostly to have been cooked with either the flowers or the seeds of the bee plant. Possibly the plant added flavor to a corn dish, though this was not necessarily the reason for its use.

HOLYOKE MUSEUM—
WISTARIAHURST
(See Wistariahurst Museum)

INDIAN HOUSE MEMORIAL

Main Street, Deerfield. Open Monday and Wednesday through Saturday; afternoons, Sunday, May 1 to Oct. 15. Admission charged.

An extensive collection is arranged by culture periods from the Paleo to historic in Massachusetts. Some unusual materials displayed include early Archaic leaf-knives and basalt axes.

PEABODY MUSEUM
OF ARCHAEOLOGY
AND ETHNOLOGY
(See Harvard University)

PHILLIPS ACADEMY, ROBERT S. PEABODY FOUNDATION FOR ARCHAEOLOGY

Main St., Andover. Open free, Monday through Friday. Closed certain holidays.

Materials drawn from the extensive collections of the museum are arranged in displays that illustrate the daily lives of people of various cultures, the techniques of archeologists who dig up and study prehistoric cultures, and the theories that finally emerge.

Exhibits from sites which cannot be visited include the Boylston Street Fish Weir in Boston, Ellsworth Falls in Maine, the Bull Brook Site in Massachusetts, which yielded much important information about Paleo people in New England, Labrador Eskimo sites, and the Debert Site in Nova Scotia.

Material on the Boreal Archaic people shows how they differed from southern Archaic people because of their heavy reliance on hunting and fishing rather than on plant foods, while at the same time they used many of the same tools.

Exhibits showing cultural influences on New England indicate the spread of burial-cult ideas from the Adena in Ohio, of copper artifacts from the Great Lakes, and of agriculture from areas to the south.

A diorama of Pecos Pueblo is based on information gathered during excavations conducted by the museum. Among other major sites in other areas represented are Etowah, Moundville, and the important site at Tehuacan, Mexico.

A Wampanoag one-family summer house, shown under construction at Plimoth Plantation. Fish are drying on the rack in the foreground. Plimoth Plantation photo.

PLIMOTH PLANTATION, INC.

Warren Ave., Plymouth. Open daily, April through Nov. Admission charged.

In an effort to show what Indian life was like before the arrival of Europeans, members of the Wampanoag tribe, sometime during August, hold a midsummer feast, open to the public. Usually they serve a stew of meat, Jerusalem artichokes, squash, and sunflower seed. In the afternoon there are bow-and-arrow contests, dancing and singing, and Indian football matches. At times there is an Indian campsite open to the public in summer. For information write to Plimoth Plantation, Box 1620, Plymouth, MA 02360, or phone (617) 746–1622.

ROBERT S. PEABODY FOUNDATION FOR ARCHAEOLOGY
(See Phillips Academy)

WISTARIAHURST MUSEUM

238 Cabot St., Holyoke. Open free, afternoons, Tuesday through Saturday; afternoons, Sunday for special programs only. Closed certain holidays.

Youth Museum in the Carriage House uses some pre-Columbian material in its North American Indian culture exhibits.

New Brunswick

NEW BRUNSWICK MUSEUM

277 Douglas Ave., St. John. Open daily, May 1 through Sept. 30; afternoons only, Oct. 1 through April 30. Admission charged.

Exhibits in this museum are changed frequently, but there are always some archeological materials on display. Of particular interest are the artifacts from shell-heap sites along the Bay of Fundy. For study purposes the museum has an extensive collection of pre-Algonquian artifacts from the New Brunswick area.

An Icelandic map, made nearly 600 years after the Vikings are said to have visited America, shows a peninsula called Promontorium Winlandiae. This tongue of land some archeologists interpret as the tip of Newfoundland Island, the traditional Vinland where old sagas say the Vikings lived. L'Anse aux Meadows is at the northern end of Newfoundland. The map shown here is redrawn from a 1670 copy.

Newfoundland

L'ANSE AUX MEADOWS
(LANSS oh meadows)

At the terminus of Newfoundland 81 on the northern tip of the Great Northern Peninsula. Open free, daily in summer.

In 1960 the Norwegian explorer Helge Ingstad found a group of mounds here. Ingstad theorized that this might be the site of an ancient Viking settlement—perhaps even Leif Ericksson's Vinland. Beginning the next year, he and his archeologist wife, Anne, together with archeologists from other countries, spent seven summers excavating the mounds. One appeared to be the ruins of a turf house nearly 80 feet long, with slightly curving walls resembling those of Norse buildings. In it they found a stone lamp and other things that seemed to be of the kind used by Norsemen. Besides other houses, they excavated what appeared to be a sauna and the remains of a blacksmith shop, where iron from a nearby bog had been smelted and made into tools.

The Ingstads reported that Carbon-14 tests of charcoal revealed a date of about A.D. 1000 for the site—which would make it contemporary with Leif Eriksson.

Two Canadian archeologists, Thomas E. Lee and Robert E. Lee, say that the Carbon-14 tests do not reveal any such thing. The Lees interpret the Carbon-14 dates as evidence that the site was originally inhabited, long before the Norse period, by aboriginal people and, in post-Viking times, occasionally visited by whalers from Europe. Thomas Lee, a Norse specialist has reported Viking remains at Ungava Bay in northern Canada. He does not deny the presence of Norsemen in North America. He merely contends that the claim that they were at L'Anse aux Meadows is not supported by the evidence. In any case, L'Anse aux Meadows is an interesting National Historic Park, developed for visitors by the Canadian government.

The Name: Contrary to popular belief, L'Anse aux Meadows does not mean "Bay of Meadows." Instead, *Meadows* is a corruption of the French word *méduses,* meaning "jellyfish." Many of the first settlers in the area were French; hence the name.

NEWFOUNDLAND MUSEUM

Duckworth St., St. John's. Open free, Monday through Saturday; afternoons, Sunday.

Collections of artifacts made by the Beothuk (bee-AWTH-uk) Indians, whose last survivor died in 1829, are being augmented by archeological materials which this museum is excavating in cooperation with the National Museum of Canada. Also on exhibit are Nascapi Indian artifacts, from Labrador.

The Beothuk, primarily coastal people, moved inland for a month or so in autumn. There they hunted caribou, by building a fence, or barrier, of fallen trees, that extended along the Exploits River for 40 miles. In spring and fall the hunters waited at gaps which had been purposely created in this fence for the migrating caribou herds to pass through. As the animals crowded into the narrow openings, hunters found it easy to kill as many as they wanted. The meat was smoked and cached for use later.

Carbon-14 Dating

An archeologist can often learn the age of a site if it contains charred wood or bone. He or she sends samples of the charred material to a laboratory where radiocarbon, or carbon-14, or C-14, dating is done.

Carbon is part of the nourishment of every living thing. Plants get it by taking in carbon dioxide from the air; animals and men get it from their food, which may be either plants or plant-eating animals. Among the carbon atoms which living things take in, some are radioactive. These radioactive atoms, called carbon-14, or C-14, are not stable. They decay, giving off tiny bursts of energy, which can be detected in a laboratory.

When a plant or animal dies, it ceases to take in food, and therefore it ceases to take in C-14 atoms. But it continues to lose them. The C-14 atoms in a dead object decay at a steady pace. Half of the radioactivity in a dead plant or animal is gone at the end of 5,730 years, give or take 40 years. Scientists say that C-14 has a half-life of 5,730 plus or minus 40 years.

By measuring the number of radioactive bursts produced by C-14 atoms as they decay in a given quantity of dead plant or animal material, a scientist can calculate how long ago the plant or animal died. Since the method does not reveal the exact year of death, allowance is made

---

PORT AU CHOIX CEMETERY (PORT oh shwah)

In Port au Choix on Newfoundland 73, on the west coast of the Great Northern Peninsula. Open free, daily, in summer; at other seasons on request.

In 1967 excavation of the basement for a new theater in this small fishing village turned up so many bones and artifacts that building operations were stopped and archeologists continued the digging. This, they found, was one of several spots along the shore where graves had been dug in beach sand. The crushed seashell in the sand had helped to preserve the remains of people who lived and died here from about 1900 B.C. to 1280 B.C.

Somewhat as did the Red Paint people, who lived farther south in New England, these Archaic hunters and fishermen deposited a pigment called red ocher in graves. They also left gifts for the dead. Their choice of gifts, however, was sometimes unusual. Instead of placing a woman's tools with her body, supposedly for use in an afterlife, and a man's tools with his body, they occasionally did just the opposite. They put men's axes and hunting charms and amulets in women's graves. And some needles for sewing were recovered from men's graves. Some of the burials of children were accompanied by lavish gifts of all kinds. Apparently an article's supposed usefulness in afterlife was not the only criterion for grave goods. these people also gave things they treasured when they buried those they loved.

Among the artifacts recovered at the site were beautifully carved stone effigies of whales, small images of birds, and other hunting charms; a wealth of harpoons, points, and daggers made from bone and ivory; and animal teeth, especially beaver incisors, which seem to have been made into woodworking tools.

To judge from the type of material found in the graves, these people may have lived inland in the winter, existing mainly on caribou meat. In summer they lived here on the coast, where they fished and caught marine mammals. The fact that they were able to venture out to sea in boats of some sort is obvious, for Newfoundland is an island, and at its nearest point the mainland is ten miles away.

The culture of these seacoast dwellers resembled that of other Archaic people and they may have come originally from the New England region. However, they also had distinctive traits of their own. For that reason some archeologists are inclined to put them in a special category, called Maritime Archaic.

Many of the Maritime Archaic artifacts resembled those of Eskimos who lived in the area at a later time. However, there is no evidence that Eskimos borrowed these implements from their predecessors. Apparently the two peoples, living in the same environment, developed the same kinds of tool for dealing with it.

The Museum. Most of the exhibits here deal with the archeology of the Port au Choix area, which is now a National Historic Site, maintained by the Canadian Department of Northern Affairs.

for error. Therefore a C-14 date is usually written this way: 5,000 ± 250. This means that the date of death falls between 4,750 and 5,250 years ago.

The original C-14 method had its flaws. It could not date back more than 40,000 years, and in order to get a date for an object it was necessary to destroy a large sample of it. As much as ten ounces of a unique bone had to be burned in order to tell how old it was. Archeologists also discovered that they had to regard all C-14 dates with caution, because research had revealed that the C-14 content of the atmosphere varied at different times in the past. Checking against dates obtained from other sources showed that C-14 dates tended to be more recent than they should have been. Archeologists had to develop a mathematical formula for use in correcting all C-14 dates obtained before 1971.

Now a new method exists, which enables archeologists who have access to a million-dollar dating machine (a particle accelerator) to count C-14 atoms *before* they decay. When atoms from a sample are run through the accelerator, the C-14 atoms shoot off in one direction and C-12 atoms in another. Then, working from the known proportion of C-14 to C-12 atoms in living matter, it is possible to determine when any *(Continued on page 344)*

Carbon-14 dating can reveal the age of things made of plant material, such as this Anasazi hairbrush.

New Hampshire

DARTMOUTH COLLEGE MUSEUM

East Wheelock St., Hanover. Open free, Monday through Friday; afternoons, Saturday, Sunday. Closed certain holidays and on weekends when college is not in session.

In addition to several permanent displays of material from important archeological sites in Central and South America, this general museum has a small interpretive display of prehistoric North American artifacts.

LACONIA PUBLIC LIBRARY

Main Street, across from the old railroad station, Laconia. Open free, by appointment. Phone: (603) 524–4775.

On the third floor of the library are displayed prehistoric artifacts from Lake Winnipesaukee and the Laconia area.

LIBBY MUSEUM

From Wolfeboro drive 4 miles north on New Hampshire 109. Open Tuesday through Sunday, July through Labor Day. Admission charged.

In addition to local Indian artifacts, this museum has on display a map of Indian trails and campsites in the area.

MANCHESTER HISTORIC ASSOCIATION

129 Amherst St., Manchester. Open free, Tuesday through Friday; Saturday; closed state and national holidays and Tuesdays following Monday holidays.

In addition to random local finds, this museum displays materials from controlled excavations near the Amoskeag Falls at Manchester. The falls apparently provided a good fishing spot and attracted prehistoric Indians from as far away as Maine and New York. Visits to the region obviously began a very long time ago, for a Clovis point was found in the excavation at the falls. Projectile points of this type found

elsewhere were associated with hunters of big game which has long been extinct. Later materials, which resembled artifacts made by the Iroquois, were also recovered at the site.

(Continued from page 343)

object ceased to live. This method has advantages. It does not destroy more than a few milligrams of the object whose age is being sought. It is more accurate and much faster than the old method. And it extends the range of C-14 dating to about 100,000 years.

For detailed technical information about early C-14 dating and about a variety of other dating techniques, see Stuart Fleming: *Dating in Archaeology,* New York, St. Martin's Press, 1976; H. W. Michael and E. K. Ralph: *Dating Techniques for the Archaeologist,* Cambridge, MIT Press, 1971; J. W. Michels: *Dating Methods in Archaeology,* New York, Seminar Press, 1973. For a popular explanation of the new C-14 dating method, see *Early Man,* Spring 1981, p. 6. For a nontechnical story of how dating techniques developed and affected our understanding of the past, see Franklin Folsom: *Science and the Secret of Man's Past,* Irvington-on-Hudson, N.Y., Harvey House, 1966. Also see "Dendrochronology" on page 000 of this book, and look in the Glossary under these entries: amino acid racemezation, archeomagnetic dating, fission track dating, obsidian hydration dating, potassium-argon dating, relative dating, tephrachronology, thermo-luminescence, and varve dating.

PHILLIPS EXETER ACADEMY, PHILLIPS MUSEUM OF ANTHROPOLOGY

On the campus, Exeter. Open free, mornings, Monday through Friday, during school year; by appointment in summer. Phone: (603) 772–4311, Ext. 214.

The Dr. P. Phillips Museum of Anthropology houses an extensive North American basket collection and a large primitive mask collection, as well as limited ceramics collections from the American Southwest and several collections of North American prehistoric artifacts. The museum acts as a repository for the New Hampshire Archeological Society.

PHILLIPS MUSEUM OF ANTHROPOLOGY
(See Phillips Exeter Academy)

UNIVERSITY OF NEW HAMPSHIRE, ANTHROPOLOGY LABORATORY

Parsons Hall, College Rd., Durham. Open free, by appointment. Phone: (603) 862–1547.

Archaeological Research Services of the Department of Sociology and Anthropology maintains an active program of field research in central New England. Visitors may arrange a guided tour of the laboratory facility on campus and view various stages of artifact processing and analysis, as well as small, changing exhibits of cultural materials from sites in the Lakes Region and Coastal Zone of New Hampshire.

WOODMAN INSTITUTE

182–192 Central Ave., Dover. Open free, Tuesday through Sunday. Closed certain holidays.

Artifacts of the Red Paint people of Maine and other prehistoric New England materials are on display here in the Annie E. Woodman Institute.

Advanced technology helps archeologists to get C-14 dates for prehistoric remains. In this laboratory materials containing carbon are first cleansed, then converted by combustion to carbon dioxide in the system shown in the foreground. The carbon dioxide is then further purified and stored for analysis in the system shown in the background which operates at very low temperatures. Teledyne Isotopes photo, Westwood, New Jersey.

New Jersey

MORRIS MUSEUM OF ARTS AND SCIENCES

Normandy Heights and Columbia roads, Morristown. Open Monday through Saturday; afternoons, Sunday, Sept. through June; Tuesday through Saturday, July and Aug. Closed certain holidays. Admission charged.

This museum has on exhibit Indian material from the Plains area, the Southwest, and the Northwest Coast, as well as a gallery on Woodland Indians. One display shows a Lenape village as it might have looked before Europeans arrived. There is also material from earlier periods.

NEWARK MUSEUM

49 Washington St., Newark. Open free, afternoons, daily. Closed certain holidays.

Included in this general museum is a gallery devoted to Indian material, some of it from the prehistoric period. Of special interest is a diorama showing a central New Jersey Indian village, the work of Dwight Franklin, who pioneered in developing this form of museum exhibit.

NEW JERSEY STATE MUSEUM

205 West State St., Trenton. Open free, Monday through Saturday; afternoons, Sunday. Closed certain holidays.

A room here is devoted to the Delaware, or Lenni Lenape, Indians of New Jersey and includes archeological material.

SETON HALL UNIVERSITY, ARCHAEOLOGICAL RESEARCH CENTER

Humanities Bldg., on the campus, South Orange. Open free, daily, when the university is in session.

As this book goes to press the museum has on display a very comprehensive exhibit on the pre-history of New Jersey, scheduled to remain until the end of 1984. At that time it will be broken up into smaller local exhibits, reflecting the museum's work along the Delaware River. In planning at this Catholic university is another major exhibit "In Search of Humanity's Roots," which will deal with the progress of humankind from about five million years ago to the beginning of civilization. The exhibit will be the answer of paleoanthropologists to Scientific Creationism.

On permanent display are the only two petroglyphs that have been found in New Jersey.

SPACE FARMS ZOOLOGICAL PARK AND MUSEUM

Midway between Sussex and Branchville on County 519. Museum open daily. Closed Dec. 25. Admission charged.

The museum includes materials collected by the owner, Ralph Space, during 60 years of amateur archeological activity along the Delaware and Navesink Rivers in New Jersey and New York, in Wythe and Smythe counties in southwest Virginia, and in Tennessee.

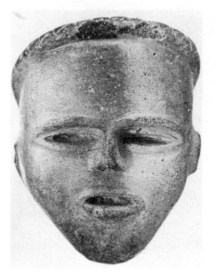

This ceramic likeness of a human face appears to have been part of a smoking pipe. It was found in 1975 in New Jersey at the Minisink Site on the Benna Kill which flows into the Delaware River. Seton Hall University Museum Archaeological Research Center photo by Herbert Kraft.

SUSSEX COUNTY HISTORICAL SOCIETY

Hill Memorial Bldg., 82 Main St., Newton. Open free, Monday through Friday.

This museum displays surface finds, made in the Wallkill Valley, of material from the Archaic through the Woodland periods. There is a life-size model of Indians inhabiting a rockshelter.

THUNDERBIRD MUSEUM

Mt. Laurel Road, east of Moorestown. Open afternoons, Saturday, Sunday; at other times by appointment. Admission charged.

A wide variety of prehistoric artifacts from New Jersey and also from other areas is on display in the privately owned museum.

WATSON HOUSE
(Abbott Farm Site)

151 Westcott St., Trenton. Open free, by appointment. Write, or phone: (609) 888–2062.

This house, which was built in 1708, now serves as a headquarters and museum for the Daughters of the American Revolution. Its grounds overlap an extensive archeological area known as the Abbott Farm Site. Prehistoric artifacts on display in the museum were recovered in 1966 by the Unami Chapter of the Archeological Society of New Jersey, from the area immediately surrounding the house.

Excavation at the site has gone on at intervals for the last 100 years and has attracted wide attention. Much of the early material recovered is in the Peabody Museum, at Harvard. A small amount of material found later can be seen in the New Jersey State Museum, Trenton.

In 1872 a physician, Dr. Charles Conrad Abbott, owner of a farm which included part of the site, published a book, *The Stone Age in New Jersey,* about the artifacts he was finding in the area. Thereafter he gave up the practice of medicine and devoted the rest of his life to archeology. Dr. Abbott put forth several theories to explain the

material, some of which seemed spectacularly old. More recent researches have not supported his ideas.

In 1936, with funds provided by the Works Progress Administration, Dr. Dorothy Cross began extensive excavation of the site, which extends for 3½ miles along a bluff above the Delaware River. She recovered materials which showed that somewhere between 8000 B.C. and 3000 B.C. Indians walked along the bluff and dropped projectile points in one small area. At about A.D. 100, Woodland people carved steatite (soapstone) bowls at the site and adorned themselves with steatite beads and gorgets and pendants. Somewhat later the knowledge of clay pottery making came to them from other Indians, who lived to the south. Soon after A.D. 350, they began to garden. Their pottery became more varied in form and style.

Although they were far from the centers of the most active Indian life, in the Ohio and Mississippi valleys, the people at Abbott Farm were not entirely isolated. They traveled and traded, and travelers came to them. One visitor from central New York

Chalk lines have been added to make clearly visible the pecked figures in this petroglyph, which is the first to be found in New Jersey. It is on display in the Seton Hall University Museum. Seton Hall University Museum Archaeological Research Center photo by Herbert Kraft.

State brought with him a variety of personal belongings which showed he was a man of importance. While he was there, he died and was buried with his exotic finery.

Material recovered from Abbott burials and large photographs showing how burials are excavated are on display at the New Jersey State Museum, in Trenton.

New York

AMERICAN MUSEUM OF NATURAL HISTORY

Central Park West at 79th St., New York. Open Monday through Saturday; afternoon Sunday and holidays. Admission by donation.

This great museum has large collections of prehistoric North American material, but very little is on exhibit. In the Hall of the Eastern Woodland and Plains Indians are some pre-contact artifacts. In the Hall of the Northwest Coast Indians one exhibit shows how the Kwakiutl Indians felled trees and split huge planks from them for house building before the introduction of metal tools by Europeans. A huge seagoing Northwest Coast boat is on display.

BEAR MOUNTAIN TRAILSIDE HISTORICAL MUSEUM

In Bear Mountain State Park, 45 miles north of New York City. Parking at the main Bear Mountain parking lot. Daily Mohawk Bus Line service and Hudson River Day Line boat service from New York City in summer. Open free, daily.

Indian artifacts, mainly from Orange, Rockland, and Ulster counties, are used in exhibits that show prehistoric shelter, food, weapons, and art in New York State. The Paleo, Archaic, and Woodland periods, from about 7000 B.C. to the seventeenth century, are represented.

Albany to Buffalo

The Mohawk Trail, another name for US 20 and New York 5, provides an easy, gently graded route from Albany to Buffalo. As the name implies, it follows a prehistoric Indian trail which once linked the villages of all the tribes belonging to what White men called the Iroquois Confederacy.

Many other modern travel routes in the United States follow old Indian trails. A usual sequence was this: First, animals made paths to and from watering places or feeding grounds or salt licks. Indian hunters followed the animals, widening the trails, some of which later proved useful as means of communication between Indian settlements. Pioneers of European origin then used the Indian paths—on foot at first, later on horseback. Next wagons went along the same trails. Still later, when railroads were built, civil engineers often found that the best routes had been followed by the drivers of the horse-drawn wagons. Finally, when automobile roads were needed, highways often took the same easy grades that the Indians discovered long ago.

BROOKLYN CHILDREN'S MUSEUM

145 Brooklyn Ave., Brooklyn. Open free, afternoons, Wednesday through Monday.

In this museum, which is devoted mainly to interesting children in science, there are exhibits that interpret prehistoric Indian life.

BROOKLYN MUSEUM

188 Eastern Pkwy., Brooklyn. Open Wednesday through Saturday; afternoons, Sunday and holidays. Closed Dec. 25.

In this large general museum are several exhibits of North American archeological materials, including Southwestern Basketmaker artifacts and a model of Pueblo Bonito, Chaco Canyon.

BUFFALO MUSEUM OF SCIENCE

Humboldt Park, Buffalo. Open free, Monday through Saturday; evenings, Friday afternoons, Sunday and holidays. Children under 18 must be accompanied by an adult.

In this museum there is a special emphasis on the Iroquois Indians, including their prehistory. One exhibit shows the cultural sequences of all five Iroquois tribes. Paintings by a Seneca Indian artist depict Iroquois legends. Four dioramas show pre-contact Iroquois life. There are also exhibits which include prehistoric life in the Northwest Coast and the Southwest.

CASTILE HISTORICAL HOUSE
(kass-TILE)

17 E. Park Rd., Castile. Open free, afternoons, Tuesday through Sunday; other times by appointment.

Although most of the material in this museum is from the historic period, some of it throws light on Seneca Indian prehistory. Three miles away, in Letchworth State Park, is a Seneca council house dating from the time of the American Revolution.

CAYUGA MUSEUM OF HISTORY AND ART
(kah-YOO-gah)

203 Genesee St., Auburn. Open free, afternoons, Tuesday through Sunday; also Saturday mornings. Closed certain holidays.

Some materials from the Owasco culture (A.D. 100 to 1500) and from the later Iroquoian culture are displayed here.

CHAUTAUQUA COUNTY HISTORICAL SOCIETY
(shuh-TAW-quah)

Main and Portage streets, Westfield. Open Tuesday through Saturday, May through Oct.; afternoons, Sunday, July, Aug. Closed certain holidays. Admission charged.

Displays of prehistoric and historic Algonquian and Iroquoian material include restored Iroquoian pottery.

This fragment of a pot rim shows how Iroquois women decorated their pottery by pressing designs in the wet clay before firing. Photo Université du Québec à Trois-Rivières.

CHEMUNG COUNTY HISTORICAL SOCIETY, INC. (shuh-MUNG)

Historical Center, 415 East Water St., Elmira. Open free, afternoons, Tuesday through Friday. Closed certain holidays.

Material from the society's extensive archeological collections are displayed in exhibits on Paleo-Indian occupation of the Northeast, Archaic period cultures, including the Lamoka Lake Site, and Woodland peoples. Contact period and contemporary Iroquois cultures are also featured.

FORT STANWIX MUSEUM

207 North James St., Rome. Open Monday through Saturday; afternoons, Sunday. Closed certain holidays. Admission charged.

With paintings, dioramas, and displays of random local finds of artifacts, this museum sketches the life of prehistoric Indians in the area from Paleo times, about 7000 years ago, to the Iroquois occupation of the historic period.

Special Interest. The museum, operated by the Rome Historical Society, is located adjacent to Fort Stanwix National Monument, the site of a fort built in colonial times. The area was important in the Indian period because it was what Indians called the "Great Carry"—the land route over which they portaged canoes between two water routes, one going south and east to the Hudson and Atlantic, the other going northwest to the Great Lakes.

FORT WILLIAM HENRY RESTORATION AND MUSEUM

Canada St., Lake George. Open daily, May through Oct.; evenings, daily, July, Aug. Admission charged.

Included with historic exhibits are displays of archeological material relating to the aboriginal occupation of northern New York and the Lake George–Lake Champlain area in particular. A diorama shows how small animals were caught in a deadfall trap.

The Indian village surrounded by a wooden stockade is a reconstruction of an eighteenth-century Iroquois settlement, which closely resembled villages of late prehistoric times.

GARVIES POINT MUSEUM

Barry Drive, Glen Cove. Open daily, all year. Admission charged.

Some of the exhibits here are devoted to the archeology of the area, with displays of prehistoric artifacts. Dioramas illustrate the daily life of Indians.

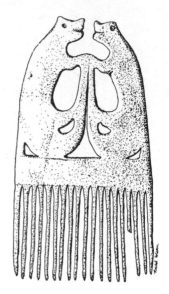

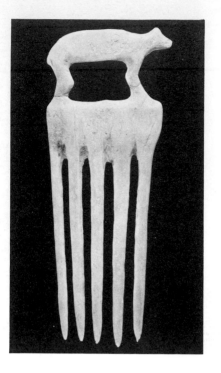

The custom of making bear effigies on combs fashioned from antler or bone was popular among the Iroquois and their predecessors in New York State. On the right is a Seneca antler comb of about A.D. 1550–1575 from a site in Livingston County. Rochester Museum and Science Center photo by James Osen. On the left is a prehistoric bone comb. Original in the Museum of the American Indian, New York.

HARTWICK COLLEGE, YAGER MUSEUM

Yager Hall, on the campus, Oneonta. Open free, Monday through Friday.

In addition to exhibits of materials from Central and South America, this museum has on permanent display prehistoric materials from the Upper Susquehanna Valley, representing the Archaic period, the Early Woodland, and the Late Woodland. Some materials from the Upper Susquehanna River drainage not yet on display may be seen by appointment.

HOWE PUBLIC LIBRARY

155 N. Main St., Wellsville. Open free, Monday, Tuesday, Thursday, Friday, Saturday, winter; Monday through Friday, summer. Closed certain holidays.

A feature of the David A. Howe Public Library is a small display of identified local artifacts from the Paleo Period to the historic Iroquois.

MOHAWK-CAUGHNAWAGA MUSEUM
(cog-nah-WAH-gah)

In Fonda on New York 5. Open Tuesday through Sunday, May 15 to Oct. 15. Admission charged.

In addition to an outdoor exhibit area, Iroquois artifacts are on display inside the museum, which is on the site of an excavated Iroquois settlement.

MUSEUM OF THE AMERICAN INDIAN, HEYE FOUNDATION

Broadway at W. 155th St., New York. Open Tuesday through Saturday; afternoons, Sunday. Closed certain holidays. Admission charged.

This museum, devoted exclusively to the American Indian, is probably the largest and most complete of its kind in the United States and Canada.

Many of the ethnologic exhibits throw light on prehistoric cultures. The extensive archeological displays contain materials from several sites which cannot be visited—for example, various sites on the Northwest Coast

A prehistoric village once stood at Nichols Pond, between Canastota and Morrisville, N.Y. It may have been this village which Samuel de Champlain attacked in A.D. 1615, as shown in this picture, reprinted from his *Voyages*. Smithsonian Institution National Anthropological Archives.

and Mimbres sites in the Southwest. Many artifacts have been chosen for their superior artistic quality.

By geographical areas, some of the special features of the museum are:

Pacific Northwest—a very large and beautiful collection of sacred and utilitarian objects;

Plains—early ethnographic material predominates;

California—important collections of basketry, stone work, personal ornaments;

Southwestern United States—especially rich collection of ceremonial objects, fabrics, and ceramics;

Great Basin—excellent ethnobotanical materials;

Eastern and Southeastern United States—large collections of materials that illuminate prehistoric ranked societies.

NEW YORK STATE MUSEUM AND SCIENCE SERVICE

Empire State Plaza, Albany. Open free, daily. Closed certain holidays.

Life-sized dioramas combine artifacts and scientific specimens to tell the story of people and nature in New York State. Films, lectures, and learning programs are offered for adults and children.

NIAGARA COUNTY HISTORICAL CENTER

Pioneer Building, 215 Niagara St., Lockport. Open free, Tuesday through Friday; afternoons, Saturday, Sunday. Closed certain holidays.

Artifacts from local prehistoric Indian sites are on exhibit here, together with a diorama showing an Iroquois Indian village.

NICHOLS POND

From Morrisville on US 20 drive north on county road toward Canastota to directional sign, then west to the Champlain-Oneida Battleground and Nichols Pond. Open free, at all times, weather permitting. Camping.

An Oneida, or Mohawk, Indian village stood at this place in late prehistoric times, and there is some reason to think that it was attacked by the French explorer Samuel de Champlain

in A.D. 1615. Champlain was accompanied by about 500 Huron and Algonquian Indians from Canada, in addition to a dozen men of his own, who were armed with arquebuses. Since the village seemed very well protected by a high palisade, Champlain tried a special stratagem. He ordered a tower built close to the palisade. Standing on the tower, his gunners could fire down into the village. More than this was needed, however, to overcome the inhabitants. They withstood the seige, and the French adventurer was forced to return to Canada. The illustration of the palisaded village which appears in Champlain's *Voyages* is probably a fairly accurate picture of the village which once stood here and which dates from prehistoric times.

ONTARIO COUNTY HISTORICAL SOCIETY

55 Main St., Canandaigua (Can-an-DAY-gwah). Open free, Tuesday through Saturday. Closed certain holidays.

Permanent and temporary exhibits include artifacts from local Seneca Indian village sites.

Owasco Indian village at Auburn, New York. New York State Department of Commerce photo by Sid Lane.

Iroquois Indians carved masks such as this in living basswood trees, then removed them and used them as part of curing ceremonies. Original in the Rochester Museum and Science Center.

OSSINING HISTORICAL SOCIETY MUSEUM

196 Croton Ave., Ossining. Open free, afternoons, Monday, Sept. through June, or by appointment.

This museum has locally collected artifacts, some of which have been dated to 5000 B.C., and some of which were made in contact times by the Sint Sinck tribe of the Wappinger Confederacy.

OWASCO STOCKADED INDIAN VILLAGE

Emerson Park, near the foot of Owasco Lake, 3 miles south of Auburn. Open daily, July, Aug.; at other times by appointment. Admission charged.

This is a reconstruction of an Owascan stockaded village as it was about A.D. 1150. The Owasco culture was ancestral to the culture of the Iroquois Indians, who lived in this area from about A.D. 1200 to 1779.

Inside the stockade are two reconstructed longhouses. One has been left unfinished, so that visitors may see how it was built and how it was used as a living area by many families at the same time. There is also a religious leader's hut in the village and a garden area. Displays show how pottery developed and how hunting and other crafts were practiced. One exhibit shows how the prehistoric Indians played lacrosse and what equipment they used.

OYSTERPONDS HISTORICAL SOCIETY, INC.

Village Lane, Orient, L.I. Open, afternoons, Tuesday, Thursday, Saturday, Sunday and holidays. Admission charged.

Local Indian artifacts on display here include a Clovis point, stone pots and tools dated at about 4000 B.C., and some material dating from 1000 B.C. to A.D. 1600.

POWELL HOUSE

434 Park Ave., Huntington, L.I. Office open, Monday through Friday; tours, Sunday afternoons or by appointment. Admission charged.

On exhibit here are materials recovered from excavations in the vicinity. The museum, which stands at the intersection of old Indian trails, is operated by the Huntington Historical Society.

ROBERSON CENTER FOR THE ARTS AND SCIENCES

30 Front St., Binghamton. Open free, Tuesday through Friday; afternoons, Saturday, Sunday.

Archeological materials of local origin are arranged according to cultural periods from Paleo through Transitional. There are also some Woodland and Late Woodland materials.

A diorama shows life in an Owasco village about A.D. 1300. Another shows how a longhouse was constructed.

Arthur C. Parker, Seneca Indian, directed the Rochester Museum for many years. Rochester Museum of Science Service photo.

This diorama in the Rochester Museum and Science Center shows an Iroquois village scene about A.D. 1600. Rochester Museum and Science Service photo by William G. Frank.

ROCHESTER MUSEUM AND SCIENCE CENTER

657 East Ave., Rochester. Open Monday through Saturday; afternoons, Sunday. Closed Dec. 25. Admission charged.

Numerous displays cover all New York State Indian cultures from the Archaic to the historic period, including Adena, Hopewell, Point Peninsula, Owasco, and prehistoric Iroquois.

Exhibits are arranged to show how people fitted into their environment and how their tools are clues to the way they managed life. Of particular interest are cases which show the sequence of New York projectile points, how wampum was made, radio-carbon dating at sites, and evidence of illness in prehistoric times. One entire alcove is devoted to the life of hunters during the Archaic, before the use of the bow and arrow. Other exhibits are devoted to the Arctic, Northwest Coast, Southwest, Plains, and Southeast culture areas.

In addition to prehistoric material, many exhibits show Indian life at the time of first contact with Europeans and later.

Dioramas show the construction of a prehistoric Iroquois longhouse, the life-size interior of a prehistoric longhouse, a Haida Indian village, the Zuni pueblo, and how an archeological site is excavated.

Special Interest. The museum achieved national prominence under the directorship of Arthur C. Parker, a Seneca Indian.

SIX NATIONS INDIAN MUSEUM

Off New York 3, 1 mile east of Onchiota. Open daily. Admission charged.

This museum, dedicated to preserving all aspects of Iroquois culture, has exhibits of prehistoric Iroquois pottery and other artifacts, as well as some pre-Iroquois material, largely from the St. Lawrence River Valley and the Lake Champlain regions. Displays show how various articles were made and used. A diorama is devoted to the carving of a false-face mask from a living tree.

Special Feature. This museum will supply on request a catalog of a series of educational pamphlets and charts which it publishes on Iroquois history

and culture. One of these publications, entitled *Six Nations Indian Monuments,* is a kind of guidebook to sites which are important in Iroquois history and legend. It covers parts of New York State, Pennsylvania, Ohio, and Canada.

TIOGA COUNTY HISTORICAL SOCIETY MUSEUM
(tie-OH-gah)

110–112 Front St., Owego. Open free, Tuesday through Friday; afternoons, Saturday, Sunday; evenings, Wednesday. Closed certain holidays.

Artifacts collected in the immediate area represent cultures from about 2500 B.C. to historic times. A special display is devoted to the Engelbert Site, which is about ten miles from Owego. In this display are materials representing Lamoka, Late Owasco, prehistoric Iroquois, and Susquehannock cultures.

Designs scratched on slate by prehistoric Indians near Lake Kidgemakooge, in Nova Scotia. Photo by Arthur Kelsall, courtesy of Campbell Grant.

WAGNER COLLEGE, MUSEUM OF ARCHAEOLOGY

On the campus, 631 Howard Ave., Staten Island. Open Tuesday through Thursday; afternoons, Sunday. Admission charged. Closed Aug. and certain holidays.

A few exhibits here are devoted to the prehistory of Staten Island.

YAGER MUSEUM
(See Hartwick College)

YATES COUNTY GENEALOGICAL AND HISTORICAL SOCIETY

200 Main St., Penn Yan. Open free, Monday through Friday. Closed certain holidays.

Locally collected material is on display here, together with artifacts mainly from the Midwest.

Nova Scotia

CITADEL HILL BRANCH, NOVA SCOTIA MUSEUM

Citadel Hill National Historic Park, Halifax. Open free, Monday through Saturday; afternoons, Sunday, Sept. through May; daily, June through Aug.

In addition to ethnological materials, this museum exhibits some Nova Scotia archeological items. One diorama shows an Indian camp at the time of contact with Europeans. Another shows a mid-seventeenth century burial.

MICMAC MUSEUM

From Pictou drive 2 miles east on Shore Road. Open daily, June 1 to Sept. 15. Admission charged.

Material recovered from Indian burials on the museum site are on exhibit here.

NOVA SCOTIA MUSEUM

1747 Summer St., Halifax. Open free, daily, all year. Closed Dec. 25.

A section of the main exhibit area is devoted to the prehistory of Nova Scotia from Paleo-Indian through the Archaic and Ceramic, or Woodland, stages.

In 1934 the Seine River band of Ojibwa Indians, in Ontario, were still building longhouses much like those used in prehistoric times. Here the pole framework of a ceremonial longhouse has been completed. National Museum of Man photo.

Ontario

ASSIGINACK HISTORICAL SOCIETY
(ass-SIG-in-ack)

Nelson and Queen streets, Manitowaning (MAN-it-toh-WAH-ning). Open Monday through Saturday; afternoons, Sunday, June through Sept. Admission charged.

Here may be seen artifacts from the nearby Sheguiandah Site, (see below) on loan from the Royal Ontario Museum.

BRANT MUSEUM

1240 North Shore Blvd., Burlington. Open Monday through Saturday; afternoons, Sunday. Admission charged.

This museum, named for Joseph Brant, an Iroquois leader on the English side during the American Revolution, features Brant memorabilia and has other material, some of it prehistoric, representative of Iroquois culture.

BRUCE COUNTY MUSEUM

Southampton. Open Monday through Saturday; afternoons, Sunday, July, Aug.; afternoons, daily, May, June, Sept. Admission charged.

Artifacts on display here are Archaic, Middle Woodland, and Iroquoian.

CHATHAM-KENT MUSEUM

59 William St. North, Chatham. Open free, afternoons, Tuesday, Thursday, Saturday; afternoons, Sunday, May 1 to Sept. 30; first and third Sundays, Oct. 1 to April 30.

The main concern in this museum is with local history, but there are archeological exhibits, which include a display of identified artifacts; a display that shows how prehistoric tools were made and used; a display on the evolution of pottery from 1000 B.C. to about A.D. 1500. A special exhibit shows the stratigraphy of a prehistoric village site.

A diorama of an Iroquois village of longhouses surrounded by a palisade, from the National Museum of Man, in Ottawa. National Museum of Man photo.

HURONIA MUSEUM

Little Lake Park, at King St. entrance, Midland. Open Monday through Saturday; afternoons, Sunday, May 16 to Oct. 12. Admission charged.

Displayed here are random finds of local prehistoric material. Near the museum a Huron Indian village has been reconstructed.

LITTLE CURRENT-HOWLAND CENTENNIAL MUSEUM
(See Sheguiandah Site)

McMASTER UNIVERSITY MUSEUM

Department of Anthropology, on the campus, Hamilton. Open free, during classroom hours.

Display cases contain archeological material from the Southwest, from western Canada, and from Ontario. These are housed in a museum-laboratory in the Arts III Building.

MUSEUM OF INDIAN ARCHAEOLOGY AND PIONEER LIFE
(See University of Western Ontario)

MUSEUM OF THE WOODLAND INDIAN

In the Woodland Indian Cultural Educational Centre, 184 Mohawk St., Brantford. Open daily. Admission charged.

Along with a wide variety of material illustrating the historic culture of Woodland Indians is a section devoted to prehistoric artifacts. The museum has resource persons and a mobile resource unit that travels widely, explaining Woodland Indian life, past and present. Also housed here is an Indian Hall of Fame.

NATIONAL MUSEUM OF MAN

Metcalfe and McLeod, Ottawa. Open free, daily May 24 to Sept. 6; closed Mondays and certain holidays in winter.

In this museum are several galleries which contain interpretations of the prehistoric as well as the more recent life of Canada's aboriginal peoples. In the Eskimo gallery exhibits show how Eskimos who lived in a harsh environment made use of whatever was available to them. They built igloos of snow. Using driftwood and sealskins they made boats, one type, called the kayak, for hunting, another type, called the umiak, for carrying freight. From seal and caribou they obtained clothing, meat, and fuel. A diorama in this gallery shows an Eskimo dwelling of 500 years ago and modern archeologists excavating that dwelling.

Beautiful art created by Coastal Indians of northwestern North America fills another gallery and indicates the kind of work these Indians did before contact with Europeans, as well as more recently.

Exhibits in the Plains Indian gallery illustrate the many uses people made of the buffalo in prehistoric times, and also show the changes in their lives after they obtained horses.

Exhibits in the Iroquois gallery suggest the remarkable political life of these Indians, who lived in palisaded

This exhibit in the National Museum of Man, Ottawa, shows how the Eskimo hunted seal. National Museum of Man photo.

villages and ruled over a very large territory. Displays show how the Iroquois obtained much of their food by farming. Special exhibits are devoted to artifacts of the Ontario Iroquois. There is also a display of prehistoric materials from the village of Hochelaga, which was on the site of Montreal.

Dioramas show the corn harvest in a Huron village in 1615, the False Face curing ceremony, a later prehistoric Huron village of 11 very large houses, the interior of a longhouse, Indians in the eastern part of subarctic Canada hunting caribou, and artifacts made and used by the Ojibwa and Cree Indians in the eastern subarctic between A.D. 900 and 1750.

Two galleries, "A Few Acres of Snow" and "Everyman's Heritage," emphasize the postcontact period and the multinational heritage of Canada.

PERTH MUSEUM
(The Archibald M. Campbell Memorial Museum)

5 Gore St. East, Perth. Open Monday through Saturday; afternoons, Sunday, April 1 through Dec. 23; afternoons,

Saturday, Sunday, Jan. 1 through March 31. Admission charged.

In addition to random local finds this museum houses some archeological material from the southwestern part of the United States.

ROYAL ONTARIO MUSEUM

100 Queen's Park, Toronto. Open daily. Closed certain holidays. Admission charged.

One gallery in this museum is devoted to Ontario prehistory. There are also exhibits on Beringia and on some archeological sites in the New World.

SERPENT MOUND

From Peterboro drive southeast to the north shore of Rice Lake. Open free, at all times.

Here about 80 feet above the lake is a mound which depicts a snake. It is 189 feet in length, and averages 5 feet in height, 24 feet in width. Near the head is an oval mound, which contained four burials.

Serpent Mound seems not to be the work of Effigy Mound people who were

active in Wisconsin. It is instead a rare example of a mound built by people who followed a lifeway called Point Peninsula. A cremation in the mound has a radio-carbon date of A.D. 130.

SHEGUIANDAH SITE
(SHEG-wee-AN-duh)

From Sudbury drive 41 miles west on Trans-Canada 17, then 43 miles south on Provincial Road 68 through Little Current to the Little Current–Howland Centennial Museum at the edge of the town of Sheguiandah. The museum is open daily, June through Aug.; afternoons, May, Sept., Oct. Admission charged.

At this site, near the museum, an excavation conducted for several years has produced considerable controversy in archeological circles. Dr. Thomas E. Lee, who was in charge of the dig, reported that he had found crude choppers and scrapers made of quartzite *underneath* several levels of deposits in which there were signs of human occupation. These crude tools had been tumbled about and mixed in what appeared to be glacial till—that is, an

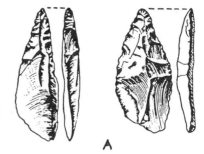

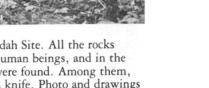

Excavation in progress, in 1953, at the Sheguiandah Site. All the rocks visible in the photograph had been quarried by human beings, and in the rubble many broken and unfinished stone tools were found. Among them, shown in the drawings were (a) gravers and (b) a knife. Photo and drawings by Thomas E. Lee.

aggregation of clay, sand, and rock deposited by a glacier. It looked to Dr. Lee—and to some eminent geologists—as if the front edge of a glacier had pushed a very ancient campsite for a short distance, thus disturbing the artifacts which had been left there. If this is what happened, the people who made these quartzite tools lived in Canada *before* the last great glacial advance.

The archeologists who believed that Dr. Lee had found very old artifacts estimated their age at 30,000 years, at the very least. According to some responsible estimates, they were much older than that. Not all archeologists, however, agreed that the Sheguiandah materials were of such antiquity.

One thing is certain. If Dr. Lee's discovery proves to be what he and others think it is, he has shown that people were on this continent much earlier than has generally been believed. And if this is so, some of the basic theories about Early Man will have to be revised.

The Museum. Some of the artifacts recovered from the Seghuiandah Site are on exhibit here, together with pho-

tographs of the dig. Visitors may enter the site, which is protected by the provincial government.

SIMCOE COUNTY MUSEUM AND ARCHIVES
(SIM-coe)

From Barrie drive 4 miles north on Ontario 27 to West Hwy. 26, then ½ mile west to museum, adjacent to Springwater Park. Open Tuesday through Saturday; afternoons, Sunday, Sept. through May; Monday through Saturday; afternoons, Sunday, June, July, Aug. Admission charged.

Materials from a number of systematically excavated sites may be seen here. The cultures represented are the Laurentian, Middleport, Lalonde, and Huron. The earliest materials have been dated at sometime between 3000 and 2000 B.C. An electrified map shows the location of the sites and clearly indicates what culture and period are represented at each site.

Two students in the 1982 Carnegie Museum field school work on a wall profile in a multi-component site the earliest level of which was C-14 dated to 5350 B.C. Carnegie Museum of Natural History photo.

THUNDER BAY MUSEUM

219 May St., South Thunder Bay. Open daily, June 15 to Sept. 15. Admission charged.

Artifacts of the Paleo and the Copper Culture periods found at a site in the vicinity are on display, together with Woodland material.

UNITED COUNTIES MUSEUM

731 Second St. W., Cornwall. Open Monday through Saturday; afternoons, Sunday, May 1 through Oct. 31.

On display here are some Point Peninsula artifacts.

UNIVERSITY OF WESTERN ONTARIO, MUSEUM OF INDIAN ARCHAEOLOGY AND PIONEER LIFE

On the campus, London. Open free, Monday through Friday.

Here are exhibits illustrative of the archeology of the surrounding area.

WOODWINDS HISTORICAL MUSEUM

From Gravenhurst drive north on Ontario 69. The museum is on the shore of Lake Muskoka at Barlochan, 2½ miles off Highway 69. Open afternoons, daily, July, Aug.; afternoons, Saturday, Sunday, June 15 to July and Sept. to Oct. 15. Admission charged.

Exhibited here are random local finds of hunting implements. The vicinity of the museum was apparently a summer hunting area, but not a place where permanent habitations were built.

Pennsylvania

CARNEGIE MUSEUM OF NATURAL HISTORY

4400 Forbes Ave., Pittsburgh. Open Monday through Saturday; afternoons, Sunday. Closed certain holidays. Admission charged.

In the main archeological exhibit of this important museum a series of cases contain artifacts from, and ex-

Archeologists at work in Meadowcroft Rock Shelter, near Avella, Pennsylvania, where 20,000 year old evidence of Paleo-Indian occupation was found. University of Pittsburgh photo.

planations of, each major culture period in the Upper Ohio Valley, from Paleo-Indian through Archaic, Early Woodland, Middle Woodland, and late prehistoric to historic. A typical site for each period is represented with artifacts, text, and illustrations. There is also general information about each period.

Special exhibits depict certain phases of New World archeology, such as Adena.. In this connection the materials from Cresap Mound in West Virginia are on display. There is also full treatment of the late prehistoric Monogahela culture. Special exhibits on various aspects of Eastern archeology change every few months.

FORT LIGONIER

50 miles east of Pittsburgh, on US 30 in Ligonier. Open daily, April 15 through Nov. 15. Admission charged.

In this reconstruction of a fort of the period of the French and Indian War, one building contains exhibits of prehistoric materials.

FRANKLIN AND MARSHALL COLLEGE, NORTH MUSEUM

College and Buchanan avenues, Lancaster. Open free, Wednesday through Saturday; afternoons, Sunday, Sept. through June; afternoons, Saturday, Sunday only, July, Aug. Closed certain holidays.

All periods in the Northeast are represented in archeological exhibits here. Special exhibits are devoted to pottery making and to the local Shenk's Ferry and Susquehannock cultures. There are also technical exhibits on Northeastern projectile points and pottery types. A diorama shows a Shenk's Ferry village.

INDIAN STEPS MUSEUM

From Airville (east of York), where Pennsylvania 74 and Pennsylvania 425 intersect, take a local road east to the museum, which is on the west bank of the Susquehanna River. Open free, Tuesday through Sunday, April 1 through Oct. 31.

In seven rooms containing American Indian material are exhibits devoted

Woodland Indians made a great variety of containers from birch bark. Some were cooking vessels, some were used for storage, others for hauling water. The practise of making such containers continued into historic time. Passamaquody Indians decorated this small round box with pictographs. Robert Abbe Museum of Stone Age Antiquities photo.

to the Susquehannock and Cherokee Indians. All periods from Paleo through Late Woodland are represented. Shadow boxes show various aspects of Indian life. One display consists of a burial from the Shenk's Ferry Site. Also on exhibit are plaster casts of petroglyphs which are now submerged under water impounded behind a dam on the Susquehanna River.

The Name. Before the dam was built it was possible to reach the river's edge by steps which prehistoric people cut in the rock. Hence the name Indian Steps Museum.

Special Interest. This museum was constructed on the site where the Susquehannock tribe, decimated by smallpox, ceased to exist, after it lost a battle with the Massowomeke Indians.

MERCER MUSEUM

Pine and Ashland streets, Doylestown. Open Tuesday through Saturday; afternoons, Sunday. Closed certain holidays. Admission charged.

Here, along with tools and implements which European settlers used in the United States before the Industrial Revolution, are tools of the prehistoric Lenni Lenape Indians.

MONROE COUNTY HISTORICAL SOCIETY

Main and Ninth streets, Stroudsburg. Open free, afternoons, Tuesday.

On exhibit are local finds, mostly of Lenni Lenape origin.

NORTH MUSEUM
(See Franklin and Marshall College)

SOMMERHEIM

In Scott County Park, 3 miles west of Erie on Pennsylvania 5. Open free, mornings, Monday through Friday, in summer.

This was the site of a Native American settlement between 1000 B.C. and A.D. 1. Some shell middens and patterns of postholes still exist, and visitors may watch ongoing excavation. There is an interpretive display in a trailer at the site.

In the sixteenth century the English artist John White painted this scene showing how Indians had made dugout canoes for centuries, using fire and stone tools. From the engraving of White's watercolor by Theodore De Bry published in *Wunderbarliche. . . .*, Frankfurt, Germany, 1590.

TIOGA POINT MUSEUM
(tie-OH-gah)

724 S. Main St., Athens. Open free, afternoons, Monday, Wednesday, Saturday; evenings, Monday.

The prehistoric Indian collection here consists mainly of random local finds, but there are materials from three systematically excavated sites—Murray Garden, Spanish Hill, and Abbe-Brennan—which provided data about several cultures. One exhibit shows the chronologic sequence of different local pottery types.

UNIVERSITY OF PENNSYLVANIA, UNIVERSITY MUSEUM

Spruce and 33rd streets, Philadelphia. Open Tuesday through Saturday; afternoons, Sunday. Closed certain holidays and Sundays, in summer. Admission free, donation requested.

This great museum has conducted many important excavations and has outstanding collections of New World

material. Important and representative artifacts from various cultures in North America are on display.

VENANGO COUNTY COURTHOUSE

Liberty and 12th streets, Franklin. Open free, Monday through Friday.

Display cases here are devoted to material from 18 Pennsylvania sites.

WILLIAM PENN MEMORIAL MUSEUM
(The Pennsylvania State Museum)

Third and North streets, adjacent to the State Capitol, Harrisburg. Open free, Monday through Saturday; afternoons, Sunday. Closed certain holidays.

In the Hall of Anthropology, exhibits give insight into the culture and technology of peoples who lived in Pennsylvania for more than 10,000 years before the arrival of Europeans. The museum's archeologists have done excavation at many sites in the state, and exhibits introduce the visitor to the archeologists' techniques. Other displays show how people made and

At the Micmac Indian Village, on Prince Edward Island, this prehistoric Indian dwelling has been reconstructed as part of an exhibit. Artifacts found in the area are also on display in a museum there. Micmac Indian Village photo.

used the objects they needed. Five full-scale dioramas depict major happenings in the life of a Delaware Indian from birth to death.

WYOMING HISTORICAL AND GEOLOGICAL SOCIETY

49 South Franklin St., Wilkes Barre. Open free, Saturday; afternoons, Wednesday and Friday.

Archeological exhibits here illuminate the prehistory of the Susquehanna River Valley from the Archaic to the historic period. Included are displays of Owasco and prehistoric Huron material.

Prince Edward Island

MICMAC INDIAN VILLAGE (MICK-mack)

Rocky Point, Prince Edward Island. From Charlottetown travel west on Route 1 to Cornwall, then follow Route

19 to Rocky Point. Open daily, June 1 to Oct. 1. Admission charged.

Here, in an outdoor setting, the proprietors have reconstructed a sixteenth-century Micmac village. Indoors is a museum with random local finds of prehistoric artifacts.

Québec

L'ÉCOLE POLYVALENTE DE LA SARRE

In La Sarre, Abitibi-Ouest. Open free, Monday through Saturday.

The museum in this school has on display an interesting collection of Archaic and Woodland material from excavations at Abitibi Lake.

McCORD MUSEUM
(See McGill University)

McGILL UNIVERSITY, McCORD MUSEUM

690 Sherbrooke St. W., Montreal. Open free, Wednesday through Sunday.

Archeological exhibits here include prehistoric Canadian artifacts.

UNIVERSITÉ DU QUÉBEC À TROIS-RIVIÈRES, MUSÉE D'ARCHÉOLOGIE

Pavillon Nérée-Beauchemin, on the campus, Université du Québec à Trois-Rivières. Open free, Monday through Friday; afternoons, Saturday, Sunday. Closed certain holidays.

The main section of the museum presents artifacts—tools of flint, polished stone, and bone, as well as pottery, jewelry, and pipes—from the Early Archaic period through the Woodland period in Québec. The material was all collected during surveys and excavations in the Trois-Rivières region. Various exhibits illustrate everyday Indian life.

Fishnet sinker from Red Mill, Québec. Université du Québec à Trois Rivières photo.

Eskimos engraved this mask in steatite on Qajartalik Island near Wakeham Bay, Québec. Bernard Saladin d'Anglure photo, courtesy Campbell Grant.

Two axes (left) and gouge (right) with polished cutting edges used by archaic people in Canada. Université du Québec à Trois Rivières photo.

One type of structure which the Inuit (Eskimos) apparently never built was this kind of beaconlike column, 13 feet high. Many like it have been found on the Ungava shoreline. If they were beacons, they could have been very useful as landmarks to seagoing Norsemen. Photo by Thomas E. Lee.

UNIVERSITÉ LAVAL, CENTRE D'ÉTUDES NORDIQUES,

On the campus, Siège Social, Québec. Open free, Monday through Saturday; afternoons, Sunday, when the university is in session.

This small but well-planned museum features material from Arctic Québec, in culture sequences as it was excavated, especially Norse remains, but also Dorset, Thule, Paleo, and Archaic.

Expecting to find remains of the Dorset culture on Ungava Peninsula in Northern Québec, Dr. Thomas E. Lee began investigations there in 1964 for the Centre d'Études Nordiques. What he found led him to suspect that the Norse had been in the area. In subsequent years he found increasing evidence that convinced him and many—but not all—archeologists that there had indeed been Norse settlements along the coast of Ungava Bay and even inland at Payne Lake.

Rhode Island

BROWN UNIVERSITY, HAFFENREFFER MUSEUM

Mount Hope Grant, off Rhode Island 136, Bristol. Open afternoons, Saturday and Sunday, Sept. through May; afternoons, Tuesday through Sunday, June through Aug. Closed certain holidays. Admission charged.

One of the best places in America to see Arctic archeology is in a modest building on a rambling estate located outside of Bristol. Here excellent exhibits display the results of Brown University digs in the Far North. Each exhibit is accompanied by a clear explanation. One display deals with beach-ridge dating in Alaska at a place where the coast is rising and ocean currents have piled up a series of beaches. The newest beach is closest to the sea. The oldest is farthest away. Be-

What the Ungava site called Longhouse #2 looked like when discovered. The same site, after excavation and partial restoration, turned out to be an 83-foot long structure of the kind that the Norse built. A fourth room at the right was left unexcavated. None of the Ungava sites are open to the public. Photos by Thomas E. Lee and Robert E. Lee

cause Eskimos are dependent on the sea, they like to live close to it. At this spot they have long built homes near the water. When a new beach formed between them and the shore, they moved to a new house site. The result is a continuous record of life over a long period of time. Archeologists have traced this story by excavating Eskimo remains on beach after beach.

Very tiny blades, from the Denbigh culture are on exhibit here, as are harpoon heads, semilunar knives, carved figurines, and other artifacts of later cultures.

Other exhibits are devoted to baskets from California and other parts of the West; Iroquois materials, including masks known as False Faces; and artifacts made by Archaic people. The displays make clear the relationships of these Archaic people to others who entered the area from the West, bringing with them knowledge of farming, copper tools, and smoking.

In many ways the museum illustrates the varied life patterns of Indians and Eskimos and the manner in which these patterns changed as people kept working out new adjustments to their environments.

Special Feature. One display is devoted to the Red Paint people, who lived along the Penobscot River in Maine about 4000 years ago. They are so called because they used the mineral red ocher in burial ceremonies, sprinkling quantities of it on the dead and over all the gifts they placed in graves. Among the gifts were familiar objects, such as knives, projectile points, and woodworking tools. Less common were net sinkers, polished slate objects that resemble bayonets, implements of flint and iron pyrite for making fire, and mysterious little perfectly rounded pebbles. Since there are no visitable Red Paint sites in the United States, the display here is of special interest (The Port au Choix Site in Newfoundland was

occupied by people who had many of the same cultural patterns.)

FORT NINIGRET

In Charlestown, off US 1A. Open free, daily, all year.

Excavation revealed at least two periods when Native Americans inhabited this site, high on a bluff overlooking a tidal lagoon. The first, between A.D. 700 and 1300, is known only from bits of pottery. The second occupation, in the seventeenth century, overlapped the period of contact with Europeans. At that time Niantic Indians built a fortified trading post on the bluff. One possible reason for the fort may have been the fact that a great deal of wampum, a form of currency, was manufactured here from shell, and its makers may have felt the need to protect it.

HAFFENREFFER MUSEUM
(See Brown University)

A grid over an area where knappers manufactured stone tools, at a site in Thunderbird Archeological Park in Virginia, makes it possible to map the exact position of each object found. Thunderbird Research Corporation photo.

ROGER WILLIAMS PARK MUSEUM AND PLANETARIUM

Roger Williams Park, Providence. Open free, Monday through Saturday; afternoons, Sunday. Closed certain holidays.

Although most of the material in this museum is postcontact, there are some items and some whole exhibits which throw light on prehistory. One case shows hypothesized routes by which Indians entered America. Another presents a chronological chart for North American archeology, with appropriate tools and weapons for each period. A third shows the differences in physical appearance among Indians of different regions. There is also an exhibit on the plants domesticated by Indians and a summary of their accomplishments in prehistoric times.

TOMAQUAG INDIAN MEMORIAL MUSEUM

On Summit Rd., Arcadia. Open Monday through Friday; afternoons, Saturday, Sunday. Admission charged.

In the exhibits on Indian culture there are limited prehistoric materials.

Vermont

ROBERT HULL FLEMING MUSEUM
(See University of Vermont)

UNIVERSITY OF VERMONT, ROBERT HULL FLEMING MUSEUM

61 Colchester Ave., Burlington. Open free, Monday through Friday; afternoons, Saturday, Sunday. Closed certain holidays.

Here may be seen selected random local finds and artifacts from other parts of the Eastern Woodland area, together with prehistoric materials from the Southwest and the Northwest Coast.

A Dalton spearpoint (late Paleo-Indian) just as excavators found it in the ground at a site in Thunderbird Archeological Park in Virginia. Thunderbird Research Corporation photo.

VERMONT HISTORICAL SOCIETY

Pavilion Bldg., State St., Montpelier. Open free, daily, July through Aug.; Monday through Friday, Sept. through June.

Exhibits here include material from an Archaic site on Isle la Motte in northern Vermont, dated at about 1800 B.C. to 1200 B.C. There are also tools, weapons, and ceremonial objects of later Indian cultures.

VERMONT MUSEUM

In Montpelier, 109 State St. Open Monday through Friday, Sept. through June; Saturday, Sunday, July through Aug. Admission by donation.

In this general museum are some exhibits of prehistoric Vermont Indian material.

Virginia

COLLEGE OF WILLIAM AND MARY, VIRGINIA RESEARCH CENTER FOR ARCHAEOLOGY

In the basement of Wren Building, on the campus, Williamsburg. Open free, Monday through Friday. Closed certain holidays.

The exhibits here are changed every two or three years. The title of the 1982 display was "Foraging, Feasting, and Fast Foods: The Archaeology of Virginia's Foodways." The subsistence activities of Virginia's inhabitants from 10,000 B.C. to the present were discussed and illustrated with artifacts and graphics. A sampling of materials recovered through Virginia's archeological survey and salvage program are also on exhibit.

COLONIAL NATIONAL HISTORICAL PARK, JAMESTOWN VISITOR CENTER

From Williamsburg drive 10 miles southwest on the Colonial Pkwy. Or from the south take Virginia 10 and 31 to Scotland, where a ferry crosses the James River to Glasshouse Point near the Jamestown entrance. The Jamestown Entrance Station is open daily, all year. Closed Dec. 25. Admission charged.

Seventeenth-century artifacts are displayed in the Entrance Station. About 300 Indian artifacts were excavated in the park, and some of these, all Algonquian of the Woodland and historic periods, are on display in one exhibit.

FLOWERDEW HUNDRED

From Richmond drive south on Interstate 95, then east on Virginia 10, then north on local road 639; or from Williamsburg drive west on Virginia 5, then south on local road 639. The site is on the south side of the James River about 5 miles east of the Benjamin Harrison Bridge. Open daily, Tuesday through Sunday, Apr. 1 through Nov. 30. Admission charged.

The plantation, which was named after the Flowerdew family from England, was one of the earliest English settlements in North America. Ex-

Excavators at a site in Thunderbird Archeological Park found an area they call a chipping floor where a great many chunks of stone revealed that it had been used as a place for the manufacture of stone implements. Thunderbird Research Corporation photo.

cavation has revealed Native American occupation of the same area as early as 9000 B.C. Artifacts from the period before 1618, when the English took over, are on display in a museum here, along with materials that range from the Colonial Period up through the Civil War. Ongoing excavation, which visitors may watch, has exposed Indian house and village patterns, projectile points, and pottery.

Several colleges and universities have conducted digs at this site, and students have taken part in them. From April to November serious volunteers may join in the work at Flowerdew Hundred where more than 60 sites, historic and prehistoric, have been discovered. Information about the volunteer program may be obtained by writing to Flowerdew Hundred Foundation, 1617 Flowerdew Hundred Road, Hopewell, VA 23860, or by phoning 804-541-8897.

HISTORIC CRAB ORCHARD MUSEUM

At intersection of Virginia 19 and Virginia 460, Tazewell. Open free, Tues-day through Saturday; afternoons, Sunday, May 1 to Nov. 1.

This museum interprets the prehistory and history of Tazewell County, with special emphasis on artifacts from a Late Woodland village located near the museum.

JAMESTOWN FESTIVAL PARK

From Williamsburg drive south 6 miles on Virginia 31 to park entrance. Open daily, all year. Closed Dec. 25 and Jan. 1. Admission charged.

In the New World Pavilion at this park are exhibited 400 prehistoric stone artifacts from Virginia. These date from about 8000 B.C. and represent Early and Late Archaic cultures and Early, Middle, and Late Woodland cultures.

In addition there are dioramas that show Indian tobacco growing at Jamestown and the kind of life that Pocohontas led.

Among the outdoor exhibits is a reconstructed Indian longhouse such as Powhatan might have used.

PAMUNKEY INDIAN MUSEUM

Pamunkey Indian Reservation, King William. From Interstate 95, Kings Dominion exit, drive east on Va. 30, then south on Va. 629. Open Monday through Saturday; afternoons, Sunday. Admission charged.

Exhibits here depict Pamunkey history from Paleo times to the present. Tools and other materials are shown as they would have been seen and used by Native Americans of various periods. Original artifacts are supplemented with replicas.

The Pamunkey Indians were part of the great Powhatan Confederacy—more than 30 tribes that lived on the coastal plain from the border of what is now North Carolina north to Washington, D.C. At the time Europeans arrived Chief Powhatan and his daughter, Pocohontas, lived among the Pamunkey.

A typical village of the 1600s is being constructed by volunteers near the museum. Visitors who want to participate in the construction should call (804) 843-4792.

Clovis points, named for the site near Clovis, New Mexico, where they were first found, appear in a very wide area. These parts of Clovis points are from a site in Thunderbird Archeological Park in Virginia. Thunderbird Research Corporation photo.

PEAKS OF OTTER VISITOR CENTER

At Mile Post 86 on the Blue Ridge Pkwy., near Bedford. Open free, daily, June through Oct.

In addition to wildlife exhibits, this museum displays materials which archeologists recovered in 1965 from a prehistoric campsite nearby. The site, which was discovered in the course of building a lake had been occupied by wandering hunters 5100 to 5600 years ago, according to a radio-carbon date obtained for charcoal from a firepit. Below this there was another occupation, which has not been exactly dated, although it is thought to have been 1000 years earlier. The site has now been flooded by Lake Abbott.

THUNDERBIRD MUSEUM AND ARCHEOLOGICAL PARK

From Front Royal drive 6 miles south on Virginia 340. Open daily, April to November. Admission charged. Camping nearby.

Almost 12,000 years of human occupation have been uncovered here. Two of a number of Paleo-Indian sites along the Shenandoah River are being excavated, as well as an Archaic fishing camp dating from 2000 to 1500 B.C. Visitors may take guided tours and watch archeologists at work during the summer season. A slide show in the museum gives an introduction to the prehistory of the area, and exhibits interpret material found in the digs, which have been conducted for more than ten years. For serious amateurs field schools are conducted in summer, and volunteers may take part in excavation. For information about either the field school or volunteer work, write to Thunderbird Museum, Route 1, Box 432, Front Royal, VA 22630.

VALENTINE MUSEUM

1015 East Clay St., Richmond. Open Tuesday through Saturday; afternoons, Sunday. Admission charged.

Although this museum focuses on the "Life and History of Richmond," it maintains some American Indian material.

Special Interest. The Junior Center of the museum has a program covering the culture of the original population of the area, the Algonquian-speaking Powhatan Indians.

VIRGINIA RESEARCH CENTER FOR ARCHEOLOGY
(See College of William and Mary)

AN INVITATION TO READERS

Do you know about a good prehistoric Indian museum exhibit that is not included in this book? Or an archeological site which is open to the public and adequately protected against vandalism? If you do, please send full information about it, including if possible the mail address of the curator or superintendent, to Franklin and Mary Folsom, authors of *America's Ancient Treasures,* c/o University of New Mexico Press, UNM, Albuquerque, NM 87131. Such information will be valuable when it comes time to update this book.

If you should discover an archeological site which so far as you know has not been excavated or may not be known to archeologists, leave it undisturbed, take a careful note of its location, and send news of your discovery to the nearest of the state archeologists or officials listed below. If you are interested in joining or working with an archeological society, you will find their addresses, too, below.

National and Regional Organizations

American Society for
  Conservation Archaeology
c/o Alexander J. Lindsey, Jr.
Museum of Northern Arizona
Route 4, Box 720
Flagstaff, AZ 80001

The Archaeological Conservancy
45 Orchard Drive
Santa Fe, N.M. 87501

Archaeological Institute of America
260 West Broadway
New York, NY 10013

Archaeological Survey of Canada
National Museum of Man
Ottawa, Ontario K1A OM8
Canada

Center for American Archeology
PO Box 1499
Evanston, IL 60204

Central States Archeological Societies
1228 West Essex
St. Louis, MO 63122

Eastern States Archeological
  Federation
Box 260
Washington, CT 06793

Society for American Archaeology
1703 New Hampshire Ave., N.W.
Washington, DC 20009

State or Provincial Archeologists; National, State, and Local Organizations

Alabama: McDonald Brooms
                Staff Archaeologist

Alabama Historical Commission
Montgomery, AL 36092

Alabama Archaeological Society
c/o Eugene Futato, Editor
1 Mound State Park
Moundville, AL 35474

Office of Archaeological Research
University of Alabama
Box BA
University, AL 35486

Alaska: Doug Reger
State Archaeologist
Department of Natural Resources
323 East 4th Ave.
Anchorage, AK 99501

Alaska Anthropological Association
University of Alaska
2651 Providence Drive
Anchorage, AK 99504

Alberta: Director
Archaeological Survey of Alberta
10158 103rd St.
Edmonton, Alberta T5JOX9
Canada

Arizona: Paul Fish
Staff Archeologist
Arizona State Museum
Tucson, AZ 85721

Arizona Archaeological & Historical
Society
Arizona State Museum
University of Arizona
Tucson, AZ 85721

Arizona Archaeological Society
PO Box 9665
Phoenix, AZ 85020

Local Chapters

Cochise Chapter
Arizona Archaeological Society
PO Box 477
Douglas, AZ 85607

Desert Foothills Chapter
Arizona Archaeological Society
PO Box 1864
Cave Creek, AZ 85331

Phoenix Chapter
Arizona Archaeological Society
9310 Briarwood Circle
Sun City, AZ 85351

Verde Valley Chapter
Arizona Archaeological Society
PO Box 1057
Sedona, AZ 86336

Yavapai Chapter
Arizona Archaeological Society
PO Box 828
Prescott, AZ 83602

Yuma Chapter
Arizona Archaeological Society
PO Box 4997
Yuma, AZ 85364

Arkansas: Hester Davis
State Archaeologist
Arkansas Archaeological Survey
Fayetteville, AR 72701

Arkansas Archaeological Society
University Museum
University of Arkansas
Fayetteville, AR 72701

Northwest Arkansas Archaeological
Society
Box 1154
Fayetteville, AR 72701

British
Columbia: Provincial Archaeologist
Archaeological Sites· Advisory Board
St. Ann's Academy
Parliament Buildings
Victoria, British Columbia V8V 1X4
Canada

California: William Seidel, Archaeologist
Office of Historic Preservation
Department of Parks & Recreation
PO Box 2390
Sacramento, CA 95811

Society of California Archaeology
Dept. of Anthropology
California State University
Fullerton, CA 92634

Archaeological Research Facility
University of California, Berkeley
Berkeley, CA 94720

Institute of Archaeology
UCLA Extension
10995 Le Conte Ave.
Los Angeles, CA 90024

Kern County Archaeological Society
PO Box 6743
Bakersfield, CA 93306

Los Angeles Archaeological Survey
University of California,
Los Angeles
Los Angeles, CA 90023

Pacific Coast Archaeological Society
Box 926
Costa Mesa, CA 92627

San Diego County Archaeological
Society
Box 187
Encinitas, CA 92024

San Luis Obispo Archaeology Society
PO Box 109
San Luis Obispo, CA 93406

Colorado   Emerson Pearson
State Archaeologist
1300 Broadway
Denver, CO 80203

Colorado Archaeological Society
PO Box 27339
Lakewood, CO 80227

Adrienne Anderson, President
Colorado Council of Professional
Archaeologists
National Park Service
Rocky Mountain Regional Office
PO Box 25297
Denver, CO 89225

State Historical Society of Colorado
Colorado Heritage Center
1300 Broadway
Denver, CO 80203

Connecticut: Douglas F. Jordan
State Archaeologist
University of Connecticut
Storrs, CT 06268

Archaeological Society of Connecticut
c/o Dr. Roger Moeller
American Indian Archaeological
Institute
Box 85
Washington, CT 06793

Connecticut Historical Commission
595 Prospect St.
Hartford, CT 06106

Albert Morgan Archaeological Society
c/o Charles Rignal
185 Hubbard St.
Glastonbury, CT 06033

Archaeological Associates of
Greenwich
Bryan Drive
Greenwich, CT 06870

Archaeological Society of Southern
Connecticut
PO Box 654
Old Lyme, CT 06371

Fort Stamford Restoration
c/o Elizabeth Gershman
86 Saddle Hill Road
Greenwich, CT 06870

New Haven Archaeological Society
c/o David Thompson
403 Bethmore Road
Bethany, CT 06525

Norwalk Community College
Archaeology Club
33 Wilson Ave.
Norwalk, CT 06854

Southeastern Connecticut
Archaeological Community
c/o Earl Claypool
23 Plymouth Road
Stamford, CT 06906

Delaware: Claudia F. Melson
Bureau of Museums and Historic Sites
Hall of Records
Dover, DE 19901

Kent County Chapter
The Archaeological Society of
Delaware
52 S. Old Mill Road
Dover, DE 19901

Minguaannan Chapter
The Archaeological Society of
Delaware
State Road, Box 310
Avondale, PA 19311

Sussex Society for Archaeology and
History
R.D. #3
Box 190
Laurel, DE 19956

Tancopanican Chapter
The Archaeological Society of
Delaware
15 Myrtle Ave.
Claymont, DE 19703

Florida:
L. Ross Morrell
State Archaeologist
Florida Department of State
Tallahassee, FL 32304

Florida Anthropological Society
Florida State Museum
University of Florida
Gainesville, FL 32611

Pensacola Historical Society
Old Christ Church
405 S. Adams St.
Seville Square
Pensacola, FL 32501

Suncoast Archaeology Society, Inc.
2216 Third St., N.
St. Petersburg, FL 33704

Tallahassee Historical Society
Florida State University
Tallahassee, FL 32306

Georgia:
Lewis H. Larson, Jr.
State Archaeologist
Room 102, Martha Munro Hall
West Georgia College
Carrollton, GA 30117

Society for Georgia Archaeology
c/o Patrick H. Garrow
Earth Systems Division,
    Soils Systems, Inc.
525 Webb Industrial Drive
Marietta, GA 30062

Augusta Archaeological Society
2206 Mura Drive
Augusta, GA 29208

Northwest Georgia Archaeological
    Society
Shorter College
Rome, GA 30161

Idaho:
Thomas J. Green
State Archaeologist
610 N. Julia Davis Drive
Boise, ID 83706

Idaho Archaeological Society
Box 7532
Boise, ID 83702

Illinois:
Margaret Kimball Brown
Staff Archaeologist
405 E. Washington St.
Springfield, IL 62706

Illinois Archaeological Survey
109 Davenport Hall
University of Illinois
Urbana, IL 61801

Illinois Society of Archaeology
c/o Tom Razmus
607 Park St.
Georgetown, IL 61846

Cahokia Mounds Museum Society
7850 Collinsville Road
East St. Louis, IL 62201

Southern Illinois Historical Society
Southern Illinois University
Carbondale, IL 62901

Upper Mississippi Valley
    Archaeological Foundation
2216 West 112th St.
Chicago, IL 60643

Center for American Archeology at
    Northwestern University
PO Box 1499
Evanston, IL 60204

Indiana:
James Kellar
Archaeologist
Department of Anthropology
Indiana University
Bloomington, IN 47401

Indiana Historical Society
315 West Ohio St.
Indianapolis, IN 46202

Indiana Society of Archaeology
590 N. Washington St.
Scottsburg, IN 47170

Indianapolis Amateur Archaeological
    Association, Inc.
Glen A. Black Laboratory of
    Archaeology
Indiana University
Bloomington, IN 47401

Northwest Indiana Archaeological
    Association
c/o Anthropology Department
University of Notre Dame
South Bend, IN 46600

Wabash Valley Archaeological Society
c/o Anthropology Department
Indiana State University
Terre Haute, IN 47809

Iowa: Duane C. Anderson
State Archaeologist
Eastlawn
University of Iowa
Iowa City, IA 52242

Iowa Archeologist Society
East Lawn
University of Iowa
Iowa City, IA 52242

Quad City Archaeological Society
4106 El Rancho Drive
Davenport, IA 52806

Kansas: Thomas A. Witty, Jr.
State Archaeologist
120 West Tenth
Topeka, KS 66612

Don Rowlinson
Kansas Anthropological Association
Route 2
Beloit, KS 67420

Kansas State Historical Society
120 West Tenth
Topeka, KS 66612

Archaeological Association of South-
Central Kansas
PO Box 52
Wichita State University
Wichita, KS 67208

Kentucky: R. Berle Clay
State Archaeologist
Department of Anthropology
University of Kentucky
Lexington, KY 40506

Kentucky Archaeological Association
Department of Sociology & Anthropology
Western Kentucky University
Bowling Green, KY 42101

Kentucky Historical Society
Old State House
PO Box H
Frankfort, KY 40601

Local Chapters

Bowling Green Chapter of the
Kentucky Archaeological
Association
c/o Department of Sociology and
Anthropology
Western Kentucky University
Bowling Green, KY 42101

Louisville Archaeological Society
Chapter
Kentucky Archaeological
Association, Inc.
c/o Lewis Soule
2906 Brinkley Way, Apartment 2
Louisville, KY 40218

Louisiana: Kathleen Byrd
State Archaeologist
Division of Archaeology & Historic
Preservation
PO Box 44247
Baton Rouge, LA 70804

Tommy Johnson
Louisiana Archaeological Society
307 Dulles
Lafayette, LA 70506

Maine: Bruce Bourque
Staff Archaeologist
Maine State Museum
Augusta, ME 04333

Maine Archaeological Society
Box 133
Stillwater, ME 04489

Manitoba: Staff Archaeologist
Historic Resources Branch
Department of Tourism, Recreational
and Cultural Affairs
200 Vaughan St.
Winnipeg, Manitoba R3C 0P8
Canada

Maryland: Tyler Bastian
State Archeologist
Maryland Geological Survey
Merryman Hall
Johns Hopkins University
Baltimore, MD 21218

Archeological Society of Maryland,
Inc.
c/o Mary Lathroum
729 Hollen Road
Baltimore, MD 21212

Massachusetts: Valerie Talmage
State Archaeologist
Massachusetts Historical Commission
294 Washington St.
Boston, MA 02109

Massachusetts Archaeological Society
Bronson Museum
8 North Main St.
Attleboro, MA 02703

Michigan:

John R. Halsey
State Archaeologist
Michigan History Division
Department of State
Lansing, MI 48918

Michigan Archaeological Association
Department of Anthropology
Western Michigan State University
Kalamazoo, MI 49001

Michigan Archaeological Society
Museum of Anthropology
University of Michigan
Ann Arbor, MI 48104

Local Chapters

Clinton Valley Chapter
Michigan Archaeological Society
c/o Don Hays
Cranbrook Institute of Science
500 Lone Pine Road
Box 801
Bloomfield Hills, MI 48013

Coffinberry Chapter
Michigan Archaeological Society
c/o Kenneth C. Nickel, M.D.
1535 Groton Road, E.
Grand Rapids, MI 49506

Kalamazoo Chapter
Michigan Archaeological Society
c/o Alice Noecker
117 Par Circle 4
Kalamazoo, MI 49008

River Raisin Chapter
Michigan Archaeolocial Society
c/o Dennis Au
Monroe Museum
Monroe, MI 48161

Saginaw Valley Chapter
Michigan Archaeological Society
c/o Bernard A. Spencer
2545 E. Moore Road
Saginaw, MI 48601

Southwest Chapter
Michigan Archaeological Society
c/o Bill Beverly
R–2, Box 529
Watervliet, MI 49098

Upper Grand Valley Chapter
Michigan Archaeological Society
c/o Donna J. Sanford
773 Raymond Road
Owosso, MI 48867

Traverse Bay Chapter
Michigan Archaeological Society

c/o Fel V. Brunett
2165 N. River Road
Saginaw, MI 48603

Minnesota:

Christy A.A. Caine
Office of the State Archaeologist
Hamline University
St. Paul, MN 55104

Minnesota Archaeological Society
Bldg. 25–27, Fort Snelling
St. Paul, MN 55111

Minnesota Historical Society
1500 Mississippi St.
St. Paul, MN 55101

Mississippi:

Samuel McGahey
Staff Archaeologist
Department of Archives & History
PO Box 571
Jackson, MS 39205

Mississippi Archaeological Association
c/o Mary G. Neumaier
115 Wiltshire Blvd.
Biloxi, MS 39531

Local Chapters

Clarksdale Chapter
Mississippi Archaeological
   Association
615 Oakhurst Ave.
Clarksdale, MS 38614

Gulf Coast Chapter
Mississippi Archaeological
   Association
115 Wiltshire Blvd.
Biloxi, MS 39531

Winterville Mounds Chapter
Mississippi Archaeological
   Association
Route 2, Box 146
Shaw, MS 38773

Missouri:

Michael Weichman
Senior Archaeologist
PO Box 176
1204 Jefferson Building
Jefferson City, MO 65101

Missouri Archaeological Society
PO Box 958
Columbia, MO 65205

Montana:

Thomas Allyn Foor
State Archaeologist
Historic Preservation Office

Montana Historical Society
225 North Roberts
Helena, MT 59601

Montana Archaeological Association
State Office of Historic Preservation
Montana Historical Society
225 North Roberts
Helena, MT 59601

Montana Archaeological Society
Dept. of Anthropology
University of Montana
Missoula, MT 59801

Nebraska: Gayle Carlson
Senior Archaeologist
State Historical Society
1500 "R" St.
Lincoln, NE 68508

Nebraska State Historical Society
1500 "R" St.
Lincoln, NE 68508

Nevada: Charles D. Zeier
Staff Archaeologist
State Historic Preservation Office
201 S. Fall St.
Carson City, NV 89710

Nevada Archeological Society
University of Nevada
Reno, NV 89507

Nevada Historical Society
1650 North Virginia St.
Reno, NV 89503

Am-Arcs of Nevada
PO Box 552
Reno, NV 89504

Archeo-Nevada Society
Box 5744
Las Vegas, NV 89102

New
Brunswick: Provincial Archaeologist
Historic Resources Administration
Research and Development Branch
Box 6000
Fredericton, New Brunswick
Canada

Newfoundland: Dr. James Tuck
Department of Anthropology
Memorial University
St. John's, Newfoundland A1C 5S7
Canada

New
Hampshire: Gary W. Hume
Staff Archaeologist
Department of Sociology &
    Anthropology
University of New Hampshire
Durham, NH 03824

New Hampshire Archeological
    Society
Averill Road
Brookline, NH 03103

New
Jersey: Lorraine E. Williams
State Archaeologist
New Jersey State Museum
205 W. State St.
Trenton, NJ 08625

Archaeological Society of New Jersey
Room 106, Humanities Building
Seton Hall University
South Orange, NJ 07079

Local Chapters

Abnaki, Salem County Chapter
Archaeological Society of New
    Jersey
Garrison Road, R.D. 1
Monroeville, NJ 08343

Minisink, Sussex and Warren
    Counties Chapter
Archaeological Society of New
    Jersey
Newton, NJ 07860

Monmouth County Chapter
Archaeological Society of New
    Jersey
407 Sunset Ave.
Asbury Park, NJ 07712

Southern New Jersey Chapter
Archaeological Society of New
    Jersey
316 Middlesex St.
Gloucester, NJ 08030

Unami, Middlesex, Monmouth,
    and Mercer Counties Chapter
Archaeological Society of New
    Jersey
95 Broad St.
Matawan, NJ 07747

New
Mexico: Curtis Schaafsma
State Archaeologist

Museum of New Mexico
PO Box 2087
Santa Fe, NM 87503

Archaeological Society of New Mexico
Box 3485
Albuquerque, NM 87110

Gallup Archaeological Society
Dr. Caroline Davis, Director
Gallup Museum of Indian Arts
Box 328
Church Rock, NM 87503

New York:

Robert Funk
State Archaeologist
Cultural Education Center, Rm. 3122
Albany, NY 12203

New York State Archeological
Association
c/o Dr. Elizabeth M. Dumont
29 Highridge Road
Monroe, NY 10905

North Carolina:

Jacqueline R. Fehon
Chief Archaeologist
Division of Archives & History
Department of Cultural Resources
109 E. Jones St.
Raleigh, NC 27611

Archaeological Society of North
Carolina
Research Laboratory of Anthropology
University of North Carolina
Chapel Hill, NC 27514

North Dakota:

Signe Snortland-Coles
Research Archaeologist
State Historical Society of North
Dakota
North Dakota Heritage Center
Bismarck, ND 58505

North Dakota Archaeological
Association
809 North 9th St.
Bismarck, ND 58501

Northwest Territories:

Coordinator of Historical Programs
Natural and Cultural Affairs
Government of the Northwest
Territories

Yellowknife, Northwest Territories
X1A 2L9
Canada

Nova Scotia:

Curator of History
Nova Scotia Museum
Halifax, Nova Scotia B3H 3A6
Canada

Ohio:

Bert Drennen
Ohio Historical Preservation Office
Ohio Historical Society
The Ohio Historical Center
I–71 & 17th Avenue
Columbus, OH 43211

Ohio Archaeological Council
c/o Martha Potter Otto
Department of Archaeology
I–71 &17th Ave.
Columbus, OH 43211

Regional Archaeological Preservation
Office
Department of Anthropology
College of Social and Behavioral
Sciences
Ohio State University
213 Lord Hall
124 West 17th Ave.
Columbus, OH 43210

Archaeological Society of Ohio
c/o Mr. Summers Redick
35 West River Glen Drive
Worthington, OH 43085

Toledo Aboriginal Research Club
Department of Sociology and
Anthropology
University of Toledo
2801 West Bancroft St.
Toledo, OH 43600

Oklahoma:

State Archaeologist
Oklahoma Archaeological Survey
Department of Anthropology
University of Oklahoma
1335 South Asp Ave.
Norman, OK 73019

Oklahoma Anthropological Society
Department of Anthropology
University of Oklahoma
1335 South Asp Ave.
Norman, OK 73019

University of Tennessee
Knoxville, TN 37916

Tennessee Archaeological Society
c/o Division of Archaeology
5103 Edmondson Pike
Nashville, TN 37211

Volunteer State Archaeological
Society of Tennessee
Tennessee Department of
Conservation
Division of Archaeology
5103 Edmondson Pike
Nashville, TN 37211

Texas:
Curtis Tunnell
State Archeologist
Texas Historical Commission
Box 12276, Capitol Station
Austin, TX 78711

Archaeology Research Program
Department of Anthropology
Southern Methodist University
Dallas, TX 725275

Texas Archeological Society
Center for Archeological Research
University of Texas at San Antonio
San Antonio, TX 78285

Local Chapters

Central Texas Archaeological
Society
4229 Mitchell Road
Waco, TX 76710

Coastal Bend Archeological Society
c/o 326 Troy
Corpus Christi, TX 78412

Concho Valley Archaeological
Society
213 East Ave. D
San Angelo, TX 76901

Dallas Archaeological Society
c/o Archaeology Research Program
Southern Methodist University
Dallas, TX 75275

East Texas Chapter
Oklahoma Anthropological Society
Box 374
Jacksboro, TX 75056

El Paso Archaeological Society
PO Box 4345
El Paso, TX 77914

Houston Archaeological Society
1706 Oaks Drive
Pasadena, TX 77502

Iraan Archaeological Society
PO Box 183
Iraan, TX 79744

Midland Archaeological Society
PO Box 4022
Midland, TX 79701

Panhandle Archaeological Society
PO Box 814
Amarillo, TX 79105

Southern Texas Archaeological
Association
132 East Crestline
San Antonio, TX 78201

Southwest Texas Archaeological
Society
620 Terrell Road
San Antonio, TX 78209

Tarrant County Archaeological
Society
413 East Lavender
Arlington, TX 76010

Travis County Archaeological
Society
1507 Lorrain
Austin, TX 78703

Webb County Archaeological
Society
c/o Dr. Leon DeKing
Texas A&I University at Laredo
Laredo, TX 78040

Utah:
David Madsen
State Archaeologist
Crane Building, Suite 1000
307 West 2nd South
Salt Lake City, UT 84102

Utah Archaeological Society
Department of Anthropology
University of Utah
Salt Lake City, UT 84122

Vermont:
Giovanna Neudorfer
State Archaeologist
Division for Historic Preservation
Pavilion Building
Montpelier, VT 05602

Champlain Maritime Society
Box 745
Burlington, VT 05402

Vermont Archeological Society
Box 663
Burlington, VT 05402

Virginia: Commissioner of Archaeology
Virginia Research Center for
   Archaeology
Wren Kitchen
College of William & Mary
Williamsburg, VA 23186

Archaeological Society of Virginia
c/o Col. Howard A. Maccord, Sr.
562 Rossmore Road
Richmond, VA 23225

Chesopiean Archaeological
   Association
c/o D. Painter
7507 Pennington Road
Norfolk, VA 23500

Washington: Sheila Stump
State Archaeologist
111 W. 21st Ave.
Olympia, WA 98501

Washington Archaeological Society
Department of Anthropology
University of Washington
Seattle, WA 98195

Mid-Columbia Archaeological Society
c/o State Archaeologist
Washington Archaeological Society
Department of Anthropology
University of Washington
Seattle, WA 98195

West
Virginia: Jeffrey R. Graybill
Geological and Economic Survey
Archaeological Section
Box 897
Morgantown, WV 26505

West Virginia Archeological Society
c/o Thomas Kuhn
2124 11th Ave.
Huntington, WV 25703

Wisconsin: Joan Freeman
State Archeologist
State Historical Society of Wisconsin
816 State St.
Madison, WI 53706

Wisconsin Archaeological Society
Box 1292
Milwaukee, WI 53201

Wyoming: George Frison
State Archaeologist
University of Wyoming
Laramie, WY 82071

Wyoming Archaeological Society
Department of Anthropology
University of Wyoming
Laramie, WY 82071

Yukon: Yukon Archaeologist
Archaeological Survey of Canada
National Museum of Man
Ottawa, Ontario K1A 0M8
Canada

GLOSSARY

Here are some words and terms that may be encountered at archeological sites and exhibits and in readily available literature about archeology. Words defined in the text of this book are not included in the glossary, but may be found by referring to the index.

abrader; abradingstone. A stone tool used in grinding or shaping tools or other articles.

absolute dates. When archeologists know how many years ago a dwelling was built or between what calendar years a pot was made, they say they have an absolute date. Absolute dates can be obtained in various ways—for example, from certain kinds of *tree rings* (see feature in text) in certain places. Dates obtained from the analysis of the carbon-14 (see feature in text) content of organic matter are considered absolute dates, although they cannot be pinpointed at an exact calendar year.

acculturation. The process by which one group of people takes on the lifeways, institutions, technology of another group with which it has close association. Usually the less advanced group is influenced by the more advanced group, but the acculturation process may also be reciprocal. Individuals as well as groups may become acculturated.

adobe. A gritty, clay-like buff or brown material used in the prehistoric Southwest as mortar, plaster, amorphous building material for walls, and occasionally as hand-molded, sun-dried bricks, called *adobes.* This type of construction is still used in the Southwest. The word comes from Spanish.

altithermal. A period also called the Great Drought, or Long Drought, which lasted from about 5000 B.C. to 2000 B.C.

amateur. One who is actively interested in archeology but has not had advanced academic training in the subject or who does not make his living in some pursuit connected with the study of prehistory. Amateurs have made important contributions to archeology, and many professionals welcome their help.

Amateurs can be useful in various ways. They can provide extra eyes to look for sites, extra hands for digging and record keeping and sorting, and extra brains, too. It does not take a college education to be intelligent, but it does take intelligence to be an archeologist, whether amateur or professional.

Amerind; Amerindian. A shortcut word meaning American Indian, sometimes used as a convenient way to distinguish American aborigines from the inhabitants of India. Some scholars have objected to the word, which was already in use at the time of a Congress of Americanists in New York in 1902. The menu for the Congress banquet included "Amerind Siouxp." When it came time for Frederic Ward Putnam to speak at the banquet, he remarked, "Amerind seems to have been placed where it belongs—in the soup."

The Amerind Foundation of Dragoon, Arizona, an important archeological research organization, obviously does not agree with Putnam.

amino acid racemization. Certain substances in living organisms are called L-amino acids. When an organism dies, L-amino acids slowly change into D-amino acids (the technical word for this change is racemization). The longer an organism has been dead, the more D-amino acids it contains in relation to L-amino acids. A comparison of the two forms of amino acid tells how long an organism has been dead. However, the history of the temperature of the soil in which the dead organism was buried must be taken into account. The rate of change of L into D-amino acid can vary widely from one place to another, depending on temperature.

Amino acid racemization dates for some skeletal material in Southern California are older than many archeologists are willing to accept, but some researchers claim the method gives dates that check well with C-14 dates on the same material. The method is supposed to work with reasonable accuracy up to 100,000 years ago.

anathermal. A period, a little cooler than the present, which lasted from 7000 B.C. to 5000 B.C.

archeomagnetism. See paleomagnetism.

articulated. Archeologists say a skeleton is articulated when the bones in it are in the same relationship to each other as they were when the person (or other creature) was alive.

assemblage. A collection of artifacts, features, and non-human-made remains that are clearly associated with each other. An assemblage may be in a dig, or may come from a dig or from the surface.

associated; association. When archeologists say an artifact was found associated with certain other material, they mean that it is necessary to assume that the artifact and the material belong together; they were probably made and/or used by the same people at about the same time.

Artifacts may be found next to each other in the earth and still not be associated. For example, in the Southwest a modern pipeline may lie within inches of the wall of an ancient kiva. The two are not in association as archeologists use the term. The pipeline is *intrusive.* Indians often dug into trash heaps left by earlier people, making holes in which to bury the dead. The burials are intrusive.

An archeologist constantly questions and evaluates the association of material in a site. Have all the artifacts been lying together in a certain layer of earth for the same length of time? Or did a tool, for example, drop through a rodent hole to a lower level? The reverse may also be true. Did a rodent carry an object upward from somewhere deep underground, and can the object therefore belong to an earlier culture than its position indicates?

Atlantis. A mythical prehistoric continent, which was supposed to have existed between Africa and the New World before sinking beneath the surface of the Atlantic Ocean. Some people persist in believing in it, although scientists have failed to find evidence that it existed, and oceanographers who have studied the sea floor say it did not.

backfill. As an archeological crew digs a site it often piles the excavated earth to one side. Later it puts the earth back to fill in the excavation. The purpose of backfilling may be simply to prevent erosion. It also helps to prevent vandalizing of unexcavated portions of a site which scientists hope to study at some later time.

biface; bifacial. A stone artifact from which flakes have been removed from both of two opposite sides.

biomass. The total plant and animal life, calculated by weight, existing at a given time on a given land area.

blade. An early kind of tool was made by knocking off chips from a stone in order to shape it into usable form. Later, people made a great technological advance when they found that they could strike some kinds of stone in a certain way and knock off a chip that had two sharp edges. Each edge could serve as a knife, and such a chip was often called a blade, if it was large, or a micro-blade, if small. A blade could also be reshaped to form a projectile point or any one of several other kinds of tool. Instead of making only one tool out of a chunk of stone, a knapper (see below) could now make many tools. The amount of cutting edge that could be obtained from one piece of stone was greatly increased. One present-day experimenter found that he could get up to 75 inches of working edge from a two-pound nodule of flint. Prehistoric people saved a great deal of energy when they adopted the practice of making blades. They did not have to mine or transport nearly as much stone as had been necessary before. Also the invention of blades led to still another invention—handles. A handle made it easier—and much safer—to manipulate a sharp, two-edged blade.

blank. A partly finished stone artifact, given rough shape at a quarry or workshop and often taken elsewhere for completion. Blanks were presumably made in quantity because they were easier to carry from place to place than heavy, unshaped lumps of flint or other stone. Caches of blanks have turned up in burials, on habitation sties, and also in places where no other artifacts are found. Some rough tools found at quarries, although they have been called blanks, may instead have been made on the spot, used, and then discarded. Close examination of the edges of these "blanks" reveals the kind of dulling that comes from use on wood. Presumably the toolmakers brought wood to the quarry and shaped it there, where they had readily available sharp flakes of stone. Laborious resharpening of a worn edge was not necessary, since a new flake could be struck off and shaped with a few quick blows.

blowout. When wind blows away topsoil in an arid region it creates a blowout. Sometimes when earth is removed in this way archeological sites are revealed.

bola. A weight, usually globular or pear-shaped, made of stone, bone, ivory, or ceramic, and grooved or pierced so it could be fastened to a thong. Bolas, tied together usually three to a group, were used for hunting. The hunter threw the bolas so as to entangle the legs and/or wings of the prey.

buck. A male deer. People who have the illusion that they are members of a superior race sometimes use this word to refer to young Indian males. The term is offensive to Native Americans.

burial. Archeologists can learn a great deal about prehistoric societies by studying skeletons and the way they were buried. In some cultures bodies were buried stretched out in an extended position; in others they were placed in the ground in a fetal, or flexed, position with knees drawn up to chest. In still other societies the dead were exposed on platforms or in charnel houses. When the flesh had been removed by decay or scavengers, the disarticulated bones were made into a bundle and buried. Sometimes bodies were cremated and the remains buried. Careful study of bones can reveal sex, age, and often something about nutrition and disease. Goods interred with a burial give many clues to the social position of the person buried and the kind of culture from which he or she came.

burin. A piece of stone with a sharp point, used like a one-tooth saw for shaping or engraving bone or shell or wood. A blade (see above) or a flake could be formed into any one of about twenty varieties of the tool.

cache. When archeologists find a group of identical artifacts buried together they call the collection a cache—from the French word meaning *to hide.* Sometimes the artifacts are finished; sometimes they are not. Often it is difficult to know whether the objects in a cache were hidden for safe keeping, for ceremonial purposes, or for some other reason.

cesium magnetometer. An operator walks across a field carrying this device, which detects large structures underground and is more efficient than a proton magnetomator (see below), which does the same thing.

chiefdom. When a group of people had an ample food supply in one place, they often developed a social structure based on wealth. On the Northwest Coast of the United States, for example, a social pyramid evolved, with the most prestigious man at the top. He was a chief, and the sedentary people over whom he ruled formed a chiefdom. Many less affluent, more mobile groups also had chiefs, but these individuals had less power and their societies are not called chiefdoms.

chopper; chopping tool. This stone tool had a single cutting edge and could be held in one hand and used for chopping. Some archeologists say a chopper is made by knocking off flakes from only one side of a piece of stone, and that a chopping tool is made by knocking flakes off both sides. But the use of this distinction is not universal.

coiling. A term used in both pottery and basketry. When a potter shapes moist clay into a long, ropelike form, then builds up a pot by winding this clay rope round and round on itself, the method is called coiling.

A basket is said to be coiled when a long bundle of fibrous material is laid up, spiral fashion. Each coil is sewed by a slender splint to the coil below it. The basketmaker pierces the fiber bundle with a bone awl and passes the splint through the hole thus made.

collagen dating. Collagen is a protein abundant in living bone. Like all protein it contains nitrogen, which makes up about 4 percent of its weight. After death the collagen remains in bone, but it decays at a measurable rate. The amount of decay can be determined by measuring the percentage of nitrogen that remains in the collagen. However, the length of time it takes nitrogen to disappear from bone varies with temperature and other aspects of the environment. Therefore the nitrogen test cannot give an absolute date. It can tell only whether two pieces of bone in the same deposit are of the same age. If, for example, the nitrogen test shows that a leg bone in one part of a dig is older than a skull found in another part, then the archeologist must conclude that the person to whom the skull belonged was buried there at a date later than another person, whose leg bone was found. In other words, by itself collagen dating can only give relative dates for different bone samples from a particular site.

core. The part of a stone that is left after chips or blades have been removed. A core may be waste material or it may itself be a tool.

cross dating. When a date for a certain type of pottery, for example, is known at one site, an archeologist attributes a similar date to another site in which the same kind of pottery appears. This is cross dating. It is not precise, but it is helpful.

cultural evolution. The progressive development of a culture.

culture. All that a group of people makes, does, thinks, believes.

culture area. A geographic area in which one culture prevailed at a given time.

culture trait. Any phenomenon that is an element in the total culture of a group of people.

dating methods. See *absolute dating, amino acid racemization, collagen dating, cross dating, deep sea core dating, fission track dating, glottochronology, magnetic dating, nitrogen dating, paleomagnetic dating, potassium-argon dating, relative dating, tephrachronology, thermoluminescent dating, varve dating*

debitage. When material is struck off a stone in order to make an artifact, the waste material is called debitage. Study of debitage can reveal a good deal about techniques used by knappers (see below).

deduction. A process of thinking sometimes used in archeology, which involves reasoning from the general to the specific, or, as one archeologist put it, "from a lucky guess" about what prehistoric people were doing "to a provable fact."

deep sea core dating. Changes in climate produce changes in the life forms in the ocean, and as sea creatures die their shells or skeletons accumulate in sediment on the ocean floor. When drilling equipment recovers sediment cores, the sequence of life forms can be studied and equated to changes in climate on land. This broad method of dating gives information about the Pleistocene, or Ice Age, during which human beings lived. So in a very general way deep sea cores can give some information about the conditions in which people have existed for the last 1,500,000 years.

desert pavement. Because some Southwestern archeological finds have been made in what is called desert pavement, the words appear in archeological literature. They refer to terrain that is thickly covered—or paved—with small rocks. Vegetation is scarce, and for this reason soil, sand, and gravel have not been held in place and have been blown away by wind or washed away by infrequent but violent rainstorms, leaving only rocks too large for wind or water to move.

desert varnish. See patination

diagnostic trait. A cultural trait that helps to distinguish one group of people from another. A diagnostic trait appears in one group but not in another with which it might be confused.

diffusion. The movement of human ideas or customs— even domesticated plants and animals—from one place to another. When people migrate they take their habits with them. This is primary diffusion. When ideas or customs, but not the people who have them, move from one place to another, the phenomenon is called secondary diffusion. The spread of agriculture across much of North America was secondary diffusion.

disarticulated. Bones out of their natural arrangement. See also articulated.

ecotone. The dividing line between two different ecological communities.

fission track dating. Spontaneous fission of minute amounts of uranium leaves tracks in obsidian, human-made glass, and other crystals. These tracks can be observed by special techniques, and the number of tracks is proportional to the time that has elapsed since the material was formed.

flake. A chip that has been forced off a larger piece of stone. Tools are shaped and sharpened by flaking. A tool can also be made from a flake itself.

flaking tool. An implement, often a piece of antler, used in tool making to press flakes off a piece of stone.

flotation. Minute bits of vegetation, tiny mollusks, and insects in the soil of a dig can tell archeologists much about the environment in which people once lived at a site which is being excavated. In order to recover these very small, often very light, bits of evidence, archeologists put soil into water which may be mixed with any one of several chemicals. The heavy particles sink to the bottom and the sought-after, light-weight material rises to the surface, where it can be removed and studied.

fluorine dating. Bones and teeth absorb fluorine when they are in the soil. The longer they are buried, the more they absorb, so it is possible to obtain relative dates (see below) for bones buried at different times in the same area.

glottochronology. A way of arriving at a date of separation between two languages that have a common origin by studying the extent to which they have diverged from each other.

graver. A tool for engraving. See also burin.

grid system. A way of dividing a site into quadrangles to make it easy to describe exactly where in the site a find is made.

hearth. A place where a fire has been built, sometimes identified by charcoal, sometimes by baked earth. Hearths often appear in one layer of soil after another as an archeologist digs down through a site, and they are an indication of a succession of camps or habitations. Charcoal from a hearth can be dated by the radiocarbon method. Baked clay in a hearth can be dated by the paleomagnetic method. Either method tells when human activity went on at the spot.

hydration rate. See obsidian hydration

hypothesis. An unproved theory. Scientists find hypotheses useful as they search for new knowledge. In a science such as archeology, which is developing rapidly, new hypotheses are constantly appearing, and hypotheses that are not very old are constantly being discarded. These discarded hypotheses are signs of growth and advance. When investigators have tried a theory and found it wanting, they have eliminated one wrong solution to a problem. They know one direction in which they do not have to go in order to find an answer. So to a good scientist it is not frustrating to have to give up a hypothesis. Indeed this act can be a source of satisfaction and pleasure. In a very real sense it turns the searcher away from illusion.

indirect dating. When object A is found clearly associated with object B, whose date is known, the date of B is given to A. This is called indirect dating.

induction. A proces of thinking much used in archeology, which involves reasoning from the specific to the general. See also deduction.

industry. When similar sets of particular kinds of artifact appear again and again, archeologists refer to these similar groups of artifacts as an industry. They are presumed to have been made by people who had a common culture.

in situ. An archeologist uses these Latin words (meaning "in place") to say that an object is in exactly the place where it was found.

knapper. One who makes stone implements by chipping.

law of superposition. In undisturbed deposits of soil the top layer is the most recent, the bottom layer the oldest.

lexico-statistical dating. See glottochronology.

lithic. Having to do with stone.

magnetic dating. Clay contains iron that is slightly magnetic. When clay is baked—in pottery or beneath a fire—the magnetic fields of the molecules of this iron are aligned in relation to the position of the earth's magnetic pole at the time when the clay was very hot. If the clay has not been moved since it was last heated, it is possible to determine where the pole was when the clay was hot. The magnetic pole of the earth is known to have wandered, and its wanderings have been charted in a general way for hundreds of thousands of years. The exact position of the pole has been traced throughout the last 2000 years. Accordingly it is possible, by determining the orientation of the iron molecules in unmoved baked clay, to determine the date at which it was last heated. This fact makes it possible to determine when a campfire baked the clay beneath it or when a kiln was last used for firing pottery. If pottery was left in the kiln after the last firing, it is possible to date the pottery. This method is also called paleomagnetic dating.

magnetic surveying. See proton magnetometer.

model. A theory that is to be tested to see if it is valid. *See also hypothesis.*

Mongoloid. A major race of humankind to which American Indians, Eskimos, and Aleuts belong.

Mu. A mythical, sunken continent supposed to have been in the Pacific Ocean. *See also Atlantis.*

neutron activization analysis. Each natural deposit of obsidian, flint, clay, and of some other lithic materials contains a unique pattern of trace elements. Neutron activization makes it possible to determine from what source an obsidian blade or a flint arrowhead or the clay in a pot comes. In a laboratory the artifact is subjected to a bombardment of neutrons. These neutrons, interacting with the nuclei of trace elements in the material, form radioactive isotopes. Each isotope gives off gamma rays with a characteristic energy. By measuring the energy of each ray, it is possible to identify the isotope from which it comes. Then, by discovering the pattern of trace elements in an object and comparing it with the patterns of trace elements in natural deposits of the material, it is possible to determine from which quarry the material comes.

For example, neutron activation analysis of certain Hopewell artifacts made of obsidian has proved that the source of the obsidian was in what is now Yellowstone National Park. This fact in turn throws light on the trade routes used by Hopewellians.

nitrogen dating. See collagen dating

obsidian hydration dating. In each specific environment, the surface of an obsidian artifact absorbs water at a steady rate, forming what is called a hydration layer. The thicker the layer, the older the artifact.

osteodontokeratic. When there is no sign that a people used wood or stone for tools, and when it is supposed that this people did make tools of bones, teeth, and horns, their culture is said to be osteodontokeratic. It is difficult to see why this jaw-breaker,

which is not found in most large dictionaries, serves any purpose except to make its user seem learned. It would be just as accurate and a lot easier to understand if scientists referred to "bone-tooth-horn" cultures.

paleo-. A prefix meaning ancient, or prehistoric. The name Paleo-Indians is applied to the earliest people who are known to have lived in the Americas. Special sciences are devoted to paleoastronomy, paleobotany, paleoecology, paeloethnobotany, paleopathology, paleopedology, paleoserology, paleozoology, etc.

paleomagnetic dating. See magnetic dating

palynology. The study of pollen. Each kind of flowering plant produces pollen that is unique, and an expert can tell by looking at a pollen grain exactly what plant produced it. Pollen grains have tough coverings that can last a long time. By studying pollen grains found in ancient soils it is possible to tell what kinds of plant were growing nearby when the soil was formed. Palynology helps archeologists find out what plant resources were available to ancient peoples at different times and what the climate was at those times.

paradigm. Archeologists make increasing use of this word, borrowed from other sciences. It means pattern, or type.

patination. The surface of metal or rock may change color and texture as a result of the action of chemicals in the soil or atmosphere. This new film on a surface is called patina, and the amount of patination is sometimes used as a very rough indicator of age. Because chemical environments vary greatly from place to place and even from time to time, the method is far from precise. The patina on rocks in the southwestern part of the United States is often called desert varnish.

pedology. See soil analysis.

Pleistocene. The million and a half years of the history of the earth that preceded the Holocene period, which began about 11,000 years ago and includes the present. The Pleistocene is sometimes called the Ice Age.

pollen analysis. See palynology

post mould. When one end of a pole or post is buried in the earth, it leaves an outline clearly visible in the soil, long after the post itself has decayed and disappeared. This outline is known as a post mould. By noting carefully the pattern of post moulds at a site, it is often possible to determine the size and shape and method of construction of dwellings or other buildings. Post moulds can reveal that a settlement was surrounded by a palisade and thus presumably had enemies. Post moulds can even reveal the plan used by ancient astronomers to observe the solstices or equinoxes or other phenomena.

potassium-argon dating. In potassium-bearing minerals, potassium decays at a known rate, forming the gas argon. The proportion of argon to potassium can tell the age of a specimen from 50,000 years back to 50,000,000 years ago. Because potassium-argon analysis only yields dates so remote from the pres-

ent, it has had little application in American archeology, although it has been useful in determining
the age of ancient human remains found in deep layers
of the earth in Africa.

problematical. Any object that presents a problem that an
archeologist admits he or she can't solve.

proton magnetometer. A device for measuring variations in
the intensity of magnetic fields in the soil. By de-
tecting such variations it is often possible to locate
buried walls, ditches, and artifacts without digging.
The proton magnetometer is one of the instruments
used in remote sensing (see below). *See also cesium
magnetometer*

quantitative archeology. By counting, by measuring, by
using statistical methods and computers, archeologists are learning much about prehistoric people that
they have not been able to learn by other means.
For example, they think they can tell the number
of people who lived in certain places at any one time
merely by measuring the number of square feet in
the area that was inhabited.

Archeologists can find what people ate, and
in what proportions, by counting the various kinds
of bones and shells and seeds found in refuse heaps.
From a tabulation of bones it is possible to go on to
making an estimate of the weight of the edible meat
that was once supported by those bones. Together
with other data this figure may indicate how much
protein, on an average, each person in a community
probably consumed in relation to other elements in
the diet.

racemization. See amino acid racemization.

relative dates. When archeologists say that event A occurred before or after event B, they have a relative
date for A.

remote sensing. Any one of several techniques for obtaining information from a distance is called remote sensing. Aerial photography, imagery from satellites,
detection of buried structures by radar or by proton
magnetometer, are forms of remote sensing.

retouch. When a cutting tool made of stone is retouched,
it is sharpened. Retouching is done in one of two
ways—either by blows that knock small flakes off
an edge (percussion retouch), or by pressure to force
flakes off (pressure retouch).

salvage archeology. The saving of as much archeological
information as possible before a site is destroyed by
construction, possibly of a skyscraper or parking lot
or pipeline or dam. In the United States the first
major program of salvage archeology was undertaken
in the 1930s, ahead of the construction and dam
building done by the Tennessee Valley Authority.

scraper. A piece of stone or bone so sharpened in one portion that it could serve as a chisel or for cleaning
hides or for smoothing wood or bone. This kind of
tool was made in various forms and was sometimes
hafted.

secondary burial. The burial of disarticulated (see above)
bones after flesh has been removed from them by
decay, predators, or cleaning.

seriation. Archeologists sometimes arrange artifacts, such
as pottery, in a progressive series to obtain relative
dates (see above). This process is called seriation.

shaman. A person who is regarded as having healing powers derived from supernatural sources. A holy person; a religious leader; a "medicine man."

soil analysis (pedology). By analyzing the soil at a site it
is possible to learn a great deal about the environment at the time when people lived there. It is even
possible to learn how densely a site was populated:
the more phosphate in the soil, the denser the population.

sterile soil. An archeologist calls soil sterile if it contains
no evidence of human activity.

striking platform. The flat surface on a piece of stone
which a knapper strikes in order to detach a flake
or a blade (see above).

surface find. An artifact found on the surface of the ground.

tephrachronology. Volcanic ash, which is called tephra, is
often deposited around volcanoes—even at some distance from them—following eruptions. The chemical content of tephra is unique for each eruption.
If artifacts lie below tephra known to have come from
a certain eruption, the artifacts predate the eruption.
If the calendar date for the eruption is known, as is
sometimes the case, a date is known, before which
the artifacts must have been made.

thermoluminescence dating. Radioactive materials in pottery decay and produce electrons and other carriers
of electric charges which, when heated, produce light.
The older a piece of pottery, the more light is produced. Measurement of the light by a complicated
process yields the age of a piece of pottery with a
margin of error of no more than 10 percent.

uniface. A stone tool on which an edge is created by chipping from one side only. *See also biface*

varve dating. A moving glacier grinds some rock into
fine powder, which is carried along by the ice. When
melt water from a glacier accumulates in a lake, the
powder settles to the bottom. Each melting season
leaves a distinct layer of powder, called a varve. When
artifacts are associated with varves, relative dates (see
above) can be obtained. When one varve in a series
can be connected with a dated event, exact years can
be assigned to every varve in the series, giving absolute dates (see above).

SUGGESTED READINGS

In the main we have tried to list publications that are in print or are likely to be available in good public libraries. However, also included here are some specialized titles on which we have drawn particularly heavily. Detailed biobliographies of technical subjects can be found in many of the publications below.

Alex, Lynn Marie. *Eastern Iowa Presistory.* Iowa City: University of Iowa Press, 1981.

————. *Exploring Iowa's Past.* Iowa City: University of Iowa Press, 1980.

Ambler, J. Richard. *The Anasazi: Prehistoric People of the Four Corners Region.* Flagstaff: Museum of Northern Arizona, 1977.

Anderson, Douglas, and Barbara Anderson. *Chaco Canyon.* Globe, Arizona: Southwest Parks and Monuments Association, 1976.

Armstrong, George. "Cahokia's 'Woodhenge.'" *Early Man,* Spring, 1979.

Bandelier, Adolph F. *The Delight Makers.* New York: Dodd Mead, 1918.

Barnes, F.A., and Michaelene Pendleton. *Canyon Country Prehistoric Indians: Their Cultures, Ruins, Artifacts and Rock Art.* Salt Lake City: Wasatch Publishers, 1979.

Barnett, Franklin. *Dictionary of Prehistoric Indian Artifacts of the American Southwest.* Flagstaff, Arizona: Northland Press, 1973.

Bass, George F. *Archaeology Beneath the Sea.* New York: Harper and Row, 1976.

————. "Underwater Archaeology: Key to History's Warehouse." *National Geographic Magazine,* July, 1963.

Beadle, George W. "The Ancestry of Corn." *Scientific American,* January, 1980.

Bordaz, Jacques. *Tools of the Old and New Stone Age.* Garden City: Natural History Press, 1970.

Boyd, Lynn F. *Toltec Indian Mounds Site: Search for the Past.* Fayetteville, Arkansas: Archeological Survey, 1978.

Bray, Robert T. "The Missouri Indian Tribe in Archaeology and History." *Missouri Historical Review,* April, 1961.

Brennan, Louis. *No Stone Unturned.* New York: Random House, 1959.

————. *Beginner's Guide to Archaeology.* Harrisburg, Pennsylvania: Stackpole Books, 1973.

Breternitz, D., and J. Smith. "Mesa Verde: 'The Green Table.'" In *National Parkways Guide to Rocky Mountain and Mesa Verde National Parks.* Casper, Wyoming: World-Wide Research and Publishing, 1975.

Briggs, L.J., and K.F. Weaver. "How Old Is It?" *National Geographic Magazine,* August, 1958.

Brody, J.J. *Mimbres Painted Pottery.* Albuquerque: University of New Mexico Press, 1977.

Brose, David S., and N'omi Greber. *Hopewell Archaeology: The Chillicothe Conference.* Kent, Ohio: Kent State University Press, 1979.

Broyles, Bettye J. "The St. Albans Site, Kanawha County, West Virginia." *The West Virginia Archeologist,* Fall, 1966.

Bureau of Indian Affairs. *Indians, Eskimos, and Aleuts of Alaska; Indians of Arizona; Indians of California; Indians of Montana-Wyoming; Indians of New Mexico; Indians of North Carolina; Indians of Oklahoma; Indians of the Central Plains; Indians of the Dakotas; Indians of the Great Lakes Area; Indians of the Gulf Coast States; Indians of the Lower Plateau; Indians of the Northwest*. Washington, D.C., various dates.

Bushnell, G.H.S., *The First Americans*. New York: McGraw Hill, 1978.

Butler, B. Robert. *A Guide to Understanding Idaho Archaeology*. 2nd ed. Pocatello: Idaho State University Museum, 1968.

Canby, Thomas Y. "The Search for the First Americans." *National Geographic Magazine*, September, 1979.

Carlson, John B. "Dead Ends in the Search for Ancient Astronauts." *Early Man*, Spring, 1979.

————. "Hopewell, a Highly Complex Way of Life That Developed in America's Eastern Woodlands Around the Time of Christ." *Early Man*, Winter, 1979.

————. "Pre-Columbian Voyages to the New World: An Overview." *Early Man*, Spring, 1980.

Carter, George F. *Earlier Than You Think*. College: Texas A and M Press, 1980.

Castleton, K. *Petroglyphs and Pictographs of Utah: The East and Northeast*, Vol. 1. Salt Lake City: Museum of Natural History, 1978.

Champion, Sara. *Dictionary of Terms and Techniques in Archeology*. New York: Facts on File Publications, 1980.

Chapman, Carl H. *The Archaeology of Missouri*, Vol. II. Columbia: University of Missouri Press, 1980.

————, and Eleanor F. Chapman. *Indians and Archaeology of Missouri*. Columbia: University of Missouri Press, 1967.

Chard, Chester S. "Routes to Bering Strait." *American Antiquity*, October, 1960.

Chedd, Graham. *The Chaco Legacy (an Odyssey Program)*. Boston: Public Broadcasting Associates, Inc., 1980.

————. *Seeking the First Americans (an Odyssey Program)*. Boston: Public Broadcasting Associates, Inc., 1980.

Childe, V. Gordon. *Piecing Together the Past: The Interpretation of Archaeological Data*. New York: Praeger Publishers, 1956.

————. *A Short Introduction to Archaeology*. New York: Collier Books, 1962.

————. *World Prehistory, an Outline*, 3rd ed. London: Cambridge University Press, 1975.

Childers, W. Morlin, and Herbert L. Minshall. "Evidence of Early Man Exposed at Yuha Pinto Wash." *American Antiquity*, April, 1980.

Clark, Grahame. *Archaeology and Society*. New York: Barnes & Noble, 1960.

————, and S. Piggott. *Prehistoric Societies*. New York: Knopf, 1965.

Clausen, C.J., A.D. Cohen, Cesare Emiliani, J.A. Holman, and J.J. Stipp. "Little Spring, Florida: A Unique Underwater Site." *Science*, 16 February, 1979.

Cleator, P.E. *Underwater Archaeology*. New York: St. Martin's Press, 1973.

Corliss, William R. *Ancient Man: A Handbook of Puzzling Artifacts*. Glen Arm, Maryland: Source Book Project, 1978.

Cotter, John L. "Prehistoric Peoples Along the Natchez Trace." *Journal of Mississippi History*, October, 1950.

Cressman, L.S. *Prehistory of the Far West: Homes of Vanished Peoples*. Salt Lake City: University of Utah Press, 1977.

————. *The Sandal and the Cave: The Indians of Oregon*. Portland: Beaver Books, 1962.

Cross, Dorothy. *Archaeology of New Jersey*. Vol. I, 1941; Vol. II, Trenton: The Archaeological Society of New Jersey and the New Jersey State Museum, 1956.

————. *New Jersey's Indians*. Trenton: New Jersey State Museum, 1965.

Daniel, G.E. *The Idea of Prehistory*. London: Watts, 1962.

————. *Man Discovers His Past*. New York: Crowell, 1966.

Davidson, D.S. "Snowshoes." In *Memoirs of the American Philosophical Society*, vol. 6. Philadelphia, 1937.

de Borhegyi, Stephan F., and Suzanne de Borhegyi. *The Rubber Ball Game of Ancient America*. Milwaukee: Milwaukee Public Museum, 1963.

Deetz, James. *In Small Things Forgotten*. New York: Anchor/Doubleday, 1977.

————. *Invitation to Archaeology*. Garden City: Natural History Press, 1967.

Denevan, William M. *The Native Population of the Americas in 1492*. Madison: University of Wisconsin Press, 1976.

Deuel, L. *Flights Into Yesterday: the Story of Aerial Archaeology*. New York: St. Martin's Press, 1969.

Dickens, Roy S. and James L. McKinley, in collaboration with James H. Chapman and Leland G. Ferguson. *Frontiers in the Soil: The Archaeology of Georgia*. Atlanta, Georgia: Frontiers Publishing Co., 1979.

Di Peso, Charles C. "Macaws . . . Crotals . . . and Trumpet Shells." *Early Man*, Autumn, 1980.

Dockstader, Frederick J. *Indian Art in America: The Arts and Crafts of the North American Indian*. Greenwich, Connecticut: New York Graphic Society, 1966.

Douglass, Andrew E. "The Secret of the Southwest Solved by Talkative Tree Rings." *National Geographic Magazine*, December, 1929.

Dragoo, Don W. *Mounds for the Dead*. Pittsburgh: Carnegie Museum, 1963.

Driver, Harold E. *The Americas on the Eve of Discovery*. Englewood Cliffs, New Jersey: Prentice-Hall, 1964.

————. *Indians of North America*. Chicago: University of Chicago Press, 1969.

Drucker, Philip. *Indians of the Northwest Coast*. Garden City: Natural History Press, 1963.

Dutton, Bertha P. *American Indians of the Southwest*. Albuquerque: University of New Mexico Press, 1983.

————. *Indians of New Mexico*. Santa Fe: Museum of New Mexico Press, 1963.

————. *Let's Explore Indian Villages Past and Present*. Santa Fe: Museum of New Mexico Press, 1962.

————. *The Pueblos*. Englewood Cliffs, New Jersey: Prentice-Hall, 1976.

————. *Sun Father's Way*. Albuquerque: University of New Mexico Press, 1963.

Eddy, Frank W. *Archeological Investigations at Chimney Rock Mesa: 1970–1972*. Boulder: Colorado Archeological Society, 1977.

————. *Metates and Manos*. Santa Fe: Museum of New Mexico Press, 1964.

Elting, Mary, and Michael Folsom. *The Mysterious Grain*. New York: M. Evans, 1967.

————. *The Secret Story of Pueblo Bonito*. New York: Scholastic Book Services, 1964.

Euler, Robert C. "The Canyon Dwellers." *The American West*, May, 1967.

Fagan, Brian. *Archaeology: A Brief Introduction*. Boston: Little, Brown, 1978.

————. *Elusive Treasures: The Story of Early Archeologists in the Americas*. New York: Scribners, 1977.

————. *Quest for the Past: Great Discoveries in Archaeology*. Reading, Massachusetts: Addison Wesley, 1978.

Farb, Peter. *Humankind*. Boston: Houghton Mifflin, 1978.

————. *Man's Rise to Civilization as Shown by the Indians of North America, from Primeval Times to the Coming of the Industrial State*. New York: Dutton, 1968.

Faulkner, Charles H. *The Old Stone Fort*. Knoxville: University of Tennessee Press, 1968.

Fitting, James E. *The Archaeology of Michigan*. Bloomfield Hills, Michigan: Cranbrook Institute of Science, 1975.

————. *The Development of North American Archaeology*. Garden City: Anchor/Doubleday, 1973.

Folsom, Franklin. "An Amateur's Bonanza: The Story Behind the Discovery of Early Man in America." *The American West*, November, 1974.

————. "An Archeological Honeymoon." *Early Man*, Spring, 1981.

————. *Exploring American Caves*. New York: Cromwell Collier and Macmillan, 1962.

————. *Science and the Secret of Man's Past*. Irvington-on-Hudson, New York: Harvey House, 1966.

————. "Space-Age Archeology." In *Science of the Times 3*. New York: Arno Press, 1980.

————, and Mary Folsom. "Sinodonty and Sundadonty: An argument with teeth in it for man's arrival in the New World." *Early Man*, Summer, 1982.

Ford, Richard I. "Artifacts That Grew: Their Roots in Mexico." *Early Man*, Autumn, 1980.

Frazier, Kendrick. "The Anasazi Sun Dagger." *Science 80*, Premier Issue, 1980.

Frison, George. *Prehistoric Hunters of the High Plains*. New York: Academic Press, 1978.

Fundaburk, Emma L., and Mary D. Foreman, *Sun Circles and Human Hands*. Luverne, Alabama: Emma L. Fundaburk, 1957.

Gaede, Marnie, and Marc Gaede. *Camera, Spade and Pen: An Inside View of Southwestern Archaeology*. Tucson: University of Arizona Press, 1980.

Giddings, James Louis. *Ancient Men of the Arctic*. New York: Knopf, 1967.

Gladwin, H.S. *A History of the Ancient Southwest*. Freeport, Maine: Bond Wheelwright, 1957.

Gorner, Peter. "Plants as Evidence for Pre-Columbian Contact." *Early Man*, Spring, 1980.

Grant, Campbell. *Canyon de Chelly: Its People and Rock Art*. Tucson: University of Arizona Press, 1978.

————. *Rock Art of the American Indian*. New York: Thomas Y. Crowell, 1967.

————. *Rock Paintings of the Chumash, a Study of a California Indian Culture*. Berkeley and Los Angeles: University of California Press, 1965.

————, James W. Baird, and J. Kenneth Pringle. *Rock Drawings of the Coso Range, Inyo County, California*. China Lake, California: Maturengo Museum, 1968.

Greenberg, Ronald M., and Sarah A. Marusin, eds. *National Register of Historic Places*. 2 vols. Washington, D.C.: Government Printing Office, 1976.

Griffin, James B., ed. *Archaeology of Eastern United States*. Chicago: University of Chicago Press, 1952.

————. "Eastern North American Archaeology: A Summary." *Science*, 14 April, 1967.

————. "The MesoAmerican-Southeastern U.S. Connection." *Early Man*, Autumn, 1980.

Haury, Emil W. *The Hohokam, Desert Farmers and Craftsmen*. Tucson: University of Arizona Press, 1976.

————. "The Hohokam, First Masters of the American Desert." *National Geographic Magazine*, May, 1967.

————, E.B. Sayles, and W.W. Wasley. "The Lehner Mammoth Site, Southeastern Arizona." *American Antiquity*, July, 1973.

Haynes, C. Vance, "The Calico Site: Artifacts or Geofacts?" *Science*, 27 July, 1973.

————. "Fluted Projectile Points: Their Age and Dispersion." *Science*, 25 Sept., 1964.

————. "The Earliest Americans," *Science*, 7 November, 1969.

Heizer, Robert F., ed. *California. Handbook of North American Indians*. Vol. 9. Washington, D.C. Smithsonian Institution, 1979.

————. *The Archaeologist at Work, a Source Book in Archaeological Method and Interpretation*. New York, Harper and Row, 1959.

————. *Man's Discovery of his Past: Literary Landmarks in Archaeology*. Englewood Cliffs, New Jersey, Spectrum Books, Prentice-Hall, 1962.

————, and M.A. Baumhoff. *Prehistoric Rock Art of Nevada and Eastern California*. Berkeley: University of California Press, 1962.

————, and M.A. Whipple, eds. *The California Indians*. Berkeley: University of California Press, 1967.

Hester, James J. *Introduction to Archaeology*. New York: Holt, Rinehart and Winston, 1976.

Hester, Thomas R. *Digging into South Texas Prehistory*. San Antonio: Corona Publishing, 1980.

————, Robert F. Heizer, and John A. Graham. *Field Methods in Archaeology*. 6th ed. Palo Alto, California: Mayfield Publishing, 1975.

Heyerdahl, Thor. *American Indians in the Pacific*. London: Allen and Unwin, 1952.

————. *The Kon Tiki Expedition by Raft Across the South Seas*. London: Allen and Unwin, 1950.

Hodge, Frederick W., ed. *Handbook of American Indians*

North of Mexico. 2 vols.; reprint. New York: Rowman & Littlefield, 1968.

Hole, Frank, and Robert F. Heizer. *An Introduction to Prehistoric Archeology.* New York: Holt, Rinehart and Winston, 1973.

Holton, Felicia Antonelli. "Celts in New England . . . in 800 B.C.?" *Early Man,* Spring, 1980.

Howard, C.D. "The Atlatl: Function and Performance." *American Antiquity,* January, 1974.

Irwin, Cynthia, Henry Irwin, and George Agogino. "Wyoming Muck Tells of Battle: Ice Age Man vs. Mammoth." *National Geographic Magazine,* June, 1962.

Irwin-Williams, Cynthia. *The Oshara Tradition: Origins of Anasazi Culture.* Portales, New Mexico: Paleo Indian Institute, Eastern New Mexico University, 1973.

Jennings, Jesse D., ed. *Ancient Native Americans.* San Francisco: Freeman, 1978.

————. *Danger Cave.* Salt Lake City: University of Utah Press and The Society for American Archaeology, 1957.

————. *Prehistory of North America.* rev. ed. New York: McGraw Hill, 1974.

Jones, Anne Trinkle, and Robert C. Euler. *A Sketch of Grand Canyon Prehistory.* Grand Canyon, Arizona: Grand Canyon Natural History Association, 1979.

Jones, T.B. *Paths to the Ancient Past.* New York: Free Press, 1967.

Josephy, Alvin M. *The Indian Heritage of America.* New York: Knopf, 1968.

Joukowsky, Martha. *A Complete Manual of Field Archaeology.* Englewood Cliffs, New Jersey: Prentice-Hall, 1980.

Judd, Neil. *The Material Culture of Pueblo Bonito.* Washington, D.C.: Smithsonian Miscellaneous Collections, 1954.

Keeley, L.H. "The Function of Paleolithic Flint Tools." *Scientific American,* November, 1977.

Kelly, A.R., and Lewis H. Larson, Jr. "Explorations at Etowah, Georgia, 1954–1956." *Archaeology,* Spring, 1957.

Kidder, Alfred Vincent. *Introduction to the Study of Southwestern Archaeology.* 2nd ed. New Haven: Yale University Press, 1962.

Kirk, Ruth and Richard D. Daugherty. *Exploring Washington Archaeology.* Seattle: University of Washington Press, 1978.

————. *Hunters of the Whale: An Adventure in Northwest Coast Archaeology.* New York: Morrow, 1974.

Kirkland, F., and W.W. Newcomb, Jr. *Rock Art of Texas Indians.* Austin: University of Texas Press, 1967.

Krup, E.C. *In Search of Ancient Astronomers.* Garden City: Doubleday, 1977.

Laughlin, William S. "Eskimos and Aleuts: Their Origins and Evolution." *Science,* 8 November, 1963.

————, and Albert B. Harper, eds. *The First Americans: Origins, Affinities, and Adaptations.* New York: Harper and Row, 1979.

Leakey, L.S.B., Ruth D. Simpson, and Thomas Clements. "Archaeological Excavations in the Calico Mountains, California: Preliminary Report." *Science,* 31 May, 1968.

Lee, Thomas E. "The Antiquity of the Sheguiandah Site." *The Canadian Field-Naturalist,* July-September, 1957.

————. "The First Sheguiandah Expedition, Manitoulin Island, Ontario." *American Antiquity,* October, 1954.

————. "The Second Sheguiandah Expedition, Manitoulin Island, Ontario." *American Antiquity,* July, 1955.

Lewis, T.M.N., and Madeline Kneberg. *Tribes That Slumber: Indians of the Tennessee Region.* Knoxville: University of Tennessee Press, 1958.

Lister, Florence C., and Robert H. Lister. *Earl Morris and Southwestern Archaeology.* Albuquerque: University of New Mexico Press, 1968, 1977.

Lister, Robert H. "Archeology for Layman and Scientist at Mesa Verde." *Science,* 3 May, 1968.

————, and Florence C. Lister. *Chaco Canyon: Archaeology and Archaeologists.* Albuquerque: University of New Mexico Press, 1981.

Llewelyn, Morgan. "The Norse Discovery of the New World." *Early Man,* Winter, 1980.

MacNeish, Richard S. ed. *Early Man in America: Readings from Scientific American.* San Francisco: Freeman, 1973.

McFarland, Elizabeth. *Forever Frontier: The Gila Cliff Dwellings.* Albuquerque: University of New Mexico Press, 1967.

McGimsey, C.R., III. *Indians of Arkansas.* (Arkansas Archeological Survey, Popular Series, No. 1) Fayetteville: University of Arkansas Museum, 1969.

McGregor, J.C. *Southwestern Archaeology.* Champaign: University of Illinois Press, 1965.

McHargue, Georgess, and Michael Roberts. *A Field Guide to Conservation Archaeology in North America.* Phildelphia and New York: Lippincott, 1977.

McKusick, Marshall. *Men of Ancient Iowa.* Ames: Iowa State University Press, 1964.

————, and Eric Wahlgren. "Vikings in America— Fact and Fiction." *Early Man,* Winter, 1980.

McNitt, Frank. *Richard Wetherill: Anasazi.* Albuquerque: University of New Mexico Press, 1957, 1974.

Mangelsdorf, P. *Corn: Its Origin, Evolution, and Improvement.* Cambridge, Massachusetts: Belknap Press, 1974.

Margolin, Malcolm. *The Ohlone Way: Indian Life in the San Francisco—Monterey Bay Area.* Berkeley: Heyday Books, 1978.

Marshall, James A. "Geometry of the Hopewell Earthworks." *Early Man,* Spring, 1979.

Martin, Paul S. *Digging into History.* (Popular Series in Anthropology, No. 38). Chicago: Chicago Natural History Museum, 1959.

————. "The Discovery of America." *Science,* 14 March, 1973.

————. *The Last 10,000 Years.* Tucson: University of Arizona Press, 1963.

————. "The Revolution in Archaeology." *American Antiquity,* January, 1971.

————, and F.W. Sharrock. "Pollen Analysis of Prehistoric Human Feces: A New Approach to Ethnobotany." *American Antiquity,* October, 1964.

————, and H.E. Wright, Jr., eds. *Pleistocene Extinctions: The Search for a Cause.* New Haven: Yale University Press, 1968.

Meggers, Betty J. "Did Japanese Fishermen Really Reach Ecuador 5,000 Years Ago?" *Early Man,* Winter, 1980.

Mewhinney, H. *Manual for Neanderthals.* Austin: University of Texas Press, 1957.

Meyers, K. *The Plundered Past.* New York: Atheneum, 1973.

Milanich, Jerald T., and Charles H. Fairbanks. *Florida Archaeology.* New York: Academic Press, 1980.

Miller, Carl. "Life Eight Thousand Years Ago Uncovered in an Alabama Cave." *National Geographic Magazine,* October, 1956.

Morgan, Lewis Henry. *Ancient Society.* Chicago: Charles H. Kerr, 1907.

Morgan, Llywelyn. "The Norse Discovery of the New World." *Early Man,* Winter, 1980.

Morgan, William N. *Prehistoric Architecture in Eastern United States.* Cambridge, Massachusetts: MIT Press, 1980.

Morris, Ann Axtell. *Digging in the Southwest.* Santa Barbara: Peregrine Smith, 1978.

Morse, Dan F. "Introducing Northeastern Arkansas Prehistory." *The Arkansas Archeologist,* Spring, Summer, Fall, 1969.

Müller-Beck, Hansjürgen. "Paleohunters in America: Origins and Diffusion." *Science,* 27 May, 1966.

Museum of Anthropology. *Pueblo Pottery, A.D. 400–1967.* Albuquerque: University of New Mexico, 1967.

Nash, Charles H., and Rodney Gates, Jr. "Chucalissa." *Tennessee Historical Quarterly,* June, 1962.

National Geographic Society, ed. *The World of the American Indian.* Washington, D.C.: National Geographic, 1974.

National Park Service. At each park and monument a descriptive leaflet is available and all these leaflets are also obtainable from the Superintendent of Documents, U.S. Government Printing Office, Washington, D.C., 20402.

Newcombe, William W., Jr. *The Indians of Texas from Prehistoric to Modern Times.* Austin: University of Texas Press, 1961.

Noble, David Grant. *Ancient Ruins of the Southwest: An Archeological Guide.* Flagstaff, Arizona: Northland Press, 1981.

Norona, Delf. *Moundsville's Mammoth Mound.* Moundsville: West Virginia Archeological Society, August, 1957.

Oppelt, Norman. *Guide to Prehistoric Ruins of the Southwest.* Boulder, Colorado: Pruett Publishing Company, 1981.

Ortiz, Alfonso, ed. *Southwest. Handbook of North American Indians.* Vol. 9. Washington, D.C. Smithsonian Institution, 1979.

Pavlish, L.A., and E.B. Banning. "Revolutionary Developments in Carbon-14 Dating." *American Antiquity,* April, 1980.

Peckham, Stewart L. *Prehistoric Weapons in the Southwest.* Santa Fe: Museum of New Mexico Press, 1965.

Pike, Donald G. *Anasazi: Ancient People of the Rock.* (Photography by David Muench). New York: Crown, 1977.

Pope, G.D., Jr. *Ocmulgee National Monument, Georgia.* Washington, D.C.: National Park Service, 1956.

Potter, Martha A. *Ohio's Prehistoric Peoples.* Columbus: Ohio Historical Society, 1968.

Protsch, R., and R. Berger. "Earliest Radiocarbon Dates for Domesticated Animals." *Science,* 19 January, 1973.

Reed, C., ed. *The Origins of Agriculture.* Denver: Morton Publishing, 1978.

Riley, Carroll L., J. Charles Kelley, Campbell W. Pennington, and Robert L. Rands. *Man Across the Sea: Problems of Pre-Columbian Contacts.* Austin: University of Texas Press, 1971.

Rippeteau, Bruce Estes. "A Colorado Book of the Dead." *The Colorado Magazine,* Fall, 1978.

Ritchie, William A. *The Archaeology of Martha's Vineyard: A Framework for the Prehistory of Southern New England.* Garden City: Natural History Press, 1969.

————. *The Archaeology of New York State.* Harrison, New York: Harbor Hill Books, 1980.

Ritzenthaler, Robert E. *Masks of the North American Indians.* Milwaukee: Milwaukee Public Museum, 1964.

Robbins, Maurice, and Mary B. Irving. *The Amateur Archaeologist's Handbook.* New York: Crowell, 1973.

Rogers, Edward S. *Indians of the North Pacific Coast.* Toronto: Royal Ontario Museum, 1970.

Ross, Edward Hunter. *Indians of the Passaic Valley.* Newark, New Jersey: Newark Museum Association, 1963.

Rowe, Chandler W. *The Effigy Mound Culture of Wisconsin.* Milwaukee: Milwaukee Public Museum, 1956.

Sahlins, Marshall, and Elman Service. *Evolution and Culture.* Ann Arbor: University of Michigan Press, 1960.

Sauer, Carl O. *Agricultural Origins and Dispersals.* New York: American Geographical Society, 1952.

————. *Land and Life.* Berkeley: University of California Press, 1969.

Schaafsma, Polly. *Indian Rock Art of the Southwest.* Albuquerque: University of New Mexico Press, 1980.

————. *Rock Art in New Mexico.* Albuquerque: University of New Mexico Press, 1975.

————. *Rock Art in the Navajo Reservoir District.* Santa Fe: Museum of New Mexico Press, 1963.

Schroeder, Albert H., and Homer Hastings. *Montezuma Castle National Monument.* Historical Handbook Series, No. 27. Washington, D.C.: National Park Service, 1961.

Schuiling, Walter C., ed. *Pleistocene Man at Calico.* Redlands, California: San Bernardino County Museum Association, 1979.

Schultz, Helen A., ed. *The Ancient Aztalan Story.* Jefferson, Wisconsin: Lake Mills–Aztalan Historical Society, 1969.

Schwartz, Douglas W. "Prehistoric Man in Mammoth Cave." *Scientific American,* July, 1969.

————. Prehistoric Man in the Grand Canyon." *Scientific American,* February, 1958.

Sheratt, Andrew, and Grahame Clarke, eds. *The Cambridge Encyclopedia of Archaeology.* New York: Crown Publishers/Cambridge University Press, 1980.

Silverberg, Robert. *Mound Builders of Ancient America: The Archeology of a Myth.* Greenwich, Connecticut: New York Graphic Society, 1968.

————. *Sunken History: the Story of Underwater Archaeology*. Philadelphia: Chilton, 1963.

Smith, Jason W. *Foundations of Archaeology*. Beverly Hills, California: Glencoe Press, 1976.

Snow, Dean R. *The Archaeology of New England*. New York: Academic Press, 1980.

South, S.A. *Indians of North Carolina*. Raleigh: North Carolina Division of Cultural Resources, 1976.

Spencer, Robert F., Jesse D. Jennings, et al. *The Native Americans: Prehistory and Ethnology of the North American Indians*. New York: Harper and Row, 1965.

Stalker, Archie MacS. "Geology and Age of the Early Man Site at Taber, Alberta." *American Antiquity*, October, 1969.

Steward, Julian H. *Theory of Culture Change*. Champaign: University of Illinois Press, 1955.

Struever, Stuart, and Felicia Antonelli Holton. *Koster: Americans in Search of their Prehistoric Past*. New York: New American Library, 1980.

Struever, Stuart, ed. *Prehistoric Agriculture*. Garden City: Natural History Press, 1979.

Stuart, George E. "Who Were the 'Mound Builders'?" *National Geographic Magazine*, December, 1972.

Suggs, Robert C. *The Archaeology of San Francisco*. New York: Crowell, 1965.

Sullivan, George. *Discover Archaeology: An Introduction to the Tools and Techniques of Archaeological Fieldwork*. Garden City: Doubleday, 1980.

Turner, Christy G. II. *Petrographs of the Glen Canyon Region*. Museum of Northern Arizona Bulletin 38, Glen Canyon Series Number 4. Flagstaff: Northern Arizona Society of Science and Art, Inc., 1963.

Tuck, James A. "An Archaic Indian Cemetery in Newfoundland." *Scientific American*, June, 1970.

Underhill, Ruth M. *Red Man's America*. Chicago: University of Chicago Press, 1953.

————. *Red Man's Religion*. Chicago: University of Chicago Press, 1965.

Viele, Catherine W. *Voices in the Canyon*. Globe, Arizona: Southwest Monuments Association, 1980.

Wallace, Paul A.W. *Indians in Pennsylvania*. Harrisburg: Pennsylvania Historical and Museum Commission, 1961.

Watson, Patty Jo. "Prehistoric Miners of Salt Flats, Kentucky." *Archaeology*, October, 1966.

Webb, Clarence H. "The Extent and Content of Poverty Point Culture." *American Antiquity*, July, 1968.

Webb, William S., and Charles E. Snow. *The Adena People*. Knosville: University of Tennessee Press, 1974.

Wedel, Waldo R. *Prehistoric Man on the Great Plains*. Norman: Oklahoma University Press, 1978.

Wheat, Joe Ben. *Mogollon Culture Prior to A.D. 1000*. Menasha, Wisconsin: American Anthropological Association, 1955. (Also appears as Memoir 10 of the Society for American Archaeology)

———. "A Paleo-Indian Bison Kill." *Scientific American,* January, 1967.

———. *Prehistoric People of the Northern Southwest.* Grand Canyon, Arizona: Grand Canyon Natural History Association, 1963.

White, Leslie. *The Science of Culture: A Study of Man and Civilization.* Garden City: Doubleday, 1969.

Willey, Gordon R. *An Introduction to American Archaeology,* vol. 1. Englewood Cliffs, New Jersey: Prentice-Hall, 1966.

———, and Jeremy A. Sabloff. *A History of American Archaeology.* San Francisco: Freeman, 1980.

———, and Jeremy A. Sabloff, eds. *Pre-Columbian Archeology: Readings from Scientific American.* San Francisco: Freeman, 1980.

Wilson, Josleen. *The Passionate Amateur's Guide to Archeology in the United States.* New York: Macmillan, 1981.

Wing, Kittridge A. *Bandelier National Monument.* Washington, D.C.: National Park Service, 1955.

Witthoft, John. *The American Indian as Hunter.* rev. ed. Harrisburg: Pennsylvania Historical and Museum Commission, 1967.

———. *Indian Prehistory of Pennsylvania.* Harrisburg: Pennsylvania Historical and Museum Commission, 1965.

Wormington, H.M. *Ancient Man in North America.* Denver: Denver Museum of Natural History, 1957.

———. *Prehistoric Indians of the Southwest.* Denver: Denver Museum of Natural History, 1961.

———. *A Reappraisal of the Fremont Culture.* Denver: Denver Museum of Natural History, 1955.

———, and Richard G. Forbis. *An Introduction to the Archaeology of Alberta, Canada.* Denver: Denver Museum of Natural History, 1965.

———, and Arminta Neal. *The Story of Pueblo Pottery.* Denver: Denver Museum of Natural History, 1951.

Wright, Barton, and Evelyn Roat. *This is a Hopi Kachina.* Flagstaff: Museum of Northern Arizona, 1965.

Zeuner, F.E. *Dating the Past.* 4th, rev. ed. London: Hutchinson, 1958.

Archeological magazines that often include articles on North America:
American Antiquity, 1703 New Hampshire Ave., NW, Washington, D.C. 20009.
Archaeology, 53 Park Place, New York, NY 10007.
Early Man, PO Box 1499, Evanston, IL 60204
Popular Archaeology, PO Box 4211, Arlington, VA 22204.
Many local societies publish newsletters and journals. For information about these write to the societies whose addresses appear beginning on page 373.

ACKNOWLEDGMENTS

The many whose courtesies and knowledge made possible the first and second editions of *AMERICA'S ANCIENT TREASURES* were thanked in those editions. To repeat the long lists of those to whom we are indebted would reflect our genuine grattitude for the continuing use we have made of their assistance, but lists can be an encumbrance in a book of this kind. We have chosen, thinking of the convenience of the reader, to thank in this edition only those who have made new and distinct contributions to it. We hope all those whose names are not carried foward will consider that we have discharged our obligation to them in the earlier editions. And we do thank them most sincerely, together with all the new people who have helped us to help the public find its way to and around in America's prehistory.

For supplying information that appears for the first time in this third revised edition, we wish to thank: Emma Adams, J.M. Adovasio, Bob Akerly, Robert Alex, Duane C. Anderson, Stephen Archibald, Bertin T. Arsenault, Peg Atkinson, Betty Bacon, Gene Ball, William D. Barkley, Grace Bartlett, Tyler Bastian, Shaun Bell, Joseph L. Benthall, Vernon C. Betts, Bruce J. Bourque, Ramona K. Bradley, Ron Brand, Claud Breede, David A. Breternitz, Robert G. Breunig, B. McDonald Brooms, William E. Brown, Bruce Bryan, Judy Bullington, Barbara Burney, Kathleen Byrd, Christy A. H. Caine, Helen Camp, Michael D. Carman, Thomas B. Carroll, Evelyn Casias, W. Dennis Chesley, Lucille E. Christie, R. Berle Clay, Kenneth W. Cole, Herdis H. Conder, Peter W. Cook, P.P. Cooper, II, Fred E. Coy, Jr., M.G. Creasey, Earle

G. Curran, Arthur Cuthair, Phyllis Daughtery, Richard Daugherty, Hester A. Davis, Eugene W. Dehner, C.L. Dill, Veronica Dolan, Margie E. Douthit, Bert C. Drennen, Frank W. Eddy, Nancy Eubank, Judi Falk, Robert P. Fay, Jim D. Feagins, Pieter B. Feenstra, Jacqueline R. Fehon, Paul R. Fish, Daniel Fowler, Judith A. Franke, Joan E. Freeman, George C. Frison, Darrell Fulmer, Frank Gachupin, Nancy V. Gauss, Catherine Gent, Jonnie L. Gentry, Jr., Pat Gibson, James Gorman, Jeffrey R. Graybill, Candace Green, Dee F. Green, Ernestene Green, Thomas J. Greene, Rhonda Groell, Alice Gryszkiewicz, Ernest Buillen, Jeff Gunderson, Lucile Hadley, Ivol Hagar, John W. Hall, M.E.A. Hall, John R. Halsey, Robert E. Haltiner, John Haney, Paul Happel, Russell P. Hartman, Thomas L. Hartman, Dennis J. Hartzell, James N. Haskett, Brian W. Hatoff, Emil W. Haury, Dorothy Heinze, Robert Heitner, Glen E. Henderson, B. William Henry, Jr., Joyce Herold, Mary Ellen Norrisey Hodges, Donald Hoffmeister, Erik L. Holland, Karen Ann Holme, Judy Horine, Loren N. Horton, Ben Hoy, William Jack Hranicky, Michael E. Humphries, R. Stephen Irwin, M. Wayne Jensen, Jr., Bernard Johnson, E.A. Johnson, Eric Johnson, Bruce Jones, Henry L. Jones, Mary D. Jones, Juan S. Juanico, W. James Judge, Eugene R. Junette, Harold S. Kachel, James H. Kellar, Roger E. Kelly, Barry C. Kent, Orion Knox, George V. Knudsen, Herbert Kraft, David Krouskop, Mrs. Carl Krueger, Carol Kruse, Mary Kwass, Alice Larson, André P. Larson, Lewis H. Larson, Jr., Olin Larson, Yulee Lazarus, Thomas E. Lee, Bobby Leverette, John D.

Linahan, John Lomoro, Bruce Louthan, Ike Lovato, Nancy O. Lurie, Carol McClelland, Samuel O. McGahey, Isabel McIntosh, R. McKenzie, Mary Mallory, J. Paul Malmberg, John Mapel, Tony Martinez, J. Mead, Larry G. Meadows, Jan Meiresonne, Claudia F. Melson, Robert L. Melson, Patricia G. Michael, Larry Mink, Michael C. Mitchel, Jimmy L. Mitchell, Roger W. Moeller, John S. Mohlenrich, Robert Moll, P.A. Moore, William Moorman, Geoffrey P. Moran, Lloyd Morris, Chris L. Moser, James W. Mueller, Vance E. Nelson, Giovanna Neudorfer, Raymond Olivas, Evaline A. Olson, Virgil J. Olson, David Orr, James V. Parker, John H. Pattimore, Eli Paul, Stewart L. Peckham, R. Percy, William Phenix, Jimmie E. Picquet, Howard J. Pomerantz, Dave Povero, Palmer Price, Larry D. Reed, Richard S. Reed, J.J. Reid, Phoebe R. Resnick, René Ribes, Bruce Estes Rippeteau, Dave Roberts, Mimi Rodden, Edward C. Rodriguez, Jr., Martha A. Rolingson, David Rotenizer, Parker Rouse, Jr., E.I. Rowland, Samuel R. Rowley, Don D. Rowlinson, J. Jerry Rumberg, Allan J. Ryan, George S. Sample, Sherwin Sandberg, John L. Sansing, Kay Sargent, Ron Sauggs, William L. Schart, George F. Schesventer, Henry A. Schoch, Robert J. Schumerth, William Seidel, Ethel G. Shanahan, Brad Shaw, Payson D. Sheets, Steve Sigstad, Ruth D. Simpson, D. Smith, Jo Davenport Smith, Samuel D. Smith, W.W Smith, Ron Snuggs, Signe Snortland-Coles, Dennis Stanford, Jack Steinbring, Robert L. Stephenson, Rick C. Stevens, Richard Alan Stout, Sheila A. Stump, Linda Suss, Thomas D. Thiessen, Simone Thomas, Caryn Throop, Jim Trott, Curtis Tunnell, Kenneth G. Ulrich, R. Gwinn Vivian, John R. Vosburgh, James P. Vukonich, Anne P. Wainstein, Harry Walters, Ward Weakly, Michael S. Weichman, Marcia K. Weinland, Jeanne M. Welch, Robin F. Wells, Gilbert Wenger, Joe Ben Wheat, George Wheeler, Susan Whiteacre, John T. Wilcox, Dan E. Williams, Thelma Williams, Douglas A. Wilson, Tom Winder, Roger Wise, Loraine E. Williams, Thomas A. Witty, Jr., Virginia A. Wulfkuhle, Thomas Wylie, Stephen Zimmer.

For courtesies rendered after the above list was set in type, we are indebted to: Pamela Barefoot, Leslie Floyd, Richard L. George, Wayne Haley, Charles F. Hayes III, Herbert Kraft, Robert E. Lee, Phyllis Marangelo, Susan F. Payne, Bruce Estes Rippeteau, Maurice Robbins, Ruth D. Simpson, Jean Walker, Don Wyckoff, and Larry Zimmerman.

To Emmy Ezzell and David V. Holtby we owe special thanks for the skill and diligence they used in transforming our typescript into a finished book.

For typing the manuscript, sometimes at considerable personal inconvenience, and for making some drawings for this new edition, we are indebted to Abby Fountain.

INDEX

Canadian Department of Northern
Affairs, 342
Canadian River, 154, 156, 160
Canaliño Indians, 108, 122
Canals, 16. *See also* Irrigation.
Canandaigua, NY, 351
Canastota, NY, 351
Canaveral National Seashore, 223
Cannibalism, 132, 260, 316
Canoe, 6, 122, 131, 134, 146, 147,
238, 327, 328, 363
Canyon de Chelly National Monument,
8, 12, 14–15
Canyonlands National Park, 91, 94, 95,
98
Canyon, TX, 202
Cape Cod National Seashore, 337
Cape Cod shell mounds, 326, 337
Cape Denbigh, xix, 139, 144, 328
Cape Krusenstern, 139
Cape Royal Ruin, 18
Capitol Reef National Park, 94, 96
Captain Cook, 131, 133, 134, 148
Capulin Mountain National Monument,
66
"Carbon-14 Dating," 342–345. *See also*
C-14 dating.
Carbondale, IL, 272
Caribou hunters, 288, 341
Caribou kill, 326
Carlsbad Caverns National Park, 66–67
Carnegie Museum of Natural History,
314, 360
Carson, Christopher "Kit," 15, 82
Carson City, NV, 128
Cartersville, GA, 212
Casa Grande Ruins National Monument,
15–16, 17
Casamero Ruins, 67
Casa Rinconada, 68, 74
Casas Grandes, Mexico, 5
Cashmere, WA, 163
Castile, NY, 348
Castile Historical House, 348
Castillo de San Marcos National
Monument, 220
Castine, ME, 335
Catawba College, Museum of
Anthropology, 238
Catlin, George, 187, 247, 294, 295
Catlinite, 21, 187, 292, 293, 294, 295
Catlow Cave, 152, 153
Cave dwellers, 9, 122, 155
Cave paintings, 15, 64, 66, 67, 113,
202, 203
Caves, 18, 24, 61, 62, 63, 64, 65, 66,
67, 78, 79, 95; Catlow, 152;
Chumash Painted, 113; Fishbone,
128; Fort Rock, 152, 153; Goat, 67;
Graham, 294, 295; Gypsum, 126,

127; Lake Lenore, 155, 156, 157;
Lehman, 127; Lovelock, 127, 128,
129; Mammoth, 285; Mummy, 334;
Painted Grotto, 67; Panther, 202;
Pictograph, 184; Roaring Springs,
154; Russell, 208, 216, 217; Salts,
285; Sandia Man, 88; Seminole
Canyon, 203; Ventana, 34;
Winnemucca Lake, 128; Wyandotte,
278
Cave Towers Ruins, 100
Cayuga Museum of History and Art,
348
Cemeteries. *See* Burial practises.
Cemetery Mound, 313
Centennial Museum of Vancouver,
146
Center for American Archeology, 265,
267
Center for Archeological Investigations,
272
Ceramic lifeway, 251
Ceramic (Woodland) culture, 355
Ceremonial center, 16, 59, 74, 235
Ceremonial lodges, 228
Ceremonial practises, 4, 28, 52, 54, 75,
230, 242, 244, 252, 253; Ball game,
6; Black Drink, 223, 224, 334; Busi,
242; Cahokian, 260; Harvest, 263;
Mississippian, 212, 213; Snake
Dance, 36; Southern Cult 216, 224,
225. *See also* Religious practises.
Cedar Tree Tower, 53, 54
Celt, 6
Cesium magnetometer, 387
Chaco Canyon, 68–75; mentioned, 10,
25, 41, 42, 334, 339, 348
Chaco Canyon outliers: Aztec, 61;
Casamero, 67; Chimney Rock 40–41;
Dominguez and Escalante, 44–45;
Lowry Pueblo Ruins, 47; Salmon
Ruin, 87; Village of the Great Kivas,
90
Chaco Culture National Historical Park,
68–75
Champlain, Samuel de, 351
Channel Islands, 119, 122
Chapel Hill, NC, 240
Charles E. Bowers Memorial Museum,
111
Charleston, WV, 314
Charlestown, RI, 367
Charles Towne Landing Site, 241
Charlotte Harbor, FL, 236
Charlotte, NC, 238
Charlotte Nature Museum, 238
Charnel house, 307
Chatham-Kent Museum, 356
Chatham, Ontario, 356
Chattahoochee National Forest, 231

Chatauqua County Historical Society,
348
Chemehuevi Indians, 117, 120
Chemung County Historical Society,
349
Cheney Cowles Memorial Museum, 155
Cherokee Indians, 217, 224, 238, 239,
330, 362
Cherokee, NC, 239
Chetro Ketl, 68, 72
Cheyenne Indians, 171
Cheyenne, WY, 207
Chicago, IL, 263
Chickasaw Indians, 214, 235
Chickasaw Village Site, 235
Chiefdom, 387
Chief Sealth, 158
Children's Museum, Inc. (MA), 337,
338
Children's Museum of Hartford, 330
Children's Museum of Indianapolis, 274
Chillicothe, OH, 249, 251, 282, 306,
312
Chimney Rock, 40–41, 42, 43, 71
China Lake, CA, 118
Chinle, AZ, 14
Chinook Indians, 156
Chippewa Indians, 291
Chippewa Nature Center, 286
Chipping floor, 370
Chisholm Trail Museum and Governor
Seay Mansion, 180
C.H. Nash Museum, 242
Choctaw Indians, 214, 242
Choctaw Trail of Tears Museum, 190
Chopper, 387
Chopping tool, 387
Chucalissa Indian Town and Museum,
242, 243
Chumash Indians, 109, 111, 122
Chumash Painted Cave, 113
Chunkey game, 240, 246, 247
Cibicue, AZ, 19
Cibola, cities of, 81
Cincinnati, OH, 301
Cincinatti Museum of Natural History,
301
Citadel Hill Branch, Nova Scotia
Museum, 355
Clara T. Woody Museum, 17
Clark, William, 165
"Classifying Anasazi Cultures," 40–41
Clay balls, 233, 284
Clay County Historical Museum, 295
Clear Creek Canyon Rock Art, 96
Clear Lake State Park, 113–114
Clearwater, FL, County Courthouse,
222
Cleveland, OH, 302, 312
Cleveland Museum of Art, 302

Fish Farm Mounds, 280
Fishing equipment, 146
Fish net sinker, 365
Fish trapping, 215, 220, 326, 327, 330
"Fish trap" settlement pattern, 107
Fish weir, 326
Fission track dating, 388
Five Kiva House, 103
Flagstaff, AZ, 24
Flaking tool, 388
Flesher, 56, 163, 388
Flint Ridge Memorial, 302
Florence, AL, 214
Florence Hawley Ellis Museum of
    Anthropology, 76
Florida, 220–224, 236; keys, 220, 221
Florida State Museum, 224
"Florida Key Dwellers," 220, 221
Flowerdew Hundred, 369–370
Flotation, 388
Fluorine dating, 388
"Fluted Points," 77. See also Clovis
    points; Folsom points.
Fluted points, xx, xxi, 77, 174
Flutes, 335
Folsom Man State Monument, 66
Folsom Museum, 76
Folsom, NM, xxx, 76
Folsom points, xxi, xxii, 46, 66, 77,
    123, 174, 186, 201, 202
Folsom Site, xxi, 76, 174
Fonda, NY, 350
Foot drum. See Dance platform.
Ford, James A., 232
Forest Service, 40, 88, 206, 241
Fort Ancient, 309
Fort Ancient culture, 277, 284, 301,
    305, 311, 312
Fort Ancient State Memorial, 303, 304
Fort Atkinson, WI, 318
Fort Burgwin Research Center, 78
Fort Caroline National Memorial, 221
Fort Clark State Historic Site, 186, 187
Fort Collins, CO, 174
Fort Collins Museum, 174
Fort Hays State University, 179
Fort Hill State Memorial, 304
Fort Ligonier, 361
Fort Lewis College Library, 45
Fort Lincoln State Park, 188
Fort Lowell Museum, 16
Fort Matanzas National Monument, 221
Fort Michilimackinac, 286
Fort Ninigret, 367
Fort Robinson Museum, 185
Fort Rock Cave, 152, 154
Fort Rock Cave Historical Marker, 152,
    153
Fort Rock, OR, 152
Fort Simcoe Museum, 155

Fort Simcoe State Park, 155
Fort Stanwix Museum, 349
Fort Stanwix National Monument, 349
Fort Sumner State Monument, 15
Fort Toulouse Park, 214
Fort Walton Beach, FL, 223
Fort Washington, 336
Fort William Henry Restoration and
    Museum, 349
Fort Worth Museum of Science and
    History, 201
Fort Worth, TX, 201
Fort Yukon, AK, 142
Four Corners area, 15
Fox Field Site, 284
Franciscans, 82, 84
Francis Marion National Forest, 241
Franklin and Marshall College, North
    Museum, 361
Franklin, Dwight, 345
Franklin, PA, 363
Frank Phillips Ranch, 195
Fraser Canyon and Delta, 146
Frederick Head, 168
Frederick, OK, 191
"Fremont Culture," 92
Fremont culture, 42, 92, 94, 96, 97,
    100, 102
Friar Marcos, 81
Frijoles Canyon, 61, 62, 64
Front Royal, VA, 174
Frost, Bartlett, 269
Fruitlands Museums, 338
Funeral practises. See burial practises.

Gabrielino Indians, 111
Gahagan Mound, 231
Gainesville, FL, 224
Galisteo, NM, 246
Gallatin County Court House, 182
Gallup Museum of Indian Arts, 78
Gambell sites, 144
Games: ball, 6, 30, 31, 36; chunkey,
    246, 247; dice, 246
Game trap, 125. See also Buffalo jumps;
    Fish traps.
Gardner, Jefferson, 190
Garvies Point Museum, 349
Gass, Jacob, 281
Gastonia, NC, 239
Gatchell Memorial Museum, 206
Geometry, knowledge of at Newark
    Earthworks, 308
Georgia, 224–231
Ghost Dance, 196
Ghost Ranch, 76
Giant bison, xviii, xxi, 46, 166, 201,
    279
Giant Desert Figures, 110, 123
Giant Ground Sloth, xviii, 126

Gila Cliff Dwellings National
    Monument, 78, 79
Gila County Historical Society, 17
Gila River, 5, 16, 30
Ginkgo Petrified Forest State Park
    Interpretive Center, 155
"Ginsburg and Margie and Paleo-
    Indians," 174–175
Gitksan Village, 148
Gitksan Village Dancers, 148
Giusewa, 82
"Glacial Kame Culture," 284
Glacial Kame people, 284, 300, 309
Glen Canyon National Recreation Area,
    17
Glen Cove, NY, 349
Glenn A. Black Laboratory of
    Archaeology, 274
Globe, AZ, 17
Glossary, 385–390
Glottochronology, 388
Goggles, 139
Goodman's Point, 55
Goodwell, OK, 192
Gorgets, 193, 275
Gouge, 365
Goulding's Trading Post, 97
Graham Cave State Park, xxiii, 295, 297
Gran Chichimeca, 19
Grand Canyon National Park, 18–19
Grand Coulee, 155
Grand Gulch Archeological Primitive
    Area, 97
Grand Mound Center, 290
Grand Rapids, MI, 286
Grand Rapids Public Museum, 286
Grand River Valley, 286
Grand Village of the Natchez Indians,
    235–236
Gran Quivira, 59, 80
Grapevine Wash, 126, 127
Grasshopper Ruin, 19, 20
Grave Creek Mound State Park,
    313–314
Grave goods, 44, 194, 224, 225, 227,
    245, 249–253 passim, 279, 283, 288,
    300, 306–311 passim, 333. See also
    Burial practises.
Graver, 359, 388
Grave robbers, 38
Great Basin and California, 105–129
Great Bear Group, 280
Great Bend, KS, 176
Great Carry, 349
Great Circle Earthworks, 308
Great Indian Trail or Warpath, 322
Great kivas, 44, 45, 46, 59, 60, 67, 71,
    72, 74, 87, 90
Great Lakes Indian Museum, 287
Great Plains, 105, 165–207

Snake Dance, 36
Snake effigy. *See* Serpent Mound.
Snake Indians, 96
Snake River, 161
Snaketown Site, 13, 21
Snoqualmie Indians, 160
Snoqualmie Valley Historical Museum, 160
Snowshoes, 327, 332
Snyders Site, 195
Soapstone. *See* Steatite.
Social classes, 194, 197, 225, 226, 227, 242, 252, 253, 254, 256, 258, 269, 274, 308, 351
Soil analysis, 390
Solecki, Ralph, 314
Sommerheim, 362
Soto, Hernando de, 213, 235, 236
Southampton, Ontario, 356
South Carolina, 241
South Charleston, WV, 314
South Dakota, 196–199
South Dakota State Historical Museum, 198
Southeast, 209–247
Southern Cult, 212, 213, 216, 224, 225, 226, 300
Southern Illinois University, University Museum and Art Galleries, 272
South Florida Museum and Planetarium, 222
South Fort, 304
South Orange, NJ, 348
South Texas Indians, 170
South Thunder Bay, Ontario, 360
Southwest, 3–103; defined, 19
Southwest Museum, 5, 123, 126
Space Farms Zoological Park and Museum, 345
Space, Ralph, 345
Spanish Conquest, 28, 59, 75, 80, 81, 83, 86, 178, 200, 213, 222, 235, 236
Spanish Hill Site, 363
Spanish Missions, 59, 84, 86
Spear throwers. *See* Atlatls.
Spiro Mounds State Archaeological Site, 192–194; mentioned, 195, 201, 217, 218, 220
Speed Art Museum, 286
Speed, J. B., 286
Spider man, 290
Spider Rock, 8
Split-twig figurines, 18, 19
Spokane Indians, 158
Spokane, WA, 155, 158
Springfield, IL, 264
Springwater Park, Ontario, 359
Sproat Lake, 147
Spruce Tree House, 48, 51
Square Tower Group, 98, 99

Squash Blossom Girl, 24
Squaw Tank, 117
Squier, Ephraim George, 249, 250, 270, 275, 305, 306, 311
Staked Plains. *See* LLano Estacado.
Stalker, A. MacS., 172
Stamford, CT, 331
Stanford Museum and Nature Center, 331
Standing Rock State Historical Site, 189
Stanford, Dennis, 174, 175
Starved Rock State Park, 272, 286
State Capitol Museum (WA), 160
State Historical Museum (MS), 237
State Historical Society Museum (ND), 189
State Historical Society of Iowa, 282
State Historical Society of Wisconsin, 322, 323
Staten Island, NY, 355
State University of Iowa, Museum of Natural History, 281
Steatite vessels, 108, 121, 124, 132, 211, 328, 332, 337
Sterile soil, 390
Sternberg Memorial Museum, 179
Stevens Point Museum of Natural History, 323
Stevens Point, WI, 323
Stonehenge, 260
Story Mound, 312
Stovall Museum, 193, 195
"Stratigraphy," 244–246
Stratigraphy, 98, 244–246
Strecker Museum, 200
Striking platform, 390
Stroudsburg, PA, 362
Struever, Stuart, 266
Stutsman County, 188
Sul Ross University, Museum of the Big Bend, 203
Sun Dagger, 75
Sun Point Pueblo, 52
Sunset Crater, 22, 35, 36
Sunset Crater National Monument, 31, 37
Sun Temple, 52
Surface find, 390
Surface surveys, 43
Susquehanna River, 350, 362
Susquehanna River Valley, 364
Susquehannock Indians, 354, 362
Sussex County Historical Society, 346
Suttles, Wayne, 134
Swift Creek, culture, 228, 230

Taber, Alberta, 172
Tablets: Adena, 301; Cincinnati, 301; Davenport, 281; Grave Creek Mound, 314

Tacoma, WA, 161
"Tales That Old Bones Tell," 196–197
Taos Indians, 41, 178
Taos, NM, 82, 90
Taos Pueblo, NM, 78, 83, 88, 90
Tarahumara Indians, 35
Taychas, 200
Tazewell, VA, 370
Teeth. *See* Dental anthropology.
Tempe, AZ, 13
Temple Mound Museum, 222, 223
Temple Mounds. *See* Mounds, by type
Tennessee, 242–247
Tennessee Archaeological Society, 217
Tennessee Division of State Parks, 243
Tennessee River, 217, 259
Tephrachronology, 390
Terra Ceia Island, 221
Tesquesta Indians, 221
Texas, 170, 198, 199–205
Texas A & I University, John E. Conner Museum, 203
Texas Memorial Museum, 168, 192, 201
Texas Parks and Wildlife Department, 200
Texas Tech University Museum, 202, 203
Texas Wilderness Museum, 203
Thermoluminescence dating, 390
Thomas Burke Memorial State Museum, 161
Thomas Gilcrease Institute of American History and Art, 195
Thompson Wash Petroglyphs/Pictographs, 112
Thousand Hills State Park, 298
Three Kiva Pueblo, 102
Three Rivers Petroglyphs, 90
Three Turkey Ruin Tribal Park, 31
Thronateeska Heritage Foundation, 231
Thule culture, 140, 141
Thunder Bay Museum, 360
Thunderbird, 189, 318
Thunderbird Museum (NJ), 346
Thunderbird Museum and Archeological Park (VA), 368, 369, 370, 371
Thunderbird Park, British Columbia, 146
Throwing stick, 89
Tillamook County Pioneer Museum, 154
Tillamook, OR, 154
Timucua Indians, 222, 224
Tioga County Historical Society Museum, 354
Tioga Point Museum, 363
"Tipi Rings," 188
Tipi rings, 184, 188
Tipis, 188, 189
Tishomingo, OK, 190

Ute Indian Museum, 58
Ute Indians, 96, 97, 175
Ute Mountain Tribal Park, 58
Ute Mountain Ute Indians, 58
Ute trail, 176

Vail Site, 326
Valentine Museum, 371
Valley of Fire State Park, 129
Vancouver, British Columbia, 146
Vancouver Island, 147
Vandalism, 38, 194, 197
Van Meter State Park, 300
Varve dating, 390
Vegetation, prehistoric, restored, 128, 282
Venango County Courthouse, 363
Venice, FL, 236
Ventana Cave, 34, 121
Verde River, 22, 23, 34
Verde Valley, 22, 23, 34
Vermilion, SD, 198
Vermont, 368–369
Vermont Historical Society, 369
Vermont Museum, 369
Vernal, UT, 96
"Very Old Sites in Alberta," 172
Victoria, British Columbia, 146
Vikings, 141, 244, 338, 341. *See also* Norse.
Village of the Great Kivas, 90
Villages, development of: xxiv, 3–11 *passim,* 108, 133, 168, 211, 252, 258, 261; earliest, 266; Mesa Verde, 47–57; Plains, 169–170; Northeast, 328–329
Vinland, 341
Virginia, 369–371
Virginia Research Center for Archaeology, 369
Virgin prairie, 291
Visalia, CA, 123
Visitable excavations in progress, 20, 42, 155, 156, 157, 158, 159, 198, 205, 219, 243, 286, 291, 296, 300, 313, 333, 362, 370, 371
Vivian, A. Gwinn, 71, 74
Volcanic eruption, 22, 31, 36, 37, 81, 152, 162. *See also* Sunset Crater; Mount Mazama.
Volunteer activities, 118, 120, 153, 158, 159, 370, 371
Von Daniken, Erick, 88

Waco, Texas, 200
Wagner College, Museum of Archaeology, 355
Wake Forest University, Museum of Man, 241
Wakeham Bay, 365

Wakemap Mound, 161
Waleska, GA, 224
Wallowa County Museum, 154
Walnut Canyon National Monument, 35, 67
Walpi, AZ, 36
Wampanoag Indians, 337, 338, 340
Wampum, 354, 367
Wanapum Dam, 155, 161
Wanapum Tour Center, 161
Wapanucket #6 Site, 336, 337
Wapanucket #8 Site, 325
Wappinger Confederacy, 353
Warfare, 197, 229, 240, 253
War Path, 322
Warm Mineral Springs Spa, FL, 236
Warren County Historical Society, 312
Washington, 154–163
Washington State Historical Society, 161
Washington State University, 157, 158, 159; State University of Anthropology Museum, 161, 162
Washington, D.C., 333, 334
Washington, George, 336
Washington Square Mound Site, 205
Washington State Park (MO), 300
Washita River culture, 170
Washita Valley Museum, 195
Water and Power Resources Service, 40
Watson House, 346, 347
Waterloo, IA, 280
Wattle and daub, 7, 42, 43, 170, 246, 260, 273, 282
Wawenock Indians, 334
"Weather Prediction," 102
Weaving, 17, 22, 23, 32, 50, 51, 57, 133, 154, 308
Wedel, Waldo R., 171
Weeden Island culture, 222, 223, 226, 252
Weeping eye symbol, 193
Weippe Prairie, 151
Weirs, 326, 327, 330
Weis Rock Shelter, 151
Wellsville, NY, 350
Western Archaic, xxiii–xxiv, 4, 8, 18, 106, 107
Western Baptist Hospital, 282
Western Reserve Historical Society, 312
Western Trails Museum, 195
Westfield, NY, 348
West Hartford, CT, 330
West Virginia, 305, 313–314
West Virginia Archeological Society, 314
West Virginia Department of Culture and History Museum, 314
Westwater Creek, 93
Westwater Ruin, 92, 103

Wetherill, Clayton, 98
Wetherill, John, 25, 98
Wetherill Mesa, 39, 49, 52, 55, 56, 57
Wetherill, Richard, 25, 48, 53, 54, 98
Whalebone artifacts, 334
Whale effigy, 116
Whale hunting, 157
"What Was It Used For?", xix
Wheat, Joe Ben, 175, 176
White, John, 363
Whitehorse, Yukon Territory, 163
White House Ruins, 8, 14
Whiteford Site, 178
White Mountain Apache Indians, 20
Whiteriver, AZ, 20
Whiteshell Provincial Park, 164, 180, 182
Wichita Indians, 191, 195
Wild rice harvest, 291
Wilkes Barre, PA, 364
William Penn Memorial Museum, 363, 364
William Rockhill Nelson Gallery and Atkins Museum of Fine Arts, 300
Williamsburg, VA, 369
Williamson Museum, 232
Williamson Site, 325
Willis Carey Museum, 163
Willow Springs, 129
Wilmington, DE, 332
Wilmington, OH, 302
Wilson Butte Cave, 136, 151
Wilson Museum, 335
Wind Cave National Park, 199
Window Rock, AZ, 28
Winged serpent, 211, 218
Winnemucca Lake Cave, 128
Winnipeg, Manitoba, 182
Winquatt Museum, 154
Winston Salem, NC, 241
Winterville Mounds State Park, 237
Wisconsin, 314, 315–323
Wisconsin Department of Natural Resources, 318
Wisconsin Historical Society, 318
Wistariahurst Museum, 339, 340
Witte Memorial Museum, 205
Wolfeboro, NH, 343
Women's activities: in Archaic period, 211; at Mesa Verde, 49, 50; at Ocmulgee, 230; in Northeast, 328; at Poverty Point, 233
Wood carving, 144, 193, 220, 221
Woodhenges, 260, 261
Woodland Indian Cultural Educational Centre, 357
Woodland culture: described, 167–169, 251–254, 328–329; mentioned, 196–199 *passim,* 211, 218, 234, 236, 239, 256, 262–266 *passim,* 272,